T0354774

Hard Times
And
Survival;
The
Autobiography
Of An
African-American
Son

WILLIAM A. JAMES, SR.

HARD TIMES AND SURVIVAL; THE AUTOBIOGRAPHY OF AN AFRICAN-AMERICAN SON

iUniverse books may be ordered through booksellers or by contacting:

iUniverse
1663 Liberty Drive
Bloomington, IN 47403
www.iuniverse.com
1-800-Authors (1-800-288-4677)

Because of the dynamic nature of the Internet, any web addresses or links contained in this book may have changed since publication and may no longer be valid. The views expressed in this work are solely those of the author and do not necessarily reflect the views of the publisher, and the publisher hereby disclaims any responsibility for them.

Any people depicted in stock imagery provided by Getty Images are models, and such images are being used for illustrative purposes only.
Certain stock imagery © Getty Images.

ISBN: 978-1-5320-6077-9 (sc)
ISBN: 978-1-5320-6076-2 (hc)
ISBN: 978-1-5320-6078-6 (e)

Library of Congress Control Number: 2018912389

Print information available on the last page.

iUniverse rev. date: 10/18/2018

To Sarah, Deloris, Barbara, William Jr.

Hakim, Acacia, Sarriah, Alainnah, Imani, William III. and Sean

PREFACE

Most of the story you are about to read is based upon the author's past experiences. Some of these experiences were so horrible that the author's psyche became thereafter plagued with unforgettable images. These images were extended as the author listened to his Mother, Grandmothers, and many of his relatives and neighbors tell and retell the tales that had surrounded the James Family's history. In this Book I, William (Billy) A. James, Sr. try to make sense out of all of the experiences I had growing up poor and desperate in rural South-Central Virginia.

The majority of the names appearing in this Book are authentic; however, some names are thoroughly fictitious for obvious reasons. A certain-minimal-amount of fiction was necessary in order to add balance to the narrative. Most events, with the exception of a few dates, occurred as is stated.

INTRODUCTION

Billy James was born June 11, 1947, in the middle of the day, in the middle of the hottest, driest, June anyone could remember. His birthday represented the road his life would travel on, in that, he would find himself, from day one, in the middle of heated controversy from the earliest days of his childhood to adulthood.

Most of Billy's pains came from his Father who despised him from birth, because Billy's birth got in the way of Henry's guitar-playing womanizing. He was a free-wheeling (twenty-six year old) blues-man and wanted to remain so. But he was compelled by his Mother, Mary Etta (A'nt Maetta), to marry a "child," (seventeen-year old) Mabel Louise Scott, who he thought "was too black and ugly for me to marry." A'nt Maetta, after seeing Baby Billy, said that the child resembled Charlie Edward James, (Unc' Charlie), its Grandfather. She demanded, with an oath, that Henry bring the baby to her for raising. She did not trust Agnes Mickens, Mabel's Mother, or Mabel, and did not think them capable of properly raising Billy as well as she could.

A'nt Maetta was a hardened woman who often took out her frustrations on whoever angered her. She felt as though she was still enslaved almost like her ancestors had been, and she was not going to let people in her community walk all over her. Hard times and horrid social conventions, forced upon any "Negro" living in the South, had fostered in A'nt Maetta a domineering nature that got coupled with a typical "Bible-Belt" regional fanaticism, motivating her to sometimes use misquoted/misunderstood Scriptural Admonitions, like in The Ten Commandments: "Honor Your Father and Mother ..." to scare Henry into obeying her; even if it meant that he had to marry Mabel to bring Billy home to her.

To allay "God's Wrath," and after Henry thought he had incurred that because of what had happened to him the night that his Mother had sworn: "You ain't go have no good luck cause you done sassed your Mamma," he decided he would go do what she had demanded him to do. He had nearly been killed by a jealous Tank Snowvall over Babe Bates Snowvall's girlfriend. Henry James had nearly stabbed this man to death. He was facing time in jail. The next day after the stabbing, he went to Richmond, Virginia to ask Mabel to let him take Billy to his Mother to be raised. Mabel said the only way she would return to Fluvanna County with Billy was if Henry married her. He planned to force her to leave him as soon as Billy was safely with A' nt Maetta. Therefore he married Mabel a "woman" he truly despised "for forcing him to marry her."

Some of what had motivated Henry was what he had witnessed growing up. He did not want to find himself surrounded by the same circumstances that he had seen his Father, called, "Unc' Charlie," overwhelmed by all of his life.

Unc' Charlie, an ill-mannered shiftless alcoholic, had just about given up on life. His liquor drinking was in reality temporary suicide. He was henpecked and disrespected by his children. He blamed all of his troubles on "the white man who take 'way ev' thin'." His hobo-roaming all over the United States before, during, and after The Great Depression gave Siegfried, a local, large, farm owner, whose farm A'nt Maetta had to live on and raise her family, an excellent opportunity to take sexual advantage of A'nt Maetta. On his return from one of his excursions, she presented Unc' Charlie with a "little bundle of joy," Siegfried's half-white baby-daughter. Unc' Charlie knew that he could not do anything to stop the seduction of his wife by Siegfried; so, when she brought Cora into the world, he just tried to drown his pains in bottle after bottle of cheap liquor. The above circumstances made Henry declare: "I'd kill my wife, her half-white child, and the child's Father, if what happened to Poppa ever happened to me." He often threatened Mabel with this declaration.

From 1950-1963, Billy somehow survived his Father's horrid brutalizing violence-including attempted murder at the age of three or four. Henry was seemingly minded to cut his oldest son in the head with a sharp axe, but tried to pull the blade back at the last minute. He cut off Billy's right-trigger finger instead of splitting open his head. Billy lived in absolute fear of his Father from age three or four to sixteen when he left home for good.

But before Billy left home he witnessed the 1950s old color caste and racial ideas in American society changing slowly, culminating in the Supreme Court's Mandate (May 17, 1954) in *Brown vs. Board of Education* that Public schools must desegregate all over America. After the public school desegregation mandate took effect, all over the South; and after the White Citizens Council of Fluvanna County had hurriedly erected a so-called, "Separate but Equal,"

Central Elementary School in Palmyra, Virginia. Billy heard that Evergreen Prep, a semi-private Black school in Fluvanna, had parents who were not willing to send their children to a school with darker-skinned children.

From the age of six he had been acquainted with the light-skin, dark-skin schisms in the Black community. He'd almost been killed for not informing on his Mother. He'd seen the aftermath of his Uncle Lin's murder of a man named Burton Gaines over his Aunt Bessie. He was slapped around and another little girl was seriously injured by an enraged first-grade teacher. A man called Bo Rabbit did permanent damage to Henry James's head with a hickory stick because Henry had threatened Bo with a knife about Mabel. Billy never witnessed Unc' Charlie ever speaking to or acknowledging his Aunt Cora. Billy knew that his Aunt grieved all of her life because the man she called "Daddy" hated her guts. All of the above grief and sorrows were directly related to Black-on-Black skin-color prejudices. Billy called the above: "The Skin Color Syndrome Among African-Americans."

Billy dropped out of school in 1963, because he had grown tired of his Father's abuse; and in his sixth year at school a teacher had told him "that you're too dark to ever become anything but a sawmill menial"; and in his tenth year, another teacher said, "You darkies in here might as well give me a break. You're never going to be nothing but a cook, maid or janitor, anyway." He made up his mind that he was not going to suffer through twelve years of painful inferior education to become some insignificant menial. He felt that he had no alternative but to venture out on his own and take a chance with what little education he had.

After five years of wandering around in the streets of Charlottesville, Virginia, Billy met and married a delightful woman, Sarah, from Madison County in 1968. They had three children (by 1975) before he decided to go back to school. He'd gone off to a Job Corps Center (Fort Custer, Battle Creek, Michigan) in 1965, and in 1966, before he met Sarah he'd earned a GED diploma from Western Michigan University through the Job Corps. From 1975-77, he attended Piedmont Virginia Community College in Charlottesville, and earned an Associate of Science degree. He went on to Virginia State College (now a University), to earn his BA (1979), and his MA in 1980-in Recent American History. He studied above a Masters degree at the University of Virginia from 1980-1983, and again in 1985-86, and finally in 1993. He did not graduate.

I, William (Billy) James, Sr. am relating to you Dear Reader what I went through in this Book, so that you will learn as I did that: "The Hard Times ... "you are enduring in life, no matter how horrible, are to force you to become a better individual. There is a Divine Plan at work moving all of Mankind forward; and some of us here on Planet Earth have been selected to bear the brunt of the evils, ill-treatments, deprivations, and racial and other-group, ostracisms, so that our suffering, sacrifices, and ordeals will make us stronger as individuals; and will push Mankind globally up the evolutionary ladder towards absolute humanitarian and egalitarian Perfection. I write to inspire you all to *keep on keeping on. For we all will reap if the chosen among us do not faint or give up the* **Primordial Struggle.**

PART I

Unto Us A Son Is Given

CHAPTER ONE

In a small room of a five-room shanty in Cumberland County, Virginia, a seventeen-year old Black child was panting and screaming from the pains accompanying childbirth. She was lying on top of a homemade mattress (tick: made from burlap bags sewn together and stuffed with straw). The tick was laid out over the rusting springs of an old iron bed-frame. Between the tick and the child several old newspaper pages had been spread.

Mrs. Cora Cooper, the local midwife, was standing over Mabel Louise Scott lying prostrate with her legs spread, her face contorted, and her body straining, as balls of sweat fell off her like raindrops. Mabel looked up at Mrs. Cooper for further instructions. The "Aunt Jemima" facsimile-except that she was a little fatter and a shade lighter than the Pancake-mix caricature-smiled docilely. Mabel's breath came out of her like little puffs of wind as she emitted them in a rapid staccato. Tears streamed down her ebony cheeks. Then she tightly shut her eyes. On this oven-hot day, June 11, 1947, at about Noon, Mabel was about to become a mother for the first time.

Mrs. Cooper got an old pillow from under the bed and slid it under Mabel's buttocks. "Push child," she whispered. Then she spoke louder, "Go-head on. You're almost there. I can see the head-it's cresting, baby. That's it. That's a good gal ..."

With her arms pulled back to her sides, with her hands balled up into hard fists, Mabel gave it all she had. "Oh, fuck ... Oh Lord!" she screamed. The head of the child came inching out of its Mother along with some vaginal bleeding and other birthing fluids.

"Push baby. You near 'bout got the job done. You only got a little ways to go fore we go have another soul in this world," chimed Mrs. Cooper.

"It hurt me like hell, though, Mrs. Cooper!" Mabel screamed.

"Yeah, I know, baby. Just push. It's go be all over but the shouting, directly," Mrs. Cooper, said.

Mabel cried and screamed even louder, then. Her voice came out in a shrill pitch as she yelled at the top of her lungs: "Damn that O' Henry James. I ain't never dreamt that I was gonna go through all this pain to have no baby." She gave a long scream, "Ah-h-h-h! Oh-h-h-h! This shit's hurting me too much. All Henry had to do was put this baby in my belly. I'm the one gotta bear all these pains." Mabel gave a final big push.

Mrs. Cooper stood very close to Mabel. She took a white handkerchief out of her white midwife's uniform-pocket, gently wiped the sweat off her brow, put it back into her pocket; then she caught a little dark-brown boy as he finished his descent into the world of humans.

Mabel's young body trembled all over. She watched Mrs. Cooper go to a large midwife's bag the size of a suitcase to get something out. She quickly went out of the room to get a basin of hot water dipped out of a twenty-gallon tub setting on the top of an old stove in the kitchen. She rushed back to the Mother and child and dropped a pair of surgical scissors into the basin of very hot water. She got the scissors out of the water with a pair of forceps, held them up until the scissors cooled enough to use by hand.

Mabel didn't know what was going to happen next. She'd never been present when her Mother or Sisters had given birth. But she was glad when she saw that Mrs. Cooper was clamping off the umbilical cord and was going to snip it to separate Mother from newborn child for the first time. Mrs. Cooper snipped the cord and slapped the baby on its rump.

The little boy screamed and cried. His cries echoed throughout the shanty, alerting everyone that he had just finished experiencing the horrors of being born.

The old midwife took a bar of Ivory Soap out of her black bag, along with two towels and two wash cloths. She went back into the kitchen taking with her the basin of hot water. Once in there, she dipped a couple of dippers of water out of a five-gallon bucket to cool the boiling water down some. She came back into the bedroom. She got out two bed-sheets from her bag.

"Raise up, Mabel. Lemme get all that old dirty newspaper and stuff out of here. I wanna make up your bed with a couple of them clean sheets the Relief Department over in Palmyra gave me for you gals round here. Gotta give a newborn baby a clean start in life," Mrs. Cooper said. After the bed had been made, Mrs. Cooper washed the baby and helped Mabel clean herself.

A little air escaped out of Mabel's lips as she opined, "I ain't go never do this again, Mrs. Cooper, I swear. I'm still hurting, a lot. I' on think I' ma ever go with another man."

A twisted little smile came to Mrs. Cooper's lips. She gave Mabel a sideway glance as she quipped: "You don't say?" Mrs. Cooper seemed very amused. "Child, I 'spects I'm go see you again real soon. They all talks like you just did, at first. But then, nature go take its course. Fore ya know it, there ya go again, baby, baby, baby." She gave a little chuckle.

Mabel was not amused. A frown eased across her face as she thought about what Mrs. Cooper had prophesied. Her thoughts were interrupted-

"Mabel, you got any baby clothes for the baby? We gotta dress 'im in something." Mrs. Cooper stood at the foot of the bed with her hands on her massive hips.

"Yes 'am. Momma got me a box together from an old White lady. Her granddaughter had a still-born baby a cup 'la months ago. The box's under the bed."

Mrs. Cooper groaned as she had to get down on the floor on her knees to get the box. Her knee print showed through her dress from the ground-in dirt on the old wooden floor boards. She tried to brush that off, but gave up knowing that it was futile.

"We go get Lil' Angel Pooh all dressed. Y'all got some nice things in this box, gal. Must've belonged to a rich White gal," said Mrs. Cooper.

"Yes 'am. It was one-a 'em Woods' gals. They own ev' thin' round here." Mabel yawned. "Yes indeed. I know you got that right, child," chimed Mrs. Cooper. "Okay, Mabel, I'm go dress this cute little rascal directly. He's a right pretty baby, Mabel-an' I done seen a lotta 'em."

Mabel's face brightened up into an ear-to-ear grin. "Mrs. Cooper, he's probably the best thing that done ever happen to me." Her eyes became very heavy with teardrops. A couple of those spilled down her cheeks.

Mrs. Cooper blinked away the emotional moment. But the whites of her eyes became a little red. She was thinking of how ironic the statement was that Mabel had made. She knew that this gal did not have a clue about what she was in for.

First, Mrs. Cooper wrapped a bellyband around the middle of the infant's body, after she had powered his little body all over with antiseptic powder. She pinned on a clean diaper. She got a pink blanket out of the box-thinking: the lost child must have been a girl, most of the blankets and printed clothes are pink or yellow. Second, Mrs. Cooper put antiseptic eyedrops into the child's eyes. She smiled tenderly at the baby now lying in her lap. She cooed: "I bet he's go make something outta hisself I just got that feeling 'bout 'im. His ears 're nut-brown. He's not go be too dark-skinned. Mabel, this boy might just have a chance. The world she is a-changing, y' know."

Mrs. Cooper handed the child over to its smiling Mother. She put the baby's mouth to her bulging bosom. He quickly seized the nipple of her left breast and eagerly nursed it.

"Move your legs over a little, Mabel." Mrs. Cooper put a couple more clean sheets at the foot of the bed. She put a summer blanket on top of the sheets. She got out a stack of new cloth diapers and laid them on top of the pile of nice bed things. "Well. There ya go. You's all set."

Mabel broke down and cried. She could not look Mrs. Cooper in the eye. "What 'cha go ...

What 'cha go charge me, ma'am?" The words finally gushed out of her anxious lips.

Mrs. Cooper's eyes grew a little wider. She did not answer at first. Then she uttered: "Mabel . . . raise your legs. Lemme spread one-a 'em sheets under you. This old tick ain't fitting for no baby to be lying on. Got to make sure he don't."

"But ma'am, I just wanna know . . . what 'cha go charge?" Mabel asked.

"Aw-ight. I hear you," Mrs. Cooper replied. She looked squarely at Mabel. She shook her head a little, and then frowned as though what she was about to say would cause her some pain. "Well . . . the usual, I guess. Three dollars ought-ta 'bout cover it, I reckon. You can have the stuff I gave ya. The County Relief Department gave us Colored Midwives a whole slew of towels, washcloths, sheets, and a few sets of baby clothes. I would've

4

given you some clothes if you didn't have any. But, you know times is hard, child. Gotta save all I can for those who really, really, need it.

"Mabel, baby. I hope you will not forget me, aw-ight. You understand now-don't ya? I know you don't have it today, but I want you to pay me when you can, though. Will ya do that?"

Tears eased out of Mabel's eyes. "I ain't got no money today is right. But I'm go see Henry in a cup 'la days. He's go give me the money you charge. He'll gimme that if no more." Mabel spoke in a whine.

"Just remember we's all seeing some mighty hard times. That's all I'm saying. It's mighty tight on a dime these days. I know you know what I'm saying?" Mrs. Cooper started gathering up some of the things she had used in helping Mabel bring her child into the world.

The sunlight started to fade. Mrs. Cooper looked up, went over to one of the windows of the room and peered out. "Mabel I b'lieves a storm is coming in here from the East. It done cloud right up out yonder, child. I can see the distant lightning."

"Yes 'am," was all Mabel could think to say. "What you go name the child, Mabel?"

"Well, Mrs. Cooper, I think I go name him William Anderson James, even though I ain't married to his Daddy. Henry and I might end up getting married one day."

"Hey, baby, I didn't mean to sound like I was trying to pry in y'all's business. Honey, all I'm trying to do is get this Birth Certificate Application filled out. It's the Law now. It'll come back to you through the mail from the Bureau of Records. It will take a few days for it to come back. That's all I mean ..."

"No-No, Mrs. Cooper. I didn't mean to sound like I was acting smart, or nothing. I want to name my child: William Anderson James. I'll appre' sate that."

"Okay then, Mabel. 'William Anderson James,' it'll be." Mrs. Cooper filled out some papers she'd taken out of her midwife's bag. "Sign on the bottom of this one, sugar." She handed a page to Mabel. She signed it. Mrs. Cooper folded up the papers, stuck them in her bag, along with the tools of her trade. She stood up and grabbed her zipped-up bag by its handles.

"Go call Agnes, Mabel. I gotta get away from over here fore that storm hits," she said.

CHAPTER TWO

"Momma. Momma. Come on in. Mrs. Cooper wanna talk to you. Momma ..." Mabel's voice sounding a little tired, echoed throughout the shanty.

"Agnes. Agnes. Come on in here. I got to get away from over here fore long," Mrs. Cooper pied.

Agnes Mickens, who was with child herself, wobbled into the room. She was a light-brown, near cream-and-coffee, complexioned mulatto, with coal-black straight hair, that hung down to her very shapely buttocks. Her skin was so smooth it appeared to be flawless, radiant, and youthful. Her petite lips seemed fixed in a permanent smile; and when she smiled, her even, pearly-white teeth sparkled. She was a very pretty woman, all five feet of her. Even though she wore a baggy dress made out of flowery-print feedbag, she wore those mini-daisies well. Mabel was Agnes's fifth child, and Mabel's Twin Brother George was her sixth. Agnes was so heavily pregnant it looked like she might have her baby any day.

Her forty-nine-or so-years did not show badly on Agnes's face, but she had outlived two husbands. She had lost John Archer in 1918 (or so) to TB, after several troubled years of marriage; and Willie Scott in the 1930s to a Stroke. These men had been ten or twenty years older than Agnes. Both men had claimed "semi-ownership" to plots of land on the Woods' Farm. At their death they left Agnes nothing but a pile of Tenant-farming debts.

Without any money, Agnes roamed all over Cumberland County to work on any farm she could during and after the 1930s. She was forced to live like a vagabond. At times, she would just work for whatever leftover food farm owners threw out, (like she had after the 1920s).

On one of the farms, owned by a black tenant farmer, where Agnes found herself working, she was forced to submit to the animal lusts of the farm owner, who was also a Deacon in a local Baptist Church. He got her pregnant and ordered Agnes and her children off his farm. This was prior to her hooking up with old man Willie Scott. Agnes gave birth to Mabel and George shortly after she married old Willie. Soon after she married Willie, Agnes got pregnant again and brought forth a baby girl Willie named, Frances Marie Scott. Before Willie's death, Agnes had gotten pregnant six times and brought seven children into the world by old men Archer and Scott and the Deacon Agnes would never name; though Mabel begged and pleaded with her Mother to tell her who her Father was, over and over again; but Agnes refused. After the death of old man Scott, Agnes had to find somewhere to go again, so she could survive and raise her children.

Sometime during the late Thirties, or early Forties, a rich-White farm owner heard of Agnes's plight, and offered her a place to stay. She jumped at the chance. She wanted to give her seven children a little rest from having to roam around all the time, and sometimes sleeping in barns and or old abandoned houses. She'd been raped or molested several times, and then the rapists talked about her like she was a "who'e." The local women hated her because she was pretty and light-skinned, and their men came right after her. Even though she resisted, some men took her anyway, and nobody gave a damn! The women just called her names. They wanted to believe that their husbands and boyfriends were as innocent as schoolboys. So, when what seemed to be a good offer from a kind White man came along, Agnes gladly said, "Yes."

She moved to Robert Lee Woods Ill's farm located in the beautiful Cumberland countryside, with great joy. His farm was situated at about five miles south of the town of Columbia, Virginia, flanking the banks of the James River. Woods owned nearly 12,400 acres of prime farmland that had been in the possession of his family since Colonial times. He produced tobacco, com, and wheat, much as his slave-holding ancestors had done during slavery. Most of the Blacks in that area with the last name "Woods" were descended from slaves who had been owned by old Robert Lee Woods

I. His main Plantation had been near Farmville, Virginia. The latter R.L. Woods III was directly descended from this humongous Original Family.

After Woods had heard of Agnes's plight, and even before he approached her, he had his farm hands build a shanty not very far from Columbia. It was actually in walking distance from that town. He invited Agnes to come live on his farm and bring her children with her. He told her all she would have to do is a little light housework, and her children who were old enough would be required to help with the planting and harvesting of the crops. That was all the payment Woods said that Agnes and her children would have to make. This sounded too good to be true to Agnes, but it was an offer she could not refuse. So Agnes agreed to all of Woods' preliminary requirements.

Early on one Monday morning at daybreak, a Black farm hand called out to Agnes.

"Agnes, Agnes ... Agnes Scott!"

Agnes came to her window. "Yeah, what 'cha want so early this morning?"

"The boss wants ya to come shuck corn with the gals in the fields today," said the Black Baby Huey in Belle Overalls. He seemed to be the size of a young elephant to Agnes.

"Okay, Hoover," Agnes replied. "Just lemme get something to eat. I just got up when you called." Hoover had helped her and her children move into the Shanty.

"Aw-ight, then. See ya in front of the main barn, then." Hoover ambled on up the path from Agnes's shanty.

Agnes got busy frying the fatback that Mr. Woods had supplied her. She fried potatoes and made biscuits. She left all of that on the back of her stove for when her children would get up. She was so proud of the fact that Mr. Woods had given her a sack of flour, one of beans, and another of meal. He'd given her four laying hens. One had set and had baby chicks already. So she had plenty of fresh eggs. She loved the two hams and shoulders Mr. Woods had given her; and what was really surprising was: *up until the morning of the shucking, he had not asked her to do a bit of work-not even housework.* Agnes felt like surely this man was a Godsend.

After Agnes ate her breakfast, she was glad to be going out to do something in return for all of Mr. Woods's kindness towards her and her children. She arrived at the cornfield. She saw a big Mansion with a veranda, with them little gable windows on all four or eight sides of the massive house. It had been freshly whitewashed and trimmed in green paint. With the smooth well-trimmed lawns that stretched far away to the distance tree-lines, and the boxwood hedges on all four to eight sides of the house, this place was in Agnes's opinion, like a King's Mansion.

Then she saw them:

Several tired-looking Black women came up a path from behind a huge red barn. They wore feedbag daisy-print dresses. They stumbled along like old soldiers returning from a war, or something. One started a chorus: **We Shall Overcome Some Day** *. . . But it wasn't a song. It was more a chant. Agnes could feel within her soul that she had a kindred spirit that was closely related to those women. She felt that spirit like it was hot-heat radiating out from them like the sun's rays. Their voices filled her with a certain kind of fear--a foreboding-but she didn't know for what? The women marched on to the corn. fields singing/chanting as they walked along like ghosts in a dream. One turned towards Agnes and cried out:* **"Oh, God Help Her!"**

"Hey. Agnes. Good to see you this morning, Gal." A baritone voice nearly scared the "Be Jesus" out of Agnes. But she knew that it was *Dear Mr. Woods.*

"Oh, yes sir, Mr. Woods. How're you doing this morning?" Agnes spoke with an almost little girl's giggle. She turned to face her kind benefactor. She saw what she thought was a very handsome middle-age White man. She backed away a little because it seemed that Mr. Woods was standing just too close to her for comfort all at once.

Agnes reflected for a moment: *This great big o' house. This's a fine farm. House got windows ev' where, I can see fine draperies from out here, even. This here place's near 'bout a palace. It can't b'long to no po' white trash. This-here gotta b'long to people of the rich Wood's family. Maybe, if I keeps my nose clean, and play my cards right, like other gals, I may be able to get my little hands on some-a that money. But I don't wanna move too fast.*

"Agnes, go into the barn over yonder and get yourself a shucking tool off the wall in there. Then come on back out here. I'll tell you what I want you to do after that, directly. All right?"

"Aw-ight, Mr. Woods," Agnes said. "Will do."

It was sort of flattering to Agnes for how Mr. Woods was staring at her.

But the voices of the weeping women she'd seen marching to the cornfields started chanting in her mind. She tried to force that to stop. Woods stood watching her walk up the hill a ways, with his eyes fixed on her butt as she entered the open doorway of the barn.

The barn floor squeaked loudly as Agnes walked over it. That unnerved her a little, but did not get the scary image of the weeping women out of her mind, nor did it quell their chanting. The smell of cow's manure hit her nostrils and the air in the barn was thick with the smell of decaying hay, silo-com, and the faint smell of souring milk-the typical odors of farm life.

On one side of the wall inside of the barn were several scythes, axes, saws, and a whole line of shucking tools of various sizes. Agnes got one of the hook-shaped contractions. She turned around, got ready to go back out to the front of the barn, and was shocked.

Mr. Woods walked slowly into the barn. Agnes was forced to take a deeper look at this tall man. He looked to be over six foot tall. He had shiny-green eyes like a cat's. Now, they seemed fixed in the middle of his head. His staring made her feel nude, totally naked. Instinctively, she put her hands over the place he was concentrating on. His ruddy skin filled up with beads of sweat. His bright-red hair seemed to stand up on his head and neck like on an excited dog. His breathing came out as short healthy spurts. His handsome appearance disappeared, and was replaced by the image of a "lustful demon." Then the muscles of his arms started to pulsate. He seemed to be flexing them like a weight-lifter, and or a wrestler. It was like he was getting ready for some powerful competition in a sport's arena. His baritone voice came out an octave iower as he spoke:

"Agnes, you're a right nice-looking Gal. As long as I gets what I wants, you and your little Picaninnies will never have to move off this place," spilled out Mr. Woods's mouth like molasses out of a bucket, thick and slow. Then, he undid the clamps of his green overalls, they dropped to his ankles. He stood before Agnes exposing a bared, huge, erection. "Gal, you gotta take it or leave it."

Agnes felt glued to the spot where she stood. Fear engulfed her to the point that she did not know what to do: to run, scream, or submit. Inside of herself she screamed: *"Why do this shit keep happening to me all the gal-darn time!"* She just stood there whimpering like a little child waiting to be spanked. Then the chant came to mind: **We Shall Overcome Some Day** . . . All of this was happening way too fast for her.

Woods rushed over and grabbed hold of Agnes. He put one arm around her waist in case she might be thinking about running away. He pulled her close to him. He reached down with his right hand and suddenly lifted her dress tail until his hand found her full bush. He violated her with his fingers. He pulled her dress up by its helm and snatched it up over her head. Agnes stood dead still, whimpering, "No. I don't wanna. Lemme go ..." She covered her vagina with one hand, and draped her other arm over her breasts to cover her nudity as much as possible. She knew to not lift her hands threateningly against a White man. She might end up dead. So, she just stood there whining, deciding to do whatever it took to survive.

Woods paid no attention to her whining. He pushed her down suddenly onto her dress on the barn's rough floor boards. He dropped down between her legs after prying them open. He guided his male member into her feminine sanctuary with decided force. Agnes felt like she was being split in-two with a baseball bat. He wasn't gentle at all.

She let out a powerful scream, but knew that nobody cared, and would not come to her aid even if they did. The rhythm of his thrusting himself into her reminded her of the swaying of the poplar, oak, and pine tree-limbs, on the trees surrounding his farm, when they are driven by a brisk wind.

Agnes was conscious, but the pain and disgust she felt made it impossible for her to remain in her body. She had to escape by using her mind to get away: *She floated up out of her body. She had become an Angel. She was among a group of women, who were Angels too, singing: **"We Shall Overcome Some Day** ..." in unison, over-and-over again. She and they were floating high above all of the pains they did not have the power to stop.*

Woods spent his final payload and rolled off Agnes. She had come back to her hurting, trembling, body. She was aware of the three times that Woods had raped her. His big, old, thing was limp and Agnes hoped it wouldn't get up again. He sat up. He laughed. His laughter reminded Agnes of the whinnying of a horse.

"Now, that was mighty good, gal-I tell you," Woods said. He had the snarl of a sly fox on his disgusting face, and Agnes hated the way he looked.

She wished there was some way she could stick a knife in him as many times as he had stuck his o' thing in her.

Woods rose to his feet. He pulled his coveralls up, and gave another one of his little chuckles. As he walked away, he allowed: "You don't have to shuck com today, now. But I expect you to come back over here next Monday. If you don't get to shuck corn, well, I'll damn sure find something ar' nother for you to do." Then he laughed out loud, sounding like a hyena, to Agnes.

Just as Woods went out of the doorway, Agnes let out a scream like that of a wounded animal. It came from the depth of her deprived soul. Tears streamed down her cheeks. Her face burned from her self-hatred. She blurted out: "I hate being a 'high-yellar Nigger!' Being good looking with no way to defend myself, ain't from shit, cause any old dog liable to come 'long an' jump right on ya, an' stick his o' nasty thing 'tween your legs. I hate being a poor 'Negro' in Cumberland County even worse." Her tears came down her cheeks like the rain.

She gathered up her dress and put it on backward in her haste. She ran from the barn like a bat out of hell. She didn't stop until she found her shanty. Her children were all outside in the woods playing. They did not see her come home. Agnes ran to a comer of her shanty, balled up in it like a cat and just stayed there until nightfall. She stayed balled up in a knot, crying softly, not daring to move, with her eyes fixed expressing her fright, and her anger. Her oldest Daughter, Dora, cooked supper, after she could not get her Mother to bulge.

In her mind Agnes screamed: *I gotta stay over here for my chillun sake. I can't keep moving 'round. Gotta just shut my mind to the bad things Woods do to my body. When that ol' sonavabitch climbs on me to do his bizzness, I just won't let my body feel nothing. Then I won't feel the pain-no-no-no-no.*

Agnes became cold, and impersonal, and indifferent to life in general, the more Woods raped her, which was often. He lusted after Agnes more than he did after the many other Black women he was abusing in Cumberland; literally all of them working on his farm. Agnes was forced to stay on his farm, he had warned other farm owners that they had better not think about luring Agnes away from him, or else!

She repressed the evil Woods did to her deep within her subconscious mind, until it rendered her conscious mind emotionless and insensitive to the assaults and insults forced on her body by him. Thus when Woods raped her she just laid there, shut her eyes tight, and dissociated from the horrid reality. When Woods :finished raping her, it was like she was awakening from a violent reoccurring nightmare.

As time went on the whole experience made Agnes's ability to emotionally interact with friends, family, and foes extremely limited. What was even worse was the fact that her repressed emotional state of mind dominated whenever serious problems confronted her.

She was chained to her situation like a hundred other Black women who were treated like they were Woods's personal concubines. It did not matter whether they were married or single. All that seemed to matter were that they were "Negroes" and in desperate need of somewhere to iive. That's the Hard Times they had to Survive.

The announcement of the death of Robert Woods III gave Agnes cause for great jubilation. He passed away sometimes during the early Forties. She danced and shouted for joy for hours. A number of Black families had heard the news and were also dancing and shouting.

What was strange, was that for the foreseeable future, no White family member came to kick Agnes out of the shanty she had been living in. She didn't know anything about who Woods' family members were. She never wanted to know. That's how bad she hated him. But the old fear of becoming a vagabond again became an overwhelming lump in Agnes's chest.

Agnes knew that she had to find a job and another means of support for herself and her children now that "she was not going to be old Woods's who'e anymore." She walked over to Columbia, at about five miles from her shanty, to go from house to house seeking a domestic job with some White family. She just wanted to be able to put food on the table for her children.

She found some day-work in Columbia with various families. They paid her ten cents per day, and all of the leftover food she wanted. She ate as much as she could on the job so that she would not have to eat anything that she took home to her children. She would sometimes steal a ham, or a chicken, or maybe a piece of beef now and then. She never got caught, or the people she worked for never questioned her about any food that was missing.

Dora knew that her Momma did not have the money to buy some of the food she brought home at various times. Agnes had told her never to steal because White folk would brand her for life if they caught her in the act.

On this evening, Agnes came home with a cured ham. Soon as she walked through the door, Dora asked, "Momma who gave ya that ham? I know you didn't steal it, right?"

Agnes beckoned for Dora to come close to her. She whispered, "Gal, listen good now. I've gotta take stuff cause them White folk don't pay me 'nough to feed a mouse. When I takes stuff from them White folk, it ain't stealing. It's taking back. Remember that, aw-ight."

Dora shook her head in agreement. She knew what her Mother meant: *Poor Black folk cannot steal from rich White folk, cause rich Whites stole ev' thing they got from the labor of slaves. That's what slavery was all about; them Crackers stealing and taking whatever they wanted from slaves. So, Negroes can never steal back what Whites owe them.*

Sometimes in the forties, a man named Charles Turpin, a married man, had an affair with Agnes, before she found out he was married. She got pregnant, then he told her he could not marry her because he was already married. She had his child and named her "Virginia (Ginia) Mea Scott."

(Dear Reader: The ages of Agnes and her children may be off by a few years or so. Most of her children did not get birth certificates filed when they were born. Nor was one filed for Agnes at her birth. I had to approximate when the above were born and how old they were in 1947 at my birth.)

Agnes's children in 1947 were Dora, at about thirty-three, or thirty-five. She had long since moved to Richmond, Virginia, leaving behind three illegitimate children for Agnes to feed. Anna Belle was around two-years younger than Dora (31-33). She was married to a man from Stage Junction, Virginia, two miles northeast of Columbia. She had five children of her own. Mary Beth was nineteen or twenty and had moved to Petersburg, Virginia to work as a Maid at the Central State Hospital for the Mentally Ill. Julius Archer was eighteen or nineteen. George Archer Scott and Mabel Louise Scott were seventeen. Frances Marie was twelve or thirteen.

Virginia was eleven or twelve. (Dora, Anna, Mary, and Julius were Archers. Mabel, George, Ginia and Frances were Scotts.)

After the birth of Virgina, Agnes met a handsome Lumberjack named Clemmon Montgomery Mickens. He worked with a construction company in the Blue Ridge Mountains based out of Albemarle County. He was helping to fell the trees and cut them up into logs for a new highway expansion of the right-of-way to widen Route 33-West through the Blue Ridge Mountains. He was away all week, living in a Lumber Camp. He came home on Friday evenings, leaving on Sunday evenings. By 1947, he and Agnes had Clarence Eugene, ten-years old; Willie Lee, was eight, and Agnes was pregnant again by June 11, 1947. (She'd been pregnant every two or so years since age fourteen or fifteen, when she was forced to marry old man Archer.)

The children and young adults had been ordered outside until after they heard Mabel's newborn baby's cries. All heard the news, "Mabel done had a Boy." They were jumping up and down rejoicing. Everyone seemed very happy except Agnes. She had been anxiously prancing back and forth on the cooler, shady, side of the shanty, with a look of almost horror on her face.

Mrs. Cooper's grating voice called out: "Agnes. I ain't got no time to fool 'round, now. I gotta get 'way from over here fore I get caught in an open wagon in the rain. Tell Julius to go get the horse and wagon hooked-up. I don't know where my no-count husband can be."

Agnes called through an open window, "Julius!"

"Yes' am, Momma. What you want?" a bass voice called out to Agnes from the woods-edge. "You go hitch up Mrs. Cooper's horse and buggy. Bring her wagon 'round so she can get going, okay," Agnes said.

A tall, lanky, dark-skinned young man lumbered out of the woods near the shanty wearing dirty blue jeans, a stained T-shirt, and dirty-white tennis with no socks. He had buckteeth, cold black straight hair cut short, and big eyes that were grayish brown. He was all brawn. In a few minutes he rode a red medium hay-wagon he had hitched to an old gray nag out of the edge of the woods around to the front of the shanty. His younger Brothers rode with him, one on either side of him. Once he got to the porch he said, "Ho-o-o!" and pulled on the reins to halt the old horse.

"Here's your wagon, Mrs. Cooper," he said. "You's read-ta-go," he added.

"Yes I am, Julius. I wonder where that Van Cooper is, though. Said he'd be back over here fore the evening set in good. I'ma set right out here for a little while. Hope he get on back fore long. A streak of lightning lit up the distant horizon. A booming thunder peal meant to Mrs. Cooper that the storm was getting really close.

Before Mrs. Cooper had finished complaining, a very handsome mulatto man came strutting up the path lined with walnut and hickory trees. He came from the direction of a spring that old man Woods had dug-out for the "Colored" help, so they wouldn't have to use his well.

Once Van got up to the shanty, he eyed Frances, who stood on the porch beside her Mother. Frances seemed very mature-looking for her age. Her bosom, hips, and figure made her look to be eighteen or so old. Van Cooper was wearing a gray double-breasted coat over a white-silk, dress shirt with black-edged ruffles. He wore thin-blue dress pants, black skinny-toe shoes, and a wide, blue, Stetson Hat. He was "sugar sharp" and the young people sniggered at him when he walked by.

The boys all figured that it was way too hot for Mr. Van Cooper to be all gussied up. But they also knew that he was Chairman of the Deacon Board at Columbia Baptist Church, and that meant that he had to keep up appearances no matter how hot it got. Van stopped when he saw Mrs. Cooper sitting on the wagon. He could see that her eyes were bugging out with anger at him because he was a little late getting back to Agnes's shanty.

Mrs. Cooper beckoned, shaking her right trigger-finger at Van. "Come here, Van. Where you been?" she almost hollered at her husband. Then in a lower voice she said: "You light-skinned Negroes ain't worth a plugged-nickel. Come on here, man. We gotta go fore we go be traveling through a big storm. Can't ya hear the thunder rolling over yonder?"

Van grimaced and frowned up his face until one corner of his waxed mustache almost touched the edge of his nose.

Julius and his Brothers were laughing until they nearly split their sides. Mrs. Cooper glared at them so sternly that they all fell silent like children in a classroom when ordered to "Be Quiet!" by their no-nonsense strict

16

teacher. The boys scampered around to the other side of the house and continued to snigger at Mr. Van Cooper.

Julius peeped around the corner and watched Van climb up on the wagon beside his disgruntled wife, who was glaring at him like he was a big old worm. "We'll see y'all later. Giddy up!" Van yelled, and the wagon was off. Soon the Coopers were out of sight rounding the curve down below the shanty.

Agnes stood on the porch of her shanty with big tears easing down her cheeks. She didn't dare look up at the Coopers until the wagon carrying them was nearly around the curve and out of sight. She exclaimed through short-gushes of air out of her mouth: "*I know I' ma be low rated like-a dog, now!*"

She turned towards Frances, who was sitting on an old built-in bench on the porch. "Cora thinks I want her man. I could 'da had 'im if I wanted 'im. I don't want that slick-britches man. Oh, but Old Cora thinks I done had 'im already. I know she do by the way she act round me when Van's 'round. She done told ev' body to watch they husbands round me. That lie fly outta her mouth like flies outta a outhouse," groaned up out of Agnes.

The Coopers were gone way out of sight, now. Cold tears came down Agnes's cheeks. Ginia came over to stand beside her Mother. Agnes turned to her and said: "Ginia, ev' body go be talking 'bout us like we's some kind-a animals. Just ya wait an' see when that 'black bitch' get through waggin' her stupid tongue. She's got mo' mouth than a elephant got ass. A lotta shit done got started cause-a her lies-she always messing in people's bizzness. She call herself a church lady, too. She go get somebody kilt one of these days. One-a her lies go be the reason!"

The Lightning Flashed And The Thunder Rolled!

CHAPTER THREE

Now that the wagon had carried them out of earshot of Agnes and her children, Mrs. Cooper let Van know what was really on her mind: "Van, it's a shame-fore-Gawd how Agnes 'nem is carryin' on," she exclaimed. She spoke through frowning lips out of the side of her mouth.

Van, a chubby fellow, sighed and kept his eyes forward, looking towards Columbia. They were on the southern edge of town. As a Hardware Depot (Holland's), and a large Grocery Store (Thurston's), came into focus, they had just about crossed the Cumberland Bridge over the James River that linked Fluvanna to Cumberland. Black thundering clouds loomed overhead flashing lightning that seemed to Mrs. Cooper to be getting too frequent for comfort.

"Van, you gotta speed up a little, now. We's too close to home to let ourselves get caught out in this storm. It's right on top of us," Mrs. Cooper whined. "It's probably go be right rough."

Van slapped the reins a little against the back of the old nag, but he knew it was fruitless. The horse went along at the same pace no matter when it was hitched to a wagon. As they wound down, Main, one of Columbia's two streets, Mrs. Cooper took her focus off the weather to attack Agnes and her Daughters again:

"Hope we don't get caught out in the middle of this storm; but Van, y' know I done delivered a many baby for them sluts over yonder in Agnes's shack. Ain't nothin' but-a shame, too. Now, I know you know what I means, Van. How do Agnes just let them little tramp-Daughters of her'n lay 'round an' pop-out baby after baby is beyond me." A brilliant flash of lightning was followed by a very loud peal of lingering thunder. All of the daylight was blotted out. It was pitch-black outside, like in the middle of a starless, moonless, night. The lightning was the only light, giving the ride home a scary feel, to Mrs. Cooper. But it was not enough to stop her from clawing at the character-or lack of it-of Agnes and her Daughters.

"Van. Think about this: Them whores in that shack over yonder in Cumberland keeps a train-load-a mens comin' an' goin' all times of the day an' night. Next thing ya know, one-of 'im got they belly full-a baby. Ain't nothin' but the Devil, Van. Sin is all it is." Mrs. Cooper spoke in a growl. The thunder roared like a lion in the jungle getting ready to prance on its prey.

"Giddy Up!" Van shouted at the old nag. He slapped the reins hard against its back, hoping the horse would get the energy to get them home quickly so he wouldn't have to listen to anymore of Cora's mess. He got a very hateful frown on his face. He was thinking: *I wish Cora would just shut the hell up!* But he kept his eyes forward hoping his wife hadn't seen the discomfort on his face. She did not shut up, however.

"Van. That Dora done had three babies. Only two-a 'em darlin' Lil' boys's still alive." Mrs. Cooper spoke with a groan that had started to sound like the mooing of a distant cow to Van. "They tell me, one-a Lil' Charlie's twin sons died-a neglect. Lil' Mabel was too young to know how-ta take care-a baby. Dora 'nem took to the one named James Frederick Scott, but didn't want the one named after his Grandfather, Charlie Edward. They let Mabel play with Charlie like he was a doll baby. Mabel fed the child unsterilized milk. She used to bathe the child in cold water. She didn't know how often she ought-a change the baby-cause she didn't know no better. The baby caught the Gripe and died. What-a shame!" Mrs. Cooper said, raising the whine in her voice up a couple of octaves. "Mabel's only 'bout nine, or so."

He was tired as could be of listening to the same old gossip, but all that Van managed to do was a loud clearing of his throat. Then he rolled his eyes as hard as he could.

"What I can't see is, how that cold-hearted Agnes could just standby and let her Lil' Grandchild suffer from Dysentery and the Gripe so bad that it upped and died? I'd a done somethin' ar' nother, Van." The words flew out of Mrs. Cooper's mouth like rapid gunfire.

19

Van turned to look at his wife. He knew she couldn't clearly see his face. A curse formed in his throat but he did not dare to let it come out of his mouth. He was really fed up with her gossip at this point. They were just down the hill from Columbia Baptist Church. They would be home soon and Van was very glad. The words were coming out of his wife's mouth nonstop.

"They name the survivor-if you can call 'im that-'James Frederick James,' hah! That baby weren't no James. Last I heard, Dora an' Charlie, Jr. never been married.

"Then, Dora started slippin' round with-a married man, let's see, name's John Mack Taylor. He's from Kents Store; you know, next to Stage Junction. She got knocked up again, yeah. She scooted on off to Richmond, left another mouth for that poor-creature, Agnes, to feed. Now, she got two-a Dora's boys, James and John, an' neither Dora nor Agnes give-a damn 'bout them boys. I 'on kno' what's the matter with Agnes 'nem?"

He could see the steeple of Columbia Baptist Church, and that meant that they were only yards away from their front door. Van was so glad. He knew that he would be able to get away from the gossip being dumped on him. But for a little while it continued.

"Mary weren't no better, no sir. She done been knocked up 'bout six times, I've heard tell. I also heard that she dropped all of them dead chillun in the toilet. Got rid-a ev' one of 'im. Van, she gotta be a demon from hell or somethin', I swear-fore-Gawd.

"Look Van, Mary's screwing Henry James. He's slippin' round with Agnes while Clemmon's 'way all week at that lumber camp; and, that's how Henry got to slip it to poor-little Mabel. That gal probably didn't know what's happening to 'er. She seen her Momma and her Sister going after Henry, so she decided to try it too.

"A Mother and her Daughters goin' round with the same man; ain't that the nastiest mess you ever done heard of, Van? Henry dropped Mary after she got rid of his baby."

Van couldn't stand it any longer, that endless gossip had to stop. "I don't want nothing at all to do with them people's business. Cora, they don't b'long to our Church. I don't even know if most of what you've heard about them people over yonder is true. People talk. They lie. Some will tell you most anything they think you want to hear. How you know you ain't just repeating some lie people done put on your mind? Now what do you think about that?" Van said. He got a little twisted smile on his face.

"You listen here, Mr. Van Cooper," Mrs. Cooper yelled at her husband. It annoyed the hell out of her to hear Van seeming to disagree with her. "Lil' Charlie and Henry James, A'nt Maetta's boys, have gone through a lotta gals over in Cumberland. I don't see what them boys see in the trash they's foolin' round with; 'specially them gals over at Agnes's shack." Tears came to Mrs. Cooper's eyes, like she may have been genuinely concerned. But Van knew that those tears were most likely crocodile tears.

"You worry too much about other people's business, Cora. That's why you stay so upset all the time. Since our college days at Virginia State Normal Institute, soon after we got married, you started worrying about this and that. During 1915, it was a lot to worry about then. You're doing all right. I'm doing fine as a Barbour, we got twenty acres to farm, done raised two children to grown, we got five Grandchildren, and they're all healthy and fine. Your hair is all gray and whatnot, cause you done got so deep in other people's business 'til you're about to worry yourself to death." Van's voice was brimming with thick sarcasm. But even that did not stop Mrs. Cooper.

"I feel so sorry for Mabel, though, Van. She just got started havin' chillun she ought not to be having. I gave her four sheets, two pillowcases, two towels and two washcloths. I didn't see none of that in her room. That room wasn't fit for no newborn baby to be coming into. I'm go tell A'nt Maetta 'bout that child Mabel had. He's the spittin' image of Unc' Charlie James. Looks just like 'im for the world; an' I bet A'nt Maetta go wanna get that Lil' boy 'way from over yonder, Van. What do you think?"

"Well, Cora, like I said before, it ain't none of my business," Van said. He was really tired of Cora's mess-real tired.

Her grimacing turned into a snarl and spread across Mrs. Cooper's face. She rolled her eyes and bugged them out until they looked like pool ques. Her voice took on a husky tone.

"I 'ma tell ev' body at Church Sunday how soft you's getting on sin, Van. If you wanna stay Chairman of the Deacon Board, and Treasurer, you go have to see things my way-is that clear?" spurted out of Mrs. Cooper's mouth like water out of a garden hose.

A grand fa9ade of timidity seemingly pervaded Deacon Cooper's face. "I just want to leave people's business alone is all I'm trying to do, Cora. I'm not trying to ruffle your feathers. You ought to know that," Van said. He was like a lamb cornered by a pack of wolves.

Mrs. Cooper was not impressed. She interjected: "Yeah, and just you remember, I can have anybody I want removed from whatever position they're holding. Do you understand that, Van?"

"Cora, I just don't want to mess ..." "Aw-ight now, Van. I'm warning you!"

"Yeah ... Cora . . . Maybe ... You're probably right-I dunno ... I ..."

"Y' bet'cha, I'm right. When did I ever go wrong 'bout them things over yonder in Cumberland?"

The lightning flashed in rapid succession, and the thunder rolled until the ground trembled from the volume of the peals. Mrs. Cooper climbed off the wagon and ran to her front door carrying her suitcase-size Midwife's bag.

Van steered the horse and wagon down a rough road to a big red barn a little ways from the house. He was thinking: *I can't stand no more of Cora's gossip for right now. I'm going over to visit with Deacon Garland Baskerfield at his house. We can go out to his barn and knock down a few shots of his good o' bootleg. The man makes a mean brew. Cora's letting what she has accomplished in this world go to her head She's looking down her nose at too many people. People mean more than money. I know Cora's money got us what we want in life. It got us that Church up the hill. We are all grateful-but she got to see reason. She just doesn't when it comes to people who she sees as coming from a lower-class than her. That's messed up. She being able to pass the "Paper Bag Test" has got her puffed up to highfalutin "Heaven."*

Van rode on the wagon to the back of the barn, led the horse and rig into a wide space in back of it, got down off the wagon and unhitched the horse. He fed the old gray nag. He gave it some water, and led it to a stall in the barn.

He headed up to the two-story brick house that had been whitewashed with green trim. It had shutters on all twelve of its windows. The front of the house facing the Church had a full porch with green and white metal porch furniture that was practically brand new. The house was surrounded by a plush lawn that was bordered by neatly-trimmed boxwood hedges.

Once Van walked through the front door, he could feel the hostility emanating from his wife. It made him want to cry or something. Another flash of brilliant lightning, followed by a loud-booming peal of thunder seemed to punctuate the moment.

I got to get outta here. I am not gonna sit around here and have Cora stare me to death.

She's putting those big o' rollers in her hair, and she's gonna sit in that green-leather end chair and just give me the silent treatment. No way. I hate the way she punishes me with her silence. That is just as bad as her gossiping, Van was thinking.

"Cora, I'm going over to see Deacon Baskerfield. I got to go over some details about how we're going to repair the Church's back steps. He's going to have to order the blocks and cement. I got to get an accurate estimate. I know it's storming out, but he's just over yonder a bit. I'm not afraid of the storm ..."

Mrs. Cooper cleared her throat and rolled her eyes. She put her roller bag on the ornate coffee table in the middle of the front room. "Van, I ain't worried, aw-ight. But lemme serve notice on ya; and God is my witness. You just go on over yonder to Deacon Garland's barn. I know what goes on over yonder. I done heard all about it. I feel so sorry for Audrey. She gotta know what Garland is doing out in his fancy barn some nights, but she acts like she don't know." "What do you think is going on, Cora?" Van's cheeks flashed red streaks, his anger mounted.

He was thinking: *Now here comes some more of her gossip.*

"I know 'bout them little high-yellar heifers that sneaks over from Stage Junction to Garland's barn. I know 'bout the drinkin' an'gamblin' over yonder, Van. I'll get through this storm all by myself. Go on to y'all's light-skinned tramps. Get drunk and do whatever-you been doing it since I married you. I know I ain't light enough for you. So, go on, Van."

Mrs. Cooper picked up a box of Kleenex Napkins off one of her two Victorian Night Tables that matched the Coffee Table. She pulled several pink napkins out of the blue box. Her nose made a loud honking noise when she blew into the napkins.

"I'm not going over yonder for none of that, Cora. You just think like that. It's all in your mind. You think because I'm a little lighter than you, that I'm going to stick-it to every woman who is lighter than you. You don't have no proof of that, just useless gossip."

Van walked around in the spacious-plush-blue-carpeted front room wringing his hands. The electric lights of the chandelier in the ceiling flickered, the storm was directly overhead and the lightning struck nearby. Van walked over to the end chair where Cora sat.

"Honey, why can't you just believe me when I say, you are the only woman for me." He knelt down before his whining wife, who had tears easing down her light-brown cheeks. "I love you now just as much as I've always loved you. But I know you don't believe that."

"Van, I can't trust you light-skinned men 'round them hot-yellar gals. It's just a bad combination. When y'all get together, in the same place, alone, somethin' is fixin' to happen. The lighter they is, the quicker they go seduce y'all. Y' know that's true, Van."

"Cora, I can see it ain't no use in arguing with you about this. You can believe what you want to. I know it's no use in arguing with you when you've already made up your mind on something. You think you're always right no matter what."

Van walked past their green Sofa and Loveseat, and headed on out the front door. The lightning lit up the horizon. He walked northeast towards the Garland's Farm that was within hollering distance of his house.

Mrs. Cooper stood in the doorway in a pink frilly housecoat. She watched her husband go around the bend in between lightning flashes. Big teardrops ran races down her wrinkling cheeks. She was thinking: *If I ever caught that man in the arms of a high-yellar gal, I'd kill 'er.* "God Help Me!" she prayed.

A large brilliant streak of lightning caused the darkness to fade away, turning it into the likeness of the middle of a sunny day. The loud thunder peal that followed the lightning made the ground tremble and quake like during an earthquake. Van thought that this storm was indeed too strange. He paused for a moment, thinking: *I better get my butt back to the house 'til God is through with His work out here.*

Van ran back to his front door. He rushed inside his home. Mrs. Cooper ran to him, grabbed him, and draped her arms all around him. *"God has a strange way of working things out. But He'll perform miracles that way, sometimes,"* Mrs. Cooper whispered. Van melted into her arms; then the lights were knocked out by a lightning strike.

Mabel looked out of the curtain-less windows of the shanty and the lightning flashed so brilliantly it amazed her. The loud thunder peals that followed the lightning made her very nervous. Big boom after big boom made the shanty vibrate and shake. She had never seen anything like that in her life. It was pitch-black outside.

Before Mabel could return to the bed to lie down beside her baby, a huge streak of lightning of unusual brilliance and size that seemed to have Seven Prongs lit up the sky all the way to the ground. It lasted for a split second or two longer than all of the other flashes Mabel had seen so far that afternoon. On the way to the ground, the lightning streak had changed colors from red to blue, and then to purple before it slammed into the ground. When it hit the ground it sounded to Mabel like planks slamming together, making a loud cracking noise. Mabel thought that it must've hit somewhere nearby.

The thunder following that lightning strike was earsplitting for a minute or two, causing the ground and the shanty to shake violently. The loud booming of the thunder hurt Mabel's ears a little. That was very scary to her. The wind blew ferociously sounding like wolves howling. That was down-right frightening. What was even more frightening was that the storm seemed to just hang overhead up above the shanty. To Mabel, it seemed like the terrible storm was just surrounding the shanty. The flooring in the shanty was trembling like a scared dog. Mabel was almost ready to cry. She picked up Lil' William to hold him to her bosom for protection. A strange thing happened then.

He had been sound asleep on the tick. He was still asleep when Mabel picked him up. Another Seven-Pronged Streak of Lightning touched the earth as before; only, this one struck very close to the shanty. William's eyes opened wide. An old Oak tree near the shanty was split from the top down. Another flash of lightning made it possible for Mabel to see the damage the lightning had done to the old tree.

Mabel's heart pounded rapidly. She feared that the lightning may have struck the top of the shanty, and because the walls of it were sealed up inside with discarded cardboard boxes used instead of sheetrock, and covered over with the pasted pages of old newspapers, Mabel thought she might have to make a run for it. She knew that the shanty would burn down in a matter of minutes. It was pitch-black outside and in the room where Mabel stood holding her baby. Her fear eased somewhat when she did not smell any smoke, or anything burning. She looked down at William for a moment.

The child in her arms had some kind of a bright-light glowing all around him. He seemed to be smiling and staring up at the ceiling. Mabel didn't know what else to do, so she laid her baby down on the tick. Lil' William fell back asleep before she had a chance to feed him. Mabel wondered: *What in the world is going on? That's the strangest storm I done ever seen.* Then she noticed that glow had gone away from around her baby when she looked at him. Mabel had to wonder if she had just imagined all that.

Then the rain came down torrentially, like a thing maddened. The wind got mixed in it, and the drought was over. Now the shanty shook from the force of the wind and rain. The usual leaks from the roof went tick-tick-ticking along like the beat of a snare drum. *I think God's trying to tell us something in this storm. It's just too strange,* Mabel thought.

She threw on an old baggy dress she had worn while pregnant. She still wobbled when she walked, but made her way to an adjacent room where Agnes was seated on an old rocking chair, smoking a pipe full of "Mickey Twist" tobacco. The pungent odor of the tobacco permeated throughout the shanty. Mabel hated the smell of it. She was excited, and thought she had something important to tell her Mother.

"Momma, I think there's somethin' or Someone, Spiritual in that storm. I don't know what it was trying ta tell us, but I b'lieves the Good Lord was speaking through that storm," Mabel exclaimed. "Maybe, God Almighty His-Self was walkin 'round in that storm.

"It probably got somethin' to do with William in there, Momma. When the lightning struck and hit that o' tree out yonder, my baby got a glow all 'round 'im. That's got to be a Sign from God. Momma, do you think that God done come and Bless my little baby for some special reason?" Mabel said. She smiled from ear-to-ear.

Agnes laid her pipe on an old dresser. She blew out a puff of smoke.

"Now that the lightning done gone, get-a match and light that lamp on the dresser, Mabel."

Mabel obeyed her Mother.

"Lemme tell ya something I want'cha ta listen too, child." Agnes rubbed her belly, her baby kicked and stretched so hard, it made her belly seem like a ball was rolling around inside her. "You oughtn't wish all that on no child. If God want 'im, let God choose 'im. The world go hate any child chosen by God. Do you wanna wish that on a 'Negro.' We's already cursed from the 'Days of Cain.' Y' know, the peoples tried to kill the Lord from the day he's born. Do ya wanna wish all that on your baby? Now, don't get me wrong. I b' lieves in God, aw-ight."

Mabel didn't know what to say, so she said nothing. She hung her head and wobbled on back to her baby. She laid down beside her son. She thought about what her Mother had said. She wondered could her Momma be right? She got up and took off her dress and put on a thin gown Mrs. Cooper had left for her. It was hot as hell, and the rain made it even hotter. The air was thick enough to cut with a knife.

Mabel concluded that there may be some truth to what Agnes had said. But if God wanted to make something outta her son, she would not try to stand in His way. She wanted William to have a much better life than she had. William woke up screaming from hunger.

Mabel cuddled her son, and breast-fed him. While William nursed her, Mabel whispered: "Billy, Momma's go make sure you don't see day after day of hunger, like I had to go through. I 'ma make sure that you get nice clothes and things. I 'ma put you through school. I'll work my fingers to the bone so you will have ev' thing ya needs. Yes, Momma will."

William looked up at his Mother after he'd drunk his fill of her milk. While she spoke to him, he smiled like he understood her. She burped him. A little milk came up and spilled onto Mabel's shoulder. Lil' Billy closed his eyes and went right back to sleep.

Mabel wept a little at the fact that God had given her such a beautiful baby. She changed his diaper and put the soiled diaper in a bucket to be washed in the morning. She was so grateful, she prayed: "Thank you Lord for such a sweet-little baby. I promise you I will do my best to raise this child up the right way." Then, she noticed that the rain was slowing down. The wind ceased, and the humidity started clearing up. Right away it got a lot cooler. She put her baby down on the tick. Then she heard heavy footsteps coming towards her room. A little fear crept up from her stomach. She was thinking: *Momma only walks like that when she's mad as hell 'bout somethin' ar' nother.*

Agnes came into Mabel's room carrying a lit kerosene lamp. She sat that on a little table in the comer of the room. It was the only thing resembling furniture-other than the bed-in the room. The look on Agnes's face was almost scary to Mabel. That look aggravated Mabel. With her hands on her hips, Agnes verbally lit into Mabel.

"Mabel, I gotta thing or two to say to you, gal." Agnes said. She paused for a minute. "I raised you chillun the best way I could. I had to beg, steal, and take abuse from dirty old mens, so that I would be able to keep food in y'all's stomachs. I did whatever it took to allow y'all a chance to grow up. Y'all who is grown, you gotta go out on ya own. Mabel, I'm gettin' tired, yes indeed, young lady." Agnes grew more nervous with every word she spoke.

"Mabel. Little gal. It's time for y'all who is having babies to carry your own weight. I got Dora's boys here. She's' pose ta be helping out, but she don't never send nothin' toll for them boys. It's all on me. Seems like I'm still begging, borrowing, and whatnot to keep food on the table for ev' body. You know that better 'n anybody. I can't go on like this. I gotta get more help from y'all than I'm gettin'." Tears ran down Agnes's cheeks.

She stood in the middle of the room facing Mabel. Mabel's eyes focused on her baby. She did not look directly at her Mother, because: The words Agnes spoke were *The Cutting Double Edge Sword of Truth.*

"Mabel, here's what I'm go do: I'm go only take in your baby, William, there, if you pays me for his upkeep. I ain't gettin' no younger. You gals of mine, y'all 's 'bout-ta fill my house up with Grand-chill 'ren. Y'all's go worry me to death. You go have to work is all. You go have to put food and whatnot here for your son, Mabel. Now, that's what I'm go do. You gotta make up your mind 'bout what you go do."

The truth cut deep into Mabel's heart. Like always, it made the hearer of it, *Madder Than Hell!* Mabel's eyes grew wide into the likeness of dotted pool ques. Her lips got ashy. Her voice came out in a shrill tremolo. "Momma, you let Dora drop three babies in this house, and I ain't never heard you fuss 'bout that. Mary, your spoilt-little-pet, done got rid of six babies. She done buried two of them right in the backyard out yonder. You didn't fuss 'bout that, neither.

"Frances's serving-it-ta boys 'round here, an' don't tell me ya don't know 'bout that. You ought ta be able to tell that by the way she smells when she comes home a lotta times; and, even, Ginia, ain' no virgin. Now, Momma, what 'cha go do 'bout all that since you so ready to jump on me?" There's *That Double-Edged Sword, again. It will cut both ways: going and coming.*

Agnes paced around the room like a chicken looking for a worm. She anxiously wrung her hands, and her eyes became blood-red. "Don't ya even mention Ginia, Mabel. She and Frances, they 's my gals. Let me worry 'bout 'em! You need ta look out for yourself. I see you didn't do no better 'neither one of them, now. No matter what they's doin', they didn't drop no baby on me to feed, now!" Agnes said. Her words came out like shotgun blasts.

"Well-don't ya worry 'bout me, Momma. I was a virgin when I gave it up to Henry. He's the only man that's been 'tween my legs. I wouldn't let the men 'round here even feel me up. Henry's my baby's Daddy. I go make him take care of his child. I'm go do that, hear? I'm go do that!"

Mabel sobbed. Her words came out in rapid succession. "I'll be glad to get a job to help support Lil' Billy. I ain't like Dora 'nem. I never was. But ... I gotta ask you this one thing, Momma. Why is it that you don't love me and George as much as you love the rest-a your chill'ren"?

That question stopped Agnes from pacing around in the room. She stood still trembling like she had been slapped.

"Ah-h-h, Mabel. Ah-h-h, Lord! You done stabbed me in the heart, child. I love all y'all the same. I suffered for all-a y'all. I stayed with y'all 'til you 's grown. I didn't lose none-a y'all. I didn't leave none-a y'all with nobody else to raise. Why ya sayin' I didn't do the same towards you an' George, baby? It ain't true." Agnes's trembling increased.

"Momma, that's how I felt-and I know, George felt it too. You wouldn't even tell us who our Daddy is. Ev' one-a your chill 'ren knows who they Daddy is, 'cept me an' George. Least ya could do that for us, Momma ..."

It was as though Agnes had not heard that last statement. Her face took on an angry fierceness. "As soon as your child is old enough to wean, Mabel, you's go leave here an' get a job in Rich-men, Peter-burg, or Charles-ville. I don't care where. You's so womanish an' sassy, an' think yourself 's so smart. Let's see if you can make it on your own. I had to do that the hardest way. Now you go have-ta find out what that's all 'bout. I ain't never had-a child sass me like you do. You little sassy wench! Now, I'm through wit' it! You hear me, Mabel?"

"Yeah, Momma, I do; and, just as soon as I can, I 'ma do what ya just said. I hope you heard that!" After Mabel yelled at her disgruntled Mother, she sit down on her bed, picked up Billy and nursed him.

Agnes rushed into an adjacent room of the shanty where she slept. Instead of going to bed, she went over to a comer of the room and balled up in it. She anxiously wrung her hands with her eyes closed shut. "Damn it . . . I'm stuck with taking care-a Dora's boys. Julius is still home eating at my table. I got three girls and three boys of my own to care for. I'm pregnant, go have my baby fore long. Iain' go ask Clemmon to feed nobody else's baby. Let Henry James take care of his own child. Billy is his'n, looks just like Unc' Charlie James his Granddaddy. Let them take care of Billy. I can't afford to take care-a no more babies in this house."

Agnes's eyes rolled back up into her head. Her body jerked back and forth in a nervous fit. She made noises like birds chirping. She got up out of the corner and laid across her tick. Her body went into a fit of convulsive trembling. She made noises like someone speaking in tongues (glossolalia). Her children were used to her lapsing into fits like that so they tried to ignore her when she did. This time her fit lasted/or about two hours, an hour and a-half longer than usual.

Mabel was too nervous to sleep. She knew that her Mother was in her room "nutting-up." She felt partially responsible for exciting her that much. But she felt too, that the truth had to be told.

Mabel placed Billy on her shoulder and patted him gently. He burped. She tried to whisper to her baby in a soft soothing voice, but her voice quivered from anger and disgust. Her guts boiled from rage and agitation. She kissed Billy and intoned:

"I'll show Momma, Mrs. Hothead, Agnes Mickens. I tried to be a good gal. I kept myself pure too, 'til your Daddy came along." She smiled mischievously. "I gave him my Cherry. That's how we ended up with you.

"I stole your Daddy from Momma. She had stolen him from your Aunt Mary. He put Mary down after she got rid-a his baby. Your Daddy's sure funny 'bout women gettin' rid-a they babies. Most-a the mens round here wouldn't care at all 'bout no baby, if they wasn't married to the baby's Momma. A gal could get rid-a one all she wanted to. Not Henry. Your Daddy's a strange one, Billy-yes he is."

Billy was fast asleep. Mabel laid him on the tick. She got lost in her thoughts. Her mind rehashed the past:

I can remember the day, as though it was yesstiddy. I knew that when O' Henry came to sneak 'round with Momma, he'd hide his jar of liquor, he always brought with him, in a stump near the riverbank. I saw him stick his quart jar of bootleg in a stump just off the spring path. It was an old Pine stump 'tween two Black Oaks. For some reason him doing that reminded me of something else-an' I got real hot in the middle.

I watched that pretty man standing there by a big old Walnut tree, then he leaned up against a Pine tree, and pee-peed I saw what Momma and Mary was crazy 'bout. It was so nice, 'specially when he shook it. I couldn't stand it no more. I'd been watching this man for a long time.

I'd never wanted to do nothin' with-a man like I wanted to do with this one. I remembered how he an' Momma went at it all up into the night. That made me so hot for him.

I got hotter when I'd seen 'im sneakin 'a look at me, checkin 'out my butt an' tits. I didn 't let on at first, but I was longing for the day when I would offer 'im what he's sneakin' a look at.

So that day came: I was out at the spring when he came to get a swig of his bootleg. He started up the shortcut through the woods. I got on that path up the hill ahead of him. I waited 'til he was pret 'near me. He saw me. He stopped I knew that I had his attention. I squatted down and made pretend I was go pee. With my panties down to my ankles, I knew he could see ev' thing. I smiled from ear-to-ear. A fat lump showed up in the crotch of his pants. At first he just stared at me. I thought he was go not do nothin'. Tears came to my eyes. A nervous look came over his handsome face. He grabbed down there 'tween his legs like he was making sure it was still there. He squeezed himself down there. I was so glad to see him smile at me. I stood up, and stepped out of my panties. He came to me slowly grinning like a sly fox.

"*Gal, what in the world you's doing? Round me, you might get hurt or somethin' if ya ain't careful,*" *he whispered*

"*I want ya to give-it-ta-me. I know it's go hurt, but I want it anyway. I been watchin' ya for a long time, an' I want to be with you. I wanna be your woman, an' I ain' married-ta nobody.*

You won't have-ta sneak 'round to see me, "*I almost shouted I wanted this man so bad*

"*Sugar, you's so young. I might hurt you too bad I don't wanna do that, now,*" *he said, moving closer and closer to me. He had a little deceitful smile on his good-looking face. He grabbed me and stuck his tongue in my mouth. That thrilled me all over. He pulled my dress up over my head, and I helped him take it completely off me. He laid my dress on the leaves, and planted me on top of that primitive bed*

He got on top of me and started to slowly grind until he got it in me. I felt searing pain. But I didn't want him to stop. He was gentle. He put his tongue in my ear. He put my breasts in his mouth an' kissed them. Soon the pain gave way to pleasure. Then it was pleasure-pleasure-and more pleasure. My body quivered as I had my first orgasm. I hadn't ever felt anything like that in my life. His kissing my whole face an' my breasts, made me feel so good He put his tongue far back into my mouth. He groaned! felt a hot-sticky spurt of fluid that came out of him, an' it warmed up my whole body. Oh, it felt so damn good! He did that a couple of times.

When he rolled off me, he smiled and said, "*I didn't think you was a virgin, Mabel. That's the best loving I done ever had I'm go always remember this. You done give me somethin' that's more precious than gold*"

What he said made me feel so damn good all over again. He kissed me long and hard I searched his mouth with my tongue, and he did the same back to me. I felt like I could-a clung to that man forever. Then Henry said something I had to wonder about:

"*Mabel, for now, you let what we just done be our little secret. Then we can do this again. If it gets out, I'll have-ta stop. Aw-ight?*"

I didn't know what else to say, so I said somethin' very stupid: "*Henry, am I just as much woman as Momma or Mary?*" *I wanted this man all to myself. I wanted him to keep on doing what he 'd just done forever. I didn't want to share him with Momma or nobody anymore.*

"*Mabel, honey, you's a whole lot more than either one-a 'em,*" *he said*

I watched him pull up his black riding britches. He stuffed his white long-sleeved-shirt down inside of them, to make sure he looked as sharp as possible. He checked his high-top brown riding boots. They were still shining like a new penny. His slicked-back hair had gotten a little out of place, but a couple of hard swipes with his hands slicked it back into place. That man looked good!

I watched the love of my life go get a swig of his liquor. Then I heard Momma call: "Mabel, where you at, gal? You must've had-ta drill a well or somethin'. Bring that water on up here to the house, we gotta cook supper." I scooped up my dress, put it back on, and hugged myself. I was singing to myself: "I got me a man today. I became a real woman; and, don't nobody know 'bout it, neither!"

Nine months later, ev' body knew what I'd done. It showed in my gut. It is why I'm a new Mother of Lil' Billy in there.

I heard that Henry bragged all over Cumberland and Fluvanna that he's some Big-o-stud! He's so proud of the fact that he had been with a Mother and two of her Daughters, all living under the same roof. I wonder how proud he'll be of this beautiful baby son I done had for him? I really wonder if he 'll ever come to see 'bout Billy, or me?

I wonder, too, how it would've felt being hugged by my own Daddy?

PART II

---

*And Charlie Begat Henry
And Henry Begat*

CHAPTER FOUR

"I sure hope Mabel don't get stuck in the mud on her way up the road today," Agnes whined. "Boy, it's rainin' cats an' dogs out yonder, yes Lord!"

"Yeah. You's right, now, Momma," Virginia agreed with Agnes. "Momma, by the way, where's Mabel's little Sambo, hiding at?" Virginia went from room to room looking under every tick in the house, calling out: "Billy. Billy. Billy, where you at, boy? Billy . . . That little Tyke can't be found, Momma. You seen 'im?"

Virginia and Agnes stopped in the middle of the kitchen. "Ginia, I bet 'cha he done gone out in all that rain. He's probably muddy as hell by now. Gal, get somethin' ar' nother on right quick an' go out yonder and find that child fore Mabel gets up here," Agnes shouted.

Virginia frowned and stomped the floor. "It's too wet out yonder, Momma."

"Go on, Ginia. I 'on kno' what Mabel liable do if she finds Billy out yonder playin' in all that rain and mud. Y' know how crazy she is 'bout that child?"

"Yessiree, I do. I don't get it, neither. You'd think she done had-a high-yellar baby, the way she's carryin' on 'bout that little-bitty Blackie of her 'n," Virginia said.

Agnes chuckled. "She thinks that little rascal's a Special Gift from God, or somethin'. She much as said so on the night she had him. I tried-ta put 'er straight 'bout that, but I didn't do no good. She's still goin' on an' on 'bout makin' somethin' outta Billy."

Agnes got her old corncob pipe out of her pocket. She broke off a piece of Mickey Twist from off a little shelf in the kitchen. She stuffed the tobacco into the bowl of her pipe, got a match, struck it against the old table in the middle of the kitchen, and the shanty filled up with the putrid smell Mickey Twist's smoke gave off. "Go on, Ginia," Agnes said, out through one side of her mouth, holding the stem of the pipe in the other side, "find Billy."

Ginia got an old sheet and wrapped that around herself. She got ready to head out the backdoor into the pouring rain. Then-

"Hello-o-o," Mabel called out in a cheerful voice at the front door.

It was too late for Ginia to go find Billy, now. Mabel was at the door, and the worst would have to follow. Ginia threw the old sheet to the floor. She got a little sheepish grin on her face.

Mabel knocked on the front door. "Hey, y'all in there, c' mon-1 got two soak 'n wet bags out here. Open the door fore I lose ev' thin' in 'em out here on the porch," Mabel said, a lot less cheerful than at first.

The rain had soaked through the two paper shopping-bags, it was a good thing she had gotten the store-baggers to double bag her merchandise in Richmond. It was raining even harder after Mabel stepped into the shanty. What was absent was her son rushing to her yelling: "Momma, Momma, what 'cha bring me?" before he jumped into her arms. She looked around for him. "Billy, Billy, where you at, son?" she called. No answer.

Mabel dropped the bags she held in both her arms to the floor. Her smile quickly became a snarl. An angry frown spread across her face after she saw Agnes rushing out the backdoor into the rain. She knew it could only mean one thing: *Billy was out in all that rain playin' or somethin'.*

In an instant, Agnes burst through the backdoor carrying Billy in her arms. She gave a little nervous laugh. "I 'ma have-ta wash this Lil' Rascal. Mabel, he done got all wet. Y' know how little boys love-ta get wet an' muddy." She said that like it was just an everyday thing.

She sat Billy down in a corner of the kitchen. She stoked the fire in the cooking stove. She went out and came back with a ten-gallon bucket of rainwater she had gotten out of the rain barrel behind the shanty. She poured the water into a galvanized washtub, set that on the back of the stove, and just stared at the floor. She didn't dare look at Mabel, eye-to-eye.

Mabel had finished picking up the contents she had in her shopping bags that had scattered on the kitchen floor when she dropped the bags.

She put the new clothes and toys she had purchased for her son, along with a couple of chickens, a head of cabbage, and some canned goods, on top of the old hand-me-down dining-room table that had been covered with a flowery print oil-tablecloth. She stood with her hands on her hips, patting her left foot. She blew a little air out of her mouth before speaking. Then Billy spied his Mother.

Billy leapt up and ran to Mabel. "Hi Momma! Hi! What' cha bring me?" He jumped into his Mother's arms. She hugged him tightly. She put him back down. Mabel refocused now on her Mother.

It was apparent to Mabel that: *My son's been out yonder playin' in all that rain an' mudan' nobody's been lookin' out for 'im! He could-a got in the branch and drowned! Could-a fell in one-a the old stump holes in the backyard an' broke his little neck. Nobody would-a knowed 'bout it! What's the matter with these bitches 'round here? Don't they know that a child can't look out for his-self?*

Her anger came gushing out of her: "Momma! Ginia! Franny! Y'all ain' from shit! Lemme tell ya." She started walking around in the kitchen shaking her head and waving her left hand at each of the women she was laying-out. "While I'm down in Rich-men scrubbin' floors, and gettin' treated like a damn slave by o' nasty White folk, y' all's up here treatin' Lil' Billy like-a puppy or somethin'!"

Guilt made Agnes, Ginia, and Franny to-at first-just stand there and take what Mabel said. "Don't tell-me, y'all been lookin' out for William. He's skinnier than an alley cat. Have ya been feeding 'im the food I leaves for 'im?" Mabel screamed. "What in the hell is the matter with y'all?"

The women Mabel yelled at in the kitchen stood like wooden statues. Mabel continued to yell at them. "I get up here today, Friday, it's rainin' like hell out yonder," she points towards the kitchen windows, "an' Billy's up to mud to his ears, and now, ya go just give 'im a little bath, an' all's go be well an' good-huh? Is that what y' all's thinkin'?" Mabel was almost crying.

"Well-it ain't never hurt you, gal!" shot out of Agnes's mouth. "You played out in that yard, got muddy, dried off, an' went on 'bout ya bizzness, Ya turned out aw-ight! You didn't catch no pneumonia. Mabel you's just actin' stupid over Lil' Billy, like ya have since that child was born," Agnes snapped at Mabel.

"I 'ma take my baby 'way from over here. I can see y'all don't give-a-damn 'bout 'im! Iain' lettin' y'all put Lil' Billy in no early grave. No-sir-reel" Mabel was so angry she spat out her words. Tears came streaming down her cheeks. She remembered her little Nephew, Charlie. She didn't want Billy to end up like that.

"See if l care, Mabel," Agnes quipped. "If ya wanna take Billy with ya when ya leaves today, go on. Leroy's the only baby I got ;round here. He's the one rm most worried 'bout. His Daddy, Clemmon go take care-a him. You let-a man get ya pregnant, but ya ain't woman enough-ta make 'im care for the baby he put in your belly. You ought-ta not be yellin' at me! You go find Henry James an' start yellin' at him. He's your problem, not us."

The words coming out of Agnes's mouth cut to Mabel's heart. Her tears ran down her face.

She stood looking at her Mother, eye-to-eye.

"You an' Dora, y'all 'spects me-ta raise y'all's chillun. I done told ya, I can't do it all by myself So, Mabel, you might as well stop yellin' an' sassin' me like you's doin' fore I put you an' your baby outta here. I don't have-ta take your sass no more. Mabel, I ain't gotta put up with your shit! You hear me?" Agnes trembled all over. Rage danced in her eyes.

Mabel couldn't look her Mother in the eye any longer. But she managed to say, "This is some real stupid shit. My own Momma talking 'bout puttin' me an' her own Grandchild out in the damn rain. That sure show me a lot, Momma, yeah! What that says is you don't give-a damn 'bout me or him. That's what all this shit tells me, Momma!"

Mabel and Agnes stood facing each other, both were nervous and trembling all over and staring one another to death. Mabel's rage had helped her overcome her guilt.

Franny ran over, got between Mabel and Agnes. She got up in Mabel's face. "Mabel, Mabel, you stop cussin' at Momma. You just leave 'er alone, now! If ya don't like the way she's treatin' your Lil' Blackie Son, take 'im on back with you to Rich-men when ya get outta this house today," she screamed.

Mabel was amazed at Frances. Never before had she been so bold as to jump up in her face like that. Mabel had beat her little butt enough to let her know better than to overstep her sibling bounds.

Frances stuck her finger up in Mabel's face. "Y' know, Ginia," Frances yelled, "I likes Stevo, Cousin Maude's little boy. He's almost White, least, his Daddy's a Whiteman. She done had a pretty baby an' ev'body says so. Nobody says that 'bout that little Tar Baby you done had, Mabel. What' cha think 'bout that, Miss Sassy Mabel Lou?"

What flashed through Mabel's mind like lightning was: *Not only is she insulting me, she's mocking God's Gift to me, my precious little Son. How dare her!*

Mabel rushed over to Frances and in one quick motion slapped her younger Sister in the mouth with enough force to knock her down to the floor. Frances jumped up off the floor. She ran screaming out of the kitchen like she might die any moment. Her mouth was bloodied. But the ordeal mostly hurt her pride.

Ginia backed away into a corner of the kitchen. She was smaller than Frances and didn't know what a lick like that from her older Sister might do to her.

Agnes ran over to Mabel. She grabbed Mabel by both hands. "Don't ya never hit one-a my chillun, again, Miss Sassy Pants. I 'on kno' what 'cha think ya go get 'round here. Cause you gone out to work, it don't give ya no right to come back in here an' hit nobody, Mabel. Have you lost your natural mind, gal?" Agnes shouted.

"You didn't hear Frances throwin' Maude's high-yellar mistake up in my face? You didn't hear what she said 'bout my Lil' Billy? You should-a been the one slapping 'er. She's using your half-White Nephew to mock your own Grandson, an' that's aw-ight with you?"

"I'm son-y 'bout what Franny said. But I don't want ya to whip no child of mine. If it go be any whippin' I'm go do it. Now, I want ya to go say you's son-y to Franny," Agnes said.

"When hell freezes over, Momma. If anything, Franny owes me a beg pardon. I don't owe her nothin'." Agnes released Mabel's hands. Mabel called out to Frances: "Franny 'Ree, come in here, gal. I gotta say somethin' to you. Aw-aight?"

Frances eased back into the kitchen towards Mabel. She was expecting an apology.

"Look Frances," said Mabel in a somewhat calmer voice, now, "lemme tell ya somethin', an' see if you still think light skin is somethin' to be so proud of." Mabel walked over to Frances.

Ginia came over and sat at the table. Then Frances sat beside her. Agnes stood over near the stove, and Mabel stood at the head of the table.

"Maude, Stevo's Momma, is dark-skinned as can be. She got pregnant by some Whiteman she won't name-it wouldn't matter no way. Maude had a very high-yellar child." Mabel walked away from the table and paused for a moment to get her thoughts together.

"Y'know Aunt Neddy had Phyllis, an' that was a poor example she set for her Daughters. Phyllis an' Stevo's Daddies were them O' Woods mens. Phyllis is almost White too. Cousin Maude an' Catherine, Neddy's Black Daughters, she had with Uncle William Archer, they's very dark-skinned like our Grandma Daisy, an' Uncle Gus. But Uncle John an' Momma is very light skinned."

Frances started to get a little squirmy, but listened to Mabel for the moment. She kept her head hung down. Sadness spread over her face, it had come up out of the depth of her young soul. Mabel saw her younger Sisters fidgeting around a little and decided to get right to it.

"Frances an' Ginia: you's brown-skinned, but most of us we's Black. Maybe that's cause Grandma Daisy got raped by one-a them old Woods. She was a cook in they Big House on a Farm in Farmville. Cause-a that, we all gotta be kin to them Crackers. But we ain' gotta be proud-a it. We don't have-ta hate one nother cause we don't show by the color of our skin that we came from some Cracker raping one-a our Grand Elders.

"I heard Great Grandma Rosa say, 'We all came from off that O' Woods Plantation over yonder near Farmville.' That's where Momma 'nem an' Grandma Daisy got their last name, 'Woods' from, fore some-a them got married to Archers, an' Scotts, an' whatnot."

Frances got a little frown on her face, as Mabel continued.

"White mens done messed up our blood so bad in slavery, 'til nowadays Negroes should never worry 'bout skin color. We ought-ta 'cept ev' body the same no matter how dark they be. But a lotta Negroes, they's stuck on light-skinned peoples. I don't want none-a that growin' up in Lil' Billy." When she said that, Mabel took a hard look at Agnes.

"Mabel, how did ya learn all 'bout what ya just said?" Agnes asked. Her eyes were getting a little bit moist. A tear eased down her cheeks. Before Mabel could answer, Agnes allowed:

"Yeah, I know what it feels like to be some Whiteman's gal. That's what I was for a time for one-a them O' Woods men. It is the onliest time in my life that I felt like a slump-down who'e," Agnes whined.

"Momma, ain' nobody gonna blame you for doin' whatever ya had-ta do to help your chillun stay alive. Any lower animal would-a done the same thing. But we can all do better an' y'all know what I mean. I met this lady in Rich-men, who's a Maid like me, but she reads a lotta books. She talks-ta me all the time an' I listen. She's teachin' me how to read. I talk to a lotta people from Fluvanna and Cumberland who works in Rich-men. We talk on the bus ride up here, an' back. They told me a lotta stuff 'bout what done happen to us 'round here."

Mabel took off her black and white Maid's uniform. She stripped down to her full under slip to keep her uniform from getting too dirty. She went outside carrying the bucket to get a little of the rainwater out of the rain barrel to cool the hot water in the washtub. She took the washtub off the stove and placed it on the floor. She got on her knees and gave Billy a nice warm bath. He was almost asleep before she could finish cleaning him. She took her son to the boys' room and put him to rest on one of the ticks in there. He had on nice-new night clothes.

Mabel got back into her uniform. "I'm ready to go, but y'all take care-a my baby. I don't wanna never catch 'im out in the rain an' mud no more."

Neither Ginia, Frances nor, Agnes said a word. Ginia went into one of the backrooms of the shanty. Frances came to help Agnes get the chickens ready for frying. It was time to cook supper. "Mabel we go have a social next week, aw-ight?"

"Yes Momma," Mabel said. She noticed that the rain had stopped. As she walked down the path that led to the bus stop in Columbia beside Thurston's Grocery Store, Mabel thought: *I hope things do get better, or least, different fore I get back to see Lil' Billy again. I swear I do.*

Mabel got up to the corner near Thurston's Grocery and stood at the Stop Sign where the Greyhound Local picked up passengers headed to Richmond.

She was a few minutes early and was out of breath, even though the bus stop is only a mile and a-half from Agnes's shanty. She had time to reflect on the place where she worked:

I hate workin' as a live-in Maid That Mr. Joseph Phillip Gault and his wife, Mrs. Sarah Ruth Gault, have near 'bout worked me to death. They all got money, them Gaults, cause they owns a Bank, but won't hire enough help. So we few Maids gotta work like hunting dogs for Mr. Gault's gut-fat wife, an' her highfalutin fat friends. Those old windbags she's always got over in her parlor is always drinkin' tea, coffee, an' high-priced liquor, an' eating tray-after-tray of them finger-sandwiches. Don't make no sense, neither. That's all them fat heifers ever do. Like a slave, I ain't got but a little time of my own. Gotta slip up here for a little while on Friday evenings, an' be back fore Mrs. Gault misses me. Just a cup' la hours every week is all I get to spend with my baby son. She'd probably fire me ifi'n she knew I had a child.

The noise of the bus's diesel engine interrupted Mabel's thoughts. The bus doors swung open. Mabel fumbled in her pockets to find the sixty cents fee. She went up the steps of the bus, paid the driver, then headed to the back of the bus. She seated her-self in the very backseat of the bus. There was no way she'd have to move or give up her seat sitting back there. One of the last things Agnes had said was, "We's go have a social next week."

Wish I could be home next week for the whole night. I'd like to see ev' body havin' a good time. Maybe, I would get Henry acquainted with his son. A Daddy's somethin' I been deprived of I don't want that to happen to my son. Iain' never got to know my Daddy. I got to make sure Henry knows his Lil' son. ...

Mabel dozed on off to sleep. The noise of the diesel engine had its usual effect on her.

CHAPTER FIVE

Henry and Charlie, Jr. hurriedly got dressed in their new suits. Each of them sported a pair of alligator shoes that they had shined so bright they could clearly see their reflections in their shoes. These young men strutted around in front of their admiring Mother, called A' nt Maetta by all who knew her (but her name was actually Mary Etta), putting on airs like two barnyard roosters. Charlie, Jr. had not long been discharged from the A1my. He had paid for the fancy clothes he and his older Brother were sporting. He wanted them to be the best dressed homeys in West Bottom. They had gone to Bradford Clothing Store in Dillwyn and bought matching Double-Breasted, black-and-white pinstriped Suits, beige Stetson Hats with red-silk bands, and silky-white Van Heusen Shirts. They even got white-silk Socks, and red-white-and-blue striped ties. On this evening both young men thought they were *"country-boy"* sharp. Lil' Charlie had spent a sizeable amount of his discharge money to make sure they were *"dressed to pull the gals at the party that night."*

A'nt Maetta, a light-brown-skinned woman, the color of brown sugar, weighed around three hundred pounds on a five-foot frame. She had a relatively pretty face and was a little past middle age. For her age, she was thought by many to be very pretty although she was a little plump. The hard work she had been forced to do all of her life had taken a toll on her physique and appearance. She walked with a limp, and often complained of a recurrent stiffness in her left leg. Her wrinkled hands looked older than the rest of her. That no doubt came from her daily milking several cows and plucking corn from cobs by hand to feed the cattle. Her limping might have come from her having to walk up and down tobacco rows hoeing for days on end and then coming home to cook and clean her own home 'til her children were old enough to help out.

Tears formed in the corners of her eyes for seemingly no apparent reason, but those who knew A'nt Maetta knew that her hard life manifested itself in her slow-silent weeping, as were the case for many women like her in West Bottom. Deep folds meandered across her brow that came from her continued frowning at the inescapable austere circumstances surrounding her life from day one.

The almost impossible task of having to raise six children practically by herself had taken a grievous toll on A'nt Maetta over the years, and had reduced her striking good-looks to a lot less than beautiful. She had a beautiful smile though, and she expressed that whenever something or someone pleased her.

On this evening, A'nt Maetta, at first, smiled brightly at her strutting handsome Sons, but her smile was followed by a little grimace. She put her hands in the pockets of her red-and-white gingham dress. She slowly walked over to her handsome Sons. First she hugged Henry, her oldest, then Lil' Charlie, her youngest child. A bit of sadness erased the smile off her face. Her watery eyes took on a very tired and worried look. She stood before, *the pride of her life,* her Sons, who were standing in the foyer of the little bungalow house she had raised them in. She was looking up at them, then sweat formed into little beads on her brow.

"Henry, you an' Charlie, Jr. better watch out now." Her voice came out in a slow whine. "Ever time Agnes 'nem throw one-a they parties over yonder in Cumberland somebody get hurt, or somethin'. I 'on kno', boys."

She turned her back to Henry and Lil' Charlie for a moment. They stood like soldiers, but with a sly grin on their clean-shaven nut-brown faces with thin mustaches. Their hair was slicked back with deep waves in the front of their heads-from stiff-grease. A' nt Maetta paused for a second or two to gaze out of the screened-door at the huge Chestnut Oak trees at the top of the hill in front of their home. She closed the brown front door, it was getting dark outside. She came over to stand directly in front of Henry.

"Henry, it ain' nothin' but the evil in them womens over yonder an' the devil that keeps 'em full-a demons that make them gals so nasty an' all over yonder in Cumberland. I wouldn't set foot in none-a they houses. I tell ya, they ain't decent Colored Folk," A'nt Maetta said.

"Ah, Momma, you just don't like Agnes, or none-a her Daughters, that's all," Lil' Charlie said. He got an even slyer grin on his face after he said that. He could have passed as Henry's twin, except that he had a slightly bigger nose than Henry and was around a half-foot taller than his older Brother.

"You sure's right on that score, Charlie, Jr. I sure don't like 'em, I ain't go lie 'bout that. But you can't talk. You let them wretched womens over in Agnes's house throw my Grand boys ta the-dogs. The one what looked like ya Daddy up an' died. James, the other 'n looks just like-ya, but I 'on kno' where that child's at. He could be with his Momma, or Agnes 'nem." A'nt Maetta's light-brown eyes filled with tears. She wiped them on her right arm. Then she focused on Henry.

"Look Henry, I want you to go get my latest Grand Baby from over yonder in Cumberland. Mrs. Cooper told me that little boy is as cute as can be. She say he looks just like his Granddaddy. Son," she paused for a second or two to snuff the tears out of her nostrils, "I wish you'd go over yonder an' get that boy. Bring 'im back here for me to bring up. I'd raise 'im right. Least he'd have a better chance to grow up to be a man. Why won't ya do that, Henry?" she said, raising her voice a little.

"Momma, I don't want no baby taggin' long after me." His response was quick and almost disrespectable. A bit of sass sounded in his voice mixed with some nervousness. "I ain't read ta-get married an' settle down. I sure ain't go marry nay gal from over yonder in Cumberland." He moved away putting some space between his Mother and himself. He knew he was treading on dangerous ground.

"Besides, Momma, I like playin' my guitar an' whatnot too much to wanna set up housekeepin' with any one gal I knows. All-a them loves the way I play, an' love me too much for me to get saddled with one. That's all I'm 'bout over yonder in Cumberland. I don't wanna lose my freedom." He hugged his Mother, who was shaking her head disagreeing with every word that came out of his mouth.

"You ought-ta thought 'bout who you's sleepin' with fore ya got 'er pregnant. It's too late after she done dropped your baby. Ain't no use in talking 'bout ya freedom now," A 'nt Maetta snapped at Henry.

"Momma, Mabel's Billy's Momma. I done been with her Sister, Mary. I done been with their Momma, Agnes. Now, y' know I don't wanna marry into no mess like that. Both Agnes an' Mary's prettier than Mabel. They got lighter skin then her, anyway. I don't wanna get stuck with no dark-skinned gal like Mabel, Momma." Henry's voice quivered a little as he spoke. He gave a little two cents chuckle to cover up the irony of his statement.

"Yeah, I know how you boys feel 'bout them light-skinned gals. But if you gets down low enough ta-sleep with-a gal, it don't make no never-mind how dark her skin was. 'Specially if ya got 'er knocked up. The child's still your baby. You ought-ta take care of it-like the Bible say ya s'pose-ta do. I'm just tryin'-ta tell ya what's right, is all I'm doin'."

"That's why I don't fool with no dark-skinned gals, no more. I'm always afraid somethin' like that might happen an' you might want me to get hitched up with one-a them, Momma," Lil' Charlie said. "Dora's my one an' only mistake. All my gals now is light-skinned as can be."

"Sometimes, you boys sound like rabid dogs, or somethin'. I didn't raise ya ta-be-like that.

But you's terrible 'bout womens." A'nt Maetta just shook her head at Henry and Lil' Charlie.

Henry knew it was time to cheer up his Mother. She seemed so sad after what they had laid on her. He dashed into the room where he and Charlie, Jr. had slept since they were born. He came back holding a Spanish Guitar. It had red and gold markings around its F-Holes. It was a beautiful instrument that sounded as good as a piano. Henry knew how to play that thing, too.

Henry played the music to the Lindy Hop. Lil' Charlie did his version of the dance. He grabbed his Mother by the hand, and she-for the moment-let go of the irony of the moment. She pulled away from her wayward Sons after Lil' Charlie said something she didn't like.

"This ought-ta get me the gals tonight." He laughed out loud, but A'nt Maetta did not find a bit of humor in what he'd said.

"Just don't ya get no more babies that y'all go leave out there in the world. A gal might get carried away listenin' to the music y'all's playin' an' the dances y'all's doin' an' she might be persuaded ta-lift 'er dress for ya. But y'all gotta refuse; aw-ight?" A'nt Maetta was dead serious.

"Yeah, I got'cha, Momma," Henry said. He winked at Lil' Charlie.

"Yeah, I sure is, Momma," Lil' Charlie said. He winked back at Henry. He was laughing, dancing and snapping his fingers as Henry played a low-down Delta Blues riff

The front door of the neatly kept bungalow swung open. In stumbled Charles Edward James, Sr. called Unc' Charlie by just about everyone who knew him. He was very drunk as usual. All five-foot of him stumbled through the door and fell to the floor of the foyer. He got back up, ran his long deep-ebony fingers through his black-naturally-straight hair, he wore in a pompadour, with long sideburns. His facial features actually resembled Caucasians'. He had a long aquiline nose, a flat face with thin lips, grayish-brown eyes, and high cheekbones. Tiny-little ears sat on the side of his head. But his skin was as dark as midnight, and as smooth as velvet. He fell to the floor again and tried to get up. Then he just rolled over and stayed where he had fallen down onto the floor. His very lean, five-foot frame in the gray and gold Zoot Suit, he wore, gave up the struggle to get up; being weighted down by several bottles of cheap liquor.

Unc' Charlie took out a silver watch he had attached to a long-gold-plated Jive Chain, and tried to focus on the face of the watch for a moment-he was trying to be funny-and allowed in very slurred speech: "I b'lieve it's time ta-go-ta-bed." He chuckled in a drunken manner. But no one else saw the humor in what he said.

His Sons just stood back staring at him even though this was a scene they had witnessed many times before. They said nothing, but knew what was about to go down.

"Charlie you ought-ta have brought your drunken ass ta-this house, already. Where have you been, anyway, for the last three days? You been gamblin', whorin' round again-just where ya been at?" A'nt Maetta snapped out of the side of her mouth.

Unc' Charlie rolled over onto his back. He smacked his mouth, and rolled his beady eyes, under very bushy eyebrows, and groaned: "I done been hackin' round, Maetta. Lookin' for some work to do to make a little money like I had-ta do all my life. You just don't trust nobody. Ya don't cut me enough slack, that's what is the matter, Maetta." His speech was very slurred.

"Why ya always on my back?" came out of his mouth sounding like he was chewing up his words.

"It ain't none-a what you's talkin'. It's just that I needed you to be with me down to Columbia today. Had-ta shop all by myself. I don't like to do that nowadays." A'nt Maetta paused while Unc' Charlie tried to get up off the floor again.

"I saw Cora, Bessie an' Cary in Columbia. They all asked 'bout you. They's worried 'bout they Daddy. I had to tell 'em the truth-I hadn't seen ya for days. Cora's minded to go look for ya. But I reminded 'er how you be. You always come back. That's how you is, Charlie."

Henry and Charlie headed on out the door. They knew where the conversation between their parents was going. They had heard it all so many times before, while growing up.

"See ya later, Momma ... Daddy," Henry said.

"We gotta run, y'all," Lil' Charlie said. The young men went out the door and got into a 1947 Four-Door Ford Coupe parked up the hill in front of the house. It was all shiny and new-looking. The exterior of the car was of a purplish-blue color with a red and white interior. Lil' Charlie thought he had gotten a good deal on it at Loco Auto Sales in Fork Union. He only paid three hundred dollars for it. The car was like a huge egg. Its backdoors swung backwards like a bird flapping its wings, and the front doors swung in the opposite direction. Henry opened the backdoor on the passenger side, plumped his guitar in the backseat, and slammed the door shut. He got into the car's front seat and Lil' Charlie cranked it up. He revved up the motor a few times and waited for it to warm up.

Lil' Charlie looked over at his older Brother and allowed: "It's go be hot in there for a few ticks, man; kno' what I mean?"

"Yeah, you got that right, man. Momma an' Daddy gotta go through it ever time Daddy get drunk. You'd think they would-ta got over that mess by now, Bro," Henry said.

"Daddy ain' go never get over nothin' toll, he's clinin' to it like stink on shit," Lil' Charlie said.

Lil' Charlie put the car in gear and gave it the gas. They sped off.

"Maetta, ever since the Depression, I had-ta go out yonder where I could an' squeeze out a little money, a buck or two, the best way I know how;

kno' what I means?" Unc' Charlie sat up and tried to look into the face of his wife who was standing over him.

"Yeah, I . . . bet. I knows all too well what ya means. What I guessing is . . . you's more tryin' to get hold-a butt or two. That's what I b'lieves ya been <loin' Charlie. I know you Zoot Suit wearin' mens. Y'all's dressed for the gals. That's where your boys get it from. Watching they Daddy. Now they's turnin' out just like you, Charlie."

Unc' Charlie got up off the floor then. He took two steps forward and two backward before steadying himself. A'nt Maetta had to catch him. He almost knocked over one of the fancy hand-me-down Kerosene Lamps resting on a little vanity table in the foyer.

"Ah ... watch out, Charlie. Lemme get ya to the bedroom." "Ah, Iain' that drunk. Lemme 'lone, I can walk all by myself"

"Get on in there, then," Maetta said. She pointed one of her nubby fingers at him, balled up her right hand into a fist, but thought better of the situation. She swallowed her anger, and forced a twisted-little smile onto her tired face. She escorted her wobbly husband to a room just left of the front door. It was where they had always slept. Within the room was a hand-me down caste-iron king size bed, a fluffy-padded armchair right next to it-that had seen better days, and a large Warm Morning Heater next to the chair. A couple of wicker rocking chairs sat in the corner of the bedroom flanking a large window with a view of the whole front yard.

Unc' Charlie plumped himself down into the armchair. A' nt Maetta sat in one of the rockers. "Well ... lemme ask ya somethin', Charlie."

"Go head on, shoot."

"Y' know Mrs. Cooper done invited us to come down to Columbia Baptist Church. It's for they First Sunday Services. The Reverend John Jasper Nicholas go be running the revival. That boy done become a Preacher. I knew 'im when he was the biggest Devil in the world."

A'nt Maetta got up from the rocker. Charlie leaned on his elbows to keep himself from falling out of the armchair. He was like a huge rubber band.

"I hope he's as hard a preacher as he was a bloodthirsty Devil. Didn't have no respect for nobody. Even shot at his own Momma one day. Shots just missed her. But he done found The Lord, now. They say he's a prayin' man," A'nt Maetta said.

"I don't b'lieve he's no different nowadays. He just do his thing in the name of the Lord. Them saved people 'll cut ya heart out cook it an' eat it. Them preachers is the worst. Some-a them got babies all over the place. You go into any church an' take a good look 'round. You'll see right off how many chillren look just like the Pastors who got 'im with a lotta the gals who be married to Brothers in those churches. That's why I don't go to no church. I can be a Devil out in the world. I don't wanna be no frustrated Devil.

"I don't b'lieve in it, but I'll go with ya Sunday. Ya just gotta wake me and remind me; aw ight?"

A half-smile came to A'nt Maetta's broad lips. "Well, the Lord say we gotta forgive. So I'm go forgive you since ya go come to the House of Gawd with me. Maybe, you'll get saved, an' stop comin' home smellin' of liquor an' strange gals-yeah, the scent gets on ya an' stays on ya for days. Sometimes, you hurt me so bad, Charlie."

"Save all that testifyin' an' carryin' on for the meetin' tomorrow. I 'ma get ta bed," Unc. Charlie said. He was sobering up a whole lot, now.

He got up and stumbled over to a piss pot sitting in a corner of the bedroom. He spat out a lump of stinky vomit into it. He wiped the drool off his neatly-trimmed beard with a handkerchief He took off his two-toned patent leather shoes, his Zoot Suit came off next, and then he was dressed down to his shorts. He fell across the bed on top of its goose-down covers.

One of the main reasons that Unc' Charlie drank so much forced its way into the forefront of his mind as soon as he started to get a little bit sober: *That big o' iron bed it's a hand-me-down from the Siegfried Farm. So is the goose-down covers. The vanity table in the hall came from over yonder too. All the tables an' chairs in this house, the stoves an' the icebox all came from over there. As a matter of fact ev' thin' we got came from over yonder.*

0' Siegfried loves to give Maetta things. He's been humpin 'er since she was nine. He only stopped cause he's too old to do it now. He done just 'bout worked an' screwed 'er ta-death. I 'on kno' why Maetta 's so proud-a the things that Family hands-down-ta-'er. Even though they done deeded this house an' twenty-seven acres of land to my wife, I ain' proud-a none-a this shit they gave ta-'er. She sold 'er soul for that hand-me-down furniture an' whatnot. Now she go tell me 'bout gettin' religion! Both she an' Siegfried claim they got religion. They call theyselves Christians.

Unc' Charlie rolled over onto his side of the bed on top of the covers and quietly cried. The tears came down and A'nt Maetta saw them. She wrung her hands in her apron like she always did when she felt anxious. She knew why Charlie was whimpering. She came to the foot of the bed. "Cora an' Cary go be at the Church tomorrow. They told me they would come. I don't think Bessie's go come. She an' Lin they's too worldly. I hope God '11 bring His peace into they lives fore it will be too late. It would be nice to see her singin' in the choir right 'long 'side Cora an' Cary. I don't wanna lose-a 'nother one-a my gals ta-the-Devil like I did Florence. You hear me Charlie?"

Unc' Charlie was almost dozing, but A'nt Maetta continued on. "Yeah, I remembers Florence like it was just yesstidy that she run off to New York to be with that Cracker. Never heard a word back from 'er after that. All I got was her body back-ta-me in a Pine Box. Somebody kilt her. It was nobody but that O' Cracker who'd begged her to pass for white in the first place. She's dead, but she'll always be my first child. I ain' go never forget her. I'll never stop lovin' 'er. Never! I know ya have-a lot of problems with that, still; don't ya, Charlie?"

Now, Unc' Charlie was wide awake. Fear came across his face, then guilt, and then hatred, and finally, hot-anger!

"Yeah-since ya done brung it up, ain't neither one-a them gals mine! Cora's Daddy was that same Cracker Siegfried that knocked ya up with Florence fore we got hitched. You all times bringin' that shit up. I get drunk to forget 'bout it. Why?"

Unc' Charlie sat up and came to the edge of the bed. "While I'm out yonder ridin' the rails tryin' to get my hands on a dollar anyway I can, you's back here givin' way the thing that's most precious to any red-blooded man. It's somethin' ya can't give back, Maetta! It's a pain that can't end. It stays with me. All I can do is get drunk, that's all!"

"You had Florence when I married ya. You promised you'd never do that again. Then you got knocked up by that Cracker again right in the middle of our lives. What was I s'pose-ta do?

I had-ta look at the face of that Cracker ev' time I looked at Cora.

She looks just like 'em. "That's what drive-me-ta drink, Maetta. It was the only way to get Cora off my mind. I don't want 'er ta-call me Daddy. I ain' her damn Daddy, Maetta. I don't want 'er ta-call me that, neither! I never want anythin' ta-do with that Whiteman's Daughter. I 've hated the sight of Cora from the day she's born!"

A'nt Maetta sat on the side of the bed beside Unc' Charlie. A few tears came down her cheeks. "Charlie, as I done told ya so many times," her voice quivered a little as she spoke, "I didn't do that cause I wanted-ta. I bring it up when you's grieving 'bout it, so we can get the pain outta our hearts an' out into the open. Inner-pain will rot the Soul. What I did was bad, I know it. But y' know I was forced-ta do it. I didn't have no choice." She turned her eyes away from her misty-eyed husband.

"Siegfried told Momma Josephine an' Daddy Jim Kingston, they had-ta send me to they Farm directly cause I was old 'nough to work on their Farm to do light housework, and cookin'. I was nine at the time. I was big for my age, an' I looked like a teenage girl. My body had developed too fast.

"Old Siegfried threaten-ta put our family off the Farm if Daddy Jim didn't send me over to his house right away. Charlie, I know y' know how it is round here. We Kingstons ain't no different than the Jameses. They been screwin' over us all, Charlie, since slavery days. If one-a they mens wants one-a our womens, they go find-a way to get 'er.

"O' Siegfried raped me right away! Tore me open like a knife does a hog. I screamed, I bled, I tried-ta run away. When I got home an' told Momma an' Daddy what that Cracker did to me, Daddy gave my ass a solid beatin' with a belt. Momma ordered me ta-go back over to the Farm an' learn ta-behave myself. I was allowed to stay home 'til the soreness healed. Then I was sent back to the Farm.

"I hid for days in the woods near the Farm 'til I got real hungry. Then I cried my way down the road back to that o' nasty Cracker's house an' he made me one-a his favorite gals. I couldn't help it, Charlie. You know that! At twelve or thirteen, or so, I got pregnant with Florence. I didn't even know what carryin' a baby was all 'bout. Nine months later I had the painful job of pushing one outta my body. She was born White with blond hair an' had the bluest eyes. The midwife wouldn't b'lieve she was

Colored if she hadn't seen me givin' birth ta-'er. I named her Florence Emma-Jean Kingston.

"She got teased all the time by Negroes. She got raped by three White boys. She got raped by an old black man, an' you hated her after ya married me. That's why she ran away. That's why she passed. Probably when that rich Jewish family she married into found out that she was a 'Nigger!' they had her kilt. That's a pain in my heart that will never go 'way Charlie."

"Maetta, it tweren't Florence that tore my heart wide open. You got pregnant with Cora after we got married. You keep tellin' me ya couldn'ta fought that Cracker off or somethin'. Lotta gals did. They didn't bring no White baby home. He attend church ev' Sunday. He's a Judge.

He didn't get all the gals workin' on that Farm. Why you, Maetta? You didn't fight 'im off hard 'nough, that's all to it.

"He got ya knocked up twice. Cora came 'tween Bessie an' Cary. Ya can't 'spect me-ta just forget all 'bout that, Maetta. How ya reek-en that made me look 'round here? People look at me sideways. I know they think I got no manhood. They thinks I should-a kilt that Cracker or you, an' I didn't do neither one. Now ya see what'cha done to me, gal?"

With tears coming down her cheeks, Maetta responded as she had many times: "Charlie ... Charlie-what'cha 'spect me ta-do? You's on the road or ridin' the rails, or just gone most the time. I had-a stay on this plot-a land so I could keep my chillun in this house that old man built for us, an' not have 'em only God knows where. Hell, I only got knocked up once-while ya was on the road. You'd leave me an' my chillun to fend for ourselves for months at a time, Charlie. What was I ta-do, when that O' Cracker told me ta-put out or get out? I had-a do one or the other, tweren't my choice.

"I only got messed up twice. Beatrice Christian had four-in-a-row while her husband was livin' right there with 'er. She only got two boys with Benjamin her husband. Maggie Ross had eight girls with a White Boss on the Bremo Bluff Farm-she ain' got none by her husband Carl. Ophelia Dabney had ten, five boys and five girls-her husband's too old to father any chillun with her. All them kids look just like they White Daddy. He owns the Payne Farm over in Arvonia.

"There ain't-a family round here who don't got at least two or more chillun by some nasty O' Cracker. It's just some-a the Hard Times we gotta endure to Survive. Charlie, Warren Bradley's wife, Dorothy, gotta go live with her White Boss five days-a-week. She come back to see her husband on weekends. She got two chillren, one by her husband, an' one by Mr. Seay. It's a fact of life. All you Colored mens be proud. All-a y'all wish it wasn't happenin' ta your wives. Ya talk 'bout what'cha go do if it do happen ta-'em; but ya fail to see that it's already happenin' ta-ev' body. I know how ya feel-hell, I feel the same way. But we gotta face the facts; right?"

"I just wish, Maetta, that I could-a kilt that White sonavabitch!" Unc' Charlie shouted. It was more like a *Primal Scream*. His face got twisted up like a Halloween Mask.

"But if ya lift a finger 'gainst one-a them White Bastards, they go lynch ya ta-death! That's what happen-ta young James Langhorne. Caught old man Courtney Payne in his house throwin' it ta-his little wife. He fought 'im off her. Next day we found 'im in the woods down on the riverbanks hangin' from an old Oak tree. James was naked. His balls was missin'. Had-a sign over his head that read: 'Don't Cut Off Your Hand To Spite Your Face.' Sue Langhorne had twins nine months later. She lost her mind.

"That's why I stayed on the road. That's why I rode the rails. I couldn't stand what was happenin' ta-my wife, an' I couldn't do nothin' toll 'bout it, neither! But, least I didn't stay' way for good like a-hundred mens from up round here. I came back ta-see 'bout y'all. You gotta gimme that, Maetta. I been with you most my life inspite of what's been shoved down my throat time-an' -time again.

"Maetta this house ain' go never feel like mine. No matter that I done lived here for most-a my life. This place came from some **O'** Cracker pawin' and gorin' you. I didn't pay for it with my work or my sweat. What's the difference in me an' a head of cattle? I may as well be a bull in your barn, Maetta-or a bull in O' Siegfried's pasture. I can't feel good 'bout that.

"What happen to me happen cause I couldn't own my own place. Old man William Bradley got his place deeded to 'im from his Daddy. His Great Granddaddy-a Whiteman's child-got the first deed ta-the-place, an' passed it on to the oldest son. So many-a them Bradleys live up yonder now they call the place Bradleys' Hollow. Ain' no White man gon go up yonder to take 'vantage-a one-a those gals. They know better'n ta-try. So, I guess, the difference is, ya gotta own ya place, be able to farm it like you wanna, an' get a good White-agent or sponsor ta-help ya get-a fair price for your crops at the Exchange in Rich-men, so you won't be dependin' on no Whiteman 'round here. Same thing is true for Old man Palmer Armstrong up in Cloverdale. So, some-a us get by-but most-a us get screwed. What I wonder though-an' I've always wondered 'bout it, is: How these White-men's wives let 'em get 'way with their foolin 'round?"

"Charlie, I 'spects it's like Mrs. Siegfried an' her Daughters. They got they nose so high up in the air till it's a wonder they don't get bird's poop in 'em. They done been told that they ain't s'pose-ta even think 'bout such things-it's beneath 'em. They can't say they like doin' it. That's not Lady-Like! They have-ta make-pretend that they hate that! Some don't even seem-ta mind they husbands gettin' it on with us gals, so they won't have-ta put out.

"Then they try not ta-notice all the little high-yellar boys an' girls the gals be havin' who works on they farms. They make-pretend some unknown Whiteman sneaked on they farms an' did all that damage, when the half-White chillun looks just like they husbands, or Sons, Brothers, Grandfathers, or Uncles. That's so damn stupid, but it's true, Charlie. But ya gotta realize that Siegfried deeded this place to me cause-a Cora. I'm shame-a that, but that don't make it untrue. So we's all caught in-a trap here Charlie. You can't hold none-a that 'gainst me. Tweren't my fault-can't ya see that?"

"Maetta you blame me for roamin' round. You hold that 'gainst me. Ya shouldn't blame me so much for that. Ya ought 'n whole that in your heart 'bout me. You's tryin' ta-make all the pain we's havin' my fault; ain't ya, gal?" Unc' Charlie said.

"No Charlie, I ain't." A'nt Maetta stood up to walk around a little. In a bit of a whine she said: "You just never let Cora forget that she weren't your'n. She wanted so bad for ya-ta-be 'er Daddy. She cried herself to sleep many-a-night when you didn't come home. She blamed ev' thin' on herself She hated her light skin. She saw you as her Father an' she'd fight like a wildcat with anyone who'd dare say you weren't. But ya never had-a kind word, or nothin' ta say ta'-er. To this day!

"It hurt Cora real bad cause ya couldn't stand her, the onliest Daddy she'd ever known. Them drunken rages you put her, an' us, through nearly drove Cora crazy. Ya didn't have-ta call her all those names ... her skin color wasn't her fault. That's why she ran away an' got hitched with-a man twelve-years older than her; and that's why I didn't try-ta stop 'er. She's a lot happier with Roy Winston. One-a the reasons she got with 'im is cause he's as dark-skinned as they come. I knew Cora's almost too young, but I imagine she's old enough. Least, she got 'way from all your fussin'. You ought-ta consider that, Charlie."

"Whoa! Hold it! Whose fault? You blammin' all that on me? All the girls left home early. They all got hooked up young. Why you want me to feel bad 'bout one who ain't even mine? You want somebody-ta blame, look in the mirror. I ain't got no babies out there by no other gal. I don't feel bad 'bout Cora. Other mens have kilt chillren like her. I let 'er stay with us 'til she decided ta-run 'way. I never pretended, or nothin' like that. I was honest with you an' her, least ya don't have no proof otherwise. So, I did the best I could, Maetta."

"Charlie, that's why I wanna take you fore Gawd! He's the only one that go soften ya hard heart. His love is the onliest thing that'll do that without fail, Hallelujah!" A'nt Maetta said, raising her left hand up towards the ceiling with her right hand over her heart. "That's why I want ya with me tomorrow, an' I hope the Holy Ghost falls on you, Charlie. Yes, Lord!"

A'nt Maetta walked around in the bedroom a little while with her left hand raised chanting: "Yes, Lord! Save 'im, Lord! Save his Sin-Sick Soul, Thank You Jesus! O' God, Come Down, Lord!"

Unc' Charlie got up, got under the covers, and fell asleep almost immediately.

Charlie and Henry sped out to Route 656 turned left and proceeded two miles to Route Six. They turned right on Six. They traveled four miles down Six to Columbia. In Columbia, at the corner of Main Street and Cumberland Bridge Road, they turned right. They traveled for about two miles into Cumberland, turned left onto a bumpy, unpaved back road that led to several shanties. Agnes lived in the third or fourth shanty on the left-side of that road.

Henry and Charlie were the music-makers for Agnes's Social. He and Charlie, Jr. could see that Agnes 'nem had put up new cardboard, and pasted new newspaper pages on top of the cardboard. All of the children too young to be at a party like Henry and Charlie were preparing to play for had been removed.

There was a table in the kitchen and Henry saw that it was full of used pop bottles that had been refilled with homemade beer. The air in the house had the distinct odor of fried chicken, and potato salad, collard greens, pigs' feet, chitterlings, and corn pudding. A loud sweetish alcoholic odor was due to the shots of bootleg (white lightning), a number of people held in their hands in paper cups. Others had cups of homemade wine, and opened bottles of the beer.

The shanty was full of people. The James Brothers were popular. People came out to hear them wherever they played. The hosts of the Socials always gave them food and drink free. They also made tips for playing the Blues Hits of the day for anyone. There was a kerosene lamp here and there that gave the whole atmosphere a dark-strange-shimmering aura.

Henry walked into the mix of people with his guitar slung over his shoulder. He gulped down several shots of bootleg, a cup of wine, and took a bottle of homemade beer to sip on between tunes. Lil' Charlie did the same.

Lil' Charlie was a piano player. Agnes had an old piano with a couple of missing keys. But Lil' Charlie could even play that well!

The James Brothers were joined by Howard Harris, Anna Belle's husband. He was a rotund, very light-skinned fellow, who had been a cook in the Navy. He stood at about six foot, and was a jolly-happy-go-lucky, 300-pound, guy. He could play the hell out of a Harmonica.

Henry and Charlie got right down to it. Howard (who would put you in mind of Dizzy Gillespie; he had the same goatee), joined in with Henry's and Charlie's rendition of a pulsating Delta Blues Score. Howard wore a belated White-On-Deck Sailor's Uniform to pull the girls.

The music filled the shanty up to the rafters. The crowd danced and vigorously humped their hips to the fast tunes, ground real slow and nasty to the slow sounds, and some of the women did what seemed like a quasi-striptease to some of the more sultry sounds the trio played. They played "Mo Jo" by Muddy Waters; "Down in Mississippi" by Robert Johnson; and, "Minnie, The Moocher," by Cab Calloway. Then they played "The

A-Train" by Count Basie. Then Henry, Charlie, and Howard took turns soloing, down-home Blues Style.

The crowd loved the musicians. The music they played set the stage for them to forget the miserable circumstances surrounding every individual at the Social. The harder anyone's life was the more enthusiastic were their participation in wild overly-exuberant merrymaking, dancing, and drinking. When the alcohol and music took full effect on some, they slipped outside, sometimes with perfect strangers, to have wild, unbridled sex. It was the ultimate release of their suppressed emotions.

All of Agnes's children still living at home, who were old enough, were at the Social except Frances. Mamie, and Neddy's (Agnes's Sister) older Daughters, Maude, Catherine, and Phyllis were dancing, and so was old Neddy, as best she could. She had gotten somewhat stiff from years of hard work in one of the Woods's tobacco fields. She soon had to find an old chair to sit in. Her girls did a variety of acrobatic Swing Moves to the delight of the crowd.

Maude, the oldest, Catherine, the next oldest, and Mamie, were Neddy's Jet-Black-skinned girls, although they were very shapely and pretty. Phyllis was the odd one out. She was as white as snow and stood out because of it. She had only a mere-hint of Negroid features.

Neddy had been accused many times by local Whites of illegally raising a White child, but she vehemently argued that Phyllis was really her Daughter. A White women in Columbia once slapped Neddy in her face for being insolent, after Neddy continued to argue that Phyllis was Colored, and was her Daughter. Even some Black Folk could not see how Neddy, being as Black as she was, could have Phyllis, an apparent White girl. But some adored Phyllis because of her very light skin. She was told that she was very pretty-even beautiful-by a lot of people.

Phyllis became very arrogant about her alleged beauty the older she became. Her misuse of the word "Darkie," and the phrase, "Ugly Nigger!" were how she often characterized other Blacks. But she saw light skin, and or, White skin as, "Fair Skin," or "Good-Looking Skin." Blond and or straight hair was "Good Hair" to her, and blue eyes were "Pretty eyes."

Therefore Phyllis was thoroughly stuck on the color of her skin. The more various people commented on how pretty she was, the more self-centered she became. She matured into a five five physical frame, had very smooth skin, shapely legs, with a very gracious and voluptuous bosom and buttock accompaniment. She had those Cupid-Bow lips that were naturally pink on her cream-colored face. She possessed piercing eyes. In short, she had a "Poker Face."

She had to constantly fight off advances from teenage boys-her own age-but also from men of every age and Race. They promised her money if she'd give in. The amounts being promised got larger and larger over time. She decided: *I may as well go-head-on an' make that money. I ain't gettin' no richer refusin' all that money these mens be willin' ta-gimme for what's 'tween my legs ... I might as well. . . .*

She charged three dollars for her services. That fee grew to five dollars as she became very popular and her sensuous skills developed. She enjoyed the attention she was getting, and that made her feel special. She loved the fact that she had been with so many of the husbands around the area, and could laud that over their straight-laced wives' heads-especially the White wives. The money she made plying her trade she used to purchase nice clothes, more expensive than the women in her community could afford. Most of them hated her. They called her "Stuck Up!" and names like, "Meal Face Heifer," and "Husband-Stealin' Who'e!" What they said about her did not matter to her. When she made an appearance anywhere, she loved that seemingly all eyes were on her. That was the greatest joy she got out of life.

On the night of the Social, the nine-by-sixteen area just to the left of Agnes's front door, where the piano sat in a comer with Lil' Charlie playing it, and Henry sat in a chair beside that playing his guitar, with Howard standing on the other side of the piano blowing his harmonica, Phyllis came in the door as the trio was playing a very sultry rendition of the "Huckle Buck." She was wearing a bright-red, full-length, gown with a gracious split on the right side of it. The top of it was so low it exposed a generous portion of her well-endowed bosom.

Right away Phyllis started shaking her hips and moving to the pulsating beat. Mamie, Maude and Catherine were the only ones who stayed in the nine by sixteen hallway of the shanty that was where the local girls had been taking turns toe-tapping, doing Swing Acrobatics, splits, and hot hip-shaking to the delight of the crowd. Some pulled their dresses up so high it exposed their panties as they danced-those who were bold enough to dare. The men cheered and applauded.

Once Phyllis got into the mix, the crowd moved back except for Neddy's Daughters. Then once Phyllis got going doing her gyrating, dirty, seductive dancing, even they let her have the floor. Phyllis had seen what the other women had been doing. She wanted to top everything that they had done.

Lil' Charlie, Henry and Howard seeing the possibilities, pumped their music up a notch or two, speeding up the beat to give Phyllis a chance to get all the way down and dirty.

The ten or fifteen people packed into the nine by twelve kitchen area and back of the hallway clapped and applauded as Phyllis danced seductively, wildly gyrating her hips in a stooped posture. She inched her dress up higher and higher until she fully exposed her thighs. She let her dress's hemline drop, but never missed a beat shaking her hips and rolling her rump. She did the Huckle Buck like a professional Burlesque Queen.

Phyllis dropped to the floor. She rolled over onto her back. Her hot buttock gyrations assimilated the sex act itself. She inched her dress up again with her left hand that exposed her black panties via the split in her dress. With the trigger-finger of her right hand, she put the tip of it to the right comer of her mouth. She groaned and moaned as she increased her sensuous moves on the floor of the shanty. She raised her legs, took her right hand from her mouth, put it in the right edge of her black panties, exposing a trace amount of pubic hair. She got up off the floor and continued her Huckle Buck antics. Some of the women out with their husbands and boyfriends had looks of disgust on their faces. Some even whispered: "Who'e!"

Agnes came out of her totally swamped kitchen area at the right of the front door. She had to push by a couple of people. She could see that all the men at the Social had leering smiles on their faces and big lumps in the crotches of their pants. Some of the women were holding onto the arms of their men. Agnes pulled Phyllis through the people to the kitchen area.

Several lusty panting men followed Phyllis and her Auntie to the kitchen. They all gazed excitedly at Phyllis. They all wanted to see more of her. They all had heard that she was a "Working Gal." They wanted some of that too. One reached out and tried to fondle her, but Phyllis slapped his hand away and in a whisper allowed: "I don't sleep with no Darkie Men. They gotta be White or light-skinned!" He said, "Bitch!" under his breath back at her.

Strangely enough none of the women offered to fight Phyllis, nor the men who were spumed by her. Her Herodias-like Dance had them so on-fire with passionate lusts until they were open to anything she suggested.

"Y'all buy some sandwiches, a dinner or two, or somethin' ta-drink," Phyllis suggested.

The men pushed and shoved each other out of the way to be the first to buy some food or drink from Agnes. She served them all with a smirk on her face as the dollars piled up in her gallon-money-jar. Phyllis slipped away.

Three Brothers that Phyllis knew from over in Fluvanna were beckoning for her to come their way. They were Broadus and Linwood, Twins, and Monroe Jackson. They were very light skinned and always paid her double for her services. She wanted to make that money. She always liked doing them. They were in her opinion good lovers, especially Broadus. He was the only man she had made love to that gave her the ultimate pleasure that any woman wanted. She slipped out of the backdoor of the shanty, got in a black, 1950 Ford Sedan, owned by Linwood. They took her back up the raggedy road to a little road that led to a pasture. They parked the car there, Phyllis got undressed, and one by one she passed the night away with these young men.

(She had been with Broadus and Linwood before, but she was introducing to Monroe what it meant *to go with a woman.* She was his first. The young teenager *became a real man early that morning.*)

Frances was next to the youngest of Agnes's girls. It was customary for the youngest girl to be the babysitter when someone gave a Social. But Agnes always let Virginia have her way. She was allowed to attend the Social because Agnes felt that she would not go with any of the men that came looking for a quick lay with a young gal. She knew that was what Frances wanted because she made no bones about that.

It pissed Frances off to the max because she knew a lot of hot young studs would be out prowling around and stopping by the Social just to get laid, and she wouldn't be able to have hot free crazy sex with one of them that night. She had to take care of Mamie's three little-Black Brats, Twins, Calvin and Charles, and Cathy, their little baby Sister; and the one she despised the most, that one they called Lil' Billy, Mabel's little Sambo. Mamie's older Son, Bernard was out spending the weekend with one of the Woods' men, his White Daddy. "He ought to be the one saddled with babysitting for Mamie, his Momma," that's what Frances was thinking.

Frances pranced back and forth in Mamie's one-room Shanty. It was twenty-four by forty eight feet in size. It was sealed up inside just like Agnes's much larger place. In the corner to the left of the door was Mamie's Queen Size Bed. Two smaller beds standing end to end followed that. One was for Bernard. The other one was shared by the Twins and the little girl. In the next corner was an old large Warm Morning Heater. It had some cracks around its middle. A Cook Stove sat over from it attached to a long pipe that was hooked to the same flu as the Heater. Then there was a little four-chair kitchen table, no bigger than a card table. The flooring in the Shanty was of rough boards with cracks in them so wide that in places you could see all the way under the shanty. Mamie had one large kerosene Lamp sitting on a small lamp table in back of the kitchen table.

Mamie's Shanty was about a hundred yards west of Agnes's Shanty. You actually came past it before you got to up to where Agnes lived. The Woods who was twelve-year-old, Bernard's White Father, who acknowledged his Son, came for his Son on weekends, picking him up on Fridays and returning him on Sunday evenings. He was educating Bernard on weekends.

Although Bernard's last name was Archer, after his Grandfather William's, he had been told that he was a Woods by blood, and that he should be very proud of that. His White Father was so proud of him that he introduced him to his White wife and his White Son and Sister, and demanded that they not mistreat or treat him like a "Nigger!" Bernard's Father was Louis Woods, a Lumber Camp and Planer-Mill owner. His wife was Margie, his Son was named Louis, Jr., and his Daughter was named Meggie. Bernard was the only "Colored" child that Louis had Fathered. Margie, Meggie and Louis, Jr. had to hate Bernard, but did not dare to express it in earshot of Louis, Sr.

Woods had given Bernard a brand-new thirty-six inch, red-and-white, Schwinn Bike. He bought him new clothes every week. He allowed Bernard to play with his only White Son, but kept his half-Sister away from around him, as much as possible. The boys came to adore each other.

Bernard looked so much like Louis, Jr. you would think they were twins, except that Bernard's skin color was closer to gingerbread than his half Brother's. Mr. Woods dared anyone who knew the truth to utter it in front of him. People in Cumberland and Fluvanna knew that he had a very quick temper. He'd beaten several White and Black men to within an inch of their lives for saying the wrong thing, or not doing the work at his Mill the right way. He had his bad and good days. It was rumored that Woods had killed a few Black men, but the evidence never added up enough for an arrest of him. He also knew the dirt on all of the local Judges and law officials. They knew to not mess with him. So he was a man to be feared. He got to do almost anything that he wanted to do.

Mamie had been working as a Maid, Cook, and Laundry gal, when she was seduced by Louis one day. He didn't rape her. He asked her to make love to him, and she always wondered what it would be like to be had by a White man. They developed a relationship that was kept quiet until Mamie got pregnant. She had her Son, and was told by Louis, that" if it's a boy, name him Bernard." It was a boy, and Mamie named him as she was instructed.

Woods built her a Shanty on the part of the Woods Plantation usually reserved for women like Mamie. That was the custom. Mamie quit working for him soon after her Son was born. She was afraid some angry White man or woman might try to get even with her for breaking their race rules. She was hired by Dr. Robert Snead as a Maid in Fluvanna near Fork Union.

On the night of the Social, the last thing Mamie told Frances was, "It's late August. It's gwine get cold after it gets dark. If it do, make a little fire in the Heater. Not a Big one, that old Heater is in bad shape. Ya gotta be careful."

Frances didn't utter a word. She was looking daggers through Mamie. But that's just the way Frances was, and Mamie didn't pay that too much mind.

Soon after Mamie left, Frances could hear the music coming from

Agnes's Shanty. There were clapping and cheering, and everybody seemed to be having a great time. She wanted to find a way to go up yonder to where all those people were partying and carrying on. She wanted to get popped real good by some hungry stud. She couldn't do none of that stuck here with these little "Tar Babies." She hated that.

Billy jumped off the bed he was sharing with the Twins and their little Sister. He ran to the piss pot in the back of the kitchen area near a backdoor. After he finished peeing, he whined, "I wanna piece-a bread, Fran." Up at his Grandmother's house he often got up in the dark and found his way into the kitchen and got a cold biscuit out of the breadbox. What he really wanted to do was go home. He had a hard time getting to sleep on a strange bed. But he also truly loved cold biscuits.

"Billy, get'cha ass back on that bed," Fran snapped at her little Nephew.

"I want my Grandma, I wanna piece-a bread-I 'on wanna stay down here!" Lil' Billy squealed back at her.

Fran's sudden move towards him made him go jump on the bed beside his Cousins. He'd been slapped by his Aunt before, and it felt like fire burning on the side of his face. He didn't want that to happen again. So he watched Fran's movements hoping for a chance to dash out the door without her seeing him.

She went over to gather some kindling from a box behind the cooking stove. She put that in the opened top of the old heater. Still Billy didn't see his chance to get away. But he kept watching Aunt Fran. She got a gallon can of kerosene from a comer in the back of the Shanty and splashed a lot of that onto the kindling, spilling a little onto the floor near the heater. She put a chunk of dried wood on top of the kindling and kerosene. She found a couple of old brown paper bags, balled them up and threw them in on top of the wood and the kindling. She splashed in a little more kerosene.

Fran got a strike-anywhere-match out of a box sitting on the little lamp table. She struck the match and stood back a little bit from the heater. She threw in the match and closed the top. The heater blazed up. Fire belched out of its grill, and its top vibrated. Sparks shot out of the cracks in its side. After throwing the lighted match into the opened top of the heater, Fran didn't look back. She turned and ran out the door hoping to get up to the Social, get popped, and return before Mamie came back to see about her children.

When Fran got up to her Mother's Shanty, she was greatly disappointed. The partying was winding down. The music had stopped. Most of the people were leaving. She saw Henry and Charlie, Jr. leaving with a couple of very light-skinned girls, probably from over in Farmville. Fran didn't really know where they were from.

"Damn! I done waited too late. Iain' go get nothin' tonight," Fran exclaimed.

Just as soon as his Aunt Fran stepped off the steps of the little porch of the Shanty, Billy jumped off the bed, ran to the door, watched his Aunt head up the rough road to his Grandma's Shanty, and then he lit-out for home. He made it, dashing through the door, he called out: "Grandma, can I get-a piece-a bread?"

"Grandma got more'n a piece-a bread for her Grand Baby tonight. C 'mere-ta Grandma," Agnes said, with a drunken slur to her voice. She'd down a couple of the homemade beers. She gave Billy a whole chicken leg-unheard of Children got a drumstick or thigh, never a whole leg.

Billy bit into the leg hungrily. He dropped it to the floor, picked it back up and asked: "Can I get-a piece-a bread too Grandma?"

"Yeah, Baby, you can ..."

Just then, bloodcurdling screams rang out: "Help! Help! Help! The house is on fire! Help!

Y'all Help! Ev' body Help! . . ."

Agnes ran out onto her porch. She trembled all over, even her eyes vibrated. "Where's Fran? Where's the chillren? Oh, Gawd! I hope they ain't in that house!" She was in a near fainting state.

Clemmon yelled to her from just in front of their Shanty: "I hope they ain' in that place now.

Can't nothin' be alive in that fire. I'm so sorry for them babies." He wept convulsively.

The whole Shanty had become a roaring, crackling, inferno; and the sound of the children screams: "Momma! Momma! Momma...."were silenced. The air had a noticeable stench to it-the smell of burning human flesh.

Maude, Catherine, Mamie and Frances were lying on the ground having emotional fits. Their eyes were rolled back up into their heads. They foamed at their mouths. They urinated and defecated on themselves.

Their stench mixed with the other smells, mimicked the odors of Hades. They were in the front yard of Mamie's Shanty.

The men and women who had not left Agnes's place futilely ran to the nearby river carrying buckets and tubs of water and threw them onto the lost Shanty to no avail. Others carried bottles and glasses of water to throw onto the fire. Their efforts only created a sizzling effect, the water soon evaporated. No adult had braved the fire to try to save the children.

Mamie screamed hysterically: "Save my Babies . . . Save my Chillun . . . O'Lord save 'Em!" before she fell into a convulsive fit. But she, nor anyone, dared enter the fire to save the children or to retrieve their charred remains.

Louis Woods was grooming his Son, Bernard, for entrance into Evergreen Elementary Prep School for Coloreds in Palmyra, Virginia. This Saturday Bernard had a premonition that he should get up and leave his room over the barn at the Woods's Farm and go home. He felt like something wasn't right. He got dressed in his Jeans, and red-and-blue flannel shirt, white-sports socks and Converse tennis, got on his bike and headed for home. The closer he got to home the greater the smell of burning wood, and some other "God-awful odor," seemed to fill the air. It made him pedal his bike faster. When he was close to his home, the smell became nauseating. Then he spied the source of the smell:

He saw that his home was on fire. He didn't see his little Brothers and Sisters standing around anywhere. A lonely bystander simply pointed towards the *flaming pyre*. Without saying a word, Bernard dashed into the flames, came quickly back with the Twins' charred remains. They no doubt had made it to near the door. He ran back into the fire and came back with his little Sister. She was nothing but a charred charcoal lump. The children were all burnt beyond recognition. Bernard had literally walked through the fire in an attempt to save his Siblings.

The fire burned all of the clothing off his body. Ugly blisters formed on his arms. His hair was scorched off his head as were his eyebrows. He had burn-blisters on the front of his legs, and his hands were burned so badly they were bleeding. He yelled at the top of his voice: "Gotta get my little Brothers an' Sister outta the fire!" Then he fainted and fell prone to the ground. He fainted dead-away. He had endured the pains of walking through the fire in a vain attempt to rescue his Twin Brothers and little

Sister. The pain on his body was horrible, but the emotional pain inside was insurmountable.

In about an hour and a half, the Shanty was reduced to a pile of smothering ashes. Agnes did not go off her porch. She got very nervous. She could barely talk.

"I'm glad ya came up here for a piece-a bread, Lil' Billy. If'n ya hadn't you'd be a little Angel right now, like Mamie's chillun. Lord-a-mercy!" Agnes moaned. She looked out from her porch. She spied Frances lying on the ground.

"Frances. Frances. Where ya at, gal? I see you's go be aw-ight. Ya didn't get caught in that fire. But ya liable to bum from it for the rest-a ya life," Agnes groaned up out of her gut.

Frances was lying on the ground with her lips shut tight. Her eyes were plastered together like those of a corpse. Her body convulsed grotesquely, trembling at short intervals, and in waves, like the ripples upon the river. She was having a fit of guilt, shame and disgust. Her mind imploded: *"Why did I set that fire like that. I thought I knew how-ta make a fire. I seen Julius doin' it time an' time again. That fire kilt them Babies! I wish I could bring 'em back! Oh Gawd, what I gonna do, now!"*

Mamie, Maude, Catherine, Frances, and Bernard were put on the back of an old Ford Log Truck. Gus Woods was cutting timber for Mrs. Hugheslette, a spinster who lived alone near so-called, "Buck Town," where Agnes, Neddy, Gus, and John Edwards had Shanties. Any number of "Negroes" lived in that place. All of the land belonged to the Woods Family.

A Dr. Allen Whitley had an office nearby, but he would only see "Negroes" at their homes. They had to pay him his fees up front. If they could not pay, he refused to see them. Dr. Snead did not see "Negroes" at any time or for any reason. The only Doctor who would see "Negroes" any time of the day or night was Doctor Samuel Josiah Yateman. He had an office in Fork Union, near the Fork Union Military Academy, and lived in a beautiful Victorian Home a mile from his office. He had retired from the Military and had been one who treated the Jewish Concentrated Camp Victims at the end of World War II. He refused no one, and broke the Law by using a First-come First-served policy. His waiting room was desegregated, and he had only one treatment room, where he treated all of his patients, Blacks and Whites.

Gus Woods knocked on the old Blond Doctor's front door early in the morning. He got dressed immediately when Gus told him who he had on the back of his truck. The Doctor came out to the truck wearing all white. He put a blanket over Bernard on top of the sheet Gus had draped over him. He gave Bernard a few shots. He treated the smelly women for shock, gave them mild sedatives, and said: "Gus, get this boy up to the University of Virginia, right away. He ought to be dead already, but he's still very much alive. God got a reason for that. Better still, I'll get Hunter Bradford to convey him up there. We got to get that boy some help right quick." Hunter can use his Hearse as an Ambulance.

"Take these gals back home, let them clean up. Take this bottle of pills I'm going to give you and tell the gals to take one of these to calm themselves down as need be. Don't bring them back up here unless they go completely wild or something. It might take some time, but judging from what you've just said, they are going to be all right."

"Aw-ight, Dr. Yateman, I will do," Gus said.

"Go on up the road to my office and wait a second and I'll be on up there. You can help me take this boy into my office to wait for Bradford to come pick him up. We got to be careful. He's pretty fragile right now, Gus."

Gus wondered: *What the hell do frag-dial mean?* But he just answered, "Yessah."

Bernard was forwarded to The University of Virginia's Barringer Emergency Room. He had suffered first and second degree burns on his legs, arms, and hands. Burns on his legs approached third degree. He was treated in the Emergency Room and was then housed on the K-Ward for Colored Patients.

He should have died, but in a few short weeks a miracle happened His skin cleared up to almost perfect. He fully recovered from his burns, leaving no visible scars except a little discoloration under his bottom lip. But he had lost his speech.

He would just sit in a corner of his Grandma's house not uttering a word He seemed to understand what people said, but he would not answer except with his eyes. After several months, he started to talk again, but only in monosyllables, and broken phrases. But if anyone asked about "The Fire," he would lapse back into silence. The amazing recovery of his skin was probably due to a Reward Divine Providence bestowed upon him for his frenzied bravery in his failed attempt to rescue his burning Siblings. Before the fire, Bernard had been a very talkative guy, but after the fire he remained very quiet and introverted He was very sad most of the time.

Bernard's White Father, Louis Woods, gave up any interest of sending his Son off to be educated after he saw what mental condition he was in. Louis did not think him capable of learning any longer.

CHAPTER SIX

The news of the fire spread faster than the fire that had engulfed Mamie's Shanty. The Gossipers had spread the rumor that "Frances had intentionally set the fire that had claimed the lives of four children; and that Agnes had planned the whole affair; and that the party at Agnes's Shanty was just a cover up of the fact that Agnes hated Mamie and wanted to get rid of her little children. One of the victims of the fire was Billy James, A'nt Maetta's Grandchild. You know she wasn't gonna just let that go"

A lot of people heard the above vicious half-truth from none other than Mrs. Cora Cooper. Everywhere she went that morning she told the story over and over again enriching it as she reiterated and exaggerated the facts about the fire and who had started it, and who were the actual victims. Anyone who would listen to Mrs. Cooper for at least a minute or two got an earful of her vitriolic tirades against Agnes and her Daughters.

In Columbia, she told Mrs. Eva Thurston, a plump owner of the leading Grocery Store in Town, (where almost everyone "Colored," made at least one stop there on Friday evenings, except Mrs. Cooper, and a couple others, was required to do her shopping), the "lurid" details. She gave the graying old widow, that seemed very proud of wearing plaid-it was the pattern on the blouses, skirts and aprons that she wore every day-her store list. Afterwards, Mrs. Cooper stood in front of the large counter, where it was customary for Coloreds to stand, and allowed:

"Mrs. Thurston, Frances, one-a Agnes's gals, is now wandering 'round in the woods like a wild animal. They say she's cryin' outta her mind, searchin' for them lost chillren that she done cause-ta be burnt up in that fire over yonder in Cumberland. If ya ask me, tweren't nothin' but-a evil spirit in them Wenches over yonder that done the deed using 'em." She looked at Mrs. Thurston who was dashing back and forth along the aisles and counters of her Store selecting the items that Mrs. Cooper had on her list, with a twisted grin on her lips. She straightened her homed rimmed glasses with her left Index Finger every now and then.

"How much ya chargin' for them pigs' feet in your case this week, Mrs. Thurston?" Mrs.Cooper asked.

"Oh, five-cents-a-pound, but the hocks are dime-a-pound this week. Cora," the old lady stood up and rubbed her hips, she had been bending over to select ten-pounds of Irish Potatoes, that she put into a paper bag, "how's Agnes really taking all this, have you heard?" She paused, and went over to a smelly barrel in the middle of the store near an old potbellied stove she never used anymore because she had a gas heater in the store, and dipped up six Salt Herring Fish. She wrapped those in white-waxed paper, and put that in the cardboard box with the rest of the items she had fetched for Mrs. Cooper. "I got some fresh Roe-Shad in for a-dollar-a-piece. Wanna try one-a them, Cora?"

"No ma'am. But I want four of the pigs' feet, an' two hocks, though. Gimme two chickens, ten slices of that country ham, and a pound of that good o' bologna I got here last week."

While Mrs. Thurston got the items Mrs. Cooper had asked for that hadn't been on the original list, Mrs. Cooper answered her previous question. "That Agnes ... she go 'round, they tell me, like nothin' done happen. Don't nobody kno' what evil done got in that old gal. Like the Devil, she can't be touched 'bout nothin' toll. That fire ought-a been for her. She more deserve it than them innocent chillren. Just wait till A'nt Maetta hear what she done-ta her Grand Baby. I tell ya, sparks go fly. She ain' never got over Charlie, Jr.'s little Son dying like he did."

Mrs. Cooper paused for a couple of seconds. "I think I will get one-a them Shad. Van loves 'em. I love my Herrings."

"Cora, it happened yesterday. I'm sure A'nt Maetta hasn't heard about the fire, yet?" She went over got a large Shad out of her cooler wrapped it in waxed paper and put it in the box.

"I 'on kno' if'n she's heard or not, 'bout it, but I know she's been tryin'-ta get Henry to go over yonder-ta Cumberland-ta get Billy fore somethin' like the fire happen-ta 'im. She been worryin' her oldest boy, Henry, since Billy was born, an' I told 'er the boy look just like Unc' Charlie, his Granddaddy. I know she go flip when she hear what done happen."

Mrs. Thurston boxed up all of the items that Mrs. Cooper had ordered. "Cora, exactly what do you think that old gal, A'nt Maetta, gonna do when she does hear about all that you're talking about?"

"Lemme tell ya what I thinks: I don't know how she's go take it, but I'm go see her at Church on Sunday. I previously invited her an' Unc' Charlie to our First Sunday meeting. She's go come even if Unc' Charlie don't. I feel like she's gotta right ta-know all 'bout it. Afterall, it's her own flesh an' blood."

"Well, Cora, I reckon you know what 'cha doing, and all. Here's your box." Mrs. Thurston put a box full of groceries on top of the large counter in the front of her Store a little to the right of the front door, along with several brown paper bags. "I'll put that on your ticket."

Mrs. Cooper went outside to the street and beckoned to Van to come help her carry her groceries out to their new 1950 Red Ford Pickup with its light-tan interior. The old nag had died, and Van thought it was time to get some better transportation. Over Mrs. Cooper's protest, he went up to Loco Motors and paid cash for his Pickup.

Van strutted into the Store wearing a dark-brown, two-piece suit, tan shoes, a blue Van Heusen shirt, a broad, red-and-white paisley tie, and a new gray Stetson hat. He was overdressed as usual. He hauled the groceries to the back of the truck that was parked over across the street from the Store. He seated himself on the driver's side and waited for Cora to finish gossiping. She had gone back into the Store.

"Well, I'm go see ya later, Mrs. Thurston. Been nice talkin' with ya. I know this: A'nt Maetta's go fix Agnes's little-red-wagon, for sure, when she hear what I go tell 'er on that gal."

"Cora, I don't have a thing to do with your business, but I gotta ask you, why do you seem to hate Agnes 'nem so much? What've they done to you?"

"Come here-ta the door. Look at that pretty man I got out yonder sitting in that truck," Mrs.Cooper said. She got out of the way so that Mrs. Thurston could get by her.

"Okay, Cora, what did she do with Van, over there. I never heard about anything ever happening between Agnes, or her gals, and your Van."

Mrs. Cooper began to pat her right foot a little. She put her white-gloved hands on her hips. "Look, Van went over yonder ta-one-a them party-Socials one night. I know he don't think I knows 'bout it, but he came home one night an' I could smell a faint scent of some funny-cheap perfume on him. I asked him, where ya been, Van? He said, he'd been over in Garland Baskerfield's barn playin' cards. They play a little poker sometimes. But Willie Payne told me, he, Garland, an' Van went over yonder-ta Cumberland to a party.

"I nearly had-a fit! More cause Van didn't own up-ta the truth, than if he had done somethin' with one-a them nasty gals over in Cumberland. But he sticks-ta his story ta-this-day. That's one-a the reasons I can't stand Agnes. As long as my husband won't level with me 'bout that night, he's puttin' them sluts above me. That's how I see it."

Mrs. Thurston frowned at what Mrs. Cooper said, but did not dare utter a response to it. Mrs. Cooper did most of her shopping at her Store, and that might change if she said anything that Cora might find offensive. *Willie Payne's the biggest liar in Fluvanna among the Negroes. I wouldn't believe a word that came out of his mouth. He doesn't like Cora either. He probably just told her what he said to upset her, cause he knows how jealous that gal is of her light skinned Buck.* Mrs. Thurston thought.

"Well, I'll see you next time, Cora. Take care, now." She waved as Mrs. Cooper went out the door. Mrs. Cooper was a little pissed, so she didn't return her wave.

Mrs. Thurston was thinking: *I wouldn't wanna be that gal, Agnes, for nothing in this world Cora Cooper's got it in for her. One way or the other, she's going to try to get-even with that gal, who probably hasn't done a thing to her. Cora's a good-old gal, but she carries and brings too much gossip. But she's one of my favorite Saturday-Morning Shopping Gals.*

"Charlie, Charlie, get up, man," A'nt Maetta shouted, "we gotta get ready fore Lil' Charlie an' Henry hit the road. We won't see them boys till late tonight if we don't hurry."

"Well ..." Unc' Charlie groaned. "The way I's feelin', maybe it'd be better if they went head-on. Can't y'all go without me, I feel mighty bad."

"No-Gawd! You's goin' with me to Columbia Baptist Church this Sunday if I have-ta drag ya all the way down there." Her words sliced through the air like an arrow launched from a bow. "I want Lil' Charlie to take us down to the Church in his car so we can get there early. You get on up, now Charlie," A'nt Maetta ordered her very hung-over husband.

"Oh, aw-ight. I 'member. I promised ya I's goin' with ya. I'm go keep my promise," but his voice was full of resignation and disgust. He didn't want to do what he had promised.

A'nt Maetta went into her kitchen wearing a flannel housecoat. She made a roaring fire in her caste-iron cooking stove. Soon the house was full of gracious aromas from frying fatback, boiling oatmeal and coffee, baking buttermilk biscuits, hot sausage-gravy, frying potatoes and scrambled eggs. She set the table with her hand-me-down, once-fancy China-that had sustained a number of chips over time. Then she called out: "Y'all come on, now. The food's on the table. We gotta eat, an' I gotta wash the dishes. I gotta get dressed so we won't be late.

"There's plenty of hot water in my big o' steam kettle so y'all can wash up. But ya gotta get a move on, now," A'nt Maetta sounded like a Boss at a Mill.

It didn't take long for the food to disappear. Henry and Lil' Charlie got dressed in cleaned sweat shirts, new Blue Jeans, surplus Black Combat Boots, and Army Fatigue Caps. Charlie, Jr. wore a green shirt and Henry a yellow one. They couldn't wait to get going. Both felt as though the best way to get rid of their hangovers was to get some more to drink.

"I feel real tough, this mornin'," Henry said in a low groan. "Momma's food helped a lot, but ain't nothin' but-a drink go fix me up."

"I heard that, Bro." Lil' Charlie opined.

"Y'all got that right," Unc' Charlie groaned. He ran outside to vomit. He came back and declared: "I feel a lot better now that I got it all up." He chuckled.

A'nt Maetta just shook her head at her house full of drunks. "Lord-a-mercy," she said. She got dressed in a blue-full-length gown, black low-heal pumps, brown nylon stockings, and a large hat that seemed to have a whole chicken and nest on it.

Unc' Charlie put on his other red and purple Zoot Suit. He got on his one pair of dressed shoes, but left off the Jive Chain.

"Lil' Charlie, go in the kitchen an' get that box an' things outta the icebox. It got days-a labor in it, I tell ya. Ain't as young as I used-ta be. Cookin' them chickens, pies, a cake, potato salad, com puddin' an' string beans done took all the starch outta these old bones."

"Yes 'am," Lil' Charlie said.

She looked over at Henry. "Y'all ain't goin' out so sharp this mornin'. What'cha go do? You could get dressed an' c 'mon ta-church with me an' ya Daddy. Wouldn't that be nice?"

"Yes 'am," Henry said, but he shook his head in disagreement. A'nt Maetta didn't see that.

Henry was twenty-nine, or so, years old Lil' Charlie was around twenty-seven. Yet they always answered A'nt Maetta in a very respectful manner. But to their Father they were almost always very disrespectful. Maybe it was because of the fact that Unc' Charlie was absent for most his children 's growing-up years, due to his hoboing around the country in search of a day's work to make a couple of dollars. Then he had the near impossible task of trying to actually make it home with some of that hard-earned money. His trips took him as Far away as Main in the summer and Texas in the winter. He would be gone several months at a time. He'd come back with a pocketful of small change, or a few dollars. What he brought home really didn't matter that much.

One thing that may have contributed to the above disrespect was the fact that when Unc' Charlie was home, he'd beat the hell out of his children-especially Cora-for the slightest provocation to show them who was Boss. Sometimes, his wife and children were glad when he decided to go on one of his incursions. At least they would have a little peace while he was away. Finally, at the same time that Unc' Charlie was so ready to jump on his children and hit them, he'd cower like a scared rabbit in front of A'nt Maetta. [A'nt Maetta didn't take any stink off of Unc' Charlie, or anyone else from her community, but she took it from the Siegfried Family.] She would slap Unc' Charlie in public, at times. People came to regard Unc' Charlie as henpecked, and said that he ought to put his wife in her place. Unc' Charlie may have cursed at his wife, but would not dare to raise a hand to her. He knew that she knew how to use a Straight Razor. She once tried to cut Unc' Charlie after she came home and caught him whipping Henry, her favorite. She slapped her husband, and he barely got away. She nearly cut his shirt off of him.

They all got everything loaded in the trunk of the car. Then Unc' Charlie and A'nt Maetta got in the backseat. Henry was on the passenger side of the front seat, and Lil' Charlie was the driver.

"Why y'all ain't dressed-ta-kill today; 'specially you, Henry?" A'nt Maetta asked.

"Well, Momma, after last night's partyin' I'm just go take it easy today. I might down a cup 'la beers an' head on back to the house. I wanna get rid-a this darn hangover," Henry said. "Well, y'all take me an' ya Daddy down to Columbia Baptist, directly." "Yes 'am," Lil' Charlie said.

A'nt Maetta twisted up her face a little. "When you boys go seek Gawd?" she asked.

She got a little smile on her face. "Why don't y'all go back, get dressed, an' c'mon ta-church with us today?" A'nt Maetta said.

"Momma Iain' read-ta get religion, yet," Henry said.

"Well Momma . . . I went overseas to fight for this country. I had-a dodge a lotta bullets, since Truman 'nem decided ta-put us Negroes out on the battlefield, like the White boys. Soon's I got back-here to home, I faced the same shit from the Crackers that I did fore I left for Europe.

"We Colored mens fought over in Europe for freedoms we ain' go never see back here at home in America cause-a all-a them Rabid Crackers over here ..."

"That's it, Lil' Charlie. Only Gawd can set-ya-free! Praise the Lord!" A'nt Maetta raised her left hand up above her head as she said that. Then she let it fall back into her lap.

"No it ain't, Momma. I love ya an' respect ya, but Jesus Christ look just like one-a them O' White Crackers 'round here. Ain't-a bit-a difference 'tween 'em. Ya-look at all the pictures ya done seen of The Lord. He seem just like the average pure-White Cracker to me. I swore I ain' go never bow down an' worship nobody that look like-a Cracker-Bastard, No Sir! An' I ain't. I seen 'im in pictures all over in France an' Germany, that same O' Faggot-looking White boy. Y'all got pictures like that right down at Columbia Baptist. Long's he looks like that, ya-can count-me-out," Lil' Charlie exhorted.

"But it don't matter what He look like, Lil' Charlie. He's The Son Of Gawd! That's what matter the most. Ya gotta b'lieve on Him ifn ya wanna be saved! Now, that's in The Good Book, somewhere," A'nt Maetta said, with tears coming down her cheeks.

"Momma, you church people is tryin' ta-follow a religion that be askin' y'all to act just like slaves-to-the-White man. Only Jesus Christ done replaced the old slave masters. That's all! Just like the slave masters ruled over our people's bodies, this Christ wanna rule over our minds by askin' us to bow down before Him, a White man. I wanna be free. Free from it all," Lil' Charlie said. "That Book ya-call good, ain't so good, far as I can see."

"Lil' Charlie, it don't make things no better for ya ta-be so full-a hate, neither. Gawd can't come in 'til ya get all that hate outta ya heart. Ya gotta forgive it all, Son, no matter how much it done hurt ya," A'nt Maetta shouted, like a preacher.

"Momma, I can't do nothin' toll 'bout what these Crackers 'round here be doin'. I know ain' nothin' that I do go make no difference, no how. But I don't have-ta go bow down fore none-a them in a Black Church.

"How the hell can it be A Black Church, and A White Church, anyhow? Is there a Black Heaven and a White Heaven, too? Do my people truly b'lieve that they go be saved cause they bowed down fore a White man draped in a sheet? I don't know what in the world y'all be worshiping. I b'lieves a lotta y'all don't know, either," said Lil' Charlie, with great conviction. "For all-a the praisin' of this God y'all be doin', it ain't made y'all no freer!"

A'nt Maetta was grieved to her heart. "Lil' Charlie. Look Son. There's peoples workin' for our freedom. These mens they's smart too. The White man go have-ta listen to'em. They's very 'portant, edge-me-cated, peoples. They been ta-them White-folk schools up North. They b'long ta-the N-A-A-C-P. I heard Mrs. Siegfried talkin 'bout it with Mr. Siegfried. Them White folk's scared-a them people fightin' for our rights. They say they don't want us in they schools 'round they young girls-'specially our young boys; but might not be able ta-stop it."

"Momma I don't know much 'bout the rest-a the NAACP," Lil' Charlie said, "but we Brothers in the Army heard 'bout the one called Walter White. He's one-a them highfalutin, edge-me-cated, light-skinned people who look out for his own kind, mostly. It's him or Booker T. Washington. Some see 'em as great. I don't see nothin' changin' that much, ceptin' they got the Crackers all stirred up in the South. We down at Fort Bragg wished they'd just stop. When I think-a the boys who lost they lives out in the battlefields of Europe an' Japan, cause the NAACP thought that was go make us equal to Whites, I hate the thought of the NAACP. I didn't wanna fight nobody in the White-man's Wars," was Lil' Charlie's stinging reply.

"Amen! Lil' Charlie!" Henry said. "I know what you's sayin' is what God Loves-the truth." "Y'all young peoples just don't know," A'nt Maetta said.

Unc' Charlie cleared his throat. Then he allowed: "Y'all see all them acres we just drove by?" He hung his head down low, then he cussed under his breath for a second. "Goddamned son of bitches!" He latched out in more detail: "All the hun'erts-a cattle, mile-an'-miles of cornfields; all them fine-bred horses on old man Siegfried's Farm came from slavery, then convict labor, an' near 'bout the slavery of us.

"Not ta-mention, all-a them many gals them bastards done ruin. Now we poor Coloreds gotta scrape-a livin' the best way we can, while them White wolves live like Kings and Queens." As they came to near the end of the Siegfried's property line on Route 656, Unc' Charlie declared, in an almost scream: "It ain't right, I tell ya. It ain't right a' toll. That's what I'm waitin' for Gawd-Almighty-ta-fix!"

With a voice brimming with sarcasm Lil' Charlie trumpeted: "When I was in Europe, some-a the White boys use-ta come over to talk with us Colored soldiers in secret. They talked 'bout us joinin' them an' formin' a group ta-fight the rich. Say we ain' go have nothin' toll till we up an' take it. I'm more with them than I am with Ya Gawd, or the NAACP. All I want is a chance ta fix things in my life the way I want 'em. I don't need no Gawd-ta-do that."

"Ya got that right, little Brother," Henry said. He slid hands with Lil' Charlie.

"Henry. Lil' Charlie. You young peoples go get into a lotta trou 'ba cause you's so uppity. Some nasty O' Cracker go get the devil in 'im, an' go shoot or stab one-a y'all ta-death. They don't like it when Colored mens stand up to 'em like y'all's talkin' 'bout. There's Cracker-mobs in Florida, Mississippi, Georgia, an' North Carolina, cause-a brave Colored mens standin' up ta them Crackers. Them Crackers be killin' the Colored mens an' gettin 'way with it. I don't want that ta-happen ta-my-boys. Y'all know, ya get them Crackers stirred up 'nough, they'll do the same things right here. I kno' y'all know what I means." A'nt Maetta issued a sincere warning.

"Now," said Henry, "we ain't scared-a no livin' Cracker. I wish one-a them suckers would come in my face an' try to put his hands on me, my wife, or one-a my gal-friends," he looked sternly at Unc' Charlie, "I'd gut 'im like-a slaughtered hog. I'm just waitin' for the day when one-a them will get the nerve to step-ta-my face. I'd go ta-the Chair for killin' 'im. I ain' lying."

Unc' Charlie hung his head. He knew that One was aimed at him like a Missile.

"Me too, Big Brother. I'm a man. That's what I go be to the bitter end," Lil' Charlie said.

In somewhat of a whiny voice, Unc' Charlie said: "Boys. If'n ya raise your hands to harm one-a the poorest Crackers 'round here, ev' last Cracker go come after ya so they can lynch y'all. Ah, they'll put ya in jail, then kangaroo court ya right on ta-the-'lectric Chair. It'll be White 'gainst Black. That's all that matters. What ya talkin' is the way ta-a quick grave."

"Well Daddy," said Henry, "They gotta bring ass to get ass. I'm go take at least two or three a them White dogs ta-hell with me. I'm ready-for-that-shit! Been ready, let 'em come on."

"You better b'lieve it!" Lil' Charlie said. "It's a new day, Momma. Poppa. Ain't nobody go take the kind-a shit y'all took off them Crackers. We done been through too much during World War One and Two. We ought-a have the same rights as ev' one else 'round here, an' all over America.

"Right up yonder in Charles' ville, I hear that they's treatin' Nazi prisoners better'n they is Ex-Colored Soldiers. The Ex-Nazis can go in a restaurant an' be served, but-a Negro Ex-Soldier can't do that-Whites Only-y' know." He had a very angry grimace on his face.

"So, that means I'm go take the Law in my own hands when a Cracker steps over the line, anytime one do."

"Oh, Lord-a-mercy!" A'nt Maetta said. She threw up both her hands for a couple of seconds. Unc' Charlie just hung his head. He had a very sad and sorrowful look on his face.

Soon Lil' Charlie pulled off Route Six onto a dirt road just up the hill from Columbia's Town limits. They turned onto Stage Junction Road.

They drove past Halle Bland's house, a two-story clapboard structure that stood across from Herman "Doc" Johnson's nice-brick-siding home. Then Mrs. Cooper's nice home came into view just down the hill from Columbia Baptist Church. They proceeded to the top of the hill and saw a number of other cars, horse and buggies, wagonloads, and log-truck loads of people arriving to the Church.

Columbia Baptist Church was a large clapboard building that had been newly whitewashed. It had a large steeple, and was surrounded by several huge Indian Oak trees. They stood on all four sides of the Church like sentries. The Church had stained-glass windows on its North and South sides. On the North side the stained-glass was meshed together so that the scene it depicted was one continuum. It had a White-blond- Blue-eyed Jesus Christ standing at a stone fence holding two little White Lambs, one in each arm. The Lambs had pure-white wool, and bright-blue eyes. A host of similar Lambs were inside of the fence. A caption on the bottom of the scene read: *THE SON OF GOD.* The Lambs looked adoringly at Jesus.

On the South side, those windows depicted a White "Glorified Savior" who seemed more like a portrait of a red-headed Irishman wrapped in red, blue and white sheets. A bright light shone all around this pontific depiction of Jesus, highlighting his rusty beard and his beady-little blue eyes. A little white dove descended out of the sky having an even brighter light shining all around it. The Christ figure had a Halo around its head seeming to faintly resemble a red, white, and blue circular rainbow. Christ's feet were standing on a cloud. Under his feet was the caption: *"BEHOLD THE LAMB OF GOD."*

Henry asked his Brother, Charlie: "Junior, man, why do Colored folk go to a Church that's painted white with stained-glass windows showing little-white sheep, and a White Son of God? That's gotta mean the Son's Father's White, too. Colored Churches got this mess painted on they windows all over America. Looks to me like our peoples don't wanna b'lieve that God might've created a Heaven for them. So they gotta b'lieve in Whiteness so they can one day be made White too, then they can get into the Whiteman's Heaven. Charlie, if that's true, the Whiteman ain't go let us Negroes into his Heaven."

"Big Bro. That's what the Whites' been teachin' us from way back. Got most-a us thinkin' that 'White Is Pure!' The Whiteman put that dumb idea in or heads an' it stuck, man. It got beat into us during slavery. Now, they got us bowing down worshiping they white skin like that was God. The problem is, ev' body in their Bible done been made out ta-look like somebody White. The Real Bible done been messed with, man. The Whiteman rewrote it. Their Pope, or somebody like that. I heard some-a our Black Muslim Brothers talkin 'bout it in the Army.

"I didn't pay much 'tention ta-what they be sayin', but I heard one say that 'the Real Jesus was A Black Man.' That's why ev' thin' ta-do with religion had-a be made to look White, Henry. White mens just won't go bow down an' worship nobody that look like-a Black man. But look at us!"

"Lil' Charlie, I hear ya, Bro. But how the hell did the Whiteman get that shit over on us so deep in our minds, man? Brother, we got some really smart peoples out there. Looks like they done all bought that White Shit lock-stock-an'-barrel. Ya gotta wonder 'bout that, Lil' Charlie."

"Henry, it's like this-here: Most Colored preachers taught they church peoples that whiteness is next to godliness. They encouraged 'em ta-b'lieve in-a White God, an' a White-Blue-eyed Jesus Christ, that resembled Old Southern Gentlemen, or Northern Abolitionists. So, our peoples got so much respect for the Old Masters, or their White Deliverers from slavery, that looked just like the Whites they saw in they Bibles ev' Sunday, they accepted worshipin 'em in churches in the North an' South.

"Henry, ain't ya never wondered why our peoples will b'tray one-nether quick as a skunk's stinks? Well, it's cause they b'lieves they's 'fessin' up ta-God when they be turnin' in one nother! We's brainwashed. It got done ta-us right by our own preachers. When we tum 'gainst one-nether, our Colored Preachers tell us we's 'Pleasin' God!' That's why Reverend Josh Bonnepart got run 'way from Columbia Baptist. He's teachin' his flock that Whites ain't no better 'n Negroes. That there ain't but one God. All had-a stand equally 'fore Him. That got 'im fired, man."

"They minds done been turned 'round backward, an' the religion our preachers be teachin' is one-a the main faults. What in the hell's we gonna do, man?" Henry said.

Lil' Charlie paused a second or two. "I'on'kno', man, but let's get on off this hill," he said. "It gimme the creeps, though, when I see Momma an' Poppa goin' into the Belly-of-the-Whale. Let's go to Parish's Cafe an' get some beer, man. I gotta 'nough for-a case of Slitz or Richbrau. Which one ya want?"

"Hey, Daddy-o. Let's get Richbrau, that's the best," Henry said Lil' Charlie cranked up the Ford, put it in gear, and the car sped off. They went back up Stage Junction Road, turned left on Route Six and traveled a half-mile east to Columbia.

Unc' Charlie and A'nt Maetta saw several new Chryslers, Buicks, and Fords full of smiling people pulling into the front of the Church. One big Old Chrysler threw gravel all over the old couple as it sped to the back of the Church. Parking was at a premium, and some drivers swore under their breath, and others out loud, at the people taking their time getting out of the way so they could quickly find somewhere to park near the Church.

"Maetta, reek-en we ought-a get on inside," Unc' Charlie said.

As Unc' Charlie and A'nt Maetta went up the seven cement steps of the Church into its vestibule, two deep-ebony velvety-skinned "Angels" wearing white gowns greeted them. They were like Cherubs. "Hello. Welcome to Columbia Baptist Church," one on the right said to Unc' Charlie. One on the left said the same thing to A'nt Maetta. They handed out fans depicting the Lord's Supper on one side and "Hunter Bradford's Funeral Services" on the other side. The Cherubs greeted everyone the same way, as a multitude of groomed and gowned people came bouncing up the steps and into the Church. Beautiful young women in white gowns were Ushers who showed them to the Pews that were fast filling up to capacity.

Once Unc' Charlie and A'nt Maetta were seated, Unc' Charlie gazed upon the scenery that was typical in most Negro Southern Baptist Churches in the Bible Belt-meaning, in Virginia, and the lower South: North and South Carolina, Florida, Georgia, Alabama, Mississippi, Louisiana, Texas, Arizona, Arkansas, and Tennessee.

In Columbia Baptist, the pews were sitting upon highly-polished hardwood floors in a semi circle pattern. Those Pews nearest to a beautiful Altar featuring an opened red-Bible to Exodus 20: 1-17 *(THE 'JEN COMANDMENTS)*, were lengthwise. The Pulpit was on an elevated stage and had a Throne-like Pastor's Chair in the middle of the stage, and one of lesser size to the right and left of it. To the right of the Throne the

20-voices Choir stood wearing white gowns with red sashes. An ornate Balustrade separated the Choir from the Throne. To the left of the Throne, was a Baby Graham Piano. Mrs. Cora Cooper sat on a stool in front of the Piano wearing a red gown with a white sash.

The walls and the ceiling of the Church were overlaid with Cedar paneling. A golden Chandelier hung from the ceiling over the Pulpit giving off a shimmering majestic light. On the

Altar a Silver Communion Set was to the right of the Bible. A'nt Maetta loved the interior of the Church. Unc' Charlie wondered: *How the hell do these peoples over here at Columbia Baptist 'ford-ta-have so much costly stuff in they Church. Ain't nothin' like that in Cloverdale Baptist, or West Bottom Baptist. On the inside, this Church is almost too rich-lookin 'for the poor peoples 'round here to be able ta-'ford it. I don't know how they done it.*

As Unc' Charlie and A'nt Maetta had been ushered down the main aisle of the Church, they walked past many familiar faces: They saw Mr. and Mrs. Baskerfield, Sr. the Black owners of the largest tract of land in the Stage Junction area, consisting of a thousand or more acres; and their Son Garland, Jr. owner of a small sawmill and a subcontractor with Kents Brothers, the largest Sawmill-Planer operation in the Cumberland-Fluvanna area. His petite light-skinned wife, who looked like a White woman, had her little nut-brown Son on her lap, Garland Baskerfield III. These were some of the Wealthiest Blacks in Central Virginia. But they still attended Columbia Baptist Church, and acknowledged people like Unc' Charlie and A'nt Maetta. They waved at the older couple as they walked by, and they returned the wave.

Next they went by Halle Bland. She was another one that could have passed for White. She had her Twin Daughters, Charlotte and Priscilla, sitting beside her. She took them everywhere she went because she was so proud of them. She'd had those with her White Boss, while James Bland, her husband of twelve years, was away fighting in Korea. As a matter of fact, she had had seven children and four of them were with that same Boss. She would proudly say, "I'm his House-Girl, and he takes care of me." She was heavily pregnant, and A'nt Maetta wondered what color this one would be? But Halle knew of A'nt Maetta's history. She grinned and waved. A'nt Maetta half-heartily returned her wave. Unc' Charlie grunted and snorted and gave her a very hateful stare, rolled his eyes, and kept on walking.

Mrs. Lee Johnson, the nut-brown, half-Indian, wife of Herman "Doc" Johnson, Sr. was there with her Daughters, Elnora and Evelyn, and a Son, Herman, Jr. Doc Johnson owned another Sawmill, but he was nowise as prosperous as the Baskerfields. Rumor had it that he knew that one of the Kent Brothers was after his wife. Doc was a man almost no one would dare to mess with. When he confronted the Kent who was the culprit, the "White dog" confessed that he thought Lee was the prettiest woman in Fluvanna, but he would leave her alone. He gave Doc the equipment he needed to get a Sawmill up and running. He also gave Doc a very used log truck and an old pickup, because he feared that Doc might stalk him, and try to kill him. Kent knew that Doc had been a Sniper in Japan who had seen action in "The Battle at Pork Chop Hill." Lee waved vigorously at the old Patriots. A'nt Maetta waved back. Unc' Charlie just smiled, but did not wave. Doc was not at Church, as usual.

Over a little ways from where the Ushers seated A'nt Maetta and Unc' Charlie were Cora's Children: Roberta (Bert), Mamie (Mae), Louise (Lou), Clarabelle (Booco), Robert (Rob), Beatrice (Bea), Miriam (Puddin'), Richard (Rich), Cornelius (Peanut), and Eugene (Gene), who was two going on three-years-old (a few months younger than Billy James). Cora had these Children one-or-two years apart with Robert Leroy Winston, Sr. (Roy). He had named his first Son after him, but everyone called him, "Rob." But they called Robert, Sr. "Roy."

Roy was seated with his Children. He stood at about five-five, wore a black business suit, white shirt and bright-red tie, and had very silky-wavy hair. His skin was very dark, like midnight. His black shoes were so highly polished until they reflected the light. He had married Cora when she was about thirteen years old. She was nearing thirty-four, or five, in 1950. Roy was pushing towards fifty. Her Mother had lied so that Cora and Roy could get a marriage license. One good thing was that Roy owned land on the North side of Route 656. He had been involved in helping the Carpenters in France who were part of a rebuilding Brigade following World War One. Roy had been a Soldier then, and was discharged soon after his Unit was through with the rebuilding projects. He had been married to Cora for over twenty years, and was building a house at about a mile up from Route Six on the left side of the road. He lived at present just up the hill from Route Six, just before you get to 656 North, within seeing distance of Doc Johnson's Mill, that had been erected just down the hill from William (Will), Roy's younger Brother, and Cary, Henry James's youngest Sister. Mimi Winston had deeded both her Sons the land they needed to build homes. Her Father, a Whiteman, had left a large tract of land to his only child with his "House Gal."

"Hi. Hi Grandpa," whispered Mamie. She was around nineteen of twenty, and was a sophomore at Virginia State Normal Institute in Petersburg, Virginia. "Hi Grandma," she whispered as loudly as she thought prudent. She wore a beautiful pink gown.

"Hi y'all," A'nt Maetta whispered back. She waved at her Grandchildren. She frowned and rolled her eyes at Unc' Charlie because he completely ignored Cora's children.

Cora had waved at her parents as they approached the pews near the Choir Stand. A'nt Maetta waved back, and tears came to her eyes when Unc' Charlie refused to look in Cora's direction.

William Augustus Winston (Will), Cary's husband, was seated not far from Unc' Charlie and A'nt Maetta, a few pews over. He was directly in front of Roy's Children, his Nieces and Nephews. Will had married Cary at or just over thirteen-years old, like his Brother had Cora. Cary was a Type I Diabetic, had developed Fibroid Tumors in her late teens, and had to have a hysterectomy. She would never be able to have children, though Will yearned for a Son. This frustration drove him to bouts of alcoholic bingeing. Cary opted to adopt a child, but could not find a boy. The only baby that became available was a little girl. So they adopted the girl and Cary named her "Mary Ann," but Will remained very frustrated.

Will Winston had grown to profoundly dislike Unc' Charlie. He felt that Unc' Charlie needed to soften his heart towards his Sister-in-Law. Will waved at A'nt Maetta, but rolled his eyes at Unc' Charlie. Unc' Charlie looked away from the hulk of a man that some called Big Will, who dared to be under the influence in Church, and wore no tie with his brown suit, white shirt, and tan loafers.

Everyone's focus was upon the Choir as it stood up with hymnals in hand. Mrs. Cora Cooper played the piano. A tall, handsome, man, rose from the illustrious Pastor's seat, wearing a beige Preacher's Robe with red, black and gold embroidery all around its fringes, and the print of a large-golden Cross on the left side of its lapel. He waved toward the Choir Leader.

A tall lean but shapely woman stood up from among the Choir members, wearing a Robe just like her Mother's. This woman was a modem version of Cleopatra. She was gorgeous without any makeup. She smiled a big-beautiful luminous smile that everyone could feel. This was Mrs. Leona Hewitt, Mrs. Cooper's only Daughter, a divorcee, a single Mother, a Schoolteacher at the Goochland County School System near Richmond, and a Voice Specialist. She stood facing the Choir. She raised both her hands toward the Choir. The members began to sway back and forth matching the rhythm of her hands and the music that Mrs. Cooper played.

The Choir sang a very moving rendition of "Amazing Grace." The Hymn moved many of the older people to stand up in the pews and shout: "Hallelujah!"

The Pastor waved his hand and the Choir sang softly. The Reverend Julius Hailstock prayed: "Father God, in the name of Jesus, bless your people this morning; come into the room and save somebody, we pray; lift somebody up outta sin; come into their lives, for God's Sake; heal somebody who is sick an' can't get well, Lord, we pray; deliver somebody from fear, and want; anoint this service so that we will know how to give You the praise, for You are our only God and Savior; All The Glory And Honor Is Thine O 'Lord God Almighty! Amen!"

After the prayer, the Choir picked up the rhythm of the Hymn again. Reverend-Doctor Hailstock waved his hand and Mrs. Hewitt signaled the Choir to cease with a quick jerk of her hand. The Choir members seated themselves.

Reverend Hailstock came to the Podium carrying a large-black Bible. He opened it and read The 23rd Psalm. He returned to the Pastor's Chair. The Choir rose and sang "What A Friend We Have In Jesus"; followed by, "Sinner Man You Better run To Jesus" then, "Oh The Blood Of Jesus That Washes Me White As Snow." That last Hymn caused a lot of people to go dancing in the aisles. The Ushers had to fan a few older people who seemed to be fainting. Some had to be helped up off the floor and back to their seats. They shouted: "Save me, Lord! Make me Whiter than Snow! I wanna be just like Jesus! Save me from the Curse of Sin!"

After the commotion had quieted down somewhat, and the Choir had sat down, Rev.

Hailstock came back to the podium and said:

"Praise The Lord! Thank God Saints." A new round of handclapping, praises, shouting and some dancing broke out and lasted for five-to-ten minutes. Then Rev. Hailstock continued: "Let me introduce to some, and reacquaint to others, a man that many of you know well, Amen. Praise God, because he grew up right here in Fluvanna. A few of you went to school with him on the hill up yonder in Columbia Elementary where Mrs. Lucy Woodson taught so many of us, God Rest Her Soul. Praise The Lord! Let the Church say Amen."

A little bit of praising broke out but soon stopped. The Pastor spoke on: "Reverend John Jasper Nicholas is our guest speaker for The Revival this week. This Minister is a dynamic Preacher, hailing from Thessalonica Baptist up in Dillwyn. God called him to the ministry, a farmer, while walking behind a mule plowing. Now, he's working in the Field of Souls for God. Let the Church say Amen. Without further ado, let us bring Minister Nicholas to you. Let the Church say, Praise The Lord!"

Rev. Nicholas came to the podium wearing a black robe without any frills or fancy embroidery. He was a short stocky man, with a round-brown face, a big nose, thick lips, busy eyebrows and mustache. He had short nubby fingers showing that he was used to hard work. He had very serious-looking brown eyes, that made him seem to be a no nonsense person. He had left his Chair beside the Pastor's almost reluctantly, with a frown on his very sober face. He stood at the podium and smiled and revealed that he had capped a couple of his front teeth with gold and a couple back teeth with silver. He spoke softly at first:

"I thank God for Pastor Hailstock's invitation and introduction, and for this opportunity to come and share the praises of The Lord with you; to take Communion at The Lord's Supper Table with you; and to say what, 'Thus Saith The Lord' to your hearing today. But first, I would like for this great Choir to come back and sing a couple of verses of "The Blood of Jesus."

The Choir did an upbeat rendition of the requested Hymn. Rev.

Nicholas exhorted: "Brothers and Sisters why don't you let go and let God bless you? Let The Lord have His way! Get up on your feet!" now, his voice was booming like a bass drum. "Turn to your neighbor and say: 'Neighbor, it's good to be God's Child! I'm one of God's Children! And God loves me! And I love you cause I know that God loves me!' Amen!" The Congregation obeyed Minister Nicholas, repeating every word he had said.

Rev. Nicholas took his Text from a Grey Bible he had brought with him from Leviticus 18: 21, and 20: 2. *"And thou shalt not let any of thy seed pass through the fire to Moloch, neither shalt thou profane the name of God: I am the Lord*

"Again, thou shalt say to the children of Israel, Whosoever he is of the children of Israel, or of the stranger that sojourn in Israel, who giveth any of his seed unto Moloch, he shall be put to death; the people of the land shall stone him with stones."

He put the Bible down on the podium and paused for a moment. He preached a fire-and brimstone message accusatively charging the congregation with parental neglect.

Most of his sermon helmed around the concept that "like those ungodly people of ancient Israel were doing when offering their little children to a god of fire, as they had learned to do during their Babylonian Captivity, when you fail to instill in a child the way of God; by not bringing him to the Lord Jesus Christ; you're sacrificing him to a modern fiery deity, a present day Moloch," Rev Nicholas exhorted.

The whole congregation had become very quiet. Some nodded in agreement with Reverend Nicholas. Others shook their heads in disagreement. Unc' Charlie sort of dozed off until A'nt Maetta hunched him awake with her elbow. Most of the women in the Congregation were with her; most of the men with him.

Rev. Nicholas ended his lengthy discourse with a call to the Altar. "If you don't know the Lord in the pardon of your sins come forward at this time. Though your sins be as crimson, God Will Make You Whiter Than Snow!

"Let the Deacons and Missionary Mothers come and lay hands on those seeking God's Grace, In The Name of Jesus," Rev. Nicholas intoned.

The Choir rose and sang, "Come to Jesus ..." Several young women and fewer young men came to the Altar to be prayed for. Rev. Nicholas waved his large hands and intoned: "Let those who have fallen away from the Church come forward and be reclaimed by God. God loves you and wants you to be saved. Confess your sins before Jesus and you shall be saved. If you need healing in your body come and be prayed for at this time."

The Choir sang louder. A small crowd of mostly older people gathered around the Altar. Rev. Nicholas laid hands on several people and uttered short prayers. Two enfeebled looking older women came up to be prayed for. They had to be helped by the Ushers. The Reverend laid hands on one and then the other. Both fell to the floor after he prayed for them.

A'nt Maetta stood up in the pews and raised both her hands over her head. She ran around in little circles, shouting: "Yes, Lord! Yes, My Gawd! Have ya way O' Lord-Gawd-Almighty! .."

Unc' Charlie looked very annoyed at all that he was witnessing. He frowned at his wife. He grimaced at the rest, especially at those old ladies who were just getting up off the floor. He was thinking: *They don't look no 'mo' healed then they was at first. I 'spects they just down on that floor gettin' ttention. I bet they's just showin' off That's all!*

Slowly the people at the altar went back to their seats, except the teenagers who had first come up to the altar.

Rev. Hailstock talked to each one of them-about seven of them (five girls and two boys) shook their hands and sent them over to the Church Secretary. These were seeking Baptism. They would have to sit on the Mourners' Bench until that coming Friday night, when they would be immersed in water and declared "Saved!" Their names would be added to the Church-rolls.

A wave of Pastor Hailstock's hand brought the morning service to a close.

Next, the Deacons came to take up the morning offering for the Church and the Speaker. For the Church a huge offering basket was passed around. A much smaller one was passed around for the Speaker. The Deacons took the money baskets through a door in back of the pulpit. The Choir sang, "You Can't Beat God Giving No Matter How Hard You

Try...." When the Deacons returned to the offering table, Rev. Hailstock waved his hand. The Choir went silent.

"If there is no mistake, God bless you for a total offering of four-hundred Dollars," Deacon Baskerfield, Sr. said. "Deacon Percy Thomas will now ask a blessing over these offerings."

A very light-skinned man that resembled one of the White Woods prayed over the offerings that were in two large envelopes on the offering table. He then handed the two envelopes to Deacon Van Cooper. He took one envelope over to a lady sitting beside the Church Secretary, the Church Treasurer, Sister Pauline Quarles. The other envelope he took up to the pulpit and handed it to Rev. Hailstock.

"Let the Church stand on your feet," Rev. Hailstock said. He walked over to in front of Rev. Nicholas, shook his hand and intoned: "Our hearts did bum, Brother Minister as you delivered the word of God to us this morning. We cannot pay you all that this is worth to us, God has blessed us to be able to present you with this token of our esteem." He handed the envelope full of cash to Rev. Nicholas. "We hope you will accept this gift in the name of Jesus and in the Spirit in which it was given."

"God bless you all. I thank God for you, and I look forward to speaking the Word of God to you all of next week, if God wills." Rev. Nicholas vigorously shook Rev. Hailstock's hand.

"If all minds and hearts are clear, 'May the Lord watch between you and me while we are absent one from another, in Jesus Name, Amen!' Church dismissed." Rev. Hailstock shook hands with Rev. Nicholas again, then the Deacons, the Choir members, and a number of the other Church members who came by to greet him and Rev. Nicholas on their way outside.

The Benediction could've come sooner for Unc' Charlie. He made it for the front door as fast as he could. He rolled himself a cigarette and lit-it-up. He figured: *I'm liable to become-a millionaire fore I repent an' be a watered-down Christian.* He found a shady spot under one of the huge oak trees. He leaned against the oak and puffed away feeling good about being away from all of the Church noise. After the first cigarette burned out, he rolled another one.

He looked over across the Church grounds and spied Mrs. Annie Woodson. The tall muscular woman with black-Shirley Temple Curls, wore a long full-length black dress, flat shoes, and a hat on top of her head that seemed like a miniature flower garden. Mrs. Woodson had her little Grand Daughter, Nancy, who was a smaller version of her Grandmother. Both had that smooth pretty skin, with a nice face to match. They were some of those who didn't have to use makeup to be attractive. Unc' Charlie had heard that little Nancy was hard of hearing.

A'nt Maetta and Mrs. Woodson were chatting it up, and laughing at something that had to be pretty funny. They hugged each other and Unc' Charlie was glad that only Maetta was heading over to where he sat.

"Lil' Charlie an' Henry gave my food to Cora an' Cary to serve. I can't stand on my left leg for very long, Charlie. Cora got plenty of paper plates, plastic forks, an' plastic cups. Cary go fix us a cup'la plates an' some Cool Aid or Lemonade. We just gotta wait a little while." A'nt Maetta was all smiles. She and Unc' Charlie seated themselves at a picnic table near the tree.

"I hope it ain't too long, Maetta, I got mighty hungry during the service. I feel like I could eat a horse. Hope we get some-a your fried chicken. Can't ev' body fry chicken to suit me."

A' nt Maetta seated herself on a rough bench of a picnic table, one of many near the oak sentinels surrounding the Church. Unc' Charlie sat across from her.

Unc' Charlie surveyed the churchyard It buzzed with the chatter of young ladies and their Mothers. All had on bouncy-pastel skirts made buoyant by crescent-slips; ruffled blouses with long sleeves; and wide brim sun hats. The way they dressed, smiled, and addressed each other in a sugary southern belle fashion, made them blend in with the whole country-like ambience. Many wore lots of ribbons attached to long braids of their hair; with lots of bright-colored bows sewn onto their dresses; and this definitely distinguished them from visitors, or outsiders. Some of them looked askew at "City Gals" wearing tight-fitting clothing, with dresses "way too short." These they called "Jezebels" under their breath.

Unc' Charlie looked up towards the Church. He saw that a lot of people had gathered around a long table that had been constructed from un-planed hardwood boards nailed to several four by four oak studs for table legs. It was attached to the oak sentinels.

Several cleaned-starched white-sheets were draped across this elongated table that stretched seventy feet long by six feet wide. The air filled with a delicious aroma from the food being brought out and assembled on the table.

Every description of good country cooking was laid out: Blackberry, sweet potato, lemon meringue, pumpkin, chocolate, coconut, and lemon-chess pies; caramel, chocolate, and coconut covered cakes; pans of golden-fried chicken, sliced-baked ham, sliced-roast beef, roasted raccoon, corn pudding and macaroni and cheese; bowls of potato salad, string beans, deviled eggs, collard greens, corn on the cob, and fruit-cocktail ambrosia. The sight of the food and the way it smelled got Unc' Charlie's digestive juices flowing. Rev. Nicholas stood at the head of the large table with his hands lifted up towards Heaven. He prayed for "God's Grace and Blessings upon the food and upon all who prepared it, and for all who would partake of it."

As soon as the "Amen" was pronounced a horde of people that Unc' Charlie didn't remember seeing in the Church for the service that morning flocked to the table with plastic plates and cups in their hands waiting to be served. These interlopers were seemingly the first to invade the feast. A special table had been set away from the larger table for the Pastor and the Guest Speaker and their wives; the Chairman of the Deacon Board, and his wife; and the Mother of the Missionary Board and her husband. It consisted of three card tables set end to end and overlaid with cleaned-starched sheets.

The Pastor sat at the head of this special "Table of Honor." Sparkling silverware and very ornate plates and glasses graced this Table. Several beautiful young ladies dressed in white gowns brought platters of local cuisine to the Pastor and his wife and the Guest speaker. They were served first. Then the young ladies came around to the rest. Once the Pastor started to eat the rest followed his lead.

Cary Winston, a short-plump, gingerbread-colored woman, with long-black hair-locks that went down her back, a jolly-smiling face, and the prettiest grayish-brown eyes, came from the back of the Church carrying two paper plates piled high with food. She carefully walked over to her

Mother and Father, smiling and giggling as she usually did. She put the plates of food with plastic forks and knives down on the table and left right away. She soon returned with two-tall plastic cups, one full of lemonade, and the other of Black Cherry Cool Aid.

With her mouth full of food, A'nt Maetta said: "Thank you, honey. Nice gown you's wearin'. How's Will an' little Mary Ann?"

"Thank you, Momma. We's all fine. I got this gown, mail-order. Saw it in the Sears Catalog. I can get one for ya if-ya-want me-ta."

"No Baby. Iain' got nowhere ta-wear-a gown like that to. I like the rose-flower pattern in it though. This lemonade is good."

"Cora made it. She cooked the chicken too. See y'all later. I gotta get on back up yonder and help serve the food. See y'all for evening service."

"Okay, baby," A'nt Maetta said.

"Bring me some more-a that 'tater salad honey when ya get time, Lil' Bit (Cary's nickname, Unc' Charlie had invented for his Baby Girl)" Unc' Charlie said.

"Okay, Daddy," Cary said. She giggled and returned to the large serving table.

Mrs. Cooper, as Head of the Missionary Board, had well eaten at the Special Table of Honor, but she had gotten another plastic plate of food and made her way over to where Unc' Charlie and A'nt Maetta were seated.

"How y'all?" Mrs. Cooper asked the old couple. She nibbled on a chicken leg then took a bite, chewed it up and gulped it down. "Maetta, as calm as you is, I know you aint heard the news, child!"

"What, Cora? What ya talkin 'bout, now?" A'nt Maetta asked. She stopped eating, so did Unc' Charlie.

Mrs. Cooper got a piece of fried chitterling and ate it up. She cocked her head to the side a little, glancing at A'nt Maetta sideways. "I'm go tell ya somethin' that's go throw ya, honey. You an' Unc' Charlie ain't never heard nothin' like it in ya life!"

A'nt Maetta put her plate down altogether. She stood up and walked around to face Mrs. Cooper. "Cora. What in the world is ya talkin 'bout?" She put her hands on her hips.

"Baby, ya better sit back down fore I tell y'all what I'm go say." Mrs. Cooper got such a serious look on her face that A'nt Maetta started to worry that this may really be serious.

"Aw-ight, Cora. I'm seated. What is it?" A'nt Maetta exclaimed.

"Unc' Charlie, A'nt Maetta, I heard from a number of 'liable peoples, that your Lil Grand Baby, William, done got burnt up in-a big o' fire that broke out at Agnes Mickens's Party last night. They tell me that four little chillren died in that fire. I'm sorry ta-have-ta tell ya!" Mrs. Cooper blurted, then she got crocodile tears in her spiteful eyes. "Y'all ain't heard 'bout it yet?"

"No-Gawd! I ain't heard nothin' toll like that, Cora. Ifn I had, I wouldn't be at Church today. Y' sure ya got-it straight, now?" A'nt Maetta choked the words up out her throat. The pain was too unbearable for her to swallow.

"Here's my hand to God, Maetta," Mrs. Cooper replied. She sat her plate on the table. She stared eye-to-eye with A'nt Maetta. She put her right hand over her heart and raised her left hand up towards the sky. "Child, y' know, I wouldn't lie ta-ya. This is too serious for me ta-be foolin 'round with y'all like that-I wouldn't do that-No Lordi"

A'nt Maetta searched Mrs. Cooper's eyes for a couple of minutes. Unc' Charlie did the same thing.

"Cora, you looks like you's tellin' the truth," A'nt Maetta said. "I just wish ya wasn't." Unc' Charlie's face took on a deep sadness. "I gotta 'gree with ya, Maetta."

"I'm just tryin' ta tell y'all what God loves, an' that's the truth," Mrs. Cooper said.

"Y'all, I figured somethin' like that was go happen. That's why I tried so hard to get Henry an' Charlie, Jr. ta-go get my Grand Babies from over yonder in Cumberland. Now Henry can't, cause Billy ain't over yonder no more. Lord-a-Mercy! I 'on kno' what I 'ma do!" A'nt Maetta's voice fluctuated from a whisper to a minor scream. "Gawd-a-Mighty, Mabel's boy done been burnt up in a fire! One-a Lil' Charlie's Chillun is dead too-Gawd have mercy. Somebody go have-ta pay for this mess." She let the tears come falling down her cheeks.

Mrs. Cooper patted A'nt Maetta on her shoulders. The two women embraced. Then A'nt Maetta brawled like a spanked baby.

"Maetta, it's neglect is all it is. It's them O' Demonic Womens over yonder in Cumberland, honey. If they ain' reckin' somebody's home, they's killin' somebody's chillren. Them sluts're fit to be kilt. Four little innocent chillren, now that's got ta-be the last straw! I tell you!" Mrs. Cooper shouted.

"Cora, I don't want nothin' else ta-eat. I don't know when I'm go have-a appetite. Y'know, I b'lieve The Word of Gawd was aimed right at me. Now I can feel that way down in the pit of my Soul. I done let my Grand Baby 'pass through the fire!' I feels sick ta-my stomach. S'cuse me, Cora, I gotta puke." A'nt Maetta went to the edge of the woods and vomited up almost all of the contents of her stomach

Unc' Charlie ran to his wife. "Maetta tweren't ya fault. Now, you ain't got no reason ta-be sick like this. You gotta think 'bout whose fault it be's. Come back over ta-the table an' rest ya self a little bit. Calm down baby, 'til we get ta-the bottom of all this, aw-ight?"

A'nt Maetta let Unc' Charlie lead her back to the picnic table. She sat down on the rough bench and hung her head.

"Charlie, I should-a drove them boys outta my house like they was mad dogs till they came back with my Grandchillren. Ifn I had, they'd all still be alive today. That's what the Word was tryin' ta-tell me this morning."

Unc' Charlie hugged his grieving wife. "I guess we's both got to bear that Cross. I should-a got on them boys too. Now I wish I had," Unc' Charlie said.

"Cora, wait till I see Agnes's ass--oh pardon me-for cussin' on Gawd's property, I'm go kill that yellar Bitch soon's I see 'er! Go send 'er right-ta-the Pit of Hell!" A'nt Maetta's voice grew to near a growl, reflecting her deeply-felt grief, anger and sorrow.

"I'm so sorry all this got dropped on ya lap like this on-a First Sunday Revival Day. But 'The Truth Is The Light.' That's all I'm tryin' ta-do." Mrs. Cooper got a pontific guise on her gossipy face.

"Well ... I'm duty bound ta-cut Agnes's ass too-short-ta-shit!' flew out of A'nt Maetta's angry lips.

"Baby, ya gotta 'member, you's standin' on Holy Ground. Ya in front of God's House.

Gotta 'spect that, now," Unc' Charlie groaned.

A'nt Maetta didn't want to hear anything of the kind coming from her wayward husband. "Don't try ta-tell-me nothing 'toll 'bout Gawd. Charlie, you ain't the one for that." Anger flashed over A'nt Maetta's face.

Now that Cora Cooper had finished serving Unc' Charlie and A'nt Maetta the **Bread of Wrath,** she gracefully exited and melted into the crowd. She melded in the crowd on the Church grounds like nothing out of the ordinary had happen.

One by one, Roy Winston and his children came by the old couple to pay their respect. A'nt Maetta barely heard or saw them. She was in a daze until, her Daughter, Cora came over to where she was sitting.

"Hi, Daddy," said Cora.

"Humph," said Unc' Charlie. He twisted his mouth up into a scary frown-like that on an angry wolf. He got out his bag of Roll-Your-Own tobacco, and a pack of Cigarette papers, rolled a cigarette, lit it up, and puffed away. Under his breath he uttered: "I ain't ya damn Daddy!"

Cora's eyes grew moist as usual when Unc' Charlie chose to ignore her. "Hi, Momma. How you doing?" she said.

"Oh, Hi Baby," said A'nt Maetta. "I ain' <loin' so well. I gotta ask ya somethin'. Want ya ta-be real truthful, now. Gotta check somethin' out I heard from Cora Cooper. I gotta see ifn you done heard the same thing."

"Momma, I know what ya go ask me. You done heard that Henry's little boy he got with Mabel Scott got burnt up in a house-fire over yonder in Cumberland: Right?"

"Yeah, Baby. Tell Momma what 'cha done heard. I seen Cary earlier, she didn't say nothin' toll 'bout it. What you heard?"

"Momma, it's all over the place. I ain't been over yonder ta-Cumberland, but some people claim they have. They say they didn't see nothin' but ashes over yonder. Couldn't no child make it through that. Billy might be dead like Mrs. Cooper say."

"So, I reek-en what I done heard's true then. Oh-Lord! I wish I had-a done run Henry over yonder to fetch Lil' Billy soon's he born-Oh Lord!"

People seeing A'nt Maetta grieving, and already knowing why, came around to hug and caress her and offered to help in any way they could. Cora, Roy, and their children came first. Tears came down the cheeks of them all.

"Oh, if I only had a chance ta-do-it all over again. I'd send Henry marchin' over yonder fore Gawd got the news. I swear fore Gawd-a-Mighty!" A'nt Maetta shouted, raising her voice like the trumpeting of an elephant.

Everyone slowly made their way back to the Church. It was nearing the time for the start of the evening service. Another local Minister would be the Speaker. The Reverend Samuel Lee from up in Buckingham County, a very dynamic Preacher, who always got people to fall out and lay on the floor in the aisles under The Spirit would bring the Word that evening. He was the Assistant Pastor of Columbia Baptist, but was also the Pastor of Bethlehem Baptist in Arvonia, Virginia.

Rev. Lee's Text that evening was *"Jesus Wept."* But A'nt Maetta hardly heard a word he spoke. People danced, shouted, fell out, and had to be fanned, but A'nt Maetta couldn't feel The Spirit. Then it was as though a lot of members of the Congregation fell into a daze. The bad news had taken a toll on them. Their melancholia put a damper on the whole Congregation. It was a great weight on Rev. Lee. He cut his sermon short. The Benediction could not have come sooner for A'nt Maetta and Unc' Charlie. They were among the first to quickly exit the Church as though they were fleeing a forest fire.

When A'nt Maetta ambled out of the Church, with Unc' Charlie tagging behind her, she sobbed softly like someone leaving the funeral of a Dearly Departed One. Vera and Charles Payne came out behind them.

The Paynes were from up in Troy, a community in Palmyra, Virginia. Palmyra was one of those quaint little places one drives by very quickly when traveling up Route Fifteen North to 250 West from Fluvanna County to Albemarle County. Washington Town, Scottsville, Wilmington, Cary's Brook, and Zion Cross Roads were others. Vera's and Charles's oldest Daughter, Alicia, had gone through Evergreen Elementary Prep, meaning the school that only the Mulatto-elitists' children could attend.

Evergreen Elementary Prep was located just off Route Fifteen at about three miles before you get to S.C. Abrams High, (the only high school for Coloreds). It was originally founded in the late-1800s to educate the children of house servants who had been fathered by White Masters. The children would then be sent North to get a high school education. Eventually they went to Colleges and Universities like Meharry Medical, Howard, Wilberforce, Talladega, Spelman, Morehouse, Texas A&M, and,

Tuskegee; also, Hampton Institute, Virginia State, and, Morgan State Colleges. Evergreen Prep was underwritten by Clubs, Fraternities, and Sororities, such as *The Bon Ton Club; The Jack 'n' Jill Club; The Boys and Girls Club; The Tri Delta Sorority, Etc.*

Promising mulattoes whose parents could afford-or who had a White to Sponsor-the tuition sent their children to Evergreen, then to one of the Mulatto-Elitists' schools. After schooling they often came back to Virginia to teach school, Pastor a Church, or to run a business. Alicia had just been hired by the Fluvanna School Board to teach at a rural elementary school,

Gravel Hill Elementary, until one of the older teachers at Evergreen Prep retired. She had been promised a position at Evergreen. She was around twenty-one years old.

Alicia stood at about Five-Six, and Unc' Charlie saw that she was well-built: shapely hips, pretty legs, a narrow waist, full bosom, and small hands and feet. Her beady eyes were gray like diamonds. Her hair was sandy like her Mother's and both had that styled into Shirley Temple ringlets. She wore a beige two-piece ladies' suit, with the skirt just above the knees, showing brown fox-stockings. Her Mother wore a very similar outfit. Both carried polished brown leather ladies' handbags. Mr. Payne looked like a picture Unc' Charlie had seen of Bob Hope. He wore a three-piece navy-blue suit and brown, highly-polished, loafers. He had darting greenish-blue eyes. His tie that he wore over a yellow dress-shirt was of a green-blue speckled pattern. But A'nt Maetta and Unc' Charlie could see the disgust in Mr. Payne's eyes.

A'nt Maetta had first met Vera when Judge Siegfried had hired her to cook for Alicia's Cotillion at Evergreen. It was Alicia's sixteenth birthday. The muck-to-muck of the Mulatto community had attended the Ball with last names like: Tyler, Fowler, Banks, Garnette, Payne, White, Jackson, Washington, Harris, Carter, Holland, Ragland, and Brown. A'nt Maetta thought that some of those people "was as rabid (racist) as them White folk."

"Hi, Vera," A'nt Maetta said. "What brings y'all to this neck of the woods?"

"Hi, Miss Maetta," Vera said. "We came to support our Pastor Rev. Lee. You know, he went to Virginia Union. I once belonged to his Church up in Buckingham. We're returning to our roots nowadays. You know, all that talk on the radio and TV about civil rights and all."

"What's a TV?" A'nt Maetta asked. "And what'cha mean, returnin' ta-ya-roots? Ya ain't never lost ya roots. I don't care how much-a money y'all got-or who gave it ta-ya, that don't make ya no different than the rest-a us; it don't matter who your Daddies is."

"Well, a TV is like a radio with a big camera-screen on the front of it. When you turn it on, you can see the people talking. It's real nice. But, I disagree Maetta with you on one thing ..."

Mr. Charles Payne got a fox-like snarl on his pale face. "I beg pardon. I have to disagree with you, Madam. My Daddy was a White man. I got a fine home, two-hundred acres of land, and a beautiful farm. I don't have to ask anyone for anything. So, there is a difference, here, between me and people who aren't like me. All my children finished college. How many of yours did?" Mr. Payne said.

"Mr. Payne, that's why I stays 'way from you highfalutin peoples. It's bad 'nough ta-be treated like dirt by them White-Crackers. But comin' from you Colored-Crackers it feels a lot worse. I don't care what'cha got, ya still ain't nothin' but-a Nigga even in the eyes of y' all's White-Daddies. No, my chillun didn't go far in school. They learn-ta read 'n' write though. But I didn't raise no fools, either. Least they ain' shame-a who we is like y'all," A'nt Maetta said. "Humph!" went Charles, Sr. "Vera, Alicia, let's clear the air by moving on. We don't have to listen to any more of this." He rolled his eyes in A'nt Maetta's direction. He, his wife, and Daughter threw their noses up in the air and strutted away to their new black Cadillac Convertible parked near the Church's entrance in a space right next to the Pastor's parking area.

As Mr. Payne walked away he uttered loud enough for A'nt Maetta and Unc' Charlie to hear him: "See, Vera, I've stressed the point to you before, that we no longer bear any affinity to those people. They're so thick-headed that only a sound beating can turn them towards anything positive. They just don't have the sense to understand anything any other way. I hope you see what your job has to be up at Gravel Hill, Alicia. I wouldn't wish it on a dog."

"Yes ... but, Charles, they're still our Blood, Dear," Vera answered sheepishly, as though she'd said something awfully bad-like a cursed word. She fell into dead silence.

"Yes, Father," was Alicia's only reply. She looked straight ahead as their car sped off. Her eyes became like those of a Great White Shark.

"Charlie, ain't it-a-shame the way them peoples look down they nose at us? Sometimes, I 'spects they hates us more'n them o' rabid Crackers," Henry hissed as the Paynes drove past them.

"Them peoples ain't like us. They ain't one-a us, Big Bro. Since slavery days, they been 'gainst peoples like us. They worked in the Whiteman's Big Houses, ate with they families, an' slept in they beds-y' know, bed-wenches and all. Man, they ain' nothin' but Chocolate Crackers, that's all they is. What they think 'bout us is the same shit as them Crackers. I don't know why they ever bother ta-come 'round us at all. I bet it gets right in they gallbladders when they have-ta face us. Ta-them, it gotta be like lookin' at-a Bogeyman," Lil' Charlie said. "We come from the Field Hands-that be the trouble, man. It was even like that in the Army."

"Yeah, Charlie, I reek-en that be right," Henry replied.

The 1947 Ford Charlie, Jr. drove kicked up dust when it slid off the pavement onto the gravel of the Church's driveway. Both of A'nt Maetta's Sons were feeling their beer a little bit. They were all smiles, when they observed the pretty Sisters still melding around on the Church Grounds. Some of the frisky young ladies waved and smiled suggestively at the cocky-young men and they smiled and waved back. But as soon as A'nt Maetta and Unc' Charlie had climbed into the backseat of Lil' Charlie's Car, an argument erupted.

A'nt Maetta lit into her Sons: "Henry, lemme tell ya that ya ain' from shit! While you an' Lil' Charlie was out whorin' 'round all over Fluvanna, an' Cumberland, last night, Agnes was burnin' the hell outta my Grand Baby, Billy, an' three-a Mamie's Chillren. Cora Cooper couldn't wait ta-tell-me 'bout it at Church today." She blurted out her compliant as though it was all one sentence.

"I 'on b'lieve-it, Momma," Henry replied. He was a little alarmed at that story being dropped on him all at once. "Charlie, Jr. an' I played for that party till way late, an' we didn't see no fire fore we left."

"We left with-a cup'la gals we picked up at the Party. It was gettin' ta-be pretty early in the mornin'. Look like we ought-a seen any fire goin' that might've kilt a bunch-a chillren," Lil' Charlie explained.

A'nt Maetta was not convinced. "Henry, ya-should-a gone an' got Billy from over yonder when I-told-ya-ta. If somethin' done happen ta-that boy how's that go make ya feel?"

"Momma, I'd feel right bad 'bout that, if it be true. I' on want the boy ta-get burnt up in no fire, he's my flesh-an'-blood. But I still b'lieve ya-gotta take what Cora Cooper say with more'n a grain of salt."

It was something about the sound of Henry's voice that made A'nt Maetta doubt the sincerity of his statement. That made her blood boil.

"I didn't let James Lewis force ya ta-marry his Daughter, Henrietta, after ya got 'er knocked up. I thought nineteen was too young ta-force ya into a shotgun wedding. Now I wish I had. I hate the way ya-done turnt out. James's gal had a girl, she named Agnes. I 'on know where Henrietta done took my Granddaughter. I heard she's up yonder in New York."

"Ah, Momma, there ya go jumpin' on that o' horse. Henrietta ran off ta-New York an' took my Baby Girl with her. Weren't my fault. I got cold feet at first. But if she'd stayed a little bit longer, I'd-a done the right thing. I had ta-come ta-the right mind, that's all," Henry groaned.

"Oh, shut the hell up, boy!" A'nt Maetta yelled at the top of her voice. "Who the hell do ya think you's foolin'? You left that little pregnant gal at the altar with her Momma, Edmonia, an' her Daddy, James, Sr., an' Rev. Hailstock-an' the rest-a her family. All-a her friends was there waitin' on you. I know 'bout it all.

"Talk had it that you's over yonder in Cumberland gettin' little Mabel Scott pregnant an' sleepin' with 'er Momma after ya did it, an' that's why ya didn't show up to marry Henrietta. Agnes Mickens is Clemmon Mickens's wife-he got ya the job with Van Yahres Tree Construction up yonder in Charles'ville--an' you's all over his wife, Henry? I heard all 'bout it. That's probably why Henrietta named your Daughter, Agnes. It had-a be ta-spite ya. That's some nasty shit, Henry. Ya know it is."

Henry rolled his eyes at his angry Mother but didn't dare to answer her back. Lil' Charlie motioned with his right hand, while steering the car with his left. He was getting ready to say something in his Brother's defense.

"Don't ya open ya mouth, Lil' Charlie. You ain't worth-a shit, neither.

Now get this whore wagon on up ta-West Bottom quick as ya can," A'nt Maetta shouted at Lil' Charlie.

"Aw-ight, Momma," Lil' Charlie said.

Once they were home, A'nt Maetta climbed out first. All of the men stayed in the car to see what might happen next. After a while all three got out of the car and eased toward the house. They all went in and carefully sat down. Unc' Charlie lit a lamp.

All that next week, A'nt Maetta's anger boiled. At one point she hissed to Unc' Charlie: "I wanna cut that heifer's throat, Charlie. When next I see Agnes Mickens's ass in Columbia, I wanna send 'er ta-meet 'er Maker! I ain't go never get over this. I ain't never kilt nobody, but I swears fore-Gawd! I's read-ta kill Agnes. I done cut one or two mens and a cup 'la womens ta get 'em off me. But I ain' never wannna kill one-a 'im"

Thursday Night rolled around and A'nt Maetta couldn't sleep. Anticipation was keeping her awake.

CHAPTER SEVEN

Mabel boarded the Westbound local at the Greyhound Station in Richmond on Thursday instead of Friday. She had been anxious and upset until then as though something bad had happened. Her fears came from deep-down in her psyche. It was like a big o' lump pushing from the bottom of her guts up to her throat. It had driven her to a state of near hysteria.

That Thursday afternoon after she had served lunch to Mrs. Gault and her chatty friends, Mabel took off her apron and allowed: "Mrs. Gault, I gotta get up to the bus station right away. Somethin' ain't right at home, an' I gotta get up yonder an' take-a look see."

Mrs. Gault took off her thick glasses and sighed. "Wait . . . I'll dismiss you on one condition, you have to be back at your station in the morning. We're having the Governor's wife over for lunch, and I want everything to be perfect. I need you then. You're one of my best gals. Is that all right with you?"

Mabel didn't answer. In a minute or two she was out of the door jogging to the street bus stop. She found herself getting off the street bus like she was in a dream. West Broad was really noisy that day. Seemed like way too many people were in the Bus Station for a Thursday afternoon-evening maybe-but not this early. She was glad that she was in time to catch the Westbound local, and she laughed out loud.

Mabel got a little upset when it seemed that it was taking way too long to get on the bus. It seemed like the bus was filling up too fast. That could mean that she might have to wait an hour for the next Westbound local; especially if all the seats got taken by the Whites. Finally, the line narrowed to her. She got on the bus and went to the back and sat down beside another fat black woman.

The bus was crowded. Almost immediately, a well-dressed heavyset White woman, wearing a charcoal grey suit, a big ladies' bag and a black umbrella came and stood in front of Mabel and the lady sitting next to her. The White lady looked to Mabel to be some office person or secretary. She stood staring at Mabel and her seatmate. A number of other people were standing in the aisle some of them were White and some Black. But this woman got a snarl on her pencil line lips. She put her hands on her hips.

"Niggers! Why aren't you getting up? Get up, I say," this facsimile of a lard can ordered, pointing first at Mabel then at the other lady. "Can't you see there isn't room enough on this bus for you all to sit while a White lady's standing? You people are getting more uppity every day. It's that Civil Rights Movement that's gone to you all's heads. I'm telling you all for the last time: Get The Hell Up!" The Elephant trumpeted. Her voice had an exaggerated tone of importance to it. But the White-Southern Drawl came across dominating the ending of each word she tried so hard to properly pronounce.

Mabel was sitting on the outside edge of the seat. She grimaced, but remembered that at the ticket counter back at the Station, the Blacks had to wait in the back of the line until all of the Whites had been served. Blacks had to go downstairs to a little "hole in the wall" waiting room to wait for their buses to arrive. It was right next to the toilets. A tear eased down Mabel's cheeks. The other lady, who also wore a Maid's Uniform, got teary-eyed too. Both got up and gave up their seats. They knew the Lard Can had no intentions of sitting beside a "Negro."

After the fat lady sat down she allowed: "Now they're some good Niggers! I like it when Niggers know their place." She smiled from ear-to-ear.

"It's because of people like you that make our good Colored people mad, and it's why they're in the streets all over the South fighting to change the Law. I hope they win," a little-White blonde lady wearing a Maid's Uniform said. She was standing in the aisle.

"You best mind your business, hussy," the fat lady said. A skinny White man sat in the seat beside the fat woman. He smelled of cow's milk, manure, and funky underarms. The fat lady snorted, coughed, and got up. She stood in the aisle again. No one would sit beside the Farmer wearing Bibb Overalls, with tobacco stains on his frizzy beard, and on his cowboy boots.

The Farmer beckoned to Mabel and the other Maid to come sit beside him. Both refused.

They would rather stand than to be subjected to White inferiority.

Mabel was very tired. She felt even worse on her way up Route Six. The bus made a stop at every nook and cranny. She hoped somebody would challenge that bus policy so tired people could just sit on the bus wherever they pleased. Finally, she got off the bus up at Cumberland Bridge Road.

On that Monday, Mabel had a nightmare. She saw Billy screaming for her. He was a little Tar Baby running towards her screaming: "Momma! Momma! Save Me!" His whole body was engulfed in flames, crackling, bubbling, and boiling. Panic swelled up in her chest making her feel as though she would burst asunder. Up until Thursday that panicky feeling would not go away.

The closer she got to home the greater the fear. Her temples felt like her brain might explode any moment. Her heart beat like a drummer's snare drum. Then her mouth became dry as powder, like it was full of desert sand. A stabbing pain surrounded her heart. It matched her heartbeat. She took off running towards her Mother's Shanty. It seemed like it was twenty miles away instead of the short distance it actually was. Mabel screamed as she ran:

"I hope Billy's all right! I hope ain' nothin' happen ta-my baby!"

Then her eyes focused on the ashes left from the fiery devastation of Mamie's Shanty. "Oh My-God! What done happen ta-my-Billy?" She increased her strides. She felt like she was floating instead of running at full-speed.

Out of breath, Mabel burst through the door of her Mother's Shanty. She screamed: "Momma! Where the hell is Lil' Billy? Where's he at? If'n one-a ya Bitches done hurt a hair on his head, you's go wish you's never born! I'll kill ya with my bare hands. Do ya hear me?"

Agnes, with a lone tear easing down the side of her right cheek, came into the hallway carrying Billy in her arms. He had on training pants and a T-Shirt. He jumped out of his Grandmother's arms to the floor. He jumped up into his Mother's outstretched arms. She laughed for a little, joyful, moment. Billy hugged his Mother tight as he could. He let go and blurted out: "Hey, Momma. I almos' burnt up in-a big o' fire A'nt Franny made in Mamie's house! All Mamie's chillren's dead 'ceptin' Cousin Bernard! What ya bring me, Momma?" The words came out of Billy in one breath.

Mabel gasped for breath. She trembled all over. This had been close enough for her. "Momma, ya get Billy's things an' toys together. I'ma take my baby 'way from over here. I ain' lettin' you trifflin' Bitches kill my Baby!

"I don't know why-in-the-hell I ever was stupid 'nough ta-leave-'im with y'all in the first place!" Mabel shouted just below a hysterical scream.

Agnes uttered not a word. She turned on her heels, went from room to room to gather some of the many clothing outfits, little toy trucks and cars, and jeans Mabel had bought and delivered to Agnes for her son. But Agnes could only find a couple pairs of pants and one shirt for Billy. There were no toys. The clothing she found was torn and raggedy.

When Mabel saw what her Mother presented to her, she yelled: "Where the hell's the rest-a Billy's clothes an' toys, Momma?"

"Mabel, Maude borrowed a few-a Billy's things for Steve. She ain't workin' no more, cause she's a little-bit crazy since the fire. Since you is workin' we figure you wouldn't mind lettin' Steve wear some good clothes, an' things . . ."

"Momma! I don't give-a-damn 'bout what Maude is or ain't doin'! You go ta-Neddy's place, get my boy's things an' bring that back ta-me so I can get my ass and my Son an' get-the hell- 'way from this place for good!"

Agnes went on out her door right away. She cursed under her breath as she trotted along the few yards to Neddy's Shanty. She burst through the door of Neddy's place. "Neddy, child, get all-a Billy's things, put that in-a box so I can take it back to my sassy-ass Daughter, Mabel. She go take Billy ta-Rich-men, directly. I hope she don't think I'm go try-ta stop 'er." The words spewed out of Agnes's mouth like the water does out of a fireman's water hose.

Neddy answered: "Lordy-Agnes, I reek-en all-a them clothes be mostly rags by now, 'ceptin' that Cowboy Suit Mabel brought ta-Billy last week. It's prob-be still fittin' ta-wear. I'on kno' if'n we can find his cap pistols, or his carpenter's set, or his little-red wagon. The bigger boys done broke those all up playin' with Stevo, an' all."

Looking around the Shanty, Needy got a sad look on her old face. "I 'on kno' what little Stevo go play with now? He ain't go have nothin' ta-wear neither. If only we could get Mabel ta-see reason." She handed Agnes a cardboard box of tattered clothing, with a fairly-new red and-white Cowboy Suit and a pair of Black Boots. That outfit was placed on top of the rest.

"I'ma take this shit back ta-Mabel. She ain' never go unnerstan' nothin' toll. We gotta raise up chillun like Stevo to be leaders, so one day he'll get us all free. Why can't Mabel see that? All our Leaders Look Like Stevo."

Agnes took the box she had been given back to her Shanty to an anxiously-waiting Mabel. "There! Hope you's happy! Ya-can take ev' thin' an' ev' body on back ta-Rich-men, Mabel."

Mabel took the Cowboy outfit off the top of the box, and the pair of Cowboy boots, dressed Billy, with her eyes getting very moist. "Here, Momma. Take the rest-a those rags back to y'all's ever-lovin' Stevo. That shit in that box ain' nothin' but-a sin an' a-shame."

After she had gotten Billy dressed she asked: "Where's Franny?"

"All last week Franny wander 'round in the woods hollerin' for Mamie's chillun what got burnt up in the fire. She, Maude, Catherine, Mamie, an' Phyllis was taken down to Peter 'burg ta-get they heads straight. Go be a while for them gals down yonder. State People been over here askin' questions 'bout the fire. They been askin 'bout Stevo, an' his little Sister, an' Catherine's Twins. Them kid 're so White-lookin'. Neddy had-a lotta trou'ba with Phyllis like that."

"Momma, though I'm pissed at ya, I gotta know somethin' fore I leave. Why was ya-so mean-ta-me? What did I ever do ta-make ya act like-a ice-Queen? Why won't ya tell-me who my Daddy is? I wanna see my Daddy awfully bad. It hurts me so bad. Do ya hate me over Henry?"

"Well, Mabel, Clemmon be gone all week long-an' sometimes, he didn't bother ta-come home on weekends. I got mighty lonely. When he came home ever Fridays, he took-a bath, got a home-cooked meal an' I didn't see'im again till Sunday nights. He be cuttin' logs all week long, an' I 'on kno' what or who he be cuttin' on weekends, most-a the time. It sure won't me. I had-a lay in my bed lonely, night-after-night.

"Henry's a guitar player. His playin' made me feel good. I 'vited 'im ta-come cheer me up one night after he an' Mer' broke up. One thing led-ta-another. I gave him what all mens wants. He must've like it, cause he's with me one night when he's s'pose-ta be off marryin' some gal up near Dixie. I know he didn't marry 'er. He's a lot younger 'n me, but I'd a left Clemmon for him any day. He said he's thinkin' bout it when you came 'long. Ya got 'im with ya young body, he's a lot older 'n you, but that's why he fell for you."

"No, Momma. Lemme tell ya what I think was the problem. It was all that blankin' out ev' time somethin' excited ya a little bit. You'd flip out an' stay that way for a cup'la days. A man wants his woman ta-be-there for 'im. Sometimes ya ain't there for Clemmon, or Henry. So ya know they go get with some-a the pretty women who is always after 'em. They's both real cute, Momma. Neither one go have any trou'ba gettin' a gal here an' there. Lonely womens are a dime a-dozen 'round here. Good mens be a lot harder ta-find. So, if not me, it would-a been somebody else."

What Mabel said cut a little deeper, but Agnes responded: "Mabel, ya didn't have-ta sleep with Henry, though. I would never fuck one-a y' all's mens while you's still goin' with 'im. That was so nasty of you. Ya screwed one-a ya Momma's mens. Now, ya know that's true."

Mabel came right back at her. "Don't judge me, Momma. You's married-ta Clemmon all the time you's goin' with Henry. Mary's ya Daughter. Least, I's fuckin' a single man-I'm a single gal. Ain't nothin' wrong with that. You oughtn't be mad at me 'bout that. The best woman just won out is all."

Agnes grew very sad. "Mabel, I can see ya ain' go lemme get-a word in edge-ways. But ya Daddy got me knocked up an' left me that way. I had ta-fend-for myself an' my chillun. I told 'im he's never go see that child in my belly. Turns out I had two-a y'all growin' in me. So it ain't no use in ya beggin' me 'bout that no-good bastard. He ain' worth-a shit. He didn't ever try-ta come see 'bout you or George. Maybe, ifn he had, I'd given in. So forget 'bout 'im. Funny thing, George don't never ask 'bout 'im. I'll never take his name in my mouth till the day I die."

Mabel didn't give up. "Momma, didn't none-a the other mens ever give ya anythin' neither.

You didn't stop them from knowin' who they chillren was. Just me an' George don't know. That ain't fair, Momma. What did Ginia's Daddy ever give ya? She knows who her Father is. Why would it hurt ya so bad just ta-tell me who mine is."

Agnes didn't want to hear Mabel asking her that question again. "No, it ain't Mabel. By Gawd! I done got mighty tire-a ya mouthin' off 'bout it. Iain' go never talk no more 'bout it an' tell ya no more 'n I done already told ya. So ya might as well drop it. It's 'bout time for your bus ta-come. Take care-a Billy an' yourself, now," Agnes said.

Mabel took Billy by the hand and set out for the bus stop. She cried as she walked away, and Agnes stood on her dilapidated porch and wept sorely as Mabel walked away. Mabel stopped and turned around once. She didn't know whether to feel sorry for her Mother, or to hate her. Then, her Mother waved bye-bye, and Mabel waved back.

"I'm glad-ta be takin' ya way from that chicken coop, Billy. We ain't never go be comin' back there ta-stay."

It dawned on Billy what was really going on then. "I don't wanna leave Grandma. N-0-0-0- 0, lemme go!" He tried to pull his hand out of his Mother's grip. He tried to fall to the ground in protest. He stuck his left thumb in his mouth.

His resistance caused Mabel to snap for a second or two. She slapped Billy up beside his head pretty hard. "I said let's go! And I mean, right now!" Mabel exclaimed.

Billy screamed at the top of his voice. The lick had caused a ringing in his ears. His Grandma had never done that before-only A'nt Franny had. He saw little lights dancing before his eyes. It reminded him of when his Cousin Maude had slapped him for insisting on coming over to her Shanty to play with the toys his Mother had left for him. He never got to play with the new toys Mabel left for him after his Mother left. Right away, they were given to Stevo. His new clothes were given to Stevo to wear, and he got to wear those clothes Stevo had messed up. He only got to wear good clothes when it was time for his Mother to come see him. Now she was beating him too. He thought he had better not resist her anymore, so he trudged along behind her away from the only home he had known thus far.

Mabel looked down at her little Son and tears came down her cheeks. The bus came. Billy was afraid of this steel monster, but dared not anger his Mother again. He got on after her, holding onto her dress tail, and followed her to a backseat on the bus.

"I's hungry, Momma," Billy whined. "I only ate bread this morning. I don't like thick 'n gravy. Grandma say she ran outta groceries. We's waitin' for Grandpa Clemmon to come bring some. He didn't come yet, so I had a lotta Buttermilk an' water. My stomach hurts, Momma."

Tears squirted out of the corners of Mabel's eyes. She grabbed Billy to her and kissed her Son all over his little face. "Momma loves you, honey. I's sorry I slapped ya like that. I'll never hit ya like that again.

"Wait till we get ta-Rich-men, ta-Mrs. Gault's place, where I works. She got plenty-ta eat. You'll be able ta-eat till it run outta ya. My Darling little Son, Momma loves her Lil' man, yeah, she do. Ev' thin' go be aw-ight, an' I promise ya I'll never leave ya again as long as I live," Mabel said. She sat Billy in her lap and rocked him to sleep.

Soon the bus came to a stop at the Bus Station in Richmond. Mabel climbed out to the loud noise of West Broad Street. To Billy, the air stank like gasoline, stale food, and rotting leaves mixed together. His Mother raised her hand and a big old yellow car came to a stop in front of the Bus Station. Billy got in the backseat of the yellow car with his Mother. The street signs and lights whizzed by until they were out in what looked like the countryside. Then they arrived at a Mansion on Parham Road. The Gault's place reminded Billy of a Doll House he had seen Linda Walton playing with at Arthur Walton's Grocery Store in Columbia.

He had never seen so many doors and windows on one building in his life. This was no Doll House though. Real people lived there. A boxwood hedge surrounded the house. Outside that was a tall brick and stone fence. Beautiful evergreen trees dotted the landscape, and the lawn was like a green-velvet carpet. The driveway even had bricks covering it. They had gone past a number of Mansions like this one on their way up to this house, but none was as large or had as many bricks as this one that his Mother worked at. He was very excited.

Billy watched Mabel go around to the side of the building to a smaller door than the rest of those that he had seen. He saw her pushing a white button on the door entrance. It made a funny buzzing noise. A very dark-skinned fat woman answered the door. She reminded Billy of his

A'nt Neddy. Only this one had on a uniform just like his Mother's. She frowned at them.

"Mabel ... C' mon in. Who's that with you? I didn't know ya had any of those. Bet Mrs. Gault don't know neither. Y'all c' mon in, it's gettin' dark out yonder. Mabel ... Y' better get ya little bundle of joy to-ya room fore Mrs. Gault sees 'im. Y' kno' how she's liable-ta act, child," came out of the thick lips of this gray-headed old Maid. Her voice was husky, but it also had a minor squeak to it too.

Mabel grabbed Billy by his right hand. She and he scurried down a long hallway to a section of the building way in the back to the Maid's Quarters. Mabel was hurrying along as fast as she could. Then-she heard footsteps behind her fast approaching. Then-

"Mabel Louise, whose little pickaninny do you have there with you in my house?" Mrs. Gault's aggravating Southern-Styled voice called out.

Mabel did an about-face to face her Boss. She saw that she was dressed in a pink-satin housecoat with ermine borders, and was wearing a matching pair of slip-ons on her large feet. Her satin-blond hair was up on large-black rollers. She covered her head in a red fishnet scarf. Her face was covered in a green-mud mask. She looked like a monster standing in the middle of the hallway with her hands on her protruding hips. Mabel knew she was waiting for an answer.

"This is William, my Son," Mabel said. Her face took on a sheepish gaze like a child caught with her hands in the cookie jar.

"What!" gushed out of Mrs. Gault's mouth like champagne out of a newly uncorked bottle. "I certainly did not know that you had one of those, Mabel Louise. I would never have hired you. Do you understand that?"

"Yes' am, I do, Mrs. Gault," Mabel whined. Her eyes filled up with tears.

"Well Mabel. How will you do your work like I demand of all my Maids and worry over this boy of yours, too? I require your services on a twenty-four hour basis." Mrs. Gault had a very scornful look on her face.

"Ma'am, I'll manage. I 'ma do very well, I promise. I'll work twice as hard for ya, just you wait an' see. Lil' Billy won't be no trou'ba a' toll. Lemme keep 'im in my room just for a little while. I ain't got nowhere else ta-take 'im. Ya ain' go put me an' my baby out after I done tried ta-do a good job for ya, scrubbin' an' waxin' all these floors, an' things, Mrs. Gault, are you?" Mabel pleaded with her Boss.

"Mabel . . . You are a good-little gal, I must say. But I'm sorry. I just can't have a little Negro running loose in my home. What would the people I entertain think? What if one of the government officials we entertain, or one of their wives, would see a little chocolate-colored child scampering about the premises? I can't take the slimmest chance of that happening. I am afraid that will never do. I mean, you will have to move away from here and find another job immediately. A person of my standing in society simply cannot take the risk you're asking me to take.

"I am, however, not heartless. I will give you a week to find another job. You can count on me to give you an excellent reference. I'll give you a month's pay, and a fifteen dollar bonus for all of the good work you have done for me so far. That should add up to forty-five dollars in all. I feel that it is more than generous-certainly more than other ladies I know would give you. Nevertheless, it will have to tide you over in any case."

Mabel cried. She was in a panic. "But Mrs. Gault, where can I go? What am I go do, now?" She hoped there was a soft spot in Mrs. Gault's heart, somewhere.

"Mabel, Mar' Lizzy, my door gal, has been with the Gault family for most of her life, since she was a gal of about ten or twelve, she's over sixty, now. She never married. She never got pregnant. That's why she's been allowed to live in this house continually. All she has to do now is answer the front door. We love her, and she loves working for us. That's the kind of service I'm looking for in a loyal gal. With a child underfoot, you cannot give us that kind of service."

Tears of defeat streamed down Mabel's cheeks. "Mrs. Gault, I swears, I'm go do ev' thin' just-ta way ya wants. I'll keep my little Son William outta sight. You an' nobody else won't never see 'im. But I wanna keep 'im in my room near me."

"Mabel," said Mrs. Gault, now frowning scornfully at her. "You just do not understand. The two gals in the washroom, Gayle and Sukie, are young but they are committed just like Mar' Lizzy too. The two cooks, Mae and Lilly, are a bit older, but are my standbys. If I give in to you, it would create quite a storm. It would break the trust I have with them.

So, I'm sorry, but I want you out of my home in a week. That's my final word, Mabel!"

Mrs. Gault turned her back to Mabel, stuck her long-pointed nose up in the air, and strutted on up her highly-polished hardwood floors that Mabel had cleaned and polished just two days ago.

Mar' Lizzy had been eavesdropping. She tipped over to Mabel.

"Don't worry sugar," said Mar' Lizzy, "It's cause-a Mrs. Gault can't have babies is the reason she's the way she is. I got a bundle of dollar bills I'ma give ya ta-help out. Now, ya take that money an' go up yonder ta-1717 Venerable Street. That's where ya Sister, Ma' Dear lives. Dora never wanted me ta-tell ya that, cause the place she's livin' in is so raggedy. But ya go find her an' tell'er Mar' Lizzy says hello, aw-ight?"

Mabel and Mar' Lizzy heard footsteps coming in their general direction. Mar' Lizzy tiptoed back to the front door to stand like a Roman Soldier so that Mrs. or Mr. Gault would never have to answer their own front door.

Mabel put the roll of bills into her uniform pocket. She went to her room with Billy. He sat on the big o' bed in his Mother's room. She slipped down to the kitchen and Mae and Lilly fixed a cold plate full of leftover assorted finger sandwiches. Billy ate until his little stomach ached. He drank nearly a half-glass of fresh milk and got sleepy right away. It had been a long day.

As Billy dozed off, Mabel whispered: "Don't worry, Darlin'. We's go find A'nt Dora up on Venerable Street in the mornin'. We got a warm bed tonight. We's go rest till tomorrow," Mabel cooed to her dozing little Son. He sank right down in the goose-down comforter on Mabel's bed, in more comfort than he had ever known. He went out like a light.

Early the next morning, Mabel awoke Billy. "Get up, baby, Momma's go feed ya somethin' good ta-eat this mornin'." Mabel carried a plate piled high with grits, bacon, scrambled eggs, toast and Jam, and hash browns. The cooks had rustled it together for Mabel. They were sad and almost crying at the heartlessness of their Boss. Lil' Billy dove into the plate of food and filled up quicker than he thought. He got sick to the stomach because he tried to eat too much.

Mabel took the dirty dishes to the kitchen. Strangely enough, she walked past Mrs. Gault.

She had ruin her mascara. She had been crying. Mabel returned to her room in a trot.

"Billy, let's go fore Mrs. Gault know we's gone. We don't need-ta let 'er have the last word." Mabel wore a pair of gray slacks a pink blouse, and a pair of black flats. She put on a light jacket Mae had given her. She had to leave her Maid's Uniform behind. Billy only had his

Cowboy suit to wear.

Then Mabel saw an envelope on the bureau in her room. It simply had her name written on the front of it. There was a note inside: "Dear Mabel Louise. Take the seventy-five dollars inside and God bless you. I don't hate you or your child. Good Luck, Mrs. and Mr. Gault."

"Billy, ma-be, she ain't such-a big o' turd after all. Could be that she just don't know how-ta act no other way. She's a Southern-White Woman."

The stack of bills that Mar' Lizzy had given Mabel consisted of a-hundred dollars. Mabel had never held one-hundred and Seventy-five Dollars of her own before in her life.

"Billy, let's go, Son. We gotta go face the world."

CHAPTER EIGHT

"C'mon, Charlie," A'nt Maetta shouted, "let's getta move on fore Walton's truck get up here. We won't make it-ta Columbia ifn we miss it. Man, you's movin' slower 'n me, an' my leg's gettin 'bout cripple. A gang-a peoples go be on the road today, mostly from up here at West Bottom. Ya always sees the same bunch, an' it's 'bout time for 'em to go-ta Town, like us."

Unc' Charlie scratched his chin that badly needed a shave. He was wearing a Bibb Jean and Jacket outfit with its insulated padding. A'nt Maetta wore a thick-cotton dress, thick stockings, a thick sweater, and an even thicker coat. She sported a pair of lace-up boots. They were ready to brave the cold. Unc' Charlie stepped in front of his wife. She stopped to listen to her husband with a look on her face that conveyed: "This better be important!"

"What you want, Charlie? It's too cold ta-be foolin' round, now," A'nt Maetta said.

"Maetta . . . Look. When ya gets ta-Columbia, don't make-a big fuss- that go just make-a ass outta yourself 'Member now, you's s'pose-ta be decent Church people."

"What!" A'nt Maetta snapped. She rolled her eyes like marbles for a second.

"Mary Etta-well-I mean," Unc' Charlie scratched his head. "Don't show off in front-a them Crackers. They like it when we act like a bunch-a wild-crazy Niggers! When we do that it please 'em more 'n anythin' in this world. They like it when we put our bizzness in the streets like that. It make 'em feel like they's so much-a better'n we is. Ya unnerstan'."

"Look, Charlie," A'nt Maetta said. She backed away from Unc' Charlie a little. "I ain't promise you that I ain't go act up when I sees Agnes's ass. No-Gawd! I feels worse ever time I thinks 'bout Lil' Billy being taken from us like he was. Now, all I got is that child's cute-little face in my heart. I's only seen 'im once, Charlie. That little gal, they call 'Ginia was holdin' 'im.

"I'm go send Agnes's ass to hell so she can feel the fire she put my Grand Baby through.

That's all ta-it, Charlie."

"Maetta, I know what'cha feelin'. But ya gotta do ev' thin' the right way. Ev' body go be down ta-Columbia today. They 'spects you's go be there for Agnes. If y'all gets ta-fightin' the Colored peoples go laugh, an' the Crackers go just think y' all's crazy. Do ya wanna be looked at like that? That's all I'm askin'."

Tears came to the comers of A'nt Maetta's eyes. "Hear that, Charlie? It's that old truck of Arthur Walton's growlin' up the road. "Let's go get loaded on back."

Unc' Charlie and A'nt Maetta lumbered up the hill to the roadside. A'nt Maetta waved her left hand. She carried an old black ladies' bag on her other arm.

"Hold it, Mr. Walton, we's goin' ta-Columbia today," Unc' Charlie yelled as loud as he could.

The driver of the truck, Arthur Walton-a descendant of the Afton Mountain's Waltons-a steady built man, with reddish-blond hair, beady-little gray eyes, and was about in his late forties-early-fifties. He wore, as always, a green serviceman's khaki pants and shirt outfit. He had on a red and white plaid jacket, and tall fishermen's boots. His thick glasses indicated that he had poor vision. He drove a green International Truck with a lattice wall around its flatbed. He picked up the people in West Bottom, Cloverdale, Gravel Hill, Stage Junction, and this side of Cumberland. People usually packed on the back of his truck like cattle. The truck pulled to the side of the road, An't Maetta and Unc' Charlie got on just in time. Walton pulled off without looking back, or giving a damn about the safety of the people he was hauling like livestock.

A'nt Maetta noticed that there weren't that many people hopping on the truck that day. As the truck made its way up through West Bottom, only ten older people had jumped on back of the truck. "Maetta, the young people 're gettin' cars nowadays, that's why they ain't catchin' the truck no more."

"Reck-en you's right, Charlie. Wish more peoples was gettin' on. We'd be a lot warmer back here. It's cold as can be this December day."

The truck came down the hill on Route Six to the edge of Town. A'nt Maetta saw a noisy horde of people at Walton's Grocery as she and the "West Bottom Crowd" got off the truck. There were loud joking, mule-sounding laughter, people gossiping and telling lies standing in front of Walton's, "cutting-the-fool" was the term local people used.

Unc' Charlie shook hands with several of the men out that day. He watched them fan out to nearby stores: Profits Dry Goods and Grocery Store; then they went past the Catholic Church and the Town Hall; to Holland's Hardware; and then to the greatest hole-in-the-wall in the one horse-Town, located in the building that housed Parish's Cafe, and Thurston's Grocery Store.

At Parish's "Negroes" could buy beer on the premises, but had to take it out of the restaurant to drink it. Local laws prevented them from drinking in the Town's limits. Unc' Charlie and a few of his drinking buddies put together enough money to buy twenty-four 12 Oz cans of Richbrau Beer. It cost six dollars. They could've bought twelve, but there were nearly fourteen of them in on the Case of Beer.

Unc' Charlie cradled the Case of Beer under his left aim like an awkward baby, and he and his bunch of smelly drunks headed for the Cumberland Bridge. Over across it, they could drink their beer without fear of being arrested by the Fluvanna County Sheriff. Such an arrest could net them a fine of twenty dollars, a tidy sum for poor folk back then, or thirty days in jail.

The second door of the building that housed Thurston's and Parish's Cafe, was the first entrance to the Cafe. Within the "White Only" side of the Cafe were grills, deep-fat fryers, reach-in refrigerators and freezers, and several newly-paneled red and blue booths. A counter separated the utilities from the dining area, and had six or seven stools for patrons to sit and casually drink a beer, eat a hamburger or hotdog, eat some French fries, and or drink a milkshake or soda. A moderate-size Juke Box sat in a corner of the Cafe featuring all of the latest Country and Western hits by Roy Rogers, Gene Autry, Patty Paige and Dale Evans. Pop singers like Doris

Day, Cab Calloway, Ella Fitzgerald, and Billy Holiday, were also featured. The interior of that part of the Cafe was newly painted green and white. Different portraits of White soldiers in unif01ms of the various Armed Forces were superimposed on the walls of the Cafe. There were big-red letters on one side of the wall: "BEAT THE JAPS"; and on the other side: "STUMP THE GERRIES." On this Friday, a couple of local White men were having a few beers with their girlfriends sitting very close to them. There were several other Whites eating fries, drinking shakes, and eating hamburgers or hotdogs sitting at tables. The White side was Gas Heated.

Around the corner from the front door of the Cafe was a little fenced-in alley with a backdrop of some seven or eight feet. A large barrel was at the bottom of the backdrop. Garbage and trash were thrown into that barrel and burned each day. The front end of the alley was open so that "Negro" patrons could get to their backdoor entrance. Once inside, they found themselves in an eighteen by twenty-four feet one-room "hole" for "Coloreds Only." There were only two falling down booths in the right corner of the place. In the farthest left comer was a huge potbellied stove. There was a two by four feet, square, cubby-hole through which Unc' Charlie had to buy his beer. The food items were priced at twice what they were on the White side. So most "Coloreds" did not buy any food items.

The booths had holes that exposed white padding all over them, their tables had cigarette burns and a thousand names cut in them. They were once painted gray, but were dirty-brown from lack of cleaning. The hardwood floor in the place was dirty and un-swept with loads of grit and soil caked into the cracks of the boards. The one window in the place had mettle grating covering the glass making it very difficult to see through it. Orange paint had peeled off the walls revealing holes in the sheetrock. The once white ceiling was brown and or black from fly specks, especially near the one huge round-globed ceiling light. The light-globe was supposed to be white, but was dark-brown from dead roaches, fireflies, and moths. There was no restroom for the "Coloreds."

The one restroom for the Cafe was for "Whites Only." When a Colored woman or man had to go, he or she had to go find relief in the woods across the Cumberland Bridge. When they would return they might see Mrs. Arlene Parish giving out a key to the Cafe's restroom to a White patron or two so they could go relieve themselves right around the corner next to the "Colored Only" entrance. As insulting as the above was, the area's poor Blacks packed into the segregated, racist, place on Friday and Saturday nights like ants in an ant hill.

Mrs. Parish was no fool. She and the other merchants of Columbia were members of Columbia's Town Council, and knew that forcing Blacks to buy beer in bulk, and passing a Town's Ordinance forbidding them the right to consume it on premises, or in the Town's limits, would cause "Negro" Patrons to buy a larger quantity of beer, and gulp it down quickly before it got warm. Therefore Mrs. Parish would sell a lot more beer that way than if she allowed them to buy a bottle of beer at a time and sit down and leisurely partake.

This is why she allowed the atmosphere in the "Colored Only" side to go to hell: She didn't want her "Negro Patrons" to enjoy the atmosphere at Parish's Cafe. She wanted them to get their beer and or overpriced food items and hit the road. The only thing modern she provided them with was a bigger than life Juke Box. On it all of the latest hits by Chuck Berry, James Brown, Fats Domino, Bo Didley, B. B. King, Nat King Cole, Lena Horne, Eartha Kitt and etc., were featured. They could get five plays for fifty cents, or ten cents for a single. This machine was kept blasting all evening long until eleven p. m. on Fridays, and ten on Saturdays. Mrs. Parish made a killing off her "Colored Patrons."

On the White side of Parish's, her patrons could sit around and maybe drink twelve beers all day long, but most just drank one or two. That side had three new table and chairs. A beer cooler had every conceivable brand of beer a patron could choose from. Very seldom did any of these patrons ever purchase a Case of Beer.

The grills and deep-fat fryers were there so that the patrons could see what was actually prepared before it was wrapped up and bagged like the food that came to the "Coloreds." Mrs. Parish's teen-aged (late teens) Daughter, Carolyn, made hamburgers with her hands, for Blacks, dressed them the same way, and served all orders to Blacks on flimsy paper plates. All drinks were served in cheap Dixie cups, hot or cold. But that was the only place Negroes could go to get served at all. White patrons were served on china and or out of glasses.

Across the street from Parish's, was Amos Cafe and Bed and Breakfast. A white sign had in large black letters: "WE DO NOT SERVE NIGGERS!"

The place was owned by Claude and Elvira Amos. They were Jews who were as racist as any of the White Merchants in Columbia. The Amoses would call the Sheriff if Negroes stood/or "too long" in front of their establishment.

Ten or fifteen minutes were "too long." Although they only served Whites in their Cafe during the day, they served Blacks out of a backdoor to their place at night. They sold them State Sealed Bootleg liquor. They jacked up the price of a two-dollar pint of liquor to four dollars. They were one-half of a two-headed bootlegging monster in Columbia whose clientele was mostly Blacks. Martha and Joe Manby were the other half. These latter "denizens of alcoholic vice" lived two doors down from the Amoses. This put them directly across the street from Thurston's Grocery. The proximity is truly ironic.

Friday evenings to early Saturday mornings were considered by Columbia's Merchants to be "special times for Negroes." It was understood by the "Negroes" that was when they would be "favorably" accommodated. Therefore, no self-respecting White Citizen would come to shop when it was time to serve "The Niggers." There was a very good reason for the above.

Mostly inferior goods were put on the shelves for sale to the Blacks. "Negroes" were not allowed to choose what they wanted to buy from the shelves. They presented a list to the merchants, and the merchants selected off the shelves whatever they thought proper, or that was "good enough for a Nigger." Blacks almost never got to see fresh produce, meats, or anything else from store to store. Blacks almost never paid for the goods and foods they purchased on the day they made the purchase. A "running ticket," or credit-line, was tallied weekly of allegedly how much they had charged. They paid "whatever they could" each week. The Blacks could not question how much they owed on any of the "tickets" the merchants held against them. So they never got to pay up their "tickets," no matter how much they were able to pay any given week.

Since transportation was a major problem for most local Blacks, the Columbia Merchants Association hired Arthur Walton to transport them. He got paid a tidy sum to make trips to West Bottom, Cloverdale, Gravel Hill, Stage Junction, and this side of Cumberland County.

Columbia's White Merchants made tremendous profits from exploiting poor-hapless Blacks by selling them cheap, inferior, goods, produce, and meats at exorbitant prices. Some of what they sold should have been thrown into the garbage. That is why the Merchants paid Walton a tidy sum to give

"Negroes" a so-called "Free-Ride" to Town and back home on Friday evenings and Saturday mornings. The inferior goods, and large quantities of beer Blacks bought from Parish's, and the bootleg they bought from the Amoses and Manbys, made the "horde of Negroes" coming to shop on weekends Columbia's most prized commodities. The Parishes, Thurstons, Amoses, Manbys, and all of the White Merchants in Columbia, became multimillionaires from their trafficking in retail chicanery.

On this Friday, Agnes and Virginia, her youngest Daughter, came up the road from Cumberland to Fluvanna. They had gotten off the truck at the Bridge at the so-called, "Jungle," an area on the riverbank near the Bridge where drinking, gambling, and fooling around took place. They wanted to see who was down there doing whatever before they went to the stores to shop. Several men offered Agnes and Virginia drinks. Both took a couple of sips of beer and a little nip or two of liquor. Some men tried to fondle Virginia and Agnes. Both slapped away their hands. Both headed towards Parish's Cafe.

Twenty-five or thirty Blacks were standing outside the "Colored" entrance to Parish's when Agnes and Virginia came around the comer.

"Hi Ginia," went some people in the crowd. "Hi y'all," Ginia said. "Hi, Miss Agnes," went some others. "Hi, yourself," Agnes said.

Agnes went over to the little whitewashed picket fence surrounding the backside of the little enclosure that led to the "Colored" entrance. Agnes could see that the Cafe was packed. There was a larger crowd than usual. A lot of people were staring at her with a sad look on their faces.

The Juke Box was playing at full blast. Mrs. Parish turned it up when there was a large crowd of people standing in and around the "Colored" side of the Cafe. With the noise the crowd made and the syncopated beat of the Soul Music, Agnes could barely make out a word that anyone said. Agnes and Virginia pushed their way through the crowd. They went in and-

"Missus Agnes ... You's gotta ... gotta get outta this place. I done heard tell ... Miss Maetta's go get ya ifn you don't run 'way. Says she go cut ya with-a razor. Go cut ... ya neck. Run ... Missus Agnes, fore she ... get up here ..." Frank Miller, the mindless, slow of speech, Town's idiot managed to say. He stumbled on back down the street after he finished speaking. He sounded retarded and Agnes was minded to ignore him.

Agnes turned to Virginia. "That fat old woman ain't got nothin' toll ta-get on me 'bout, Ginia. Iain' done nothin' to 'er. Her husband's way too old for me or y'all. It can't be that. Let's get some food. I got a cup 'la dollars for that. I wanna hamburger; what you wants?"

"Okay, Momma, I'll put in our order."

Just after Virginia finished speaking, A'nt Maetta burst through the crowd, into the door and rushed towards Agnes-bad leg and all. She was pushing and shoving people out of her way. Those who saw her coming got out of her way, quickly. She dropped her ladies' bag. She had drawn a pearl-handled Straight-Razor. A couple of people screamed. A couple others cried. Everyone moved away from Agnes and Virginia.

Agnes saw Maetta stalking her like a cat does a mouse. Virginia backed up and plastered herself against the wall near the Juke Box. Instead of running, Agnes froze and started trembling and shaking like the ground during an earthquake. She stood defenseless in the middle of the Cafe.

A'nt Maetta's lips were pouted and curled at the edges. Her eyes had become little beads of hate. She came over and stood face to face with Agnes. She growled: "Dammit, Agnes, ya stupid Bitch! I'm go send ya shitty ass to hell this day! All them little chillren ya done kilt, an' my Grand Babies's gone cause-a you. You's the one ought-a burnt up in that fire over yonder. Ya can't bring my Lil' Billy back, so I'm go send ya where he's at," A'nt Maetta shouted.

The music had stopped. The crowd got very quiet. You could almost hear a pin drop on cotton, except for a lone whimper or two from people who were afraid for Agnes.

Agnes got presence of mind enough to whimper: "Maetta . . . A'nt Maetta. I ain' done nothin' toll ta-ya Grand Baby, Billy. He's...." Agnes could barely speak. Fear had a stifling hold on her vocal chords. The words got all choked up in her throat.

Virginia started screaming: "Don't ya hurt my Momma! Don't ya hurt Momma! Ya O' Crazy Woman! Leave my Momma 'lone!"

Neither Virginia nor anyone else would dare to approach A'nt Maetta. Everyone stood glued to the spot he/she stood on. Mrs. Parish got on the phone and called for the Sheriff

A'nt Maetta couldn't make out clearly what Agnes tried to tell her. She walloped Agnes up beside her head. The lick knocked her to the floor dazed. A'nt Maetta climbed on top of a pitiable Agnes. She was nothing but a mass of whimpering morass. Maetta grabbed hold of one of Agnes's locks. She drew the razor back. The dimmed light flashed off its shining blade.

Virginia ran towards the two women on the floor. She did not get close enough to be slashed with the razor, though. She screamed: "Momma, wake up. Ya gotta get 'er off you!"

Agnes was struggling against "schizzing-out." She remembered that her life was in grave danger. She heard Virginia yelling at her to resist. She got her mind to work enough so that she could strain against Maetta. Then she strained as hard as she could. Momentarily, she upset Maetta's balance toppling her to the floor.

A'nt Maetta took a swipe at Agnes as she tried to quickly crawl past her for the doorway. The razor missed Agnes's whole body, but the blade hung on the skirt of her dress. It cut her bellowing skirt, making a loud "rip!" sound as it parted the pastel fabric. Agnes made it to the door with her dress hanging half off her. In her excitement she ran the wrong way. Instead of heading for the street, she ended up against the fence enclosure. A'nt Maetta was right behind her brandishing that Straight Razor. Agnes was trapped. She screamed: "Help! Somebody Help Me! Hel-1-1-lp! She's go kill me!"

Nobody would dare to come near her or A'nt Maetta, until, Unc' Charlie and some of his drinking buddies came running towards Parish's. They spied A'nt Maetta holding that razor readying to cut Agnes.

Unc' Charlie ran to his angered wife. Before he could reach Mary Etta James, she had slapped Agnes again. Agnes laid prone on the ground praying: "Gawd Help Me. Save Me Lord. I didn't do it...." Then Agnes schizzed right on out. She tried to escape the horrible reality the only way she knew how.

Maetta slapped Agnes again. She grabbed a lock of her hair again. She got ready to bring the razor down to slice Agnes's throat again.

Virginia had figured out what this shit was all about. She screamed: "Billy's down-ta Rich men with his Momma. We ain't done nothin' ta-'im. You's wrong! He didn't get burnt in no fire set by my Momma. You's dead wrong. Oh ... don't hurt my Momma!"

Being in a frenzy, A'nt Maetta was still going to bring the razor down to its intended target.

Unc' Charlie screamed: "Maetta put that blade down, woman! You's too old for prison. Stop this foolishness, gal! Didn't ya hear Agnes's gal? Lil' Billy ain't dead!"

A'nt Maetta had Agnes pinned to the ground. Unc' Charlie slapped the hand she held the razor in. It flew over the fence and fell down the backdrop into the incinerator barrel. It had landed in a pile of still-hot ashes.

A'nt Maetta jumped up off Agnes. She fired an open-handed blow up beside Unc' Charlie's head. It stunned him. He fell to the gravels for a couple of seconds. His nose was bloodied.

Agnes had gotten her senses together enough to run for her life. She and Virginia took off like two bats out of hell. They turned the corner and were crossing the Cumberland Bridge in what seemed like seconds. As she ran past A'nt Maetta, Virginia had screamed again: "I done told ya, Billy's down ta-Rich-men with his Momma. He ain't dead!"

Unc' Charlie got up off the gravels. He wiped his nose on a red bandana. "See, Maetta, you's wrong as can be. If n ya had kilt Agnes, you 'da kilt a innocent person. Seems ta-me, you's the one who's full-a hate. I may not be a Christian, but I ain' never tried-ta kill nobody even those who needed killin'. Lil' Billy's down in Rich-men with his Momma. Ya just don't listen ta-nobody," Unc' Charlie chided his disgruntled wife.

A'nt Maetta walked across the gravels, dusted herself off and just whimpered a little. She sat down into one of six white-wooden chairs along the picket fence of the enclosure. She put her face in her hands, then she shook her head. Tears streamed down her cheeks. "I'll never do anythin' like that again, O' Lord have Mercy! I'm glad I didn't kill nobody," she whined.

Unc' Charlie quickly went down to Walton's Grocery Store. He was shame of the fact that his wife had bested him in public again, but proud of the fact that he had saved an innocent person from being killed for something she hadn't done.

The few people left of the crowd had all gone their separate ways. The County Sheriff showed up and just asked a few mundane questions. He had no intentions of arresting anyone if nobody had actually gotten hurt.

There were only two other couples on the truck home that evening. Everyone was silent and kept his eyes on the flatbed. A' nt Maetta was thinking of how she might get Henry to go get Billy and bring him to her house so she could raise him.

CHAPTER NINE

That weekend neither Henry nor Charlie, Jr. came home. They stayed in Charlottesville like they did sometimes. A' nt Maetta knew they were spending up their pay on the girls that hung around that place she had heard so many rumors about: "Vinegar Hill." She made up in her mind that she would get on them as soon as they set foot in her yard.

On this Friday, A'nt Maetta and Unc' Charlie went right to Thurston's. On Walton's truck to Columbia, twenty-five or thirty older people hopped a ride. Unc' Charlie and A'nt Maetta got right in the middle of the crowd so they were a little warmer than those on the outer edge of the bunch of cold and trembling people.

A' nt Maetta gave Mrs. Thurston her store list. The silence was deafening as Mrs. Thurston went around the shelves of her store selecting the items she could understand on the list. She crossed those out after she had gotten them and placed them in a cardboard box. She could understand most of A'nt Maetta's scribble, but she pointed to something she did not understand every now and then. A' nt Maetta told her what that was. Pretty soon she had fetched every item on the list and added that to their ticket.

While Mrs. Thurston got the things on the list, A'nt Maetta and Unc' Charlie stared anxiously at the floor. They felt ashamed. The angry stare on A'nt Maetta's face let Mrs. Thurston know not to say or ask too much.

What A'nt Maetta was feeling was:

Me 'an Agnes roll 'round on the ground fightin' like two mad-bitch-dogs. Yet no one tried-ta stop us. Somebody-prob-be, Mrs. Parish-called the Law. He came. Stood over yonder near his car watchin' us fight. Didn't raise a finger. We could-a kilt one-nother. Charlie's right. White peoples feels good when we acts stupid like we did I'll never 'mit it-ta'im, but he's right. If'n I had it ta-do it over, I'd make sure of the story fore I let it upset me like that, and I'll never act like some wild-crazy bitch again. My Grandson is in Rich-men. That makes Agnes in-a-cent. Gawd! I'm glad I didn't cut that gal.

Tears eased out of the corners of A'nt Maetta's eyes; but she uttered not a word to Mrs. Thurston or to Unc' Charlie. She was unusually quiet for the rest of the evening. Unc' Charlie slipped away for a little while to visit the Jungle. He had to see what was going on down there.

He saw a big old fire going in a barrel. There were men sitting around playing Poker on four large wooden spools left behind after the Virginia Electric Power Company had finished wiring the area around Columbia. These were being used as card tables. Tree trunks had been cut down to size for stools. In the woods near the barrels a Crap game was in session. Several men were shooting Crap.

Herman "Doc" Johnson was there selling pints of his homemade bootleg liquor (called, White Lightning). Unc' Charlie bought a pint of the booze from Doc Johnson. He gave him a dollar, took a swig of the liquor, gave it to Doc to "prove it," and turned and walked away when he saw that Doc swallowed the liquor on down. That meant that it had to be good.

There weren't as many people on the truck as there were that morning. At least, there were not as many men. Their wives caught the truck back up the road with their boxes of groceries, but many of the men stayed downtown in the Jungle. Not only were they gamblers, and were willing to brave the cold to get their game on, some women came all the way from Albemarle County, not to mention, Fluvanna, Goochland, Cumberland, Louisa, and Powhatan Counties to ply their trade. These "Fancy Gals" made a lot of money on weekends. (Phyllis Archer had been one of these.) The men gambled by gasoline torch-lights. Some, as soon as they had a good hand at Poker, pulled away from the game and spent their winnings buying what the "Fancy Gals" had to sell. The Crap Shooters did the same.

When Unc' Charlie and A'nt Maetta got off the truck that evening, Unc' Charlie carried the grocery box. He walked along for a minute or two. Then he said: "Maetta, wait-a-minute." He put the box down on the ground. It seemed like he had a hard time straightening up.

129

"What now, Charlie?" A'nt Maetta asked. "I just wanna get down ta-the house. My hips'sa sore as can be. Must've sprain 'em last week. I ain't young as I use-ta be, y' know."

"That's just it, Maetta. I know' ya don't wanna hear 'bout it, but I'm go have-ta say it anyway."

"Yeah, Charlie. Go-head-on, get it off your chest." She rolled her eyes. "We'll both feel a lot better; aw-ight." She avoided eye contact with Unc' Charlie.

"Maetta, didn't ya see that the Sheriff drove up an' got outta his car, and just watched y'all down on the ground? He didn't lift a finger. None-a the White folk what came outta Parish's did either. They all stood 'round watchin' you draw that razor back, hopin' you'd bring it down an' cut Agnes's throat.

"See Maetta, you'd be <loin 'em a big favor. You would-a kilt a gal, an' then you would have-ta spend the rest-a ya few days, or years, in prison. That's killin' two birds with one stone. Do ya see what I'm sayin'?"

"What ya want me ta-say, Charlie James," said A'nt Maetta in an angry shout. Her eyes shed a few tears. Inside of her the guilt was almost overwhelming. But all she managed to say was: "Let's go-on-in-the house, man. That is, ifn you's through runnin' me down ta-the ground.

"The only thing I wished was, it would-a been so good if Agnes had come to Town today. I would-a begged pardon of her right in front-a ev 'body. Then I'd feel a lot better 'bout it all."

With her black ladies' bag dangling from her arm, A'nt Maetta let the tears come down her cheeks. "I ain' go never put-a-nother razor in this bag or my bosom again, long as I lives. It's stupid, Charlie, I know that, now!"

A'nt Maetta bent down picked up the box of groceries and limped on down the hill to the house. Unc' Charlie eyed her walking away. The liquor and beer he had drunk started coming up on him. He got a little dizzy. He staggered towards the house. When he got to the house, A'nt Maetta had lit several kerosene lamps. The bootleg on his stomach bubbled up and made Unc' Charlie feel sick to his stomach. He ran outside and vomited it all up.

When he came back into the house, A'nt Maetta had changed into house clothes. She had taken off her sweater and had replaced it with a flannel housecoat. She started putting away the groceries into the pantry, cupboard, and the icebox. Then the sound of a car motor caused A'nt Maetta to scramble towards the front door.

"Charlie, the boys 're up the hill. They's comin' home this week. I'm so glad," A'nt Maetta said. She was mad as hell with them, but just as glad to see them. They always gave her ten or fifteen dollars-a-piece; and, they were her favorites.

Henry and Lil' Charlie came through the door and burst in laughing and joking with one another. Both carried a sack where they kept their personals: soap, washcloths, towels, and Mum Deodorant, and dirty clothes. Lil' Charlie had bought a couple of those sacks at the Charlottesville Army, Navy, and Athletic Store. They headed to the boys' room an' dropped those sacks in a comer. Lil' Charlie gave A' nt Maetta a box of assorted chocolates and fifteen dollars. Henry gave her a small bottle of perfume, and ten dollars.

"Hi, Momma," Lil' Charlie said.

"Hey, Momma," Henry said. "What ya know good?"

"Hi, boys. Things ain't goin' all that good; but I's glad you's home. I gotta talk with both-a ya'll 'bout-aver 'portant matter."

"Hold it, Momma," said Henry. "If you's worri'd 'bout us not comin' home last week, don't.

"We's up at The Blue Diamond Cafe on Vinegar Hill havin' a couple beers, an' some guy who knew us went into the back-a the place came back an' shoved a guitar in my lap. They gotta pretty-good piano, too. Me an' Charlie stayed an' played 'til the place closed. They'll stay open long's peoples keep buyin' wine an' beer. Hell, we played for most-a the night.

"It was too late to get-a ride down here, so the cats up there knew-a cup'la gals who put us up for the night. That's why we didn't come home. Sorry."

"Y'all go on-ta the kitchen an' sat at the table. I'll be in directly," A'nt Maetta said. "Ah-h-h-h, shit," said Henry under his breath.

"This go be some tough shit, Bro." Lil' Charlie answered Henry in a near whisper.

Henry tried to stall things a little. "Momma, let us get sponged off a little first. We smell like-a cup'la Bull Minks. We'll be able ta-listen a lot better then."

"Aw-ight, y'all go-head-on. But don't ya try-ta leave 'thout talkin' with me first; especially you, Henry," A'nt Maetta said. "There's a hot fire in the stove an' the water's good an' warm."

Henry and Charlie, Jr. got basins and dipped hot water out of the stove's tank with a dipper used especially for that purpose. They both returned with the basins to the boys' room. They took their time scrubbing up. They came out of the room wearing two-piece charcoal-gray flannel suits they had bought at Tonslers Clothing Store; and black-dress shoes at Tillies Shoes, all on Vinegar Hill. Henry had on a thick-blue cardigan Sweater, and Lil' Charlie had on a green one. They had their hair all slicked back and waved in the front. Both wore starched-white shirts that they had gotten cleaned at Leeches' Cleaners on Vinegar Hill, and gray dress hats purchased at McGinness Tailors on Vinegar Hill. They waited for A'nt Maetta to applaud their "sugar sharpness," but she didn't.

"Y'all go on back an' sit at the table for a spell. I want ya ta-listen carefully at what I'm go say to ya."

"Yes' am," Henry said. Some annoyance eased into his eyes. "Yes'am," Lil' Charlie said. He wondered what this could all be about.

"Y'all boys been real good ta-me an' ya Poppa. We can't complain. But I nearly cut Agnes's throat last week."

"What, Momma?" Henry asked. "Why?" Lil' Charlie asked.

"It's cause I thought she'd been 'sponsible for the death-a Billy, your little Son, Henry," A'nt Maetta spoke in a rant. "I want ya ta-go get William from Rich-men. Bring Mabel Scott back here with Billy anyway ya can. I wanna take care-a my Grand Baby, so he'll live.

"You too, Lil' Charlie. I want ya ta-go get James an' put 'im over here with me an' ya Poppa.

I don't want no more my Grand Chillun ta-be lost, no Gawd!"

Lil' Charlie got that twisted frown on his top lip again. 'Ton kno', I gotta look at that one, well . . . ma-be. I gotta see 'bout that, now."

Quick anger came to Henry's face. "Momma, I don't wanna get hitched. An' I don't want no ready-made family when I get marri'd. Not after what I done seen round y'all marri'd peoples. White mens comin' in an' takin' over. I 'ma kill somebody-that's what I'll liable-ta do! Looks like ta-me, when you's hitched, ya might as well be in jail. Then ya gotta take care any half White bastard the Whiteman dumps on you"

"Henry," Ain't Maetta shouted, "Don't ya never use that word 'round me no more. Hope ya ain't talkin' 'bout Cora, she's your Sister-no matter who her Daddy is. Don't ya forget that."

"Yeah, Momma, I know," said Henry, "I'm sorry 'bout that." He paused, and took a very deep breath before going on.

"Momma, the only way I'm go be able ta-bring William back ta-ya is for me ta-marry Mabel Scott. She done already said that much.

"I don't love Mabel. I wouldn't be able ta-stand 'er. I'm sorry I ever messed with her," Henry said, in a low groan.

A'nt Maetta got up from the table. She came around the corner of the table to right directly in front of Henry. She pointed the trigger finger of her right hand to just an inch from her Son's face as she spit out:

"Henry, I love ya. But ya get-ya-ass outta this house tomorrow. Ifn ya come back without Billy, I'll get Poppa's shotgun down off the top of the door over yonder," she pointed towards the front door, "an' I'm go put ya outta ya misery.

"I don't care ifn ya gotta marry Mabel. You got 'er pregnant didn't ya? Next time you's stickin' it ta-a-gal, ya better think 'bout what might happen down the road. You unnerstan'?"

"But, Momma"

"I'm through with it, Henry," A'nt Maetta shouted just below a scream.

A'nt Maetta's eyes were full of rage at both her Sons. She turned to look in Lil' Charlie's direction.

"Momma. Queen Anderson's got knocked up. She been foolin 'round with me, lately. It's her second child. She got a little girl named Shirley. She say the baby's mine. I been meanin' ta-tell ya, but I wanted ta-see what the child look like before I did. If her baby's a James, I'm gon marry'er, an' I'll go get my boy James, they call Stumpy. Queen already said she don't mind him come live with us. See, I'm tryin' ta-do right."

A'nt Maetta turned back to Henry. "Why can't you be more like Lil' Charlie?" she asked. Henry stared at Lil' Charlie like he was a traitor. "What ya talkin 'bout, now, Lil' Charlie?" "Reck-en I better go do my thing, Big Bro. I gotta date with Queen tonight. See ya in the mornin', aw-ight." Lil' Charlie slipped on out the door while the getting out was good.

A'nt Maetta was glaring down on Henry who was still sitting at the table. She hoped he'd reverse his opinion like his younger Brother had.

Henry jumped up from the table and backed away from A'nt Maetta to a safe distance up the little hallway. His Mother's gaze followed him like a spotlight.

"I ain't Poppa! You can't order me 'round like ya do him. I'ma do what the hell I wanna do!

Ain't no natural woman-'cludin' you, Momma, go tell me what ta-do an' run over my life. Hell no," Henry shouted.

A'nt Maetta tried to quickly limp towards Henry. Her facial muscles twitched. Lil' Charlie pulled off ahead of Henry coming up the hill. Henry wondered if he should run down through the woods. He looked back for a minute towards home.

A'nt Maetta came out on the porch and shook her left fist at her fleeing Son. She yelled at the top of her voice:

"You ain' go have no good luck tonight. You hear me? Ya done sassed ya Momma. You done gone'gainst the Bible, now, Oh, Gawd!" Then she limped on back inside the house and cried like a whipped child.

Lil' Charlie doubled back to pick up Henry. "I hate it when old folk try-ta scare young peoples with they Bible mess, man," Henry said.

"Henry I'm with ya on that, man. Let's get goin' fore somethin' bad happen. Momma could shoot right up here."

"Charlie, take me down ta-Columbia, man. I may as well go and hustle the Jungle tonight as long as I can. It's gettin' late, but a cup'la babes might be down there. I see you got the guitar in the backseat. You can come on back up ta-Cloverdale an' pick Queen up. You owe me, Bro. I got ya on at Van Yahres. We good-ta-go?"

Charlie dragged hands with Henry. "Yeah, we good ta-go."

Lil' Charlie pulled his car across the Cumberland Bridge, turned it onto a little rough path, and cut off the engine and the lights.

"Henry, my-man. I'm go marry Queen. I know she's carryin' my child. I like that little yellar gal, man. She's almost White. Unc' Wayland Anderson hate 'er just like Daddy hate Cora. Queen's sorry 'bout that like Cora. She still call Unc' Wayland Daddy. She won't go out with nothin' but dark Negroes like me, man. I guess I ought-a be glad-a that. That little gal'sa cutie, man, ya kno' it."

"Yep," said Henry, he was all smiles. "Yeah, I know A'nt Nola, her Mother, an' Unc' Wayland. They been marri'd a long time. Got Dorothy,

Queen, Cookie, Timothy, and Wayland, Jr. I never thought 'bout it much, but you gotta wonder how Queen got so light-skinned?"

"Henry, that's cause she's that old White Rutherford Ross's child. Nola cooked for the Ross Family. It done happen ta-us all, man." Lil' Charlie said.

"You don't mind her being like that, man? You trust her?" Henry asked. "No, man. I likes 'em high-yellar. The lighter the better," Lil' Charlie said. "Have fun, man," Henry said.

Lil' Charlie looked over in front of his car and saw a 1950, red and white Chevy 4-door Sedan by moonlight. "Who the hell's drivin' that, Henry?" Then he cranked up his car.

"I' on kno, but I go find out in a jiff, see ya, later, Bro.

Lil' Charlie turned on the lights, backed out on the road and was gone into the night.

CHAPTER TEN

Even by moonlight Henry James noticed who the driver of that new Chevrolet was. It was Tank Snowvall. He had Barbara (called Babe) Bates sitting close beside him. When Snowvall saw Henry he blew his car horn playfully at him. "C'mon, homes, let's go boggie-woogie, aw ight!" Snowvall yelled. Then he laughed like a clown at a circus.

Henry wanted to get next to Babe, so he slid into the front of the shiny-new Chevy, noticing that it had a gold-colored interior overlaid with large silvery flowers that resembled roses. "Ya gotta fine 'chine here, man" Henry said. He eased as close to Babe as he could. He thought he would crack a little joke.

"Babe, you's gettin' prettier-an'-prettier ev' time I see ya." He got a sly grin on his lips. "What ya doin' with this chunk of wood, Tank, here?" He followed that statement with a laugh.

Tank didn't laugh. "Watch it, sucker," was his quick reply. He got a grin on his face that was more a snarl like an angry dog did when aroused.

"Man, I'm just foolin 'round," said Henry. "I didn't mean no harm." He licked his lips in the dark at Babe. She was a real-life "Betty Booper," a very shapely "Fancy Gal" with beautiful lips, eyes, bosom, hips and legs. She had a reputation for being "too Hot to Trot." Henry wanted her right away. Her perfume set him on fire. Her long-black hair was up in a French Roll with dangling ringlets on either side of her attractive head.

When Henry gave her the compliment, she smiled from ear-to-ear, showing pearly-white teeth.

Henry glanced over at Snowvall and he just couldn't figure what the hell Babe could see in that chump. He was tall and lanky, at about six foot. He was a cream and coffee light-skinned guy, with straight-ish, dark-brown hair. His sandy goatee was kinkier than sheep's wool. His big hands were even bigger than his feet. The greasy coveralls he wore meant he came from working at a saw mill to pick up Babe in the Jungle without bothering to go home and bathe. He sure smelt like it anyway. He reminded Henry of poor-white trash. His pointed chin certainly resembled theirs. The bulbous nose that he had was way too big to belong to a Whiteman. His beady-little gray eyes were like theirs though. His big o' car-door ears were like bird's wings. Henry could not believe that Babe, a "gal" that all the fellows wanted, could really be tight with Tank Snowvall, an ugly duckling.

Babe pushed the soft-right side of her gorgeous rump tightly against the left side of Henry's hip. She slyly moved her rump so as to create a hardly noticeable sexy motion against his hip. Henry tried to be cool, but got a very salacious grin on his face. Then, he got erected, he couldn't help it.

Even though it was good and dark outside, out of the corners of his disgruntled eyes, Tank didn't like what he thought he saw. "Aw-ight. I want 'cha to get back off my lady, man. I know ya want 'er. I can't blame ya, there. But, homes, lemme warn ya. I ain' lettin' that gal go with nobody but me. I'm her 'Ace Coon Boon!' Dig? I'm her big daddy-o. I hope ya can dig where that's comin' from. I just came back here from D.C. a couple of months ago. Don't think you's go get over on me, now, homes. Dig?"

Henry smiled. "Look, man, I ain' tryin'-ta cut-in on ya. She's a looker, though, but I'm go be cool. I know you an' ya family. You's A'nt Connie Belle Tolliver's an' Unc' Lou Snownvall's boy, though ya don't look much like them."

Henry's last statement went straight to Snowvall's heart. He got out of the car immediately. He said: "Henry. Let's go across the street to Manby's an' getta drink. I'm buying," Tank whined, fighting back the tears.

Before Henry got out of the car, and because it was good and dark outside, he quickly slipped his left hand up Babe's red skirt. She bent over his way a little and bumped her left breast against his face. They thought Tank couldn't possibly have seen them doing that.

Henry got out of the car with a two-cent grin on his face. "Tank, I reek-en you's right. But I'ma go half on the liquor." He took out his wallet and popped out a five-dollar bill.

Snowvall all but snatched the money out of Henry's hand. "You c'mon, follow me, I'm not stupid," Snowvall snapped.

Henry followed Tank to Joe Manby's steps. He watched as Snowvall climbed the tall steps to the screened-in front porch. Snowvall knocked on its screened-door. A tall, skinny, Whiteman came to the door wearing a blue-Dodgers Baseball cap over rusty-blond bushy hair. He wore faded jeans, a dirty sweat shirt, and black and white cowboy boots. He held in his right hand a Thirty-Eight, Long-Barrel, Smith & Wesson. He snatched the screened-door open. "What 'cha you boys want now?" he yelled at Tank. His voice sounded like a transplanted deep-North Carolina-drawl. He was pointing his pistol out in front of him like he was ready to shoot.

Henry spoke up. "I'm Unc' Charlie's an' A'nt Maetta's oldest Son. We wanna Fifth of Old Crow, is all." He held his hands up so that Joe could see them. Tank did likewise.

Joe looked them over for a minute. He lowered the barrel of the gun. "Uh-huh. Yeah. I know A'nt Maetta an' Unc' Charlie. Y'all stay out yonder for a minute. I'm going back an' see what I got. Be back, directly. Go cost ya ten dollars; all right?"

"We got you covered," Tank said.

Through the door, Henry and Tank could see all manner of debris and old stuff scattered all over the porch. Henry figured that Joe must be a pack rat.

Joe came back to the door carrying a Fifth of Old Crow in his left hand, and the gun in his right hand. He gave the bottle to Henry. "There ya go, boys. Ya can see that it's still sealed. That's more 'n I can say you boys would get over at Amos 'nem. An' they charge fifteen dollars for a Fifth."

"Thank ya, Mr. Manby," Henry said. "Yeah, right-on," Tank said.

Tank gave Joe the ten dollars. Joe took the money and said: "Y'all got somewhere to go, right? I'm goin' back to bed. See ya'll later."

Both Tank and Henry headed on back to the car. When they got back to the car, Snowvall got in first. Henry got in next. He started to get into the backseat.

"Hey, daddy-o, let's all sit in the front seat." Babe spoke in a very sensual voice.

"Snowvall eyed Henry jealously. "Yeah, let's act like one big happy family. Right-on, my man."

Henry wanted some of Babe so bad that he would never blow a chance to get as close to her as he could. He got in beside Babe again. She played footsy with him for a couple of seconds. Snowvall saw that, *and didn 't like that shit at all.*

"Let's pop the seal on that bottle, dude," Tank said. He almost growled. "Right-o daddy-o," said Henry. "The night air's makin' me thirsty as hell." Babe cajoled Snowvall. "See that suit the cat's wearin', ain't it sporty, man?"

"Yeah, I see it. I can't 'ford nothin' like it. I'm too busy puttin' ev' thin' I make on ya back, an' in this car. Takes ev' penny I can beg, borrow, or steal ta-keep ya little hot-ass happy, Babe," Snowvall quipped.

"I think I can dig where ya comin' from, homes. Look, I put all my dough into my clothes and keepin' a new guitar. That's me. I gotta look good when I play for the ladies, man. Hey, that's all that I am." He winked at Babe, and she winked back. Snowvall saw them. Snowvall took the top off the Old Crow. He took a big swallow. He handed the bottle to Henry. He took a bigger swallow of the liquor. He handed it to Babe. She poured herself a small-paper cupful.

Babe handed the bottle back to Henry. Henry took a gulp of the liquor. He frowned as that one went down the hatch. He wiped his mouth on his right coat sleeve.

Babe got another plastic paper cupful and this time drank it right down. She threw the empty cup up to the ceiling and gleefully shouted: "Let's go do the boogie, I wanna dance, man." She laughed loudly and followed that with a sultry giggle. She shook her hair loose, and it fell down to nearly on her shoulders.

Henry was feeling the liquor he had gulped down. He watched Babe jiggle her breasts until one tit came out of her bra cup and popped up out of her low-cut blouse.

"Let's go down to Hacknette Cafe, baby." Babe squealed like a giddy-little schoolgirl. She pulled up the hem of her dress so that her legs were exposed up to her thighs. Snowvall' s eyes grew large and bugged out.

He cranked up his car. He sped out onto Route Six, turned right and headed down Six towards Richmond. He was angry and driving like a mad man. At one time he topped one hundred miles per-hour. He saw Babe taking another sip of the Bourbon, this time, out of the bottle. She tried to hand the bottle to Tank, he refused. He just wanted to get to Hacknette Cafe as fast as he could. Then Babe gave the bottle to Henry.

Henry drained the bottle. The split in the side of Babe's skirt revealed a lot of her body. She guided Henry's hand up her right leg. She quickly fondled the crotch of his pants. She slid over as close to Henry as she could. *"Baby, I'm gonna give-ya everythin' . . . I wanna give ya my candy ..."* She brushed a brief kiss on Henry's left cheek after whispering.

Tank could not stand too much more of what Babe was doing. He thought she was way overdoing what she was supposed to be doing. She was supposed to help him play "Rolly Poley." That's all. He knew that he had to get rid of Henry sooner than he had the others.

Just then, Snowvall and company pulled into the loose-graveled parking lot of a fairly downtrodden hole-in-the-wall beer joint. The parking lot and the falling down building were packed with wall to wall people and cars. It was located at about ten miles from Columbia.

Some people were dancing out in what space they could find outside and likewise inside. The place had the latest Juke Box blasting at full volume. When Babe saw the crowd, she dashed out of the car and disappeared in the crowd inside the Cafe. She had just climbed on over Henry.

Henry got ready to stagger out of the car. "Hold it, homes," Tank said in somewhat of a slur. "I wanna run somethin' down to ya; aw-ight?" he growled.

"Okay, my-man. Shoot. Go-head-on, run it down ta-me," Henry replied. "You don't get it, do you?" Tank asked.

"No, ta-be honest with ya, I ain't followin' ya too well, my-man," came out of Henry's mouth in a long slur.

"Look Henry, I love that gal, Babe. I kno' she ain't no good. But I still loves the ground she walks on, homes. You got that?"

Henry got a sheepish grin on his face. "Hey, I ain' go mess with 'er, man. I'm just foolin' round, my-man. Hey, but I ain' go let it get outta hand. I know how you feels 'bout that gal. "Look, man, let's go on in the Cafe. I'll buy us a cup 'la pitchers-a beer; aw-ight?" Henry still had that sheepish grin on his face.

They got out of the car and went up the four steps to a little porch in front of the place. They had to push their way through the crowd. The loud music seemed to make even the whole clapboard building vibrate, especially the pounding bass coming from the Juke Box.

Once inside, Henry pushed his way up to a counter that flanked the right side of the Cafe. His nose was slammed with cigarette smoke, pickled pigs' feet, and with the stale odor of alcohol. Snowvall followed close behind Henry.

"Give us a pitcher of draft an' two glasses, please," yelled Henry over the noise of the crowd, to Don Hacknette, the Cafe owner.

"I got ya, daddy-o," said Hacknette, a tall, cream-and-coffee colored, man, wearing a food stained apron over black slacks and a cook's tunic. He had a fat beer-belly, a thick, black, mustache, a right-side glass eye, and wavy-black hair. The glass eye was a little browner than the other. It made him cock his head slightly to the side when he looked at Henry and Tank. The guy did not look like somebody anyone in the place would want to tangle with. He had a double-barrel shotgun mounted on the wall behind the counter.

After looking Henry and Tank over for a few minutes, Hacknette picked up a dingy pitcher from among many sitting on a stand behind the counter. He ran it full of beer until a thick head of foam ran down the side of the pitcher. "That'll be sixty cents," he said to Henry.

Henry smiled and slapped the coins down on the counter. "Let us have two glasses."

Hacknette got two tall beer-glasses off the same table he had gotten the pitcher. He brought the beer and glasses over to Henry. He had a grin on his hard-chiseled face. "Good luck in finding somewhere to sit down in this place tonight."

Just then a couple of young people got up to slow drag. Henry and Tank rushed over and sat at the table they left behind. "When ya move ya lose," Henry said.

Henry poured one glass full of beer and shoved that over to Tank. He poured himself one next. Then they both spied Babe out in the middle of the place putting on her imitation of Ma Rainey's sultry dance moves. Babe shook her hips, grinding her buttocks, with the split of her dress laid open up to her pink panties. Men were taking turns to get near her to dance with her.

In a bland attempt to outdo Henry, Tank went over to the counter and ordered two pitchers of beer. He came back to the table, shoved one in front of Henry, and kept the other for himself. He took a sideways glance at Babe, and Henry saw the muscles of his jaws tighten. "Drink up, Henry," Snowvall said.

Henry drank glass after glass of beer. He was like a hog sucking up slop. His pitcher was empty before Tank could finish two glasses of his pitcher.

"Wanna 'nother pitcher, Henry? I got ya covered, my-man." Tank said.

"Sure, homes. Don't mind ifn I do," Henry slurred. His head was bobbing up and down. After he drank two glasses of that last pitcher his vision blurred a little and his speech was thick and slurred. He squinted through one eye, and tried to avoid double-vision.

Upon seeing how drunk Henry had become, Tank whispered: "That's it, you greased-haired dog. Now ya right! I'm go take all ya money now, sucker. I'm go leave ya ass in the Jungle broke an' disgusted. An' ya ain't go get into Babe's pants, neither! I kno' that's what you's thinkin' ."

Snowvall called out: "Babe! Babe! Bring ya little-hot ass on over here!" He beckoned to his dancing siren. "Let's go pretty mama. We just 'bout got this sucker in the bag."

"Yeah, daddy-o, I got ya," Babe yelled back at Snowvall. "Lemme order a quart of beer fore we leave, though, honey."

That annoyed Tank a little. "Go-head-on, now. I gotta help this cat outside an' put his drunk ass in the car. I hope he don't puke. Babe, hurry up, now!" he yelled at Babe.

"Don, gimme-a quart of Paste Blue Ribbon Beer ta-go, please," Babe yelled to Hacknette. "Look, Babe, I kno' what y'all be about, aw-ight. Your crap b'longs in the toilet. It's go backfire on y'all one-a these nights. Here, there's ya beer. That'll be sixty-cents." He slid the quart of beer over to Babe.

Babe giggled. "Now pop the top for me, daddy-o. Gimme three paper cups. An' thank ya very much. Hope you'll stay outta our bizzness, though." She jiggled her breasts at him, shook her hips, and went through the crowd on out the door. The wanton way she swished her hips got the attention of a lot of men. They stared at her like fixed statues as she swayed her hips on out onto the porch, then to Tank's car. Hacknette picked up the change Babe left on the counter.

Tank was waiting for her. He stood on the driver's side. "Get in the car, Babe, damn! Ya sit in the middle cause I want Henry to sit near the window in case he start pukin'. I done roll down that window. The scent-a drunk's puke's hard as hell ta-get outta a car. I don't wanna be doin' that all day tomorrow."

Babe giggled. "Right-o daddy-o." She came around and got in the car on the driver's side. She sat beside Henry, but squeezed as close to him as she could. She threw the cups out of the window. She turned the bottle of beer up and drank from it and that caused her to spill a little beer onto Henry. She brushed her hand on his coat, then his pants, and then she fondled him a little. She spilled more beer when Snowvall sped off She brushed Henry off some more.

Drunk as he was, Henry managed to respond to Babe's come-on. He touched her breasts and her leg for a minute or two. He had forgotten all about Tank.

Tank zipped the car up route **Six. He** wanted to get to Columbia back to the Jungle as quickly as he could. That was where he was going to dump Henry after he had rolled him. He almost lost control of his car when he looked over and saw Henry's hand up Babe's dress. He pulled the car to the side of the road and came to a complete stop.

"Babe, help me get this black sonavabitch outta my gott dam car. I'm go shake his ass down right now." Tank was so angry and excited that he was shouting like a mad man.

Babe scampered around behind Snowvall like a bunny rabbit. She grabbed Henry's right arm, and Snowvall grabbed his left arm. "C'mon, sugar-baby, lemme help ya outta the car. It's time for you ta-go-o-o. I wish ya didn't have-ta go," Babe said.

"Whoa. What's goin' on?" Henry groaned.

"Nigga, I saw ya hand up Babe's dress, feelin' her fury kitten. Ya done had ya hand on 'er like that more'n a cup 'la times. You slicked-back scion. Did ya think I was just go let ya get 'er right in front-a me? Coon, who the hell do ya think you is?" Snowvall growled.

Henry could sense that danger was not far away and he was trying to get his head together. "I'm sorry, man. Man ... I just forgot where I was. That's all. Just lemme go, I won't do it no more."

"I'm go let ya go aw-ight! I' ma let ya go right ta-hell!" Snowvall shouted.

Snowvall ran around to the back of the car to the trunk. He stuck his key in the lock. He got out a single-shot Twelve-Gauge Shotgun. He broke it down, stuck in a Number Four shell. He clanked it shut. He ran around to the driver's side of the car. He sort of laid the gun down over the top of the car opposite Henry, who was leaning his head on the roof of the passenger's side of the car. He was sobering up by the minute. He could feel that danger was getting closer.

"I ain' go let no chocolate-Nigga like you get over on me like ya tryin' ta-do. Up in D.C. you'd be dead already. They don't play that shit up yonder." Snowvall was snorting like a Bull.

Snowvall cocked the hammer back on the gun. He eyed Babe for a second. Then he paused a couple of seconds. "Babe you ain't shit, neither! Ya whorin' bitch! I ought-a shoot ya ass too!"

Babe cried out: "I do what ya want me ta-do. You ain't got no right ta-call me names, an' ya sure ain' got no reason ta-shoot me. Why you so mad at this man?"

"That ma-ther been all over you since we picked his ass up. You just s'pose-ta jazz them suckers. You ain' s'pose-ta be read-ta-give-it up. Henry could-a got in your pants tonight. Ya wanted 'im to." Snowvall aimed the cocked gun at Babe for a couple of seconds.

"Tank, don't shoot me, baby. I'm with you. We's in this together, right? You's just jealous, is all. You thought I was really gettin' hot for Henry. The guy's cute, but you's my man, that's all that ya gotta remember. Don't do nothin' stupid. We'll both end up goin' down the road, baby," Babe whined.

Snowvall pointed the gun towards Henry again.

"Baby, don't do that, put the gun away. Let's roll the man an' get the hell outta here," Babe screamed.

Henry started to get a little more sober. He sensed that he was in danger, and it was right around the comer. Then he saw the shotgun pointed right at his head. The barrel of the gun was almost on his forehead. Then, he grabbed the end of the barrel of the gun, and "BLAM!" it went off. He had raised the barrel of the gun just slightly high enough so that all of the pellets whizzed just over his head. He could hear the pellets whine behind the sound of the explosion. Henry sobered right up after the shotgun blast.

"Damn! I can't b'lieve I missed that Black sonavabitch!" Snowvall exclaimed. He dashed back to the trunk of the car. He rummaged around in the trunk searching for another shell to reload. He found one. Foolishly, he had left the gun on the car's rooftop.

Henry met him as he was coming around to the gun. He hit Snowvall a straight-right to the chin. The lick stunned Snowvall, knocking him to the ground. Snowvall shook his head. He tried to get his bearings back.

Henry drew his switchblade knife. It had a six-inch blade. He hit Snowvall again with his left hand. That lick was like a mule's kick. Snowvall was out like a light. Henry fell upon Snowvall screaming: "Ya go try-ta shoot me. Ya go try-ta kill me"

Babe yelled: "Y'all stop! Stop fore somebody gets hurt real bad. Stop, please"

Henry stabbed Tank in his shoulders, on top of his head, his jaws, and both his arms. He didn't penetrate deep enough into Snowvall to kill him, but blood spewed from the gashes Henry made on tank.

Snowvall came to screaming like a dog barking. He wiggled but he couldn't get loose from Henry, who had him pinned down between the car and a ditch. The way that Henry was slicing and cutting Snowvall was like he was trying to peel the man.

"You high-yellar dog. Ya think ya can just kill me like-a dog? I'll cut ya ta-death!" Henry screamed like a maddened animal.

Henry drew the long knife back with the intention of stabbing Tank in his forehead. Tank had fainted. Babe, hysterically, ran over and hit the knife with the empty beer bottle she had retrieved out of the car. It dislodged the knife from Henry's hand. It rolled down into the ditch. Henry couldn't find it. He jumped up and slapped Babe to the ground with one blow. She laid on the ground whimpering. "Don't kill 'im. Don't kill me," Babe pleaded.

Tank came to again. He jumped up off the ground. Like a wounded animal he ran down through the woods screaming like a barking dog. He was out of his mind. He was so bloody he looked like he had been through a meat grinder. Babe took off after him. Snowvall didn't know whether Babe or Henry was after him, so he ran like a scared deer. Then he heard her calling: "Tank. Tank. Tank, baby, I gotta get ya-ta-a doctor ... Tank. ..." He finally stopped, but still screamed.

Henry watched Babe catch up to Snowvall. She grabbed him and with some determination was able to push him back towards the car. By the time she got back to the car she was as bloody as Snowvall. She angrily shook her finger at Henry. "You's goin' ta-jail for this, Nigga!" Babe hissed at Henry.

Babe's shaking her finger at Henry reminded him of his Mother shaking her fist at him. "Ah, that's the Jinx that Momma' s talkin 'bout. It became clear to Henry what he had to do to get himself free of the "Curse of Sass," that was upon him. He hated it, but his Mother had won that argument. Henry knew: *I ain 't go never get outta this curse till I go ta-Rich-men an' get Billy, bring 'im back and let Momma have 'er way raisin 'im. That's what I gotta do, an' that's what I'm go do. I don't wanna marry Mabel, but I'll do that if 'n that's the only way to bring 'im from Rich-men.*

With the shotgun lying in the ditch, Henry watched Babe shove Snowvall into the front seat of the car. He had calmed down enough so that he didn't want to do neither Babe nor Tank any more harm.

The car lights disappeared around the bend. Henry knew that Babe was carrying Snowvall to the University of Virginia's Hospital. He knew too that those people at the UVA would have to report the injuries Snowvall had sustained to the Law Officials of Fluvanna. He figured he would get charged with assault and attempted murder. He hoped because this was his first reported offense, against a Negro, he would just get probation. He realized that by the landscape he had to be only about two or three miles from Columbia. He could walk home, so he struck out for home with his head aching and ears tingling from the shotgun blast.

Henry stumbled home at near daybreak. His new suit had been torn. Blood streaks were all over his clothes. A'nt Maetta was sitting in a rocking chair watching out of her window half asleep. When Henry staggered through the door his appearance shocked his Mother.

"Henry . . . Boy, what done happen ta-you?" Her voice was hoarse from shock. "Have ya been hurt? Who done this ta-ya?"

"I ain' hurt, Momma. That stupid-ass Snowvall, A'nt Connie's an'

Unc' Lou's oldest boy, tried ta-shoot me over Babe Bates, tonight. He shot but just missed the top of my head.

"I kno' I'm goin' ta-jail. I cut Tank all over his face and head. I laid 'im out for dead. If'n it hadn't been for Babe knocking the knife outta my hand, I 'da kilt Tank. I'm sorry, Momma."

"Onliest thing I can do, is talk with the Judge . I know that family. I've cooked for 'em. When I tell the Judge that you's my son, I b'lieve he'll go easy on ya. Ain' go promise ya that ya go get outa all that ya done Scot-free, but you'll get the least that he can give ya.

"But, Henry, I have-ta have your word, that you go get down ta-Richmen an' bring Billy back here ta-me ta-raise. Will you do That?"

Since Henry had already made up his mind he told her, "Yeah, Momma, I promise."

"Oh, thank Gawd!" A'nt Maetta shouted. "Henry, Lil' Charlie done got up all his things an' moved out. Says he's goin' over ta-Cloverdale ta-live with some gal named Queen. He go marry her after she drop her baby. He wanna see the baby, first. I don't blame 'im there."

"Yeah, Momma, Charlie told me 'bout that yesstidy. Good for 'im if'n that's the gal he wanna be with. I'll do it if I have-ta, if that's the onliest way I can get William from Mabel to bring ta-you ta-raise." Henry groaned like he had a pain in his stomach.

A'nt Maetta smiled. She whispered a little prayer: "Thank You Lord!"

CHAPTER ELEVEN

Standing on the corner of Routes Six and 656, on this morning, one week after his violent assault on Tank Snowvall, Henry felt like his world was about to come to an end. While he waited for the Eastbound Local to Richmond, the thought of why he was going to Richmond made his stomach ache. He hated the prospect of possibly having to marry Mabel Scott. The thought of staying on the bus and proceeding to North Carolina passed through is mind. But the fix he was in had probably come from his disobedience to his Mother, so running to North Carolina would not be of much help to him, he thought. It seemed like it was taking the bus forever to come.

His mind whiled away the time by focusing on where Mabel and William were in Richmond. He knew very little about the streets of Richmond. A'nt Maetta had heard through the grapevine that Mabel was staying with her Sister Dora, and her address was at 1717 Venerable Street or something like that. Henry wondered where in the hell that could be? He figured it had to be in one of the poorest parts of the "Colored" Neighborhoods, because that was probably the only place Dora could afford.

Henry heard the roar of a diesel engine coming down the road. He looked up and the bus came to a stop. Because of where the bus was going to take him, it seemed more like a mechanical monster, than one of the main modes of convenient transportation. He boarded the monster, paid his fare, and headed to the back of the bus. He slumped down into one of the last seats in the back. He was very tired and hung-over.

The horrible things he had been compelled to do to Tank Snowvall came to mind. He was sure Tank deserved what he got because he was trying to kill him. It was self-defense after all. But he had nearly killed another human being, and had permanently disfigured Tank for life. So he felt like getting ready to go to jail was all that he could expect. He believed that he deserved some jail time.

Henry was mindful of the fact that he would do whatever it took to undo the *jinx* that he had brought upon himself by *sassing his Momma*. He had come to grips with the idea that he may have to get hitched to Mabel, and stay with her long enough to convince her to let him take William to A'nt Maetta to bring up. He would try to talk her into just letting William go. But if that failed, and if Mabel insisted, he'd do the unthinkable. He would marry her.

He settled back in the last seat on the left side in the back of the bus and dozed off. Before he knew it, the bus pulled into the Station in Richmond. The bus driver announced the connections for farther South, and West. He opened the bus doors and the busload of people unloaded. Henry saw a Porter standing on the Franklin Street side of the Bus Station: "Sir, where's Venerable Street?"

The tall dark-skinned man, wearing a black and white uniform, pointed to Broad Street and alluded: "It's up yonder a ways up Broad on the western edge of Church Hill. You can't miss it. Just keep walkin' that way, an' readin' the street signs."

"Thank ya, sir," Henry graciously replied.

The farther Henry walked up East Broad the slummier the housing and surroundings became. He came to a bent and twisted black and white street sign that said, "Venerable Avenue." He turned left onto Venerable, and noticed immediately that the sidewalks ceased to exist. Only primitive curb and gutter remained on both sides of the Street. It reminded him of the worst part of Vinegar Hill in Charlottesville. Every building Henry saw was in a decadent state nearly falling down. The decay got worse and worse the farther he walked down Venerable. He finally came to a gutted two-story building with a twisted sign that said, "1700" on one side, and "Venerable Avenue" on the other side. That building at 1700 and Venerable was crumbling down. Henry wondered why the State hadn't condemned this building and demolished it. The 1700 Block had a smell like garbage.

There were heaps of that in back of some of the buildings. Henry wondered how anyone could live in this part of Richmond and still be healthy.

Seemingly half-way down Venerable, Henry came to the unpainted-elongated, wooden two story cracker-box building, surrounded by a rotting-down remnant of a once-proud veranda that probably dated back to the 1800s. The entrance of this building-nightmare was nearly gone, leaving behind a huge-square hole that may have once been two fine ornate doors to a mansion. On the left side of the door frame was a print where "1717" had once been nailed.

There were steps that led up to the second floor. The apartments on the first story were empty. No one lived in these barn-like places. Sheetrock and peeled paint littered the floors.

Henry saw the notices written in big red-letters on white paper, "CONDEMNED," on a couple of the doors nearest to the stairway. All of the doors on the first floor were ajar or hanging open. *How the hell do "Colored" peoples keep alive in shitty places like this?* was what Henry had to wonder. He just shook his head in disgust.

The air of the whole area stunk like a mixture of cow's manure, an outdoor toilet, burning coal, kerosene, gasoline, and burning wood. Then the worst of all was the stench of garbage piled as high as a tepee behind several of the abandoned buildings on the 1700 Block.

A huge black cat howled. It came running from behind one of the heaps of garbage in hot pursuit of a rat that was more than half its size. The cat caught the rat, tore it open exposing some of its guts, but let it go when the rat went limp. The bleeding rodent took off when it thought it had gotten by the cat's notice. Henry didn't know whether the rat made good its escape or not. But a large gray dog came from behind another heap of garbage and gave chase after the cat. This scene coupled with the rest of the sights and smells of 1717 Venerable made Henry feel glad that he lived in the country. While still standing near the doorway, Henry heard a shrill voice call out to him.

"Hey ... Hey, man," Dora yelled. She was now a smooth-skinned, ebony beauty. She ran down the rickety steps of the stairway and grabbed Henry in a bear hug. She almost picked him up off the floor. She seemed too strong for a very skinny, but shapely, woman. "What 'cha standin 'round down there for? C'mon, let's go on upstairs. Mabel an' Lil' Billy go be so glad ta-see ya. Billy's always askin' bout his Daddy. C'mon man, let's go on up."

Henry wondered how anyone forced to live in a place like what he was seeing and smelling could be so jolly? He climbed the stairs behind Dora. He was afraid each step might cave in, or something, but Dora paid them no mind. Once they were at the top of the stairway, they came to a door that was covered in scratched-up varnish. The door handle had been removed. The door was kept shut by a piece of folded cardboard wedged in the crack of the door's edge and the doorsill. Henry just shook his head. He wondered how safe could that be?

Dora removed the cardboard and the door flung open. Henry saw that the interior of her apartment was the same as some of those he had seen downstairs. A causal glance revealed that all of Dora's furnishings were half-broken, or barely standing, even on down to the huge kitchen table and the chairs around it. Henry saw large cracks in the flooring, where boards had separated, with dirt caked in there for years. Henry stood in what was the front room grimacing, but trying to cover that with a deceitful smile.

"Don't mind the place, Henry. We's go clean it today, I reek-en," Dora said.

Henry found that statement almost ludicrous, because he thought to himself: *There just ain't no way she'd ever be able ta-do that. This pigpen's past her being able ta-clean it up in-a month a days.*

After hearing the voices and determining who were doing the talking, Mabel came running from a pitiful backroom with Billy in tow.

"Henry! Henry! I'm so glad ta-see ya. You came-ta see 'bout us. I's hopin' you'd get the message. I'd tell ev' body I knew would see ya, that me an' Billy's down here in Rich-men an' we need ya. Did ya hear 'bout us?" She tried to kiss Henry, but he almost brushed her off.

"C'mon in my room or lemme go in the kitchen an' cook ya somethin'." Mabel sounded like a little girl who was very glad to get a visit from her Daddy. She had that kind of gleam in her eyes. She put her arms around Henry and looked up to him like a Daughter would.

"No, Mabel. You, me, an' Billy's goin' ta-a-little rest'rant I passed on my way to this house. I think the place's called Smokey's Cafe. Okay?"

Henry said. "Y'all go on get ready, I'll just stay on out here in this front room an' wait till ya get ready."

Mabel pecked Henry on his cheeks with a little "sweet" kiss. He didn't return that. "Okay, honey," Mabel chimed. "I'll get Billy and myself ready as quick as I can."

In a few minutes, a little-brown smooth-skinned Billy peeked from behind his Mother's bouncy gray skirt. She had on a thick blue sweater over a yellow long-sleeve blouse. "Is he my Daddy, Momma?" Billy asked. He had on a heavy winter two-piece sailor suit and a pair of brown high-top shoes. Mabel wore black high-top ladies' boots.

"Yes . . . Billy, this is ya Daddy." Mabel was full of enthusiasm.

"Yipee! Momma he's the best's Daddy in the whole-wide world," Billy said.

Henry didn't grab his little Son up and hug him. He looked at him like he would a worm that had crawled out from under a rock. Billy could feel the distance between his Daddy and himself It made him feel fretful.

"Mabel, y'all ready? I want ta-get up yonder to the comer of West Broad and Venerable Avenue. That's where I saw this rest'rant," Henry said.

"Yeah, I once worked at Smokey's. It's a nice place," Mabel said.

Henry looked a little disappointed at the fact that Mabel already knew about Smokey's Cafe. "Look, Mabel, let's go on up yonder an' get somethin' then. I'll tell ya my plans after we gets up there."

Mabel's heart bubbled with joy. Billy eased over to hug his Daddy's leg. He had his left thumb in his little mouth. He had never been that close to his Daddy before. He wanted his Daddy to touch him. He wanted him to pick him up and do Daddy-loving things, like kissing his little face all over, and telling him how much he loved him. But instead, Henry yelled:

"Mabel, get Billy off my leg!" Henry ordered.

Mabel grabbed Billy up into her arms. Billy cried out loudly. He didn't want his Mother to hug him. He needed his Daddy to do that. He screamed louder the more Henry ignored him.

Henry got mad. "Mabel, tell that boy-ta shut up that noise. I can't stand no child yellin' like that. If n he don't stop, I'll give 'im somethin' ta-cry 'bout."

"Sh-h-h-h, Billy. Daddy don't want 'cha ta-cry. Hush, now," Mabel cooed to her little Billy.

Her loving voice calmed Billy down for the moment. Mabel put her Son on her hip.

The three of them went towards the stairs. "See y'all, Mabel, Billy. Henry y'all comeback an' see me soon's ya can."

Mabel turned, and with tears in her eyes, said: "I hope-ta see ya as Mrs. James the next time I sees ya." Her voice trailed off into a hoarse whisper.

Henry grunted, cleared his throat, and grimaced. His voice had a little-boy's nervous sound to it. He could barely get the words out: "Yeah, I'll see ya 'round. I hope things turn out better for ya."

Mabel went out the door and Henry followed her. She pulled Billy along after her. Henry looked on. It was like he couldn't stand to look at Billy very long. They came out on the street. Mabel hoped Henry would help carry Billy up the seventeen blocks to West Broad to the corner where Smokey's stood. But Henry carried Mabel's night bag with Billy's and her meager belongings inside. Henry had a look on his face like a convict would have on his way to the electric chair. By the time they arrived at Smokey's Mabel was completely exhausted.

Mabel walked into the Cafe first. Henry was right behind her. He saw several nice tables in the dining area. These were covered with starched-white tablecloths. Each table had four red vinyl-padded chairs. The wood of them seemed to be mahogany. There were red-cloth napkins on the tables, and shiny-clean silverware already set on the tables. Henry was impressed. He'd seen something like that at the Cavalier Inn off of Vinegar Hill in Charlottesville, but nothing like that for "Coloreds" in Fluvanna County. The red wall-to-wall carpet in the place was immaculately clean. The whole place had an aura of newness about it, from its freshly painted walls, to its cleverly placed photos on those walls of Billie Holiday, Cab Calloway, Count Basie, and Josephine Baker; to paintings of African scenery featuring elephants, giraffes, and gorillas; to Africa's open savannahs and tropical rainforests.

Henry had seen nothing like the interior of Smokey's before in his life. Mabel had seen it only after moving to Richmond. The music of Charlie Byrd came from speakers mounted on the walls.

Henry was wearing a two-piece imitation sharkskin suit, a gray Stetson hat, highly-polished brown wing-tipped shoes, a red-and-white polka dot tie over a brown Van Heusen shirt. He better blended with the ambience of Smokey's Cafe than Mabel and Billy. He took off a grayish brown full-length overcoat, an imitation London Fog, and he meant to drape it over a chair at a table he had selected. He didn't know that was not appropriate.

A tall smooth-skinned ebony beauty came over to Henry and asked: "Sir, may I take your hat and coat? I will be happy to." She had on a starched-white waitress uniform with a black apron.

"No," said Henry. "They go be fine right here."

"Sir, I'm sorry, but our policy is that there are to be no outer garments of our customers at the tables. I will be happy to secure these for you," the pretty waitress said. She blinked her big eyes and crinkled her prominent nose. But there was no smile on her red cupid-shaped lips. Henry decided not to make an issue of where his coat and hat hung while he ate.

Mabel stood near the checkout counter at the entrance of the place, because she knew to wait to be seated.

Henry gave his waitress his hat and overcoat. Mabel and Billy did the same. Their waitress took their overcoats to the coatroom. Mabel went over and got a high chair for Billy. All three got seated at their table.

"May I take you all's order, please?" Henry didn't utter a word. Mabel said: "Yes ma'am.

Gimme coffee, some pancakes an' sausages ..."

Henry interrupted her: "Dammit, Mabel. Lemme do the orderin'. I'm the one payin'. When yall's out with me, lemme do the talkin'."

Mabel's eyes clouded up. She wrinkled up her face. Tears eased down her cheeks. In her mind she thought: *I guess he's startin' ta-act like-a Daddy. He knows best. He's ten-years older 'n me. I'm more like-a Daughter to 'im. This must be what it feels like ta-have a Daddy scold ya.*

"Go-head-on, honey, you order for me an' Billy," Mabel whined.

"Gimme two eggs over hard, two over easy, an' one scrambled. Gimme two coffees, one small orange juice, an order of bacon and one-a sausage, and a short stack," Henry said.

"I'll bring your drinks out first," the waitress said. She rolled her eyes at Henry. She strutted on behind the counter through a door that led to the kitchen.

The waitress brought out the coffee and juice, and then the food. Mabel broke the bacon up into little pieces, and stirred them up into the one scrambled egg for Billy. She set the glass of juice in front of Billy.

Billy took a little sip of the juice. He picked up a plastic spoon that the waitress had brought out with the food, got a little of the egg and bacon on the spoon, and managed to get that into his mouth. Fear beat along with his little excited heart. The look in his Father's eyes was to Billy something very ugly, scary, and threatening. Billy lost his appetite.

"Eat your food, boy!" Henry ordered. "Go-head on, baby, eat," Mabel pleaded.

"Mabel, that boy's go need a lotta correctin', I can see that. We'll have-ta get 'round ta-that." Henry sounded like a prizefighter threatening to knockout his opponent.

She kept her eyes on her food. Henry's anger made her feel choked up inside. Mabel didn't want to eat either, but she didn't want to anger Henry any further.

Henry finished eating, wiped his mouth, and took a couple of sips of his coffee. "Mabel, here's what I think's go be best. Why don't ya lemme take Billy there back up yonder ta Momma, an' she'll give 'im a proper up-bringin'?" he said, in a very matter-of-fact way.

The look on Mabel's face bordered on panic. "Henry . . . The onliest way you's go ever get Billy is for ya ta-take his Momma as your wife.

"I ain' got no job. The last money I made on my last job is all gone. I need you. Billy need ya. Don't ya have no feelin's for us at all? Don't ya 'member how good we was together when we's gettin' Billy. Don't that count for somethin'?"

"Mabel, I gotta level with ya. I don't wanna get marri'd to ya. But if ya force me to hook up with ya ta-get Billy ta-my Momma, I'll do it, but I don't love you.

"Look, Mabel. I's once s'pose-ta get marri'd ta-a gal named, Henrietta (Henny) Lewis. I got cold feet at the last minute. I went over ta-see ya Momma. It was how I first got ta-lookin' at you. I never showed up for the marriage. Left all of Henrietta's peoples standin' at the Altar with the preacher, while I was over to see ya Momma. Henrietta never forgave me for that. She's pregnant then. Later on she had a little girl she named, 'Agnes,' to spite me. Henrietta never allowed me to see my little girl.

"Henrietta's the onliest gal I'm go ever love, an' I didn't marr' her. She took my only Daughter to New York an' kept 'er from me ever since 1940. That's what ya go be up against."

"Henry, Iain' never seen or heard who my Daddy is. I know we gotta lotta problems to work out, but I'm willin' ta-try ta-do that with you. I love you. I loved you from the first time I ever saw you, long before we got together. I still wanna marry ya," Mabel said.

Henry allowed her to give him a peck on his cheek that gravitated towards his lips. He pulled way at the last second.

"It's settled then. All we gotta do is go back an' get ev' thin' you left at up at Dora's hut, aw ight?" Henry's remark made mockery of Dora.

"Henry, Dora may live in-a hut, but that's all she can 'ford. Don't make fun of 'er for being poor," Mabel whined.

"Mabel, I don't wanna hear that crap. Let me go pay the ticket, an' y'all get-read-ta go."

Mabel knew she would have to carry Billy all the way back up the street. Mabel wondered how Henry could despise his own flesh and blood like that. A person's blood-relatives: Parents, Grandparents, Brothers, Sisters, Aunts, Uncles, and Children are all that anyone has in this world.

"Don't worry, Henry, we don't have-ta go back to Ma 'Dear's (Dora's) place, I got ev'thin' b'longs ta-me an' Billy right here in my night bag. We can just go-ta the Bus Station."

Henry replied: "Aw-ight, then, let's get our stuff an' get on up yonder-ta the Bus Station."

CHAPTER TWELVE

Mabel had to carry and or drag Billy all the way to the Bus Station. Henry tried to completely ignore his little Son, except when he wanted to scold him. At the Station, Mabel stood back, thinking: *I gotta let 'im take care-a the bizzness cause he wanna Be The Man! Guess I' ma be just Mrs. James standin' behind 'er man. He's go be my Sugar Daddy. After all, I's a virgin when he got me. So, I can be a lady if'n I wanna be. I ain'go do nothin' toll to upset this man. I 'ma be a Perfect Wife. He's go have-ta love me. When he see how good I'm go be, he's go wanna make me an' Billy real happy.* Mabel smiled at her thoughts. Then, Henry came back from the ticket counter with a terrible frown on his face.

He hated standing in the long line behind all of the White customers before he was allowed to buy tickets. There were just two or three other Black customers. He and they had to wait until all of the White people bought their tickets. By the time Henry got to buy his tickets he was cussing under his breath, like the other "Coloreds" waiting behind the long line, because every time a White person came up to buy tickets, he inserted himself in front of the Blacks in back of the line. {That's the way it was.)

While boarding the Westbound Local, Henry, Mabel, and Billy, had to stand in back of a long line of Whites before being allowed to board the bus. Soon the twisted-face bus driver took Henry's and Mabel's tickets, Billy rode free, and they proceeded to the very back of the bus, as was required. *I hate all of this shit!* Henry thought.

Mabel got a little bit nervous after seeing the frown on Henry's face. She knew that Henry had a terrible temper. She figured that Henry was not going to let too many Whites mess with him before he got mad and did something stupid.

Finally, the bus was loaded. It pulled out of the Station onto West Broad and headed out to 250 West to Route Six. Up Route Six the Bus made a stop, letting several White people off the bus, and several got on at this stop in Goochland County. One of the boarding passengers was a tall-skinny Whiteman. He came to the back of the bus. He had to stand in the aisle because the bus remained full to capacity. Other Whites had gotten on the bus with this man, and stood in the aisle without complaining, but only this one made a bold demand.

The Whiteman standing in the aisle ogling Mabel annoyed Henry. Henry looked him up and down. He decided that he was looking at a "Poor-White Trash" farmer acting crazy as they sometimes did.

Mabel hated the way this White farmer was staring at her bosom and her legs with a salacious grin on his flat Quarter-Moon face. He was long and lean with blondish hair. He had beady little blue eyes. His face had a five o'clock beard. He wore a red-plaid coat and a pair of faded green overalls, a thick-red sweat shirt, a pair of tall-black fishing boots, and a brown safari hat. He had a plug of chewing tobacco in his jaw. He smiled at Mabel and winked at her with his left eye. Mabel returned him a very hateful stare.

Henry saw the come-on on the farmer's face and the wink he had dared to do right there in the bus aisle. Henry's blood boiled. But as long as this farmer did not put his hand on Mabel in front of him, he was not going to take matters into his own hands. Henry thought this man smelt like cow's manure and soured milk.

The farmer stood directly in front of Henry's and Mabel's seat. "Y'all Nigga's knows better 'n this. White people get to sit first. Tain't right for y'all to be a-sittin' while I' ma standin'. Why, boy, it's agin the Law. Now, you get your Black hide up, directly, an' let-a Whiteman sit down. If you don't get up, I'm gonna have your ass 'rrested."

Henry wondered why this White Sucker had singled him out? There were other Black people on the bus, why was this "Cracker" picking on him? Thoughts about his Momma and Poppa came to mind. His temper exploded. He stood up.

"Cracker, ifn ya thinks you's man 'nough ta-take my seat, you's welcome ta-try. Otherwise, carr' ya stinky ass somewhere else, fore I kick-a mud hole in it," Henry growled. Henry had lost his switchblade knife in his attack on Tank Snowvall, but he carried a pocketknife he used at work in his front pants' pockets. He drew that, opened it, and stood facing the farmer.

White-racist arrogance quickly turned to fear as the jaw muscles twitched on the farmer's face. His eyes trembled. Then his hands shook. Finally, his whole body trembled.

"Don't ya worry, boy. I'm go see you 'round. I ain't scare-a no Nigga. I gotta mind to get the driver on your insolent ass. The only reason I'm not all over you is cause of that cute gal with you, and her little pickaninny. If tweren't for them, I'd make you wish you's never born!" the farmer said. His voice sounded like the croaking of a frog.

"You's a red-head liar ifn ya thinks ya go do anythin' ta-me. I'll gut ya like a hog, White boy," Henry said. He moved a little closer to the farmer.

The farmer blinked his eyes and moved on up towards the front. The bus made another local stop. A couple of seats were emptied. The farmer took one of those. He uttered: "We got ourselves a uppity Nigga right here on this bus." He aimed this nonsense at the Whites sitting nearest to him. None of them said a word, but most of them stared back towards Henry with racist hate emanating from their fearful eyes.

Henry closed his knife, put it back in his pocket and sat down. He was thinking: *They fucked over Poppa an' Momma all they lives. I be damned if'n I'm go take that shit from them Crackers. I'll cut 'em ta-death, or die tryin' fore I let 'em mess over me.*

The Whites up front could see that Henry was a defiant Negro who would not take any crap from them. Since World War Two had ended, a lot of the "Good Colored Boys" had changed. But Mabel was so scared she was nearly wetting her panties.

"Henry," said Mabel, with fear vibrating off every word that she spoke. "Ain't we s'pose-ta give up our seats ta-Whites? Ain' that the Law? That's what Momma 'nem always told me."

"Mabel, long's we do that, the longer we's go have-ta do that. We's already sittin' way in the back of the bus. Hell no, I won't give up my seat to no Cracker 'thout-a fight." The muscles of his jaw jumped up and down from his anger. "Don't ya be no fool for-a Cracker, an' they won't be able-ta treat ya like no fool! See, they knows who they can push 'round an' who they can't. They can tell by the look in my eyes that I ain' one-a them pushover Negroes."

At another stop more Whites got on the Westbound Local. Some seated themselves near Mabel and Henry. "Hush your fuss, man," a man that looked a lot like the farmer Henry had had a run-in with, said to another one that looked very similar to him. "Cute little gal, though," the farmer allowed. The one sitting next to him said: "I wish I could get over yonder, um-um-um." Both men were looking straight at Mabel.

Henry put his hand in his front pocket on his knife. "Mabel, I wish that big-mouth Cracker would c'mon over here. I'd slaughter 'im like a pig. He better keep his ass up yonder!"

At a stop just before the bus got to Columbia, several White women got on the bus. The bus was very crowed again. The women started complaining very loudly: "Why we got to stand up? Them Blacks are sitting there in seats that ought to be given to us. We're tired"

The bus driver had had enough. He stopped the bus and went to the back where the Negroes were sitting, and where the commotion was coming from.

His blue uniform and matching cap, with a Thirty-Two Automatic Pistol strapped to his side made the driver look like the consummate authority figure on the bus that day. The driver saw Henry yelling at Mabel. She was nearly in tears. Whites standing near the back of the bus were murmuring and complaining about there not being enough seats for them to sit down, and the Negroes weren't getting up and giving up their seats. So the driver thought he would end the melee by simply putting the "Uppity Negro" in his place. He pranced back to where Henry and Mabel were seated.

"Boy, y' know the Law," the driver yelled. "What're you doing sitting down there while these nice White folks are standing? Y'all gotta get up and offer your seats to one of the Whites standing around in the aisle. If y'all don't get up I'm gonna have to ask you to get off this bus, directly." The driver placed his hand on his gun.

Mabel was so afraid tears came down her cheeks. "Henry, let's get off," she said. "Sit still, Mabel. I'll handle this," Henry replied.

Henry stood up and came out into the aisle to face the driver. He thought the driver resembled "Porky Pig." Henry's eyes got an angry glaze on them. He started to look like a cornered animal that was ready to defend itself to the death. He had a little nervousness about him, but showed very little real fear.

"Son-a-va-bitch!" Henry shouted. He drew his knife and clicked it open like a switchblade knife. He had learned how to do that from some guys he had met from North Carolina who worked with the Road-Right-Of-Way Crew. The knife came out of his pocket opened. His lips were ashy. His nostrils flared. "If'n ya touch me, or my girlfriend, or my child, it'll be the last thing you go ever do in this world, Cracker. You got that?"

Henry was thinking: *This's what Poppa ought-a done years ago. Should-a been a lot more dead Negroes, or a lot more dead Crackers. One-a us go meet his Maker today if'n that Cracker makes any funny moves.*

The driver looked Henry up and down for a moment. "Ah, to hell with this shit!" he said. "I'm not gonna get myself all cut up or killed over some stupid segregation Law. That stupid shit ought to be over anyway." He walked away and quickly took his place in the driver's seat. He looked back at Henry and just rolled his eyes as Henry took his seat again. All eyes of everyone were on Henry.

"Mabel, I b'lieve I saw ya crack a little smile when that redneck said you's cute. He's up yonder starin' at ya like he knows he's go get some. He's lookin' through ya clothes."

"Gal, lemme tell ya somethin'. The onliest thing that'll make me kill ya fore Gawd get the news is, ifn I see ya, or ifn I find out ya been sleepin' with-a Cracker-man! If ya do an' I find out, ya better get lost for good," Henry said, loud enough for all in back of the bus to hear.

"Henry, ya don't have-ta yell at me like that. I ain't had the hots for no Whiteman. One of 'im took 'vantage-a Momma. I never let none-a them touch me. When they tried to catch me in the woods, I outran them. I always got away. They caught Ginia, Mary, Dora, Frances, Maude an' Catherine; A'nt Neddy, an' Grandma Daisy, too. But, I stayed clean away from them all. So ya don't have-ta worr 'bout that," Mabel said. She cried like she had been slapped.

The bus finally came to a stop in Columbia. Billy was tired of his Father fussing at his Momma. After all of them had gotten off the bus, Billy started whimpering. Henry thought it best to get off the bus in Columbia because the murmuring and complaining got louder and louder. One shouted: "I'm gonna report this to headquarters." Another one shouted: "You should've dealt with that boy properly." Still others shouted: "You're letting an 'Uppity Nigga' get away with too much sass!" An older Whiteman quipped: "What the hell's this country coming to now? Why didn't you shoot the bastard?" They yelled at a bus driver that kept his eyes on the road and his pedal to the metal. He was glad to see Henry and Mabel getting off in Columbia. A fat White woman spat on the floor when Henry walked past her.

The whole affair was upsetting to Billy. He didn't fully understand what he heard but the sound of things made him whimper, even after they had gotten off the bus.

"Mabel, shut that boy up," Henry ordered. "I 'ma go down yonder ta-the Jungle. I bet somebody's over there who will give us a lift up the road. You an' Billy stay on the comer till I get back . . . Tell that boy to quit cryin', Mabel," Henry said.

"Billy . . . Hush, Son. Don't make Daddy mad," Mabel whispered to her Son.

The harsh sound of his Father's voice made Billy even more fretful. He wanted a kind touch from his Daddy. He reached out to Henry. He wanted his Daddy to pick him up. He figured crying was the way to make that happen. It had always worked with his Mother. He wanted Daddy to say, "I love you." But instead:

Henry undid the buckle of his belt and snatched it off in one quick motion. He walloped Billy on his tender-little back, twice. The belt made a snapping sound each time it landed.

"I said shut that whinin' an' cryin' up, boy!" Henry barked at his little Son.

Billy squirmed in pain. He let out a half-muffled shriek. He'd never been whipped like that before. He tried covering his mouth with his little hands to stop the sounds that had aggravated his Father so bad. The best he could do, however, was muffled whimpers and half-yells. He was too afraid to cry out any louder, but the burning pain forced him to defy the odds.

"Now, dry up that cryin' an' don't ya make another sound; you hear?" Henry shouted. He drew the belt into the air again. But Mabel had had enough for right then.

"Henry I don't mind ya correctin' Billy like-a Father ought-ta, but

don't whip my baby like you's whippin' a mad dog! I won't stand for ya
ta-hurt my boy like that," Mabel screamed at Henry.

Henry was thinking: *Now that ought-ta 'vince 'er-ta forget' bout marryin'*
me. That let's 'er see what livin' with me go be like. Should change 'er mind
'bout gettin' hitched ta-me.

"Mabel dammit, don't never argue with me bout nothin' toll. I 'ma
man you an' that boy's go have-ta respect. I want y'all ta-get that shit
straight right now," shot out of Henry's mouth like a shotgun blast.

Like a little girl, Mabel hung her head and answered: "Yes sir." She
whimpered and trembled all over. She grabbed Billy and pulled him close
to her. Both of them looked up at Henry with teary-eyes blinking, waiting
for what Henry might do to them next. They watched Henry put his belt
back on. Then Mabel started to cry like she had been beaten. Billy clung
to his Mother and she held tightly to him. Mabel's night bag was the only
thing between them and Henry. She knew that she could pick that bag
up and go across the tracks and head home and take Billy with her. But
she just stood there, clinging to her little Son, hoping "The Devil" would
change for the better.

"I can't stand no more-a this shit. I 'ma go to the Jungle an' see who
I can find to give us a ride up the road ta-Momma's. Y'all can stand there
cryin' like Hyenas, but I ain' go stand 'round an' watch y'all do that," came
out of Henry like sarcastic vomit.

Henry turned towards the Cumberland Bridge. He paused for a second
or two. Looking back at Billy and Mabel standing on the comer, he wished
they would disappear before he could get to the Jungle and return with a
ride up the road. He was thinking: *If Mabel is still there when I gets back,*
she gotta be the Dumbest Bitch I done ever seen. Why would she still wanna
marr' me? He walked towards the Bridge.

Just then, Lin Jackson came across the Bridge in his new 1950 Ford
Four-Door Sedan. It was black and shiny with cream-colored interior, with
red-plaid seat covers.

"Y'all get in my car over here. Cut out that damn glarin' nose, Henry.
It ain't good for ya to be fussin' like I hear ya doin', with your cute-little
gal-friend, fore y'all get hitched. Bessie told me that she heard from A'nt
Maetta, that you's gettin' hooked up with one-a Agnes Mickens's gals.

"C'mon, y'all, get in the car. Lemme give ya a lift up the road. Henry …

You's a long way from Route 656. Why y'all got off down here 'stead-a up yonder?" Lin said.

"Man, them Crackers on the bus was read-ta-lynch me. So I got off while the gettin' was good," Henry said.

"C'mon, Mae, or what's'ever your name is ..." "It's Mabel, Mr. Jackson," Mabel interrupted him. "Nope, just call me Lin, Mabel."

"Okay, Lin it is," Mabel said. It felt good to hear a kind voice for a change. Henry frowned at Lin like he was doing something wrong.

"Y'all get in the car. I gotta get up the road an' take the two cases of beer I got in the trunk fore it gets too warm. I sold a cup'la jars of my 'White Lightning' ta-the boys in the Jungle. Got a cup'la cases of beer, now I'm goin' back ta-the house an' make-a little money," Lin said with a hefty laugh.

Mabel and Billy got into the backseat of the car. Henry sat up in front with Lin. In about five minutes Lin had driven the five or six miles up to his tum off. "Henry, you wanna go to ya Momma's, or to see Cary an' Will 'nem? I know Cary wanna holler at ya fore you get ta-be all marri'd and whatnot," Lin said.

"Well, Lin, I think I will go by an' holler at Cary 'nem. We'll take the back path up ta-ya house after we finish vistin' with them. I know she'll be glad to see who I 'ma marry. I know she thought I'd never get hitched ta-no gal 'round here. She an' Cora go be surprised as can be 'bout who I'm go marry, Lin. They thought I'd get marri'd ta-one-a them light-skinned gals from over in Louisa, or Farmville," Henry said.

Lin, a very light-skinned person himself, just laughed at Henry's remark. "Well, Henry, y'all go on up the hill there. Cary's been dyin' ta-see O' Henry. I gotta get back ta-the game at the house."

Henry gave a sly laugh. "You an' Bessie still trimmin' them suckers, man?" "Yep, that's our hustle," Lin said. He winked at Henry.

Mabel got out of the car with Billy in tow. Henry got out last. Lin gave him a bottle of his bootleg liquor, and he took a big swig of that before he got out of the car. "Let's go up yonder," said Henry, pointing to a five-room bungalow up the hill from where Lin had let them out. It was down a little east of 656.

Mabel saw the house that stood on a hill overlooking Herman (Doc) Johnson's Sawmill. A large branch of the Rivanna River ran by the Mill then under Route Six, and then flowed parallel to it for about two miles towards Columbia. Will Winston was Doc's saw man. The Johnsons were close-kin to the Winstons. Will's Mother had given Doc permission to run his Mill at that location for as long as he would give Will the right to be his saw man.

As she approached the house, Mabel saw that its eaves were boarded up with planed whitewashed lumber. The rest of it had been overlaid with red brick-siding. The window-and door-frames were trimmed in green. The windows had screens and the front and back door-ways had screened-doors.

Henry knocked on the front-screened door gently at first. Nobody answered. Then he hit the door pretty hard with an opened hand. Mabel and Billy stood directly behind Henry.

Mabel saw a fat, four or five foot woman come to the door. She had on a pink bathrobe, with her hair up in large blue rollers. She had on a pair of red bunny-slippers. Her big, light-colored eyes filled up with tears when she saw Henry, Mabel and Billy. She stood on the stoop in front of the front door holding it open, but seemed to be trying to think of some reason not to let her Brother and his girlfriend, and their baby, come in. She looked to weigh 250 pounds.

The house was immaculately clean. New daisy-print draperies were hung at all of the windows. The red and white blocked linoleum on the floors had a waxed sheen on it. Mabel figured because Henry had told her that Cary worked for the Waltons in Columbia, she was not going to let her house look dirtier than her employer's. All of the walls were newly painted white, or beige. The house had been wired and had electric lights in the ceiling. Mabel couldn't figure out why Cary was not inviting them in to sit for a spell.

"Henry, y'all c'mon back tomorrow when Will go be feelin' a whole lot better, I reek-en," Cary said in a whine. She was wringing her hands a certain way. "Will's been workin' real hard at the Mill an' he's too tired to entertain y'all. So, y'all come back, tomorrow; okay?"

With a frown on his face, Henry allowed, "Aw-ight, Cary. We's goin' ta-see Bessie 'nem. Lin just let us out a minute ago. See ya, Sis." Henry was a little annoyed, though, at Cary's lying to cover for Will. "Y'all follow me," said Henry. He looked back at Mabel and Billy.

"Y'all, we's gotta go up yonder through the woods a ways." Henry pointed northward to a broad path through the woods that meandered past several Beechnut trees, a bunch of Poplar trees, and a stand of Huckleberry bushes. On the hill surrounding the house were several huge Indian Oak and Pine trees, and Dagwood trees grew like weeds on that hill. The trees shaded the path and made it seem darker than it should be at that time of the evening.

"Mabel, Will ain't too tired to see us. He's drunk as a skunk, that's' what's wrong with that O' Boy. Cary lie 'bout 'im all the time. Cary's shame of the way Will drank. Most weekends, he's dead-drunk."

Mabel was curious. "Why he's drinkin' so much, Henry?" Mabel asked.

"He can't get over the fact, Cary ain't able ta-get knocked up. Took Will years ta-gree ta adopt-a child. That's the onliest reason they got Mary Ann; but Will wanna Boy. They can't 'ford-ta adopt no more chillren. So Will get drunk ev' week," Henry said.

Mabel didn't say anything more about that subject. But she wondered how miserable Cary had to be living with a man who was drunk all the time and resentful of the fact that she couldn't give him a Son?

Mabel carried Billy on her hip then she pulled him along when she got too tired to carry him on her hip. As they went up the long path through the woods, Billy started to whine.

"Momma, my legs hurt. Can we rest, Momma. I 'on wanna go up yonder, Momma. Can we go back to Ma' Dear's house, Momma? I wanna eat. I'm tired ..."

Right away, Henry tore a switch off a Maple sapling. He raised it high above Billy. 'Whap up!" it went as it cut into the tender flesh of Billy's neck. It cut a gash around the back of Billy's neck. He screamed and fell down to the ground and rolled around in the leaves for a minute or two. A large bloody welt rose on the left side of Billy's neck.

Mabel was hysterical. "Henry! why don't ya stop hittin' that boy like that? Man, what's the matter with you?" She grabbed Billy up and hugged him to her bosom. She tried to comfort her little son: "I know it hln1, baby, but it go be over soon. The pain gonna go 'way. Gawd go take it all away, Darlin'." She turned to Henry.

"Nigga, what in the hell's the matter with your stupid ass?" Mabel exclaimed.

"I want y'all ta-know I'm the boss 'round here. I want both you an' that boy to know that!" Henry snapped. "I'on want no whinin' an' shit when I say let's go do somethin' ."

After he finished yelling at Mabel he cut Billy with the switch again. This lick took the skin right off of Billy's neck. Billy screamed as loud as he could because the pain was almost unbearable. Then everything went black for a few minutes. Billy fainted.

Henry eyed the boy for a second or two. He yelled: "If ya want some more I don't mind givin' it ta-ya, boy."

Mabel stood there crying worse than Billy. "Henry, ya oughtn't hurt our Son like that. Don't ya love 'im at all? That pain's go grow up in 'im an' he's go hate you one day. It ain' go be nobody's fault but your own. Whatever you's mad 'bout, it ain't Billy's fault, an' y' know that.

You's a grown man beatin' up on-a little-bitty child. What in the hell do that make ya? Is you outta ya mind, or somethin'?" Mabel said.

The truth hit home. A little mist came to Henry's eyes. He wiped that away very quickly.

He tried to justify himself

"Mabel, I wanna get it straight fore we get tied-ta one-nother. I swears, I can't let no woman run over me with no Whiteman, they chillun, or nothin' else. I'm go make the decisions 'bout ev' thin', my word come first. You go have-ta lemme be the head of the family all the time. When I scold Billy you can't come 'tween me an' him. I gotta teach that boy how-ta mind me. That's all to it. Ifn ya can't go 'long with that, then it'll be better if ya go your way, an' I go mine." Henry said.

With tears in the corners of her eyes and some coming down her cheeks, Mabel yelled at Henry as loud as she could. "Henry, I ain't go let ya beat my Son like ya been doin'. I'm Billy's Momma. I gotta protect him, even from you if need be. Now, ya stop hittin' him, or I'm go get one-a them hickory sticks on the ground over there an' knock some sense into ya head, man.

"Much as I wanna marr' ya, if ya hit Billy like ya did again, I 'ma go back down that path ta the road ta-Columbia, an' I'm go end up in Cumberland. Billy's my flesh-an'-blood, an' your'n too. I'll leave right now ifn that's the onliest way I can protect my baby. Stupid Nigga, ya got that?" Mabel shouted.

Henry stood still in the path. He didn't utter a word in response to Mabel. He was thinking: *I don't want Momma shakin' her fists an' pointin' her finger at me ta-jinx me no more. I gotta 'nough trou 'ba. Mabel ain' go give up no matter how bad I treat 'er, or Billy. I might as well take 'em on up to Lin 'nem an' see what go happen.*

"Be quiet, Billy. I ain't go hit ya no more," Henry whispered. For the first time he looked directly at his little Son. But he still didn't pick the child up to show him any kind of affection, or emotional connection. Henry walked in front, Billy came behind him, and Mabel brought up the rear.

Mabel looked at the ground as she walked along. She was thinking, was it the right decision to come get tied down with this brute? She wondered if she could change him. Would he ever love and cherish her and her Son? Then she remembered the longing inside of herself for her Daddy. She didn't want to ever subject Billy to the horror of not knowing who his Father was. So she hoped that her "Love [Would] Cover The Multitude Of [Henry's] Sins"; and she walked on up the "Path Of Life."

Henry, Mabel, and Billy came to an open field. It was on the edge of the Jacksons' property line. Bessie's children: Monroe (Ton), the youngest; Madeline (Matt), the next youngest; and the twins, Broadus and Lil' Lin, came running down the path to meet them. Lin, Sr. had told them Henry's Bride to be, was on her way to the house.

Ton was about seventeen, Matt was about nineteen, Broadus and Lin, Jr. in their twenties.

The children were all very light-skinned like their Father, who was White enough to pass. Ton had blond hair and blue eyes. He was what was commonly referred to as a "Red-Bone Negro." His skin was like a lighter tinge of the color of an orange-peel. He had a long pointed nose, a flat face, and very thin lips. He was often mistaken for "hey, that's a White boy." He was often teased by other Blacks. He hated being too Black to pass for White, and too White to be taken as a "Down-Brother." He was six-one and very lean.

Lin Jackson was a happy-go-lucky kind of guy. He cracked a lot of jokes about how many children he had fathered all over Louisa-where he was from-Fluvanna, Cumberland, and Buckingham Counties. He was five-five, weighing about 200 pounds, and was solid as a rock. He had a lot of hair on his arms, chest, and on the back of his neck. His hair was blondish-red and straight. He let it grow wooly-like because he very seldom combed it.

After he had married Bessie, he purchased a 100-acre tract of land from Walter Mosely, a wealthy landowner, who had inherited his wealth from generations of slave owners, who had collaborated with the Yankees during the Civil War, and were allowed to keep all of their property (minus the slaves) after the War.

Lin had come back from World War One with thousands of dollars. No one knew how a poor, illiterate, cook could have gotten his hands on so much money, and Lin would not discuss it. He'd just laugh and say: "I got my Mo Jo workin'." The land that Lin had purchased was mostly all that he owned.

Lin cut logs and pulpwood, with the help of his Sons, for a living. He was slick enough to steal a log or two now and then, or a few trees or two, from his White farm-owning neighbors. He called that, "Gettin' over on Mr. Charlie." Lin came down the back road just as Henry, Mabel and Billy had come up the path. He had been in the woods getting a jar of bootleg.

Bessie heard her children greeting someone and came out on her front steps to see if it was Henry's Bride to be. She was short, five-one, and weighed 250 pounds. Her skin was of a smooth-very-Black complexion. Her hair was short and thoroughly kinky. She didn't like putting a hot comb in her hair because she had a tender scalp. It was said that she had a very pleasing personality, until someone riled her.

When Henry heard his Niece and Nephews calling out to him, he threw the switch away that he had kept in his left hand. He carried Mabel's night bag in his right hand. As Matt got closer to the trio, Henry picked Billy up for the first time. He tried to conceal the welts on Billy's neck from Bessie's children, by turning Billy this way and that. Billy tried to pull away from Henry because the welts on his back were sore and hurt when his Father tried to move him around.

Matt spied the cuts and the ridge the switch had made on Billy's neck. Matt had her Mother's temper. She became instantly furious.

"Uncle Henry, what in the hell you done to this little boy? You did it-ain't nobody done it but you. Why you wanna hurt this cute-little child?" Matt screamed.

"Matt, I's just tryin' ta-teach 'im some manners, is all," Henry said.

"Mabel, why'd you let my fool Uncle hurt your little boy like that?" Matt asked Mabel.

Mabel gave Henry a scornful glance. She rolled her eyes, and allowed, "I ain' let 'im do nothin' toll." She shouted back at Matt. "This's all on him."

"Man-man-man, wait till Momma see what Uncle Henry did to this child," Ton said, with a deceitful grin on his young face.

"I wouldn't wanna be Uncle Henry for nothing," Broadus said. He chuckled.

"Me neither," Lil' Lin said. He was thin and sickly. Broadus was stout and muscular like his Daddy. Madeline was short and curvaceous. They all had on blue Jeans and heavy white sweat shirts. The twins wore brogans. Ton and Matt wore Chuck Taylor tennis. They glared at their uncle grimacing.

Bessie, wearing a black dress that went from her neckline to her ankles, and no shoes, even though it was a little cool out that evening, came strutting by the stand of Pine, Gum, and Chestnut Oak trees along the path from the house, until she got to Henry, who was standing there holding Billy. He had a sheepish look on his face, like a little boy who had gotten caught misbehaving. She could clearly see the wounds on Billy's neck.

Henry put Billy down and the child ran to his Mother. Mabel scooped him up. Henry had sat the night bag on the path. Matt had taken that up.

"Henry, ya stupid bas'sard," screamed Bessie. Her open left hand came up out of nowhere and walloped Henry up beside his head. It happened so quickly he didn't have a chance to duck. He stumbled back two or three steps. He fell to his knees for a couple of minutes. He grabbed his right earlobe. He got behind Mabel and Billy; and to Mabel's surprise, he stood back of her and cried. He was boohooing like a whipped child. He didn't draw his knife, or try to hit Bessie back.

"Now-ya big-ass, stupid Negro, hit me! Ya wanna hit somebody, try me. Ya my Brother, but I'll blow ya way, Henry! This ain' nothin' but some bullshit!" Bessie shouted.

Henry stood there trembling fighting back the tears. "I'm sorry, Bessie. I's just tryin' ta correct the boy like Poppa did ta-us. I'm go marr' Mabel in the momin'. I just want'er ta-know who's the boss, like Poppa use-ta do when he came back off'n one-a his trips." Henry whined like a little boy.

"Listen, Henry, and ya better listen, good!" said Bessie. "Ya, like Poppa did, ain' got no right ta-take ya spite out on no in-a-cent child. Ya got that?" Bessie shouted.

"Yes ma'am,' Henry said. "I reek-en ya got that right." The young people were laughing out loud.

"Bessie," said Henry, "I'm go have-ta marr' Mabel tomorrow. See, I didn't plan on this happenin' ta-me. It's all Momma's <loin'. I got jinxed, Big Sis. I ended up cuttin' Tank Snowvall up real bad. He's tryin' ta-kill me over Babe Bates. I's just protectin' myself Momma shook her finger an 'er fist at me for sassin' 'er. All this bad luck done come down on me cause-a Momma's jinx." Henry was trying to justify himself.

"Henry, that ain' nothin' but a lotta shit you's talkin'. I heard 'bout that run-in ya had with Tank Snowvall. All-a that happen ta-ya cause you an' Tank's full-a bullshit. You's fightin' over the underpants of some high-yellar gal who didn't care nothin' toll 'bout nay one-a y'all. Babe's one-a them 'Fancy Gals,' you an' Lil' Charlie use-ta sleep with up in Charles'ville on Vinegar Hill. I think the place is 'Margarita's Place.' Was a place for White mens, but y'all got slipped in the backdoor cause you's musicians. Or y'all went over on Preston Street ta-Calvin's Inn, or Cav 'lier Inn-ah, you know where I mean. Broadus and Lil' Lin been up yonder too. I done told 'em ta-stay 'way from up yonder 'fore one-a them gals get 'em kilt, like Babe almost did for you.

"Babe left Snowvall in the hospital. She done taken up with a man old 'nough to be her Granddaddy, name's, 'Harold Dale Allen.' They live up yonder in Palmyra. Now Snowvall's outta his head. They took 'im down ta-Pita 'sburg. He's in the nuthouse. Ain't that a damn shame?

"Ifn Snowvall had-da blew ya brains out, Babe wouldn't give-a-damn! That slut wouldn't care," Bessie said.

Henry took out a white handkerchief to wipe his face and to blow his nose. "You's right, Bessie. I 'ma fool, I know it. But it ain't too late. I can change. I'm just trapped, though. That's all."

Hot anger came into Bessie's eyes. But she decided to make the most of the situation. "Look, Henry. Lin an' I gon go with you an' Mabel tomorrow. I 'ma be lookin' out for all-a y'all. I'm go stick 'round till this show gets on the road; aw-ight?" Bessie said.

"Why ya so hard on me, though, Big Sis?" Henry asked.

"Henry, I can't stand-ta see 'Colored' mens beatin' on they womens. I'm the only one who ever beat ya ass when you's misbehaving. To-this-day, ya still respects me. I once shot at Lin cause he's tryin' ta-beat me. The shots hit a side of that big oak down yonder 'stead-a Lin's head, or else he'd got kilt.

"I never hit one-a my Chillun. I always talk things out with 'em. They ain' turn out no worse than them chillren peoples always beatin' the hell outta 'em. I won't let Lin hit 'em neither. You gotta stop hittin' ya Son. That's all to it." Bessie turned towards the house.

Matt carried Mabel's night bag. Ton carried Billy. It was getting dark outside. They all walked very slowly like everyone was trying to absorb what had just transpired. Mabel broke the silence.

"Bessie, I'm tired as can be, an' hungry. We ain't had nothin' ta-eat since this mornin'.

Right now, I just wanna lie down. Is that aw-ight with you?" Mabel asked.

"Yes, honey," said Bessie. "Matt, you an' Ton take their stuff up ta-the house. Let 'em use Matt's room tonight.

"Broadus, you an' Lil Lin get the keys from ya Daddy. Go down ta-Colombia an' getta mess offish from Arthur Walton's. We go have-a fish-fry tonight."

Mabel and Billy followed Matt and Ton to the house. Henry stood near Bessie.

"Henry, it's 'bout time for ya ta-grow on up. Momma done spoilt ya ta-death. That's what's wrong with you. The world don't owe ya no livin'. Just like Daddy an' Momma had-ta do, you go have-ta step up ta-the plate. You can't go 'round gettin' babies all over the creation an' goin' on 'bout ya bizzness. Now, that boy Mabel's got looks just like Daddy. Y 'know it's your 'n. You might as well get read-ta take care-a this one.

"Sorry ... I hit ya so hard. I had-ta knock some sense into ya head, man.

You's too old to be actin' like a spoilt brat. That's why I did it." Bessie gave Henry some Motherly advice.

Henry got his handkerchief out again to wipe his eyes. "Aw-ight, Big Sis. But I wish you'd not done it in front-a Mabel or Billy. Looks bad. Aw-ight?"

Bessie eyed Henry scornfully for a minute. "When ya act like a ass in public, I 'ma go to ya ass in public. So, you keep that in mind."

"You ain' never hit ya Chillun. Yet, you don't mind hittin' me, an' I's ya Brother-how come?"

"I trained my Chillun never ta-mess with me. They know how ta-behave 'round me. All I gotta do is look at 'em, they go stop doin' what annoy me. But you's grown. Ya thinks you's a big-bad man. I gotta knock the shit outta ya fore ya go be able ta-hear me. But-a little child, I'll never hit like that. I can get 'em ta-listen by just yellin' at 'em. Don't never hit ya Son 'round me; aw-ight?"

"Aw-ight," Henry said.

Henry followed Bessie up the path to the house. She took him around to the backdoor. A card game had come to a close. Lin had a pile of small change in front of him, and a smaller pile of dollar bills beside of that on the kitchen table, a table that Lin had built with his own hands, using tongue-and-groove lumber. It was painted white. The six chairs around it he had built also. He was a good carpenter, but didn't like doing that kind of work regularly. He liked hustling.

"Clean they butts this evening in a hurry. I 'specially got that Burton Gaines. It was like takin' candy from-a baby. Wayne Nicholas got up an' left right quick. He lost 'bout three dollars in change. Got O' Toad [Sherman] his Brother, an' Sherwood, his younger Brother outta most-a the money ya see here,' Lin said with a chortle.

"What's all the noise y'all's makin' out yonder. Thought I go have-ta get my gun down.

What's the matter?" Lin asked.

"I gotta get use-ta being marri'd, is all," Henry said.

Lin laughed. "Ya may as will keep-a stiff upper-lip on that one my-man. Cause it ain' go make no difference if 'n ya don't." Lin laughed at Henry like there was a joke in his statement somewhere. Henry didn't get it.

"Lin ... Gimme a shot of somethin' strong, man. I need some bootleg, y' know what I mean," Henry whined. His voice sounded so sad it seemed like he might cry.

"Sure," said Lin. "Bessie go over yonder an' get that jar outta the pantry. I's go set 'er on the table, but the boys didn't last long 'nough to get-a free drink. I must be gettin' better at this shit."

Bessie gathered up the money from off the table. She got out a little galvanized-gallon bucket out of the pantry. She raked the change into it. She stuffed the dollar bills into her dress pockets. Her pantry was small and was next to the backdoor. She got a jar of white lightning off one of the shelves in the pantry. She brought it back to the table and seated herself in one of the birch-branch homemade chairs at the table.

Lin got up from the table and went over to the homemade cedar china chest he had built to get three tall glasses. He plopped them down on the table. "Want some ice an' RC soda to chase this boot with, man?" he asked. He was looking at Henry.

Henry didn't know why they called the liquor 'White Lightning?' The stuff in the jar was brown, not white. "Yeah. I'll take some ice an' the soda."

"Bessie, if'n ya don't mind, get us a little bowl-a ice an' a cup 'la RC's outta the frig'rator." Lin said.

"I 'on need no chaser," Bessie said.

"Me, neither," Lin said. "But I go socialize with Henry here." "Y'all suit yourself. Let's drink," Henry said.

"You gotta pour your own 'round here, Henry," Bessie said.

The drinking went on all night long. The drinkers sung songs. They argued about baseball games, Joe Louis's fights, and the trouble the N-A-A-C-P was going to cause poor Negroes like themselves. By morning all three were drunk as hell. The smell of fish was in the air. Bessie's boys must've come home and deposited them in a big dishwashing pan with water and ice. The ice had melted. All three drunks were snoring loudly.

The sun rose bright and beautiful that morning. The air outside had the feel of Indian summer even though it was almost wintertime. Some fall birds uttered their distinctive sounds, and the chickens and hogs clucked and grunted. A rooster did its job of crowing over and over again. Billy had become unused to the country sounds. It woke him right up.

"Gotta pee, Momma," said Billy. He got up holding the crotch of his training pants. There were no toilets to run to.

He woke Mabel up. "Go on in back of the kitchen. There's a washroom. They gotta piss-pot in there. Ya can pee in that. Nor ya go on outside an' piss on the ground. You's in the country. Nobody's go care," Mabel whined. She got up and put on a thin bed-robe.

She watched Billy scurry out of the little room where they slept. He went past where Lin, Bessie and Henry were drunk with their heads down on the table. He opened one door, and Lil' Lin, Ton and Broadus were asleep in beds in there. He closed the door. He couldn't reach the slip-knot latch of the washroom's door to get to the closet where the piss-pot was kept.

Billy came back to the kitchen table and turned up his little nose. The sleeping drunks gave off a smell that reminded Billy of a rotting tullle he'd smelt while living at Grandma Agnes's house. He was playing near the edge of the woods and ran right through a wormy turtle shell.

Billy crept up closer to the edge of the table with his fingers up his nose. "Oh, pee ewe-e-e!" he said. "They stink!" He had forgotten about his need to pee for the moment. He saw a little of the brown liquid in the bottom of his Daddy's glass. A'nt Bessie's glass was half-full, and Unc' Lin's glass was empty and lying down near his left hand on the table. After looking the sleeping beauties over for a moment, Billy wondered what the brown liquid would taste like, to make grownups stay up all night drinking it in their good clothes. He made up in his little mind that he was gonna taste that brown stuff, and see what it tasted like.

Slowly Billy crept over to the table as quietly as he could. He grabbed his Father's "heavy" glass and tried to gulp the liquid down. The foul, hot, taste of the liquor made Billy gasp for breath. He felt like his mouth, throat, and insides were on fire. He got sick to his stomach. He felt dizzy. He ran out of the kitchen door and vomited the liquid back up. It stunk coming up his throat and out of his mouth. He swore: "I'm never gonna put any of that stuff in my mouth again!" He had peed in his training pants. "Ump-ah-0-0-0-oh, I hope Momma don't slap me," Billy whined.

He ran back through the kitchen to his Mother. Billy was still a little bit dizzy. He was scared of getting punished for wetting his pants. "Bo-o-ho-o, Momma, I had-a accident," Billy exclaimed, walking a little wobbly.

Mabel grabbed her Son up and felt his training pants. "Boy, what I go do with you? Ya gettin' too big ta-be doin' that. Ya can't keep on wettin' ya pants," Mabel said.

"Yes ma'am," Billy said. He stuck his left thumb in his mouth for self-comfort. He was glad his Momma didn't give him a slap on his bottoms.

Once Mabel had gotten dressed, and put a clean pair of training pants on Billy, she headed for the kitchen. Billy followed close behind her holding onto her dress tail. The smell of the sleeping drunks made Mabel a little queasy in the stomach. She was actually too hungry to throw up anything. She soon recovered.

Mabel knew that the three drunks would feel pretty rough when they finally woke up. She'd heard how her Brothers, Stepfathers, and other men in her family said they felt like the day after a drunk. They all craved lots of food.

Billy stood back and watched his Mother make a roaring fire in the huge cook stove in the kitchen. She sliced country ham, cleaned the fish out of the dishwashing pan, battered the fish, and got the ham and fish frying in lard in two large frying pans. She made biscuits, and scrambled a dozen eggs, fried potatoes, and made a little gravy for the ham. She put on a pot of coffee to percolate.

The noise Mabel made in the kitchen rattling pans woke Henry up first. Mabel hoped he'd be pleased that she could cook and didn't mind doing it. She knew she was in another woman's kitchen, but she was going to be her in-law soon, so, she shouldn't mind so much. She was just taking over for a little while till Bessie sobered up.

Henry ran out the backdoor. He got into a fit of vomiting in the backyard. Mabel was all smiles when Henry finally came back into the kitchen. He went back to the table like he was in a daze. For the moment he hung his head, staring directly in front of himself like a zombie.

Bessie and Lin work up simultaneously. They stretched themselves the same way at the same time. Bessie got a couple of clean glasses from the china chest. She went over to the refrigerator, poured milk out of a jar into the glasses, came back to the table, gave one glass to Lin, and she kept the other one. Lin tapped his glass on hers, and they gulped the milk down. Both burped and laughed out loud.

Lin jumped up from the table, went to the pantry, came back with a quart jar of bootleg. He sat it on the table. "Nothin' go fix up a hangover better'n 'nother good-stiff drink, Henry," said Lin. He poured a half-glassful of the brown liquor.

"Dam-right," Bessie said. She poured herself a quarter-glassful.

Henry got a clean glass from the china chest and filled it to about halfway full.

Mabel watched them gulp down that liquor like it was water. It almost made her sick just looking at them.

"I got y'all's breakfast. Y'all wanna eat somethin'? Ya ought-a, I reek-en," said Mabel. "I don't see how y'all can drink this early in the mornin' on-a empty stomach. That stuff '11 eat up y'all's guts."

Mabel set the table with dishes, and silverware. She put a plate of biscuits on the table next. She got a towel and went around the table pouring out four cups of hot coffee. She got cream out of the refrigerator, and sugar out of the pantry. She put platters of the food she had cooked on the table next. She wanted the compliments to flow. But not a word came forth.

Her feelings were hurt when no one said a word of praise to her. All at the table dug in and stuffed their mouths with food. She cried softly as she took a plate of food back to Matt's room to share with Billy. She was thinking: *those half-drunk ungrateful bas'sards.*

The tinkling of silverware on the plates had stopped. Mabel knew they were through stuffing themselves. This reminded her of Mrs. Gault and her minions. Mabel cleared the table of dishes, dipped the dishwashing pan full of hot water out of the stove's water tank, and washed the dishes. Henry, Lin and Bessie were well on their way to getting drunker. She took out her anger and frustration on washing-the-hell-out-of-those-dishes. She was like a mad ox snatching a load up the hill in a hurry. She pasted a deceitful smile on her face, until the job was done.

Henry stayed at the table after Lin and Bessie got up. They went into their bedroom-living room combined, and got dressed. Lin put on a two-piece black suit. Bessie undressed near their King size bed near the front door, and put on a long-white dress, and a pair of black flats. The dress came down to her ankles. Henry was still wearing his shark-skin colored suit, that he had worn to Richmond to fetch Mabel and Billy. Bessie topped her outfit with a wide-blue fedora. They were all cracking jokes and laughing out loud, except for Mabel.

The closer it got to the time to go get married to Henry, the more nervous Mabel became. She paced around in the kitchen until she found a flatiron. She put that on the stove. It took a few minutes for that to get hot enough to iron out the wrinkles in a white-cotton dress she had stuffed in her night bag. She borrowed a pair of Matt's pumps, and a blue hat she saw on the shelf in the closet in Matt's room. She had a pair of Fox stockings in her bag. She got those on, knotted them at the knees and was all dressed up. She sat on the bed in Matt's room and boohooed for a little while. The excitement, and all, was almost too much for Mabel.

Then Mabel remembered Billy. "Billy," she called. "C'mon in here, Son. I gotta get ya read-ta-go."

"Aw-ight, Momma," Billy called out from the kitchen. He ran through the door into Matt's room. The little black jacket and white knickers, tall socks and shoes, his white shirt with a fixed bowtie were ruffled and had red mud on them. He had gone outside and gotten dirty.

"Oh, Billy, I told ya, don't go get dirty. Now look at ya. You's dirty as can be," Mabel whined. "Now, what I go do with you?"

Henry was in the front room area and heard Mabel complain. He ran over to Matt's room and yelled at his little Son. "I ought-a cut ya with my belt!" he shouted.

"No, Henry, you won't," Bessie said. She had heard Mabel's complaint, and had followed Henry. She figured he was up to no good. "Get back out the way, man. Lemme clean Lil' Billy up. He don't need whippin', he's just-a boy, like you was one day. Ya got dirty when ya wasn't s'pose-ta. Momma didn't beat ya ass then, an' ya ain't gon beat Billy, now."

Bessie looked sorrowfully at Mabel. "Calm down, Mabel. We go get that boy all cleaned up in-a jiffy. Just get-a basin of water outta the water tank. Rinse the mud off'n his little outfit. Rang it out, put it in the oven for-a minute or two, then iron it dry-then ya good-ta-go." Bessie actually went through the steps herself after she instructed Mabel.

Mabel grew even more sad and sorrowful. She sat in a chair in the kitchen watching Bessie.

She was quiet like a little mouse. Her eyes were moist like she might cry any moment.

Henry and Lin were sitting in the living room area smoking cigarettes. "Henry, let's go outside. I wanna holler at ya 'bout-a cup'la things," Lin said. He patted Henry on his shoulders as they both went out the front door and down the four steps of the front stoop. "I ain' got nothin' ta-do with ya bizzness, but ya go have-ta be a little more tender with that gal. Or ya might end up with'er in the nuthouse, or somethin'. I know ya don't want that, man, b'lieve me now. James Lewis's goin' through that with his wife Edmonia, man. It ain't pretty, okay. Ya don't have-ta go that route. I bet that little gal in there go make ya a right-good wife. All ya gotta do is treat'er with a little-bit of kindness. But, ifn ya go on 'busin 'er, ya go make ya bed way too hard. I know all 'bout that now, Henry."

"Yeah. Yes. I got ya," said Henry. "But we's all different, an' the same things ain' go be the same for ev' one-a us." He got out another Pall Mall and lit that up, took a deep puff and exhaled it.

"Aw-ight, now. Don't say I didn't try-ta tell ya, when things get tough," Lin replied.

Mabel sat at the kitchen table. Bessie got Billy all cleaned up. "Billy ya sit at the table an' don't go no-where. A'nt Bessie gotta talk with ya Momma for-a spell." Bessie sat in a chair across the table from Mabel.

"Mabel. We's gettin' read-ta go-ta Columbia an' me an' Lin go witness you an' Henry's gettin' hitched. Now, little gal, ya listen ta O' Bessie, cause ya life might be dependin' on what I's 'bout-ta tell you.

"Mabel, honey, ya gotta stop Henry from 'busin' you an ya little Son. Ifn-ya don't ... one a these days, he's go really hurt y'all. Listen, sweetheart, Henry once cut Poppa on his hand over a fishin' pole. That was the last time Poppa tried-ta whip Henry's ass. That man can be very handy with-a knife. You see how bad he cut Tank Snowvall up," Bessie said.

"Bessie, I heard people say he'd cut ya, but I didn't know he'd cut his own Daddy. What 'bout 'Honor ya Father an' Mother?' With him, I guess that only count for his Momma."

"Baby, what I'm sayin' ta-ya, is, you go have-ta stand up to 'im one-a these days. Use a fryin' pan, a butcher knife, or whatever; but ya go have-ta stop that man from comin' at ya like he do," Bessie said.

Mabel looked confused but answered: "Aw-ight, Bessie, I hear ya."

"Let's go on out ta-the car. Lin an' Henry's already out yonder," Bessie said. "Aw-ight, then, Bessie," Mabel spoke with a nervous tremble in her voice.

Henry leaned against Lin's car smoking another cigarette. Lin allowed: "Henry, ya dam-sure get the best lookin' gals 'round here." He watched Mabel come out the front door in front of Bessie. "Now Mabel's a little skinny, but she's stacked in the right places. Nice shape. I likes them dark-skinned gals. Man, they's the best. That's why I's so crazy 'bout Bessie." Lin laughed. "Man, Henry, ya look so sad. Ya could-ta done a lot worse."

"Lin, I passed up a slew-a pretty gals I might've marri'd ifn I's lookin' for-a wife. Man, my first flame was Adlai Bradley, old man Ray Bradley's daughter. She came from up in Bradley's Hollow, was a Redbone gal, and was hot as ya like 'im ta be. I use-ta meet 'er down the spring path from our house. She lived through the woods a ways in back of our house.

"That gal was short, stacked in the hips, big tits, cute legs, man, all that-a man want. I called 'er Alice, cause Adlai sound so much like-a boy's name. Her older Brother, Joseph, marri'd my youngest Aunt, Lilly Belle. Joe didn't know that I was on his Sister ev' chance I got.

"We's both 'bout twenty. I got 'er pregnant, man. She didn't wanna get marri'd, an' I didn't wanna do that neither. So, she seduced old man Albert Ross, who's lonely an' wantin' a young gal. She slept with 'im an' lied. She said he's the Father-a 'er baby. So he marri'd 'er. They named my oldest Son, 'Albert Ross, Jr.'

"Lin, I can get any-a them pretty, yellar gals. Ifn I was lookin' ta-get hitched, it'd been with Alice, or some gal like that," Henry said.

"Henry, that's what's wrong with ya. Ya too-big-a dog. Now, ya gotta stop runnin' rabbits all over the dam-place, an' settle down, man. Ya should-ta done run the wild outta ya by now. Here comes Mabel, Billy an' Bessie.

"Henry, that boy's the spittin' image of ya Daddy," Lin said.

Henry frowned, then looked at the ground. "I don't see it, Lin. Looks more like his Momma," Henry said.

Lin and Henry climbed into the front seat of the car, Bessie and Mabel got in the backseat. Mabel held little Billy on her lap. Soon the car was traveling up the back road through mud holes, rough tire tracks, and big humps in the road to Route 656. Lin turned the car south onto 656, gave her the gas, and sped down to Route Six. After a mile he turned east onto Six. He had them all in Columbia in what seemed like a minute to Mabel.

What bothered Mabel more than Lin's reckless driving was the fact that all she could smell was the rotten stench of liquor in the car. Henry had a pint jar of the mess, sipping it like it was the "Water Of Life." Bessie took a couple of sips of the putrid liquid, and sat in the comer of the car singing the lyrics of Billy Holiday's "MY MAN." Mabel felt that this was not how it ought to be for a woman before she made the most serious decision of her life.

Lin parked the car in front of The Holy Comforter Church of our Virgin in Columbia. It was located right next to Walton's Grocery. Lin knew the Pastor, Father Jerome Abbot, who was also Assistant Justice of the Peace, Assistant City Manager, and Part-time Magistrate. Lin, Mabel and Henry entered the Church through a side door. The trio was ushered into the Father's private office by one of his Nuns, Mother Magdalena Bella. Father Abbot, after briefly listening to why Mabel and Henry needed to get married, instructed other Nuns to type up a marriage license right away. When he heard that Mabel and Henry already had a healthy Son, the Father said, "I am going to make legal in the eyes of men what already is morally legal in the eyes of God. I require all marriages to be performed before The Altar of God. We are about to have Morning Mass. You will have to attend if you wish to get married on this day. Agreed?"

Lin said, "Yes, sir."

"You may refer to me as 'Father.' I am ordained of God in that capacity," said Father Abbot. "Yes, Father," Lin said. He frowned a bit over that one, but knew not to argue.

"Yes, Father," Mabel said.

"Hell yes, Father," Henry drunkenly uttered.

"The fee is an offering of five dollars," said Father Abbot. He left his office shaking his head in disgust at Henry for his lack of respect for the Church. The Nuns took the fee and handed over the license to Henry. He gave it to Mabel.

"You all may go get the others who came with you and go into the Congregation through the front doors and wait until you are called up before The Altar of God. God through the Father, and our Holy Virgin, will join you in Holy Matrimony," Mother Magdalena instructed them.

Lin, Mabel and Henry went out of the office and back out of the side door. Lin beckoned to Bessie. "Bring Billy. We's goin' in the front doors this time," said Lin, with a chuckle.

Once he was inside of the Church, Billy looked around at all of the gigantic portraits, and huge statues of the Saints, and one statue of a Lady in a flowing-hooded gown, with a cross seemingly dangling from her waist at the end of a chain. The woman was beautiful, and her robe was too, but Billy didn't know what all of this meant. He had never seen anything like that before. He wished he could go home to A'nt Ma' Dear's house.

After the Morning Mass was over, Father Abbot called out: "Mabel Scott, and Henry James, please come up to the Altar. Bring your witnesses with you at this time."

Mabel got up and gingerly made her way to the front of the Church. Henry got up and stumbled forward behind Mabel. Lin and Bessie brought up the rear with Bessie holding Billy by his hand.

Lin and Bessie stood behind Mabel and Henry. Father Abbot searched Henry's and Mabel's eyes for a few minutes. Then he began: "Henry Anderson James, do you take this woman, Mabel Louise Scott, to be your lawfully-wedded wife; to have and to hold; in sickness and in health; for richer or poorer; forsaking all others; until death you do part?"

Henry bobbed and weaved for a second or two. "You dam-right, I do," Henry said.

"Mr. James, a simple, I do, will suffice," Father Abbot said. "Ya dam-right I do!" Henry repeated louder this time.

"Well ... Yes ... Let us proceed." He looked towards Mabel. "Mabel Louise Scott, do you take this man, Henry Anderson James, to be your lawfully-wedded husband; to have and to hold; to love and obey; in sickness and in health; for richer or poorer; until death you do part?"

With tears running down her cheeks, Mabel said, "Yes, I do!" loud and clear.

Father Abbot announced: "Now by the authority invested in me by Almighty God, and The Holy Mother of God, and her Son, Jesus; I now pronounce you Man and Wife."

He looked at Bessie and then Lin. He looked out over the seated Congregation of about thirty people, and asked: "If anyone objects to this union, let him speak now, or forever hold his peace. And, whosoever God has joined together, let no man put asunder. Where are the rings?"

Henry drunkenly shrugged his shoulders. Bessie removed her own ring. She gave it to Henry. Mabel had to help him slip the ring onto her ring-finger. Henry got a twisted-little smile on his inebriated face. Lin gave Mabel his ring, and she had no trouble slipping that onto Henry's finger.

Father Abbot intoned: "Now repeat after me: with this ring, I do wed." Mabel repeated what the Father had said. Henry made some garbled noises.

Father Abbot intoned: "You may now kiss your Bride, may Almighty God grant you peace, joy and happiness."

Henry was so drunk by then he not only missed Mabel's lips, he nearly fell down to the floor. Lin and Bessie helped Mabel carry Henry out of the Church back to the car. Bessie consoled Mabel after they got back to the car. She patted her back. "Mabel, just 'member what I done already told ya. Take control now of ya family. Don't let nobody fool 'round an' mess with ya chillun." She looked scornfully at a disheveled Henry James. The liquor he had drunk had turned him into a limp dishrag. "Even against they Daddy, don't even let him hurt your babies. That's your job. You gotta protect your chillun."

Mabel hugged Bessie tightly. She let out her frustrations in a good cry. Bessie let her get it all out on her broad shoulders.

Lin had deposited Henry in the backseat. Bessie opened the backdoor on the opposite side of the car so that Mabel could get in beside her new drunk husband. Bessie got in the front seat beside her husband. Bessie silently wept for Mabel. She knew nothing about this marriage was getting started on the right foot. Lin just shook his head at the mess he had witnessed. Henry fell down in the seat until his head lay on Mabel's lap beside Billy.

"Let's take 'em up yonder-ta A'nt Maetta," Lin said. "I know she's waitin' for Henry-ta come home with his new bride an 'er Grandson. Well ... here we go."

Bessie swallowed the lump of disgust that had built up in her throat. "Y'know, Lin, I probably didn't tell ya before. Fannie Watkins from over in Cloverdale had a Son with Tank Snowvall. Tank took care of 'im while he could. But since Henry cut 'im up so bad, he been down-ta Pita'sburg.

Fannie call the boy, Lawrence. With Snowvall down tryin' ta-get over being nearly kilt, Fannie fell into hard times.

"Fannie done took up with Bay Washington, one-a Jo-Jo Washington's Sons. Bay don't want nothin' toll ta-do with Lawrence. Told Fannie she gotta get rid-a her Son. See, Lawrence's too light-skinned for Bay 'nem, they being so Black an' all.

"It'sa dam-shame too, Lawrence's goin' on eight or nine. He cries for his Momma all the time. Momma done took 'im in, old as she is now. Lawrence wanna little Brother, now he's go have one. He didn't have one while he's with Fannie, but Jo-Jo's other five gals, all still livin' at home, had-a bunch-a chillren his age. So he thought of them like Brothers an' Sisters. But with Momma, all the other chillren's way up the road. So Lawrence's lonely."

"Lin an' Bessie, ain't it funny how things turn out?" said Mabel. "She's kind 'nough-ta take in-a child of the man her Son ruined. She go raise that child up an' give 'im a normal life. A'nt Maetta sound like she gotta heart of gold. I can't wait-ta meet 'er," Mabel said.

"I wonder, Mabel ... what-in-the-hell is-a 'normal life?' "Bessie asked.

The carload of drunks, and one sober bride, with one scared-little Son, turned onto the road up the hill from A'nt Maetta's. Lin parked his car up the hill.

"I ain't go take my car down that rough path-ta the house. You'n Henry, an' Billy, y'all can make it down-ta the house aw-ight from here, I reek-en," Lin said. Bessie just chuckled.

Before she got out of the car, Mabel spoke softly to Bessie: "I'm a little-bit scared 'bout all this, Bessie. I's scared-a gettin' cut by ... "She pointed at Henry, who was slumped down in the backseat. "He cut up Snowvall. He cut his own Daddy. Ifn somethin' go wrong, what's gon stop 'im from cuttin' me up?"

Bessie frowned. "Like I done told ya, ya gotta get this bugger straight from the start fore he ups an' try-ta do somethin' like that ta-ya. It's all on you now, Mabel. Take care, Baby!"

Lin cleared his throat, harked and spat out a lump of thick phlegm that fell harmlessly on the ground, and did that again out of the drivers-side window.

Mabel's eyes quivered from her nervousness. She got out of the car, and sat Billy beside a big Oak tree. She got hold of Henry's arm and pulled as hard as she could. He became semi-awake. Mabel was able then to get him out of the car. Henry was still, however, pretty limp and lethargic. He had his left arm around Mabel. She had to half-carry him down the hill towards his home. It was late in the evening.

A'nt Maetta saw Mabel struggling with carrying Henry, with little Billy in tow, and with a burst of excitement, she limped as fast as she could up the path to meet her new Daughter-in-law. She waved both her hands.

"Hi, Bessie. Hi, Lin, How y'all doin?" A'nt Maetta called out. "How's all my Grandchillun? Why don't you an' Lin come down an' sit with me for-a spell?" Maetta said.

''Ev' body's fine, Momma," said Bessie. "I's sorry we can't stay much longer. We's been 'way all day-long." She got a sheepish grin on her face.

''Aw-ight, then. Y'all kiss my Grandchillun for me. Tell'em come see they old Grandma. I ain' never seen Ton but-a cup 'la times. He gotta be near grown, now." A'nt Maetta said.

''If'n I can catch up with my wild bunch, Momma. They stays gone all the time. They's courtin' an' all, Momma, y'know," Bessie said. "Tell Poppa we said Hello. We gotta go, we got bizzness-ta tend to goin' on at the house. We been gone long 'nough. Sorry we can't stay longer, we love ya."

A'nt Maetta waved vigorously as the car sped away. The sunset was brilliant making the skyline a reddish purple. A'nt Maetta and Mabel seized Herny and carried him down the hill to the house in a full-Nelson grasp. Each held him in a-half Nelson.

"Mabel . . . Momma . . . Billy . . . I ain't drunk. um--where we goin'?" Henry mumbled. His eyes were closed. Spittle oozed out of the comers of his mouth. His head bobbed up and down.

Billy was nervous as could be. He couldn't make sense of what he had seen. He wondered why he and his Momma were going to this strange house? Who was this fat woman helping to carry his Daddy down the hill? He walked behind his Momma with his left thumb in his mouth. He was too afraid to cry round "his mean Daddy." It might get him another mauling.

After they got inside of the house, Mabel and A'nt Maetta led Henry into the other bedroom. Right away, A'nt Maetta scooped Billy up into her large-soft arms. She hugged her Grandson tightly. She had tears of joy streaming down her cheeks. 'Thank ya Lordy. Thank ya Gawd," A'nt Maetta said in a sing-song way. "Gawd is good, Mabel!"

Billy was not familial with this new person that had been thrust into his life so abruptly. He'd heard about her, but had never met her. He didn't know if'n he could trust her or not. He cried and squirmed against her. But he suddenly felt the love emitting from her like electricity, then Billy relaxed.

He realized intuitively that what was happening between this Grandma and him was something he needed to savor. It was the greatest feeling he had experienced up till then. Billy felt like Grandma Maetta's love was something he had to give right back. He never had felt that safe and secure before. Right then, on the first day he met Grandma Maetta, Billy got a feeling inside that he never wanted to leave this wonderful person's loving embrace.

Mabel seeing Billy hugging his Grandma back instead of struggling against her turned her attention to Henry. She had left him in his room fully clothed. When she went in the room the smell of him made her turn up her nose. It was the alcohol that stunk. She noticed that Henry had managed to get up and undress. He was lying across the bed in his t-shirt and undersholts.

Mabel swished her hips very wantonly and allowed: "This could be the best night of our lives. But you's drunk on ya ass. Ya ain' no good ta-nay gal tonight. Go on sleep that stuff off so we can get our marriage started," Mabel said.

A'nt Maetta called, "Mabel, child, c'mere for a minute. I got lot 'sa good food on back-a the stove. Ya can tend-ta Henry a little-bit later. I wanna talk with ya for a tiny bit, just-ta get-ta know ya a little better."

Mabel came out of the bedroom and went into the kitchen where A'nt Maetta had a plate of food in front of Billy, and no way was he going to eat it all. The :flickering of the lamplight gave the place a romantic feel, but Mabel's eyes had become accustomed to electric lights, and lamplight made everything seem dull. She sat at the table across from A'nt Maetta and Billy, who wasn't even looking at his Mother right then.

"Mabel," said Maetta, "any way, Lil' Charlie done got hitched too. He married a gal from up'n Cloverdale, one of the Anderson gals. Her name's Queen. You know her?"

"No'am, can't say I do," Mabel said.

Tears came to Maetta's eyes. "Mabel get yourself some-a my collard greens, an' some-a my fried chicken. They tell me I make the best macaroni and cheese in West Bottom. Get much as ya want-I-got plenty, honey," She talked in a kind of groan like a Dove's moaning.

Mable wondered what in the hell was that all about? So she got a chicken breast, a helping of the other entrees, and a glass of Lemonade. A'nt Maetta had crushed some of the ice from her icebox to make the drink iced cold. Mabel was enjoying the food and the refreshing drink.

"Mabel, honey, I wan'cha ta-brace ya-self, now," A'nt Maetta said. Mabel wondered, what now?

"The Law's go come for Henry in the mornin'. They's go be here fore he gets up ta-catch a ride up to Charles 'ville to his job with Lil Charlie.

"Mabel, that Babe Bates gotta warrant out on Henry for slappin' 'er. She's mad as hell cause the lick put-a little knot on 'er pretty-little face for one day. Didn't leave no scar. But ya know them wannabe's, they'll do what they wants, but don't want us darkies to do nothin' back. She an' Snowvall was tryin' ta-rob an' kill Henry.

"I thought Henry's just 'fendin' his-self. Snowvall tried-ta shoot Henry in the head with a shotgun. Babe's tryin' ta-knock the knife outta Henry's hand with-a beer bottle. That's why Henry slapped 'er. Now Henry's go have-ta face assault charges," A'nt Maetta said.

Mabel's heart seemed like it had come up into her throat. It got to beating like a drum in a parade. "Oh, shit!" she exclaimed. "Why'd Henry have-ta slap that slut?"

"Child," said A'nt Maetta, "Henry cut Snowvall all over his face, arms, his back, an' head. He would-a kilt him had it not been for Babe knockin' the knife outta his hand. That's why Henry slapped 'er. He wanted-ta kill Tank Snowvall for tryin' ta-kill him. The shots went over Henry's head. He said he could hear them whine. Would-a blown his brains right out. All charges 'gainst Henry ought-a been dropped. I talked-ta the Judge. He said things was outta his hand. They had to serve the warrant. They gotta try Henry." A'nt Maetta looked at the floor. She wrung her hands in her apron.

"I took in Lawrence, Snowvall's boy he had with Fannie Watkins. That gal got with Bay Washington, Jo-Jo Washington's Son. Bay ain' want no child that light-skinned living in his house. So, Fannie asked me ta-raise the boy. After what Henry did, I was happy to help Fannie out. Snowvall's crazy now, Mabel. He's down in Pita'sburg," A'nt Maetta said.

"Yeah, Bessie told me 'bout that. I gotta try-ta get Henry awake. We won't have much time together. The Judge's go give 'im some time ya can bet on it," Mabel said.

Mabel had lost her appetite. She got up from the table and A'nt Maetta stood also.

"Mabel, honey," said A'nt Maetta, "I got somethin' else I gotta 'fess up ta-ya. Mabel, baby, sit back down. Get some more Lemonade. Some crushed ice is still in the icebox."

"No--I'm good. Iain' got no taste for nothin' toll right now. What'cha wanna say?" "Mabel, I gotta beg ya Momma' s pardon. I hope ya will forgive me too."

"What'cha do ta-my Momma an' me, A'nt Maetta?"

"The other week, me an' your Momma got into it down in Columbia. I thought she's 'sponsible for killin' little Billy. I heard a lie from Cora Cooper that Agnes had let my Grand Baby burn up in that fire at Mamie's house. It kilt three-a her Chillren, but Billy had escaped an' gone up ta-Agnes for somethin 'nother. He weren't hurt.

"Then, Mabel," said A'nt Maetta, "you came up an' took Billy ta-Rich-men. I didn't know Billy's with you. I's go cut Agnes's throat. Mabel, forgive me for actin' like a dam-wild fool. I beg ya pardon." She burst out crying like a spanked child.

Mabel thought for but a moment or two. She took a big gulp out of her cool drink. "I forgive ya, A'nt Maetta. Look, I can forgive ya cause I threatened Momma myself I would've been in prison today if Billy had been in that fire. I's mad 'nough-ta kill ev 'body in that house when I thought Billy had died in that fire. So I know how ya felt."

"Get up Mabel lemme hug ya, gal. I don't care what, you's one-a my favorite peoples. I'm go beg Agnes pardon. I would-a done it Friday, but she didn't come-ta shoppin'."

Mabel and A'nt Maetta embraced. Then there were heavy footsteps on the porch.

A tall, thin, boy walked through the door. Mabel could see that he had very light-orange-colored skin, and reddish-brown curly hair-that was not kinky. He had very large hands and feet. He seemed to be dirty from head to toe literally covered in greasy motor oil.

"Mabel, this is Lawrence," A'nt Maetta said. "Hi, Lawrence," Mabel said.

"Hi ma'am," Lawrence said. His voice registered in at an immature baritone level. "I'd shake ya hand, but I got motor oil all over mine."

"That's aw-ight," Mabel said. "I've had my hands in worse 'n that."

She shook Lawrence's hand and noticed how strong his grip was for a nine-year old. "Lawrence, get some water outta the tank an' clean up for supper. Boy, ya almost been up yonder too long. I likes for ya ta-be home fore dark," A'nt Maetta said. "Yes 'am," Lawrence said.

A'nt Maetta turned towards Mabel. "I know where he's been, Mabel. He's been up the road a-piece at Irving Washington's house. Irving is Jo-Jo's younger Brother. He marri'd Lulu, Unc' Charlie's younger Sister. You go learn who Billy's kin to up here pretty soon.

"Lulu had-a little gal, Belinda, fore she marri'd Irving. Then she an' Irving had Irving, Jr. Catherina, Joanna, an' Rayland. They's all Billy's Cousins. They live just up the path a-ways. Irving's teachin' Lawrence how to fix car motors. Says the boy's gotta knack for learnin' how motors work. Says he go be a find mechanic one day. That's good, cause Lawrence ain't never been ta-school a day in his life. His Momma Fannie didn't try-ta send 'im no-wheres so's he could learn his numbers an' write his name. We's go do our best-ta give'im a way ta-make-a livin'," A'nt Maetta said. "Ifn he go-ta school now, the kids'll tease 'im so bad."

After washing his hands and face, and changing into a clean pair of jeans and a sweat shirt, Lawrence came into the kitchen. He sat down at the table. "You's my Momma, now, A'nt Maetta. I wanna just call you Momma. Can I do that?" Lawrence asked.

"Yeah, Son, you can, but I don't want'cha to forget who ya real Momma is. She brought ya into this world. While ya livin' in my house, you can call me Momma, though, I don't mind that," A'nt Maetta said.

Lawrence filled his plate up a couple of times and cleaned it. A'nt Maetta cuddled and played with Billy. She had him laughing and giggling like he'd never done before.

"Lawrence, you sleep in the hallway tonight. Get that little fold-away bed outta the back of the hall closet, make it up an' use it tonight. Get the bed linen off the shelf. I 'ma let Billy sleep in my room. I doubt if Poppa go come home tonight. He's up playin' poker at Jo-Jo's house. He prob-be go be up yonder till daybreak.

"Mabel, you can stay in here long's ya wanna, but I'm goin' in ta-bed. Good night, Mabel.

Good night, Lawrence. Y'all have-a good rest, now." She winked at Mabel. "Good night, Momma," Lawrence chimed. "Good night A'nt Mabel."

"Good night," Mabel said to all, but Billy paid her little attention. It bothered her a little.

CHAPTER THIRTEEN

Mabel slept nude beside her new husband all night long. She hoped he'd wake up, take her in his arms, and make their wedding night special. But Henry just snored drunkenly along till Mabel drifted into a disgusted bout of fitful sleep: no dreams, just bland, restive sleep, without the refreshing properties of REM. ...

Bright and early the next morning a loud knocking on the front door woke up A'nt Maetta. She knew who was doing the knocking. The time had come for her to yield up Henry as she had promised. She scrambled out of bed, where she had slept beside Billy, put on a heavy cotton robe and limped out to her front door. She cracked the door to peek out. The shiny gun and holster of the County Sheriff first came into view.

A'nt Maetta opened the door. A young Whiteman named Bobby Hughes stood on the porch that morning. He wore a typical uniform for the County Sheriff: a dark-blue western-style jacket with a gold star pinned to its top-left pocket; and a pair of light-gray slacks that had a dark-blue stripe on the outside of each pants leg. He sported a highly-polished pair of black military boots; a gray Stetson hat with the County emblem on its crown; and he was armed with a Forty-Four Smith & Wesson, Revolver. He rested his right hand on the gun-handle. He stood at six foot-three, was slim but very muscular. His clean-shaven face had a chiseled roughness that gave him a no nonsense appearance, like he would not mind shooting if he had to.

He appeared to be ready to draw his gun at any moment to A'nt

Maetta. He spat out a thick lump of snuff-spittle. Then his voice rang out in a crisp tenor.

"Maetta James, I'm Sheriff Bobby Hughes, I've come to arrest your boy, Henry. Is he staying with you? If he is, tell him to come out and present himself for arrest at this time. I have a warrant for him to appear before the County Judge. Will you do that?"

Tears came to A'nt Maetta's eyes. "Aw-ight, Mr. Hughes," she said. "I'll go get 'im up." She turned to the door to the room where Mabel and Henry had spent the night. She gently knocked on the door.

"Henry ... Henry. Son, get up. Y'all gotta get up in there. The Sheriff's out here. Don't worry, Son. I got ev' thin' fixed with the Judge. Ya just c'mon get read-ta go with 'im. This mess '11 be over fore ya know it."

Henry tried to roll out of the bed but fell to the floor instead. "Oh, Lardy, I'm sicker 'n a dog. Ah, man-I swear an' hope ta-die," Henry complained. He dragged himself up off the floor, put on a pair of his blue work overalls, a red-and-blue plaid shirt, and slipped on a pair of thick woolen socks into a pair of oxford-colored brogans. He got a plug of chewing tobacco off the bureau and stuffed that into his left pants pocket. He got a flat-red canister of Sir Walter Raleigh smoking tobacco and stuffed that in his left back pants pocket. He stuffed several packs of Pall Mall cigarettes on top of the plug of chewing tobacco. He put his tobacco pipe in his right front pocket. He turned and left the room without kissing, touching or acknowledging Mabel. He came out into the little hallway of the house.

Henry stood in front of A'nt Maetta and paused for a moment. He hugged her tightly for a moment or two. "Momma, send me some Half and Half or Sir Walter Raleigh smoking tobacco soon's ya can. Charlie's go bring ya my last check from up in Charles'ville. I'll see ya just-a soon as I gets outta jail. Use what money's left as ya see fit. Hope ta-see ya soon," Henry whined. He kissed his Mother and headed for the door.

"Don't ya worry none Son. I 'ma take care-a ev' thin'. Ya just be good an' get 'way from down at the State Farm as quick as ya can-an' that shouldn't be long."

"Aw-ight, Momma. Lemme go meet the Man," Henry said.

Henry slowly stepped out onto the porch. Right away Sherriff Hughes pulled out his Forty Four. He pointed it at Henry's head. He had a scary snarl on his reddish face. "What's that you got in your front pants pocket, boy?" Hughes yelled. "Now, you take that out of there real slow," he ordered.

"Yes sir," said Henry. He reached into his front right pants pocket, got hold of his pipe, turned it around in his pocket, so that its stem would come out of his pocket first. He moved very slowly and then quickly dropped the pipe onto the porch so that Hughes would not mistake his pipe for a 22-pistol, and shoot to kill him.

Sheriff Hughes glanced at the pipe lying on the porch. "You can pick that up and put it back in your pocket, Henry. But you got to be careful, now. Someone might make a fatal mistake if you move too swiftly in the wrong direction."

He put his gun back into its holster. "Turn around Henry I'm going to cuff you."

Henry did as he was ordered. He felt trapped like a rabbit. He hated going to Court where he would most likely end up going to jail. He truly hated the thought of that.

Sheriff Hughes took Henry with his hands cuffed behind him up the hill from his house to a Blue Plymouth with the Gray Logo, "Fluvanna County Sheriff Office," printed on both sides of its front doors. Henry was ushered into a backdoor to a backseat. A steel grate separated the front from the back. The Sheriff shoved Henry very roughly into the backseat, slammed the backdoor of the car and got in the front driver's side. He cranked the car up and shot up the road like he was in a great hurry.

A'nt Maetta watched the car speed away until it vanished out of sight. "I ain't never seen one-a my chillun goin' off to jail before. Ah, that hurts me so bad," she whined. Her crying came out like she was witnessing one of her children going off to be executed.

Mabel got up that morning crying for a different reason. She got dressed, thinking: *Henry done hurt me more 'n a lick could do. Didn't feel me, kiss me, or do nothin' ta-me on our weddin' night-not even a quickie fore he went off to jail. He didn't even say goodbye ta-me or Billy, neither. He lay'side me all night long, a hot, naked gal, an' got up 'thout lovin' me. I feels like the ugliest gal in the world*

A'nt Maetta came into the room whimpering. She sat on the bed. She tried to comfort Mabel. "Don't cry, baby. He'll be back soon. I'm go make sure that he take care-a ya an' his Son in there," A'nt Maetta said.

There is a thin line between Love and Hate. Things were not going in the direction that Mabel had hoped they would. Her powerful emotions and lusts for Henry were becoming a great desire *to kick 'im in the balls 'til he bleeds.*

On Wednesday of the next week, Henry was taken before Judge Siegfried, a descendant of that original family. The Fluvanna County Court is located in Palmyra, Virginia. He pleaded guilty to one count of criminal assault and battery. He received a sentence of two years with one year suspended. He was taken to the Buckingham State Farm Prison.

When A'nt Maetta heard how much time Henry got, she said to Mabel: "Mabel, y'know, Henry got too much time for slappin' Babe. Most-a time, stuff like that get throwed outta Court.

"But ... Mabel, honey, you can 'bout figure out why it all happen like it did. Babe '11 sleep with-a White one just as soon as she would-a Colored one. Them Siegfried Mens likes them light-skinned Wenches-you know-them Fancy Gals. The Judge prob-be knows more 'bout Babe than meets the eye. That's what I thinks really's goin' on. Henry up 'n slapped one-a his Fancy Gals. Now, the Judge got 'im down on the State Farm. He want 'im to think 'bout what he done, so's he won't do that no more."

"Now, I hear ya loud an' clear," said Mabel. She got a basin of water and bathed herself, and took that basin of used water outside and dumped it in the backyard. She came in, got another basin out of the stove's tank, and bathed Billy. Billy got dressed in his Sailor Suit. He and Lawrence went outside to play.

"A'nt Maetta, lemme come in the kitchen an' help ya get breakfast ready," Mabel said.

"No, baby, I don't want no help in my kitchen. It's the onliest place in life where I's the Boss. One day you go unnerstan'. But for now, ya just rest over yonder an' listen to the radio or somethin'. I got a new battery the other day, so it ought-a play fine."

Mabel found a light jacket in the little wardrobe closet in the boys' room. She went outside to observe Lawrence and Billy playing. Lawrence had built a bicycle out of spare pants. He had painted it green and yellow.

He had attached a basket to its handlebars. He put Billy in the basket and rode up the hill from the house and back. Billy laughed and squealed with glee. He was having so much fun. Mabel watched Lawrence play with Billy day after day. A'nt Maetta wouldn't let her help when she made a couple of dresses and blouses for Mabel on her old Uniroyal foot-pedaling Sewing Machine. The clothes fit perfectly. A'nt Maetta made all of her clothes, except her coats, and she had plenty of extra cloth to work with. But this lifestyle was completely boring to a young woman, even though A'nt Maetta made Billy a lot of clothes.

As a matter of fact, Mabel was bored as hell. Day after day, the same routine of watching A'nt Maetta do everything, even caring for Billy, caused Mabel to have too much time on her hands to remember and fret about how Henry had left her frustrated, flustered, unsatisfied and full of loathing the morning he got taken to jail. Her feminine desires grew stronger as the days went by, and her anger grew even stronger.

Mabel decided: *Henry don't love me or my Son. He think I go stay up in his Momma's an' Poppa's house an' wait till he gets outta prison. We said our vows, but he didn't finish the job that night. I still ache for his touch. He left me hot, wet, an' mad as hell. Now, he's in prison. He's prob-be forgettin' all 'bout me down there. Who knows, he may find one-a them gal-men, or somethin'. Henry's ass's in the can, I'm out here, I wanna man, I'ma woman. He's poppin' Gawd kno' what down yonder. I may as well go get me a man on the side, since Henry don't care nothin 'toll bout me nohow.*

Around thirty days after Henry was gone, Mabel rose up early on this Friday morning, before daybreak. She got dressed in one of the gray wool dresses A'nt Maetta had made for her. She put on a thick cotton sweater A'nt Maetta had cut-down and sewn for her and a coat that had been taken apart and put back together to fit Mabel. A'nt Maetta had purchased a pair of ladies' boots for Mabel with some of the money Henry had left. Mabel got out to Route 656. She traveled north. She figured she'd walk the two or three miles to Bessie's house for a little change of pace. She knew that A'nt Maetta would take good care of Billy.

"Hop on, child, lemme give ya a lift down the road," said the old scratcher. He wore Bibb overalls, a thick-insulated Levi coat over that and sported a pair of fishing boots. He was very dark-skinned with a head full of frizzy white-hair and a broad frizzy beard to match. He had the reins to an old horse in his hands and he was sitting in a seat of the buckboard of a wagon with several pieces of planed lumber on back. He beckoned for Mabel to come sit beside him.

Mabel looked the old guy up and down for a couple of seconds. She decided that he was harmless. She climbed up the steps of the wagon and sat down beside the old guy.

"I'm Mabel Louise Scott-James. I'm goin' to Route Six ta-visit with Bessie Jackson my Sister-in-law. I just marri'd Henry James, A'nt Maetta's Son," Mabel said, sounding like a little songbird.

"Yeah, I know A'nt Maetta and Unc' Charlie an' all they chillren. I helped Unc' Charlie build his house when he marri'd Maetta. How long ya been hitched-ta Henry?

"People call me O' Man Pat-that's for Patrick Patterson. There's lot'sa Pattersons up the road in Cloverdale, I reek-en I's kin-ta 'em all. Right now, I'm just-a old bachelor. My wife, Viola's been dead for years.

"Ya must be some kind-a gal. Lotta'em been tryin' ta-catch that boy, but none-a them got lucky 'nough-ta land 'im."

Mabel smiled, she was getting to know more about O' Man Pat then she wanted to know. "Well, ma-be, those who didn't catch 'im was the lucky ones, who did 'n marr 'im," she chirped. "Mrs. James, I ain' got nothin' toll ta-do with ya bizzness, an' all. But ifn ya ever need-tagetta house built, look me up. I can still build 'em. I ain never had no complaints.

"Well, little lady, you's down here to Route Six. Guess I gotta let ya go. Tell Lin and Bessie I said Hello. By the way, I helped Lin'nem build parts of they house, too. Henry know where I live at. When he was-a boy, he helped me betimes."

Mabel climbed down off the wagon. "Thank ya, Mr. Patterson, nice ta-make ya acquaintance. Maybe, one day, we might hire ya to build us a house-if Henry ever get outta prison," Mabel said.

"Ya done told me too much. See ya Mrs. James, take care ... Gee Yeah," O' Man Pat said to his horse. The horse and the rig it pulled ambled up the road and turned onto 656 North.

Mabel waved goodbye to the old guy. She thought he was such a nice old man. She walked down the road eastward for a few steps, went across the bridge at Doc Johnson's Mill and on up the hill past Cary's house. She picked up her steps because she didn't want to deal with Will or Cary. It was round about 9:30 AM. She got up to Bessie's house in about fifteen minutes.

Mabel heard a lot of noise coming out of the house even though it was very early in the morning. Bessie's RCA Combination Radio and Record Player was on at full blast. Billie Holiday was singing: "God Bless The Child ..."

She stood at the front door of Bessie's house knocking on the door as loud as she could.

Bessie finally snatched the door opened. "I've come to visit," said Mabel.

"C'mon, in child, it's cold out them doors," said Bessie. "I hope ya don't mind, but we runs a Card and Crap game on Fridays. The boys came a little early this momin' ." Billie Holiday's, "My Man...." came out of the Record Player, and it saddened Mabel because she identified with the woman Holiday was singing about in that song.

"Aw-ight, Bessie. I don't mind if I do. I grew up 'round card games. My Uncle Gus an' John ran Crap games on weekends all the time down in woods 'round back-a the house."

As soon as Mabel came into the house, she heard every swearing and cussing word imaginable. The group of men swore when they rolled the dice, got a card dealt to them, when they bet, and when they had to fold a hand of cards. The Crap Shooters really swore when the dice they rolled turned up a two-and-a-one; or double-sixes; and or, double-ones. Lin, Sr. ran around to the roller, grabbed up some money off the Crap Table, and laughed as loud as he could. (That's called "Cutting the Craps." The roller loses the amount he had bet.)

For some strange reason, the tenor of the swearing and gambling stirred a deep-primitive desire in Mabel that she didn't initially know she had. She felt a little discomfort at the level of profanity that came out of the mouths of the gamblers, but their passions translated inside of her into an intense sexual desire.

The need that Henry had failed to satisfy intensified. When she got a little wet between her legs, even though no one could possibly know that, she felt embarrassed. She was afraid, too, that her juicing might actually drip down her legs. She mentally tried to control herself and make Nature go away for the moment. But she wanted a man to touch her, and that was what it was.

Burton Gaines, a tall, muscular man, with long-black braids he wore like some American Indians, sported a blue cowboy shirt, a pair of burgundy Levi Jeans, and a pair of tan cowboy boots, took one look at Mabel and knew intuitively her secret. He smiled invitingly at her.

Mabel looked admiringly at his dark-copper-colored skin, and his nut-brown, broad, lips, and wondered what it would be like to kiss him.

"Hi, Honey," Burton said in a chortle.

"Hi yourself," said Mabel, she grinned from ear-to-ear.

Burton sat at a card table with another man, Wayne Nicholas, Jr., Rev. Nicholas's Nephew. Mabel took a closer look at Wayne than she had Burton. She saw him as a tall, thin, man, with a few wrinkles in his face. He was very light-skinned with reddish-brown hair, grayish-green eyes; and had long fingers and big feet-Mabel knew what they said about men with long fingers and big feet-they had "Big Things" too. Wayne had on black Levi Jeans, a thick-yellow woolen pullover shirt, and brown penny loafers. Mabel thought this man was "Pretty."

He took his eyes off the card table for a moment and said: "Hi, Miss Pretty." Wayne smiled. "Hi there," Mabel said. She noticed that Wayne seemed to be staring right through her dress.

She got really excited and her panties got even wetter. Mabel tried to wish her inner-feelings away, but she wanted to see what this man had, and that was that. "Henry done left me alone, he don't care 'bout me. Why not go after another man?" Mabel thought.

Bessie saw the look in Mabel's eyes. She knew it was schoolgirl's lust. "Mabel, come go with me ta-the kitchen." She beckoned with her left hand. When Mabel came over to her, she hugged her with her right arm. Bessie walked Mabel to the kitchen.

"Aw-ight," said Mabel. She was having a hard time tearing her eyes away from the hypnotic grip Wayne Nicholas's eyes had on her.

"What ya want, Bessie?" Mabel asked. They were standing near the cook stove where Bessie had pieces of chicken frying in one pan, some pork chops in another, and fish in still another. "What ya go tell me?"

"Mabel, lemme tell ya a little secret 'bout me. I didn't wanna marr' Lin Jackson. Momma 'nem just 'bout gave me ta 'im when I's nothin' but a little gal of thirteen. I weren't no virgin, but I didn't know that much 'bout mens neither.

"Baby, fore I knew it, I's carryin' twins. I can see that you marri'd up with Henry for some other reason than deep love. You's scare-a than hell of Henry, I can see that. Why'd ya get hitched-ta 'im?"

Tears came to Mabel's eyes. "I guess you's partly right. I always wanted my chillun-ta be with they rightful Daddy. That's what I's tryin' ta-do with Henry. I want him an' Billy ta-get close an' be Father an' Son. I wanna love Henry, but he's makin' that awful hard ta-do."

"Lemme get right down ta-it, Mabel," Bessie said. "Don't mess with that O' Burton. That man's just too nasty. Fools with anythin' that gotta hole. He ain' no good, baby. Might give ya the 'Claps.' Now ya don't want that do ya?

"Now, I knows these mens 'round here. I know all-a 'em in there this mornin'. Lemme tell ya: ifn ya wants what a good gal needs, try *Wayne Nicholas*. My boys, they's too wild, an' I wouldn't shake-a stick at the rest-a 'em pigs. They'll root in any gal's bizzness. Okay, Mabel? Look, honey, O' Bessie knows what's fake an' what's real."

After Bessie said that, she tended to the food cooking on the stove. Mabel returned to the card table. She watched Burton win hand after hand of Poker. He had a pile of coins in front of him, and a smaller stack of dollar bills. He bragged: "Ya buggers round here, can't beat me at nothin' toll. I'm the Ace Coon Boon 'round here, yeah!" bellowed out of his thick-kissable lips. Wayne Nicholas slid his chair back from the table. He cussed: "Son-a-va-bitch! Ya must gotta a lucky 'Coon's Dick' in ya pocket, man. Or, ya got's-ta be cheatin', or somethin', damn!" "The same way ya gets all them pretty gals, Pretty Boy, I'm smooth like that with them cards," Burton said.

One after the other all of the card players declared: "I'm all in, man." Wayne walked away from the card table shaking his head. Right away, he turned his focus to Mabel. She stood near Matt's old room, leaning against the door. Wayne eased over to her, looking directly into her nervous eyes.

"Hi, Baby Girl," Wayne crooned letting a little air come out of his mouth into Mabel's ear. "What ya doin' standin 'round all by yourself. Let's get-ta know one-nother a little better."

The hot air that Wayne blew into Mabel's ear stirred the fire of lust already burning all over her young body.

"First of all," Mabel uttered in a whisper, "tell me a little bit 'bout who you is."

"Well, little lady, I'm Wayne. That skinny kid standin' at the door is Sherwood, we call 'im Bird. Cause he gotta nose like a woodpecker. The other one, Sherman, we call Toad, cause that's what he look like. My close friends call me Way-Way. I got two Sisters, Courtney, the oldest one after Toad, and Gladys, next to her. I'm the oldest, and Bird's the youngest. Momma's name is Marr' Dee. My Daddy died in World War One. I'm his Jr"

"Whoa, hold on. I didn't mean for ya to tell me ya life history. I's just curious, is all," Mabel said.

"I know a lot 'bout you already, Sugar," Wayne said.

Mabel looked surprised. "Is that so? Tell me what ya knows."

"Well ... I know that you's Agnes Woods's gal. Ya gotta Sister named Dora, another'n, named Mary, then Anna Belle, Frances, and Ginia. Your oldest Brother is Julius. Then there's your Twin, George. Your Momma hooked up with Clemmon Mickens. She got Clarence, Willie an' Leroy-who's a little younger than your child, Billy."

Mabel gasped for breath. "How'd you get-ta know so much 'bout my family? Have ya been with my Momma?"

"No, Mabel, though I didn't find ya Momma to be ugly at all. I saw Mary a cup'la times. I really wanted Dora. She had this thing 'bout light-skinned mens. I got this thing 'bout light skinned gals. We both like 'dark chocolate.'" Wayne chuckled.

"Well, I don't 'member ever seein' ya 'round our house, or nothin'. Ya must've met my Sister in the woods," Mabel said, with her voice brimming with sarcasm.

"No, we use'ta meet down at Hacknette, y'know, an' well ya can figure the rest. I had-a old piece-a car, then. But that ain't how I learn'bout ya family.

"Your Uncle Gus an' I go way back. We's hangout buddies. I first met'im down at the State Farm. We hooked up an' stole corn from old man Winthrop Woods up near Oak Grove-up the road from where y'all's livin'. Y'know Gus ran a still. He never bought corn, didn't raise it neither. We'd take it from the White farmers. We made some fine liquor with that corn.

"Baby, we got caught. We gotta year-a-piece. We couldn't pay the fine.

I leant 'bout y'all from sharin' a cell with ya Uncle Gus. So, we's already closer than ya thinks."

"I don't do much drinkin', but let me have-a cup'la drinks ta-clear my head," Mabel said. "Why sure. Ya can have those on me," Wayne chimed.

Mabel went into the kitchen. "Bessie, I need-a drink. I got this feelin' in the pit-a my stomach, I gotta get-a hold on it. It's like I's afraid-way down inside-of what I's 'bout-ta do. You ever feel that way?" Mabel asked.

"Yeah, once, I guess, the first time. I got over that real quick. Then, I figured, Lin can't miss what he can't measure," Bessie whispered. "But Mabel, you's goin' ta-a place of no return, if ya go down that road, it'll come back up a thousand times; an' ya go have-ta lie time-an'-time again. Ifn ya don't leave Henry, ya life might be in danger if'n he finds out'bout what ya get read-ta do. I ain't got nothin' toll ta-do with ya bizzness, I just wanna warn ya."

Mabel whispered back: "I don't know what-ta say. I know what I want right now. I know it's wrong. But I know I'm go do it anyway," she whined.

Every one of the gamblers had left except for Burton and Wayne, Jr. Burton bought a chicken dinner for himself and a pork chop dinner for Wayne. Bessie let them eat those at the kitchen table. They both ordered a tall glass of homemade Plum Wine to wash their meals down.

Lin saw that his supply of bootleg had just about been bought up. He called out to Lin, Jr. and Broadus: "Boys, y'all come an' go with me ta-the Still, we gotta run off a gallon of liquor. We go be gone for two-three hours fore the evenin' crowd get over here, an' we get the games goin'." When Lin, Sr. cut that gallon of liquor with water, he'd have eight quarts of 80-90 proof bootleg, that he would be able to sell.

"Yeah, Pa," Broadus said. "Okay, Pa," said Lil' Lin.

Monroe slipped out of the backdoor and headed down the path to his A'nt Cary's house. He didn't want anything to do with the Still, or cutting the liquor with branch water. He hated the smell of bootleg. He hated the fact that his Father sold it.

Lil' Lin, Lin, Sr. and Broadus headed out the front door. They got in Lin's car and left, leaving Burton and Wayne behind, whom Lin, Sr. trusted. He knew they were scoundrels, but he figured they knew better than to get over on him, a bigger scoundrel.

Five minutes after Lin and Sons went out of the front door Bessie put all of the food in pans and shoved that in the oven. She winked at Mabel.

Burton finished eating and drinking got up from the table and allowed: "I gotta go down yonder an' take me a good dump." He looked over at Bessie with a broad smile on his face.

"I gotta go take me a pee myself," Wayne said.

Both men got their jackets and went out the door. Mabel got her sweater and coat and followed Wayne out the backdoor. It was just moderately cool out that afternoon. She followed Wayne a short distance down Bessie's spring path. He turned, pick her up, and tongue-kissed her passionately. They were well out of the sight of the house. He let her down onto the path.

Wayne's kiss took Mabel's mind completely off the slight chill in the air. She put her tongue in his mouth and played with his tongue. Wayne lifted her dress, pulled her panties down to her ankles, and allowed: "Ifn ya tell anybody 'bout this I'll lie an' deny it." Then, he went down on her.

"Oh Wayne, that's nasty. Should ya be doin' that?" She groaned and panted, then she squealed out in delight: "Wayne, don't stop! Oh, Wayne, I never felt like this before, oh, don't stop!"

"I ain't stoppin' gal, I'm just changin' positions. He turned Mabel around, bent her over, and pulled the hems of her dress and underskirt up and let those rest upon her rump. "I been lookin' at you all day long. I wanted ya the moment I set eyes on ya. Now, work-it back ta-me, back it on up," Wayne crooned.

Mabel backed up and down on Wayne. Wayne's thrusting elicited, "Ow, Wayne, Iain' no cow, now," from Mabel. "Take it easy." Wayne worked on her like a battering ram.

"Sorry, Baby. Ah, you's so good. Oh, gal, I love you. O-o-o-oh! Ah-ah-ah-ah! O-o-o-oh!" Wayne shouted. His lips trembled and saliva eased out of the comers of his mouth. His super hot release warmed Mabel's entire body, the heat radiated from her vagina up to her breasts to her head. Thrills ran through her head like fingers through her hair.

"Wayne, we gotta do that again. I love what you did for me. I wanna see more of you.

You's the kind-a man I'm lookin' for. Is all you go gimme is a quickie?" Mabel whined.

Wayne removed his large placid penis from Mabel. He got a handkerchief out of his pocket, wiped himself dry, and tossed it to the side of the path. "We could go on for the rest-a the evenin', but ev' body go know, then. Lin would run me 'way. Henry's his Brother-in-Law, now. He ain' go lemme get over on Henry like that.

"I gotta get back up to the game. It's my hustle. Me an' Burton, we got game, now. I hustle an' stack the deck so Burton win an' he do the same for me. We give Lin a cut at the end of the night." He smiled and tried to kiss Mabel again. She wouldn't let him.

Mabel got a ladies' handkerchief from her coat pocket. She wiped off her feminine area. She tossed that down beside of Wayne's handkerchief. She pulled her panties up and sat down on an old oak stump. She put her elbows on her thighs, and clasped her hands under her chin and on her jaws. She looked up at Wayne.

"Yeah, I gotta get on back up-ta the house, too. I 'ma have-ta 'splain where I been, an' what I been doin' out here. I prob-be don't smell good neither." Mabel groaned at the prospect.

"Don't worry, Baby. Round here, we all got secrets. Ya go sho' nuff find that out right early," said Wayne. "An' lemme tell ya, I know Henry James. I know he cut Snowvall near 'bout ta-death. He ain't go bother me. He ain't go even b'lieve I'd step-ta his gal. Even though he got hold of Mary many times when I's seein' that gal. Henry's guilt won't let 'im come for me. Look, I got outta a murder beef Henry know I ain't go let nobody put they hands on me like that; he knows how that's go end. So, he won't step-ta me like that," said Wayne with a little sarcastic chuckle.

'Ton kno'," said Mabel. "I'm thinkin 'bout leavin' o'crazy Henry James. I'm 'fraid he might cut me up, or hurt Billy, my little Son. I'm scared-ta hell of that man-it's the truth."

"Baby, just keep quiet 'bout what we just done, an' what else we might end up doin'. Let that be our little secret, okay?"

"Aw-ight," said Mabel. "If Henry find out 'bout what we did, I'll lie my ass off. I can't run 'way cause then he'll sure know somethin' sup. Guess I'm almost stuck-ta that man."

"That's the spirit," said Wayne. "Let's go on back up yonder, we been gone long 'nough." Wayne chuckled, but Mabel got an anxious frown on her face. It was one thing to get laid, but quite another to live with the guilt that would follow the act. She had been with men in Richmond, but didn't have "I'm marri'd-ta Henry James," bothering her conscience. Wayne bounced on up the path like nothing had happened, Mabel came behind him. The couple of shots of bootleg that had burned all the way down her throat to her guts were finally making their way back up to her head, and making her a little dizzy. She pasted a smile on her guilty face and followed her latest "Father Figure" on up the Path of Life.

They only got a little ways back up the path before they heard Bessie's ecstatic moans: "Baby, give-it-ta-me, oh, yeah! I love ya, Burton! O-o-o, Oh, ump, um-um"

Mabel's eyes bugged out from the shock of what she saw. She understood now why Bessie had seemed nuts when she low-rated Burton. Bessie was afraid that Mabel was going to steal Burton away from her.

Wayne just chuckled. He whispered: "I told ya, people 'round here got secrets. Ya just gotta know how-ta keep ya mouth shut 'bout people's bizzness. See what I'm talkin' bout?"

Burton had Bessie leaning over an old tree stump left after Lin and his boys had cut a tree down. Burton was doing his work on her from behind. She had her dress up and she held the hem of it in her hands. He had pulled her panties to the side enough to enter her. When Mabel and Wayne came up the path, Burton was all but picking Bessie off the ground with every thrust into her. His pants and shorts were down to his knees. "Yes, Lord!" Burton shouted as he ejaculated. He removed his penis, turned Bessie around and kissed her passionately. Then Bessie and Burton spied Wayne and Mabel standing in the path grinning at the sideshow.

Burton snatched his pants and shorts up quickly and took off running for the hills. His jacket was flapping in the breeze as he ran, like he was running for his life.

Bessie smoothed out her dress and her thick sweater. "Mabel Gal, this ain't what it look like. I'm-I was-well," she said. She shrugged her shoulders, and pied: "Y'all, don't say nothin 'bout this ta-Lin. I don't wanna have-ta kill Lin ta-keep 'im from hurtin' me. He can't talk, though. He's gettin' laid all over Fluvanna an' Louisa. But them mens think they own us womens. We's they property. They rather kill us than let any other man have us."

"Iain' like that," Wayne said.

"Bessie, honey, you don't need-ta s'plain nothin' toll ta-me. I'm just as guilty as you could ever be. I feel so bad. I gave it ta-Wayne. It felt so good, but I feel so nasty, now. I don't know what I go do," Mabel said.

"Mabel, I feel like an o'bitch in heat. Long's nobody catch ya it'll get easier to keep <loin' it.

I don't love Lin, baby"

Wayne had heard all that he cared to. "Y'all, I'm goin' back up yonder-ta the house." He walked up the path shaking his head as he went along.

Bessie continued on: "Mabel, I never loved Lin. When I got with Lin, I didn't know what love was. Then I met a man I love. He's Burton Gaines. I wanna run 'way with 'im, but we both know Lin would hunt us down like we was deer of somethin'."

"So, what ya go do? Ya just go keep on slippin' 'round? S'pose Lin hear 'bout it. Won't he still kill y'all then?" Mabel's voice was full of exasperation.

"Gal, that's why I's so sad when ya marri'd Henry. You's hitched up ta-nothin' but sad days, lonely nights, an' being 'fraid for ya life. Lin done emptied his double-barrel shotgun down through the woods at me lots of times, till he learnt I could shoot back. It'sa wonder one-a them lead pellets didn't hit me even though I's hidin' 'hind the trees, scared nearly-ta death. I done slept in the woods many-a night waitin' till Lin cooled down," Bessie whined. "I shot at 'im one time, an' he never raised a gun at me agin."

"Bessie, I might leave Henry. What if that man find out 'bout Wayne? Now, I know he don't love me, he prob-be go be just as jealous anyway. All mens be jealous of they womens, even ifn they don't love 'em. Too many mens done kilt womens they didn't love over in Cumberland where I come from, I know 'bout that. Henry treat me mean as hell-like Billie Holiday say in her Song. Bessie, we gotta swear-ta keep what we both did a secret 'tween us. I know Burton an' Wayne ain't go tell nobody-they lives would be in danger. Do ya swears, Bessie?"

Bessie paused a second or two, then she allowed: "I swears not-to-tell-not-a soul what ya told me, if ya swears not ta-tell a soul what ya seen me an' Burton doin'."

"I swears, Bessie," said Mabel. She hugged Bessie tight as she could.

Bessie laughed and said: "I ain't worri'd 'bout Wayne. Lemme clue ya in on-a little secret. Long ago, I gave it up ta-Wayne. But I only did it that one time. I don't like mens who is oversized, Mabel. I want pleasure, not pain. So, Wayne will never tell."

Mabel had a little chuckle and then she grinned. "I likes big mens. The bigger the better's what I always say. I knew somethin' was strange 'bout you an' Burton, though. I know now, you's jealous of the way he's lookin' at me. At first, I couldn't figure it out, but now I know.

"Bessie, what kind-a man's Wayne. I could really go for 'im. I wanna get with that man some more. I could leave Henry for him."

Bessie shook her head. "Don't count on that old guy, sugar. Wayne's always been a rollin' stone. Henry might let ya go ifn ya 'gree-ta let Billy stay with Momma. But that's the onliest way," said Bessie. "Wayne might shot-off his mouth, but he's scared as hell of Henry James most-a 'em 'round here's scared-a Henry. They saw what happened-ta Snowvall, even after that man pulled a shotgun an' all. Wayne would disappear ifn he thought Henry knew you an' he had been together. Ya can't 'pend on that old scratcher, Mabel."

"Aw-ight, then, Bessie," Mabel said.

"Child, let's get back up yonder-ta the house. Lin an 'nem prob-be back from the Still an'-a bunch-a mens up at the house gamblin' they lives 'way. My boys gotta be wonderin' where they Momma's at. I don't want 'em-ta have-ta come lookin' for me," Bessie said.

The two women hurried back up the path. Bessie carried two buckets of water to the house to be used to cut the bootleg liquor. Mabel let Bessie go into the house first. In a few minutes she burst through the backdoor. She went over to where Bessie had seated herself at the kitchen table. Mabel spoke loud enough for all to hear: "Sorry, Bessie, I took so long out yonder. I couldn't find the john in the dark. I had-a go in the woods. Then I almost got lost in the woods. I wandered 'round for a little while. Got ready to start screamin' when I found the path that led me-ta the backdoor."

Bessie smiled. "That's all right, child. Did ya get it done?" "Yes," Mabel said, with a twisted smile.

"That's all to it, then," Bessie said.

Wayne stood around a group of men who were shooting Crap. When Mabel came into the house he winked at her. Neither she nor he uttered a word. After about fifteen minutes he pranced over to where Mabel stood. They were trying to act causal.

Wayne whispered into Mabel's ear: "C'mon over ta-the sofa. I'm gonna put-a bug in ya ear Mabel Louise Scott-James." Then he chuckled.

"Aw-ight, Sugarboo," Mabel whispered back. She followed Wayne to a sofa next to Bessie's bed over against the wall. It was behind the card tables. She sat in the far corner of the sofa, and Wayne squeezed close beside her.

Mabel noticed that Burton was nowhere to be found. Lin, Sr. was in the kitchen selling twelve-ounce cans of Budweiser Beer to thirsty gamblers. Lil' Lin was selling shots of Moonshine to other gamblers, and Matt had come back from her visit with her Lover, Joel Miller, Frank and Marie Miller's youngest Brother, and was helping Bessie heat up sandwiches for some hungry gamblers. Broadus had hit the road in search of a lonely woman. Monroe was in the boys' room reading a History book.

"Mabel, I know your Unc' Gus real well," said Wayne. "We got-ta talkin' the other day, an' he told me 'bout a plan-a his'n that might get our hands on some big money, real fast.

"See, I don't care nothin' toll 'bout pullin' time, or gettin' in trou'ba takin' back from the Whiteman. Gus hate them Crackers badder'n I do. He's talkin' 'bout yokin' O' Man Jacob Stiles, the owner of Stiles's Antiques in Columbia. He ain't got nothin' but-a Junk Store, but he ain' no po' White Cracker, now.

"We know he don't b'lieve in no banks. He lost-a a lotta money in the Stock Market Crash, an' ain't put money in no bank, ever since. Gus figure he got all his money stashed in his old home-place in Stage Junction. His store done been broke in too many times, so he wouldn't hide his money in there. His house gotta be the place where he's keepin' it hid.

"Joel get-a government check ev' month. He got gassed durin' World War One. Iain' never seen none-a his peoples-don't know ifn he got any. He cashes his check at the Post Office cross from City Hall. He walks outta there with the money. Now, cause he don't b'lieve in banks, ain' got no gal-cause he too old-he gotta be storin' all that money in his house somewheres.

"Gus say all we gotta do is break in his house in the middle of the night an' beat 'im till he give up that money. Ifn he don't wanna cooperate, we can cut his throat. Gus wouldn't mind, an' I sure wouldn't. He may be lying, but your Unc' Gus claim he done shot-a many Crackers out in the woods durin' Huntin' Season, soon's he run 'cross one out by his-self. That's how bad he hate 'em, Mabel."

Mabel's eyes took on a sorrowful gaze. "Wayne," she paused, "I ain't got nothin' ta-do with y' all's bizzness, but you's go end up in prison or the 'lectric chair. That's all to it. I know Unc' Gus's full-a hate 'gainst all White folks. He hates what White mens done ta-our family. He's crazy like that. He's go end up dead or in prison one-a these days. I hope-a good man, like you is, don't go the same way-especially after what we shared."

"Mabel, Baby, I's born-ta be 'lectrocuted, or locked up in jail or prison, for :fuckin' up some Crackers. Look at me." Wayne points at his face with his right hand. "I got this shit-color on my skin cause some nasty Cracker raped one-a my Grandmothers. I'm go get even with ev' one a them sons-a-bitches fore I leave this damn world."

"Wayne, I was hopin' you an' me go be able ta-hook up an' stay together, an' it'll be us 'gainst the world. Ain't that better'n throwin' your life 'way over some dumb shit?" Mabel said.

"Little gal, I love what'cha done for me. Ifn I was lookin' for-a gal ta-settle down with, you'd be my first choice. But, the truth is, we ain' go never be together like ya talkin' 'bout. I's sorry if'n I led ya down that road. I enjoyed how juicy and delicious you was, but I got a battle ta-fight, an' I can't have no gal ta-answer to. I don't wanna put ya in that kind-a danger. I do 'spect ya that much," said Wayne, he stared at the floor looking like he may be fighting back the tears.

Mabel hung her head, got up from the sofa, put on her sweater and coat, and headed for the front door.

Bessie didn't run after her, she knew what had happened. Wayne had been honest for once in his shameful life. She appreciated that much, anyway. She hoped Mabel would not end up like she had.

Mabel ran down the path that night through the woods crying, her mind conjured up nothing but illusive shadows of ghostly apparitions, that the trees had become, that seemed to be laughing at her.

She soon ran past Cary's house. After she crossed the makeshift bridge over the branch at Doc Johnson's Mill, Mabel went up to the STOP sign at 656, and let her tears come falling down. She was thinking: *I got knocked up by doin' it one day, one time. Got marri 'd ta-a man that don't even like me. Now, I don't think I like him, neither. Met 'nother man, I could love, but he'd rather go hate White folks than be with me. Maybe I ought-a let A'nt Maetta bring Billy up. I prob-be wouldn't be the kind-a Mother I ought-a be.*

It was her luck, that O' Man Pat was coming down 656 to Route Six with an empty wagon. He saw Mabel standing at the STOP sign and was surprised to see her out so late that evening.

"Hop on little lady ifn ya need-a ride back up the road. Didn't 'spect-ta see nobody out here this late," O' Man Pat, said.

Mabel hopped on back of the wagon. "It is gettin' mighty dark out here," said Mabel. "Hope A'nt Maetta ain't gettin' too worri'd 'bout me."

"Well, I 'ma have ya up yonder fore ya know it. A'nt Maetta go be so glad ta-see ya it won't matter 'bout the rest," Pat said.

There was nothing but the sound of the horse's hooves hitting the unpaved road, "clip-clop, clip-clop ... "along that dirt road. Then Pat said: "Here's ya turnoff Child, take it easy, now."

"Thank ya, kind sir," said Mabel. She jumped off the wagon and watched it go around the bend.

When Mabel walked into the house, A'nt Maetta was up rocking Billy in a rocking chair in her bedroom. Lawrence was asleep on the cot in the hallway. Billy clung to his Grandma like he would never let her go. Mabel was a little perturbed because Billy didn't run to meet and greet her like before. This made her a little jealous. William seemed to be stuck to his Grandmother like he had been glued to her. He had only met her a few weeks ago.

"Hi, Billy. Hi, Sugar. How's Momma's baby?" asked Mabel. She waved at her Son. He got down out of his Grandma's lap, came over to his Mother, hugged her briefly, and scampered right back to A'nt Maetta's loving embrace; then he hugged her tighter than before. Mabel didn't really like that at all, but she said nothing.

"Get'cha a plate, Mabel. There's plenty of ham, cress salad, an' baked yams on the stove. I b'lieves it's still warm. I figured ya be back 'round suppertime. Ya gotta eat somethin' ta-give that liquor you's been drinkin' somethin' ta-eat on 'ceptin' ya guts. I can smell it on ya," A'nt Maetta said. She got a little deceitful grin on her wise face.

"A'nt Maetta, I'm go be workin' for Bessie 'nem. I can make five-dollars-a-week. I'll just be doin' a little cookin', especially on Friday and Saturday nights. Would ya mind lookin' after Billy while I'm doin' the cookin' for Bessie 'nem?"

"Well, I reek-en it's aw-ight. Ya gotta watch out down there, though.

Bessie 'nem gotta lotta shit goin' on in they house. She's my Daughter, but I'm tellin' ya what Gawd loves-the truth.

"I don't blame ya for lookin 'round for somethin 'nother ta-do till Henry get outta prison, but ya gotta be careful, Mabel. Try-ta stay outta trou'ba, aw-ight-y'know what I mean," A'nt Maetta said. "Here's a clean towel an' a washcloth." Mabel took those to her room.

"Aw-ight, I sure will," said Mabel. She got a plate of food and ate it right up. She got a basin of warm water out of the stove's tank. She sponged off, changed underwear, and plopped down on her Goose-Down bed. She decided that she would leave tomorrow. She figured she'd let Henry have his way. She wanted to try to persuade Wayne Nicholas to come be with her one more time. She would slip away and leave Billy with his Grandma. He'd see his Daddy often, and she'd visit him regularly. If she could get Wayne to act right, everybody would be happy.

Bright and early on that morning, Mabel got up and packed her things in an old black suitcase she found under the bed. She got dressed in one of the dresses A' nt Maetta had sewn. She had also made her cotton underskirts, and a crescent half-slip. She had three other dresses and a couple of blouses. All were pastels, and all were like newly-bought clothes out of a store. A'nt Maetta was an excellent seamstress.

Mabel tip-toed into A'nt Maetta's bedroom to kiss Billy goodbye. When she bent over and touched him he awoke. He got up and hugged her tightly. A'nt Maetta seemed still asleep.

"Goodbye, Baby. Momma's go see ya soon. Behave yourself. Momma loves ya," Mabel whispered.

"Bye, Momma," said Billy. He got in the bed beside his Grandma and fell fast asleep. Tears came down Mabel's cheeks. She hated to be leaving Billy all the damn time. She made up in her mind that she was still going to do everything in her power to see that Billy and Henry knew each other well.

Mabel hustled out of the house without saying anything to A'nt Maetta. Because A'nt Maetta had given her the washcloth and towel, she had to have known that she was doing more than drinking at Bessie's house. That's why she had given Mabel such a dire warning.

As luck would have it, again O' Pat and his horse-drawn wagon came "clip-clopping" down the road. "Hop on, little lady. I'm goin' down the road this mornin'. Gotta 'nother job ta-do today. You's welcome to come ride if'n ya want to."

"Mr. Pat, I's goin' ta-Bessie 'nem again. Y'know, my Sister-in-Law, Bessie Jackson," Mabel said.

Mabel saw rolls of tarpaper and brick-siding on the wagon. Soon O' Pat let her off at the STOP sign and got down off the wagon to help her with her suitcase. Mabel crossed the little bridge over the branch. She got up to Cary's house and she spied her out of her front window.

Cary wondered why Henry's new wife was heading up through the woods carrying a suitcase. Cary hated that Mabel was headed to Bessie 'nem house, "A Den of Satan." She hated, too, the fact that Mabel didn't even stop to say hello, or anything.

Mabel wasted no time. She shot up the path as fast as she could. She got to Bessie's house out of breath. She knocked on Bessie's front door.

Matt answered the door. She carried a plump, light-skinned, two or three-year old girl in her arms. The child had nappy, sandy, hair and was pretty as it could be. Mabel was shocked.

"Come on in, A'nt Mabel," Matt said. Mabel came into the house and sat her suitcase down on the floor.

"Matt, where ya get a little gal from? I didn't even know you's knocked up. Ya must've carried that one real low, an' whatnot ..."

"A'nt Mabel, I'm gonna have-ta let Momma explain that one to ya. It's grown folk bizzness," said Matt with a little chuckle.

Bessie came out of the kitchen. She quickly took the child out of Matt's arms. "This is one-a my Son's baby. Though I don't think it could be Ton's. He only cut that gal one time. That was just months ago. Too soon for-a gal ta-drop his baby. 'Sides, this child's goin' on three."

"Bessie, who's the gal we's talkin 'bout?" Mabel asked.

"Ya Cousin Phyllis slept with all three-a my boys the night of the fire. Lin, Sr. wanted 'em ta-make-a man outta Ton. Lin thought he's too sissified. Wanted Broadus and Lil' Lin ta-make a man outta 'im by puttin 'im on-a hot gal.

"Phyllis had been foolin 'round with Lil' Lin an' Broadus for a while. She done got knocked up, had-a baby, an' kept it secret. The State's gettin'-read-ta-clean up places like where you's raised. They go make the farm owners fix-up them shanties, and tear others down. They go have-ta pay the peoples what been livin' on they farms a hourly-wage. Most-a the young peoples gotta leave, cause-a the farmers' claims that they can't 'ford-ta put out all that money.

"The fire that kilt all them chillren got the State 'ficials all riled up. They's all over Cumberland. Gal, you ain't heard? They took Catherine an' Maude's Chillren. Put'em in foster care. Them Chillren's so White-lookin' they got 'dopted by White peoples. Both Maude an' Catherine's outta they minds. They's down-ta Pita'sburg, with ya Sister, Frances.

"Unc' Willie an' A'nt Neddy is the onliest peoples who go be able ta-stay on the place. The White Woods's family go take care-a them. Your Momma's go be given time-ta find-a place ta go. They say Clemmon's lookin' ev' where for-a place. Then they go have-ta move.

"Imagine how surprised I was when Phyllis showed up here early this mornin' knockin' on my door. Ya Unc' Gus brought 'er in his old Chevy truck. She go stay in Cumberland for right now, but she didn't wanna be draggin 'er baby 'round all over the place."

Mabel was aghast at what she had heard. "Bessie, how do ya know that baby's your Grandchild? What make ya so sure 'bout that? Phyllis slept 'round with a lotta mens."

"Mabel, look at little Alize, here." The child was wrapped in a pink blanket. "She's one-a my boy's baby. Either Broadus or Lil' Lin is 'er Daddy. The little gal got sandy hair, but it's nappy as can be. Just like mine. Look at 'er closely. She looks just like me.

"Both Broadus an' Lil' Lin claim they's 'er Daddy. It don't matter. I know she's my Grand Baby. I'm go raise 'er. I'm go raise 'er as Alize Archer Jackson. I'll make Broadus an' Lil' Lin help support 'er. In-a way, she'll have four Daddies: Broadus, Lil' Lin, Big Lin, an' Ton; an' three Mommas: Me, Matt, an' Phyllis."

Mabel was stunned at what she had just learned. Phyllis had gotten pregnant, had a baby, and Mabel had not heard anything about that. But because of the difference between the way that Mabel carried herself, and the way that Phyllis had carried herself, such a secret could easily be kept. Mabel liked Phyllis. Phyllis liked her back. But they didn't mess around in each other's business.

"Well . . . the child do look a lot like ya Bessie-she's just light-skinned. Prob-be go end up lookin' more like Matt," Mabel said.

"Bessie, I got somethin' ta-ask ya."

"Come go-ta the kitchen, Mabel. Let's get-a cup-a hot coffee an' we can talk in there; aw ight?"

Bessie gave little babbling Alize to Matt. The baby was all smiles. Matt kissed her all over her little fat face. "Ah-h-h, I gotta change you," Matt said. She took Alize to her room. Mabel and Bessie went into the kitchen.

Bessie poured coffee out of a white-porcelain pot into two-tall brown cups. "Have a seat, Mabel. What ya wanna talk 'bout? I see ya got a suitcase with ya."

"Bessie, I told A'nt Maetta I's go come cook for y'all. I'on kno' ifn she b'lieve it or not. But I'm askin' ya, can I stay with ya a little while till I get things straighten out?" said Mabel, in a near whisper.

"I'on kno' Mabel ... I'on wanna get in no shit with Henry when he finds out you's been fuckin' Wayne Nicholas while you's stayin' here. That's what you's tryin' ta-get straight, ain't it?" Bessie put in four teaspoons of sugar in her coffee, and a spurt of cream, and stirred that all up. She took a sip and looked across the table right into Mabel's eyes.

Mabel put in two teaspoons of sugar and a small amount of cream. She stirred that all up.

Without looking up she whispered: "Burton Gaines."

Bessie's eyes got big as hen's eggs. She almost hissed: "What-so-never happens, it's go be all on you, gal!" Her face took on a sarcastic appearance. She pasted a smile over that.

"C'mon, gal. Sure ya can stay with us a little while till Henry gets outta prison. Ya can stay in the boys' room. Ton can stay in Matt's old room. And, we'll be One-Big-Happy-Family," said Bessie in an almost growl.

"What happen-ta Broadus an' Lil' Lin?" Mabel asked. She had a deceitful grin on her face. "Broadus got Barbara Wells pregnant, we call 'er Boopsie. She's Ton's gal-friend, but Broadus manage-ta get into 'er panties. He say just one time-but that's all it takes. She's growin' in the middle now. Her family's Catholic. They go-ta that Church in Columbia.

"Umpster, her Daddy, go press charges on Broadus ifn he don't marr' Boopsie. The gal's only sixteen. So Broadus gone-ta live with them. He could face five years. He left this mornin'. "Lil' Lin done moved in with Marie Miller over in Stage Junction. He ain't go never marr' that gal though. But they's shackin' right now. He left this mornin' too.

213

"The gal Broadus was courtin' was Shirley-they call 'er Beauty-Boopsie's Sister. Bean, or Umpster, Jr., don't like Broadus one bit. He's they older Brother. Nor do Elaine-they call 'er Missy-either. She's the youngest. Broadus-a be livin' in-a house where nobody cares for 'im."

Mabel sipped some coffee and said: "That's how it be sometimes. Bessie we can be the best of friends. Lemme get my suitcase an' come on in the house fore ya hit me with much more."

Mabel went to near the front door and took up her suitcase. She took it to the Boys' room. Ton was nowhere to be found. She was thinking: *Matt's gettin' right round in the middle. I wonder, is she knocked up?*

She came back to the kitchen table and took up her cup of coffee. Matt had laid Alize down.

"Matt, lemme look at ya, gal, what'cha ..."

"Fore ya ask, yep, I'm caught, A'nt Mabel. That dam-Joel Miller. That cute-little Sambo was s'pose-ta be wearin' a rubber. Whenever we did it I'd check. He must've slipped it off an' I didn't notice. He thinks I'm gonna marry him cause-a this baby. He's begging me to get hitched with him."

Mabel was puzzled. "Don't ya wanna give ya baby it's Father's name?"

"A'nt Mabel, yeah, that's one thing to consider, but here's another. He's good in bed, got a good job, and got some land. His parents left all three-a their kids some money and land. But, Mabel, Daddy's folk over in Louisa got a lotta money. They's not poor. Skin color makes a difference. If you're too dark, you just can't get but so far in this world. Joel's jack-black.

"That's why Lil' Lin ain' go marry Marie, she's too Black. Don't get me wrong, I love myself some dark-Brothers, now, but I won't get married to none-a them."

Mabel frowned. "I'on kno' why ev' body puttin' so much stock in they skin color. Matt, you's givin' Joel ya body. But ya won't marr 'im? I wouldn't fool with nobody too light or too dark for me. Why y'all's doin' that?"

Bessie laughed out loud and clapped her hands. Matt rolled her eyes a little bit at her Mother.

"A'nt Mabel, ta-tell ya the truth, I don't know how-ta answer that. Jeol's awesome as a man, but dark mens ain't goin' nowhere. Now as a Lover, he makes me feel good all over. But I'm gonna stay single, cause if I really wanna get hitched, I'm gonna have-ta catch a light-skinned man. That's how it is. A lotta young girls feel like I do."

Mabel just shook her head. She heard a car coming up the road.

"Goodbye, Momma. Goodbye A'nt Mabel. I gotta go with Joel. He's out yonder, I don't wanna keep him waiting."

Matt got a black fur-edged leather coat, slipped that on over a red-velvet dress, and said: "Come, y'all gimme-a hug."

Bessie hugged her first. Mabel hugged her next. Matt got a big leather Lady's handbag, and headed on out the door. Mabel followed. She saw Matt getting into a new blue Buick Sedan.

"He's drivin' a nice car," Mabel said. She was standing at the front door.

"I know," said Bessie. "I don't know what Matt's talkin 'bout. What more could she want from any man? He gotta nice home, nice car, nice job, he's right handsome, and he loves the ground Matt walk on. But she won't marr 'im."

"That's them youngin's," Mabel said.

Bessie looked at her real hard, and laughed out loud.

"Bessie, where's Ton? Ya sure he ain't hidin' round here readin' or somethin'?" Mabel asked. "Mabel, he prob-be done run 'way an' join the Army. He's the onliest one-a my Chillun tamake it his bizzness to go-ta school ev' day. He got eleven years of schoolin' now.

"Lin an' Ton ain' never got 'long. He thought Monroe's a sissy. Ton like readin' books an' stuff Lin want his boys ta-be tag-alongs. He didn't make 'em go-ta school, or nothin'. I try-ta tell 'im that was wrong, but he paid me no never-mind. Broadus, Lil' Lin an' Matt can't read an' write. Ton's ashame-a all-a us.

"Lin done beat the shit outta Ton before, when I wasn't 'round-like Poppa use-ta do ta Henry when Momma wasn't 'round. Now, that Broadus an' Lil' Lin's gone, Big Lin was thinkin 'bout makin' Ton carry the load, but Ton ain' havin' none-a that.

"So, Mabel, I'm glad my Baby Son's gone. The boy just wanna make somethin' outta his self," said Bessie. She fought back the tears.

"Ya can't fault nobody for wantin' ta-make somethin' of himself," Mabel said.

"Ton told me he was goin' into the Army. I just hope he don't go 'gainst being Colored. He hated what Broadus did ta-his gal-friend. Big Lin an' Broadus made fun of him over that till Boopsie showed she was knocked up. Light-skinned as Ton is, and he done said a lotta times, he wish he was White, I ain't sure he won't pass. I'll love him the more, no matter what color he be," Bessie said.

"Bessie, I 'gree. Hope it come out all right for Ton." (Bessie and Mabel saw Wayne and Burton often after Ton ran away. The Crap games went on as before, no one was the wiser about the affairs-or no one said much about them at that time.)

During the First week of January 1951, during a Crap game, Bobby Hughes came to Bessie's house on a Saturday morning. He nearly kicked the front door in. When they saw it was the Law, men scrambled to conceal the small piles of change and dollar bills they had accumulated for most of the previous night until that morning. Lin ran to grab his shotgun he had mounted on top of the door frame. Then he spied the Sheriff, and he backed away.

The Sheriff didn't seem to mind that he had broken up a Crap game. His red face was livid with anger. He swaggered into the house and spat out a hunk of Snuff Spittle right on the floor. He came over to Wayne Nicholas, who was grinning at the Lawman. The Sheriff put his hand on his Revolver.

"Ya yellar bastard! Get the hell up!" shot out of his mouth thicker than the snuff-juice had. "Get up, and don't ya make no false move, Nigger! I'd love to fill ya ass full-a lead. If I had my way, I'd save the Sate the trouble. This-a be it for you, ya Coon!" Hughes yelled.

"Fuck you, Bobby Hughes!" Wayne screamed. "Fuck you and ev' one-a you nasty-White sons-sa-bitches." Wayne retorted. "Go-head-on, shoot, Cracker. See ifn I give-a good Gawd dam!"

Everyone, including Lin, Bessie, Burton and Mabel got as close to the wall as possible out of the path they expected the shots to fly.

"Your ass ain't getting outta this shit that easy," said Hughes. He rushed over to Wayne and slammed his left fist into the side of Wayne's head. The lick knocked Wayne to the floor.

"Get up, you dirty Tawdry bastard. Get up slowly, boy!" Hughes shouted.

With his head ringing from the lick from Sheriff Hughes, Wayne got up slowly. He faced his nemesis defiantly.

"Wayne Nicholas, I'm charging you with the murder of Jacob Stiles. You're under arrest," Sheriff Hughes shouted. "Turn around and put your hands behind you."

Hughes rushed over to handcuff Wayne. He moved quickly and methodically. He shoved and half-dragged Wayne out of the front door. He had put his gun back into its holster after handcuffing Wayne to free up both his fists.

Once Hughes took Wayne out of the front door, he walloped him up beside his head again and again. He threw Wayne into the back of the patrol car like he was no more than a bag of rags. Then, he kicked Wayne several times. Each kick was harder than before. His licks to Wayne's head, and the kicks, grew heavier and heavier. Wayne lost consciousness.

Mabel's lust for Wayne drove her to the front door to see what was happening to her "Sugar Daddy." She gasped for breath when she saw the blood and spit oozing out of Wayne's mouth, and he was slumped over in the backseat. She wanted to run over and comfort him. Then, Hughes spat snuff-spittle on Wayne's forehead. He slammed the backdoor closed. He swaggered around to the driver's side of the car, got in, and soon sped away.

She came back into the house barely able to walk. Mabel found a chair in the corner of the front room and slowly sank into it. She felt like her insides were sinking even farther. She was silent for the rest of the day. All hopes for a relationship with Wayne were dashed.

Lin suspended the games for the rest of the day. "Y'all come back next week," Lin said. Bessie, Lin, and Mabel sat around for the rest of the day silently sipping beer. Lin lit-up a Camel cigarette. "Gimme one," Mabel asked. He gave her one. She lit-up and choked on the smoke but kept on trying until she got a little bit of the smoke inhaled. Then, later that evening, on the seven o'clock news came a startling report:

"A grisly murder took place yesterday at the home of a man named Jacob Stiles of Stage Junction, Virginia. He was the owner of Stiles Antiques in Columbia. He was shot in the head three times by what the Sheriff's Department says was likely a Thirty-Eight Pistol. Investigators found shell casings matching the alleged murder weapon. Stile's home had been ransacked, though nothing seemed to have been stolen. Sheriff Hughes described the

crime scene as the bloodiest he has ever seen in the area. He further states that attempted robbery was the most likely motive for the crime. A suspect is in custody. His name is Wayne Nicholas of Gravel Hill. Anyone with any information about this crime, or the whereabouts of any other assailants involved with this crime, should call the Sheriff's Office at 555-1113 and talk to Sheriff. I Bobby Hughes. A Reward is available for credible information. Now, a word from our sponsors"

Mabel ran outside to vomit after she heard the news. Bessie got up and walked around in the front room shaking her head.

"That Wayne Nicholas ain' had-a lick-a sense. Old man Stiles gave 'way all his money ta-peoples in need. He been doin' it since he came back from the War. That fool, Wayne, just had it in his head that the old man had money hid in his house somewheres. I heard 'im runnin' off at the mouth one day an' tried-ta tell 'im. But once Wayne got some stupid shit in his head he ain't gonna listen-ta nobody. Now, look what he's gone an' done," Lin said.

Mabel went outside. She stood behind the house weeping. Her insides ached. She wondered: "Why the hell do I fall for old-shitty-mens like Wayne Nicholas and Henry James?"

Mabel's involvement with two men so far had merited her nothing but more loneliness. Her Mother had been raped repeatedly. But fate itself seemed to be raping her.

Bessie complained about pains in her stomach. "Mabel, in a couple of months, I'm go swell up like I's pregnant. You're be 'round. You'll see. I must be havin' female trou'ba, or somethin'. I reek-en that's all-it 'tis. I just startin' ta-feel it a little bit right now. But by late-March I'll look like I'm pregnant. My gut's go hurt more 'n more ev' passin' day."

Henry was released from the State Farm the fourth week of January, 1951. He had gained some weight. He got out in the morning. He had to hitch a ride up from Powhatan to Fluvanna, some twenty miles or so. He went straight home arriving on a Friday, late afternoon.

After bursting through the door, he yelled, "Hi, Momma! I'm home."

A'nt Maetta met Henry at the door and picked him almost off the floor in a mighty bear hug. "Boy, don't scare me ta-death, sneakin' up on me like that. Lemme look at ya. O'mi-Gawd! Ya done got fat. Or, ma-be it's them jail clothes you's wearin'.

"Lawrence an' Billy's gone up the road ta-visit with Lynn an' Albert, Jr. They go be back 'round suppertime. Mabel's down ta-Bessie's. Ya Poppa's up at Jo-Jo's house playin' cards where he spend most-a his time these days."

Henry asked: "Lawrence, he's Snownvall's boy? Why you still keepin 'im? Wasn't that just s'pose-ta be till Snowvall got his-self together?"

A'nt Maetta frowned a little, then smiled. "Yeah, but Snowvall didn't get his-self back together. He's still crazy. Fannie done took up with Bay Washington. They's all jammed up in Jo-Jo's house. Wall-to-wall peoples is in that house. So, I 'ma keep Lawrence cause Bay don't want that child livin' with them."

"I be damn," said Henry. "Now, ya got one more mouth-ta feed."

"I don't see it that way," said A'nt Maetta. "I see it as one more soul to love." "Yeah, okay," Henry said.

After taking a sponge off, Henry found a pair of pants in his closet that were once too big for him. He was glad he hadn't asked his Mother to cut those down. He put on the jail-issue white shirt he had worn home, and got an overcoat out of the closet that used to be bulky, but was now very tight. He got dressed. He took off the coat, came into the kitchen and seated himself at the table across from A'nt Maetta. He got a heaping plateful of collard greens, fried chicken, potato salad, and cornbread. He dug in. After he finished eating he burped. He got a satisfied smile on his chiseled face.

"Momma, how long' s Mabel been gone?" Henry asked.

"Well ... 'bout the second week after ya went down the road-I reek-en. She say it was too quiet up here. Ma-be ya can just let 'er go now. I got Billy. I love that child like he was my own. He's my Grand Baby," A'nt Maetta said.

"So, she been gone since I been down the road, huh?" Henry grunted. "Well, it's what ya want ain't it?" A'nt Maetta replied.

"Momma, I ain' never own one-a them gals I been with. You ain't gettin' no younger. How ya go keep up with Billy an' Lawrence?"

"I's down the road long 'nough-ta think 'bout things a little bit. Could be what I's meant-ta do. I gotta go fetch what's mine. I'm goin' down-ta Lin'nem an' see ifn I can take Mabel 'way from down there. I know she might've slipped up, but I 'ma go to 'er an' see what is what," Henry said. "Ma-be one day I might really feel somethin' for 'er. Right now, she's just mine."

A'nt Maetta couldn't believe her ears. Henry was sounding more like a real man instead of a spoiled child. But, still her oldest Son did not ask about his youngest Son.

Henry got his coat on. It was cold out that evening. He walked fast and jogged down-hill until he ended up at Bessie's. He knocked on Bessie's door. A Bobcat growled. It frightened Henry a little. He knew that if one of those things was sick with the rabies, it'd launch a savage attack on him. It growled louder. It was quiet in the house. Henry didn't hear any voices or music.

Bessie came to the door. "Henry, you rascal you! C'mon in the house, boy. We cleaned the suckers out early. They's gone."

Lin ran from the kitchen. "Damn, Henry, ya done got fat, man. Come on in the house."

Henry went over to the potbellied stove. He warmed himself. Then he asked Bessie a startling question: "Is Mabel down here?" Bessie hoped she'd hide until Henry left.

Mabel came from the kitchen with her hands clasped together behind her and with her eyes downcast. She assumed the posture of "a little girl presenting herself to Daddy after a long absence."

To Mabel's surprise, Henry kissed her like he had the first time she was intimate with him. He tried to kiss her hard and long, it didn't feel right to Mabel anymore. He tried to put his tongue in her mouth, but she withdrew. It almost made her sick to think about being with Henry like that. "What's the matter with ya gal?" Henry asked.

"Nothin's the matter with me," said Mabel, sheepishly. Her body trembled all over. "Oh yeah it is," Henry snapped. He could feel that something was up.

Mabel tried to lie in her own defense. "I just . . . I just gotta get use-ta ya again," she whined.

"Aw-ight. Let's go over-ta Matt's room an' fix that right now," Henry demanded. Henry turned to Bessie an' Lin. "Can we use Matt's room tonight, y'all?"

Bessie saw the tears in Mabel's eyes, and she knew why she was crying.

220

The man she really loved was gone away to jail. He was probably going to be sent down the road for twenty years or more; and that, if the State didn't electrocute Wayne.

"Henry, she's ya wife. Y'all gotta right-ta be together. Sure, use the boys' room-I'on care," Bessie said. Lin just shrugged his shoulders and winked at Henry.

That night, Mabel was dead-weight. She couldn't get hot for Henry. His touch was not what she wanted anymore. She wanted Wayne! But Henry was what she had to settle for or have no one at all. She imagined that was what her Mother had been forced to endure. Sex like that was very painful, though.

Henry was not gentle. He was not-like he had been at first-loving and sensuous. He was not caring about pleasing Mabel. He just wanted to get those painful rocks out of his balls. A month in the State Farm seemed like a long time to him who was used to a lot of women.

It didn't matter to Henry whether Mabel wanted it or not. He was getting what he wanted. And, if someone else had been plowing her fields, he was at the helm of the plow now. This was his "Cow," and he was going to milk her to his heart's delight. She was his, and he owned her, and now, he was going to possess her.

PART III

And Henry Begat Seven Sons

CHAPTER FOURTEEN

Henry had what would seem to be what he once wanted. He was not a religious man, but when A'nt Maetta, his Mother, invoked EXODUS 20: 12, 21: 17, demanding that children honor their parents, and that they are not to curse (sass) them for fear of God's wrath, he became a quasi-believer. He thought that what had happened between he and Tank Snowvall was related to the above. In actuality, it was just Henry's and A'nt Maetta's superstitious misunderstanding of the above Scriptures. But once Henry had married Mabel, he wanted to treat her like a purchased "farm animal." Instead of running away, like he had done from Adlai and Henrietta, he decided he'd stick around this time despite his previous misgivings.

Lin, Sr. got Henry a job with Kent Brothers Sawmill. Henry got tired of listening to Lin grill him about accepting life's circumstances "like-a man!" Since Henry had decided that he was going to stay married to Mabel, even though he didn't love her, he thought he had better make the most of what he was facing.

Besides, Henry had gotten tired of trying to be "That Devil-May-Care Blues-Man." He couldn't even wear his old "slick-britches" outfits. All he could wear was his work clothes. He was maturing intuitively. He didn't want to continue to be the "Cut-Up" he had been. The incident with Snowvall and Babe had scared Henry. He knew that things could have been a lot worse. So he thought, "What the Hell! I may as well take the bitter with the sweet."

Bessie was worried to death now that Henry was out of prison. She feared that Mabel might tell Henry about Burton Gaines. She wanted Mabel and Henry to at least be out on their own, so that she'd have a better than even chance of denying anything Lin might hear about her affair with Burton. It was in late March, 1951, and Bessie's gut-pains were growing along with her stomach and were reaching excruciating levels.

A woman, named Caroline Anderson, on her deathbed, had claimed that she was a "Black Witch." She also claimed that she had been involved with Lin, Sr. before Bessie had come along. Since Bessie had been visiting Caroline several days of the week to listen to the Soaps on CBS Radio, Caroline confessed that, "Gal, I done fix ya in-a cup-a tea, an' some homemade cookies. I wanted revenge cause ya stole my Linwood from me. My Charms, strong as they was, weren't strong-a 'nough 'gainst ya young-Black-beauty. He chose ya over me. That weren't s'pose-ta happen." That happened at bout seven years ago.

Bessie didn't put much stock in Caroline's claims. She listened to the dying old woman and later exclaimed to Matt: "That old woman's just crazy as hell, is all."

But Bessie remembered that on one evening after coming away from one of the many times she had visited Caroline's home, she did get really sick to her stomach. She vomited up what looked like little red, black, blue, and green worms, or something. Her stomach started to rise up every spring and it ached something awful. It got worse every year. On her deathbed, Caroline had said: "Your stomach go rise with the sap in the Great Oak Trees, an' you's gon go to many doctors an' they ain' go be able ta-help ya. Ya gotta go-ta-a Special Black Doctor, he's the onliest one go be able ta-help ya."

Lin and Bessie's children had taken Bessie to the UVA Hospital several times. The medical doctors up there could not help her or diagnose what was the matter with her. One even suggested that she go to Petersburg and let the doctors at Central State Hospital see and treat her. But Bessie said to Lin, Sr. and her children, "I don't b'lieve 'n that Black-Magic shit. I don't b'lieve in no Black Doctors or Root Workers, neither. I thinks I got female trou'ba, that's all. It'll go 'way by itself I damn-sure ain't goin' ta-no nut-house."

After Bessie had gotten sick eating cookies and drinking tea at Caroline's house, she asked Lin, Sr. to buy her a Radio so that she could listen to the stories at home. Lin didn't want her spending that much time with one of his ex' s, so he agreed. He bought Bessie an RCA Combination Radio and Record Player.

In 1940-or 41, Caroline sent for Bessie to come to a house the Witch rented from a woman named Molly Briggs. Molly asked Bessie to come hear an old lady's confession on her deathbed, because the old lady said she owed her pardon. Bessie went with Molly to hear what Caroline had to say, and then the old Witch died right away. Molly cleaned up the house, but no one would rent it. People in that part of Fluvanna were very superstitious.

On this Friday, Bessie saw Molly in Columbia while shopping. She asked her to come by early the next morning. "Gal, I got some people's who's in need-a house ta-rent. It's Henry, my Brother. He an' Mabel Scott done got hitched. They gotta child, an' I'spects, one on the way." Molly, a rotund, jolly, woman, laughed. "What'cha want me ta-do?" she asked.

"C'mon by the house in-a mornin' early. Just show up. We go give a cup'la young people a chance ta-get started on they own," Bessie said.

"Aw-ight, then. See ya in the mornin'," Molly said. She went in the direction of Walton's, and Bessie went to Thurston's.

Molly knocked on Bessie's front door early that next morning. She was a middle-aged woman graying around the edges of her thick-black hair. She wore a full-length white-dress, a thin-black overcoat, and brown lace-up boots. A "flower-garden hat" rested on top of her head.

Bessie got out of bed and put on a flannel robe. She rushed to the door, knowing who was paying her a call. "Molly, how're ya doin'? C'mon in the house, child. Good ta-see ya this mornin'."

Molly came into the front-room area of the house. Mabel and Henry were in the kitchen area.

Henry sat at the table eating breakfast. Mabel stood at the stove sipping out of a cup of coffee. "Molly, I want ya ta-meet my Brother Henry, an' his little wife, Mabel," Bessie said. "Please ta-meet y'all," Molly said.

"Likewise," said Henry. He got up from the table and came over to touch hands with Molly. "How ya <loin'," said Mabel. She came over to shake Molly's hand as well.

"I hear that y'all's lookin' for-a place ta-rent?" Molly said.

"I'on kno' where ya heard it, but ya right on the money," Henry replied. "Yes, ma'am," Mabel seconded him.

"Molly, wanna cup-a coffee?" Bessie asked. She had a righteous grin on her broad lips. "Don't mind ifn I do," said Molly. She followed Bessie into the kitchen. Mabel and Henry followed them.

Once Molly got the cup of coffee, she sat at the table. So did Bessie, Mabel and Henry. Lin had gotten up earlier and made the fire in the kitchen. He was out feeding the chickens and hogs. He came into the house and took a seat in the front-room area.

Molly took a sip out of her cup of coffee. "Henry-Mabel, the house's near 'bout-a mile straight up the path an' cross the road up yonder. Rev. Nicholas's house's right next ta-it, an' Marr' Dee's house's on the next hill. Gimme five dollars now, an' y'all can move in it anytime ya wanna. Ya gotta clean the place a-little, an' paint an' whitewash it a bit; but other'n that, it's good-ta-go." Molly smiled. "It'll cost five-a month. What'cha, say?"

Bessie smiled even wider when Henry took out his wallet, got out a five-spot and handed it over to Molly. "Thank ya, Mr. James," Molly said. "I just happen-ta have the keys ta-it right here in my pocket on a little chain. There ya go," said Molly. She handed the keys to Henry.

"We go be movin' in directly," Henry said. Mabel frowned a little. She hadn't had a say at all before Henry made the deal for them both.

Bessie was glad about what had just happened, thinking: *I'm glad Mabel's go be leavin '. I ain'go tell'em'bout that Caroline-mess. They might b'lieve in that Black-Magic Shit! Then they won't move out. They go be fine- ain't nothin' toll ta-that shit, nohow. Now, if'n Mabel tell Henry anythin 'bout Burton, I ain't go own-up-ta-it.*

Molly, a nut-brown woman, with seemingly Native-American features, stood up. All at the table stood up as well.

"Thank y'all, very kindly, for the coffee, the rent, an' all, but I gotta go," Molly said. "Aw-ight," said Mabel and then Henry.

"I'll see ya ta-the door," Bessie said.

Lin whispered as Molly and Bessie went over to the door: "Bessie, ya didn't tell 'em'bout the house?"

"No-Gawd, Lin! We'd never get rid-a 'em, then. They gotta 'root little pig' just like we had da do," Bessie whispered.

"Goodbye, Molly. See ya round. Take care," said Bessie. She waved as

Molly walked briskly down the path towards Cary's house. Bessie figured that her boyfriend, or common-law husband, Jeffrey Buggs, was waiting down on the road to take Molly back home to Kents Store, over near Stage Junction. He drove a brand-new Buick.

Bessie called Henry to the front-room area. "Henry, did ya kno' that they's auctionin' off stuff from old man Stiles's store today? Ya heard 'bout that?"

"No, Big Sis. I ain't heard nothin'toll 'bout that," Henry said.

"Well ... I heard they got a lotta furniture, dishes, pots an' pans an' stuff-some-a it's good as new. I seen-a a cup'la beds an' mattress sets that looks pret' nice. Y'all ought-a get down-ta Columbia today fore too many peoples beat y'all ta-the punch. Arthur Walton's go be in charge a the auction. You's workin' for Kent Brothers. You're be able ta-get most-a what ya needs on time-I bet," Bessie said.

"Bessie, I reek-en I better go on down yonder, then. Lemme finish eatin' an' I 'ma get right on down there. It couldn't come at-a better time, too," Henry said.

"Lemme go with ya, Henry," Mabel asked.

"No. Me an' Lin go have-ta barr' a truck from the Boss. We gotta walk down yonder to the Mill. The Boss's house's just up the hill from it. That's three-four miles. I got the keys ta-the house. Lin an' I can swing what I buys right on over ta-the house. What' ya can do is, get our stuff read-ta-go, so when I come back we can get goin'," Henry said.

Mabel wished Henry had given her a chance to help decide on what they were going to do with the rest of their lives. Then she got sick to her stomach. She ran outside to vomit. She, Bessie, Henry, and Lin *knew-Mabel's Pregnant Again!*

Bessie gave Mabel a set of silverware, some curtains, draperies, sheets and pillowcases, and a couple of quilts. Lin had given them a set of homemade knives, he had made. Late that evening, Henry and Lin returned in the truck. Henry was driving. They had delivered a load of furniture and things to the old house up the road. Mabel asked: "What 'cha ya buy, Henry?"

"Well ... Mabel, I gotta King size bed, four chairs an' a old kitchen table-in good shape though-an' one-half-a double-bed set for Billy. I gotta Warm Momin' Heater, a cup'la blankets, a set-a used dishes-good as new-an' a set of used fryin' pans, two cookin' pots an' a cup'la servin forks an' spoons. Walton gave us a set-a drinkin'-glasses. I's able ta-charge-a week's groceries from Walton. We got flour, lard, bakin' powder, fatback, coffee, ten-pounds-a brown beans, an' a lotta canned fish; an' ten-pounds of onions, an' taters. We good-ta-go," Henry said. He gave a little chuckle.

"Guess, all we's gotta do is go get ta-goin'," Mabel said.

Lin shook hands vigorously with Henry. "I's proud-a ya decision ta-give Mabel an' Billy a chance, Henry," he said. "I gotta feelin' you's go be glad ya did."

Bessie hugged Mabel. "Mabel take the bull by the horns, gal, an' handle ya bizzness, now," she said.

"Oh ... Mabel, Henry, I gotta little surprise for y'all. Henry c'mon go with me ta-the back a the house. I's go need ya help, boy. I ain' strong as I use-ta be," Lin said.

Mabel watched as Lin and Henry came from behind the house carrying a Cedar Chest Lin had made as a house-warming gift. She jumped up and down with glee. "Thank ya, Lin. Thank ya, Bessie. I 'ma cherish this piece-a furniture for the rest-a my life."

Lin and Henry loaded the Chest onto the back of the truck. Lin hugged Henry and patted him on his back. "You take care now," Lin said.

"I got ya," Henry replied.

Henry and Mabel got into the truck's cab. Mabel rolled down the window on her side. She shouted as Henry cranked up the motor: "Bessie, I'm go come listen-ta the stories with ya some a these days till I getta radio-a my own."

"Sure, Sugar. Come back an' see me anytime ya wanna." Bessie's stomach started hurting like something awful. Maybe it was because it was bigger than in previous years. She just whined to Lin like before. (Or maybe, it was just psychosomatic guilt?")

In about fifteen minutes Mabel and Henry arrived at "their new home." It was dusk dark, but Mabel could see the once whitewashed building with a rusty tin-roof The house seemed to look like a huge, erected, penis to Mabel. The gable hole in front of the house was strange indeed. It seemed like an "Inverted Star" or something to her. All or most of the whitewash had peeled off the two-story edifice, showing corpse-gray boards with red streaks coming from the nails in them-that looked a lot like they were bleeding. Two gable-windows under the Star seemed like large-vacant eyes. The front door was like a twisted mouth on the left side of the building, next to a window to the right of the doorway. Mabel thought she saw a pair of reddish-yellow cat eyes staring out of the window. She wondered how it could've gotten in there. What was once shutters on that window were dangling and tom almost off the house. Then, the cat eyes disappeared. So far, Mabel had a bad feeling about that house.

Henry turned off the motor of the truck. Mabel thought the wind started to pick up right away. It got her a little nervous. The wind in the trees seemed to her to have a distinctive voice. It seemed to be saying: "Be-e-e-e, Wa-r-r-r-e-e-e!" But Henry didn't seem like her heard it.

Henry did notice Mabel's fear. "Don't be 'fraid, Mabel. The wind-a blow up that hill down yonder kind-a hard, betimes. It ain't nothin'. Round old houses it's like that, I think. Houses's like peoples, they gets myster'ous when they's left-ta theyselves."

Henry got out of the truck first, then Mabel. Seemed like, to Mabel, that when they approached the front door, it opened all by itself.

"Mabel, I gotta key, here. Oh, I must've left the door unlocked," Henry said.

Mabel wondered did Henry see that door opening by itself?" She figured, too, that he should've noticed how unnerving the squeaky noise it made while opening was, but he seemed not to have.

Henry had a flashlight. "Mabel, there's a bunch-a lamps already in here. Lin an' I filled them with kerosene, earlier. We ain' gotta buy none-a them. I 'ma light-a cup'la them."

After Henry lit the first lamp in the hallway on a little table beside some steps that led to the upstairs area, the bright orb that it cast lit-up the stairway that was only about five foot from the front door. There was a little foyer in that area around the stairway.

When Henry lit another lamp on a table near the back of the foyer, that light shone on the stairway as well. Mabel was alarmed at what she thought she saw. There were what seemed like pine-knots that went in a line from the front of the ceiling at the door straight to its edge at the top of the steps. The steps of the stairway and the ceiling were of rough-pine-lumber. The pine knots perfectly resembled a human's hand-print. The walls of the foyer were of planed, tongue and-groove pine-boards that seemed like they had human eyes all over them.

Mabel was shocked at what she saw. The hand-prints and the eyes on the boards even got Henry's attention. He went to the back of the foyer to the door to an open room, got a lamp out of there and lit it. Lin and he had set up the beds and heater in that room.

"Mabel, Lin an' I set up the heater, did a flue sweep with rags on-a pole, and set up the bed frames. I don't 'member seein' all this shit up in the ceilin'. This's strange as hell. Ma-be, the builder found-a tree with the markin's we's seein', but I ain' never seen nothin' like it, have you?"

"Me neither," Mabel said.

"Mabel, let's go upstairs an' see what the hell's up yonder."

Mabel followed close behind Henry. They slowly climbed the squeaky stairs. At the top of the stairs, they saw an old, rusty, cast-iron bed with white-sheets, a black goose-down quilt with a replica of the star, in red, that Mabel had noticed was the gable-hole. The bed was directly under that gable-hole with covers folded back like somebody had just gotten up and was going to shortly return. There was a little walkway that led to another open room. There was nothing in that room but a hole in a flue for a heater's pipe, rough-boarded walls, and bared hardwood floors. The moonlight was shining through the gable windows giving the room a scary haze.

"Henry, this room, smell, bad. It's mighty stuffy in here," said Mabel. "It stinks!"

"Yep, I know it. We go have-ta get our elbow grease-ta workin' on the mess in this house. "Mabel, look over in the middle-a the floor. What's that? Iain' never seen no drawin' like that before," Henry said.

"Me neither," Mabel replied.

"I wonder what that thing-that drawin'-is? It gotta big O' circle with-a star in it, an' a goat's head in the middle-a the Star. I ain' never seen that kind-a writin' that's all round that circle. It must be foreign language, or somethin'," said Henry. "Now, that's some strange shit. I' on kno' what that mean."

"I wonder who the hell live-in this room in this house?" Mabel said, with a profound frown on her face. "I bet who-so-never it t'was, was-a-strange-bird!

"Let's go down an' make up the beds downstairs. We gotta turn this house into-a home," Mabel said. But for some reason, she was as nervous as could be.

Henry lit all four of the lamps in the open room on the first floor. Mabel got busy unpacking the boxes full of bedding and other things they needed to get started. After making up the bed they would sleep in on the right side of the room after coming through the door, Henry, who was always very full of energy, got undressed very quickly, got into bed, and fell asleep right away. He immediately started snoring loudly, like the noise of a boar-hog grunting.

While Henry was snoring, Mabel blew out one of the lamps. She undressed down to her panties and brazier. It seemed like someone, or something, snatched her dress out of her hands. It fell to the floor. To Mabel, the room's temperature dropped suddenly to near freezing all at once. It was like a little wind blew through the windows-but they were not up-and blew out the remaining of the lamps. By the pale moonlight, Mabel dashed to the bed and got in it beside Henry. He seemed dead to the world. The chill Mabel felt went all the way to her bones. Her chills made her teeth chatter. She had a hard time getting to sleep after that experience. When she did, she slept restively, awaking often to what sounded like someone walking around upstairs. But it was like in a weird dream, or nightmare.

The next morning, the sun came up very bright and beautiful. It shone through bared windows because Mabel hadn't had a chance to put up any draperies or curtains, yet. Her morning sickness revived. She ran outside to vomit. A huge Black Snake came out of the woods, slithering up the path that led to another house on the hill north of where Mabel stood. It was not time for the snake season. That was in May. This was late March. The Snake had blood-red eyes, and it stopped in the middle of the path, raised its huge head, and let out its red forked-tongue at Mabel. It hissed, then, disappeared.

Mabel was thinking: *I 's more 'fraid-a things I can't see. Long's I can see it, I can deal with it!* But an annoying fear emanated from down in her stomach. She knew she was a couple of months pregnant. With Billy, morning sickness only lasted for a couple of weeks. But here she was puking again with this baby, after going on three months. She had to wonder about that.

When Mabel came back into the house, she saw cobwebs, and dust bunnies everywhere. The place seemed like some place decorated for Halloween. She got on a pair of Jean shorts that came up to just below the knee, a bulky sweat shirt belonging to Henry, and no shoes.

In the kitchen, Mabel saw a large cook stove. It had eight eyes, an oven, and a big warmer on top. It appeared to be green overcast by yellow, under an inch of baked-on grease. The eyes had a thick layer of soot on them. The oven was dirty gray with baked-on grease on the bottom of it.

Mabel went to the spring down a path south of the house, got a bucket of water, came back and used lard, Octagon Soap, and elbow grease to clean her stove. She got it fairly clean after some frantic work. There was a shine on it that she was proud of. She took the ash-pan outside to dump it. It had a lot of animal bones mixed into the ashes. Mabel wondered, what the hell was that? She had gotten so dirty she had to change into one of the pretty dresses that A'nt Maetta had made for her. Then it was time to cook breakfast for the first time for her husband in "their new home." She made a roaring fire in the stove.

Mabel heard Henry getting up that morning. He called out to Mabel: "Mabel, c'mere."

She took her hands out of the pan she had sifted a mound of flour into. She was getting ready to make biscuits, using a jar of clabbered milk she had brought along the day before. "Okay, Henry, I'll be right in," Mabel said. She dusted the flour off her hands using an apron she had made for herself while staying at Bessie's. She came into the bedroom. Henry sat on the side of the bed in his T-shirt and undershorts. She hoped he didn't "want-ta fuck!"

"Mabel . . . I had the weirdest dream last night: *I dreamt that A'nt Leah, Poppa's Aunt, came an' hugged me. Her hands and arms were ice-cold She whispered: 'Boy, you's go be aw-ight. Take care-a Mabel's Chillun, now. God's go give ya a Special Blessin'. Ya go be the Father-a Seven Sons!'*

"I could see 'er Mabel, plain as day. She was Black as the night, but a white light shone all 'round 'er, like the sunlight. She's one-a Poppa's oldest Aunts who died from TB, back in the twenties. She's a woman of God, though, Mabel. Never been with-a man that anybody knowed 'bout. She said: 'I's marri'd-ta Gawd!' Some peoples thought-a 'er as a Saint. Least they saw 'er as 'Truly Holy!' Mabel that dream must've mean somethin'. A'nt Leah was wearin' a-long white-gown. I's one-a her favorite Nephews. She told me that all the time, an' again last night."

Tears came to Mabel's eyes. "C'mon, then, let's get this place cleaned, and all. We can see that the Spirit 's with us. That dream is a good sign."

"Aw-ght," said Henry. It seemed like several neighborhood dogs started barking. Then one howled too loud for a dog. It sounded more like a wolf. A cat screamed like it was the scream of a she-cat when a Tom gets lucky.

Henry got dressed in a blue and plaid flannel shirt, Bibb overalls and brown Brogan shoes. He came into the kitchen, got two, two-gallon, buckets and headed to the spring to get more water to cook with and to wash his hands and face.

He was back from the spring in a jiffy. Mabel said: "Oh, good, now I can make gravy." She had fried some fatback in a cast-iron skillet, breaded and fried slices of hog shoulder in the fatback grease, and made a paste by stirring in flour in the hot grease until it browned. After Henry gave her the water, she poured in water out of a dipper and stirred slowly until she had a brown gravy. She then put in the slices of browned shoulder and let that simmer until they were very tender. She scrambled some eggs Bessie had given her the day before, baked the biscuits she had made; and, Mabel had cooked her first breakfast in her "new home."

While sitting down at the breakfast table, Mabel got a faraway look in her eyes. She was almost afraid to say what was on her mind. Seemed to her, Henry was still resentful of her, or was scornful of her, still. He wasn't looking her directly in the eye. He was looking past her, or something. She thought she had heard him cussing at her under his breath a couple of times.

She figured, nothing would fail her but a try. "Henry, now that we's in-a house, less go get Billy, so he can be with his Momma an' his Daddy," said Mabel in somewhat of a whine. I know that A'nt Maetta done took good care-a 'im, cause she love 'im so much; but, I kno' it's best for-a child-ta be with his real parents-an' A'nt Maetta ain't gettin' no younger."

Mabel expected Henry to blow his top. When he cleared his throat, took a sip of coffee and smiled, it shocked Mabel to the good.

"Guess you's right, Mabel. I got the truck for the whole weekend.

May as well go on up yonder-ta West Bottom an' get Billy an' bring 'im on down here with us. That boy's named for his Great Uncle, William Anderson James. Ev 'body calls 'im Unc' Billy. He's Unc' Johnny James's Older Brother, on Poppa's side. Ev' body thinks Billy look like Poppa, but I thinks he looks more like Unc' Billy James, my Uncle. Most people say his whole name when they's talkin 'bout 'im: 'Unc' Billy Jeems,' they say."

"Well ... I be," said Mabel, with a little chortle. "I'm go have 'nether baby soon. I'm go name it 'Charles Edward James,' ifn it'sa boy, an' ifn it'sa girl, I'm go name it, 'Mary Etta James.'"

Henry looked her in the eyes, but said nothing. He had a good laugh. "Aw-ight," Henry said. "But lemme tell ya this: I gotta Brother named 'Charlie Edward.' Poppa's named that, too. Then I gotta Cousin named 'Charlie Edward Ross.' I got 'nether one named 'Charlie Edward Dabney.' Joe Bradley gotta Brother named 'Charlie Edward Bradley.' Then there's a 'Charlie Edward Anderson; an', Charlie Edward Armstrong'; and, all-a them is kinfolks."

"Y'all sure loves that name," said Mabel. "It'sa cute name is why. I likes it." "Dam-straight," said Henry. He had a serious tone to his voice.

"Aw-ight, then," said Mabel with a tone to her voice signaling that "It is done." "Let's go on up yonder than Mabel," Henry said.

Mabel and Henry got in the truck and he cranked it up. Mabel hoped Henry would never hear about what she had been up too with Wayne Nicholas. Wayne was in prison and probably would never get out. But although things were seemingly going her way for the moment, the joy she hoped she would feel was not there. The feelings of doubt and fear grew worse for some reason, the closer they got to A'nt Maetta's.

Henry stopped the truck up the hill from his childhood home. Both he and Mabel bounced out of the truck at the same time.

"Lordy! Lordy! Lord!" A'nt Maetta shouted. She limped up towards the truck dragging her left leg behind her with a lot of effort. Henry noticed that his Mother was slurring the endings of some of her words. It was like her tongue was getting too tired to function correctly.

"Hi, Mabel. Hi, Henry. How y'all doin'?" A'nt Maetta called out. "Momma, why ya limpin' so bad?" Henry asked. He frowned a little. "A'nt Maetta, you been sick?" Mabel asked. She frowned a little more.

"I's feelin' right poorly since I last seen y'all. I'ma little bit stiff on my right side, an' my lip's-a little bit stiff on that side too. My left leg's gettin' a little worse, but that's due-ta old age, y'all-that's all."

Tears came to Mabel's eyes. "A'nt Maetta, did any-a this come on ya 'fore now," she asked. "Yep. I got sore on my right side all up an' down some time ago. But it went 'way by itself.

Even the pain got better. Left a tingle in my lips an' tongue. I ain't worri'd though. Gawd's go take-care-a me till my time come. He ain' go put no more on me then I can bare.

"'Nough 'bout me. Y'all c'mon-ta the house. I got Carp bakin' an' some collard greens, sweet 'taters, an' peach cobbler." Tears formed in the corners of A'nt Maetta's eyes. Her right eye dripped a little more teardrops than her left eye.

All three went down the hill to the house. Lawrence and Billy were seated at the kitchen table. Billy ran to his Momma. Mabel scooped him up and planted kisses all over his little face. He went to A'nt Maetta next. She picked him up and he hugged her tightly. She put him down. He tried to follow behind Lawrence. They were headed to the boys' room.

Henry allowed: "Ya-don't see nobody but ya Momma, boy? I'm ya Daddy-y'know that don't ya?" He was looking through Billy, and he was scared stiff

"Uh-huh," said Billy. He put his little left-thumb in his mouth. He reluctantly inched over to his "mean Daddy," sucking hard on his thumb.

Henry pulled his little Son roughly to him, but kept him at arm's length. He ordered: "Now, get ya little ass on in that room, an' don't come out till I call ya."

A'nt Maetta and Mabel stared angrily at Henry. A'nt Maetta pointed her left trigger-finger at him and said nothing, but just shook her head. Mabel spoke in muffled terms: "Stupid bas'sard!"

Lawrence sat on the bed in the boys' room. Billy came in and sat beside him. He had taken to calling Lawrence "Big Bra."

A'nt Maetta came into the room and picked Billy up. She realized that it was time for Billy to go with his parents. She cried out: "I's hopin' y'all would lemme keep 'im. He's more like my own son, now. I'on kno' what I 'ma do without 'im being up here with me. Can't y'all leave 'im with me for awhile?"

"A'nt Maetta I knows ya loves'im. I knows you'd take good care-a Billy. But I'm of-a mind that a child's parents's go raise 'im best," Mabel said.

A'nt Maetta turned to Henry with tears streaming down her cheeks. "Boy, you's s'pose-ta lemme take care-a this child. Why' d ya change?" she asked.

"I done turn-over-a new leaf, I reek-en," Henry said. He walked over and put his arms around his sobbing Mother. "Momma, A'nt Leah came-ta-me in-a dream the other night. Saw 'er plain as day. She's wearin' all white. She tol' me: 'Don't ya worry. God's go give ya Seven Sons with Mabel.' That-sa Blessin' by itself I ain' much for no 'legion, but I pays 'tention-ta dreams. I b'lieves Gawd send those."

A'nt Maetta sat down at the kitchen table. "Poppa's A'nt Leah's Holy. People knowed that 'bout Leah James. She gotta be up yonder with Gawd-Almighty. But it hurts me so bad ta-think 'bout Billy leavin'. I'll get his things read-ta-go, but I don't wanna do that. I wish y'all would just lemme keep 'im."

She got up from the table and limped over to her bedroom. She got Billy's clothes out of there, and the rest out of the boys' room. She put those in a couple of paper shopping bags. She handed those to Henry. "C'mere, Billy."

He came over to his Grandma. "Ya gotta go with ya Momma an' Daddy, Son," A'nt Maetta said.

Mabel picked Billy up. She held him against her stomach that was beginning to protrude.

Billy squirmed to get down and away from his Momma. But Mabel held tight to him. He reached out for "Grandma," even though his Momma and Daddy dragged him away towards the truck. Once they reached the truck, Billy yelled out: "Grandma . . . Grandma . . . I love you, Grandma. I love you, Grandma ..."

After Henry slammed the door to the truck he snapped: "Ah, shut the hell up, boy. I can see that Momma done spoilt you."

Mabel went silent. She stared at the truck's flooring. She tightly clung to Billy. She had one baby kicking in her stomach and another one squirming in her arms.

Henry drove the truck towards Gravel Hill. Billy continued to softly whimper. "Boy, I done told ya ta-shut that shit up. Mabel, ya better quiet that boy down ifn ya know what's good for 'im."

Mabel's nerves got the better of her. "Henry, stop the truck, I gotta puke," Mabel warned. Henry stopped the truck. Mabel jumped out to the side of the road and vomited into the ditch.

She got back into the truck, and there was silence for the rest of the way home.

When they arrived at the house, it looked like a horrible place to Billy. The house looked like a balled-up fist with a thumb sticking up into the air. Henry went into the house first. Then Mabel and Billy followed behind him. A strange wind came up the hill and blew the front door shut, "Blam!" it went, behind them.

Billy clung to his Momma's skirt tail for a while after entering the house. A nervousnessinside of Billy made him feel as though something bad was going to happen at any moment.

(If thou doest well, shalt thou not be accepted? And if thou doest not well, sin lieth at the door. And unto thee shall be his desire, and thou shalt rule over him.) GENSIS 4:7, KJV.

"Mabel, you finis' cleanin' up, I 'ma take the truck back, an' I'm go be right back," said Henry. That strange wind started blowing again. It suddenly stopped. Henry stood for a moment staring at the ceiling. His facial appearance changed. His eyes got a deep-yellow glow to them. His voice came out in a kind of growl.

"Y'all kno' what-ta do 'round here-now, go do it!" Henry ordered. He headed out to the truck in great haste. It was like he was being chased by something he feared. He got in the truck, cranked it up, and sped away, scratching a wheel and kicking up a lot of dust. When he got up to the rough unpaved road (656), he pressed the button on the steering column for the horn and it blew loud and long. He turned right onto the road and stepped down hard on the gas pedal. He sped up the road like a teenager on a joy ride. He felt like he had to get away from something, but he did not quite know what it was. Then he couldn't remember what the hell was going on-or had gone on.

The last few minutes of Henry standing in the house before leaving had eluded him. He could only remember driving down the road to the house. He couldn't place what had happened next. It made him feel very strange. It was like he was awakening from a nightmare, daydream, or day-mare. Then he noticed that his whole body was hot and sweaty like he had a fever or something. He felt like he needed a drink to cool down-a cold beer maybe.

Mabel didn't know what to make of what had just happened. She saw a little smile come to Billy's face. She knew he was glad that his Daddy had gone away for the moment. She hoped Billy and his Daddy would grow to love and respect each other.

Mabel got into a pair of Henry's rough pants and one of his old shirts and went to the nearby spring to get two buckets of water. She got busy scrubbing and cleaning the downstairs of the house. She didn't want to go upstairs again to clean or do anything else. She got both beds properly made-up, and cooked supper. She made Mackerel Fishcakes, mashed potatoes, and warmed up a couple of cans of spinach. She baked rolls and put a pot of coffee on the stove. She moved the Fishcakes and potatoes onto the back of the stove, and put the rolls in the overhead warmer-oven. Billy ate and fell asleep in Mabel's lap. He had stayed close to her all evening. Sometimes he clung to her skirt tail like he was afraid to let go. Mabel undressed him and put him to bed in his undershirt and trainer-briefs. She lit the four lamps between the kitchen and the open-room area where the warm morning heater and the beds were. In a wicker chair Mabel sat near a lamp to try to read a True Story Magazine. She had been practicing reading for a couple of years, and was getting so that she could make out what a lot of the words meant. It was easier with True Story because Mabel loved reading about romance in magazines.

It was getting late, but there was no sign of Henry. Mabel wondered where he had to drive that truck back to-Africa of somewhere, maybe. She got undressed down to her panties and brazier, blew out the lamps and slipped into bed. Then, the front door creaked open and slammed shut all by itself. Mabel got out of bed. Sounded like somebody, or something, was walking up the steps. Mabel got a strike-anywhere match, struck it and lit a lamp that sat on a little mantle over near the heater. Then-

Mabel looked out the window. She saw an old woman dressed in a black dress and wearing a black-hooded cloak. There was some kind of amber-glow around this old woman. She was in no hurry. She seemed to be gliding down the road like a feather on the wind. A small cloud blotted out the full-moonlight for a couple of seconds. When it passed, the woman had disappeared.

(It was said that Mabel and her Brother George were born with veils over their faces that made them psychic, and enabled them to see ghosts. Mabel had seen Dora's little Son, Charlie, after his death many times. When a couple of little-poor-White children who had lived just up the road from Mabel got struck by lightning and killed, when Mabel went past their home-place on any rainy night, she said she could see the little boy and girl playing in the mud at the edge of the riverbanks, like they had been doing on the evening they were killed)

So, seeing a ghost did not exactly scare Mabel as it would have some people. As a matter of fact, now that she had seen it, she was not afraid of it at all. Mabel went back to bed and drifted off to sleep.

In the wee hours of the morning, Henry stumbled through the front door of the house drunk as a skunk. He staggered over to bedside. Mabel had left the lamp she had lit, burning.

"I been over-ta Bessie's. I gotta cup'la drinks," said Henry. The lit lamp seemingly made Henry mad-as-hell!

Henry yelled: "Bitch, why ya usin' up all the damn-oil, for? Ya scared-a the dark, or somethin'?"

Mabel squinted up her eyes so that she'd be able to see her drunken husband clearly. "Nawh, I heard strange noises in the house. I just wanted-ta see what it was. I'm aw-ight if'n I can see what tis; and ya don't have-ta call me no Bitch!"

Henry got a twisted snarl on his lips. "Now, ya sound like ya slut-Momma. She's stupid as hell, an' so's you."

"I ain' done nothin' toll to ya for ya ta-be cussin' at me like that, Henry. What ya mad at me for?" asked Mabel in a whimper. She was becoming very nervous.

"Lemme tell ya what I thinks," Henry growled. "I want ya ta-carry ya ass back over yonder ta-Cumberland. I'd take Billy back up yonder ta-Momma's, an' ya go your way an' I go mine."

"Henry ya ain't gotta be so mean-ta me in my del'cate condition. You knocked me up again.

This one's your'n, too. I ain't goin' nowheres, an' Billy ain't neither," Mabel replied. "I'll show ya how del' get I thinks you is," Henry shouted.

Henry undid his belt, let his pants fall down to his shoes, sat down in the wicker chair and untied his shoes, then, he threw his pants and shoes aside with a quick motion. He practically tore his shirt and underwear off and threw them across the floor. He grabbed Mabel and pulled her to his side of the bed. He tore her panties off He was snorting like an enraged beast.

He suddenly pried Mabel's legs apart. He dropped down between them all at once; and, without any foreplay, he guided his rigid penis into her un-lubricated vagina. He thrust himself deep into her by pushing hard all at once. He paid no attention to the pain he was causing Mabel. "Oh . . . Henry, ya don't have-ta be so damn rough! Just lemme get ready. Ow-w-w-w, I wanna give-it-up ta-ya. Sto-o-o-op! you's hurtin' me real bad. Ya don't have-ta jam ya dick in my dry pussy like that, Henry. What ya doin' that for, ya crazy-ass fool?" Mabel screamed. "Bitch, I'm go show ya what-a who'e like you is, is for," Henry said out of the comer of his mouth, then he snarled like a dog. He sucked the nipples of Mabel's breasts, then he bit her left one, hard.

Mabel grimaced and screamed out: "I hate ya for that, Henry. Ya can get this any time ya want it. But ya don't have-ta never hurt me like that again. I don't mind ya being a little rough, but you's actin' crazy like-a wild dog, or somethin'. Ya know I's pregnant, ya want me ta-lose it?"

What she said must've just made Henry madder, because he rammed deeper inside her harder and harder like he may have been trying to abort her baby. "Shut the hell up, Bitch!" he snapped at Mabel.

Billy was awakened by his Mother's cries. He wanted to run to her, to try to defend her, but he was too afraid of his "Mean Daddy." He was scared to move or to breathe too hard. So, he cried himself back to sleep, after letting go of his piss.

Mabel was near fainting when Henry rolled off her. He went fast asleep like he had done nothing to anyone.

Weeping was all Mabel could do. She hurt real bad down there. Her "pussy" was on fire. It felt like someone had cut into it with a dull knife. She felt like killing Henry. When he had "busted her cherry," it hadn't felt that bad-it surely hadn't hurt that much. She wondered what in the hell

242

had gotten into her husband. He was like a brute beast, or a mad dog-or a Wolf. Mabel bled some, but did not miscarry her baby. She was "grateful to God," for that.

The next morning Henry got up, put on his work clothes, and went into the kitchen, made fire in the cook stove, and went outside to the woodpile to cut-up enough firewood for Mabel to cook breakfast and supper that day. He was acting like he didn't remember what he had done to Mabel the night before.

When Henry came back into the house, Mabel got out of bed. It pained her to stand up. She watched Henry, with a puzzled look on his face, get the water buckets and go to the spring to get the water needed for cooking and drinking. Mabel sat on the side of the bed crying softly. A little crimson circle stained the sheet she was sitting on. Henry came back into the house and put the two water buckets on a stand in the kitchen. He saw Mabel sitting on the side of the bed whimpering.

"Gal, what's the matter with you? Why ya ain' up?" Henry asked. "What ya whinin 'bout, now?"

"No, that ain't the question. It's mo' what's the hell's the matter with you last night?" Mabel said.

"Nothin' toll," said Henry. "I's just a little drunk is all. Whatever, I didn't mean no harm.

What I do?" Henry asked, feigning innocence.

"Rape! That's what ya did ta-me. Iain' never been raped before. Iain' think it's go be by my own husband, neither. I don't know what I'll do ta-ya Henry ifn ya ever try that shit again. Much as I love ya, I'll do somethin' bad ta-ya in ya sleep," Mabel snapped.

Billy got out of bed and got the nerve to run over to his mother. Henry spied the piss-circle on Billy's training-briefs. He snatched off his belt. He seized Billy's left arm and slung the child to the floor. He began whipping the child like he was beating an offending dog.

"Daddy, don't kill me," Billy screamed. "Momma, help me!"

Mabel ran over to Henry. He was standing over Billy with both of his fists balled up. He was eyeing his Son like he wanted to pummel him like a boxer would a punching bag. He had dropped the belt to the floor. Mabel became hysterical.

"Don't ya hit my baby no more, Henry. She grabbed a cast-iron poker and came at Henry swinging it wildly. She put the poker down and got one of the knives Bessie and Lin had given them, and came running towards Henry. She had a crazed look in her eyes.

"I'ma get the hell outta here an' go-ta work. I'll get somethin' ta-eat in Columbia. I'ma go up to the road to catch the Truck-ta work. Ya better get that little piss-ant of your'n trained," Henry said. He dashed out of the front door. Mabel hadn't packed him any lunch or anything like that.

Scenes like the above occurred weekly. Henry's hostilities always got started over Billy: his wetting the bed; the way he ate or didn't eat his food; and, the stupid look he had on his face, that made Henry think he was off-or crazy. But Mabel stayed with him. He never raped her again, but never showed any kindness or tenderness to her as a lover. Everything that Mabel said about anything, Henry considered that the most stupid thing he'd ever heard.

The day came for Mabel to be delivered of her Second Son. Henry got his Brother-in-law, Roy to take him in his car (a Model-A Ford), to get Mrs. Cooper. A boy was born in September, 1951.

Mabel named the child, "Charles Edward James," as she had promised. From day-one his nickname was, "Dick." After looking at Dick's hands a couple of days after his birth, Henry declared: "This boy's go play music. Bet he go be a 'Lady-Killer' too. He's go be a chip off'n the o' block."

Mabel and Mrs. Cooper just laughed at Henry. He seemed very proud of Dick, a nut-brown boy with a head full of wavy-black hair and sparkling-brown eyes.

In July of 1952, Mabel had a Third Son. Henry took one look at this light-brown baby that looked just like his Father, and named him, "Henry Levi James." Henry never liked his middle name. It was from the poorest, darkest, segment of his kinfolks. So he replaced "Anderson" with "Levi." He nicknamed his newborn Son, "Bug." Bug came into the world with orange tinted-brown skin, greenish-brown eyes, and a head full of very-nappy reddish-brown hair. He was a chubby baby that had taken after Unc' Johnny James's (his Great Grandfather), side of the family.

Billy didn't like the fact that his new Brothers took up most of his Mother's attention. He found a "Friend" in an "Imaginary Dog" he played with. It was black, and came up out of the ground one day and barked for Billy to come out and play with it. No one else seemed to be able to see the "Dog." It would never let Billy touch, or pet, it. One day, it howled: "B-e-e-e-ware e-e-e!" and disappeared never to appear again.

CHAPTER FIFTEEN

In May, 1953, when Dick was a year and eight-months old, Bug was just over eight months old, and Billy was nearing six, Billy was outside playing with another imaginary dog that had just suddenly popped up out of the ground. It too would not let him pet it. This one was brown, almost light-skinned. It would vanish as soon as an adult came along. But it came back to play with Billy every day.

During the day, Billy would sometimes come inside to ask his Mother for a cold biscuit to snack on. He loved cold biscuits.

On this day, Billy meant to run into the house to ask for a cold biscuit. The sight he ran into scared and shocked him.

Marr' Dee's Son, Bird had been coming over each day to listen to the new battery-operated radio that Henry had bought to listen to the News in the evenings, to listen to the "Stories" with Mabel. Mabel had cautioned Billy, "Don't tell ya Daddy 'bout nobody comin' round ta-listen ta the radio with Momma-aw-ight?"

"Aw-ight, Momma," Billy replied. He made up in his mind: "Iain' go tell my 'Mean Daddy' nothing about Momma."

When Billy came into the bedroom area, he saw his Mother lying on top of the bedcovers with no clothes on. She had her legs wrapped around a tall man, who had his Jeans and underwear pulled down to his ankles. He was pounding a pole that resembled a "Big Nail" m and out of his Mother. The "Nail" went in and out of a red-hole between his Mother's legs that was just below a patch of thick-black hair.

Each time the tall man pushed the "Nail" into his Mother, Billy heard

246

her groan like it was hurting her. Her face twitched and her tongue came out of her mouth. She had her eyes shut tight. Billy thought that Bird was attacking his Mother. He misunderstood her passion and pleasure for pain.

"Leave Momma alone," Billy shouted. "Get off her." He ran towards Bird with his little fists balled up, crying so loud he woke Bug and Dick up. They started to cry too.

Bird, a gangling young man, Mabel's age, rolled off Mabel, pulled up his undershorts and blue Jeans. He was wearing a yellow sweatshirt. He smiled. "I-I-I go-go-go see-see-see- ya lay lay-later, Mabel," he stammered. He dashed into the little hallway then went outside.

Billy ran to the window to watch the man go down the path towards Marr' Dee's house up on the north hill from his house. He turned to look at his Mother.

Mabel rolled herself up in the bedcovers. Her eyes trembled a little. Her lips quivered. She gently bit her bottom lip. Her eyes became moist. The guilt of being caught even by her little Son was great.

"Did he hurt ya Momma?" Billy asked. He watched her scramble out of the bedcovers to get a dress and pulled that on over her nude body. She got a pair of black panties off the floor and slid those on and pulled them up under her dress.

"No, Baby. Ya can't never tell ya Daddy what ya seen, though, honey," Mabel said. "What was you doing?" Billy asked.

Mabel searched her mind for just the right answer. Then she opined: "We's <loin' the 'Huckle Buck.' It'sa dance grown peoples do. It's bad, so ya can't tell nobody,'specially ya Daddy. This gotta be our little secret, Billy-aw-ight?" Mabel said.

"Uh-huh. Daddy's real mean to me. Iain' go tell 'im nothing about you, Momma. He might hurt us again. I don't want 'im to hit me no more," Billy whined. He stuck his left thumb into his mouth. "Momma, can I get a piece-a bread, please?"

"Aw-ight, go head on into the kitchen. It'sa pan-a it on the back of the table leftover, get all ya want. Henry's just go give it ta-the hog, anyway," Mabel said.

Billy skipped away to the kitchen got two pieces of bread, one for himself, and one for his "Dog Friend."

Mabel pondered the facts: *I hope Billy don't understand what he seen me doin'. Cause Bird's so light-skinned, Henry'l! prob-be kill us both. If'n Henry weren't so mean ta-me, I won't do that with Bird or nobody else. He never told me he love me. He won't even kiss me no more. He just get in the bed, get on top of me, get his nuts, an' forget 'bout me. I never get pleased I need-a man ta-love me. I wanna feel like-a woman, not a thing just there ta-get fucked.*

Bird came by less often after Billy had caught him on top of Mabel. Mabel and he were much more discrete after that mishap. When Bird would show up Billy would think that "Momma's <loin' the 'Huckle Buck' again." He stayed out of the way until Bird left, smiling and winking at him. But Billy thought too, "The 'Huckle Buck's' nasty!"

Billy wandered on this day to the house next to his on Route 656. It was a two-story green and white edifice belonging to Rev. Nicholas, Bird's Uncle. When Billy came running up the narrow path through the woods to Rev. Nicholas's house, a fat, jovial woman, with light skin, big lips, and big eyes came over to the edge of the woods where Billy stood. "Hey, little boy, you is Mabel's James's youngin'?" said the woman wearing a dress that came all the way down to her ankles. It had all kind of daisies all over it. She had on a white apron, and her hair was very nappy and a little bit red. She reminded Billy of his Grandma Agnes.

"Hi, little boy, I'm Edna Nicholas. I'm Rev. Nicholas's oldest Daughter," said the fat lady. The way she talked kind of reminded him of his A'nt Bessie. She had lips like her too, and the only difference was she was a lot lighter than Billy's A'nt Bessie.

"I'm Billy, Mabel's boy. I got two Brothers, Charles and Henry. They's at home with Momma. Bird's over yonder too. He's doing the 'Huckle Buck' with Momma," Billy blurted out.

"Hush, Billy. Don't say things like that. People might hear you. You gotta be careful 'bout that. Bird may get into a lotta trouble. Your Momma might disappear. You wouldn't want that to happen, would you?" said Edna.

"No ma'am," said Billy. He covered his mouth with his little hands. "I'm sorry, Edna. I don't want nobody to know, 'specially my 'Mean Daddy.' He might beat me."

"Aw-ight, but don't let nobody hear what you just told me, Billy. Be a good boy, now," Edna said.

"Okay," Billy replied.

Edna's oldest Brother, Wilbur was home on leave from Fort Bragg. He had on his olive green fatigues. He had a sharpshooter medal pinned over his left pocket, and a couple of brown stripes on each sleeve. He had a close-cut head of wavy-black hair. His lips were like those of Duke Ellington's. He had that same "Pimp-styled" mustache on his top lip. When he smiled he looked like a little-browner version of Cab Calloway. His black combat boots were spit-shined, especially the heel and toe of them. He stood erect looking at his Sister.

"Wilbur, this little boy wandered off from over yonder at Mabel James's house, over where old lady Caroline use-ta live years ago. You're a 'brave soldier' an' ain't afraid of nothing, so take this child over yonder to his Momma. I'd send Harvey an' Annette, but they's over at A'nt Marr' Dee's playin' hide-an'-go-seek with Courtney an' Gladys. Those gals are too old to be runnin' 'round in the woods. A 'Black Bear' liable to catch 'em and tear it open, or somethin', ifn you get my drift." She winked at Wilbur. She knew that he knew what kind of Black Bear she was referring to.

"Got'cha covered, Sis. I better go catch that 'Bear' before he do some real damage," said Wilbur with a laugh.

Wilbur, a six-foot muscular man took Billy's left hand with his right hand and said: "C'mon, my-man, let's go over yonder to your house." His voice was deep and mellow.

Instead of doing what he had promised Edna, Billy whispered: "Wilbur, I heard Momma an' Bird doin' the 'Huckle Buck.' Oops! I ain't s'pose-ta say that." Billy put his left hand over his mouth. Then he giggled.

"Sh-h-h-h, don't tell everybody about that, little dude. You might get somebody burnt." Wilbur saw tears come to Billy's eyes. "Why you crying, little Buddy?"

"My Cousins got burnt up," Billy whined.

"No, I didn't mean it that way ... Oh, never mind. You'll understand one day. Less hurry up and get to your house," Wilbur said.

(Wayne Nicholas told Wilbur about Mabel. Bird and Toad wanted her too. Wilbur saw taking Billy back home as an excellent chance to get what Wayne had said: "Man, that's the best piece I done ever had Soon's ya getta chance, get that gal.")

Wilbur came ditty-bopping up the path to Billy's house whistling, "Misty"

Mabel came out on the stoop in front of the house and yelled: "Bill-0-0-0. It's time ta-come home, Son. Bill-0-0-0-0. Oh." Wilbur startled her.

Wilbur came over to Mabel took a little bow and said: "Don't worry lady. I got'im. He just wandered off a little bit. He's safe. He was over with Edna, my Sister. We are Rev. Nicholas' s kids. I'm Wilbur, I got Brother and Sister twins Harvey an' Annette, an' a little Brother in Washington D.C., John, Jr. We call 'im Sonny Boy."

Mabel sat on the stoop. She extended her hand up to Wilbur. "Thank you, soldier. Now, that's so sweet of ya," said Mabel. She looked Wilbur up and down. "Where ya stationed an' what do ya do in the Services?" Her eyes came to rest at the center of his manhood.

"I'm private second-class, and I'm going to be shipped to Maryland to be trained as a Military Policeman. I ain' afraid-a nothin'. I will be stationed in Korea one day." Wilbur was all smiles. Mabel did not bite her tongue. "Wilbur, I'm marri'd-ta a man what don't love me. I'm lonely for the love of-a hot-young man like you is. You's drop-dead handsome. Could ya go for-a gal like me?"

"I heard how cute you are. Wayne told me. Me, an' my Cousins Bird an' Toad all want to be with you, honey. Henry James's a fool if he don't love you to death, baby-girl. I know I will if you let me.

"And, don't worry. I heard what Henry did to Tank Snowvall. I'm not Tank. Iain' scared-a nobody. I was trained in the Army at Fort Bragg to handle men-bad men-killers, if need be. Ain't nothing that'll stop me from making love to you."

Mabel smiled. "Ya can make-it with me right now if you want to. It'll be awhile till Henry get from work." Mabel was on-fire for Wilbur. She let her dress slide open. She cleverly undid the buttons of her dress, so that when she moved a certain way, a little of her legs at a time became completely exposed. She wanted to set him on fire, and she succeeded.

Wilbur spoke in hushed tones. "Look ... I don't wanna get it on with you in another man's house--because if my Rev. Daddy found out, he'd kill me himself But meet me down the hill at the spring."

Mabel stood up and buttoned her dress back up. "Okay, sugar," she said. "I got a cup'la things ta-do. Ya just wait till I get down there--be patient. I'll be there 'fore ya kno' it."

"Okay, Baby-cakes," said Wilbur. He jogged down to the spring and hid behind a big Oak tree shading the branch that led to the spring. It was on the left side of a path that went up the hill out of sight through the woods.

Mabel got busy cooking supper. She fried a rabbit Henry had shot that morning; she smothered it in thickened gravy and onions; she opened a canning jar of green beans; and threw together a batch of cornbread and put a pan of it in the oven. She figured the bread would be ready by the time she got back from the spring.

She called Billy inside. "Baby, Momma gotta ask ya ta-do 'er a little favor. You's big 'nough now ta-watch Dick an' Bug till I go get us some water from the spring. The babies's sleep right now. So all ya gotta do is watch 'em till Momma get back; aw-ight?" Mabel said. "Will ya do that for Momma?"

Billy looked up at his Mother and said: "Yes 'am, Momma."

Mabel pushed the cooked food to the back of the cook stove so that it would stay warm until suppertirne. She instructed Billy, "Stay outta the kitchen till Momma get back from the spring, unnerstan'?"

"Yeah, Momma," Billy said.

Even though there was fire still burning in the stove, and in light of the fact that Mabel knew how the fire that killed Marnie's children had gotten started, her lusts compelled her to leave a five-going-on-six-year-old in charge of looking after her precious children. She shot out of the backdoor in a hurry to get her joy-bells ringing.

In a minute she arrived at the spring. "Wilbur . . . Wilbur, Wilbur-ah-o-o-oh," said Mabel. Wilbur had tipped up behind her. He picked her up, kissed her all over her face, and put his tongue in her mouth. After a long probing kiss, he said: "I think you're a sweet-country rose, baby-girl, as pretty as Billy Holiday. You may be a little more on the chocolate side, but, hey, I love dark-chocolate the best."

Mabel giggled like a teenaged schoolgirl. She thrilled to the feel of Wilbur's hands touching every part of her anatomy. Then he asked a question only one other man (Wayne Nicholas) had asked her. "Would you mind if'n I go downtown, sugar?" Mabel knew what that meant.

"Well ... that feels real good, but it's so ... nasty," Mabel whispered.

"That's why it is so much fun. I feel like it was part of my basic training at Fort Bragg in Fayetteville, North Carolina. Some of the gals that came on Base to be with us soldiers wouldn't have it any other way. You had to do that first, or do without. One-a the gals showed me how to really please a woman. Lemme show you." Wilbur's voice came out like a rushing wind.

Mabel's desires reached a fever pitch. "Go ahead, then. Do it."

Wilbur took her dress off to find that she had on no underclothes. He laid her dress in the leaves and laid her on top of her dress. He dropped to his knees. Then-

Mabel uttered little screams signifying she was experiencing great orgasmic joy. Her joy intensified when Wilbur entered her suddenly. He built his lovemaking in fervor and velocity to a point where all Mabel could do was yell, "Good! Good! Don't stop ... Good" Wilbur nearly took her breath away. And even after Wilbur had gone as far as he could for the moment, she laid there still experiencing an elongated hot-orgasm. After the pleasure subsided, Mabel began to weep.

"Wilbur, what ya just gave me I needed it. I wish I could get it from my husband. He treat me like-a who'e. He get what he want, an' don't care nothin' toll 'bout me. I get mad as hell when he get to snorin' an' I can't get-ta sleep. If'n he'd show me the kind-a lovin' ya just gave me, I'd stick ta 'im like glue," Mabel whined. "Iain' tryin' ta-be no bad gal. I just wanna be loved-that's all." She burst out and cried. Tears streamed down her cheeks.

"Hush, don't cry. I can't stand it when women cry. At some point, I'll soon be sent to probably Fort Detrick up in Maryland to learn to be a Military Cop. But, before I leave, I'd like to see you again, sometimes. I hate to see you so unhappy," said Wilbur. He pulled his pants back up, stood up, and redid his belt. He watched Mabel put her clothes back on.

Wilbur tried to kiss Mabel goodbye. She refused to kiss him in the mouth. She gave him a little peck on the jaw. He laughed. He knew it was because of the oral sex.

"Omigod! The time done gone. I gotta get back ta-my babies up at the house. See ya later, Wilbur. If'n we don't get together again, take care, Baby." Mabel got into a swift jog.

Wilbur watched her run to the spring, and get two buckets of water, then, up the path she scampered. He had a self-satisfied smile across his clean-shaven GI' s face.

While Mabel was down the spring path getting laid, Billy heard Bug crying. He thought his little Brother was screaming at him because of something he'd done wrong. He wanted to make Bug stop yelling. He jumped on the bed beside Bug, turned him over so that Bug rested on his stomach. Bug's little left arm got tangled up in an awkward angle. It "popped." Billy started shaking the bed fiercely to put Bug back to sleep. Bug seemed to be asleep, but he had actually fainted. His arm had been dislocated. The next moment, Mabel came through the backdoor carrying two buckets of water.

Dick was wide awake. Billy, thinking that Bug was fast asleep, began playing with Dick. He was glad that his Mother had come back. Looked like it took a long time for her to just get two buckets of water, since it never took her that long before.

Mabel called out to Billy. She too thought that Bug was fast asleep. "C'mere, Billy Boy. Give Momma a hug. Thanks, for lookin' after the babies. Ya can go on out an' play, now."

Billy skipped on out of the backdoor. Mabel got a little warm water out of a steam kettle off the back of the stove. She got a clean washcloth out of her cedar chest, a bar of Dial Soap out of the cupboard in the kitchen, and sponged her feminine parts as quickly as she could. She put on a pair of clean panties and a brazier. She sprinkled on some Cashmere Bouquet Power, and figured that she was flower-fresh. She thought her little secret was safe. Then Henry rushed through the front door. Mabel ran to the backdoor and threw out the water she had used.

"I can smell that rabbit an' gravy an' that cornbread," said Henry. He got some water in the basin out of the steam kettle, quickly washed his hands and face, dried them on a towel that had been hanging behind the backdoor, and got ready to come to the table to be fed.

"Where's Bug?" Henry asked. He got up from the supper table, went into the front-room area, picked Bug up, and his left arm dangled. Henry could see that it had been broken.

"Mabel-ya low-down Bitch! What ya done-ta Bug," Henry yelled. He was almost screaming. "Ya been sittin' 'round on ya ass listenin' ta-them stories; ya let Bug get hurt like this. I's sorry I ever got you that damn radio! Ya weren't worth-a shit at first, now ya ain' worth-a damn! Gal, ya better have-a good explanation, dam-ya!"

Tears eased down Mabel's cheeks. Guilt made her tremble all over. Well," she groaned, "I's just down ta-the spring ta-get a cup'la buckets of water for supper. I left Billy up here, the babies was sleep. I don't know what could-a happen," Mabel lied to defend herself

Henry turned his attention to Billy. "C'mere, ya little bas'sard,' Henry yelled. He seized Billy by his right hand, and "Wallop" went Henry's fist up beside Billy's head. It knocked him down to the floor. He blinked out after that. He heard his Mother yelling: "Don't hit."

Then he was out like a light. "Bitch, I go deal with you later-b'lieve that, now," Henry said.

Henry grabbed up Bug, wrapped him in a heavy-blue baby blanket, and jogged to Roy Winston's house carrying his "favorite child" with tears running down his cheeks. He said out loud: "If somethin' else bad happen-ta Bug, I'll kill 'em both!" He meant Mabel and Billy.

Roy loaded Henry and Bug in his Model A, cranked it up and "Put-put-putted" them up to Dr. Yateman's in Fork Union.

"Bring that baby boy on in the examining room, Mr. James. You and Mr. Winston can sit out in the waiting room. This won't take long. Happens all the time. I'll pop-it back into place, put a cast on it, and in no time at all, it'll be good as new-that's the way it is for babies. They heal from those kinds of breaks quickly. He'll be all right. Calm down, Mr. James.

"After you leave here, watch him for a couple of days to see if he develops a persistently high fever. If he does, bring him on back. I'm going to give him a shot of antibiotics; that ought to do the trick.

"I know you don't have any money. I am going to bill you like this: you bring me one of your hog's shoulders after you cure your meat this fall or winter. That ought to be payment enough. Is that all right with you, sir?"

"Yes sir, Mr. Yateman. I will do," Henry said. He reached to shake Dr. Yateman's hand.

Dr. Yateman seized Henry's hand and allowed: "I call you, Henry. You can call me Dr. Yateman, or just Doc. Or you can call me Josiah. But I want you to know I don't feel superior to you or anybody else. I feel like you are equal to any Whiteman in America. See you, Henry. Don't forget me come hog-killing time, now."

"Aw-ight, Doc, see ya, then. Thank ya so much," said Henry. He noticed that Bug was fast asleep, and was all wobbly.

"Henry, don't worry. I gave him a very mild sedative to help him stay still while I set the bone in his arm. He's going to sleep that off in a little while. That's why I got him in an immobile cast. He may re-break that arm if he gets to moving it too much.

"Now, for a couple of days, he's going to be a little worrisome. But that arm will knit back together by then, and Baby Henry will be good as new."

"Thank ya, Doc for ev' thin'," said Henry. He grabbed up Bug and took him to Roy's car.

Roy had gone out to it already.

When Henry returned home with Bug, Billy, with an egg-size knot on the right side of his head, couldn't bear to look at his little-baby Brother. Bug's arm was fixed in a cast and Billy felt guilty like it was his fault. It seemed like too, that his Daddy's eyes were looking through him. The bubble of fear in Billy's guts grew and grew. He popped his left thumb in his mouth and started sucking it as hard as he could. He sat in a corner rocking back and forth staring at the floor.

Day after day, when Henry came from work, that bubble of fear inflated in Billy's stomach. He went outside to play with his imaginary dog. This big, brown, dog spoke to him: "I love you, Sonny. I love you, Sonny. Let's go to the woods and play"

Mabel decided that she would not see Wilbur or Bird again. Fooling around had got her baby hurt. If Henry had come back and beat the hell out of her after he brought Bug back home, Mabel was prepared to take it like a criminal should. When Bird came by Mabel told him, "It's over 'tween us. I got my baby hurt. I'm go cool my little hot-ass down." She said the same thing to Wilbur. They stopped coming by to see her. After all, she was just another piece they were getting. Strange enough, Henry never laid a hand on her. He stared her to death.

Marr' Dee heard Wilbur bragging to Bird and Toad. "I gave it to Mabel real good, homes.

No man ever did her like I did her. She even said that to me."

Bird got a little testy. "Hell no, Wilbur. She screamed out my name when I last got 'er. I can get'er any time I want'er."

Wilbur replied, "You little piss-ant, you ain't dry behind the ears, yet. I 'ma GI. I know how to get the job done. What you know?"

Marr' Dee came into the kitchen where all three young men were stuffing themselves with plate-after-plate of cooked-down brown-beans. Wilbur cleared his throat. So did Bird.

Marr' Dee spoke to Toad: "Was you mixed up in that mess?" she asked Toad, pointedly. "No'am, Momma. I ain' been near 'Henry Jeems's' wife, no-sir-ree. I wanna live."

"Wilbur. Bird. Have y'all been over foolin' with 'Henry Jeems's' wife?" Marr' Dee asked. She blew a little air out of the side of her mouth. She stood in her kitchen with her hands on her hips, patting her left foot, waiting for an answer from her Nephew and her youngest Son.

Both just threw up their hands over their heads. Bird got a twisted-guilty-smile on his face.

Wilbur got a grimace on his.

"Well, that says all to me," said Marr' Dee. "I'm gon go over yonder an' have-a little talk with that hussy, Mabel. I ain' go let 'er get my Son kilt. Henry near 'bout cut Tank Snowvall to death over some gal what didn't even care 'bout neither one-a them mens. What'cha think he go do to Bird ifn he find out he's been over to his house with his little wife?"

"I ain't scared," Wilbur said, defiantly. "I'm just as much man as Henry James, or anybody else. I wish some 'mother' would fade me with a knife in his hand. That'll be all he rode. He better check that shit at the door, A'nt Marr' Dee."

"Ya trainin' in the Army may have boosted ya confidence, but you don't wanna stand in front of one-a them 'Jeems's' boys. Maybe, I ought-a talk to your Daddy. Wilbur, you go get'cha self kilt foolin' 'round here like ya doin'," Marr' Dee said.

"Yeah, aw-ight, Auntie. I gotta go on home. I wanna be there if you're gonna drop the bomb," Wilbur said. He got up from the kitchen table. "Thanks for the supper, Auntie. I'm go see you later. Catch y'all later, Bird and Toad." Wilbur went to the front room and on out of the front door to the front porch. He got ready to cut across the field to home.

"Got'cha, my-man," Bird said. He had come out onto the porch. Toad stood beside him. "Take it easy," Toad said. Inside of himself, Toad burned with lust for Mabel. After what Wayne, his oldest Brother had told him about Mabel, he wanted to have a similar experience with her. He felt like he wouldn't be a man if he didn't at least try. He gulped down a piece of fatback he had taken from his plate of brown beans. He returned to demolish the heaping helping of beans still piled on his plate. He got up from the table, and without saying a word, he hit the backdoor like Marr' Dee and Bird knew what he had on his mind.

Now, Toad was the "Ugly Duckling" in Marr' Dee's family. He was unlike the rest of her children in that they were considered to be light-skinned and handsome or beautiful. Toad's eyes were very large. He had only a trace of eyebrows. His nose was very pugnacious and seemed to be sitting right down on his top lip that was very thin. He had a pronounced bottom lip. His head and body made him seem like a mammoth "Humpty-Dumpty" character. He had too tiny earlobes. He was about four-foot tall and partially bald.

Toad's skin color was ashen-gray, or greenish-gray. He had webbed-like feet, and very short nubby fingers. His arms were seemingly disproportionally short for his rotund body. Rumor had it that "Marr' Dee was frightened by a bull frog while she was pregnant with Toad." After his birth, she nicknamed him Toad because as a baby he did resemble a frog. The name stuck with him because as he grew up he retained his relative appearance.

On this day, Toad figured that he would have a chance with Mabel because she was just too hot to refuse him. He wasted no time. It was the same evening that Marr' Dee, his Mother, had admonished Bird and Wilbur, "Y'all stay 'way from that little-hot gal, now"

Toad hid in the woods near the house where Mabel lived. He saw Mabel come outside. She stood behind the west side of the house, in back of the kitchen area. She pulled up the hem of her dress until it was up to her panties. She pulled her red panties down to her ankles. She pulled her dress back up, squatted down and took a generous piss. Toad saw it all. He tipped up and stood behind a huge Indian Oak tree near the back of the house on the edge of the woods. He got very excited. He watched Mabel pull her panties back up and let her yellow-and-green plaid dress-tail drop back into place. Toad came from behind the Oak tree.

"Mabel ... Mabel. Ya' pretty gal, you," Toad said. "Lemme get some.

Mabel. Lemme do it-ta ya like my Brothers an' my Cousin did. I need-a gal like you. I'll fuck ya real good. I'll pay ya too. I done that before with other gals. I save all my money-I'll give that to you; just lemme get."

Mabel jumped back. She couldn't believe the spectacle that was presenting himself before her. "What the hell!" she exclaimed. "Who the hell told ya that I wanna give ya any." Toad had pulled out of the fly of his pants a "big-o'-hard-mule-Dick." He tried to pull Mabel's dress up, as he begged her.

"Nigga, I'll never let ya get on top of me. You's too ugly. It ain' none-a ya bizzness who else I been with-you ain't gettin' any!" Mabel shouted.

Toad grabbed Mabel and pressed his rigid penis against her dress and pressed it hard between her legs. He held her in a vise-like grip. He had tears in his eyebrow-less eyes. He pushed Mabel back against the Oak tree. He started grinding against her. He struggled to pull up Mabel's dress and got it up so that he was grinding his penis against her panties. He slipped her panties to the side, then picked Mabel up and was ready to guide it home. He was holding her with one arm draped around her and the other fighting to get what he wanted.

Mabel struggled and got out of Toad's grip. "Stupid, ugly, Nigga, get the hell 'way from me. Ya frog-lookin' bas'sard. I wouldn't give ya any pussy if'n ya was the only man left alive, an I's the only woman. Get ya o' nasty thing off me. Ya smell like-a horse. Ya touch me one more time, an' I go scream so the whole neigh-ha-hood go come runnin'. Don't ya never come by this house no more. If'n ya do, I'm go tell my husband, Henry James. He'll cut ya ass too short ta shit-now get the hell 'way from outta my yard!"

Mabel's threat of telling Henry what Toad had done, scared him back to reality. His Dick went flaccid. He stuffed it back into the fly of his pants. He headed down the path towards his home, crying like Mabel had slapped him. He stopped half-way down the path at a little grove of Spruce-Pine trees. He hid among the trees, looked to see if anyone was coming down the path; seeing no one, he got his penis out into his little hands and it grew rigid again. In his mind, the image of Mabel's naked "pussy" became a virtual reality. He stroked himself faster and faster, and then, harder and harder. "I'll make Mabel wish she had-a given that thing ta-me. Oh-oh-oh! 0-o-o-o-ah!

"I'm go make that gal, Mabel, wish she's never born. I 'ma put'er bizzness in the streets."

The image of Mabel's nudity grew larger and larger in Toad's mind. His masturbation intensified. Every muscle in his body quivered. His male member pulsated and vibrated and jerked up and down in little motions. Stream after stream of semen squirted from the head of it onto the pine needles in the woods, spurt after spurt in a multiple orgasm. It was like a volcano erupting, spewing hot-lava every which way; but it was not the release that Toad really wanted.

Toad dropped to his knees at the end of the experience. He uttered aloud: "Why do womens hate me so bad? I didn't ask to come here lookin' like this. I gotta pay 'em a lotta money for a little nooky. They don't treat Wilbur, Bird an' Wayne like that. Oh ... sometimes I wish I's dead!" Then he cried like a whipped child.

Just south of where Mabel and Henry were renting, Gerry Coleman Anderson lived with his wife, Bella Mazy, and his oldest Daughter, Arlie Ann-and her baby Daughter, Eugenia Ann and his youngest Daughter, Rena Ray. Gerry and Bella sold beer, bootleg liquor, and homemade wine. They ran an open-house on weekends-Friday night through to Saturday night. All kind of gambling went on in the house on weekends, but in the woods edging the fields surrounding the house the rest of the week. Gamblers just needed to ask Gerry for permission.

Anyone could buy beer, wine, or liquor any time of the day or night, just for the asking. Wild men and loose women frequented the two-story house on Friday and or Saturday nights. Sometimes these came by the carload. A lot of them came to try to find some "sucker" that they could hook, or crook out of all of his money. (It was one of the places that Tank and Babe had once hung out at.)

Everybody knew about Gerry's and Bella's place, that it was the place to be on weekends to get a gal, get a man, or to gamble and win some money; and or to while away the blues. Bella cooked good fish, chicken, pork chops, and Bull-burgers (a thick slice of bologna with grilled onions and cheese on a hamburger bun). She also made great potato and macaroni salads. Anyone could get a sturdy paper-plateful of a piece of fried chicken, potato, or macaroni salad, and usually collards or, curly kale salad, with a

Pepsi, cool aid, or some alcoholic drink, for three dollars. Teenagers hung out at Gerry's and Bella's. They stayed mostly outside in parked cars at night, doing what came naturally, as did Gerry, Jr. Bella's and Gerry, Sr.'s only grown Son.

Henry came home this Friday, dropped off the Herring Fish for Saturday morning breakfast, and Shad for that evening's supper, changed clothes and left without saying a word to Mabel.

The "funny thing" about Henry was: he didn't love Mabel, and didn't really want to be married to her; but he didn't want any other man to have her either. But he was up at Gerry's and Bella's house every Friday night looking for some "strange." He'd take a gal to the woods and get laid for two or three bucks. This he called: "unwinding from the week at the mill."

Henry came up the hill to Gerry's and Bella's this Friday evening. The place was packed already. Several young woman were wearing very short dresses and sipping homemade wine, or beer, and or liquor out of paper cups. The music was loud and sexy with the sounds of James Brown and the Famous Flames pumping up the crowd. Henry heard, "Please, Please, Please! ..

." And he saw many of the people in the house, and on the full-porch, and in the wide hallway in the house slow-dragging and grinding on each other like the act itself

Henry reached the front room, he saw two sofas, and three end-chairs, and a number of card players gambling at three fold-away tables with four portable chairs at each one. In the middle of the room was a beautiful English coffee table. It was covered with a green blanket to make a smooth surface for several men shooting Crap on it.

The crowd "o-o-o-oed," and "aw-w-w-ed," as a young smoothly-Black man, in a pink Gaul shirt, a pair of grease-covered Jeans, and a pair of dirty-white "Chuck Taylors," threw the dice and hit several "Sevens" and "Elevens!" His name was George Mayor from Cumberland County. He hit pass-after-pass with the dice. Then he threw a Ten. "Bet, you mo' fookas, I'ma make that Ten or Four, next roll, Ten Dollars-who go fade me?"

A fat baldhead man yelled, "Bet."

George threw the Ten the next roll. He won the ten dollars and the pot. "I bet twenty. Who go fade me?"

Another slimmer man yelled, "Bet!" George's next roll was "Seven!" He won.

Henry shook his head. He whispered: "What-a bunch-a dam-fools. They just givin' they money ta-that slick fool."

"Bella. Bella. Can I get a quart-a Slitz Malt Liquor, please?" Henry asked. "Gimme-a cup'la paper cups with that."

As Bella left the front room, Henry watched all that delicious-looking rump of hers shake and shimmy as she walked away, and he followed behind her. He was thinking that "this gal got Billy Holiday and Mae West beat. She got them pretty lips, painted red, that stays in a smile. Those long Indian braids she got is so nice. That tight-white dress she's wearing, I can almost see through it. It shows off all of her curves. I would go for some of that, but old Gerry'd blow my brains out-he's so jealous of that gal. But ifn I ever getta chance, I'm go get me some-a that."

They went into another room where Rena sleeps when she could. Most of the time she had to go upstairs until the wee-hours of the morning, when everyone went home, to get any sleep at all. Bella had an electric, RCA Combination, blasting the music. They came to a relatively small kitchen. Bella went into one of the two refrigerators in it to get Henry a quart of beer. She popped the top off the beer bottle, and gave Henry two twelve-ounce Daisy Cups. He gave her two dollars. "How you doing, Henry?" Bella asked.

"I'm doin'," Henry replied.

"Honey," Bella leaned over on the table in the kitchen and Henry could see her voluptuous breasts, all the way. "Y' still pickin' that guitar of your'n?" A delightful twinkle flashed in her eyes. Her gingerbread complexion brightened up a little as she spoke.

"I sure 'nough can, baby cakes," Henry said. He grinned from ear to ear, with his eyes glued to Bella's abundant bosom. He saw a gracious smile come to her pretty face. She flexed her long braids and stood up straight, and wiggled her shapely well-endowed buttocks.

"Well ... Big boy," Bella uttered imitative of Mae West, "maybe sometime, ya can c'mon up here an' pick that thing for me. Maybe, gimme some private lessons. Can ya use ya instrument that way, Big boy?"

Henry gave a sheepish chuckle. "I'on kno 'bout that. Gerry's mighty jealous-a ya. An' I don't blame 'im. But y'know, maybe ..."

Bella interrupted. "Ya just gotta wait till Gerry's gone-ta work," she whispered. She swished her hips suggestively. She winked. "Now, ya go enjoy ya drink, but think 'bout what we talked 'bout." She-on purpose-knocked a dishrag off the table, and it fell to the floor. She exposed her legs up to her panties while squatting down to pick it up.

Henry saw the outlines of her full-bush through very thin underwear. It set him on fire. He knew he better get out of that kitchen before he ended up giving Gerry plenty to want to kill him. He was so hard he could barely walk. He took the beer and cups and went back to the living room.

Henry whispered: "I 'ma get me some-a that just-a soon as I getta chance. It's almost staring me right in my face." Just as he entered the living room where all the action was taking place, he spied "O' Simple Toad." The dude was staring at him really hard. He sat over beside an electric lamp in an end chair, nursing out of a quart of beer that was almost empty. Toad had some scratches on his arms and hands, and three larger scratch-marks just under his left eye.

"C'mon over here ta-my-chair, Henry Jeems. I won't bite," Toad said, motioning with his frog-like arms and hands to Henry. "Got some right-bad shit ta-lay on ya!" He croaked like a Bull-frog sitting on a lily pad. His speech was one-long drunken-slur.

"What'cha want, Toad, Man?" Henry asked. He really didn't want to hear from the neighborhood retard right then. He was out to get some "play." He frowned and allowed: "I ain' got time ta-listen-ta ya right now, Toad."

"Ya go wanna hear what I gotta say ta ya, my-man," Toad said. "The shit's goin' on right on ya doorstep. Yes 'tis. I swear fore Gawd! An' hope-ta die!" He crossed his heart with his right index finger, and raised his left hand up towards the ceiling.

"What-so-never ya gotta say to me, go-head-o, man-an' it better be good," Henry replied.

Toad grinned. "Lemme getta sip or two of ya beer. Then I's go get into some real stinky shit what's go mess with ya nerves, Henry Jeems. It's 'bout ya wife, Mabel, homes."

"Look, Toad. What ya talkin 'bout, now? What in the hell's Mabel <loin'? Here, take the whole quart-a beer," Henry snarled. "Now, drop it on me, or I'll cut ..."

Toad put the mouth of the quart of beer up to his lips and turned it up and gulped down half of the quart of beer. He burped, loudly. He rolled his frog-like eyes, cleared his throat, and some hateful words croaked up out of his mouth.

"Henry Jeems, most days after ya go-ta work, one-a two light-skinned mens be comin' ta- your house ta-get into Mabel's panties. I done seen it with my own eyes," Toad said.

"Man-ya better be factin'." Henry's every nerve was on edge. "This's some bad shit!"

"It is. It is," Toad said. His voice took on a bass-like croak like a large Bull-frog.

Henry put his hand in his right pants pocket on his knife. "I 'ma get-ta the bottom-a this shit right quick. Iain' lettin' nair 'nother Nigga plow with my Heifer! That's all to it. Who're the hell's them sons-sa-bitches fuckin' my wife 'hind my back? What's they names, Toad. Don't be fuckin' with me, now," Henry asked in a muffled yell.

"I'on kno' they names, homes-I swear I don't," Toad lied. "I passed by ya house one day an' I could see through the window, one'er 'im was throwin' it to 'er. I just kept on walkin', tweren't none-a my bizzness. I don't mess in people's bizzness, much."

"That nasty Bitch!" Henry said, with a dog-like growl. "I 'ma cut that who'e ta-death! Go cut'er throat from ear-ta-ear. Damn 'er!"

Having fulfilled his desire to get even with Mabel, Toad got up out of the end chair, stumbled out into the hallway and on out onto the porch. He disappeared into the night.

Henry went into the kitchen to where Bella was fixing a couple of young foxy women paper plates of a pork chop and a chitterling dinner. They paid her and were gone.

"Bella, gimme a pint-a Beefeater's Gin. I 'ma head on home. I 'on need no cups. I 'ma leave right 'way. I don't feel too good in my stomach. Feels like somebody hit me in it," Henry said. His eyes danced from nervous rage.

Bella went back into her pantry, came back with the pint of Gin. "That'a be three-fifty, Henry."

Henry gave her the money. He went outside through Bella's backdoor. It was like he thought that everyone up at Gerry's and Bella's had to know about Mabel. Henry quickly made his way to the edge of the woods. He popped the top off the Gin, took a big swallow of it and gulped it down. For some reason, he knew he was feeling a powerful bout of jealous rage about Mabel, even though he didn't really give a damn about her. It didn't really make any sense even to him, but he felt it just the same.

He talked aloud to himself: "I cou'da marri'd one-a the good gals, like Henny or Alice, who wou'da never ran 'round on me. Now I's stuck with the slut-daughter of-a who'e. I bet-like-a Momma-she's fuckin' half the County. I'm in it worse than Poppa was. I's the biggest dam fool in the whole world-I'd be even a bigger fool ifn I don't kill that Bitch soon's I see 'er."

Henry came half-way down the path to the branch that led to the spring. He walked along the branch's bank to the trunk of a large oak tree. He took the top off the bottle of Gin. He took gulp after gulp of Gin straight from the bottle. It burned like fire all the way to the bottom of his guts. He thought about how good it would feel to cut Mabel's throat. He finished off the bottle of Gin, sat down and leaned against the trunk of the tree. He meant to just get himself together, but fell into a drunken stupor. He closed his eyes, and, the next thing he knew-

Early that Saturday morning, Henry awoke feeling sick to his stomach. He stood up and vomited at the roots of the tree where he had spent the night. Puking made him feel a little better, but he was still pretty drunk. He stumbled back to the spring path. Soon, he burst through the door to his bedroom.

His speech was slurred. "Billy . . . Billy . . . Get up, boy. Daddy wanna talk-ta ya. I gotta question I gotta ask you," Henry said.

Billy's heart got to beating fast. His Daddy never got him up in the mornings except for when he had peed in bed, and he wanted to whip him. But Billy's briefs were dry.

"Aw-ight, Daddy," said Billy. Henry was glaring over at Mabel with his right hand in his right front pants pocket, on the handle of his closed-up pocket knife.

Mabel yawned, rubbed her eyes, and sat up in bed. "What'cha want with Billy this time-a mornin', Henry? He ain' wet the bed in a long time, now. What's the matter?" Mabel asked.

"Who'e, that's aw-ight. I ain't talkin' ta-you! I 'ma get ta-ya Black ass in-a minute-ya can bet-a fat-man on that, now." Henry shook his left fist at Mabel.

The sun came up over the horizon brilliantly brightening up the morning. Mabel's shame, fear, and guilt became a painful knot in her inner-being. She trembled all over. She wondered had Henry found out what she had been up to. Mabel got out of bed, put on a pair of black slacks, and a white T-shirt. She stood at the foot of her bed watching Billy get dressed in his yellow and green shorts, a dark-green shirt, and a pair of red Kid's tennis. "Where we goin' Daddy?" Billy asked.

Henry grabbed the child's right hand and led him on out through the kitchen out the backdoor, and on down to the woodpile. Fearing that he may be getting a whipping, Billy started to whimper.

Henry stopped right near the chopping block where an axe was stuck in the top of that. He stooped down so that he would see directly into Billy's eyes.

"Boy, I ain' go whip ya. Unlessen ya don't tell me the truth. Now, who the hell's been comin 'round here-ta see ya Momma while I'm at work?" Henry asked Billy.

Billy stuck his left thumb in his mouth and tears formed his eyes. But he uttered not a word. He knew better than to tell his "Mean Daddy" anything about what his Momma had been doing while he was at work.

Henry snatched off his belt. "Did ya hear-me, boy?" Henry yelled.

Billy trembled all over, whimpered and cried, like he had been slapped; but he only looked at a pile of woodchips on the ground, and did not say a word.

Henry figured threatening the child was the wrong approach. He decided to use the sugar sweet, candy-dandy, approach.

"Hush up ya crying, Son. I'm goin' ta-Columbia today. Tell-me 'bout the mens that been comin' ta-the house ever days when Daddy's at work. I'll bring ya a lotta candy-a whole bag, an' ya can eat all ya want. I'll give ya cookies too," Henry promised. He put his belt back on. He grinned wolf-like at Billy.

The offer was tempting, but "Don't tell Daddy what ya seen Momma <loin'..." came to mind. Billy would not give up his Mother's secret. He just cried like he was being whipped. Henry figured that: "The boy's cryin' ta-cover up for his Momma." He got out his knife, turned and ran

to the house in a bloodthirsty rage. He went around the house meaning to enter it from the front door. He saw Mabel topping the hill up near the road, screaming: "Help! Help! He's gotta knife. He's go kill me! Help! ..." Her fear made her move faster, even though she was dragging two young children after her, so she was soon out of sight.

With the glistening blade of his six-inched pocket knife shining in the sunlight, Henry yelled: "Ya Black Bitch! Ya nasty who'e! I 'ma get ya ass. I 'ma stick this knife clean through ya."

Henry walked around the woodpile ranting and raving for a few minutes. He took a hard look at Billy, but closed the knife and put it back into his pocket. Billy was scared almost to fainting. He didn't want to stay with his Daddy that morning, but he didn't run away.

Mabel rushed along to Bessie's house. She burst through the door crying as she came into the Jacksons' sleeping area. "Bessie! Bessie! Help me. Henry came home drunk as a skunk. He's outta his head. Say he go deal with me. Bessie, he's gotta big o' knife in his pocket. I's 'fraid-a that man when he's been drinkin'. He may cut me ta-death!

"I had-da leave Billy behind. Oh, Gawd! We gotta go get my baby. I'on trust Henry with 'im sober. So ya kno' I don't trust 'im drunk. Henry's mad cause-a what Toad done told him or he might've beat somethin' outta Billy-I'on know."

Bessie said: "What can Toad say 'bout ya?"

"Bessie, I wouldn't let Toad get any the other day. He even tried-ta take it, but I fought 'im off He swore he's go get even with me by tellin' Henry 'bout Wayne. Now, ya Brother, say he go kill me. I hope he don't hurt Lil' Billy. It'll be all my fault, Bessie!"

Bessie got Lin's shotgun off the top of the front door-frame. She looked through the chest of drawers for some shotgun shells, got a couple of Number Fours and put one into the shotgun. "C'mon, Mabel, we gotta go get that child 'way from over yonder. I'd send Lin, but he's gone-ta Columbia this mornin' ta-do the shoppin'."

Henry James's eyes fluttered. His lips quivered. His eyes shone like shiny hens' eyes. His voice came off like the growl of an angry dog.

"Billy we gotta go over yonder an' find some lightwood so we can get a fire gonin' in the cook stove. I gotta cook the damn breakfast. Ya slut-Momma ain' here ta-do nothin 'toll. Let's go," Henry said. They were at the woodpile. Henry got the axe out of the chopping block. He rested the axe on his shoulder. He got a fox-like snarl on his wicked-looking face.

Billy didn't know what to do, to run, cry, scream, or what. His fear of his "Mean Daddy" won out. He followed behind him shaking like a leaf on a tree. He had his little left thumb stuck in his mouth. Then he whined: "I want my Momma." They were in the edge of the woods.

"Don't ya worr 'bout her. I 'ma send 'er ass-ta ya soon's I see 'er. Both y'all's the cause of all my trou'ba.

"Why ya taggin' long so far 'hind me, for? Let's get on in the woods, boy. We can't get no lightwood right here."

Henry grabbed Billy's right hand and half-dragged his little Son deeper into the woods. Several Pine stumps leftover by those who had cut pulpwood a couple of years ago were rotting away leaving their inner-essence. This inner-essence was highly combustible and was used in lieu of kerosene. Poor people who could not afford kerosene bust these Pine stumps opened with an axe to get at their core. This core was called lightwood. This was the excuse Henry was using to take his innocent-little Son into the woods that morning.

Henry came to a Pine stump near a brief clearing in the woods. He stopped. Henry turned around to glare at Billy. Not knowing what else to do, Billy started pointing to a couple of other stumps that might have lightwood in them.

"There ... there's one Daddy. There's another one." With his left thumb in his mouth, Billy, pointed at the stumps with the trigger finger of his right hand. He put his finger on a particular stump, and turned sideways to look up at his Father ...

He saw that Henry had raised the axe high into the air. His Daddy had a dreadful look on his face. Billy saw the blade of the axe coming down towards his head. Because he was aware that the axe was aimed at his head, instinctively he moved his little head out of the direct path of the sharp-edge of the axe. The blade missed his head and arm, but landed on his trigger finger. It went right through, leaving the end of his finger dangling from his right hand. The finger had been severed at the knuckle.

Billy frowned. His face became contorted and his eyes enlarged as he let out a high-pitched scream. The pain was like a burning fire that spread from his finger up his arm and then all over his body. His whole hand, arm, and the right side of his body ached. His head ached. Even his eyes ached. Blood spurted out of the wound. Billy raised his right hand up above his head, and blood ran down his right arm.

"I want my Momma ... Momma! Am I go die! Aim I go die, Daddy?" Billy screamed at the top of his voice.

Henry dropped the axe to the ground. He dropped to his knees. He could not believe what he had done. "Oh-My-Gawd! Oh-My-Lord! What-Have-I-Done? We done had-da bad accident," Henry said. He was unable to accept the fact that he had almost killed his little Son. "I gotta get ya ta-a doctor right quick," he yelled.

He grabbed a bandanna out of his back pants pockets, it was somewhat soiled, but he wrapped it around Billy's bleeding hand, picked Billy up in his arms and ran to the house. Once he got to the house, he took the old work handkerchief off Billy's wounded finger. He got out his best dress handkerchiefs out of the chest of drawers and wrapped one around Billy's finger and two others around his hand. The handkerchiefs soon bled through and turned red. He grabbed Billy up into his arms. He ran up to the road to the path through the woods that would take him to Lin's and Bessie's house. "We's go go-ta Unc' Will's house-he go take us ta-the doctor's office," Henry whined. He ran as fast as he could.

Mabel and Bessie came outside that morning with Bessie carrying Lin's single-shot shotgun with one round in the barrel and a couple more in her dress pockets. The sun was up high. A little fog lingered as the heat of the sun rapidly warmed things up. It had been a little cool that night.

Bessie saw her little Nephew in Henry's arms, as soon as he got close enough to her. Bessie dropped the shotgun and ran to meet them. She spied the blood-soaked handkerchiefs on Billy's right hand. "Henry, what the fuck have ya done ta-this child? You dam-fool!" she screamed.

"We had a little accident, Bessie, is all," Henry said. Tears came into His eyes.

"Ya stupid asshole, ya done went on an' done it. Didn't ya? I knew ya would if'n Mabel didn't stop ya ass. I told Mabel ta-watch ya. Now, ya done gone an' hurt this inn'a-cent child. God Help Us all!" Bessie yelled. "I ought-a put-a load-a lead 'tween ya eyes. Sometimes, ya ain' worth-a shit!"

Mabel ran over to where Bessie and Henry holding Billy stood. She took one look at Billy's bloody hand and screamed: "Henry, get Billy ta-a doctor right now. What the hell ya donin' comin' all the way over here 'stead-a takin' him ta-Roy's house? Would-a been closer. Ya stupid bas'sard. How the hell did Billy get hurt?"

"I's just gettin' a little lightwood when William got in the way-I cut 'im by accident. I didn't see his finger on the stump," Henry lied.

"Stop wastin' time-get ya ass in gear. Get Billy ta-a doctor, right now!" Mabel yelled. She passed out for a few moments. She knelt down on the ground hysterically puking.

Bessie got the shotgun, aimed it at Henry, and cocked the hammer back. "Nigga, get ya ass on the move an' I mean right now." Bessie fired up in the air. "BLAM!"

Henry trotted off down the path towards Will's and Cary's house. In a few minutes he arrived. Billy had fainted. That day Will was home, and even though he was a little drunk, the sight of the bloody handkerchiefs sobered him up sufficiently. "Put that boy in the cab of the truck, Henry," Will ordered.

Henry glared at Will Winston, but did not utter a mumbling word. He saw the muscles on Will tensing, and the hulk of a man snorting and grimacing at him. He had seen Will pick up the backend of a car once, and fought four strong men and knocked them out at a party. Even with a knife, Henry knew he would not be able to handle Will, who killed a hog one time with a blow to its head from one of his massive fists. Will's hateful stare at him, made Henry very nervous.

"I kno' what it look like, but Will it'sa accident," Henry said. He spoke out of the side of his mouth.

"I' on know who the hell ya think I am, but I kno' ya ass too well to hear any bullshit from ya. A'nt Maetta done spoiled the hell outta ya. But I don't give-a damn' bout you, ya Poppa, ya Great Uncles, Fitzhugh Lee James, or Raymond James, neither. A'nt Maetta's the onliest one-a y'all I got any respect for. She marri'd a James, but she ain't-a James," Will said. He didn't bite his tongue.

"Will, you's goin' on 'bout nothin' toll. My boy's hurt, we gotta get'im up ta-the doctor. We ain' got no time to be fussin' over a lotta bull," Henry replied.

"I wish ta-God that Cary could have-a boy for me. I wouldn't letta damn thing come 'tween that boy an' me. I'd kill the hell outta any son-of-a-bitch who'd do anything ta-'im.

"But you, an' ya Poppa fore ya, ain' that kind-a man. Y'all don't care 'bout nobody but ya selves. See, that'll make ya try-ta kill-a little boy that got in ya way. A wife an-a family might force ya ta-act like-a man 'stead-a blues-playin' asshole." The words shot out of Will's toughen lips like a mortar out of a cannon.

"Will . . . Will, I done said, what happen-ta Billy was a accident. I didn't mean-ta hurt my Son like that. He's already bled a lot, we gotta get 'im up yonder ta-Doctor Yateman's. Aw ight?"

Will looked Henry up an' down for a moment. Then they all climbed into the cab of the truck. Out of fear, and instinctively, Henry put his right hand on the print of his knife in his pocket. He was holding Billy with his left arm.

Will gritted his teeth at Henry. "Go-head-on, Nigga. Pull ya Gott-damn-knife on me, O' Will. Ya cut Snowvall near 'bout ta-death. See ifn you'll get ta-cut me. I'd kick-a deep mud hole in ya sorry ass. That's what you need anyway-that's what'cha didn't get 'nough of growin' up. I'd love ta-give ya some, now. I heard you's so fast an' bad with ya knife an' all. I been dyin' for one-a ya James boys ta-come at me with a knife opened in ya hand. That'll be the damn-day."

"Y'all stop it right there!" Cary shouted through her front screened door at her husband and Brother. "Will, carry that hurt child on up yonder ta-Fork Union ta-the doctor."

She yelled at Henry: "You ought-a be shame-a yourself That's all I got ta-say ta-ya right now, Henry."

"Cary. You's wrong 'bout this. It was all a accident-that's all. Didn't mean-ta hurt Billy, or nobody," Henry whined. His voice had grown very sorrowful. He couldn't look Will or Cary in the face. He stared out the window at the ground, almost crying. Inside, he felt guilty as a dog caught eating the chickens' eggs in a henhouse.

"Both-a y'all get that boy ta-a doctor right away. And, Will, and Henry, don't y'all say another word. Drive the hell off; aw-ight?" Cary had heard enough.

Cary watched the log truck roll fifty feet to Route Six. Will turned it right and headed for Fork Union. Cary just shook her head at both of the men inside the truck.

Henry was silent all the way to Fork Union. Will cussed under his breath the whole ten miles.

"Mabel, Mabel, Mabel, ya with us yet? Ya passed out. Wake up, Baby, or we go have-ta take you ta-the doctor. Ya got babies of ya-own ta-care for. Wake up," Bessie pleaded with Mabel lying on a coat and covered with a blanket.

"Bessie, oh Bessie. It's all my fault. I's the cause-a all this mess. My little Son's hurt cause a somethin' I did. Bessie-oh God-he's near 'bout got kilt over somethin' I done. Lordy, Bessie, I gotta get home fore Henry come back an' finish killin' 'im. I don't care what he do-ta me, I deserves it. But not my chillun," Mabel screamed like she had in childbirth while bringing Billy into the world.

"Ya sure ya wanna go back over yonder, Mabel? Ya can move back with us till ya get some other place-ta stay. Or, ya can go back over yonder-ta ya Mother's. Momma would take ya in too. Ya don't have-ta take no more shit from Henry ifn ya don't want to," Bessie said.

With tears running down her cheeks, Mabel whined: "Bessie, thank ya so kindly. But I'm the guilty one. Ya don't kno' the whole story."

"Mabel," said Bessie, "I ain't tryin' ta-mess-in ya bizzness. Some things's best left unsaid ifn it might cause ya even more trou'ba. I ain' go tell ya all my bizzness, an' I don't wanna know all-a your'n. But you's gotta get ya act together. Ya gotta get things straight so that ya can still live with my Brother. That's a fact, honey."

"Yep, I hear ya," said Mabel. "So, I's goin' back. Come hell or high-water, I go be doin' my best ta-make up for the stupid shit I been doin'. I ain' go do none-a that no more.

"I go be leavin' so when Henry bring Billy back home I wanna be there. I'm go see ya, Bessie." She cried like a whipped child. She got Dick and Bug ready to go.

Bessie came over and bear-hugged Mabel. They both held each other tightly. Then Bessie said: "Baby, the last time Lin hit me, I nearly kilt 'im.

I shot at 'im three or four times. That may be the only way for ya ... ya may have-ta do that at least one time."

"Bessie Iain' got the nerve ta-shoot-a gun at nobody-even ifn my life depended on it." "But Mabel, it ain' ya life I's worri 'd 'bout. It's the lives of ya Chillren I's more concern 'bout. Sugar, ya go have-ta teach that man-ta'spect ya. Or somethin' worse go happen-ta y'all."

Mabel dried her eyes. "Bessie, I'm go have-ta think that one over a few times. We's goin' on up the path ta-my house. I'm ready-ta face-up ta ... anythin'." More tears eased down Mabel's face as she trudged up the path toward home.

Bessie followed for a little ways. Her last statement was: "Baby, I'll go with y'all if'n ya want me to. I'll take Lin's shotgun if n ya want. What-"

Mabel turned and replied: "No, Bessie, I gotta fight this battle alone. See ya."

Will got into his red-Ford truck, first. He watched Henry bring Billy out of the doctor's office with his hand in a cast up to his elbow, and that arm hung in a slang. He'd watched until Dr. Yateman shoot Billy's hand and arm full of painkiller. He saw the Doc cut the dangling end off Billy's finger. Will, a big muscular man who had no fear of any other man, fainted when he saw the raw-end of Billy's nub. He had to be given smelling salts. When he came to, he dashed outside to his truck, got behind its wheel and lit up a cigarette.

"Henry," said Dr. Yateman, "here's a bottle of pain pills, and another one of antibiotics. You're going to have to give the child one of the antibiotics every day until they're used up. But only give him a pain pill when he complains. It'll be worse at night for a little while."

"Yes . . . Doc. What do I owe ya?"

Dr. Yateman smiled at Henry. "Well, this normally cost twenty-five dollars; but I know you don't have that. But I know you're raising a couple of hogs. Add a ham along with the shoulder you already owe me-that ought to do it. All right?"

"Yes sir, Dr. Yateman. That's aw-ight with me."

Henry took the bottles of pills, put one in each of his front pockets, picked up a sleeping Billy James, and went out to the truck where Will sat puffing away on cigarette after cigarette.

"Henry, ya owe me a pint-a liquor for helpin' ya out today," Will said, after Henry got into the truck with Billy.

"Yeah, aw-ight," Henry said. He was annoyed, but constrained. "Take us home, Will, aw ight."

"Ya bet'cha!" Will replied. He rolled his muscle-bound eyes and cranked up the truck.

Henry arrived home that evening carrying his little Son that he had injured for life. He had thought that he would have to go over to Bessie's and beg Mabel to come back home. Then he saw the lamplight flickering. That was somewhat of a surprise to him.

With a snarl on his rough-hued face, "You's home, I reek-en ya know how ta get the hell outta my truck," Will shoved the words out of his mouth, hoping they would slap Henry up beside his head-like he wanted to do."

"Aw-ight, Will," said Henry, "but you's wrong 'bout me. I ain' as rotten as ya think ..." "Henry, I ain' go never buy that shit!" Will cranked up the truck and sped off

When Henry walked through the door, he spied Mabel sitting on the side of the bed holding Bug in her lap, and Dick stood with his little head leaning on her left leg. Both children were almost asleep. Henry put Billy down on the boys' bed.

After sitting the bottles of pills on the bureau, he stood in the middle of the floor, and for the first time, Mabel saw tears come down Henry's cheeks. But he didn't say he was sorry. He didn't ask her pardon. He took out his bloodstained bandanna, wiped his eyes, blew his nose into it, put that back into his back pants pockets, and took a seat in a rocking chair near the Heater.

Mabel laid Lil' Henry on the bed beside Billy, then Dick beside of them. She read aloud the dosages for the medications-as best she could-and burst into a fit of crying. She scooped Billy up off the bed as gently as she could. She was filled with self-loathing and damning remorse. The painkiller still affected Billy and kept him sound asleep. The silence of the adults spoke volumes.

Mabel was thinking: *This's all my fault. It's cause-a my foolin 'round I feel like the who'e Henry's been callin' me. My baby, Henry, gotta cast on his arm. Billy done lost-a finger. I wonder if 'n Billy told Henry 'bout what I been doin'? Or was it that o' ugly Toad? All them boys might get into trou'ba for foolin 'round with me, a marri 'd woman. If 'n Henry find out who they be, he's go kill 'em. Then I go have they blood on my hands. I's go cool my-little hot-ass down ta-cold as ice. I'm just go stay still an' take care-a my boys from now on.*

Henry went out to the woodpile. He sat on the chopping block, thinking: *I's wrong as hell. I near 'bout cut the head off'n my Son, my own flesh an' blood What-in-the-hell's wrong with me? I'm doin' the same shit that Poppa did, and Grandpa Johnny did I got that shit in my mind an' J's actin' just like 'em. But even they didn't try-ta kill nay one-a they chillren. I ain't go never hurt 'nother one-a my chillun like that again.* Henry stayed out at the woodpile all night long. He wept until his eyes became bloodshot-red.

Billy was the one caught in the middle of it all. He hadn't told on his Mother, but she left him with his "Mean Daddy," who tried to take his head off. But he couldn't face *The Truth.* He shoved "The Truth" way down into his *psyche.* He created a comer in his *Subconscious Mind* Mentally, he closed that comer of his mind as tight as he could. That place in his psychological self he came to label it as: *"The Subliminal Lock Box."*

Once Billy had shoved something into that Box, he pretended that the "Bad Thing" was part of a "Bad Dream." He then mentally invented a better reality that he rehearsed in his mind until it seemed to make sense. Thus, *"I cut my finger off while playing with an axe"*-not that *"my Father accidentally cutoff my finger while trying to kill me. Daddies just don't try to kill their little boys."* The above fabrication was what he said whenever anyone asked him how he lost his finger.

Billy's nightmares, however, would not let him forget what had really happened. Almost every night he dreamt that he was being chased by a big O' Nameless Animal-that defied description. It was behind him chasing him through the woods. He always awoke before it caught him. He knew that if it had caught him, it would gobble him up like a dog would a biscuit. His dream was an attempt to mentally cope with the repressed anger he felt for both his Father and Mother.

"Bird, bring ya ass on in this kitchen, boy. You mannish-little asshole. Ya think ya grown, but ya still ain't nothin' but-a boy to me. Now that Henry Jeems done hurt his own little boy, I kno' he'd go-ta ya ass ifn he found out it was you screwin' Mabel. I know them Jeems boys. They's all quick as can be with they knives. They done cut-up a bunch-a mens. What in the hell's the matter with you? Ya can get plenty gals 'round here-why Mabel?" Marr' Dee spoke with great conviction.

"Momma, I 'on kno' what in the Devil got into me. I wanted that little gal from the first time I ever saw 'er. I don't know why.

"She's kind-a cute. One day she was sittin' on her stoop when I's on my way up to see Gerry Coleman. He owed me for cuttin' the grass off the edge of his cornfield. Mabel asked me for one-a my Camels. I got the pack outta my shirt pocket an' shook one out for 'er. The wind blew her dress up 'er thighs. She ain' had-da thing on under that dress. I just stood glued ta-my tracks. She crooked her finger an 'vited me to come in the house with 'er. That was the first time. She asked me to come listen ta-the stories some days cause she got lonely. So I went by as many times as I could."

Marr' Dee got a plate out of her pantry. She put a couple of boiled hog's ears on it. She spooned an ample helping of collard greens and some friend potatoes. She served that to Bird along with a big slice of cornbread and a tall glass of iced tea. She smiled.

"Eat, Bird. An' fool, lemme tell ya what'cha go do, next week."

Bird dug into the plate of food. "Aw-ight, Momma. What'cha want me ta-do?"

"You's goin' ta-work with Jack Tyler, Jr. from over in the Town of Mineral in Louisa County. He gotta lumber camp an' he cuts logs, an' stuff. Ya go be home only on weekends when Henry Jeems go be home too.

"I'm goin' over ta-Mabel's house an' have-a talk with that gal. I 'ma tell 'er ta-leave my boy 'lone-fore somebody get cut-up or kilt." Marr' Dee snapped at her Son, who kept his eyes on the plate of food in front of him.

"Okay, Mom." Bird emptied his plate ... and got seconds.

"Bird, Rev. Johnny sent Wilbur up-ta D.C. He go stay with his Step-Momma, Lily, till time for 'im ta-report ta-the Army Base in Maryland. Ya Uncle Johnny's 'fraid-a what go happen-ta Wilbur ifn Henry Jeems got wind-a what that boy's been doin' with Mabel. Ain' no tellin'. I's glad

Johnny sent that boy 'way. I 'ma go up an' speak with Mabel, directly," Marr' Dee said. She got her third plate of food and gulped it right down.

On this Monday morning, Marr' Dee came up the path to where Mabel and Henry rented a "haunted house." She saw little Billy playing with Charles in the sand in front of the house. Charles was still crawling around on one knee and one leg. He was sort of scared to take a chance on actually walking. But it was about time for him to be walking quite well. He would only walk when Mabel or Henry held his hand. It was late morning, and Henry had gone to work.

"Billy, Billy, Billy boy. It's A'nt Marr' Dee. Is your Momma home? I wanna talk ta 'er." Then-she became speechless. She pointed towards the south-side of the path, shaking her right hand. Her light-skinned face turned bright-red from panic. Her wrinkles smoothed out. Her eyes got big as ho-cakes. She screamed; "Chillren, y'all run-run ta-the house-run!"

Billy, seeing A'nt Marr' Dee take off like a Jet, yelling, "Run! Run! Run y'all," took off after her. He left Charles out in the sand.

Charles, seeing his older Brother running for the front door screaming as loud as he could, thought it was about time for him to start walking-and or running-right then. He ran right behind Billy, grabbing a hold to Billy's shirt.

Once all three were in the house in front of Mabel, Marr' Dee forgot all about what she had come to talk to Mabel about. Instead, she talked about something else, entirely.

"What's the matter with y'all?" Mabel asked.

"Mabel, I just seen a ghost-a haunt! It was Old Lady Caroline. She once rented this house from Molly Briggs. She's a witch, Mabel. They say, she fixed Bessie Jackson cause she took Lin away from her spells."

Marr' Dee's face became ashy-white. Her fat body was shaking like a leaf on a tree. "Mabel, Caroline put-a spell on Bessie ta-make 'er gut swell up ev' spring. It go down in the summer, but it cause Bessie a lotta pain.

"Now, Bessie don't b'lieve in that kind-a thing; but her gut swell up anyway. Must've been a powerful spell," Marr' Dee said.

"Hold it," Mabel said. "You's sayin' Bessie been conjured? Is that what's goin' on?"

"Yea, that's what they say. Mabel, the Old Witch had a lotta mens 'round here under her spell. She fixed old Jon-Jon Briggs, Molly's Daddy. She ruled over that man. That witch cou'd near 'bout get any man she want; White-men, Black-men, preachers, deacons, rich mens an' poor ones. Nobody's husband was safe.

"They said she fixed Bessie in-a cup-a tea an' a batch-a cookies." Marr' Dee sat in the rocking chair near the Heater. "Mabel, them cookies might've been cooked in that stove right in the kitchen." Marr' Dee got more nervous after she said that.

"Marr' Dee, how did-a witch get Bessie over here so she could fix 'er?"

"Mabel, Caroline's one-a the first womens round here to get a battery-run RCA Radio. She 'vited Bessie over here to listen-ta the Soaps. That's how it all got started. I's 'fraid, one-a these days, Bessie's gut's go burst an' kill 'er."

Mabel was amazed at the story she had just heard. "Bessie never told me nothin 'bout no conjure woman fore we moved in over here. I ain't scared for myself, but I done moved my boy into this cursed house; an' two was born right here. What's that go mean for them?"

"If'n I's you, I'd get my family outta this doorway ta-hell, Mabel. Have ya had any strange things goin' on over here?"

"Yep. I've seen that Old Witch. But if'n I can see 'em, I ain 'fraid-a 'em no more. I just thought the haunt I saw was just a stray ghost."

Marr' Dee got up and headed for the door. "Nice ta-meet ya, Mabel. I go see ya later. I gotta go. I wanna get 'way from over here."

Mabel watched the 200-pound woman run out the door like she was light as a feather. Mabel wondered had Marr' Dee ever seen the "Ghost of Caroline?" The way she was acting, she hadn't. Now that she had, it scared the hell out of her. Mabel had to smile at Marr' Dee. She stood in her window watching the green dress she wore billow in the wind as the rather large woman ran down the path towards her home with her little feet barely touching the ground. She panted like a working mule. Mabel was thinking: *I ain 'fraid-a haunt if'n I can see it. But even more if'n I knows it name. This house's a doorway ta-over yonder-ta the "Other Side." I's born with-a caul over my face-so's my Brother George. We can sometimes see ghostes. I only hate it when I don't kno' they names. A haunt gotta 'spect ya when ya knows they name. So, Caroline gotta show me some respect.*

In a couple of weeks the agonizing pain in Billy's finger subsided. The skin healed over his nub. He started going over to Reverend Nicholas's house to play with eleven-year-old Twins, Annette and Harvey, Rev. Nicholas's youngest children at home. Billy had grown tired of playing with his imaginary dog.

On this morning, in June, Billy was six. He scampered over to find Harvey and Annette. He first encountered Edna out in the front yard swinging a serrated Swing-Blade cutting the grass, with a hand-sickle lying nearby.

"Hey, Billy boy. Let's go inside an' get us a cup'la glasses of Lemonade. It's hot as the Devil in hell out here today-too hot for this time of year-feels more like July or August. C'mon, honey." Edna motioned for them to go onto the green and white porch with metal furniture to match. They walked through the door to the entrance-hallway past the door to a large front room. He saw two brown sofas in there and two end chairs, a Baby Graham Piano, an ornate coffee table, and a little bed in the right comer of the room.

To the right as Billy came into the entrance-hallway he saw a stairway that led to upstairs. He heard Annette giggling and playing up there.

"That's a cute nub ya got, Billy boy," Edna said, to see if Billy was sensitive about that. Edna knew how he had gotten that nub, but wanted to see if Billy would say it. She asked: "How'd ya get your finger cut off?"

"I's playin' with-a axe, an' it slipped an' I cut my finger off." He put his left thumb into his mouth and stared at the stairway. He saw what seemed like a stack of coat-hangers floating down the stairway by themselves. They suddenly disappeared. A little fear clumped up in Billy's stomach, but he just got closer to Edna.

When they got to the kitchen, the Brown dog that Billy had seen many times in his own yard appeared in the middle of the floor. It seemed to be smiling at Billy.

"Edna, I know that Dog's name. One day it told me it was 'Kit-Kit.' See it standin' over yonder near the backdoor?" Billy said.

"No, Billy boy, I don't see it now, but I done seen it before. I know who that is. It's my Momma, Kitty. She come 'round now and then to show her love for children. She died trying to bring'er last child-ta the world. It t'was more'n Mrs. Cooper could handle; they died."

"Edna," Billy had a puzzled look on his young face. "How do Mrs. Cooper bring-a child into the world?" he asked.

"She bring'em," Edna searched for an answer-just the right one. "She bring'em in'er big o' midwife's bag." Edna chuckled.

"Oh-okay," Billy said, with a sigh.

Billy tried to pet the dog. He said, "Hi, Kitty." It frowned, then blinked down into the floor. "Don't be disappointed little buddy. She will only let me, Wilbur, or Harvey an' Annette see 'er an' pet her. But she loves every child that come over here. She'll let'em see her, but she won't let'em pet her."

Edna got a tall glass out of the cupboard and a smaller one for Billy. She got a cold pitcher of lemonade out of the refrigerator and poured them a couple of glasses full. "There ya go, Billy boy," she chimed.

Edna sipped her drink and then gulped the rest down. "You can go play with Harvey an' Annette. I gotta get that lawn clipped fore Daddy gets home from Columbia. He'll go to my hide ifn it's not done when he gets back-he's like that."

"You's too big to get whipped," said Billy.

"Not for my Daddy. The only one he don't whip, an' ain' never whipped, is Wilbur." Edna went on out the backdoor. Annette came down the stairs and ran into the kitchen.

"Billy, gimme some-a ya Lemonade," Annette said with a giggle. She was a tall gal, seemingly to Billy. He only came up to her shoulder. She was dark-skinned, and resembled his Mother in appearance.

Billy gave her his glass of Lemonade, and she gulped it down. "Thanks, sugar-pants," she said. Billy didn't know what that meant.

"Where's Harvey at?" Billy asked.

"He's gone over to Bird 'nem. They're goin' fishin' today. Edna's out yonder. You an' me can play 'Momma an' Daddy.' Want to?"

"Yeah. What's 'Momma an' Daddy?'" Billy asked.

"I'll show ya in a minute. Your nub look just like a little 'Peter.' It is so cute." "What'cha mean? What's a little 'Peter'?" Billy asked.

"What-ya don't know? It's that thing down there." She pointed down between Billy's legs. "Boys have those. Some people call'em 'Dicks,' an' girls have 'Pussies.' I can't believe how dumb you are.

"Let's go to the front room an' I'll show ya all about it," Annette said.

Once they got into the front room, Annette pulled down her brown shorts and then her white panties. Billy saw the lips of her vagina. Some hair was around it, but not as much as he had seen around his Mother's. A strange thing happen, too. When he got up in the morning his little thing was hard. Now it was hard from looking at what Annette showed him.

Annette took her panties off. The cute lips of her femininity were the prettiest things Billy had ever seen on a girl. He saw her light-brown mound with some black hair darting the landscape here and there. There was a tiny-little tongue-or something-at the top of av-shaped opening.

"Billy, feel it," Annette said. She giggled and led his fingers to that little tongue.

He did as was suggested. It felt warm and sticky. He let her lead him to the little bed in the comer. She sat down on the bed. She pulled him to her so that he was standing between her legs. He looked down at that beautiful place between her legs. His little thing got more rigid.

"Now Billy, this is how you play 'Mommas an' Daddies.'" She pulled Billy closer to her, pulled down his shorts and briefs. She fingered his little thing for a couple of minutes. She raised her legs and hugged Billy tighter. With her right hand she guided his thing into her.

Billy felt his rigid thing slide into a warm, wet, best-feeling-in-the-world place. She pulled Billy on top of her so that they were both on top of the bed. "Hump it, Billy!" Annette said.

She moved her body to and fro. She grabbed Billy's buttocks and helped him grind it to her. This felt so-0-0-0 hot, and so-0-0-0 good to Billy. He wanted it to never stop. He heard Annette groaning. "You go be my little Nigga," Annette said. She got really wet down there after she said that. Then-

"Hi Daddy," Edna said, loud enough to let Annette know it was time to get her act together, no matter what she was doing. She figured she was as usual up to some devilment.

Annette pushed Billy off her, and they both rolled off the bed to the floor. Billy put on his shorts and briefs and Annette put on her panties and shorts.

"Billy, don't tell nobody that we been 'Fuckin'. Go out the backdoor an' run home. Don't tell ya Mom about this, an' don't let my Daddy see ya," Annette whispered as loud as she dared.

The urgency in Annette's voice made Billy understand that this "Fucking," or as his Mother called it, "Huckle Buck," felt real good, but made people real mad. He made up in his mind that he would never tell anyone about what he and Annette had done. But he knew he would never forget about it, and he wanted real bad to do that again-if not with Annette, than with some other girl.

Life went on. Billy tried to stay outside when his Daddy came home. He was scared to even look-hard at him. He took to playing more and more with an imaginary Dog. He never saw Bird or any other man come by to visit Mabel; and, Annette would not let him touch her, or come at her like he had done before. It was like she wanted him to forget all about it. But he wanted to do it some more. He cried, begged, and pied, but she quietly said, "no." He tried to feel her one day, and she slapped him, pretty hard, up beside his head. All he had for a long while was a terrible longing for something he couldn't even dare to ask another girl to do.

CHAPTER SIXTEEN

"Henry," Mabel whined, being pregnant as she was, everything she said came out in a whine. "Marr' Dee came over here an' dropped a load of shit on me."

Henry was sitting at the supper table eating his chicken-livers smothered in brown-onion gravy, over rice, with pickled beets on the side, and didn't want to hear nothing at all about what Marr' Dee and Mabel had been gossiping about.

"What'd that O' windbag belly-ache 'bout this time?" Henry asked. He dove into his plate. "Ya got any more-a that pear preserves Cora gave us?"

"Yeah," said Mabel. She got a canning jar out of the pantry, wobbled back to the table and set the jar on the table. She took a seat. She watched Henry pop the top off the preserves and scoop out a tablespoon of it onto a slice of cornbread resting on a saucer. With a fork, he broke off a piece of the bread and preserves and put that in his mouth. He chewed slowly.

"Henry, a Conjure Woman, named Caroline, use-ta live in this house awhile ago. That's what that drawin' is upstairs-it'sa magic circle.

"Marr' Dee say, ya Sister, Bessie got fixed by the Witch right here in this house. Marr' Dee heard the story but ain't never seen a ghost-a Caroline-though a lotta other people claim they done seen Caroline's haunt. The other day Marr' Dee came up to visit with me, ta-get to know me. She saw that O' Witch comin' up the spring path. It scared the hell outta 'er.

"It wouldn't bother me too bad, ifn Billy hadn't see the haunt along with Marr' Dee; but Billy an' Charles came runnin 'hind Marr' Dee cause they saw that ghost too. Dick even learn-ta walk."

Henry stopped eating. He got up from the table. He went into the bedroom area. Mabel followed him. "Mabel, old folk use-ta say, it' sa ser'us thing when-a child see-a ghost. It's aw ight ifn it'sa Angel. But a haunt ... Well that mean, somethin' bad's fixin' ta-happen. We go have-ta talk-ta Lin an' Bessie 'bout this conjure mess." Henry sat on the edge of the bed. Mabel sat in the rocking chair near the heater.

Mabel could see a little fear in Henry's eyes. She wondered at that. She watched him go over to a little table near the bed to turn on the radio.

"This is the Evening News with Edward R. Murray," the announcer said. Mabel watched Henry and he watched her. Both were wondering what to do about the house.

Murray's big voice began to broadcast the News: "Lawyers on both sides of the Negro Civil Rights Issue converged on the Capitol today to file briefs for or against the Desegregation of Public Schools in Greensboro, South Carolina, Farmville, Virginia, and Topeka, Kansas. The Class Action Suit is the largest such Case since Reconstruction. . . ." Mabel went into the kitchen to get a little food on a saucer. She came back with a biscuit and some gravy.

Henry turned the radio off He got a very disgusted look on his face. "Hey, ya didn't have-ta turn that off," Mabel said.

"This-here mess ain't 'bout y'all 'Colored womens.' It's 'bout our 'Colored boys' bein' put in-a school with White gals. Boy, that shit ain' go be 'bout nothin' good. Ifn it go through," Henry grew more agitated as he spoke, "them Cracker-mens go lynch the hell outta our boys.

"Just look-a what they been doin' ta our boys: hangin 'em, burnin 'em alive, an' cuttin'-out they balls. What'cha think go happen ifn our boys end up in school with them o'nasty White gals? I'ma tell ya. They go screw. Our boys go get blamed. Them gals go holler, 'rape!' Then we go have-ta standby an' watch o' rabid White-men kill our boys. I don't wanna see that go through, Mabel."

Mabel got a somewhat worried look on her face. "Well ... Billy's go be startin' school this fall. He's six now. Hope this mess-a be over by then. I don't want my boy in no school with White folks. I want 'im ta-go ta-a 'Colored' school. I too hope that Civil Rights shit don't pass." Billy came in from playing with his imaginary dog. Bug and Dick were playing with wooden toys on the floor. "Billy go in the kitchen. I go feed ya, now. Watch ya hands in the basin of water on the stand in there." "Yes'am, Momma," Billy said.

Henry had built a makeshift baby chair for Bug, and Charles sat on a makeshift extension at the table. Mabel spooned the food into Bug's mouth. Charles spilled a lot of his food, but managed to get a sufficient amount into his mouth. Mabel fed Bug, and watched over her other Sons. She called out: "Henry, c'mere, a moment. I wanna ask ya somethin'."

Henry came into the kitchen. "What'cha want?" he asked.

"Henry, I'on kno' ifn it's cause-a this house, but Billy's playin' with-a dog all the time that can't nobody see but him. He done even gave it a name-'Kit-Kit.' What we go do 'bout that?" He scratched his head for a second, then allowed: "Ain' nothin' go fix that but-ta get 'im a real dog," Henry said. "Old man Judah Langhorne gotta bitch that just dropped a litter of puppies. I helped him get up hay one evenin'. He said I could have my pick-a the litter when his dog delivered. I'm go pull his chain on that offer. That'll fix Billy's problem." "Where he live at?" Mabel asked.

"He live up yonder beside-a Gerry 'nem, just down the path from 'em. One time the Langhorne Family owned a lotta land up yonder. I on' kno' nothin' 'bout them much. Talk got it that they's the chillren by a White Father an' a Black Mother. When the old Whiteman, Langhorne, died he left all his land ta-his House gal. He gave his name-ta his boys, an' deeded a plot-a land to each one. So Neil, Gilliam, an' Judah got right-smart-a land, livestock, an' farm 'quipment; an' I heard, a whole-lotta money, after they Daddy died years ago. All-a them boys is Deacons in some Churches 'round here. One named Walter 'sa Deacon at Columbia Baptist."

On this morning, Henry woke Billy up and handed him a little white-beagle puppy with black spots on his face and back. The dog was so tiny, immediately Henry called him "Rat." When Billy saw the dog he squealed, "Thank you, Daddy. Thank ya so much. I 'ma take the bestest care-a of 'Rat.' Thank you, Daddy."

Little Rat curled up beside of Billy on his Bed, snuggling close to him like they were meant to be together. "I go build-a nice doghouse for 'im, though Billy. We can't let no dog sleep in the same room with us-like them White folk-exceptin' on really-cold winter nights, an' really bad weather.

I gotta catch the truck-ta work. Ya look after Rat while I'm at work. He's a Beagle Hound, he's go be a good Rabbit Dog."

Billy and Rat became fast-friends from the start. The dog seemed to grow in leaps and bounds. By the end of August, Rat was a big dog. Billy's imaginary Dog-friend disappeared for good.

What was strange about Rat and Billy's relationship was Billy thought he could hear what the Dog was thinking and vice-versa. On this afternoon, they were in the woods near the house at a little deeper end of the branch to the spring. Rat said to Billy: *"Jump high. Go on, you can do it. Let me show you how."* Rat ran and jumped over a mud puddle, and beckoned with his snout for Billy to do the same.

Billy ran and jumped up high as he could, but landed in the mud puddle. It caught hold of his feet. He started to sink. Mud came up to his waist. Rat barked frantically. He tore Billy's shirt off trying to get him out of the mud. He grabbed Billy's hand and bit into it in a frantic effort to get his friend out of the mud.

"Don't worry, Billy, I'll go get the Madam. I'll be right back," Rat said.

"Hurry, Rat," said Billy. He watched his friend gallop towards the house barking as loud as it could.

Rat came up and put his front paws on the windowsill nearest the comer of the house. He got into a hysterical fit of barking. It was very unusual for Rat, and that alone startled Mabel. She had been lying down after frying chicken and making com pudding. "Go 'way, Rat, I'm tired."

Then Mabel became alarmed when Rat barked even louder and growled like he was in a fight with a rival dog. Mabel got up and went outside to see what was wrong with Rat. He grabbed her skirt tail and pulled her towards the bushes. Mabel didn't see Billy anywhere.

"Where's Billy at, Rat?" Mabel screamed. "Bill-0-0-0! Where you at?" Rat pulled her skirt tail even harder until it started to tear. He ran to the edge of the woods and came back and grabbed hold of her skirt tail again. Mabel understood.

Rat led her to the deep end of the branch near the spring. Billy had sunk up to his shoulders in the muck. He was screaming: "Momma. Momma. I want my Momma," when Mabel came to his rescue.

Mabel had a heck of a time pulling Billy out of that sinkhole. Rat kept getting in the way by trying to help her pull his buddy out to safety. Soon, they got him free. She scooped her Son up and took him to the house as fast as she could, being as pregnant as she was.

Once they were to the house, Mabel gave Billy a hot bath. She scolded him: "Billy, how'd ya get in all that damn mud? Why'd ya have-ta go find-a mud-hole-ta play in? Honey, stay outta that part-a the woods from now on."

Billy just sucked on his left thumb. As soon as Mabel got through bathing him, Billy got as sleepy as he could be. Mabel laid her Son on the boys' bed. Rat got on the bed and put his snout on Billy's chest. He would not let Mabel run him off the bed. He growled and showed his teeth, and even after she got a switch, he let her beat him, but only yelped when she hit him with it; but he was not going to leave Billy's side.

"Aw-ight, Rat. I 'ma let ya stay with Billy for the moment so you's go know he's aw-ight. That dog's crazy as can be 'bout that child. He didn't take-ta Dick or Bug like he done with Billy. He won't lemme whip Billy. He bit Henry's hand for slappin' Billy. That dog's Billy's best friend."

Early this morning in late-August, Frances came to visit Mabel. It was just after Henry had gone to work. Billy was still in bed, but waking up. Frances looked fully grown, with a large bosom, very curvaceous hips, and silky-smooth cream-and-coffee colored skin. Mabel felt like she resembled a darker-version of their Mother when Agnes was younger. Frances was just around eighteen or nineteen years old. Mabel could see her coming down the path to the house.

Mabel could see she had on a black dress, black flats, and she had a black scarf on her head.

She wondered why Frances had on all of those black clothes. Frances knocked. "Franny, c'mon in, the door's unlocked," Mabel said.

Franny came into the room where Mabel was slowly getting out of bed. "How ya doin', Mabel?" she asked.

"Hi, Franny. I's <loin'," said Mabel. "Iain' seen ya since" Mabel stopped short of reminding Frances of"The Fire!"

She came in, took off her light coat, and sat in the rocking chair near the heater. Frances had a sad faraway look on her face. Her eyes were red, almost bloodshot.

"What brings ya way up here, Franny? I ain't seen ya for a long time.

How'd ya find out where I's livin'? Ya can lay ya coat on the foot of the bed."

Franny got tears in her eyes. "Some time ago Phyllis told me you's livin' up here in Fluvanna, Bessie Jackson told me you's over here. Mabel I hate-ta drop some bad news on ya ..

. seein' as how you's pregnant an' all, but . . . Go lay back down on the bed fore I hit ya with it," Franny said.

Mabel did what she was told. "Franny, what's the matter? Somethin' wrong with Momma'nem?" Mabel asked.

Frances got up out of the chair slowly, went over and stood over the bed where Mabel rested and started sobbing. She laid her coat on the foot of the bed.

"Franny, what's the matter, gal, what's happen ta-ya?"

Frances wiped her eyes and snuffed her nose. "Mabel, first lemme say I's sorry 'bout the bad things I said 'bout Billy an' you awhile back. I done come-a ways since then. I been down-ta Pita'sburg an' they gimme a lotta pills. They don't make me feel no better 'bout killin' all them chillun, but I don't go runnin' in the woods lookin' for 'em, neither." She sobbed again.

"Franny, I forgive ya. Iain' holdin' no grudge 'gainst ya. Ya have-ta forgive ya-self, though.

That's the onliest way ya go ever feel better." Mabel spoke in a very soothing way.

"Mabel, it's prob-be go take me the rest-a my life ta-get over what I's done. But, I'm go try, I swear fore Gawd!" The tears came down her cheeks again.

Mabel knew she needed to let those teardrops fall to purge the pain and self-loathing out of her Soul. "Franny, honey, I kno' ya didn't come all the way up here on ya own just-ta 'fess up-ta me. What else's the matter?"

"Ya ain't heard, Mabel?"

"Heard what?" Mabel exclaimed. "Phyllis's buried last Sunday."

"What!" Tears came quickly into Mabel's eyes and down her cheeks.

"Yeah, Mabel. She got burnt up in-a fire after one-a Momma's parties. Only, this time, it was at Unc' Gus's house. Momma had ta-move outta the house we grew up in. She live-in-a old house too small-ta have-a party in. Gus had-da bigger place up the road from where Phyllis 'nem live."

"Franny, tell-me-how-the hell-did-it-happen," Mabel shouted.

"Aw-ight. Well, on the night of the party, I heard that Phyllis was told by Unc' Gus, he ain' go take 'er ta-the party. Unc' Gus came by to load up some food an' stuff for the party. Phyllis told 'im she had-da be at that party that night.

"While Unc' Gus's in the house gettin' the food and stuff ta-load in his car, Phyllis must've fix the lock on the trunk so it wouldn't close tight, so she could get in an' get ta-the party that way."

Mabel shook her head. "Why didn't Unc' Gus want Phyllis at the party? She's always the life-a the party."

"Mabel, Phyllis quit drinkin', smokin' cussin' an' fuckin 'round after 'The Fire.' She join over at Columbia Baptist, got Baptized, an' went-ta Church ev' first Sunday. That's what was wrong. Peoples got ta-seein'er as a Church woman. Unc' Gus figured that ifn she was at the party, peoples wouldn't kno' how-ta act 'round 'er. They'd have-a cold party, then. But she wanted-ta be at this party-her last one. It's like she knew it was 'er time ta-go.

"When Unc' Gus got up-ta his house, an' open the trunk of his car, out jumped Phyllis. She said, 'I's sorry, Unc' Gus, but I gotta be at this party tonight.'

"He unloaded all-a the stuff an' took it inside. Phyllis went ta-a backroom an' they said she laid down on a cot Unc' Gus got in there. The party went on. Peoples said that Phyllis didn't drink, an' couldn't dance cause she had-da ulcer on her ankle that was 'fected. She laid back there in a dead sleep. I'on kno' why she wanted-ta be at-a party ta-do that."

Frances got to sobbing again. "Mabel, nobody had-da idea. Didn't know how that fire got started. It just did. It burnt the house up, right quick. Peoples was runnin' an' screamin' ta-get outta the fire. The house's full-a thick-smoke-they say. Nobody-not even Unc' Gus thought-ta call for Phyllis. The people that got out checked for ev'body. That's when Unc' Gus an' A'nt Neddy realized Phyllis wasn't standin' outside.

"The damn old house burnt-ta the ground fast as a brush fire. Tum-ta ashes cause there weren't no water close 'nough-ta the house. Only-a well was nearby. Ya kno' that ain 'nough water to do nothin' with.

"They found Phyllis's bones crouched in the opposite corner from the front door. She's just-a step-a-two 'way from the door. It's like she won't meant-ta get outta that fire alive."

"Oh-My-God!" Mabel shouted. "I's so sorry-ta hear 'bout this. Phyllis's such-a pretty gal.

She's carefree, had some bad habits, but we all got those."

"Hush, Big Sis. You's too knocked up-ta cry like that. It'sa strain on the baby. Lemme hug ya. I never realized till later, how much I love ya an' all my peoples. We go get through it all aw-ight?" Frances said.

"Frances, I hope she forgave me for not being at 'er funeral. I didn't even kno' she's dead!

Gawd knows I'd been there."

"Mabel, I b'lieves she knows. 'Member, she's 'Saved!' She's go be one-a God's Angels, ya go see 'er again."

"Franny, I guess that's the 'Good News.' Ya kno' Franny, ya gotta take notice-a how ya may be seein' a person for the last time any time ya seein 'im. Life's short."

"Mabel, I know what ya mean. Ya gotta mind what ya say an' do, an' who you's sayin' it ta, an' who ya <loin' it with. Wish I had-da knowed that a long time ago."

"Franny, y'know though, peoples like Unc' Gus, nothin' bad never happen-ta them. It's the good what die young. Seems like somebody like Phyllis, that just got 'legion, would have-a long life. No-she didn't get long ta-be good-cut short. That's how it is."

"Mabel, that's why we gotta watch what we's <loin', I reek-en." "How ya go get back home, Franny?" Mabel asked.

"Well, I go hitch-a ride down to Route Six. I 'ma catch the Eastbound Local ta-Columbia. I can walk the few miles-ta Momma's place. She gotta get outta that place. The State done condemn all them places over there. Calls 'em, 'Pe-ans, Pe-uns, Peons,' or somethin' like that. I'on kno' what that mean. But ev'body over yonder gotta leave off that property. Momma's lookin' ev' where for-a place. Neddy's sick. Unc' Willie's dead. So, she ain' gotta move.

"I just came up here to tell ya 'bout Phyllis. Folks say you's livin' in-a haunted place. Say the ghost-a witch's hauntin' this place over here-is that true?"

"Well, I did see a old woman that cou'da been-a ghost, or spook-a somethin'. But I ain't scared-a nothin' like that ifn I can see it, an' knows its name. Her name's Caroline, an' Iain' seen 'er since I learnt 'er name. Lemme hug ya fore ya go," Mabel said.

"I'ma see ya soon, Mabel. I gotta go back home an' take a dose-a medicine. I's startin' ta hear the chillun cryin'. That mean my medicine's runnin' low in my blood. Guess I's go always be like that. But, I knows it's all in my head. So, I can deal with it, that much. See ya Big Sis. Take care'a ya-self an' them Chillren of your'n. I love y'all."

Frances left out of the house. She was soon on up the road and out of sight. Mabel followed her to the front stoop. She waved bye-bye, and returned to sit on the edge of the bed. She turned on the radio. She turned to WRVA, "Search For Tomorrow" was just coming on. Mabel figured she'd listen to that Soap, and then get up and cook supper. She just wanted to hear the latest dope on Helen Trent. The story got started.

Somewhere between consciousness and unconsciousness, Mabel slipped into another Realm:

A small circle of light came from the center of the door. Then the circle grew larger and larger until it assumed the features of a woman standing at nearly twelve-foot tall. Her spectral head reached all the way into the ceiling. She was wearing a burial shroud. Her whole body glowed like the sunlight. Mabel recognized her-it was Phyllis.

Mabel had a hard time speaking but managed to utter through trembling lips: "What happen?. . . Why ya look like that? She asked.

"I am Phyllis," the illuminated person's voice echoed. "I want you to know I have forgiven you for not coming to my funeral. Please don't worry about me. I am going to be with The Messiah and His Angels, and they love me unconditionally, as they do you. Beware of the Demon in this house. This house is a doorway to Hell and Perdition. It is a Portal that both Good and Evil Spirits can enter and exit at will. Move you and your loved ones away from this cursed place. Tell your children about their Heavenly Father-especially those born here.

I must go now. Beware of the Seducer of your Sister, Virginia. He may come after you.

Beware . . . Beware . . . Beware. Bye, Mabel."

The ghost of Phyllis quickly became an orb of light that grew smaller and smaller until it completely disappeared. Mabel had not been frightened by Phyllis's appearance. But what Phyllis had said about the house scared the hell out of her. Spooks and things were coming and going through the house all the time and Mabel couldn't see them and didn't know their names. It had become crystal clear to Mabel that something very evil was alive and undead in that house, and she had to get her children out of that place.

Mabel didn't know anyone who was dating her Sister, Virginia. She had made up in her mind that she was not going to be fooling around with any man on the side again. She felt like the Ghost of Phyllis had to be wrong about that. That part didn't make any sense at all to Mabel.

During supper that evening Mabel was sullen and sad. She at first did not utter a word.

Henry thought she was mad at him for something.

"Mabel, what's wrong with ya? Why ya lookin' at me like that? Tell-me what's the matter, now, gal," Henry said.

"No Henry, I ain't mad at you. It's this house. There's somethin' evil in this house, an' we gotta get our chillun outta here for the sake-a they bodies an' they Souls. We gotta go someplace safer for they sake. Y'kno' what I means?" Mabel said.

"Aw-ight. I'ma give ya that much. I spects you's right. I wanna go talk-ta Lin an' Bessie 'bout this house, Mabel.

"I done heard some strange stories 'bout-a **O'** Gal what'll get rid-a baby an' then cook an' eat its body. Say that Witch could float through the air, an' disappear in-ta thin air. Say she slept with-a own Son, an' got knocked up by 'im. That's the nastiest shit I done ever heard."

Mabel got really nervous, she shook like a leaf in the wind. "Edna Nicholas will look after our chillun till we get over to Bessie's an' Lin's an' have-a talk with them. Henry this is some mighty-powerful shit that we gotta get-ta the bottom of Not just for our sake, but for the sake-a our boys."

It was late in the evening when Mabel and Henry arrived at Bessie's house. Lin was in the kitchen eating a meal of sliced Deer Shoulder and gravy, candied yams, and fried cabbage. Bessie was listening to the Edward R. Murray's News Hour.

"Mabel, Henry. C'mon in. Have some supper with us. We got ..."

"Bessie, we done ate at the house," Henry said.

"No thank ya, Bessie, I ain't hungry," Mabel snapped.

"Sure," Bessie said. She coughed and cleared her throat. "I'ma go in the kitchen an' get a drink-a Kool Aid. Y'all c'mon in there."

Bessie led them to the kitchen table. She got a bowl out of her cupboard, filled that with chocolate pudding, handed that to Henry, who took it with a boyish smile on his face. He sat down at the table and started spooning the pudding into his mouth.

"Bessie, on second thought, I'ma have some-a that Puddin', it smells so good," Mabel said. Bessie got her a bowl of the dessert. Mabel sat down at the table and so did Bessie.

After a couple of teaspoons of the delicious Pudding, Mabel said: "Bessie, it's been told to me by Marr' Dee, that the house we's rentin' is haunted by the ghost-a Witch named Caroline. We gotta right ta-know 'bout that. Marr' Dee say ya been fixed by that Witch. Is that so?"

Lin got up from the table, looked over at Henry, and they both cleared their throats. "Henry let's you an' I go outside for a cup'la minutes. Got somethin' I wanna tell ya," Lin said.

"Sure, Horse," said Henry. "You lead the way." He followed Lin out the backdoor.

As soon as Henry closed the backdoor, Bessie frowned. "Mabel, that's what they say. Now, I don't b'lieve in none-a that shit. All I kno' is my gut swells up in the springtime. It aches.

"Old lady Caroline claimed on 'er deathbed that she done fixed me. She's just-a crazy o' woman who's mad cause Lin marri'd me 'stead-a her. She just wanted me ta-be vexed an' scared-a nothin' toll for the rest-a my days.

"Some peoples claim they's seen 'er ghost after she burst into flames one day while layin' on'er bed an' burnt up. Ifn anythin' her magic ought-a saved her. That's why I don't b'lieve in that shit. Do you?"

"I guess I do," said Mabel. "I's seen things that make me b'lieve in it. I wanna get outta that house. It's cause-a my chillun. I don't want no curse on me or them. I had-da vision, too.

"Ya know' Phyllis's dead, now, an' her ghost came ta-me in the middle of the evenin'. She said the house's evil. Told me ta-get outta that place. She'd been dead for-awhile, but was on her way ta-Heaven ta-be with Jesus an' the Angels ..."

"Phyllis's dead?" Bessie asked.

"I see ya ain't heard. She's been dead a cup'la weeks or so. Frances came up ta-tell me 'bout it. Break it ta-Alize softly. It's her real Mother, ya know."

"Mabel, what happen-ta Phyllis?" Bessie asked.

"Bessie, she burnt up in-a fire," said Mabel. "It was after 'nother one-a Momma's parties." "Now, that'sa shame," Bessie said. "Well . . . My stomach bother me mighty bad sometimes. I done been ta-a lotta doctors, who can't do nothin' for me. It's female trou'ba. Cary had it. Got tumors. They took out ev'thin'. That's why she can't have no babies. But ta b'lieve in witches, ghosts an' goblins's crazy. I try-ta stay 'way from all that shit. I want-it ta stay 'way from me, too."

"Bessie, I know that there's some real-live Conjure Womens. Ma-be, Caroline's one-a them. I just hope ya find peace. The Devil ain' go be 'vided 'gainst his-self So, goin' ta-a Conjure Man or Woman ain' go do ya no good. Gawd's prob-be the onliest answer. Phyllis's ghost told me ta- teach my boys what was born in that house 'bout Gawd. I wanna get outta that house badder'n ever, Bessie."

Lin and Henry came in from outside. Henry was smiling like a chess cat. He came over to Mabel. "Mabel, Lin just sold me three acres-a land 'cross from Cora 'nem. Just forty dollars's all he's askin'. Mr. Kent go lend-me that in a heartbeat ta-build-a house. The trees on the piece a land is all we go need for the house. Ain't that good?"

Mabel got a pleasing smile on her worried-looking face. "Yep, that's great. How soon will we get the house up?"

Bessie hugged Mabel. "See, ev' thin' go workout just right for ya."

"Bessie, we gotta go. We left our chillun with Edna Nicholas. She prob-be think we's gone ta hell an' back. It's gettin' late. We's gotta be goin'." Mabel said.

"Yeah, we gotta see y'all later," Henry said.

"Henry, I'll give y'all-a ride up the road. 'I'ma use the money for the land to get-me-a power saw. I seen-a STHIL for just forty dollars down-ta Holland's Hardware in Columbia. Mr. Kent go sell me a pretty-good old truck. I'ma be subbin' for him for-awhile."

"See how ev'thin's comin'long, Mabel?" Bessie said.

Henry and Mabel got into Lin's car. "Mabel, I know Old Man, Pat up in Cloverdale. He's the one I's go hire ta-help me build my house. Ya know who he is?" Henry asked.

Mabel grinned a little bit in the dark. "Yeah, I's heard that name mention somewhere," she said. She smiled as Lin drove off.

The mailboxes for all of the families living on the north side of 656 were situated on Route Six across from 656. This evening, instead of riding up the road to his turnoff, Henry got out at his mailbox. He got a large-brown envelope with an official-looking seal on it. It was addressed "To The Parents of William Anderson James."

Henry opened it. He read: "The Fluvanna County School Board has information that indicates, that according to our records, William Anderson James, a Negro boy, six years of age, The Son of Mabel Louise Scott, and Henry Anderson James, is of School Age. He must be registered with the School Board in Palmyra, Virginia on or before, September 1, 1953. He must show that he has been vaccinated, and be enrolled at Gravel Hill Elementary at Gravel Hill, for classes that will commence, in September, 1953-54. If you have questions write or call."

Henry wondered where do these peoples get all they "infar-mat-son from?" He said aloud: "Damn. It's that time already. I'll give this shit ta-Mabel. She can get all that done. I gotta go ta-work at the Mill, an' on the house ever evenin's."

He rushed on up the road past the place where he would build his future home as soon as he got the load or so of lumber from the Mill. He got to "the rented haunted house," pretty soon. He gave Mabel the envelope.

"I's been lookin' for this letter for days now. I'll get Rev. Nicholas ta-take me an' Billy up-ta Palmyra ta-get him registered. There's a clinic for the shots in the County Buildin'. We can get ev'thin' done the same day. When's our house go be ready, Henry?"

"Way it's lookin', go be next June, or so. The Boss's got Lin an'nem cuttin' the trees right now. They gotta take the logs-ta the Mill. We's go get the lumber after that. Then Old Pat can come with-a cup'la his boys an' they can go-ta work on our house.

"Mr. Kent done cut all the timber off'n the piece-a land, but he's slow as hell 'bout givin' me the lumber I need-ta get goin'." Henry's face filled with contempt. "That's the way them Crackers always do us."

"Ain't that the truth," Mabel agreed with her husband.

Billy came into the kitchen. "Billy, ya go have-ta walk-a-mile your first school year," said Mabel. "I'm go get Rev. Nicholas ta-take us ta-Palmyra to get ya red-ta-go-ta school. We go get ya some clothes too. We go make it somehow, we go get it all done," Mabel whined.

CHAPTER SEVENTEEN

Billy was glad that his Daddy was getting a new house built just up the road from the Bus Stop. At first he would have to walk a long ways to catch a bus to school. It was the Labor Day Weekend before school was going to start.

He had gotten his shots that made a little bump on his arm. The needle the doctor stuck in his arm hurt going in and coming out, but he hadn't cried. The doctor gave him a red sucker. So Billy was happy about going to school for the first time. He was sad because he wouldn't be around to look out for his Mother. She was getting so fat in her stomach she could barely walk.

His Momma had told him that the White kids' bus came up the road to pick them up. Black kids had to walk a mile down the road to catch a bus to school. Billy wondered about that.

His Momma and Daddy had fussed at each other because his Daddy didn't have money to buy new clothes for him to wear to school. His Daddy finally gave up and bought him a pair of green-khaki shorts, a yellow sweat shirt, and a pair of red "Kids Tennis" for the first day of school. Billy was so proud of his spanking brand-new clothes. He was up early that first day.

Billy watched his Mother pack a bag lunch. She put slices of ham in, his favorite, biscuits. She wrapped those in waxed paper. "Son, this's for ya lunch. Don't eat it 'fore then. An' don't give it ta-none-a the bigger kids. Is that clear?" she said. She handed him the brown bag.

"Aw-ight, Momma," Billy said. Mabel got her little Son dressed, stood back and admired him, with tears in her eyes, and allowed: "Now, don't ya look handsome?"

Mabel got a little red-book bag in a paper bag from under her bed. "Ya gotta pack of pencils an' a pack of 'Lucky Star' lined-paper in that bag. The Teacher's go give ya a booklist. Don't lose it. Put it in ya book bag, bring it ta-me, so's we go kno' what'cha go need, an' all."

"Okay, Momma," Billy said.

Mabel took her little Son's hand. Henry had gone off to work. "Billy, I 'ma take ya up ta-the road. Harvey an' Annette go come by an' walk ya down the road for the first day."

A big yellow bus full of white kids whizzed by them as Billy and Mabel got up to the road. But they did not see hide-nor-hair of Annette or Harvey Nicholas. Mabel anxiously looked around to no avail. Mabel felt too tired from just walking the short distance from the house up to the road. She knew she wouldn't be able to make it up and down the road a mile to the Bus Stop. She thought she saw a possible solution.

Rena, Gerry's and Bella's gal was just coming out to the road. "Momin' Rena," Mabel waved at the young girl.

With her pinkish-nose turned up, she replied: "Sure!" Mabel saw that she wore a gray bouncy skirt, with a large pink-poodle embroidered on the front and back of it, over a Crescent Underskirt. She sported white Bobby Socks, two-toned, black-and-white shoes with pink shoelaces. She had on a fluffy-white blouse with pink-edged ruffles. Her black hair was styled in a short ponytail with ringlet sideburns. Her complexion had an orange-hue to it. Her eyes were light-brown, and she had brown freckles on her nose and cheeks. She seemed to be twelve or thirteen-years-old, but was maturing way above her age, in that, she had a very shapely body.

Rena stood at about five-foot tall. She meant to do an "About Face" and pivot away from Mabel and Billy. But Mabel asked her: "Would ya be so kind as-ta let Billy walk with ya down ta-the Bus Stop? I can't in my condition."

"Yep! He can walk behind me if he wanna," said Rena. She threw her face up in the air like she smelled something foul in the air. She strutted on off

"Go with 'er, Billy," Mabel said to her little Son. He took off after a fast moving Rena. He turned to wave bye-bye to his Mother. Mabel stood watching her Son go off to school for his first day. Tears came to her eyes.

As soon as they were up the road out of the sight of Mabel, Rena said, "Look, Sambo! Don't get too close to me. I don't want people to think you're kin to me or nothing. Stay your Black ass far enough from me so nobody 'll know you're walking with me. You stay way behind me."

"What!" Billy exclaimed. "What'sa 'Sambo?'" His eyes got teary-a little. "I ain't Black.

I's brown," Billy snapped.

Rena stopped for a moment to let Billy catch up to her. "Come here," she ordered. Once Billy caught up so that he stood next to her, Rena put her arm next to his. "See, there's a big difference between yours and my color. You're a 'Blackie. A Sambo. A Dumbo Negro.' You will never be nothing because of your color. You Blackies are born dumb, and you can't be any other way. Now, get your little darky-behind away from around me." She swished on up the road.

With tears of disgust in his eyes, Billy followed behind Rena all the way down the road to the Bus Stop. He whined: "I want my Momma."

At the Bus Stop, he was shocked to see the way the children-including A'nt Cora's grouped themselves. The very light-skinned ones stood over by themselves. The dark-brown ones stood in another place. The very dark-skinned children stood together in yet another group. The first two groups were making grievous fun of a few of the darkest people who looked like they might cry any moment.

The other two groups threw rocks at this last demi-grouping and called those children: "Black Sambos. Tar Babies. Blue Jesuses. A'nt Jemimas. Uncle Bens. Nasty-dumb-Niggas."

The darkest children retaliated by calling the members of the other groups names like: "Shit Face Negroes. Meal-faced Niggas. Cracker Bait. Half-White Bastards. Wannabe Whiteys. Octoroons; Quadroons; Mongrels."

They sounded like a crowd at a sporting event. Now and then, somebody got a knot on his head from a rock. Billy saw at least two bloodied noses. He was glad when he saw the yellow school bus rounding the curb. The stupid teasing and taunting stopped. But the kids got in lines according to their previous groupings. The bus came to a stop.

A very light-skinned boy got off the bus wearing a light-blue, long-sleeved, shirt, a pair of dark-blue woolen slacks, and a pair of white-high-topped Converse Tennis. He had a white sash that went across his left shoulder and around his waist. Up near his left shoulder a shiny badge was pinned to the sash. It had "Safety Patrolman" engraved on it-but Billy didn't know what that said-he couldn't read yet.

The Safety Patrolman carried a stick with a wide-red-flag at the end of it. He got off the bus and stood at the door. He beckoned with a wave of the flag for the children to start boarding the bus. When the last group got on the bus, he got on behind them. He sat directly behind the Bus Driver.

Harvey and Annette were among the darkest group, even though they weren't really that dark skinned. They stood among the group everyone else was picking on. When Billy got on the bus and tried to find a seat, the light-skinned children would not let him sit beside them, even when there was enough room. His own Cousins shunted him. A'nt Cora's children weren't "High Yellow," but they stood with that group. It seemed like to Billy, they were ashamed of him that morning. They didn't offer him a seat either. He made his way to the back of the bus to where Harvey and Annette had taken seats. Their Cousin, Maria Antoinette, was sitting between them. She was their age; next her Twin Siblings, Brandy and Clyde sat, they were Billy's age. A Sister of Maria and the Twins-a year younger than Harvey and Annette was Terry Mae. She was a blonde, blue-eyed, very White girl who looked out of place on a bus full of "Colored" people.

Annette snapped at Terry Mae: "You go let your light-skinned friends treat little Billy like that? Take that boy up front, and Make one-a them yellar-highfalutin assholes give'im a seat."

Terry Mae shook her head, grimaced, and cleared her throat. "Y'all save my seat, now." She got hold of Billy's hand. She was a sholl girl with some muscles. Her eyes were blue with a gray tinge to them. It made her look mean. She wore a gray and green plaid dress that came to her ankles, brown penny-loafers, and a large brown ribbon in her hair. She took Billy to near the middle of the bus.

"Slide over Elnora Johnson. There's room enough for one more between you an' Evelyn. Slide your little narrow-ass over, okay," TelTy snapped. Elnora was Annette's and Harvey's age. Evelyn was Billy's age. Terry was no one to mess with. So the nut-brown girls didn't dare screw with her. The bus couldn't pull off until everyone was seated. The Patrolman was getting ready to come back to near the middle of the bus. But after Billy, the last one to be seated had sat down the Patrolman sat back down. Elnora rolled her eyes and whispered: "Blackie, Sambo." Evelyn poked her tongue out at Billy.

Mr. Garland Baskerfield, Sr., the Bus Driver, closed the doors of the bus and got it moving on up the road. A commotion got started in the back of the bus. Someone had thrown a spitball that even hit Mr. Baskerfield. The kids all laughed. Priscilla Bland laughed and pointed at Harvey Nicholas. Annette slapped Priscilla up beside her near-White face. Priscilla had thrown the spitball. Hai-vey and Annette and Priscilla and Charlotte, two sets of Twins, got into a rolling around fight.

"Whoa. Whoa!" Mr. Baskerfield, a six-one two-hundred pound muscleman shouted. He and his Grandson, Melvin, the Safety Patrolman, got the Twins separated. "If y'all don't stop it right now, I'm go write y'all up the first day of school. I'ma put y'all off my bus for two weeks." He had stopped the bus and pulled to the side of the road.

"Now, get back to ya seats, and I mean, right now!" Mr. Baskerfield yelled.

"Yes, sir," went a little chorus of the guilty kids. They flipped the bird to each other. But no more licks were thrown. The bus got underway again.

It didn't take any time for the bus to reach Gravel Hill Elementarily. It was only a mile west up Route Six, on a little left-turn side-road. It was just past a Civil War Memorial that had a Chapel near the Memorial for those who wanted to Honor their long-dead Confederate Ancestors.

The School sat on land donated to the State by an Old man Josh Willis. In the late-1940s, he had deeded the land to the School Board and Dr. Samuel Christopher Abrams had helped to found the School, making use of funds made available by The Julius Rosenthal Fund. The County had given matching funds to help the "Coloreds" build a one-room schoolhouse for Grades One-through-Three.

The School had been named after the place where Governor H. Byrd in his "Good Roads Projects," in the 1930s, had construction crews dump loads of gravel at a site near where the School would later be erected. They used the gravel to widen the back trails and old roads to make them more passable. Thus, they named the School, "Gravel Hill Elementary."

On this morning in September, 1953, Billy climbed down off the bus, but he wondered why

Harvey and Annette weren't getting off the bus too? Evelyn Johnson, Priscilla and Charlotte Bland, their younger Brothers, Lawrence and John, and a little, very dark-skinned girl, Billy got to know as Nancy Lou, all got off the bus. The Patrolman got back on the bus, the bus-door closed, and it went on back to the main road. A bunch of children headed towards a clapboard building with a porch expanding across the front of it.

As he walked in the group of students, Billy saw Great Oak trees, huge Pines, and massive Poplar trees, whose limbs seemed to reach up to the sky. These gave way to a sandy clearing around the School. Then a tall iron rod came into view. It seemed to reach up into the sky too. A flag with red and white stripes and a blue square full of white stars flapped in the wind at the top of the iron rod. Billy wondered what that all meant.

He got to the porch that was half the size of the rest of the building with banisters that seemed to go all the way to the ground. Four wide-green steps were the way up on the porch. Blocking the way was what looked to be a "White woman," wearing a gray two-piece lady's suit, with a skirt that came down to her ankles, a light-blue blouse, a pearl necklace, matching earrings, and black pumps. Her eyes reminded Billy of ice. She had her black hair up in a French Roll. Billy thought she was pretty, but scary-looking. The little dark-skinned girl walked past her, and the Teacher glared at her like she was a roach bug. The Teacher stood at about five-five. She had a thick Yardstick clasped to her left side that she gently slapped against her leg, while gazing at all of the students coming up the steps.

Once the students had all come into the School and had seated themselves wherever they saw fit, the Teacher walked around the room, with a large potbellied stove in the middle of four rows of students.

"You students who don't know me, I'm Miss Alicia Payne. My name is written on that second blackboard. The first one up near the entrance has a list of Readers and Workbooks my First Grade pupils will need. I will give you a copy of that list for you to take home to your parents at the end of classes for today. Is that clear?" Miss Payne said.

Billy had sat behind Nancy Lou. She was very dark-skinned, but Billy thought she was a very pretty girl. She was shy and talked a little-bit funny, but was nice. She showed even pearly white teeth when she smiled. Then Miss Payne said: "All students get out of your seats, take all of your belongings with you, and stand against the walls. I'm going to reassign you to my new seating plan, according to your grade-level, and other considerations."

The students did as she had ordered them to do. Miss Payne stood in front of her large-brown desk. "You First-Graders will be seated to my left. You Second-Graders in the middle; and, you Third-Graders to my right. The Second and Third-Graders all answered in unison: "Yes 'am." They got seated in accordance with some pre-conceived seating-plan Billy didn't know about right then.

He was in that "infamous" classification that was going to be the "fun" for that day. Miss Payne said: "When I call your name, you First-Graders began seating from the back of your rows to the front.

The names of the First-Graders were called one by one. They were thusly conducted to their perspective seats. Then it became painfully clear to Billy that all of the light-skinned students were being seated in the front of the classroom; and all of the dark-skinned students were being seated in back of them. The children like Priscilla and Charlotte, got smirks on their faces. It was as if they knew a terrible secret the First-Graders did not know.

Miss Payne gave those students on the front of the First-Grader rows a stack of the booklist for them to take home. "Take one of these and pass the stack back to the others," she said. "Tell your parents you must have the readers and workbooks on the list in order for you to move on to the next grades."

After everyone in the First Grade had a booklist, Miss Payne went on to other matters: "Now listen up. Never refer to me other than as 'Miss Payne,' regardless of the reason you may wish to get my attention. When you call my name, you must wait for me to ask you to speak. If you speak to me before then, I will whip your legs with a switch.

"In this classroom, or out on the schoolyard, you will never use words and phrases such as, 'you is, or we is, and ain't.' I will not tolerate those 'Niggerisms' at anytime at this School."

Billy started to get really nervous. Miss Payne walked around the classroom between the rows, slapping that thick yardstick against her leg, hitting herself harder and harder. Then Miss Payne went to the second blackboard, on the left of the classroom, and erased her name. She rewrote it, slowly and carefully. The two blackboards were on the left side of the classroom next to each other. They took up most of the entire left side of the wall. She went over to a closet just inside of the front entranceway and got out a box of lined paper. "Marvell Briggs, come up here, please."

A tall boy, that seemed to be too old to be in the Third Grade, lumbered up to where Miss Payne stood in front of her desk. "Marvell, give each one of the First-Graders two sheets of this paper, and one of the sharpened pencils out of the pack on my desk. Is that clear?" Miss Payne ordered.

"Monty, you come over here and help your Brother," she ordered Marvell's Brother, a year younger than Marvell to come help out. Both boys snickered, a little.

Marvell was a cream-and-coffee-colored type, who kind of resembled Joe Louis in appearance. His Brother, Monty, was of a smaller build, a shade darker, and kind of resembled a smaller version of"The Brown Bomber." They were both in the Third Grade.

Once every First-Grader had the writing paper and a pencil on his or her desk, Miss Payne ordered: "Now, write your full names on the top-line of one of your pieces of paper. I will come by to help you in a few moments." She continued to walk around the classroom slapping that yardstick against her leg.

Billy panicked. He had run from his Momma. When she finally caught him, he kicked and screamed and fell out onto the floor, whenever she tried to show him how to write his A-B-C's.

Mabel warned: "You's go be sorry. Ya go wish ya had-da leant-ta write ya name, count ya numbers, an' say ya **A-B-C's.**"

Billy watched carefully as his Mother drew the letters of his name, but would not dare to even try to draw them himself He had only a vague idea about how to write his name. He had copied the letters of his name one day when Mabel had given up on trying to make him do that, using very laidback drunk-looking characters, that were barely legible. But that was it.

He picked up his pencil with his right hand. He stared at the two pieces of writing paper on his desk. He was shaking like a leaf, because Miss

Payne was still creeping around in the classroom slapping that yardstick against her leg. He didn't want to get whacked with that thing. "You Second-Graders take out your Readers and study chapter six. Be ready to read aloud to me when I call your name. You Third-Graders get out your Math Books. Go over the problems on page thirty-five. I will ask some of you to go to the blackboard to work a similar problem after I finish helping the First-Graders. Is that clear?" Miss Payne said.

Billy nearly peed in his pants when-lo' an' Behold-Miss Payne came right back to him and little Nancy. The benches for the desks could accommodate three students. Billy sat right close to Nancy. Miss Payne stood directly over Billy.

"William, write your name on that piece of paper in front of you-Nancy, you do the same," Miss Payne ordered. You could hear a pin drop. The Second and Third-Graders knew what to expect. They had seen what was to happen for two or three years.

"I can't write my name," Billy replied.

Miss Payne snatched his pencil rudely out of his hand. "Let me show you," she snapped.

"W-i-l-l-i-a-m A-n-d-e-r-s-o-n J-a-m-e-s: now, you do it," Miss Payne ordered. "Write it on that top-line like I've shown you." She had taken her focus off Nancy.

A couple of Second and Third Grade pupils let go of a hushed giggle or two. Miss Payne's angry stare quieted them right away.

She wrote Nancy's name on the top of a piece of paper on her desk.

"I'on kno' how ta-do it," Billy whined. He figured Miss Payne would give up like his Mother had when he had acted very stubborn.

"William, you aren't trying to do what I asked you to do. You're insubordinate. When I give you an order, you do that right away, is that clear?" Miss Payne snapped at Billy. He continued to stare at the piece of paper, but made no move towards writing his name. He meant to look up at her so she would see the tears in his eyes, and would leave him alone.

Billy felt a fiery "Wallop!" land up beside his head. He stuck his left thumb into his mouth, and Miss Payne backhanded him on the opposite side of his head. This lick felt more like a "Wham!" Billy's whole head felt like it was on fire. He saw little stars dancing around his head. He had only been hit like that by his Daddy.

"Now, write your name, William," Miss Payne shouted, with her right fist balled up. "Do you hear me?"

"Yes ma'am. Yes ma'am," Billy said. He whimpered. Just like he had put the pain he felt when his Daddy walloped him, he threw what he really felt after Miss Payne had mauled him into his "Subliminal Lock Box." The fear he felt and the pain inside reached a sublime point of creativity that got expressed as a miracle. Billy didn't know how it exactly worked, but it did.

Before Miss Payne's hand-or fist-came down to strike him a third time, Billy wrote his name--roughly-for the first time. As a matter of fact, he wrote it several more times until it looked excellent. He hysterically filled up the whole page with his name. The more he wrote it the clearer it became.

"I'm amazed at how well, and how quickly, you have learned to write your name, William. I think I may have discovered a smart one," Miss Payne said.

But with Nancy, it was a different story. Miss Payne's yelling at this fragile child, who had grave hearing impairment issues, made her withdraw into a psychological shell she had mentally invented to shield herself, when she had to face frightening circumstances. Miss Payne started to sound like a bunch of barking dogs to little Nancy. She stared at the desk and whimpered. The more she whimpered, the more Miss Payne yelled at her, and that went on until Miss Payne snapped.

Miss Payne hated being forced to teach at Gravel Hill Elementary. She never wanted to have to teach little "Tar Babies" like Billy and Nancy. She saw them as the most inferior of the "Negro Race." Now she saw this little "Black Hellion" as one who was defying her in front of the whole class, when all she was trying to do was get her to write her "stupid name."

"Nancy, you little hellion, I told you to write your name. You have to obey me just like William has. Now, get that pencil in your hand and write your name," Miss Payne ordered.

Nancy laid her little head on her desk. She looked at Billy with a pleading in her eyes, as though she was sending him a signal to help her. Billy could see that Nancy was too afraid to even breathe hard.

"Wham! Wallop! Slap-slap!" the licks sounded off as Miss Payne got carried away on little Nancy. Nancy's tongue came out of her mouth. Her eyes looked dazed. She had a little foam on her lips. She seemed like she couldn't hold up her head. Billy saw a little-bit of blood easing out of Nancy's nostrils. He also saw a little piss easing down her left leg.

"I don't have any more time to spend helping you Nancy; but when I come back to you, you better have your name written on the top-line of that piece of paper on your desk," Miss Payne snapped. "You better fill the page up like William did."

Miss Payne checked around the rows of First-Graders, she only found one other person who could not write her name. This child was as light as a paper bag. Her name was Joan Gray.

Joan's skin-shade bordered between medium to light-brown. She also had reddish-to-dark brown hair. Her piercing black eyes gave her a look that pointed towards potential glamour one day.

Miss Payne approached Joan. "Joan, why haven't you written your name?" she asked.

Billy expected a wallop to land up beside Joan's head. But instead, Miss Payne stooped down so that she could see right into Joan's face. Joan smiled on top of her understandable nervousness.

"I need somebody to show me how," Joan said. Her little frame shook as tears came out of her eyes, easing down her cheeks to wet her pretty-red dress.

Miss Payne smiled and stood up. She looked around the classroom, then, called out: "Priscilla Bland."

"Yes ma'am," said Priscilla. She flicked her light-blondish locks. An arrogant sparkle flashed across her light-colored eyes, that seemed to be bluish-green because of the sunlight hitting them just right that came through the huge windows.

"Come over here, please. I want you to work with little Joan. She looks like she's going to be a smart little girl. Show her how to write her name. I'll check back with her tomorrow to see how she's coming along," chimed Miss Payne.

"Yes ma'am," said Priscilla.

Billy thought that was just "Dandy!" He and Nancy had been "beat-to-death" for not knowing how to do the same thing that Joan couldn't do. Miss Payne didn't get anybody to help them. He wondered was it because he and Nancy were dark-skinned?

Priscilla got up and swished over to where Joan sat, which seemed to be "a million miles away from him and his little dark-skinned group" to Billy. To add insult to injury, she poked her tongue out at Billy, Nancy, and those sitting next to them, when she strutted by their desks. Billy heard her whisper: "Jiggerboos," under her breath. He didn't know what that word meant.

Priscilla went around to a number of other children with the same skin-shading as Joan to help those First-Graders better write their names. Miss Payne did not hit any of them. She was all "Smiley-Whiley" around them.

Billy wondered too, why Miss Payne never came back to see about little Nancy. The girl kept her head down on her desk. It was like she couldn't wake up, or something. One of her eyes was partially open, but the other one was shut-tight. It was approaching lunchtime.

Miss Payne, while sitting at her desk, rung a little bell. "You all stop what you are doing. Get out your lunches at this time. You First-Graders who have them in your desks today this is the last day that will be permitted. You will store your lunch bags, and pails, in the coatroom on the shelves in there after today.

"Second and Third-Graders you may go to the coatroom to get your lunches at this time, quietly now. Return to your seats after you have retrieved your lunches, but do not open your bags or pails."

The children did as they were ordered. They came back to their seats and waited until everyone had been seated again. Then, Miss Payne, said Grace! After that, she ordered: "You may begin eating your lunches at this time."

Billy opened his lunch bag. All of the children did likewise. He looked around to see what the other First-Graders had brought for lunch. He saw that they had sandwiches made with slices of light-bread filled with peanut butter and jelly, or bologna and cheese, or some other spread. All eyes were on Billy. He got out his biscuit and ham sandwiches and un-wrapped one. One pupil laughed, then another and another. It seemed like the whole school was laughing at him. Miss Payne did not stop them. She had an arrogant grin on her "high-yellar" face. Billy watched her bite into a bologna and cheese sandwich and she chewed it up slowly. He lost his appetite. He rewrapped his sandwich and put it back into his lunch bag.

Judging from what he saw of the other children's sandwiches, light-bread was the only accepted bread to bring to school.

It was a good thing he hadn't eaten his sandwiches. When he could not bear his hunger any longer, Billy slipped into the coatroom and meant to woof down his lunch out of sight of anyone. He saw that a mouse had eaten a hole in both his sandwiches. Billy was hungry as a hog, but was not going to eat food leftover by a mouse. He balled the bag and sandwiches up and threw that into the trash. Then-He remembered: Nancy hadn't left her seat through lunchtime. Miss Payne didn't seem to care about the little girl at all. She shot Nancy an angry glance or two, but never went over to see about the child. Most of the other children would not dare go near Nancy for fear of offending Miss Payne, except for two of them.

Becky Lewis, the Daughter of Jack and Jemima Lewis, a Third-Grader, and Katherine Willis, Betsy and Prince Willis's Daughter, were two light-skinned people who hated Miss Payne. Both girls had failed to move on to the Fourth Grade. Both had failed two times. Both were ten going on eleven. (Both were Agnes Lewis's cousins.)

Becky could not bear the fact that little Nancy seemed to be in a bad way, after Miss Payne's attack on her. The girls came over to hug Nancy and asked her, "How you doing, honey?"

It only took Miss Payne a second to notice that Becky and Kathy were paying too much attention to Nancy. Miss Payne ran over first to Kathy. She slapped her and left the red print of her hand on the left-side of Kathy's cheeks. "You need to pay more attention to your reading skills. Let me do the teaching around here," Miss Payne shouted at Kathy.

Becky stood there with her arms folded. She was big for her age, and was not that much smaller than Miss Payne. This red-boned, red-haired, green-eyed child stared Miss Payne right in the eye. She wore blue Jeans and a red and black plaid shirt, when all of the other girls wore dresses. She did have on a pair of black and white two-toned girl's shoes. Miss Payne came over to Becky. She watched Kathy run to her seat crying, but Becky just got an angry scowl on her face.

"Becky Lewis, take a seat," Miss Payne shouted. "If you don't, I'll send Marvell out to get a switch so that I can whip your legs."

Becky spoke in a very sassy way: "You ain't gonna do nothin' to me.

You got that?" Miss Payne tried to ignore her. "Put your hands on me and see what's go happen to you."

Miss Payne got tears in her eyes, but knew about them Lewises. She knew nobody messed with them or their children. She was glad it was time to ring the bell for recess.

Billy noticed that Miss Payne stayed in the school during recess. He ran out to where a lot of the children were playing ball using a softball bat and a rubber ball. Two ringleaders were choosing team members from among the various groups standing around a concrete block being used as home-base. Other rocks marked first, second, and third bases.

The kids had grouped themselves according to their skin-colors. The darkest children were getting picked last, or not at all. Some of the oldest-looking kids gravitated towards the edge of the woods.

Monty and Marvell, Billy found out later, didn't start school until they were nearly eight or nine years old. Here they were, ten, and or, eleven, and just in the Third Grade. In the late thirties, when localities were able to erect and build local schools, a sanguine problem still remained. There was little money left to buy enough buses to bring all of the children to school. Localities had to come up with half of the funding to buy buses, pay drivers, and pay for part of the fuel to run the buses. Fluvanna was one of the last Counties to provide adequate funding so that a bus could run up Routes, Six, and Fifteen, to bus children to Gravel Hill, and Shiloh Elementary-Shiloh was twenty-seven miles from Gravel Hill; and, S.C. Abrams High was fifteen miles away; all of the above were way past several White schools.

Many parents, like Molly Briggs, would not let their children walk the roads to school for fear that something awful might happen to them. That's why Bessie Jackson didn't send her kids to school at all, like many other Mothers.

(At the end of World War II, Garland Baskerfield, Sr. provided half the money to buy a second-hand bus for the kids living on Routes Six and Fifteen. He volunteered to drive it. He only required that the State pay for the fuel. The first couple of years, the Fluvanna School Board refused to pay for the fuel. Garland asked the local Black Churches to help out.

They did, and many more children were able to attend school because of Mr. Baskerfield' s efforts-and hundreds of others like him in the State of Virginia. In the 1950s things changed.)

Monty and Marvell wanted to make it all the way through school, and they went every day, even though they were teased for their age. But their presence in the lower grades presented somewhat of a problem: they were too wise about some things.

Billy tipped over to the edge of the woods to see what the giggling was about. What he saw brought that feeling he'd had while "doing it" with Annette that one day. Priscilla had her left leg up on Monty. He was holding it with his right arm. Her pink panties had been pulled down to her ankles. She had taken one leg out of them. Monty had positioned himself under Priscilla's blue dress, and was "Playing Mommas and Daddies" with her, up against a huge Oak tree.

Monty kept repeating, "O-o-o-Baby. O-o-o-Baby." Then he put both of his arms around her waist. He picked her up off the ground so that her legs were wrapped around Monty. He moved his young buttocks in short, jerky, motions. He laughed out loud.

Priscilla had what seemed to Billy a cross between a grin and a frown on her immature face. "Ow-ow-ow-ow, Monty," she exclaimed. "O-0-0-0-oh, ump-ump, ah-h-h-h, 0-0-0-0-oh!" Billy was about to think Monty was hurting her until he saw her working her hips just as fast as Monty, and hugging him as tight as she could. Then-Monty put Priscilla down. She stepped into her panties and pulled those up very quickly. Billy didn't see anything under her dress because of the way she had pulled her dress down so quickly. "What you looking at, Monty?" she asked. Then she giggled.

"Oh nothing," he said. Then Billy saw Monty do something he thought was weird right then. He took a white handkerchief out of his back pocket. While Priscilla looked away, Monty squeezed some white-pasty stuff out of the end of his "thing." He wiped it off with the handkerchief, and tossed that onto the leaves. He put his thing back into his fly. He kissed Priscilla in the mouth. He allowed: "Baby Girl, please don't tell no-body 'bout this. They go put me in jail if anyone find out-especially your Mother."

Priscilla giggled. "Honey, I won't tell, if you don't. You stay here for a couple of minutes, let me show up first; okay?"

Once Priscilla got out of the woods, Monty went out another way.

Billy was left alone in the woods with his little "thing" as rigid as could be. He was getting ready to head back to the schoolhouse when he saw another spectacle. Marvell had one of the very light-skinned girls, who looked to be twelve-years old, lying on a pile of leaves. He was doing to her what Billy had seen Bird doing to his Mother. Billy's little "thing" grew even more hard and rigid when he saw what Marvell was doing with Jewel Patton.

Jewel seemed to be pretty and shapely all over like a grown woman. Marvell was pounding it to her with his eyes closed. Her dress was all the way up and Billy saw that she had a full-bush. She had nearly fully-grown breasts. All Jewel said was, "Um-um-um, oh, um-um-um." Then, the bell started ringing. When Jewel stood up, Billy saw that she had a tiny waist, big hips and buttocks, and her long, pinkish, hair came down her back. She had pretty almond-shaped eyes. Her irises were blue-black. Her lips were like "Mona Lisa's."

Jewel picked up her black-silk panties, stepped into them and buttoned up her green dress, real quick. She ran towards the ringing bell. Marvell pulled up his pants, redid his belt and ran too in a slightly different direction than she had. His shirt tail stayed outside of his pants.

Then Billy came to realize what the children standing on the edge of the woods were really doing. They were lookouts. Marvell and Monty were giving them all a dime or two for watching out to warn them if Miss Payne came to check on her students.

So then, Billy, on his first day of school, had seen what he thought then was how older boys ought to act towards girls. But Billy remembered what had happened to him and his Momma because of that "Mommas and Daddies," or as Annette called it, "Fucking." He knew not to tell any adult about what he had seen going on in the woods. He got in line, but was still "hard up."

Billy strode by Miss Payne, who was standing on the porch slapping the yardstick against her left leg. She pranced through the doorway after the last student.

"Marvell Briggs, go get me a good Dagwood switch. I got some correcting to do before we get started on our afternoon classes. Well ... go on, boy. What are you waiting for?"

Marvell hoped he wasn't the one who was going to be singled out that afternoon.

There was a scary hush in the whole school. Every pupil wished he or she could run away to safety. Then, Marvell returned with a healthy Dagwood switch.

"Come up here, Genevieve Andrews," Miss Payne ordered.

A tall, dark-brown-skinned girl stood up. She was around twelve-years old. She had a little bit of a speech impediment, and was a little-bit crossed-eyed. She was on the overweight side, wore her hair un-straightened and naturally fluffy. She had on a dark-gray dress with a hemline that nearly touched the floor. She wore a pair of thick-white socks in black penny-loafers.

The older students in the Third Grade knew her as the younger Sister of Goethe Andrews. Her Twin Brothers, Kenneth and Hansel, were the same age as Billy, and were in the First Grade. Goethe was the same age as Harvey and Annette Nicholas. Two children were too young to attend school. They were Arbudella, and baby, Glynn. Genevieve was one of six children of Pete and his wife, Arbudella Andrews.

All of the kids knew Pete. He was the Janitor who cleaned the school at night and made the fires on the cold mornings. He would be leaving as the bus arrived to drop them off. He was a very nice, tall, handsome man. He had bucked teeth that he smiled to show often. He always had a cigarette dangling from the corner of his lips. His wife, Arbudella, was a Member of a Primitive Baptist Church. They did not believe in women wearing clothing that exposed any part of their bodies. They wore no makeup. They did not believe in straightening their hair, and or putting on anything false, such as deodorant, or perfume. Soap and water had to do the trick. They did not believe in ironing their clothes-they saw that as "Vainly Showing off." Mrs. Andrews did not drink of smoke. So, their little Daughter was not one of Miss Payne's favorite people.

Genevieve walked slowly past the potbellied stove in the middle of the classroom. She whimpered because she knew what to expect. The light-skinned contingent giggled, a little. They anticipated the "fun" to come.

As Genevieve got up to Miss Payne, who had seated herself at her desk, and had a wicked grin on her hateful lips, the child cried out: "Miss Payne, please don't beat me. I'm sorry I misbehaved. Whatever I've done I'm sorry"

Miss Payne, while still seated at her desk, turned her swivel chair so that she could grab a hold of Genevieve and pull her onto her lap. She had the little girl face-down. She pulled up her dress exposing thick cotton drawers that went half-way down Genevieve's thighs. She started whipping Genevieve's bared legs. She rolled off Miss Payne's lap to the floor.

"Come here to me, little girl. I'm not through with you yet," Miss Payne yelled.

Miss Payne got up so that she stood over her helpless victim. She pulled up the child's dress again and commenced to whipping her bared legs again.

Genevieve screamed: "Ma'am, what did I do wrong?-O' Lord-God Help me!"

After three licks laid-on-thickly, Miss Payne stopped brutally whipping the little girl. "I heard you playing out there today. I told all of you all never to use 'Ain't' at this school. I heard you say, 'Nah I Ain't,' The correct pronunciation is, 'No, I am not.' Is that clear?"

"Yes 'am. Yes 'am. I won't do it no more," Genevieve screamed.

"Now, get up and go in the back and get in the 'Dunce' chair for the rest of the day," Miss Payne shouted.

"Yes ma'am." Genevieve scrambled up off the floor. She ran to the back of the classroom to a tall stool that sat in the corner. She climbed on top of it and sat facing the wall.

Priscilla laughed out loud. She whispered, "O' Jiggerboo."

The ordeal with Genevieve and the long-extended lunchtime had used up most of the available hours for that day. Miss Payne looked at the pretty-shiny watch on her left wrist and said: "Classes stop what you are doing. Gather up all of your belongings. Get ready to go meet the bus. You all, who live nearby, may leave at this time. Classes dismissed."

Becky and Genevieve lived just a-half mile away. Their houses were situated on opposite sites on the north and south boundaries of Gravel Hill Elementary.

All of the children scrambled together their belongings very quickly. They were more than ready to escape from "That House of Horrors," they had been subjected to that first day of school in 1953.

Billy noticed that Nancy was not getting ready to get going. "Nancy, get up. We gotta meet the bus. Miss Payne says it's time to go. Where is your things?"

Nancy stared at Billy with a sad-distant-look on her cute face. "Huh?" she asked. "Girl, we gotta go catch the bus," Billy said.

"Aw-ight. I'll try to get up," Nancy said.

Nancy tried to stand up, but fell back into her seat. Billy helped her stand up. "What's wrong, Nancy? Why you can't stand up?"

She stood up and held onto Billy. "My head hurts really bad, Billy. I'm dizzy. I can't see good. Help me to the bus; okay?" Nancy said. She staggered towards Billy. He hugged her and they both had tears coming down their cheeks. He helped her up the road to the where the bus had dropped them off that morning.

Nancy had forgotten book bag, pencils, schoolbooks, and all. She had managed to only put on her light beige sweater. Billy noticed too, that the rest of the children going up to the Bus Stop steered clear of he and Nancy, like they were afraid of catching some disease by coming too close to them.

Little Nancy just clung to Billy. He thought she was trying to fall asleep on his shoulder. "Wake up, Nancy. Honey, wake up. You can't go to sleep now. The bus's coming.

"Nancy, Baby Girl, you got to get on the bus. It's here," Billy whined.

Miss Payne came cruising by in her black two-door, new Buick, with the white-walled tires and red hubcaps. She slowed down to shake the second finger of her left hand at Billy. At this point, it didn't matter to him. He had the most precious-little girl he had ever seen in his life in his immature arms. He was not going to let her go for nothing. Nancy whimpered, and clung tightly to Billy.

The doors of the bus swung opened. The Patrolman got out. Upon seeing Billy and Nancy, Mr. Baskerfield parked the bus. The Patrolman and Mr. Baskerfield took charge of Nancy. Billy started to resist. He clung to Nancy, shaking his little head, "No," he protested; fearing, that if he let her go something worse might happen to her. Mr. Baskerfield pulled Nancy out of Billy's arms. He dropped to the side of the road and cried like someone had given him a beating.

"Who did this to this child?" Mr. Baskerfield yelled, looking at the whole group of students standing around little Nancy and Billy. The children hurriedly got loaded onto the bus to keep from saying anything for fear that what they said might get back to Miss Payne the next day.

Mr. Baskerfield yelled: "I'm go write all y'all up ifn someone don't tell me who hurt this child."

Evelyn Johnson nervously spoke up: "Will James sat beside her in class today. He can tell you what happen to her."

Mr. Baskerfield grabbed the shoulders of Billy's shirt. The Patrolman took control of Nancy.

She was barely there. "Boy, what did you do to this little child?" He almost screamed at Billy.

His heart beat like when he was being confronted by his "Mean Daddy." He didn't want to say anything, but the "Subliminal Lock Box" kicked in: "Miss Payne beat her. She hurt her like that," shot up and out of Billy like vomit. "I didn't do nothing to Nancy."

Nancy came to enough to say: "Yes. Billy's right. He's ... my boyfriend. He didn't hurt .

. . he didn't do it. Don't ... fuss at-him." Then she fainted.

Mr. Baskerfield went over and picked Nancy up off the side of the road. "Little baby, I know your Grandmother. She go get-with that bitch. She done 'bused the right child, now. Y'all pardon my French. That nasty woman whipped my Sons Garland, Jr., Melvin and Clarence. I felt like killin 'er. Wait till I tell Mrs. Annie Woodson 'bout this."

After Mr. Baskerfield carried Nancy onto the bus, she came to and struggled to get loose from him. She made her way back to where Billy sat. She got in the seat beside him, and Annette and Harvey moved to let her sit beside Billy.

She put her little head on Billy's chest. She closed her eyes tight. She called Billy's name: "William, William, William ... Don't leave me."

"Nancy, I'll never do that," Billy replied. Tears eased down his cheeks all the way to where he had to get off the bus. He rubbed his friend's head, very gently, until the mile was up, and he had to get off.

Annette and Harvey Nicholas; Rena Anderson; Elaine and Umpster Wells, Jr; Robert,

Richard, Cornelius, Clarabelle, Beatrice, and Miriam Winston got off the bus at the same time. Billy had a little bit of a challenge to get loose from Nancy. But finally did after the Patrolman plied her fingers loose and told Billy to get off the bus.

Billy watched the bus drive away. He waved until it went out of sight. He had to run to catch up with Rena.

Harvey and Annette were gone on up the road almost out of sight. But Billy had found out where Rena had gotten her stupid ideas about skin-color making her better than dark-skinned people. Miss Payne had put that stuff in her head. Billy just hung his little head as he walked along a good distance behind Rena.

He felt that he also knew where Annette had gotten her "doing nasty" from. It was probably from boys like Monty and Marvell. But he knew he couldn't tell his Momma and Daddy about what he had seen. His "Mean Daddy" might beat the hell out of him.

Billy was glad when he reached the turn that would take him home. After coming through the door, Billy blurted out the entire day, except for the things he would not dare to divulge.

"What did ya do ta-make the Teacher beat ya?" Mabel snapped at her little surprised son.

"I couldn't write my name at first, Momma. I didn't know how to do it. So, I got slapped," Billy said in a whine.

Mabel lightly slapped Billy up beside his head. "Iain' sendin' ya ta-school ta-do things ta-get beat. Ya gotta get your learnin'. That's what you's at that school ta-do. You hear?"

"Yes ma'am," Billy said. He stuck his left thumb into his mouth. He thought that you can't tell grown peoples nothing. They's always beating somebody.

Henry came home that evening full of sawdust as before. He took off his work clothes and changed into some clean overalls and went over to pick up Bug. It was like no one else in the house mattered as much as Bug. Dick came over to his Daddy next. He got the proverbial pat on his head, as usual. "Mabel, that boy looks more like Poppa ev' day," Henry said, admiringly.

But, Billy always shied away from his Father, especially when he had just come home from work. To defray anything bad from coming up too soon, Billy got the piece of paper full of his attempts to write his name. He showed that to his Daddy, hoping for a pat on the head too.

Henry gave the piece of paper a quick glance. He grunted, turned away from Billy, and said: "Let's eat."

"Henry, wait-a-minute. Billy gotta whippin' at school, today," Mabel said. "Is that right, boy," Henry asked. He yelled like a peal of thunder.

"Yes sir. I couldn't write my name. Miss Payne hit me," Billy whined.

Henry undid and snatched off his belt. Billy ran and tried to get under the bed. He did not get under there in time. Henry grabbed his left arm. He pulled the rest of him from under the bed. He whacked Billy on his back six times. Each blow was harder and hurt worse than the one before it. Henry screamed: "We ain't sendin' ya ass ta-school ta-act up! I don't wanna hear that ya ever gave the Teacher no trou'ba. Is that clear?"

While his Daddy was flogging him, Billy wondered who was the greatest monster his Father or Miss Payne.

Billy shoved that beating into his "Subliminal Lock Box." He had a hard time with that one. But he had to push it out of mind so that he could feel like a normal little boy. He replaced the memory of that beating with thoughts of Look how good I can write my name now; I'm so smart. That night, he dreamt that he was being chased through thickets in the woods by a "Mean-Black Horse." He had trouble running away from its snorting closer and closer behind him. Instead of running fast away, he floated like a balloon in mid-air. He tried to scream to call his Momma, but the words wouldn't come out of his mouth. He just mouthed: "Momma ... Momma ... Momma"

The sun came up on that next cool, September, morning, lighting up the horizon. Its rays glistened on the dew on the dying grass and browning leaves of the trees and shrubbery. It was a clear, crisp morning. There wasn't a cloud in the sky. Billy got up and put on the same clothes he had worn the day before.

Henry had gotten up earlier, made a fire in the warm-morning heater, and in the cook stove in the kitchen. He went to the spring to get a couple of buckets of water for cooking and washing up with. Mabel was frying some Herring Fishcakes. She also had a pot of oatmeal boiling, some biscuits baking and coffee percolating. Henry came into the backdoor with the buckets of water. He was wearing his overalls including a thick jacket. The wind felt a little cooler when it blew outside.

"Henry, I done looked at Billy's Booklist. What he go need costs 'bout ten bucks. He go need-a Primer Reader, an' a Workbook that go with it. He go need-a Writing Workbook, too. He go need-a Twelve-Inched Ruler, an' a Arithmetic Workbook. We ought-a be able ta-get"

"I'on kno 'bout all that. Mabel, Cora's Chillren might have some-a those things. Billy can use them. We pass-down the same books when we went-ta school. Momma barr' ed 'em from somebody. She ain't never had-ta buy no schoolbooks," Henry said. He got up from the breakfast table, got a pipe full of smoking tobacco, lit it up and puffed away.

Mabel followed him into the sleeping area of the house. "Henry, all I got ta-put on Billy is a flannel shirt, an' some Bibb Overalls. That's aw-ight for 'im ta-play-in in the yard, but not-ta wear ta-school. He's go get teased." Mabel's voice was filled with pleading.

"Mabel-look! I had-ta wait till I's eleven an' Lil' Charlie's nine or ten, fore I ever went-ta school. We had-ta walk from West Bottom ta-Columbia ev' day. That's four-five miles goin' an' comin', rain or shine, hail, sleet, or snow. A lotta days it was too cold for all that.

"All any-a us boys had was Overalls. Clothes didn' matter. We's there ta-learn-ta write our names, read a little bit, and count some. Why we gotta get in debt dressin chillun so good today for schoolin'? Billy gotta wear what we can'ford-ta buy," Henry preached.

Tears came down Mabel's cheeks, but she didn't say another word. She felt inside that Henry didn't realize what day this was. He didn't realize that his children had to go to school looking good every day. She remembered being laughed at whenever she dared to go to school. Kids called her bony. They teased her because she had to wear the same homemade dress all the time. They made her want to stay home, so she finally did. She wished she had toughed it out, though.

Mabel made a couple of ham biscuits for Billy's lunch. Again she wrapped those in wax paper and put them into a brown paper bag. "Here's your lunch, Baby," Mabel said.

She fixed Henry's lunch bag. She put in two ham biscuits, two boiled eggs, a pickle cucumber, and a slice of chocolate cake. She wrapped those in wax paper and put them into a much-larger brown bag. Henry took his bag and said goodbye to Bug and Dick. He walked past Mabel and Billy like they were statues, not real people.

Henry did notice that "Dick ya done piss the bed again. Boy, ya' scion you. I'm go have-ta beat ya if'n ya don't stop <loin' that, Son," Henry mildly scolded Dick.

To Billy, it seemed like his Daddy never hit Bug or Dick for anything. He guessed he took out all of his desire to beat little boys out on him. It was something else Billy had to shove into his "Subliminal Lock Box." He pasted a smile on his lips and over the wound in his little heart. Then he wiped away the tears that came easing down his little cheeks. He broaden the smile on his trembling lips, headed on up the road to catch Harvey and Annette before they went down the road. He never wanted to walk with Rena anymore.

When Billy had come out of the door, he saw a strange thing. Edna Nicholas waved at him. She was carrying a stuffed carpetbag with her right hand. She waved at Billy with her left hand. Billy figured that she might be bringing Mabel some of Harvey's old clothes for him to wear. Billy hoped not. He went up to the road and caught up with Harvey and Annette.

Mabel looked out the window. She went to the door to let Edna in. "Edna, what'cha doin' out so early this mornin'. Gal, c'mon in," Mabel said.

"Mabel, I'm leaving from over yonder in that house. I done found me a man, finally, who go marry me. I'm goin' off with him," Edna whined softly.

"What's the matter, honey?" Mabel asked. "I thought y'all was in-a good o' place over yonder. You's carryin' that old suitcase, child. Now that look bad-what's wrong?"

"Mabel, Daddy's a Preacher, I know," Edna said. "But sometimes he's meaner than a junkyard dog. He slapped me 'round the other day like I's a little gal."

"What riled 'im up like that?" Mabel asked.

"He heard 'bout me seeing the man I'm go marry. He wanna know his name. I figure it ain't none-a his bizzness-I'm a grown woman, Mabel. I'm not his little gal no more. He ain't got no reason to be slappin' me 'round like that, neither. I can't take that no more, Mabel."

Mabel hugged Edna. "Hope y' know what'cha <loin'."

"Mabel, I finished the Seventh Grade and graduated but my Daddy didn't see fit to send me to Virginia State to finish school; but he sent

Wilbur, his precious Son. He didn't b'lieve us gals need no education. So, I been cookin', cleanin' washin' clothes, and lookin' after Harvey and Annette like they was my children." Edna coughed, cleared her throat, and her eyes became very red and irritated.

"That don't make no sense, Edna, where's his wife?" Mabel asked.

Edna coughed again. "Mabel, yeah. He's marri'd-ta Lily Brown. They gotta Son, right." Edna coughed even harder like she had something in her throat. "We call 'im Sonny Boy. He an' his Mother lives up in D.C. He's high-yellar like his Momma. He's about Billy's age.

"Lily comes down here during the summer. It's like she vacations down here. Come late August, she and Sonny Boy go right on back up north. She never come back here but once-a year, not even at Christmas time. Daddy gotta go up yonder if he wanna see her or John Jasper Nicholas, Jr. Daddy get right lonely sometimes-he ain' too old for that. He got other gals."

"What'cha mean, Edna?"

"I mean, Mabel, Daddy's a Preacher, but he ain't no Saint. Lily weren't neither. Fore Daddy ever got hitched with her, she had a baby with Hamlet Lewis, Jack Lewis, Jr.'s Cousin. Lily is Umpster Wells and Tom Wells, Sister. Lily named her Son, Burly Brown. His Uncle Tom raised Burly because he was too dark-skinned for Lily. Umpster Wells and Lily was almost White cause they Daddy's White. I don't know nothin 'bout they Momma-don't nobody know. Some say it was a White woman who done had children with a Black man. Others say it was a Black woman who done got children with a White man. Tom was 'Paper Bag' but darker than the other two.

"Tom Wells live up near Gravel Hill School next to a woman ev' body call, A'nt Betty Lou. She's marri'd-ta a man name, Harry Lee Anderson. Daddy hooked up with Lily right after my Momma dropped dead-some peoples thought it was too soon."

"Edna, what'd ya Momma die from?"

"Mabel, Momma's Ellie's Bishop's Sister. Her name was Kitty Bishop fore she marri'd Daddy. Their Sister's name was Marr' Julia. Mom took in washin', milked two cows by hand. Did the runnin', and Daddy made her keep 'The man of God's House, spic' an' span.' She got TB and died when she tried to bring another child into this family, the baby died too.

"Maybe that's why Daddy's so mean to us. He takes his spite out on us. I gotta work like Momma did. Iain' go let 'im work me to death so he can go an' so-call, 'Preach the Gospel,' Mabel."

Mabel was aghast. "Edna, honey, I wish you'd think 'bout all this fore ya make up your mind like ya <loin'. Afterall, it's ya Daddy ya talkin 'bout. He's the onliest Daddy ya go ever have. I wish I knew who mine was," Mabel said. "Where ya go live at?"

"Yea. My man got us a big o' house already built. I'ma move in it soon's we get hitched. We go fill it with children that we go love more'n anythin' else. I can't tell Daddy cause he'll run me down an' beat the hell outta me an' my husband. An' he might shoot my husband.

"He worked Momma to death. Mom had to make up for what a Preacher's salary brought in. Daddy didn't make that much money. The work an' worry was too much for Mom. So I'm go disappear."

Mabel hugged Edna tightly. "Baby, take care-a ya-self. It's been so good meetin ya an' listenin' ta-the stories with ya. I know ya ain' go tell me where ya goin' so I won't ask. But, Edna, come see me sometime, sugar," Mabel said in an almost whine.

Fireworks exploded that morning as soon as Billy had gotten to school and had been seated. The students said the Pledge of Allegiance, and sung The Battle Hymn of the Republic. Then they were seated.

A smooth-Black-skinned woman suddenly came through the door. She wore black high heeled shoes, a two-piece green Lady's suit, with the hemline up to her knees. She had on a pink blouse, a red fedora, and a red Lady's handbag. The short, four-eleven woman got all up in Miss Payne's face.

"What's this Becky told me? Say you threaten to whip her legs in front-a the whole class the other day. Who the hell do you think you is, Alicia?" Jemima Lewis yelled.

"I was just trying to do my job, Mrs. Lewis. I want to educate these children ..."

Before she could finish that sentence, another angry woman stomped through the school doors. This one was almost two-hundred pounds, or more. She had big eyes, a large nose, on a full-moon face. She had her hair un-pressed and tucked under a rounded blue hat featuring a long-white feather, that went from the front of it to down the woman's back. She wore a grayish gown with a hemline down to the floor. Its sleeves came down her arms to her wrists. On her feet were black laced-up boots that shined like patent-leather. Her skin color was the same as her Daughter, Genevieve's. She came up and stood beside Jemima.

"I heard what you did to my Daughter. You high-yellar heifer. You pulled my baby's dress up before all of these boys in this classroom and exposed her underclothes. You beat the only child in my home that has never misbehaved or talked back to me or my husband. I'm going to send a letter to Mr. S.C. Abrams on the School Board. He'll know what to do with your light skinned snobbish butt," Mrs. Andrews blurted out at Miss Payne.

"No don't ... I didn't mean ..." Miss Payne whimpered like a spoiled child. She sat at her desk with her eyes downcast twiddling her thumbs.

"There's another petition circulating around here again. This time we're going to get rid-da your crazy ass, Alicia," Mrs. Lewis yelled. "I'm gonna be the first to sign it."

"Me too," Mrs. Andrews snorted. "We live down the road insight of this school. If I so much as think you're going to put your hands on my children again, I'm coming back up here with a shotgun. Do you hear me heifer?"

Miss Payne didn't answer Mrs. Andrews. She stood as the two ladies strutted on out of the school through the door. Billy could see through the windows that the ladies went around the school building shaking their fists as they walked along.

In a trembling voice, Miss Payne announced: "Classes will now come to order." But instead of standing before her desk dictating where each Class was to start working, she ran outside. Billy heard her loudly crying.

He wondered why Miss Payne was crying like a whipped child. Well, maybe it was because she knew she had done little Nancy wrong. Billy hadn't seen her on the bus. He wished he knew how she was doing. He hoped her parents would come up to Gravel Hill and jump all over Miss Payne like Mrs. Lewis and Mrs. Andrews had. Then, Miss Payne came back inside.

She got her thick yardstick again, and started slapping that against her left leg again. She walked around the schoolroom prancing like an enraged Peacock. Then she said something Billy would never forget:

"You all don't have to understand what I am doing. I know what I am doing is the best for all of you. It is the best for us all. I know who among you will become leaders; and who among you will have to be their backups. That is how God meant it to be. We can't all be the same. That is why God made us all different Colors."

Miss Payne pointed to the back of the schoolroom to the light-brown-skinned people in the middle of the room. She frowned and said: "These are our go-betweens, just like the people in front of this schoolroom are the go-betweens for us and the White Race. See, there has always been a separation between the very light-skinned people and the very dark-skinned ones. From the days of slavery, that is how our White Masters wanted it to be. That is how it remains today.

"We of the Colored Race must fight against what the Whites want. But right now, we have to train leaders who they will listen to. Mr. Booker T. Washington, our Great Negro Leader taught us that while he was alive."

She stopped walking around the schoolroom. She stood behind her desk. She sat down, and laid the yardstick down. "Let me tell you exactly the way it is, pupils. It is no use in me using what limited resources the White-run School Board shoves at us to try to educate those who don't have a good chance of becoming Negro Leaders. The darker your skins are, the less likely it is for you to become a Booker T. Washington; like Walter White; or even like A Phillip Randolph; or Mr. Walter Friend, Principle of S.C. Abrams High. Not to even mention, Dr. Samuel Christopher Abrams, who is on the School Board, and is the founder of the High School named after him.

"Gravel Hill, Arvonia, Kents Store, and Shiloh Elementary Schools all owe their founding to the efforts of S.C. Abrams. What if this light-skinned man had been left behind? We wouldn't have public education facilities for any of you all today."

Katherine Willis raised her hand. "Yes Katherine, what do you want?" Miss Payne snapped. "Daddy told me to give you this note," Katherine said. "I almost forget. May I come up and give it to you?"

"Yes, you may." Miss Payne's reply was almost vitriolic.

Katherine walked slowly up to Miss Payne's desk. She held a folded piece of paper in her right hand. She didn't dare to look Miss Payne in the eye. She dropped the note on Miss Payne's desk, and ran back to her seat.

Miss Payne unfolded and read the note very quickly. Tears came to her eyes and spilled down her cheeks. She threw up her hands, with the note still in her left hand.

"Your Parents don't seem to understand. I'm just trying to do for you all what Hampton College and my Dear Father taught me. I'm taking the best route to educating Negroes. That is all that I run doing. Oh God, help me," her last sentence came out like a scream.

Billy could not understand why she ran outside and rant and raved again. She stayed out for a long time before returning. After she returned, Billy was nervous. He wondered was she going to find some dark-skinned person to take her spite out on. He had heard light-skinned people using "Ain't" and "We is," and Miss Payne was standing close enough to them to hear them. She didn't send for a switch to beat their bared legs. But as soon as a dark-skinned person did the slightest thing wrong, Miss Payne jumped right on him or her.

Miss Payne laid her head on her desk for most of the rest of the day. She cried softly without saying a word. When lunchtime came around, the children went through the motions without being told to do so. Miss Payne just kept her head on her folded aims. Then she raised her head and took a glance at her watch. It was time for the classes to be "dismissed." A bloodshot eyed Miss Payne announced: "You all get in line and go to meet the bus," she whined in a whimper. Billy wondered what she had read in that note.

That evening, when Billy got home, his Momma had some sad news. "Billy, Mr. Pat died this morning. The dear-old guy was 'bout 'round in his eighties. I reek-en it's his time. He done went on to be with his Heavenly Father," Mabel said. She wiped the moisture from her eyes.

"What is a Heavenly Father, Momma? Do I got more'n one Daddy?" Billy asked.

"Billy, honey, the Bible say there's a Big O' Whiteman sittin' on-a White-Throne way up yonder in the sky in Heaven. He's all-a our Heavenly Father," Mabel said.

Billy wondered at that saying. "What do he look like, Momma?" he asked with great excitement ringing in his voice.

"He's a Burnin' Fire. He made ev'thin', an' we's all His chillun. So that makes us all Brother an' Sisters down here on the earth. One day, when ya get ta-readin' better, ya can read the Bible we got an' see for ya-self. That's what the Bible's all 'bout." Mabel got a pontific smile on her lips.

It all sounded very confusing to Billy. He wondered: "how can all of us peoples be Brothers and Sisters down here on the earth. Is White mens kin to all the rest of us? Is light-skinned peoples the same as dark-skinned ones?" Billy thought. Now, he was surely confused about everybody and everything. Then he heard his "Mean Daddy" coming into the house. Billy scurried into the kitchen, got a cold biscuit from the bread box, and shot out of the backdoor. He heard his Daddy say: "Since Old Man Pat's gone, I gotta finish boardin' up the kitchen myself. Gotta finish the roof fore winter sets in. Lin an' Roy's go help me ever evenin's an' on weekends. Roy an' his boys's puttin' a new-white Cement-like sidin' on they house. They got them new asphalt shingles on they roof. Mabel, that make that house look good.

"A'nt Mimi an' Unc' Peter left them boys in good shape money-wise. That's how Will got that new truck. Go on feed me. I gotta head back down the road an' get up a few boards before it get too dark."

Mabel got busy putting Henry's supper on the table. "Henry, don't forget ta-ask Cora'nem for the books you go barr' from 'em," Mabel reminded Henry for the umpteenth time.

"Hump," was Henry's only reply. He gulped down his supper and a couple of cups of coffee, got his makeshift carpenter's box filled with various nails and a hammer, a handsaw and ruler, and he hustled up the path and on down the road.

When Henry got to the house site, Lin was already working alone. "Sorry I's late, Horse," Henry apologized.

Lin had cut several boards that were just the right length. He and Henry got busy nailing those boards to the kitchen walls. The remainder of the boards on the roof had been nailed into place. Henry had a brown tobacco pipe in his mouth. Lin had a Pall Mall dangling from his mouth. Both of them worked up a full head of steam.

"Lin, I gotta question I wanna ask ya. Don't want ya ta-think I's crazy, now; but tell me, what in the hell happen 'tween you and that Caroline gal?" Henry asked. "What Mabel an' Marr' Dee's sayin' don't make no sense. B'lievin' in witches is crazy, man. Ain't nothin' toll ta-that shit, Lin.

"I don't mean ta-be gettin' in ya bizzness, now. But y'kno' ... what I mean?"

"Yep, Henry I do. I'on like talkin'bout that shit. Lemme tell ya what-for 'bout it as I see fit," Lin said. He threw his cigarette out of a window frame. He got a plug of chewing tobacco out of his pocket and bit off a piece of it and started to chewing on that. He put the piece he'd bit off back in a comer of his jaw. He went to the windowsill and spat a glob of tobacco-spittle out onto the ground.

"Look man, I ain't tryin' ta-mess in ya bizzness. Forget I asked," Henry said. "Aw-ight, Homes. I kno' what'cha askin' me. I'm go tell ya. Here goes:

"Years ago, I came over here ta-Fluvanna from Louisa ta-build-a house. I'd seen a little gal in West Bottom. She caught my eye, man. I want-it ta-get a place 'fore I approached A'nt Maetta an'ya Poppa. That gal was your Sister, Bessie.

"Fore then though, I got hold of-a quick piece, man. Henry, this yellar gal put it on me like I ain't never had it. I got-ta givin 'er a lotta my money. Look like I couldn't stop comin' ta-see that gal. I put off gettin' hitched-ta Bessie for a spell.

"One day when I's still in my right mind, I hauled-off an' marri'd Bessie. That broke that gal's spell on me. She sent her Son, Waldorf, over to tell me: 'Momma say she go get ya ass an' that little tar baby ya done got hitched-ta. 'I done heard that shit from gals before. I didn't pay it no never-mind I didn'pay no 'tention ta-it.

"But on 'er deathbed, Caroline fessed up that she done fix Bessie in some cookies an'a cup a tea. Henry my Sister-in-Law's 'vangelis' Susan Jackson, b'long ta-a Pent'a 'costa Church over in Louisa. She's a Minister, she marri 'd my Brother, Thomas Lee. They claim there ain't nothin' toll ta-witchcraft. Sometime Bessie's gets a lotta pain.

"Bessie don't b'lieve none-a that witchcraft shit. She put all-a 'er pains on female trou 'ba.

So, 'cause she don't b'lieve in it, ain't nothin' the Doctors or witch-doctors can do for 'er."

Henry shook his head in disbelief. "I don't know nothin' bout no witchcraft neither. I done heard 'bout Conjure Womens. Some-a them might would work-a root on ya. That's what Momma 'nem say. A cup'la them gals live over yonder in Cloverdale. I wouldn't go nowhere near 'em, man. That was your mistake, Lin," Henry said.

"I guess ya right, Homes," Lin said. "Let's get these boards nailed up fore it get too dark to see by flashlight."

Henry eventually brought home a tattered "Dick and Jane Primer/Reader," and an Advanced Reader." One of Cora's children lent it to him. Billy still didn't have the workbooks. What was even worse was that Henry insisted that Billy wear Bibb Overalls and Brogan shoes to school every day.

The children made him the laughingstock every time he came to school dressed like they teased him: "Farmer Bill." Billy had to push the teasing and disgust he felt down into his "Subliminal Lock Box." Sometimes he'd go off to himself into a comer and cry. Then he studied his Readers and became the best First-Grade Reader in the whole school. But he hated going to school.

In the middle of October Billy got a pleasant surprise. Nancy was on the bus when Billy got on. She had saved him a seat beside her. Right away, Billy saw the thick-lens of her eyeglasses. On the left side of her head there was something big and brown that went around the back of Nancy's ear that looked funny to Billy. It looked a lot like an earlobe.

Nancy's eyes lit up when she saw Billy. "Billy, I'm back here. Come sit with me."

Elnora and Evelyn Johnson snickered. "Two ugly ducklings in the same pond," Elnora said. "Hi-i-i-i, Billy," Nancy yelled, almost too loud. She was bouncing up and down in her seat.

She still chewed up her words a little bit, but could talk just fine.

"Hi Nancy. How're ya doing. You look so nice. You talk good too," Billy said.

She touched that funny-looking thing on her ear. "I can hear you real good now, Billy. I can hear everybody. At first, I had trouble getting to sleep. I could hear too much noise," Nancy said. "I never wanted to take my Hearing Aide off."

"Why you got that thing on your ear?" Billy asked. "What'sa Hearing Aide?"

"Grandma took me up to see Dr. Yateman after Miss Payne hit me.

I was seeing double. Had a bad headache too. It made me real dizzy. I couldn't walk. Doc Yateman sent me to Charles' ville to a big o' hospital ..."

"Nancy, where's that at?"

"Way up yonder in the mountains . . . somewhere--I'on know," Nancy said, shaking her little head.

"What'd they do to you way up yonder," Billy asked.

"They put me in a bed. Made me stay still for a long time. Took x-rays all over my head and body. Gave me a whole lotta medicine, too.

"A White Nurse helped me walk again. Took-a few days. Then, William, This big O' Doctor put-a lotta instrumen's all over my chest, stomach, and neck. He listen to me several times every day. He came back one day and he and another man put that thing on my ear. They say it'sa 'Hearing Aide.' That's when I started hearin' loud noises that didn't make no sense. Took me a week to hear good."

Billy didn't know what to make of what he was hearing. "Nancy, why didn't what ya heard make no sense?" he asked.

"I had to learn how to make the noise make sense. The longer I listen, the better sense I got," Nancy tried to answer Billy the best she could. "My Momma and Daddy came down here to take me back to D.C."

"Why you comin' to school today for, then?" Billy asked. He was a little puzzled.

"Grandma told me not to tell nobody, Billy, not even my boyfriend," Nancy said, with an ear to-ear grin on her dark-chocolate, beautiful face. "You gonna see when you get to school; okay?"

She hugged Billy. The children on the bus giggled. Even though her tiny-little arms felt real good, Billy frowned and in a boyish manner, eased out of her embrace. Then he turned back to her and gently hugged her back.

He was so glad Nancy was back. He didn't care what the others thought, he wanted her to be his girlfriend. He thought maybe he'd get to do what he saw Monty and Marvell doing-only he wouldn't let anybody know 'bout it. He imagined sticking by Nancy's side for the rest of the year. He even imagined fighting Miss Payne to protect Nancy. Then Nancy smiled up at Billy like she understood what he was thinking. He could feel her smile deep inside. For some reason it almost brought tears to his eyes. Then he did something "really dumb." He got a quick kiss. He planted his little lips on Nancy's. It felt so good. She giggled; but the entire back of the bus broke out in a big laugh. Annette even said: "Ugh!" But Billy didn't care. He decided, however, to not let anyone see him do that again. There would be plenty of time for him to steal a kiss during the year. (He had forgotten that she was going to D.C. soon.)

Nancy and Billy got off the bus and Billy got hold of her hand like he had seen Monty doing with Priscilla. He wanted to eventually imitate Monty's every move, one day. Then, Nancy could clearly hear the bell ringing for the first time. She yelled: "Last one there is a rotten egg!"

Nancy beat Billy and all of the rest of the bunch of students racing to the porch of the school. They were all giggling and laughing. Then Miss Payne appeared on the porch with her thick yardstick. There was a sudden hush of the laughter.

After the children had filed past Miss Payne, and were seated in the schoolroom, Miss Payne did her usual roll call. Billy noticed that nearly half of the fifteen very dark-skinned students were not present that morning. Each day more of them stopped coming to school altogether.

Just as Miss Payne called out, "Nancy Mason," the front door slammed open. In walked Mrs. Annie Woodson. The rotund woman wore all black like she was going to a funeral: a black coat, dress, fedora, and black shoes and stockings. She took off black ladies' gloves and put those in a large ladies' handbag. Billy thought that handbag hung down like there was something very heavy in it like a brick, big knife, or a gun. Mrs. Woodson strutted slowly up to Mrs. Payne's desk.

"May I help you this morning, Mrs. Woodson? It's so good to see you. I see that Nancy is back with us at her desk. I have kept all of her things up here on my desk. What can I do for you this morning?" Miss Payne said. Each word tumbled out of her mouth stumbling over her nervous disposition. Her eyes trembled and her lips quivered a little.

"Ya yellar-Bitch! How dare ya talk-ta me like nothin' done happen. Who the hell do ya think you is? What the hell did ya call ya-self doin' beatin' up on my little-sweet Granddaughter like ya did? Ya put'er in the UVA Hospital. I want ya ta-know that the damage ya did ta-my Grand Baby ain't go never go 'way. She gotta wear glasses so she can see straight. The State won't even arrest ya half-White ass ... Even Deacon Prince Willis couldn't get that done!"

"Mrs. Woodson. I can explain ..."

"G'wine, then, s'plain, then! I'm listenin'." Mrs. Woodson shouted. She had her left hand on her hip, but had her right hand down in her handbag that hung from shoulder straps.

"I was taught in college that children descended from Field Hands were least able to learn, and . . ." Miss Payne whined.

"What!-What kind-a shit's that ya talkin'? What in the hell do ya mean? And ya better make good sense ta-me gal," Mrs. Woodson growled. She still kept her hand in her handbag.

Miss Payne was nearly crying. "Well, because their fore-parents couldn't legally get an education in the South on Plantations, the Field Hands were forced to learn by the whip. They got used to learning that way. It got so most educators believed that that was the best way to get them to learn. I am just doing what I've been taught to do."

"That's the dumbest shit I done ever heard!" Mrs. Woodson yelled. But she took her hand out of her handbag.

"Mrs. Woodson, the children of the Field Hands were always behind the children of the house servants. That is a proven fact. It has been proven even further at Hampton College and at Tuskegee Institute in modern times.

"I was taught that the darker the child, the more punishment needed to be administered to get him in a position to learn anything. That was all that I was trying to do over here. I have the tough job of teaching the worst kind of students with no resources to work with-unlike what they have over at Evergreen Prep."

"Alicia Payne, that's about the dumbest shit I've ever heard come outta the mouth of any teacher I's ever known. Bitch, we ain't in slavery no more. You ain' dealin' with no Field Hands, or they Chillren. We's free Negroes.

"An' furthermore, ain' all them house slaves was light-skinned. My Great, Great, Grandmother was one of 'im. Her name was Annie too. She's Black as a Ace of Spade. She's off-a the Holland Plantation. She's a House Maid.

"They say she could read and write when tweren't legal for Negroes to be taught to read an' let the Whites know she could write. Annie Lee practically ran the plantation house.

"Alicia, you think ya yellar-hide gives ya the right ta-be cruel to little dark-skinned chillun cause ya hate the fact that ya got some-a that blood in your veins too," Mrs. Woodson said, pointing to the back of the classroom.

"Gal, how do you know. One-a them chillren you's turnin' ya nose up at might be the One we's all been lookin' for ta-come an' Lead us Ta-The-Promised Land. Ya just need ta-get up and get ya stuck-up head outta ya stupid ass. It's peoples like you that's keepin' us Negroes down."

Mrs. Woodson was standing close to Mrs. Payne's desk. "Alicia, the time done come an' gone for dumb bitches like you is ta-be let loose on our in-na-cent chillun. I'm goin' over yonder ta-Palmyra and file-a complaint with the Chairman of the School Board 'gainst you, gal.

"I hope ta-see ya ass outta this school come next year." Mrs. Woodson turned to face the schoolroom. "Nancy, come here, Baby. Get all your things. We's goin' outta this shithouse," Mrs. Woodson shouted at her smiling Granddaughter.

"Mrs. Woodson," Miss Payne whimpered. "Save yourself some time. Mr. Prince Willis has already beat you to the punch. I will be leaving Gravel Hill after this year is over. I hope to go to my grade-school alma mater Evergreen Prep to teach. It is a more civilized school. They understand me over there. You all will never be able to do that."

Nancy came to Miss Payne's desk and collected her things left from that first day of school. "Bye, Miss Payne," the sweet-little Darling said.

Miss Payne rolled her eyes at Nancy like the child had insulted her.

"Ya could've at least say you's sorry, Hussy," Mrs. Woodson said. She came to behind the desk with her hand down in her handbag. "If tweren't for my havin' ta-look out for Nancy, I'd end your sufferin' right now, gal," Mrs. Woodson shouted.

"Go head on, I wish somebody would," Miss Payne hissed out of trembling lips. She cried out loud. She didn't watch Nancy and Mrs. Woodson go to the door of the schoolroom.

Nancy stopped at the door of the schoolroom and ran to where Billy sat. She grabbed Billy in a bear hug. "I'll see you one day, Billy. I'll come back and visit you. Bye-bye, Honey."

"See ya, Nancy." Then, Billy kissed her for the second time. Right after that tender kiss, Nancy was gone--to a waiting car-on up the road-far-far-away. Billy stood on the porch waving at his "First Girlfriend." That was the end of that.

It was early on a Saturday morning in early-November, 1953. Lin and Roy helped Henry unload several rolls of black tar-paper, and several more of green-roofing, and even more of asphalt brick-siding. Henry was ready to put the finishing touches on the house so that he and his family could finally move in.

Henry had purchased on time and installed a cast-iron heater, a warm-morning heater, and a cook stove from Walton's Grocery and Dry Goods. (Arthur Walton had taken in all that was left of Jacob Stiles' s Antiques.)

Gus and John Edward Woods had laid the cinderblock flue in the middle of the house a week ago.

The cast-iron heater and the cook stove were connected to that flue. The front room and the children's room had no heater at that time. So, Henry got ready to work alone. Roy and Lin got into Lin's truck.

"Henry, soon's we get that tree we gotta cut down on its ass, we go be back to help ya put the finishin' touches on ya house, Horse. Then ya can move in," Roy said.

"He's right as money," Lin said. "Roy's go cut 'er down, an' I'll do the rest."

The big Old Oak Tree Lin and Roy were talking about was just up the road from Roy's house a couple-hundred feet, and down in the woods for another fifty feet or so. Henry went to work hauling up the black tar-paper. Then he spread out a roll of it. He figured it wouldn't take them long with the tree. Then the three of them would get that roof done right away.

Lin put his truck in gear, and he and Roy were off. A slight-chilly wind whined then smoothed out blowing steady at about ten miles per-hour. Henry heard the truck motor stop, and the truck doors slam shut. Roy and Lin were laughing from mutual jokes, and Henry clearly heard their voices.

Then the grating noise of Lin's power saw cut through the air, getting louder and louder.

Then it suddenly stopped.

Burton Gaines happened by and offered to help Henry do the roofing if he'd buy him a couple of beers later on. Henry agreed. He got on the roof with Henry.

"Burton, Roy an' Lin s'pose-ta be cutting that big Oak Tree up Tom Well's path. It's been a few minutes, man. I don't hear no noise. We better go on up yonder an' see ifn somethin' bad done happen. I know the way right to it through the woods, there," Henry said.

Lin came running down the road out of breath. "Henry, Burton. Y'all come see what done happen-ta Roy, man-O' My-Gawd!" Lin screamed.

Henry and Burton ran behind Lin up the road and down through the woods to a stand of oak trees. Down in a little ditch, Henry spied Roy. He was lying in a pool of blood. Blood was everywhere around Roy. He got sick to his stomach when he saw bits and pieces of his Brother in-Law's brains mixed up in a bloody-mess around Roy's head, and around the split trunk of a huge Oak tree. Roy's head had been cracked opened. His body still quivered, fighting to cling to life even though death was inevitable. His eyes were wide-open, his mouth seemed like it was trying to utter something. But that was impossible.

"What the hell happen, here, Lin?" Henry screamed for an explanation.

"Man, Roy notched the tree the way we saw it leanin'. He got down in that ditch an' that crevice not payin' it no never-mind. Henry ... when he got deep in that tree, man ... damn! That bitch split. It jammed right back half-in-two. Oh, Gawd! Hit Roy on the side-a his head, man. He fell back. I'm go be sick.

"Henry, y'all tell Cora'nem. I ain' go be able ta-do it, man. I can't man. I can't!" Lin got into the truck, took a shortcut through the woods, and ran into his home. He got in a comer beside his bed. He wept like a madman.

"Burton, go tell Mr. Jasper Furman, Roy got kilt over here on some-a his property. That's who Lin was cuttin' that tree for, I think. Tell 'im to call Bradford Unde11akers, and the Coroner's Office. Ain' no need for no other doctors ta-come 'round here. Roy's gone ta-be with his Gawd!" Henry said. "I'ma go tell Cora'nem." Henry's voice was just one-long groan.

Bm1on ran up 656. He turned northeast away from where the accident happened. He then turned down a winding dirt-road at about three-quru1ers of a mile from Roy's house. He dashed down that road at full speed. He came to a two-story Victorian-styled house. Burton bounced up on the Furmans' huge porch. He knocked on their front doors.

Henry sprinted towards Cora's house. Tears came down his cheeks as he ran along. He climbed up the steep hill to the road. He slowed his pace when he thought about the task before him.

Cora was standing in the yard, sensing something intense had just happened up the road, when Henry ran up to her. Lou, Miriam, Rob, Rich, and Peanut were standing beside their Mother. Gene was playing with a new-red wagon his Father had just bought him that Friday evening. Cora got very teary-eyed when she saw Henry hurrying towards her, crying.

"Henry," Cora spoke in her soft voice, "where's Roy an' Lin at?"

"Cora, let's go in the house. You's go have-ta sit down for this one." Henry looked at the ground. He couldn't stand looking at the fear in Cora's eyes. Henry had a hard time fighting back the tears knowing the pain he was about to lay on Cora's life.

A siren could be heard whining in the distance. Clarabelle came running from the outhouse that was located a few yards down the hill in back of the house. "Lou, what done happen?" she asked.

"Uncle Henry, what done happen?" Lou, a spitting-image of her Mother, asked.

Bea came running from upstairs to the yard. "Uncle Henry, what's everybody so excited about?" she asked. "Is Daddy an' Uncle Lin all right?" Everyone wanted answers.

A certain weary knowing came across the faces of everyone. Rob began pacing around in the sandy-barren front yard. "Uncle Henry, tell us. Is Daddy all right?" The words came out of Rob like the air being let out of a car's tires. The siren in the distance got louder and louder. Everyone knew it was coming down Route Six. Cora started to whimper a little.

"Daddy must be bad off," Lou screamed. She was trembling all over.

"Henry, c'mon in the house, we go sit in the front room. Roy got me some-a the nicest sofas an' end-chairs in there. He wanted us ta-be comfortable. You go be comfy, you'll see ..."

Henry watched Cora tremble all over. She had a look on her face that said, "I wish this would go 'way." But it couldn't.

"Cora. Hold it. Roy's ... Roy's right bad off," Henry said. He followed Cora through the front door into the front room. Once they were in the house, Cora held up her hand.

"First, this is grown-folk bizzness. Y'all chillun go on upstairs till I call ya," Cora said. She cried softly. She stood at the foot of the stairway until her children had all run up the steps.

Cora went back into the front room. "What 'cha tryin' ta-tell me?" she whined. "Is somethin' done happen ta-my husband? Oh God, help me!"

Henry seated himself on a plush-green sofa. "Cora, Roy done had-a bad accident up yonder down the hill a-ways. He didn't make it. I's so sorry," Henry said. The whining siren came off of Route Six screaming by the house up Route 656 north to just uphill from the accident.

Henry ran outside. He saw a Whiteman wearing a long-white smock getting out of a blue ambulance. A "Colored" man wearing a white jacket helped Mr. Bradford carry a stretcher down the hill to get Roy's remains. Another white-panel truck came up the road. It had Fluvanna Coroner's Office in bold-red letters on the side of it. A fat Whiteman got out and shook his head. Mr. Bradford and his helper had Roy's remains in a plastic bag lying on the stretcher.

Henry came back into the house. "Cora, ya go have-ta go see 'bout Roy's remains. Ya know Bradford's got 'em. I'm so sorry. Sorry as I can be," Henry said. "Ifn it's anythin' I can do just lemme know."

"Ah-h-h-h-h! God Help Me! Lord Have mercy On Me! I Can't Stand No More! I can't do it, Lord!" Cora screamed. She fainted dead away and fell to the floor. Her girls ran down the steps and started screaming too. The boys came after them. They all got Cora up in their arms and took her to her bedroom.

Rob came back to talk with his Uncle Henry. Henry was crying and wringing his hands together. "You's the man of the family, now, Rob," Henry said. Rob was crying out like the rest of his Brothers and Sisters.

"Yeah, Uncle Henry, I'll do my best. I will," he said.

"I'll go get Aunt Bessie an' Aunt Cary ta-come help y'all. Mabel ain' able-ta right now," Henry said. Then the tears came streaming down his cheeks.

When Henry came back to the front yard, Burton was standing out there.

"Mr. Furman done called the Sheriff. I reek-en Mr. Hughes go be comin' up here real soon," Burton said. "Just lemme know when ya go work on ya house again."

"Aw-ight, Homes," Henry whined. He walked over to Lin's and Bessie's house. He jogged the half-mile or so to get there. It was getting to be late in the evening. He knocked on the front door. Bessie opened the door.

"C'mon in Henry." Bessie was crying softly. She wore a white-full slip. "I's just gettin' read-ta-go ta-see 'bout Cora 'nem. Lord, honey, I know she's got ta-be a mess. She grew ta love that man a powerful lot. She prob-be can't see bein' alive 'thout 'im.

"Ya go have-ta talk ta-Lin. He's mighty upset. Say he ain' never seen nothin' like that since he been in the military. Henry, he been pukin' since he came home today. Can't keep nothin' on his stomach.

"I thinks, he blames his-self for what happen-ta Roy. I'ma go on over ta-Cora'nem, you talk ta Lin. I'll take the shortcut through the woods."

Bessie put on a black dress and a pair of black slippers, and went out the front door. Henry watched her scamper through the woods towards Cora's house. He turned his attention to Lin, who sat on the floor near his bed, staring blankly into space.

"Lin. Lin. It might've been somethin' s'pose-ta happen today. I ain't all that 'ligious, but ..

. sometimes Gawd-A-Mighty, want things like that ta-happen. An' it's go happen. It don't seem right ta-us, but ma-be 'twas Roy's time, man," Henry said. His eyes were brimming with tears. "It ain' nothin' we can do 'bout that."

Lin covered his face with his hands. He wept bitterly. Then he removed his hands from his face. He looked Henry straight in the eyes. "Henry, I ain' go never cut no more logs or pulpwood, long's I live, man. I don't wanna never see 'nother power saw. I won't use one again.

"I'm goin' back ta-work for Mr. Kent'nem at the Mill. Bad as Sawmill work is, it's better'n gettin' kilt by a fallin' tree; or watchin' ya friend die like that."

Henry shook his head, but said: "Hope ya get over this aw-ight, Homes. I didn't go-ta-Old Man Pat's funeral. I hate funerals. But this 'un is family. I'ma have-ta be at this one-go be-a mighty sad one too. Ev'body love Roy."

The graveside funeral for Roy was held on the edge of his property in the middle of an Electric-Right-of-Way, up the road from his home. He did not belong to a Church. He believed in God, but did not trust any of the Preachers. He attended Columbia Baptist most often but would not join it. The Rev. John Jasper Nicholas preached the brief sermon. Hundreds of people came to pay their last Respects to Roy. Then his coffin was lowered into the ground and it did rain. Cora fainted again after she screamed: "God, take me with him! Take me, too!"

Henry stood in the rain watching the undertaker's helpers shovel dirt in the hole in the ground onto Roy's "Fine Casket." He wondered why Negroes never got to rest in such finery until after they were dead and buried. He made up in his mind, "I'm gonna go get so 'fuckin' drunk'!"

CHAPTER EIGHTEEN

On this morning, May 18, 1954, came the following early morning radio news: *"Yesterday, the Supreme Court in the Topeka, Kansas Desegregation Case, ruled that segregated public education is no longer Constitutional. The Highest Court heard the Case argued before it by Lead Civil Rights Attorney, Thurgood Marshall. A Majority of the Justices led by Chief Justice William H. Rehnquist struck down the Plessy vs Ferguson's 'Separate-But-Equal Doctrine' established in 1896. Dr. Colgate Darden, President of the University, and the Dean of the Law School, Dr. Neil V. Sullivan, concurred that the Ruling would prove to be bad for Negroes now and in the future. Senator Harry Byrd said that the Ruling will be massively resisted in Virginia and in the South in general. More on this Ruling after a word from our sponsors. This is WRVA Morning news"*

Henry sat down at the breakfast table. "Mabel, I's 'fraid-a what that go mean ta-our boys.

It's go put 'em all in danger."

"Yep. I see them White Bitches starin' at our mens with-a sly grin on they faces. Them little gals in high school can't wait ta-get close to 'em. I heard Arthur Walton's gal, Linda whisperin' ta 'er little Sister, Nan, after a speech she done heard on they TV, "bout do ya want ya Daughter Ta Marr' one?' She say: 'I might not get-ta marr one, but I'ma sure get-ta fuck one.'

"Mr. Wilfred Kent's Daughter, Marilyn was sittin' in-a red-Ford Convertible with her Cousin, Wally Kent's gal, Marion. She hollered out at me: 'Mabelle,' she call me, with 'er womanish little ass, 'how old's ya biggest Son? He is so cute, Mabelle. Oh, I wish he's White.' Then Marion say: 'It doesn't matter to me.' Marilyn was drivin'. She scratched-a wheel an' took off. Both them gals were laughin' like they thought I's gettin' some fun outta what they's sayin'."

"We gotta start with Billy. Tell'im stay 'way from them hot-assed little gals as far 'way as he can. They don't mean 'im nothin' but death!" Henry said.

"I'm sure go tell'im ev' day. I 'ma get his stuff read-for school," Mabel said. "I'm go talk to 'im right now."

Mabel came back to the kitchen. "I'm go let Billy go up ta-the road a little early. I want'im ta-walk with Harvey an' Annette cause Rena is color-struck, Billy say."

"Lin go lend me his truck. He's sorry as hell 'bout losin' Roy like that. But ... Mabel, he asked me somethin' the other day I act-like I didn't know nothin' 'bout," Henry said.

"What he ask ya?" Mabel asked. Her heart beat faster than her baby's inside of her womb. "Mabel, he wanna kno' ifn I knowed anythin' 'bout Burton Gaines foolin' 'round with Bessie?"

"What ya hear?" Mabel asked.

"Mabel, it's all over the place. Ev'body done heard 'bout it. I didn't tell Lin, though. It ain' none-a my bizzness. So, I lie-ta Lin. Told 'im, no I ain't heard nothin' toll."

"I ain't heard nothin' toll neither," Mabel lied. She was thinking: *"Ah hell. The shit done hit the fan, now I"*

Henry went on out to catch the truck to work. Mabel wished she wasn't so heavily pregnant. She wanted to go warn Bessie as quick as she could. She was afraid that Henry was going to tell Lin about what he had heard about her sooner or later, maybe while they were out getting drunk, or out hunting or fishing together. Then, Lin would tell Henry the names of the men she had been with. The shit would get started all over again.

Mabel figured she would ask Harvey to go fetch Bessie. Tell her to come give her some advice about the baby she was carrying. She was so afraid that things would get all messed up if the covered-up shit got stirred up right now.

By the last week in May, Mabel and Henry had moved everything they had to their new house. Billy had taken note of the fact that his Mother's stomach was getting fatter and fatter every day. She seemed to be in a lot of pain most days. She was really very fat, almost as big as A'nt Bessie. Then one morning, instead of her getting up and cooking breakfast, she cried out in a scream: "Henry, go get Mrs. Cooper. It's time!"

Henry ran up to Rev. Nicholas's house. He took him to Columbia to fetch Mrs. Cooper. In about forty-five minutes, Mrs. Cooper came to the house carrying a brown-leather Mid-wife's bag.

"Y'all take little Billy on off to school. I got to get to work, Henry," Mrs. Cooper said.

Mabel was crying out loudly when Mrs. Cooper arrived with his Daddy and Rev. Nicholas. It scared Billy real bad to hear his Momma screaming in pain. She never hollered like that before, when Mrs. Cooper came to visit her, "Carrying Her Mid-Wife's Bag?"

Henry got busy, fixed breakfast, got Billy ready for school, and said: "You go on down the road with Cora's chillren. They's walkin' with Harvey and Annette Nicholas. Go on, now."

"What's the matter with Momma, Daddy?" Billy asked.

"Boy, don't be so mannish. Go on ta-meet the bus. Lemme worr' bout ya Momma this mornin'." Henry said.

"Yes sir," Billy replied. He took two peanut butter and apple jelly sandwiches. They were made with light bread. That made Billy very happy. "See ya this evening, Daddy," he chimed.

With Mabel still yelling every now and then, Billy went out to meet Harvey and Annette.

The ranting and raving his Daddy and Momma had been doing came to mind. He had heard his Daddy saying that White Children were evil, especially the girls, and "White mens they's just waitin' ta-put-a rope'round little Colored-boys' necks." Now, that Negro and White children had to attend school together, Billy was more scared of that situation then he was of Miss Payne's beatings. He decided he'd ask somebody he trusted.

While he walked the-tenth of-a-mile or so to Route Six, where he waited to catch the school bus now, Billy moseyed over to Harvey and Annette. "Harvey and Annette, ain't y'all scared of going to school with White kids next year?"

"Billy, Iain' scare of nobody; certainly not none of them Crackers 'round here," Annette said. "Besides, these Whiteys 'round here ain' go let their kids go to school with us for nothing in this world-you can bet on that."

Harvey gave a little sarcastic laugh. "Billy, I think Annette's right. Man, them Crackers are fightin' with everything they got to stop us from going to school with their little Peckerwood children-they Fathers are scared of ... Umph, I can't tell you 'bout that yet," Harvey said. "So, don't ya worry too much, little Billy."

Billy was puzzled. "Daddy heard on the radio that that 'seg' gat-ton' passed. Say Black mens gonna get hanged-or tinned, or something 'bout White gals. He says they's tryin' to do that to some 'Scotch-Berry Boys', an' they been after them boys for a lotta years. What y'all hear 'bout that?" Billy asked.

Annette chuckled. "Billy, you mean 'The Scottsboro Boys'-there're nine of them. In Georgia, 'down in the Deep-South' they were accused of a crime they didn't commit. They're in jail for 'raping' two White Womens. The other word you missed is 'lynched'; okay?"

Billy was even more puzzled, now. "Where's the 'Deep-South?' And what's 'raping' a woman?" he asked.

"Billy," said Annette, "you go have to let your Momma and Daddy tell ya about that one, little man." Then she winked at him. He didn't know what that meant. But he knew it was time to stop asking "Silly Questions." But there was one question still weighing heavy on his expanding little mind: "Annette, Miss Payne use-ta beat us real bad for sayin' 'We is,' an' 'You is,' y'know, like regular peoples talk. Why'd she do that for?"

"Billy, the right way to talk is: "I am, you are, and, he, she, or it, is; we are, you are, or they are. That's the way you are supposed to talk-especially if you are at school or in public. Then you will be using correct English.

"Whenever you say I, you have to say, am, or was. When you say, you, you have to say are or were, and so on, understand?" Annette explained.

"Yeah, Annette. But it would've been a lot better if Miss Payne had-da told us that 'stead-a skinning us alive. 'I am gonna 'member what'cha just taught me.' Momma, 'she is sick.' Mrs. Cooper and Daddy, 'they are in there helping Momma.' Annette, 'you and Harvey are my best friends in the world.' Y'all truly is," Billy said. Then all three laughed out loud.

"You got a long ways to go before you get to using correct English, but you're making a good start," Harvey said.

That evening, Annette and Harvey stood out on the porch of Billy's house. Lucy and Clarabelle stopped by to visit as well. Billy eavesdropped a little and heard Mrs. Cooper saying in a near whisper: "Mabel, ya water didn't break. You ain' read-ta-go yet. I bet it's go be a week or so fore then, Sugar. I'ma go back home. Ifn it breaks, call me right away. Okay, Baby?"

Mrs. Cooper spied Harvey and Annette. "Little gal, Annie, go tell ya Daddy ta-come take me down to Columbia. I'm here too early."

"Yes'am," Annette said.

After Mrs. Cooper left, Mabel suffered three agonizing weeks of pain, especially at night. Then her water broke. Henry got Rev. Nicholas to go fetch Mrs. Cooper. Three days after she returned to help Mabel, she had her Fourth Son. It was June 16, 1954. Henry named this Son, John Oliver James.

It was hot as hell outside. As soon as John cried in a squeal, it clouded up outside and a brief storm ensued. It rumbled through Gravel Hill for all of fifteen minutes. Then the sky cleared up. John's descent into this world had succeeded at about midnight. Mrs. Cooper announced, with sweat and tears running down her wrinkled face, "It's a big o'baby boy!" She weighed him on a portable scale. John weighed eight pounds and fifteen ounces.

John had a very big head. He had done some damage on his way out of his Mother's womb. Mrs. Cooper told Henry: "Ifn her fever don't break in a few days, rush'er ta-the doctor's office. I got some pain pills. Give'er one ev' four hours. They's strong, an' go make'er sleep a lot. Let'er rest an' keep 'er quiet as possible. Let'er nurse Baby John as much as she can tolerate it. Keep a lotta pads I'ma give ya under her for a few days. Keep'er an' the baby as clean as possible. I'ma be here for-a cup'la days. You do what ya see me doin' after I leaves."

Two days later, Mrs. Cooper sent for Rev. Nicholas again. Mabel's fever had broken. Rev. Nicholas took Mrs. Cooper away in his new red-and-white Ford four-door Sedan.

In a week, Mabel grew very strong. In two weeks she had gotten back on her feet and was cooking breakfast and supper, as well as, taking care of John, who she started calling, "Johnboy."

On this Saturday morning, after Mabel had gotten her basic health back, Billy came in from playing outside. He had been upstairs at A'nt Cora's house playing "Mommas and Daddies" with Booco and Bea. Only they did not let him feel them "down there," like Annette Nicholas had. They didn't pull down their panties either. They let Billy lay on top of them between their legs for about ten seconds. Though he could feel their warm sweet-smelling perfumed-bodies through their panties, that was as close as he got to "doing it," with them.

"Billy, you're so mannish," Bea said. She hunched Booco and pointed at Billy's little swollen middle-member.

"Ah-h-h-h, he's trying to act like a big boy. I ought to tell your Momma on you," Booco said. She turned to Bea. "I bet he could do some damage with his little 'Peter.' Ifl was nasty like that I'd try him and see-but no." She laughed and so did Bea.

Bea hugged Billy tightly. "You're so mannish, for such a little boy," she said. Booco hugged him also.

Billy noticed that both girls had their dresses up to their panties. He thought they were just making fun of him, because they were giggling and laughing when they saw how hard he was. He could see the dark outlines of their feminine parts, and had seen and experienced what that could lead to, but he knew Bea and Booco were not going to go that far. He decided that he had better go back to his house. "Bye Bea. Bye Booco," Billy said.

Both girls came to him, hugged him, and kissed his little face. Billy didn't like that. He turned and ran on home. He wondered why A'nt Cora stayed in her room all day.

Billy was filled with wonderment. He walked into the kitchen to find his Momma breast feeding little Johnboy, who was lying in Mabel's lap, wearing a cloth diaper, and little blue booties. He had on a blue gown. Billy stared at the baby and at his Momma for a few moments. A look of real puzzlement came to his face when he noticed that his Mother had lost all of the weight she had previously gained. He wanted to know "where do babies really come from?"

"Momma," Billy paused for a second. "Mrs. Cooper didn't bring no baby in her midwife's bag. Nope. Your stomach got big, and now it's back to small. Did that baby come outta your stomach?" Billy asked. He didn't know that he had asked a forbidden question.

Mabel was appalled at his question. She had been slapped in the mouth for asking similar questions of her Mother while she was growing up. "Boy, carry ya little ass on outside an' play. I'ma tell ya Daddy what ya asked me when he get back from helping Mr. Furman'nem get up hay. You's gettin' too mannish for ya little britches," Mabel snapped at her dismayed little Son.

Billy hurried out of the house scared as could be that his "Mean Daddy," would surely kill him, now. He wished he hadn't asked his Mother that "stupid question." He hid behind the smokehouse and woodshed, whimpering because he was too scared to play. He hoped his Daddy would be too tired to whip him when he got home.

His anticipation ended when, seemingly out of nowhere, Henry brought a long, healthy, braided switch down on his back until it raised several welts. It hurt Billy awfully bad.

"Don't ya never ask ya Momma nothin' toll like that again, boy, long's ya live!" Henry yelled at Billy.

Rat, a full-grown spotted, black-and-white beagle hound, dashed out of his doghouse, beside of the woodshed, jumped up in the air, grabbed the switch out of Henry's hand and took off for the woods behind the smokehouse. Henry ran after Rat for a minute or two, but the dog outran him by miles. Henry gave up the chase.

He came back to yell at Billy. "Shut up all that damn noise, boy. I didn't whip ya that much. Poppa'nem beat the hell outta me when I asked Momma that question. That's grown folk bizzness. Ya don't need ta-kno' that."

Billy got up off the ground and ran into the woods after Rat. The dog ran to Billy. Rat stood up and hugged Billy. He tried to lick the welts on Billy's back, whining pitifully as he did so. Now and then, Rat barked with his head turned towards the house, but resumed licking Billy's welts. "Seems like my dog cares more about me than my Momma and Daddy do," Billy whined. What the ordeal caused Billy to think was: *I can't trust Momma, and I can't trust Daddy for nothing. I wish I wasn't their little boy at all. Wish I had another Momma and Daddy. I just asked Momma a simple question. Why'd she have to tell Daddy on me, and make him come and beat me? What was he beating the hell outta me for? They've been lying to me about where babies come from. I'm gonna ask my Cousins about it. Maybe they'll tell me the truth.*

The above beating shut the door of meaningful dialogue between Billy and his parents. He couldn't ask his Momma or his Daddy about things that had happened to him at school or with older kids in his own neighborhood.

Billy couldn't tell his parents that one day Peanut and Gene had tried to get him to "Suck my Dick, Billy, it'll taste like Candy." Or when Peanut begged him to let him pull down his shorts and briefs so he could "stick his Dick in his ass," Billy feared that he would get the worst for telling his parents about what they tried to do to him. Billy refused to let them use him. But one day while he and Peanut were sitting near the woodpile at A'nt Cora's house, he decided to ask Peanut where babies came from.

"Peanut, where do babies come from?" Billy asked.

Peanut cleared his throat and smiled, showing buckteeth. "Well, Billy. You gotta put your Dick in a gal's Pussy-hole. You work it to her 'til you bust-a-nut. Nine months later she drops-a baby outta her ass," Peanut said. He cleared his throat again. "You unnerstan'?"

Billy scratched his head. "No. How ya gonna bust-a-nut? What's that? Where's a gal's pussy-hole? How can a baby come outta a woman's ass?" Billy asked.

"Well, Billy, you gonna have to get a little older before ya can dig that," Peanut said. "Dig that? What you mean by that, Peanut?" Billy said.

"Ah, forget it, Billy. I got better things to do with my time. Go on somewhere and play," Peanut angrily snapped at Billy.

Billy spent that summer trying to sneak a peek up every girl's or women's dress he could. Peanut's answer to his questions about Sex had created a burning curiosity in his mind, and he wanted to get to the bottom of all of that.

His voyeurism only revealed to him that grown women had a lot of hair in their pubic regions, but he didn't see any "Pussy-Hole." The more he peeked, the more confused he became. When his A'nt Bessie came to visit with his Mother, Billy caught Alize in the children's room and pulled her panties aside to see if he could find what Peanut had said was where babies came from. She didn't have any hair down there, only red lips. But there was no "Pussy-Hole."

Billy determined that maybe it was only something grown-ups knew how to find. So he would wait until he had grown up. (He had forgotten about his experience with Annette; at least he did not know to associate that with "where babies came from.")

The summer was over seemingly too soon for Billy. He would have to get up early again. He'd heard that the White people were fighting to keep the public schools in Virginia separate. Judging from what his Father preached about the matter, Billy didn't mind the schools staying the way they were. Billy hated the idea of attending school with White kids.

(In August, 1955, a Chicago youth named, Emmett Till was murdered in Mississippi by two white-racists for allegedly whistling at a White Woman. One of the men Roy Bryant was the woman's husband. The other was J.W. Milam, Bryant's half-Brother. Carolyn Bryant was the woman in question. An all-White-male Jury, acquitted the "Murderers."

The above newscast reverberated around the Globe. Till's casket was opened at his funeral in Chicago, and most Americans got to see the ugliness of racism in America, and Henry James got ample fuel to bombast Billy and his younger Brothers with dire warnings. "Y'all stay 'way from them White Bitches. Ya see what can happen-ta ya if'n ya don't. Them Crackers 'round here will do the same thing-ta y'all if'n they catch ya messin 'round with one-a their o' White gals!"

"Ma-be them White peoples go keep our Chillun outta they schools-an' that will be that," Mabel said. "Least, that's what I's hopin' go happen.")

But, in September, 1954, Billy waited on the front steps of the front-porch for Harvey and Annette to come down the road. He was afraid that as soon as he got on a bus with White children all hell was going to break loose. He didn't want to be alone not for a moment.

Strangely enough, the children got into their color-based groups like they had the previous year. Billy felt some relief when he saw a school-bus load of White children speed by him. That meant that at least they would ride separate buses. White children on the Whites' bus "flipped the bird" at the "Negro" children standing waiting for their bus. Billy asked himself: "Don't the Crackers hate us enough? Isn't that a good reason for us to stop hating ourselves?"

A brand-new school bus came around the curve. Mr. Baskerfield was still the Driver. But the Patrolman was now a very dark-skinned boy. He wore black trousers, a white Banlon shirt, and black penny loafers. He wore a nametag bearing his name: "Fermi Payne." He had a full-head of straight-ish black hair. His nose was prominent like an Australian Aborigine's. He had African lips, like those of Ancient Africans. He was short and stocky, and as dark-skinned as the middle of midnight on a moonless, starless night.

Unlike the previous Patrolman, Fermi repeatedly greeted many of the students boarding the bus with, "How you're doin'?"

Billy was glad when the bus again turned onto the road leading to Gravel Hill Elementary. He was even gladder to see no White kids getting off any school bus. At least for the time being he felt he was safe from the dangers White kids would pose.

After getting off the bus Billy walked along in the mix of students to make sure he would not be one of the children charged with being tardy for that morning. To Billy's surprise when he got to the porch of the School, no one stood out there slapping a yardstick on her leg like Miss Payne had. He followed the rest of the students on up the steps and into the school.

Once Billy was inside of the School, he saw what seemed to be the Prettiest Negro Woman he'd ever seen up close. Only in EBONY Magazine had he seen her like. She was not too fat or too slim. She had a pretty dimpled chin, a cute-little nose, on a rounded face. Her eyes were like large Hazelnuts. She had reddish-brown skin, and black hair that she wore in a French roll.

The new teacher, because Billy figured that was who she had to be, because he didn't see hide nor hair of Miss Payne, was like a fairy tale come to life. Billy was only seven, but could not help but notice that this new teacher had the prettiest, shapeliest legs he had ever seen. They seemed so smooth, like brown velvet, or silk.

When she walked, the motion of her hips, and upper body gave her the most graceful appearance. She wore a tight-black skirt, that came to her knees, a pink-ruffled blouse over that, and a thin-white sweater tied by it arms around her neck and shoulders. When she spoke, her voice came out in a delicious-sounding tenor-soprano range. She smiled showing very white even teeth contrasting the bright-red lipstick she had on her luscious lips. For the first time, Billy wished he had been grown up so that he could talk to this beautiful lady like a girlfriend.

"Classes, my name is Miss Clara White from Caroline County, Virginia. I am your teacher for this year. Good morning to you all."

Billy and the entire schoolroom responded: "Good morning, Miss White."

"This is my first school, and you are my first set of classes. I feel that I come very well prepared. I was educated at Virginia State Normal Institute in Petersburg. I want all of you to stand at this time and sang 'The Star Spangle Banner,' after which we will say 'The Lord's Prayer,' and then, 'The Pledge of Allegiance.' You will remain standing after our devotion and be seated as I call your name. Be seated from my left to my right.

"If I do not call your name, I will talk to you later about placing you in a school with kids more appropriate for your age group."

Billy sung the songs, said the pledge and took a seat when his name was called. Soon most of the students had been seated. He noticed that the entire schoolroom was seated by classes, and in alphabetical order.

Miss White went around to all of the students whose names she had not called. She gave each one of them an official-looking letter. She said: "Take these letters home to your parents. Have them read them and sign them.

"Some of you will stay on the school bus tomorrow until you arrive at Shiloh Elementary up in Palmyra. A couple of you will be placed at S.C. Abrams High. The teachers and principals of the schools where you are being sent will test you and place you in the proper grade and or age group.

"You all with the letters please go to the back of the schoolroom and be as quiet as possible so that I may get to know the children better that I will actually be teaching. Pick one of the extra books I have brought in today to read silently. At the end of class today, please leave these books on my desk. Thank you."

One thing that stood out with Billy was the fact that Miss White on her second day of school brought in extra sandwiches in a small picnic basket. She announced that kids who were hungry could come up at any time and get a sandwich. On occasion, Billy took advantage of her generosity. She also had the Monticello Dairy of Fork Union to deliver a couple of crates of pint-size cartons of chocolate and white milk to the school at lunchtime. Miss White knew hunger made it more difficult to teach a child anything.

The second major thing about Miss White was Billy never saw her hit a child with a switch of any kind. She used "Time Out!" or writing on the blackboard, as ways to discipline her students. Students that had been too shy to say much in class became very talkative and participated in the academic activities enthusiastically and effectively. Billy excelled in the Second Grade. The extracurricular activities Billy had seen going on in the woods at recess under Miss Payne's nose, he never saw happening under Miss White's watch. Kids were there to learn, because Miss White was there to teach.

In the Third Grade with Miss White, Billy experienced more of her kindness, and efficacy, above-board care and concern for slow students, and her selfless love that radiated from her like rays do from the sun.

On Fridays, Miss White brought in extra books to read to the entire schoolroom. For the first time, Billy heard full-stories about Abolitionists with names like Harriet Tubman and Sojourner Truth; about the great educator, Booker T. Washington; about Dr.'s George Washington Carver, and Charles Drew, Luther P. Jackson, and the founder of Negro History Month, Carter G. Woodson. She taught her little students, "I want all of you to be very proud to be Negroes. It does not matter what people say about you if you have done well. If you have done your best to be the best that you can be. Now, stand with me and all of you sing one stanza of 'The Negro National Anthem.'" After the Song she would then dismiss class.

What Miss White taught Billy stuck with him. Instead of hating to go school every day, he loved waiting to catch the bus to school. The germ of wanting to learn had infected Billy's mind.

Miss White passed Billy on to the Fourth Grade with reservations. On this day in late May, 1956, she kept him in at recess. He wondered what he had done to be punished.

"William, you have improved so rapidly in your Reading, Writing, and English skills, as well as your Mathematical computations, and social skills, I'm going to take a chance on you. I will send you up to Shiloh to Mrs. Ottilia Bland the Principal up there. She and Mrs. Blanche Phallison and Miss Pauline Gaines will help you go on to do great things, and you might be one of our next Negro Leaders.

"So, honey, this is the last year I'm going to see your sunny face in my classroom and I am going to surely miss you. I will always remember you and will love you like you were my own-like I do all of my students. So go on up to Shiloh and do me proud, next year, son."

Billy was so proud of Miss White he could not hold back the tears. He jumped up out of his seat, ran over to Miss White's desk, leapt into her arms and cried real tears of joy for a minute or two. She put Billy down. He saw big o' tears coming down Miss White's cheeks. She got a napkin out of her ladies' bag, blew her nose into it, and allowed: "You may be excused William. You can go out and play, now." She spoke in an almost whine.

The next couple of weeks just floated right on by. The second week of June came and Billy got his Report Card. He held that emblem of achievement out in front of himself like it was the most important thing he had ever achieved. When he burst through the door at home he yelled at Mabel. "Look Ma, I passed!" He danced all around. "I'm going on to the Fourth Grade."

"I'ma be able ta-help ya a little bit. I been readin' them books ya barr'd from Cora's chillren. I gotta big old dict-shun-na'er an' I's ed-i-catin' myself I'ma be able ta-help ya some Momma's so proud-a ya Billy. Ya keep up that good work," Mabel replied with glee and joy.

Henry came home in a mood that evening. He bounced through the backdoor. He didn't say Hi. He just blurted out, "Mabel. Them Whites ain' go be able ta-do nothing 'toll 'bout the school thing. We go have shit ta-pay fore long. Lemme go feed the hogs, then we gotta figger 'bout what we go do this win'er."

Mabel ran out the backdoor behind her disgruntled husband. "First, look at Billy's Report Card. He go be goin' on ta-the Fourth Grade. Ain' neither one-a us never did that," Mabel's voice rung like a bell.

"I ain' got no time ta-be lollygaggin 'round with no 'port card," Henry grunted like the hungry hogs in the pen anticipating their evening slopping. He hated the fact that he had to raise his Son up in schooling. He had only gotten to learn how to read and write. He figured that was all that a Negro boy needed to know how to do. He wondered what in the hell was he going to do with a "Smart Aleck Son?"

Henry fed his chickens and hogs in a rant. He said aloud: "I hate all of this school shit. I hate the hell outta it. Look what it's <loin'. We ain'

go be able to keep bread and beans on the table ifn we keep on stirrin' up them nasty O' Crackers with that equal-school shit!"

Henry came to supper that night frowning and snorting at Billy. He didn't say anything, but the disgust he felt was seemingly aimed at his oldest Son, and at Mabel. Then-

That fall, Billy attended Shiloh Elementary. He got on the bus as usual, but stayed on it past Gravel Hill Elementary. The bus picked up kids up Route Six to Route fifteen. At the fork in the road, where Six continues to Fork Union, at a place called "Dixie," the bus took a right turn onto Fifteen. It did not stop to pick up any more children.

The bus traveled for fifteen miles to Palmyra where Route 673 intersects with Fifteen. It took a left onto 673 and traveled to 649, took another left and proceeded on for a-tenth of a mile. It made a stop at a middle-size one-story brick building, with a maroon neon sign with the yellow letters: "S.C. ABRAMS HIGHSCHOOL," prominently featured right next to a tall flagpole. Most of the older people got off the bus, including Harvey and Annette Nicholas, and the Winstons. Billy was among those who stayed put. (At this time, Route 649 was unpaved.)

The bus got on the way up 649, traveling west for another ten miles to Route 647. It turned right onto a very narrow unpaved road that was very rough and raggedy. It traveled for about another five or six miles to a white-one-story clapboard building with a sign stating: "Shiloh Baptist Church." Across the road from the Church was another larger clapboard building with a tall flagpole in front of it. There was no neon sign or other signs with the School's name emblazoned on it.

Unlike Gravel Hill, the three-room building had windows all around it. And, unlike Gravel Hill, Billy saw wall-to-wall students walking to school; arriving on various buses; and some were being shuttled to school in their parents' cars. Trucks, and hay wagons. Billy got off his bus and noticed that the schoolyard was jammed. He had to wonder how three teachers were going to teach all of those people.

Billy walked around the schoolyard wondering. He thought this School must have been built in the middle of a pasture. It was built way back in the woods. It had to be a lot of falms nearby because Billy heard the cattle mooing. All around the edge of Shiloh Elementary were huge

Oak, Popular, Pine, Birch, Weeping Willow, and a number of Hickory, Walnut, and Chestnut Oak trees. Billy kind of liked the way Shiloh looked.

His attention was diverted by something he hadn't seen anybody doing at Gravel Hill. A couple of older students were very carefully unfolding, the American Flag. They connected it to tall ropes, not daring to let it touch the ground, and hoisted it up the Flagpole. Then a five-six or so very beautiful woman, that resembled a picture Billy had seen of Billie Holiday in his Father's EBONY Magazine, came out onto a little platform in front of the School. She rang a large bell.

Most of the students got into lines and filed up the steps of the platform past her. She announced: "You new students, wait until you are assigned to a teacher. I am Mrs. Ottilia Bland, your Principal. When your name is called assemble in front of doorway one, two, or three."

Billy noticed that most of the other students were gone inside already. Then he heard: "You Fourth Graders go around to the doorway to my right. You will be in Miss Pauline Gaines' homeroom. She teaches the Fourth and Fifth Graders. Those of you who are First, Second or Third Graders, go to the doorway in the middle of the building with Mrs. Blanche Phallison. Six and Seventh Graders follow me inside, you will be in my homeroom. You may proceed."

Billy went around to where Mrs. Bland had pointed. He noticed how Miss Gaines resembled his Aunt Cary. She had pinkish-brown skin. She stood at about six foot tall. She was short but was a very nice-looking woman, with long-black hair, that she wore in ringlets. She had on a brown dress with a hemline down to her ankles. On her feet were bright-red slippers. The strange thing about Miss Gaines was that she had big-bright-green eyes. Her legs seemed enlarged from the knee to her ankles. When she had escorted her classes into the building, and had seated herself on the edge of her desk, Billy saw that her legs seemed oddly miss-shaped. She kind of limped when she walked.

"Good morning, students. I am Miss Gaines. You all look lovely. I hope you feel as good as you look. We're going to learn a lot this year. I love to teach, and I hope you all love to learn new things. As I call you all's names please answer present."

Billy loved the sound of her accent. It was certainly different sounding than what he'd heard people sounding like all around him thus far. Then

Billy heard her say: "In case you are wondering what I sound like to some of you all, I am from Durham, North Carolina. I've been teaching here at Shiloh for about six years, and I love every minute of it. I want all of my Fourth Graders to stand and I will place you by alphabetical order over to my right. You Fifth Graders will be over to my left. Soon her roll call was over and everyone was seated. Billy smiled at how she pronounced her words.

During recess, Billy got a closer look at Mrs. Phallison. He wondered why that "White Woman" was teaching at a Negro School. She was very tall-around six-foot or so. She was stout, and had big-bone features, but was a very-shapely lady. Her hair was golden-blond like the sunlight. It was pulled back so that her locks fell down her back. Her deep-blue eyes sparkled as she carefully watched over her youngsters, seemingly more of them than in all of the rest of the classes combined.

Mrs. Phallison wore a dark-denim dress that went from her neckline to her ankles. It set her cream-colored skin off and emphasized her Aryan-like resemblance. Billy could not believe this woman was a "Negro." Then he remembered his A'nt Cora, and his Cousin Phyllis.

On this first day of school the teachers were out on grounds among their students. Billy noticed that the one with the least amount of students was Mrs. Bland. She seemed to have about ten or fifteen students in her two classes. Fermi Payne was in her Seventh-Grade class.

Because of the love Miss Gaines showed her students, Billy loved coming to school every day. She would not let the other better-dressed students tease him about his "Farmer John" clothes. So they did that out of earshot of Miss Gaines. When she caught them, she made them stay in at recess. Miss Gaines had a number of extra books poor students could borrow.

Billy borrowed most of his textbooks because he could not afford to pay a modest book fee.

Shiloh Baptist purchased a number of books for people like Billy.

As did many of the other students, Billy qualified for a free (five cents) carton of milk each day. The Monticello Dairy had an arrangement with Shiloh. For a half-crate of extra milk the Diary was allowed to set-up an ice- cream freezer in the School. At lunchtime students could purchase a four-ounce cup of ice-cream for five cents; an eight-ounce cup for ten cents;

and a full cup for a quarter. Mrs. Bland sold these at the beginning of the lunch recess. She often gave away free ice-cream to the poorest students for good behavior, excellent work habits, and or for earning the highest grades on a test. Then there were chocolate-coated popsicles, as well as those with a vanilla, orange, and or banana mixed-flavor; ice-cream sandwiches; and various single-flavored solid popsicles for fifteen cents apiece. Billy hated plain white milk but loved chocolate. Like Miss White, Mrs. Bland brought a picnic basket full of sandwiches to school every day. Pupils who did not bring a bag lunch could get a sandwich and a carton of free-milk as well. Billy did so most days. Sometimes, he got the "free lunch" and some ice-cream for his good academic performance.

The problem was that Shiloh Elementary was drafty and cold in the winter and hot as hell in the summer, because the School's opened windows were the only air condition available. The toilets were outside on the edge of the woods. On a cold rainy day going to the bathroom was a tough ordeal.

Miss Gaines had about seventy students in her two classes. Therefore keeping order was a great triumph for her. She had the impossible task of getting and holding the attention of thirty five or forty nine-years old, and the same number of ten-year olds, who were cold and or hot depending on the season, and were uninterested in doing any schoolwork for the most part. (Bless Miss Gaines for her good job regardless of the hardships and emotional upheavals she faced.) Billy excelled at Shiloh. His Report Card was filled with "S" grades with "A's and B's" in Reading and Math, and "C's" in English.

(In the meantime, Mabel gave birth to another boy, June 8, 1955, Henry named Samuel Lee. On October 5, 1956, Mabel had another boy, Henry named David Leon.)

For Billy, the 1956-57 school year went by uneventfully. He was glad he did not have to go to school with white kids, and he loved Mrs. Bland and Miss Gaines. Billy passed on to the Fifth Grade. He saw that his Mother was pregnant again. As the school bus came by S.C. Abrams, Billy saw construction workers laying the foundation for a massive building. It was across the road from Abrams High.

On October 20, 1958, Mabel had her first girl. She named her Julia

Mae. Charles had started school at Gravel Hill that September. Nearing the end of the 1957-58 school year, Billy was so happy because he had heard from Miss Gaines that he would pass on to the Sixth Grade and would be in Mrs. Bland's homeroom. He wanted to be one of the few who stuck around long enough to graduate from the Seventh Grade.

On this day in April, 1958, Billy was outside playing at recess with some of his friends. A young man named Chick Christian, a very light-skinned Seventh-Grader, who was fifteen years old, came around to the back of the School. He sneaked up to Billy, and his friends, Michael Matthews, Pauley Martin, and Lloyd, Pauley's younger Brother, who were shooting marbles.

(The Public School Ordinance in Virginia stated that any child between the ages of six and sixteen years of age had to be enrolled in school or his parents would be in violation of Virginia State Law. Prior to the 1950s, that Law was all but ignored as it pertained to Blacks. But in the 1950s, Black children who could not or would not try to learn just stayed in school until they were sixteen. They could then legally dropout of school.)

Chick (Warren Christian, Jr.), and Horace Fowler, Jr. were fifteen. Roger Fowler was fourteen. All three had languished in the Seventh Grade waiting to become part of the high dropout statistics among "Negro Grade-School Students." All three of the above were very light-skinned, and had "middleclass" parents, who were in the Pulpwood Industry, or were Sawmill owners. So getting a real education was not very high on their agenda. Little dark skinned students were thought to be disgusting "Tar Babies" to them. Words like "Jiggerboos," and "Blackie" were often hurled at Billy and his little circle of friends by Chick and his pals. There was one more who looked like them but hung around them to prevent them from actually hurting one they had targeted as a "Sambo" too "Ugly" to live. He was Genie Payne, a blond, blue-eyed muscular youngster, who was also waiting to drop out of school.

Billy was down on his hands and knees shooting marbles. Horace and Roger came up behind Billy and teased him.

Roger, a tall-lanky, boy, quipped, "Man look at this nappy-headed Negro. He's so Black he's 'bout to shine," he said to his older Brother.

"Yep. Yep. You's right 'bout that Bro," Horace replied with a lot of laughter. "That Billy Bob Negro is so dark he deserves to get his ass kicked.

That's what he go get anyway. I'm already in trouble for kicking they asses. Ifl wasn't I'd get into trouble right now."

Chick, was just a little bit darker than Horace and Roger. When they turned their focus to him, he felt he needed to show who he favored. All three of the culprits were wearing Blue Jeans and sweat shirts, and Chuck Taylor Tennis. "I wanna see what this Coon's blood looks like, anyway, man," Chick hissed out of the side of his mouth. He looked at his Cousins, Roger and Horace, and all three slicked back their very-straight, black hair.

"How ya gonna do that, Chick-cut 'im?" Harold Dale Allen, another one of their pals asked. He was a very stocky sort, who wore a tie and shirt every day. He had on black trousers, penny loafers, and had his hair conked slick. He was nut-brown with grayish eyes, and hated that he was not as light-skinned as Roger and Horace.

"I got my knife in my pocket, but I ain't gonna cut nobody. But I can make 'im bleed without cutting 'im. I don't wanna go to jail over Billy-Bob, there," Chick said. He ran his hand through his slicked-back hair.

Then-Billy realized that he was their main target for that day. His friends knew too, and all got up and scrambled away from around him.

Billy ran as fast as he could to get around to the front of the School, but Chick ran him down. "You little bugger. You're making me run too hard to catch ya ass, I'm gonna kill ya when I do catch you; ya hear?" Chick shouted.

Chick caught up to Billy, tripped him up and he fell and hit his head on a large rock. He heard Chick laughing, but could not move a muscle for a few minutes. He heard him say: "Damn! That Black Negro's got red blood. I thought it would be Black too. See, it's coming all down his Tar Baby face."

Billy blacked out for about fifteen minutes. When he came to, Genie Payne had carried him to Shiloh's front entrance. He sat Billy down on the steps. Genie sat beside him.

It had not long been past lunchtime. His lunch came gushing up his throat and spilt all over the steps. His head throbbed. His vision was blurred. He was too dizzy to walk. A hen-egg size knot formed on the right side of his temple. Billy blacked out again.

When he awoke again, he was in Mrs. Bland's new green-and-white Chevy Impala sitting on the front passenger side. She had put a lot of old newspapers on the seat and the floor in case Billy got sick to his stomach again.

Billy opened his eyes to a swirling world. He couldn't remember what had happened to him.

Then he blinked out again.

Mrs. Bland "put the pedal to the metal." After they got up to Billy's house, Mrs. Bland pulled him out of her car. She struggled to get Billy up on the porch. A very pregnant Mabel came wobbling towards Mrs. Bland and her wounded son, lying on a homemade bench in the middle of the porch.

"Mrs. James. I will take William to the doctor or hospital if you want me to. But the Law requires that I call you before I do so, but you all have no phone. So all I could do was bring him here as fast as I could to see what you want me to do."

Mabel trembled all over. "What happen to 'im?" she asked.

"I don't have all the details right now, but he took a nasty fall and hit his head. He has a big knot on the right side of his forehead. It may not be much . . . or it could be very serious. So far, all I've heard is that he slipped and fell while playing outside at recess. He came to for a couple of minutes, but doesn't remember what happened to him. If I find out more I will let you know right away."

Tears came to Mabel's eyes. "We ain' got no in-sho-ance. We couldn't 'ford the Pilot, an all. Billy's right strong. I think he's go be aw-ight. I'ma just let'im rest awhile. Ifn he shows any signs of gettin' worse off, I'll get Rev. Nicholas ta-take 'im over yonder ta-Charles'ville to the Univer'sy Hospital. Thank ya for bringin'im home."

Mrs. Bland cried. "I'll get to the bottom of all this right away Mrs. James. We're right fond of William up at Shiloh Elementary. He's one of our promising students. Can I go in with you and hug him goodbye, Mrs. James?" Mrs. Bland said.

"Yes'am, you can," Mabel said.

Mrs. Bland helped Mabel carry Billy to the children's room. They laid Billy on one of the two beds in there. Mrs. Bland bent over and hugged Billy gently pulling him to her bosom. He was semiconscious. Tears came down her cheeks. "Son, you get well soon now. I promise you, I'll get to the bottom of this as soon as I get back to school. I love you."

Mabel hugged Mrs. Bland as she turned away from her Son. "Thank you so much for being so nice," Mabel whined.

"You are welcome, Mrs. James. If there's anything else I can do for you, just let me know."

Mabel watched Mrs. Bland run out of the house and get into her car. She turned it around in the road that leads up to the house and sped off. In the house her perfume lingered.

Mabel had a hard time undressing Billy. He was as limber as a dishrag. She got a pan of warm water ready and bathed her Son. "Wake up, Baby. Tell Momma where it hurts." Mabel whimpered louder when her oldest Son did not respond.

Then Billy slowly opened his eyes. It seemed as though he had just closed them for a moment. He had a blinding headache. He remembered playing marbles with his buddies at School. He didn't know how he had gotten home in bed.

He blinked his eyes and the headache eased a little. He could hear his little Brothers playing outside. Then his Momma came into the room.

"Ma, what happened to me?" Billy asked.

"Mrs. Bland brought ya home knocked out. She say ya might've slipped at school, or somethin'. Ya prob-be hit ya head. Ya don't 'member nothin' bout it?" Mabel said.

Billy got a puzzled look on his face. "Last thing I remember is playing marbles with my buddies. The big boys came 'round teasing us and we all ran away. Then I ended up here in bed." Billy grimaced a little because his head started to throb with pain, then he shut his eyes as tight as he could. The pain eased up a little.

"You's been in bed for two days, honey. I had ta-clean ya like-a baby. Thought we's go have-ta carry ya up yonder to the hospital, but ya seem ta-be pullin' outta it now. Did somebody hit ya on your head?" Mabel asked.

"I don't know, Ma. But, Chick Christian was laughing and making a lotta fun of me, like in a dream, or something. Then somebody was calling out my name. Then I woke up in bed. Ma, how did I get home?"

Tears eased out of Mabel's eyes. "Mrs. Bland brought ya home in 'er new car. That teacher's like-a Angel. She helped me tote ya like a sack of 'taters. She's a good woman."

"I love 'er, Ma. I'm gonna be in her homeroom next year. It's gonna be the best year of schooling for me," Billy said.

"Aw-ight, Sugar," Mabel said. She kissed Billy all over his face.

Fermi and Genie Payne (not related) told Mrs. Bland about what they had seen Roger and Horace Fowler, Harold Dale Allen and Chick Christian saying and doing to Billy. The next week after the incident, Mrs. Bland told Billy: "I'm sending home a letter to your Mother. I have expelled Horace and Roger Fowler from school. Harold Dale Allen quit before I had a chance to. Chick Christian tripped you up and you hit your head on a rock. He's in jail.

"The School Board is filing assault charges against Warren Christian, Jr. That's what is in this letter. These boys will never hurt you again. If your parents want to take any legal action I will do all I can to help them. You May be excused, it is time for recess."

The main threat was gone. Those boys had always been the ones teasing him all the time.

Now they were out of there. He was glad he didn't have to see them again, ever.

The May 17, 1954 Supreme Court decision outlawing public school segregation shocked a lot of people in Fluvanna. Henry and Mabel, and many like them, objected to the very thought of ever trusting their children to White teachers; or having their Sons too close to White girls.

Cora Winston had purchased a 21-inch Black and White TV. She had a large antenna installed on top of her roof Henry would go up and watch the Walter Cronkite News Hour on Sunday Evenings. He saw newsflashes of screaming hysterical White parents protesting the integration of their schools with Blacks. He hated being called a Black. Little Negro children were being spat upon, hit with eggs, and barred out of schools in Alabama. Henry saw how Emmet Till's murderers got away Free! Shortly after the Till murder and judicial debacle that followed it, Henry witnessed something just as sinister happening right there at home.

He saw the White Merchants of Columbia announcing that they were forming a branch of the an organization called "The Defenders of State Sovereignty." He heard State Senator Harry Byrd of Winchester proclaim, "All right-thinking White Virginians must join the DSS and 'Massively

Resist' the Mongrelization of the White Race through Public School integration." Thus "Massive Resistance" became a rallying cry of racist resistance to school desegregation in Virginia.

By 1956, the Columbia members of the DSS had reorganized The White Citizens' Council (WCC). This subgroup was tied to others throughout the South, with many members also a part of the Ku Klux Klan. Henry could see Whites banning together all around Virginia and the rest of the South to circumvent the implementation of the Supreme Court's Desegregation Mandate.

The grapevine had given Henry the 4-11 on a meeting presided over by Mr. Wilfred Kent. A large group had met at City Hall in Columbia. Wilfred and others at the meeting expressed fears that "Nigger-Blood" would run like water in the streets if Whites were forced to send their children to school with the "Darkies." His Brother, Wally, had a proposal. He didn't want to see all of the "Niggers" killed. That would kill the money they were able to make off them. So he made this proposal:

"I have twenty-thousand dollars, and my Brother has another twenty, that we will donate towards a fund to build the 'Niggers' fine schools so they won't wanna send their kids to ours. I say, let us build them equal schools."

The whole standing room only crowd cheered loudly at Wally Kent's proposal. Right away, checks for five-hundred-to-five-thousand dollars were written and collected by the treasurer. Thousands more were pledged by those who were caught off guard that evening.

In the days following the above initial meeting, Columbia's WCC formed strong subcommittees that met often with the Kent Brothers, and with members of other community chapters of the DSS. Hundreds of thousands of dollars were hurriedly collected. (If they had done that, years before, they would not be facing what they feared most: INTEGRATION.)

Architects, construction firms, and planning commissioners were called into speedy action to create blueprints for a new Elementary School with all of the modern conveniences in an elementary school anywhere in Virginia; and to modernize S.C. Abrams High School, so that Blacks would have equal schools. Plans were submitted to the Virginia General Assembly that voted unanimously, giving them the go ahead, and to match funds that the Fluvanna Public School Building Fund Drive had raised.

All told, the WCC and its DSS auxiliaries raised nearly a million dollars. Undisclosed funds came in to match the above monies creating a huge nest-egg that grew into over four million dollars.

The Fluvanna County School Board purchased land directly across from S.C. Abrams High. In the fall of 1957, a massive foundation had been erected. It went up fast like magic. A two story, multifaceted edifice was built seemingly like overnight.

The New School had spacious classrooms, equipped with the most modern educational tools like overhead projectors, beautiful green-boards, and shiny-new desks. The classrooms also had florescent lights and boxes of chalk and crayons. There were lockers for every child.

Central air and heat were something that even Abrams did not have, but the New School did, as well as a clean-spacious cafeteria that served a hot lunch daily. Then there was a teachers' lounge with sofas and end-chairs, soda machines, and a newspaper machine. There was an intercom system that could be heard all around the school emanating from the Principal's office.

The school was surrounded by beautiful shrubbery, and a huge asphalt tarmac. The tarmac was marked so that games like volleyball, shuffleboard, tennis, and portable basketball could be played on it. There was a softball field with the markings for football as well.

The School Board named the New School, "Central Elementary." At this point it was one of the most modern Elementary facilities in the State built to circumvent the Supreme Court's Public School Desegregation Mandate. Mosby Court Elementary, on Church Hill in Richmond, was the other.

When Henry James heard that Central Elementary had been built and was ready for occupation in 1958, he was elated. Black and White children would still have their own schools, he thought.

By the time the Fluvanna County School Board had finished building Central Elementary, and stocking its new spacious library with the latest in elementary-school media, it had little left to modernize Abrams High. Only enough funding was left to construct one seven-stool, four urinal, two hand-sink restroom for the boys; and a twelve-stool, and four hand-sink restroom for the girls. Central air was added to its small auditorium, as well as to its shop and home economics classrooms; and to its small cafeteria-that was inferior to Central Elementary's cafeteria. After the rudiments of a bio-lab were added, Abrams had to do without. It could not renovate its inferior library, build a gym, or an English lab as had been requested.

In July of 1958, Henry came by Thurston's Grocery on his way to the Jungle on this Saturday evening. He heard some loud White woman say: "Now that the 'Niggers' got better schools than us, they ought not wanna force their kids in our schools. Maybe our good Negroes will turn their backs on that old N-A-A-C-P, and all of this dam-integrationist foolishness will go away."

Mrs. Thurston answered: "If the Coloreds don't calm down 'round here, they gonna have hell to pay. They won't be able to get a crumb from my store, or none of the stores down here. That ought to make them fight them integrationists like a pack of wolves, hah-hah."

"I hear you, child. Now, you take care. I'll see you at the town meeting tonight," the first woman said.

Henry ran down the hill and across the bridge before the woman could see that he had been eavesdropping. He worried about where he would go, or what he would do, if the merchants in Columbia cut-off his credit.

Billy got on the school bus for the sixth time at the beginning of a new school year without knowing when or if he would be forced into integrated education. Fear gripped his innards causing knots in his stomach.

The bus came as usual with Felmi still the Patrolman. One good thing was that Billy knew if he had to go to school with Whites they would be getting on the same bus with him and they were not doing so.

Up at his A'nt Cora's house, Billy had seen what happened on September 3, 1957, when Colored children tried to go to school with White children in Little Rock, Arkansas. Daisy Bates, the NAACP President escorted nine Black children to Central High, and all hell broke out. Arkansas Governor Orval Faubus posited National Guardsmen at the school's entrance to keep the Black children out. On September 251 President Eisenhower sent in the 101st Airborne Division, and ten-thousand federalized national guardsmen to finally escort the Colored children to class.

Billy and his Mother saw screaming White-mobs yelling: "Niggers go home! Go back to Africa! ..." Billy didn't ever want to be confronted like that just to go to school.

On this morning, when the bus pulled off 673 onto 649, it turned onto a paved road. The road had been widened. It made Abrams look very different or something.

The east end of the building had been expanded, or something. The cafeteria area was new looking. A new building had been built beside of the cafeteria. Then Billy glanced across the road.

The bus door closed and Mr. Baskerfield put the new air conditioned bus in motion. He drove it across the road to a massive new brick building. A huge sign out in front of the building read: "CENTRAL ELEMENTARY SCHOOL." The bus parked in one of six or seven unloading lanes on the tarmac. "Grades One-through-Seven please exit at this time. We are no longer going to transport you all to Shiloh. Be quiet and walk slowly," Mr. Baskerfield said.

Billy was glad that this new school had no Whites unloading there. This was the "equal" school he'd heard that the State was building for "Negroes." He figured that it was the best school in Fluvanna County. It was the newest one anyway. Billy still hoped he would be in Mrs. Bland's homeroom.

When he had finally exited the bus, Billy noticed that the air was still very summerlike. It was nearly eighty degrees. He also noticed the lines and lines of children unloading onto the tarmac and heading up wide concrete sidewalks to the main entrance of the school. Billy followed the lines of students.

Once he had gotten up the steps of the school and ventured inside of the massive entranceway, the brightness blinded him. The lights were flashing off light-colored tiles. His eyes were used to kerosene lamps. When he visited his A'nt Cora's house, the bright electric light-bulbs took him a minute or two to get used to. But at Central-this was something else.

Once Billy's eyes adjusted to the lighting, he found himself in a great lobby. The green and white tiles were so beautiful. There were endless hallways like tunnels intersecting here and there, with a number of doors to rooms on every side of them. A number of very light-skinned teachers led groups of students away from the overwhelming crowd of grade-schoolers. And then-

"Sixth Graders, this way," quite startled Billy. The bass voice came from a man dressed in a navy-blue suit, with a red tie over a white shirt. He wore shiny-brown shoes. He was very light skinned. "I am Mr. Pressley Edwards, your Assistant Principal. When your name is called, form a line, or get in line with your homeroom teacher. You will either be in Mrs. Lowsy's or Mrs. Thompson's homeroom. Be good, students." Mr. Edwards walked briskly on down the hallway towards the principal's office near the main entrance.

"James Anderson, Tony Anderson, Garland Baskerfield III, Melvin Baskerfield, Jr., George Bland, Jr., Charlotte Bryant ... William James" The names were called until a five-eleven teacher wearing a red and blue flower-print dress, fox-colored stockings, and black flats had assembled her group of Sixth Graders.

The teacher had a nut-brown skin tone. She had very straight-looking black hair that was curled at the ends but hung down to her shoulders. She had a pointed nose, small grayish eyes, and thin-lips covered with bright-red lipstick. She was shapely and blinked her eyes a lot when she talked. "Georgette Vowels," had been the last name the teacher had called. Billy quickly counted the students around him. He got a count of about twenty-nine. This surprised him because he was used to being in class with from fifty to sixty students assigned to one teacher.

"Students, listen up. Let's go to the auditorium for your first assembly this morning. Stay in line, walk slowly; girls in one line; and boys in the other; and, now, begin. I am Mrs. Thompson, your Sixth-Grade homeroom teacher for this year." Billy thought her voice had a squeak to it that reminded him of--well, he'd forgotten whom.

Billy and his classmates marched in the direction that Mrs. Thompson pointed towards. He thought that he may as well forget about Mrs. Bland-about being in her homeroom, anyway. He didn't see Miss Gaines of Mrs. Phallison anywhere in the hallways. But-he hadn't seen Mrs. Bland either.

Soon Billy was seated in a massive circular-shaped auditorium along with thousands of other students. The place was magnificent. It had new padded red and white chairs, blue stage curtains, a huge stage, with fifty or so spotlights in the ceiling.

Mr. Edwards was sitting beside a tall, heavyset, very smoothly dark-skinned man, that wore a black and white pinstriped suit, blue wing-tipped shoes, and a red tie over a blue shirt. His head was shaved clean. He wore a pair of silver-horn-rimmed glasses. He smiled showing that he had no teeth in his mouth at all.

"This assembly will now come to order," said Mr. Edwards. He had come over to a new podium. "We will now stand and sing 'The Star Spangle Banner.' Miss Gaines, would you be so kind as to come to our new piano to accompany us this morning?"

Miss Gaines got up from the back of the auditorium, pranced past the four or five isles or so to the front of the stage area. She seated herself at a Baby Grand Piano just offstage to the right. She played and the audience stood and sung. She had tears in her eyes, Billy could clearly see that. He wondered why she was almost crying.

After the Song, Mr. Edwards returned to the podium. "I want to introduce to some and reacquaint to others, an outstanding scholar, theologian, Pastor of Cumberland Baptist Church, and our Principal, Mr. Paul Robinson Spraggs. He is also a retired Quartermaster General from the Army.

"He is a graduate of Hampton Institute, Virginia Union, and Howard University. He holds the PhD in Social Studies and High School Administration. He is certified to teach Math, General Science, and American History. He is on the Boards of Virginia State College and Norfolk State Teachers' College.

"So without further ado, I bring to you, Dr. Paul R. Spraggs."

The entire audience stood and clapped their hands as the intelligent-looking gentlemen who was also a scholar and a Man of God, strode to the podium, like an African Prince might have in Ancient Ghana, back in "Our Ancient-African History."

Billy heard Dr. Spraggs say a lot of very important things that morning that he didn't fully understand because he used so many big words. But he clearly heard him say: "We are fortunate to have the benefit of several new teachers who were formally with Evergreen Prep. Since that school no longer is in service, we have onboard, Mrs. Felicia Thompson, and Mrs. Margaret Lowsy, Sixth Grade teachers; and Mrs. Dorothy Wiggins, a Seventh Grade teacher.

"Ladies, please stand."

Mrs. Thompson stood. Then a rotund woman in a section of the auditorium stood. She was as fat as Billy's A'nt Bessie, was as light-skinned as his A'nt Cora, but had a take-no-foolishness look on her face. She was Mrs. Wiggins. A thin lady stood up a little father over. She was as White as Mrs. Phallison, and had the same blue eyes, blond hair and flat-faced features. She had a broad smile on her thin-lips. She was a handsome woman. She was Mrs. Lowsy.

The audience applauded as Dr. Spraggs pointed out each teacher. He asked, "Miss Gaines come back to the piano and we will sing one stanza of our National Anthem. After which you all are dismissed from this assembly and you are to follow your respective teachers."

Billy walked past a group of older-looking students following Mrs. Bland. Another group followed Mrs. Wiggins. Billy figured that Mrs. Bland must be teaching the Seventh Grade. Miss Gaines walked behind Mrs. Bland. Her nametag had "Substitute Teacher" written on it. Mrs. Phallison was nowhere to be seen. Billy walked past several sections of the First, Second and Third Grades on his way-with his class-out of the auditorium. He did not see Mrs. Phallison.

"Class, follow me," Mrs. Thompson said. Billy and his classmates followed Mrs. Thompson up the hallway from the auditorium to a flight of steps right across from the front entrance in the lobby. She went up the stairway to the second floor, turned right and proceeded to near the end of a long hallway. She stopped at a doorway that was two-doors away from the boys' restroom. She turned left, put a key on her keychain into the lock of the doorway, unlocked the door and pulled it open. She stood aside and let her students file into the new classroom. Billy and all of them took seats where they will or may, that first time.

On the green board, that was taller than any black board Billy had ever seen, and went from the front door to the windows on the other side of the room, were words written in large cursive letters: "WELCOME TO YOUR HOMEROOM, 214. I AM Mrs. Felicia Thompson, YOUR HOMEROOM TACHER THIS YEAR, 1958-59." Inside of the room were thirty-six shellac covered desks with metal under-hens. Billy had never sat at a desk that was not all cut-up and full of initials and salacious phrases. In back of the classroom was a table with six chairs that were very similar to the desks. Billy took a glance at the floor tiles that were of a mercurial-tan red blend. The walls were covered with light-brown plaster, and the ceiling was hung with white ceiling-tiles. The classroom was beautiful with the blue and white-tasseled curtains hanging at its multi-windows. The room was air-conditioned and was very comfortable. Billy never remembered being in a room as fine or as well-lit as that classroom up until then.

The classroom had the scent of Pine Sol, new paint, and fresh cement. There were no scars or scratches on the walls, doors, or windowsills.

Mrs. Thompson pranced into the room after the last student had entered. She slammed the door shut. She stood behind a huge brown desk and looked her classroom over before getting out her roll book. Then, she said: "All of you please stand at this time. Move into the aisles nearest to the walls. When I call your names sit in the next seat behind the last person whose name I had previously called. Is that clear?"

Once all of the students had been seated, Billy almost got sick to his stomach. There were seven students seated in three rows, leaving two desks in those rows vacant. There was a fourth row with eight students seated in it, leaving one desk vacant. Mrs. Thompson moved one desk from the end of the first row and the last one to either side of the back table. She placed a conical-dunce cap on each of the desks she had separated from the rest.

What made Billy ill was that he could not help but notice that Mrs. Thompson had positioned her students with light skin up in front of the classroom. The row with eight students Billy sat in that row. The people all around him went from nut-brown to deep-ebony. That feeling he had gotten in the First Grade came bubbling up out of his gut, like Lava out of his "Subliminal Lock Box." All he could think of was, "Great Balls of Miss Payne!"

Mrs. Thompson pranced around the classroom clasping her roll book to her stacked bosom.

Billy trembled all over when she made her speech:

"Class, I'm one of the teachers who lost their jobs at Evergreen Prep. Many of the people who had supported that great private grade school withdrew their support because of the trouble the NAACP has been causing. The school board hired most of the teachers who lost their jobs and some of us are over here at Central.

"I'm going to do my best to teach many of you who are un-teachable. Some of you are better suited for sawmill work, or farm hands, and no amount

of hard work with you will change that." She looked towards those in the dark row.

She got out of her book bag a Journal depicting pictures of "Negro Leaders" created by EBONY Magazine. She held it up before the classroom and turned pages showing various leaders.

"See, Dr. Booker T. Washington was a very educated man. He was very intelligent because of his breeding. There's Congressman Adam Clayton Powell, Dr. Thurgood Marshall, and Carter G. Woodson, who are credits to our Race. They were all the result of proper breeding.

W.E.B. DuBois has made that very clear in his many writings. The above went to schools like Harvard University and they have moved us all forward I feel that my job is to seek out people like them and to give them an intellectual boost so they can become our future proud leaders."

Again, she took a snide glance at the dark-row of students.

Billy thought that he would almost choke to death on his own saliva. That was the same shit Miss Payne had shot at him and people like him at Gravel Hill Elementary. "Farmers ...

Sawmill hands? What the hell am I doing in school if all I can become is a damn farmer or sawmill worker? I won't do none of that shit when I get outta school-that's for damn sure," Billy whispered to himself

He was seated in the front seat of the infamous "dark row." Billy made an acquaintance with the one sitting adjacent to him in front of one of the "light rows."

He spoke to a very light-skinned freckled faced, red-haired, guy. "Hi. I'm William James.

What's happening?"

"Hey. I'm Herman Tolliver III from Cloverdale. My Dad just moved us back there. He's a Sergeant in the Army. He was stationed in Germany, and me, my Mom, and my baby Sister Delora were over yonder too. I like it here in America better-it ain't so cold all the time like in Germany. What do your Dad do?" Herman said. Billy ignored that question.

Billy liked Herman from the start. Herman drew pictures he had seen in the funnies of the newspaper like "Handy Andy," and "Popeye The Sailor Man," exactly like those appeared in the paper. And, Herman was generous.

"Lemme borrow a couple pieces of paper and one of your extra pencils, my-man. I gotta see ifI can draw them pictures like you're doing," Billy said.

"Sure, man," Herman said. "But don't worry if you can't draw like me right away. Took me a while to learn. I took art over in Germany at the Base School. We went to school with White children over yonder, William."

"What!" Billy exclaimed. "How'd y'all do that?"

"Nobody cared about that in Germany. Some of my good buddies were White boys. We got along pretty good. It'll get like that around here in a little while, my Mom says. She told me to watch out for White people over here. So I do that. Know what I mean?" Herman said.

"Yep. I know, man. Round here you can get lynched for looking at a White girl, man. I'm scared to death about that. Emmett Till from Chicago got shot to death while he was visiting down in Mississippi. Been in all the papers. You heard about it?" Billy frowned.

"Yeah. Dad mentioned it. Said it was good we were not in the deep-south. But told me not to try to have White girlfriends even up here in Virginia like I had in Germany. So I keep away from them," Herman said.

"You had White girlfriends?" Billy asked. He was shocked at the very idea of what Herman had said.

"In Germany all the Black guys had White girlfriends. Most of the Black girls had German boyfriends. It was no big deal, man. You get used to seeing that. You get so you don't pay that that much attention," Herman chuckled when he saw the puzzled look on Billy's face.

A harsh voice stabbed Billy's ear. "I'm not going to tolerate this talking and passing notes you're doing in my classroom, William James," Mrs. Thompson shouted right at him.

"Mrs. Thomson, I wasn't talking-and I didn't pass no notes, neither," Billy snapped. He was not going to let her treat him like Miss Payne had. He was thinking about getting up and busting her in the mouth if she tried to hit him with her hand or anything.

"Don't talk back to me, William James! You go back to the back table for time-out for fifteen minutes. Next time, I will send you to the principal's office. Is that clear?" Mrs. Thompson said, in her shrill voice. Her light-colored cheeks grew to light-pink, then to rosy-red.

"Yes 'am," Billy said. He could see that what she was doing was aimed mainly at his dark skin. She hadn't reprimanded Herman at all. He was actually the one doing all of the talking. For the rest of the day, Billy laid his head down on the table and whiled away the hours. Out of his "Subliminal Lock Box" he conjured up images of himself being a Star Baseball Player like Jackie Robinson, or Duke Snider.

But Billy noticed that the rest of the "dark row" must have known "What Time it was." They stared out of the windows while Mrs. Thompson spent the day teaching her so-called "Future Negro Leaders," and neglecting the rest.

On the way home that evening on the bus, Billy couldn't get what had happened out of his mind, but knew that shit was way bigger than anything an eleven-year-old-like him--could do anything about. But it made him sad enough to almost cry. Once he had walked up the road with his little Brother Dick tagging along, they were surprised to see that an electric pole with wires attached to it had been installed in their backyard. The wires ran from the pole to the side of the house. Billy was glad that they were finally going to get electricity.

A few minutes after the boys came into their yard, and Mabel came out pregnant as usual, a truck loaded with furniture came up the road straining against every gear it had. In the cab of the truck were Aunt Ginia and Grandma Agnes. George Mayor drove the truck.

Mabel waved at the occupants of the truck. She turned to Billy. "They's movin' in the ol' house we moved outta. Ginia gotta little gal in 'er aims an 'nother one on the way. She named the one she got, Hazel Bernese Scott, she's 'bout 'round three. I heard tell that George's go marr' Ginia, but I wouldn't count on it. He got them that spooky place up the road, there.

"Momma 'nem ought not trust in George Mayor. I heard tell he ain't nothin' butta gamblin' man. He ain' go get hitched-ta no one gal. I know Ginia thinks givin'im chillren go make'im change. I knows better'n that. All she had-da do is ask me. She just go be stuck in that ol' ghosty house haunted by a nasty witch. I done seen 'er," Mabel said.

"Ma, I asked Miss White about ghosts and haunts and things during Halloween. She says it ain' no such thing as haunts and ghosts," Billy opined.

"Billy, I done seen 'em-an' you have too. You just don't 'members. But ya seen one," Mabel snapped at her doubting Son.

"Ma, I don't 'member seeing none of them, and I don't wanna start seeing any of them," Billy exclaimed. "It's bad enough to have to deal with real people. Then we got to deal with invisible dead ones too. That's way too scary, Ma."

A few minutes later that same evening, another truck came up the road straining against all of its gears. This time a very light-skinned woman sat in the cab holding a little girl in her lap, that resembled her. A dark-skinned man wearing a Brown Army Uniform drove the truck. It was a huge truck and was heavily loaded down.

"Tilly Langhorne died last week. Herman and his wife, Faith, an' they chillren go be rentin' the place near Gerry'nem," Mabel said.

"O' goody," Billy said. "I met Herman, Jr. at school. He's real nice. But Ma, what happened to Old Man Judah?" Billy asked.

"Oh, he's been dead, Billy. You's too young to worr 'bout such things, so I didn't say nothin' toll," Mabel said.

Billy changed the subject. "When they gonna finish wiring our house?"

"Well. Mr. Jasper Furman go do it this Sat'day. He say he gotta get a bail of wire he done ordered from down-ta Holland's Hardware. Then we go have lights. Henry gotta TV laid 'way at Profits Dry Goods Store. It's almost like Cora's, with a antenna and ev'thin', Then we can watch the soaps and the news at home. We won't have-ta worr' Cora ta-death," Mabel said.

Billy, a boy of eleven, wondered a lot about what he had been hearing and seeing on the radio and TV about the "southern sexual taboo." The death of Emmett Till was large in his mind. The Scottsboro Boys were fighting for their freedom when everyone assumed they were innocent. Yet, all around Billy, in every "Black" family, was any number of near-white people. Their fathers had to be White men. Now and then a story of a White woman being scorned, whipped, and or, killed for sleeping with a Black man was whispered about by Black people. And Billy knew of Black men who claimed they had slipped around in the woods with a White gal or two; and that a number of these women were married to White men.

Jasper Furman was a tall gangly man in his thirties. He had buckteeth, sandy hair, and a pair of sneaky-looking grayish-blue eyes. He knocked on the front door early this Saturday morning. It had to be about 6:30 A.M. Henry got up to answer the door in his long johns.

"Oh, how're ya doin' Mr. Furman. We's just'bout read-ta get up," he lied. "C'mon in an' wait-a minute. I gotta get fully dressed."

"Aw-ight, buddy," Furman said. "Be right here in ya front room."

Henry went into his bedroom. "Mabel, get up. It's Mr. Furman. He's come-ta wire the house," He said to his sleeping wife.

"Oh shit. Didn' kno' he's go come so early. Lemme get up an' make-a pot-a coffee. All White folk like coffee." Mabel rolled out of bed. She put on a flannel housecoat. Furman was peeking through a crack of the door that separated the front room from Mabel's and Henry's bedroom. He had seen her naked body.

Billy, after being awakened by Furman's knocking on the door, got up and peeped at him because he did not trust any White man. He saw the "nasty Joker" ogling his Mother and wanted to go in and bust him in the mouth.

Mabel went into the kitchen and started rustling pots and pans. Henry had made a roaring fire in the cook stove. Henry came back into the front room carrying a hot cup of coffee in his left hand. He handed that to Furman. "Ya want sugar or half-an-half, Mr. Furman?" he asked.

"No, Henry. I like mine 'Black' as can be." He got a snide little smile on his thin lips. He moved his utility belt around to cover his frontal area. He had to hide the obvious.

"Mr. Furman I'm go feed the hogs and chickens. Then I'm go get some breakfast. Ya can get started where ya want to. Aw-ight?" Henry said.

"That-a boy," Furman said.

Billy and the rest of the children got up to watch Furman wire the house. At about eleven o' clock Furman beckoned to Billy. "Go tell ya Daddy I need to speak with him."

Billy obeyed the khaki-clad farmer. When Henry came in to see what Furman wanted he said: "Look Henry. I need a part I left down at Holland's. It's a little fixture, but I'm go need it to finish wiring your house. Look, I got a couple other things to do, so take the keys to my truck and go down to Holland's. He'll know what you came for."

Henry shook his head in agreement. "Aw-ight, Mr. Furman. I'll be right back," he said.

"All you'll have left to do is call Mr. Ziegler to come turn on your electric juice. You go have lights and whatnot," Furman said with a little grin on his face. Henry went on out the front door.

Soon after Henry pulled the truck out onto the road and took off, Billy came in the back door to get a cold biscuit.

"Mabel. I swear I won't tell Henry nothing at all about it if you want to give me a little bit. I see you're pregnant, I'll be gentle. You can gimme a little piece your blackberry pie. I've done good wiring your house," Billy heard Furman say as he suddenly pulled Mabel towards him.

She pulled away from Furman, got a very devilish look on her face and shocked Billy to no end. She didn't know he was peeping at them.

"Look!" Mabel pulled back her baggy flannel housecoat, exposing her fury mound at the base of her protruding stomach for a couple of seconds. "Your eyes may shine an' your teeth may grit. But none-a this you go get," Mabel rhymed. She swished her hips in a very sexy way as she walked away from before Furman's shiny-eyed gaze.

"Bitch. Bitch. You're all bitches," Furman whispered loudly. "Why gal, when it comes to 'poontang' I don't discriminate-nor did my Daddy before me. I bet I got half-White Brothers and Sisters all over Fluvanna, not to mention a-hundred Cousins or more. Well Lavinia Anderson, Eve's gal, that's my half-Sister. I know that there's tons of Colored people all over the South with White Daddies. So, you won't be doing nothing out of the ordinary by giving me what we both want. I ain't go tell Henry if you do," Furman said a lot louder.

After all, Mabel could not believe what this "White Devil" had the balls to say to her. "Furman, ya White son-a-va-bitch! Y'all fucked over my Momma for years. Y'all fucked over Henry's Mother and gotta cup'la babies by her. That broke Unc' Charlie, her husband's heart.

"Iain' go never let no White man get 'tween my legs. Now ya go on an' wire this house like Henry's payin' ya to. Don't never come in my face again. I ain't got no pussy for ya," Mabel hissed at Furman. "Ifl tell my husband what ya ask me, he'll kill ya White ass!"

Furman scratched his head. "Well ... what ya think he'd say if I tell 'im ya pulled ya dress up and showed me all ya got?" he said.

"Ya best do what ya came here ta-do. I'll stay outta ya way, an' you stay outta mine." Mabel got busy in the kitchen. She heard Furman's truck coming up the little pathway to her house. She acted as though nothing had happened out of the ordinary when Henry walked through the door and handed Furman a brown paper bag with some kind of fixture inside.

Billy was glad he had eavesdropped on the conversation between Furman and his Ma. That was how he felt Negro women ought to act when White men tried to take advantage of them.

Billy and Herman Tolliver III, called Junnie, became fast friends. Herman never laughed at Billy's clothes, and didn't make Billy feel like a piece of shit like Tony Anderson, Melvin Baskerfield, Jr. and Garlard Baskerfield III. Then there was a crippled student named Lee Hawthrone, who teased Billy incessantly.

Lee had one of his legs in a slang that went around his shoulders. He had broken it and the bones were slow to heal. He had to use a crutch to get around. He was light-skinned and had very straight-black hair. His physical appearance was much like the above culprits. They could do no wrong in the eyes of Mrs. Thompson.

When a reprimand came at all from Mrs. Thompson it was directed at Billy. She made him sit in the Dunce seat, or at the back table. As long as he just sat back there and did not raise any protest, he was left alone. So Billy withdrew. He imagined that he was a teacher who was very egalitarian. He showed every student the dignity he or she deserved. Billy became a "knot on the log," for the remainder of the school year.

What shocked Billy was that on his Report Card in early June, 1959, was: "William Anderson James, has made satisfactory progress in the Sixth Grade, and is therefore 'Promoted' to the Seventh Grade." Since he had not been allowed to do anything at school in terms of academic work, how the hell could he have made "satisfactory progress?" So far, Mrs. Thompson-as a teacher-had been the biggest zero in Billy's educational life-even worse than Miss Payne.

Mabel never told Henry what Furman asked her. She feared what that might provoke him to do to the "White Devil." In mid-June, Henry asked another local White-farmer to come and plow his garden spots so that he would be able to plant sweet and Irish potatoes, late-com, tomatoes, and pole-beans.

Jesse Chase Shelby, a Porky-Pig looking man, wearing a denim pants and jacket outfit-in June-with a thick-red sweatshirt, and a pair of black combat boots, drove a Ford tractor and plow-rig into the yard. Billy was outside batting rocks with a stick bat. Henry had not too long ago gone off to work. Billy had gotten up early to see a tractor up close.

Billy watched the plow turn over virgin furrows across the road from the house. It was exciting to watch the tractor do its job. The morning grew hotter and hotter. Mabel came out of the house carrying a quart canning jar of iced water. They hadn't too long ago gotten a refrigerator.

As soon as Mabel had handed Shelby the water, Billy heard "that Dog" say: "Gal, I got a lump in my pants for you that won't quit. Let us get a little bit right over here. We're close to the woods anyway. You're already knocked up. We can't get into trouble that way. I love dark meat." Shelby grabbed the crotch of his pants and squeezed the lump sticking up there.

Billy got mad as hell. He was standing behind a cedar grove over from where Shelby was sitting on the tractor with both legs on one side of it. He watched his Ma put her hands on her hips.

"What'da ya asked me, Cracker? What would ya do ifn ya heard that Henry ask ya wife the same question ya done ask me? Huh? What would ya do?"

Suddenly the sneer on Shelby's lips became a twisted-looking snarl. "I'ma tell you what I'd do. I'll get a bunch of the good-old-boys together and we'd go hang ourselves another Nigger that's what will be done."

Mabel snapped back at him: "Then Henry ought-a get his gun out an' kill ya butt. Ain' no more for one than the other 'n."

Jesse harked up a thick lump of phlegm and spat that out almost too close to Mabel's feet. He got out a plug of chewing tobacco and took a bite. His red hair seemed to fizz up like the hair on the back of an angry dog. His two-day old beard followed suit. He had a thick dark-brown mustache. His piercing green eyes grew narrower and narrower. He spat out some brown juice.

"Gal, let me get something straight right now. We White men are gonna protect our women from you all's men. But you Nigga gals don't want no protection from White men. I'm talking from experience. I had my first gal when I was only ten. She was a grown woman.

"So you ain't gonna tell me nothing. You just trying to put on some Nigga airs. Now the truth is you want me just as bad as the rest-a them gals round here I done been with-and I tell you that's been a lotta them."

Mabel was angry but astonished. "First of all, I ain't no Nigga gal. Sucker-Cracker, ya can call me Mabel or Mrs. James. And ... Ya can't tell me that ya been gettin' in the pants of all the womens round here ya been plowin' for. Second, some-a they mens would-a done kilt ya sorry ass by now."

"Okay, Mabel ... ah, Mrs. James. What ya better do is face the facts of Southern life, and how you want your family to fare. If you secretly give away a little poontang you will go a long ways round here. Lotta gals know this and take advantage of that. That's what you don't know. Shit, your husband can't miss what he can't measure," Shelby said.

Mabel shook her head in disgust. She turned and walked on back to the house sorry that she had been nice enough to bring Shelby a cool drink of water on a hot day. For that, he wanted her to become his Black Whore on the side. She went on up to her house. Jesse cranked up his tractor and got back to plowing like that was that.

Then Billy's mind fixated on a program he had seen on TV. "A Black man named Mack Parker was found hanging from a bridge in Poplarville, Mississippi on the morning of April 15, 1959. It was stated by local law enforcement that he had raped a White woman while her husband was in an adjacent room. He pleaded to the mob that lynched him that he was innocent to his end. He had been dragged from a local jail, brutally beaten, and hanged with a rope from the bridge in the middle of town. An investigation is underway to determine who the assailants were in the commission of this heinous crime. So far, police have no leads "Damn! Billy thought.

Now, this son of a bitch, Shelby was saying that it was right for him to take advantage of Black women, but Black men have to be killed for just being near a White woman at the wrong time. Shit! Billy thought.

Billy was glad when Governor J. Lindsey Almond decided to close Venable Elementary and Lane High Schools in Charlottesville, and schools in Farmville and Prince Edward County in Virginia in 1959, to prevent them from being desegregated that fall. He was glad that public education would remain "Separate but Equal." He reasoned that it was bad enough to go to school with light-skinned people and teachers who hated him. It had to be worse to go to school with Whites who hated Blacks worst of all. The thought of being in school with the likes of Jasper Furman and Jesse Shelby or children with their kind of mindset was a scary one.

By the end of summer, 1959, Billy's hormones were exploding inside of him. He'd wake up in the middle of the night with a rigid hard-on. He'd dream about sexy girls and have wet-dreams. He wanted to ask questions about what was happening, but was afraid to ask his Father or his Mother about the changes taking place in his body. He was afraid of getting a mad beating.

Mamie (Mae) Winston was the lightest one of Cora Winston's children and the first one to go to college. She attended Virginia State Normal Institute at Petersburg in the late-1940s. Some people said she was Roy's and Cora's prettiest child. She had a perfect figure, had dreamy-gray eyes, and long-black flowing, naturally-straight hair. She was an exotic-Black Venus, who stood at five-six, with well proportioned, voluptuous breasts.

The boys in and around the neighborhood knew not to approach her because she had declared herself a "lady" and a "Virgin," and that she would remain "pure" for her husband. Mae did very well at Gravel Hill and Shiloh Elementary, and at S.C. Abrams. She maintained an "A" average. She did the same at Virginia State Normal. Her declared major was French Literature. Her main professor was a Frenchman from Paris, France. It did not take long for him to zero-in on Mae.

Many of the young and old women at Virginia State were romantically attracted to the idea of being ravaged by this Frenchman. But he spurned most of them.

He pursued Mae vehemently. The more she refused him the more he wanted this young, Black-Country-Mademoiselle. He wanted her so badly he could almost taste her. He told her so quite often. But Mae still resisted his every advance. She did notice that he was "Drop-Dead" handsome, though. He gave her exotic-French chocolates, expensive-flower bouquets, and bottles of some of the most costly champagne. He told her often, "I love you. I want to marry you. I want to take you back to Paris with me."

Mae's grades never fell below "A." So, on this day, after class, when Dr. Pierre Ramon said: "Mae, Darling, I'm keeping you after class today to discuss a very important aspect of your educational future. Your good grades will not be enough."

With a smile on her pretty lips, Mae said, "Yes, Dr. Ramon. What is it?" She was wearing a tight-fitting beige dress with pink, scarlet, and silver roses down its front. A large red rose was sufficiently in the middle of the dress. After the remainder of the fifteen students filed out of the classroom, Dr. Ramon fixed his gaze on Mae.

"Yes, Dr. Pierre Ramon, how may I help you?" Mae asked.

"Darling, I am keeping your lovely self after class today to," he dropped to his knees, "ask you Mamie, will you marry me?" Tears came to his large-sexy French eyes. "I truly want to take you back to Paris after this year is over. Will you come with me?

"Over there you will not be treated as a Negress. You will be my sable lady, Mrs. Ramon.

My love, please tell me you will marry me--or I will kill myself."

Mae smiled down on Pierre. "Yes, Darling, I will man-y you. I admired you from the first day I laid eyes on you. I grew to love you, but I didn't want to throw myself on you like the other girls were doing. Yes, I will be willing to go back to France with you. I hate being treated like a Negress. I hate being mistreated by everyone all around me. But ... I am not going to be your Colored Slut. You have to understand ..."

Then-Pierre slipped a large ornate Diamond Ring on Mae's finger. It sparkled in the light giving off a dazzling brilliance. Mae was blown away.

Pierre stood up. He reached for Mae's hand and guided it up, pulled her close to him. "Kiss me my sweet. Let me taste the sweet nectar of your beautiful lips," Pierre crooned.

"I love you back, Pierre. I want you just as madly as you want me. I've never felt this way about another man," Mae was breathless.

"Let me take you to my Chalet on Crater Road. We will share our love in a most magnificent way." He picked Mae up into his muscular arms, kissed her long and hard, put her down, and felt the length of her body with both of his hands. "Let's go to my place, love, and finish what we have started," Pierre said.

"Yes. Darling, yes. I'm all yours," Mae said. She followed the Professor to his BMW. They climbed inside. In ten minutes he had her in bed with him. He took the flower of her Virginity.

When Mae came home that next May, she showed signs of having gained a tremendous amount of weight in the stomach area. As the summer progressed, it became obvious that more than fat was responsible for the weight. She was pregnant. Cora was appalled. Mae was the last one of her Daughters that she would have believed would drop out of school to have a baby.

Bell slipped around with a married man, Horace Fowler, Sr. from over in Wilmington, near Louisa. She got pregnant and had a Daughter she named Belle. She ended up marrying another young man she had been dating before she got pregnant named Hal Franklin. Belle got the last name Franklin, but she was really a Fowler. Cora and Roy were relieved because they did not have another mouth to feed.

Louise (Lou) had gotten pregnant in high school. She had a little girl she named Ella. She went to work in Richmond at The Medical College of Virginia (MCV) as a Maid. She paid for her Daughter's upkeep. She got pregnant again in a year and had Mick, and the next year she had Dan. Two years later, she had Christine. Lou took her girls to Richmond to live with her. She supplied the boys, but left them with their Grandmother Cora.

Billy eavesdropped and heard the above when A'nt Cora unloaded her frustrations to Mabel. Cora declared: "I's through with raisin' my gals' babies. So, I told Mae she was go have-ta give me a lot ta-take care-a her child, Michelle Antoinette. So, Michelle's here to stay with me. She's 'bout goin' on nine. I love 'er like my own."

By 1959, Rob, Cora's oldest boy, had graduated from high school and had gone to Richmond to be a Mortician Apprentice. On this Friday evening, he was struck by a drunk driver on Broad Street. He was paralyzed from the waist down. He only retained the use of his left arm and hand. He went to live at a Hospice in Henrico County.

Booco and Bea had graduated from high school and had been employed at The National Bank and Trust Company on West Broad and Franklin Streets in Richmond.

Richard (Rich) was getting ready to graduate from high school. He couldn't make up his mind whether to go into military service, or work in one of the menial trades in Fluvanna. Billy was getting ready to find out just how dangerous ignorance can be.

Billy was twelve in June of 1959. Michelle was nine. Gene was almost nine. Billy was ignorant as could be about Sex, but was curious as can be. He had heard that "fucking, getting some, doing it," was what Sex was. He was having nocturnal emissions quite often. So, that left no one but Peanut to ask the all important questions.

"Peanut, my Dick gets real hard at night and sometimes something sticky and wet squirts out of it and makes my briefs stick to me. What am I supposed to do about that?" Billy asked Peanut.

He laughed. But what Peanut said would have profound implications. "You're about near a man, Billy. You s'pose to go get some pussy from any gal you can. That's what mens do. That stuff that you have in your sh0l1s ever mornings is Come. It's called having a Wet-Dream. Put your Dick in a gal, man. Work it to her 'til you Come. Man, try it, you gonna like it-all mens do."

A couple of weeks later, Billy and Gene were playing and Michelle came out to play with them. They were shielded from view because they were in back of the smokehouse near the edge of the woods.

Gene suggested: "Billy I heard what Peanut told you yesstidy. I can show you what he was talking about."

"Okay, Gene, go ahead and show me," Billy said with a lot of excitement.

Gene smiled a sneaky smile. He came over to Michelle, a skinny pink-skinned girl with long legs, auburn hair, big-pretty brown eyes, and nice lips like A'nt Cora's. She smiled showing even pearly-white teeth. "Let's go down the path a little," Gene said.

"Okay, Gene," Michelle said. "Aw-ight," Billy said.

As soon as they had gotten a little ways down the path, Gene pulled Michelle's green and yellow-striped shorts down to her ankles. He exposed her white panties. He pulled down her panties and those fell down on top of her shorts to her red tennis. Michelle stood there with her little brown-vulva exposed. She got a mischievous look on her face. She put her left hand behind her head, and her right hand she entangled in her white T-shirt.

Gene zipped the fly of his jeans down, pulled out his rigid cock, and with a sly grin on is immature face he came very close to Michelle. "C'mon, Michelle. Let me do the bootie with you. Come on, girl," Gene said.

She eased to as close as she could to Gene. Billy saw the pink lips of her vaginal-split. He thought that was the prettiest sight he had ever seen on a girl up until then. He noticed that Gene could not get his hard thing to go into Michelle. The lips of Michelle's Vagina grew fatter as Gene tried to enter her, but he could not. "You try, Billy," Gene said.

Michelle eased over to Billy. She had a little comical grin on her face. Billy failed like Gene had. Michelle laughed. Billy watched her pull up her clothing and she skipped off to the house.

Peanut was peeping at Gene, Billy and Michelle. When Michelle went into the house he laughed out loud. He went into the house behind his Niece.

Miriam had graduated from school the previous year. There were no other girls close-by that Michelle could play with, so she did whatever she could to be able to hang with the boys. Miriam was in Richmond with Booco and Bea searching for a job.

A day after Gene and Billy had tried to "rape" Michelle, she came down with what seemed to be a bad cold. She stayed indoors for about a week. When she came back out to play, she led Billy and Gene to the back of the smokehouse. Once they were in the woods, Gene again pulled down Michelle's shorts and panties. She stood there in a red and blue T-shirt, this time with her Vagina exposed.

Gene got close to Michelle. This time his rigid penis slipped up into her. "I saw Peanut doing this," Gene said. He ground it to her for a minute or two. Then he closed his eyes and picked her up off the ground. He groaned. "Oh, man, that feels good," he said. He put Michelle back down on the ground. He pulled his thing out. Billy's penis grew hard as a rock.

"Lemme do it, Gene," Billy shouted. But they all could hear Mick, Dan, Henry and Charles coming down the path with Charles calling out: "Billy. Gene. Michelle, where is y'all at?"

Billy didn't get his chance, and that made him determined to "do it" with Michelle as soon as he could. That's all he could think about after seeing Gene "doing it" with her.

A couple of days later, Billy went up to play with Gene and Michelle again. They waited until Dan and Mick went inside for Nap-time. Billy,

Gene and Michelle ran across the road from A'nt Cora's house, to a stand of Plum Bushes.

As soon as they were out of sight in a back path next to the plum trees, Billy asked Michelle, "C'mon, Michelle, will you give it to me like you did to Gene and Peanut, please?" His penis was hard again. The image of Gene raping his Niece was still fresh in Billy's mind.

"All right, Billy, but I'm not gonna take my clothes down like I did at first," Michelle said.

She stood looking up at Billy with a half-smile on her beautiful face.

She wore a pair of tan-baggy shorts and a white sleeveless blouse. Billy raised the left leg of her shorts until that exposed her black panties. Michelle stood still while Billy felt inside of her panties then moved the crotch of them aside. Her felt her naked vagina.

With his left hand, he pulled out his throbbing penis and managed to grind it up into Michelle as both of them remained in a standing position. He had to sort of stoop down a little to accomplish that. Michelle raised her left leg some, and Billy held it with his right hand. Then Billy slipped his penis all the way up in her.

When Billy entered her like that, Michelle closed her eyes. She got a strange grin on her face. She whispered: "Do it, Billy. You feel good; oh-Billy-Boy!" She pushed herself down on Billy's penis. Billy responded by returning her short thrusts, slow at first, then faster. He pushed up as hard as he could and picked Michelle up off the ground.

Thrills started somewhere down on Billy's spine. These grew and grew until they centered right on the tip of his penis. Then a spurt of something squirted out of his thing. It felt so good that he understood what Peanut had said, and what Gene had experienced that day. He tried to kiss Michelle all over her face. She pulled away from him.

"Stop. Billy, don't kiss me like that. If you don't stop, I will never do it with you again. I'm going to the house and wash myself I feel nasty after you all do this to me. I don't feel like kissing you all."

Gene stood over in the path laughing at the look that had come over Billy's face. The glistening vaginal secretions on his penis, well, that was kind of nasty. He had to admit.

Before school started in September, 1959, Billy did it with Michelle two more times up in the path behind the Plum Bushes. He had managed to sneak her away from Gene and had her all to himself One day she took her shorts and panties and all off. He was able to pick her up and hold her tightly to him. Then, it occurred to him, that there was something wrong with what he was doing. Michelle was his Cousin. He felt like stopping what he was doing, but he just as ardently wanted to continue being with beautiful Michelle. But she would never let him kiss her.

Billy was home playing in his yard one day when A'nt Cora came to visit with Mabel. His heart was in his throat. He hid under a window to eavesdrop to see if his goose would get cooked for "raping his Cousin."

"Cora, we gotta watch them boys of our'n. Billy gettin' ta-be mannish as can be. Child, he's spottin' his sheets. I kno' he think he's a man. He's just mannish 'nough ta-get some gal knocked up. But he ain' man 'nough to take care-a her an' er baby," Mabel said.

"Yes indeed, Mabel," Cora said. She sat down in Mabel's living room. "I raised several boys. They go be mannish, an' your gals go be womanish. That's what they all do when they's too young ta-know any better. But Mabel, ya can't worr' too much 'bout that. Won't do nothin' but give ya white hairs too soon," Cora said.

"What's worst, Cora? Is it harder to raise boys or gals?"

Cora picked up a Walter Drake Catalog and began flipping through it. "I'on kno' Mabel. Ain't none-a my boys got no gal knocked up. But I got three gals what got knocked up fore marriage. I spects if ya go by that, it's a lot harder ta-raise gals.

"I thought Clarabelle or Beatrice would've been the first ones to get knocked up, but it was my quietest gals: Lou, Bert, an' Mae. Booco an Bea finish school, got good jobs and they's read-ta-get marri'd ta-mens what's crazy 'bout them. I hope Miriam follow they examples," Cora said.

"How ... what happen ta-Mae?" Mabel asked.

"Gal, lemme tell ya 'bout that," Cora said. "Get me somethin' cold ta-drink, lemme tell ya all 'bout it," Cora said.

"I got lemonade, Kool Aid, or water," Mabel said. What'cha go have?"

"I likes lemonade best," Cora said. "Ya gotta chocolate cake on the table in there, I can see it.

Gimme a slice of that."

Mabel brought in two tall glasses of lemonade and a couple slices of cake on saucers. She gave Cora a glass of lemonade and a slice of cake off a portable tray.

Cora took one of the forks off the tray that held the saucers with the cake. She got a piece of cake on her fork, ate it, and washed it down with a sip of lemonade.

"Mabel, Mae came home with child from down at Virginia State College. She got expelled. They say she showed bad conduct. She couldn't go back. She was on scholarship. Lost all of that.

"She had a pretty ring on a chain 'round 'er neck. Said she's 'gaged ta-a Frenchman. She thought he was go send 'er tickets so she could go to Paris. She's really lookin' ta-marr' that man. That's the darn foolish thing I done ever heard Mae say. Of all the nice boys down at that school, she had ta-pick a "French Poodle," who licked her all over her face an' all, then he ran away. I thought I raised that gal better'n that. Ring was nothin' but-a fake.

"That White rascal was a 'fessor down to Virginia State. They fired his ass for screwin' round with so many of the Colored gals. Now, Mae's workin' as a Maid at MCV."

Mabel ate her cake hurriedly. She had been craving chocolate cake of late. "So I reek-en Mae ain' go never see that White boy again," Mabel said.

"Mabel, I guess no," Cora said. "I reek-en she ain' go never see 'nother man in her life. She say she hate all mens. That ain't no 'count, now. It ain' natural for-a gal not ta-have a man ifn she's young 'nough to."

"Yep, Cora. That's strange, now. Cora, I'm gonna get me one, ya wanna 'nother piece of cake?" Mabel asked.

"Nope, Mabel. I gotta go back up yonder an' see what my mannish boys 're up to. But it's been nice visitin' with ya. Mabel, ya go have 'nother little gal. See how ya gut's pointin' up, that mean ya go have a girl," Cora said with a hardy laugh. "See ya honey."

"Cora, fore ya leave, tell me: How do ya chillren take-ta Michelle?"

Cora stopped in the middle of the floor in the living room. "Mabel, that's somethin' I went through most-a my life. Peanut, Rich, Gene, Miriam, all-a'em, call'er names, like Meal-face, Yellow-gal, Half-White, Mongrel, Shit-color, or White-gal. All Michelle want is ta-be treated like ev 'body else. She can't help who her parents is.

"I spects she'll do almost anythin' ta-be'cepted like ev'one else. I had-ta do that, Mabel," Cora whined. "Go see ya later, Mabel gal." Cora's eyes filled with tears. She rushed out on the porch. She was in the yard before Mabel could catch up with her.

"Cora ... Cora. Cora ... wait-a minute. Cora ..." Mabel called out to her crying Sister in-law. But no doubt she had shared with Mabel all that she cared to for that day. Mabel watched her top the hill.

Billy was dumbfounded at the last thing his A'nt Cora had said. He knew why Michelle had given in to Peanut, Gene and himself so easily. She was just trying to get them to like her. Gene 'nem had made her feel so bad about herself that she would do anything to get them to accept her. She had learned that boys liked what she had between her legs, so she let them fondle and rape her again and again. He was sorry he had been a part of that nasty deed. He decided that he would not do that to Michelle again. Oh, God, he was so sorry.

The first week of September, 1959, meant that summer was over for school children. The hot, sticky, days would soon give way to cool, crisp mornings, then iced-cold, frosty, mornings. The leaves on the trees started to tum red, yellow, and brown. Cold winds found their way down from the Blue Ridge Mountains even to Fork Union and Gravel Hill. Anyone living in the area knew that Jack Frost was just around the corner. Billy was getting ready to brave another school year, when his Daddy came home with some horrid news.

"Mabel, Momma had a stroke last Friday. I gotta go help Cary an' Cora pick-a coffin for 'er. Poppa an' Charlie ain' in no shape. We go burr 'er Sunday up in Cloverdale on Unc' Jim's place in that yard up yonder. Momma went ta-church but she ain' never joined none-a 'em. Mabel, ask Billy ifn he wanna go ta 'er funeral. I can't let ya go cause ya knocked up an' that'll be bad luck for the baby."

Billy didn't want to hear about going to no funeral. He said: "No!" right away before his Mother had a chance to ask him. He wondered why the good always die so soon; and the wicked seemed to live forever? White people down in the deep-south killed innocent Black people all the time. They lived long-prosperous lives. Why were they not falling down dead? Life seemed so unfair to Billy.

He grieved inside so hard that his insides ached. He didn't go to his Grandma's funeral because he had heard that he would see her again one day in the Great Beyond. He wanted to not remember her as a dead person. He wanted to remember her as being alive, like he would see her one day in Heaven.

During devotion at Central Elementary Miss Gaines was not called upon to play the piano that morning. Instead, a young man by the name of Carl Timothy Atkins, Jr. (Tim), the seventeen year-old Son of Carl Timothy Atkins, Sr. (Duke), and Lacy Glee Atkins, was called upon by Rev. Spraggs to play. Tim's Dad was called Duke because he could play the piano like Duke Ellington. He had been in Special Forces in the Army. He played in a Jazz Band. After World War II, he was just discharged. Piano players who could imitate Duke Ellington were a dime-a dozen. So Duke returned home to Fluvanna and courted and married Lacy Glee Fields, a Cousin of the Kingstons from New Canton, A'nt Maetta's home area.

Lacy could play the guitar, sing, and play the piano. She and Duke had a Daughter the same age as Billy, named Peggy Lee, another Daughter two-years younger, named Judith Jade and a Son a year younger, than Judith, named Aaron Leo. They were all musically gifted offspring.

Tim had self-taught himself to read and to write music just from the rudiments taught to him by his father. He could play the Flute, Trumpet, the Piano, Guitar, Bass Viol, Drums, and Violin and read the music written for all of the above instruments.

The Fluvanna School Board had elected to pay for Tim to attend Goochland High in Goochland County because S.C. Abrams did not have a Musical Department or Band. Tim was a musical genius. Various local schools sought him out to come and inspire their students to be the best that they could be. This is why he was at Central Elementary on this morning.

Billy was elated that his handsome, genteel, Cousin was there to play the music for that morning's first-day assembly. At roll call that morning, Billy found out too that he was in Mrs. Bland's homeroom that year. His sadness at losing his Beloved Grandmother gave way to tears of joy when he heard Dr. Spraggs introducing "Mr. Carl Timothy Atkins." Then-

On October 26, 1959, Mabel had given birth to Henry's second Daughter, she named, Janice Marie (called Jenny 'Ree forever after). At twelve years old, it did not matter that much to Billy that one more sibling had come into the world. So, he had two Sisters, now. The house was filling up. He didn't know what his Ma and Dad were trying to do. He wished they would put on the breaks a little-God, man!

Lin Jackson, after hearing rumors he could no longer ignore, and suspecting that most of those rumors had a truthful basis, decided he'd find out for himself, "what the hell is going on between Bessie and Burton Gaines." He decided to pick some days at random, pretend that he was going to work, but instead, watch the house all day long. He started his spying on Bessie in November, 1959 to March, 1960. He would pick a Monday, or a Friday, or any other day of the week to watch the house, but did not catch Burton sneaking around to be with Bessie.

On this last Friday in March, 1960, Burton made an appearance at Lin's house, and Bessie greeted her paramour at the backdoor. She laughed a husky, cheerful chuckle. "Hi, Baby. Long time, no see," Bessie said. Lin was looking right at them from the woods on the edge of the spring path.

In a bass voice Burton allowed: "Had-da lay low. Peoples be runnin' they mouths. Why don't ya come be with me for good, so we can stop sneakin' 'round?" Burton said. "Ya say ya loves me. Ya don't love Lin. Ya just stuck with that Old Man. You's the onliest woman I loves Bessie. Ya make me feel good all over. That's what love's s'pose-ta do. I can't stand ya being over here with O' Lin." He kissed Bessie long and hard in her mouth. They were still standing at the backdoor.

Lin nearly puked seeing "that Black Bas'sard stickin' his tongue in his wife's mouth!" Tears came to his eyes. He wanted to rush out of the woods like a Bobcat would on a rabbit. He wanted to stab Burton to death. But he felt that he needed to know it all. So he watched Burton follow Bessie into the kitchen area. He softly cried in the woods waiting for a terrible half-hour. He heard Bessie laughing loud and happily. He whined to himself "She never laughed like that with me." He pulled out his switchblade knife, but closed it back up and put it in his pocket.

He burned with jealous anger. He raged inside like angry hounds surrounding a fox. His eyes grew wide. His lips quivered. He trembled all over. His body ached from the strain of having to come to grips with the fact that another man was in his house, "Fucking His Wife," at this very moment.

He tipped around to a side window with a view right into the bedroom.

He looked in and became sick at the stomach. He saw Burton on top of Bessie, down between her legs, and they both were stark naked. Burton was humping it to her with all of his might. "Oh, Gawd, no!" Lin whined.

Backing away from the house, Lin slipped into the woods. He found an old Oak stump, sat on it and wept. The end of the world must be just around the comer, he thought.

First, Lin thought about all of those times that he had been unfaithful to Bessie. With tears running down his cheeks, he realized that fate was dealing him out a hand in life that was precisely what he deserved. Secondly, he had suspected that something was coming between him and Bessie for a long time. She had grown so distant from him, at times, and so dull to be around, most of the time, that Lin wondered what was the matter with her.

Lin grimaced at the thought of Burton coming over to his house and how his presence seemed to cheer Bessie up. Lin declared: "I'ma give that scummy bas'sard one chance to get outta my bedroom. Ifn he don't, I'm go blow his Black ass away."

The Jungle in Columbia was like one of thousands in southern states but also in the north wherever train depots were located. Hobos rode the empty gondolas and freight cars to a Jungle nearby. There they learned where they may find a barn or other makeshift shelters, gambling houses, whore houses, and or bootleggers. Such a place was the Jungle across the Cumberland Bridge in Columbia. (It was at places like that that Unc' Charlie spent a number of years in his travels to various Jungles in or near southern or northern cities.)

On this Saturday afternoon in early April, Lin spotted Burton in Columbia in the Jungle shooting Craps with the local cutups. Lin kept the rage inside bottled up. He truly wanted to give Burton a chance to walk away alive like a man, instead of being killed like a mad dog.

Lin got in the Crap-Shooters circle opposite Burton Gaines. Burton rolled the dice and one die fell on six and the other on one. He needed to make eight. He had to give up the dice. He'd lost a fifty dollar pot.

George Mayor took up the dice next and declared: "Shoot that twenty ya Muthers.

Somebody fade me!" Somebody dropped two ten-dollar bills on the ground.

Lin raised his left hand to summon Burton. He beckoned for Burton to come talk with him for a minute or two.

Burton swaggered over to Lin with a sly smirk on his face. "What's goin' on my-man?' Burton asked.

"Let's go over yonder near the Birch trees. I gotta tell ya a thing or two 'bout ya gettin' ya act together, Homes," Lin said. He had a very sarcastic look on his face.

"Aw-ight, Homes. What'cha wanna talk 'bout?" Burton asked. He put his huge hands on his hips and stood towering over Lin. He looked down on the man with the rights to the only woman he had ever loved.

"I'ma give ya chance ta-leave Bessie 'lone. I ain' go share that gal with you or nobody. I done seen ya on 'er with my own eyes-ain' no need in ya tryin' ta-deny it."

"POW!" Lin found himself on the ground writhing in pain. Burton had cold-cocked him up beside his head and the lick had knocked Lin down. The gambling ceased. The gamblers came over to see who would win the fight. Bets were made on Lin and some on Burton.

"Yellar nigga, don't ya never run up in my face again an' cuse me of fuckin' ya woman! I'll kick-a mud hole in ya natural ass." Then Burton added insult to injury. He kicked Lin four or five times on his thighs, in his balls, and in his face.

Lin hated that he had been beaten down in front of all the boys. He knowing that he could not win in a fight with Burton picked one so that he would have ample witnesses that he had been outraged by Burton. Lin hobbled up off the ground and scurried off to avoid more licks from Burton.

Burton feeling like he had put Lin in his place left the Jungle, but he didn't leave Columbia. He went up to Main Street, sat on a chair outside of Parish's Cafe, and lit up a cigar. The Cafe was closed by then, but Burton was so full of himself at this point that he just wanted to pause and savor the moment. What he wondered was how he could get Bessie to leave Lin for good.

After a little while, Lin left the Jungle, especially after the guys teased him about letting Burton kick his ass so bad in front of everybody. Lin stumbled across the Cumberland Bridge determined to get even with Burton for humiliating him in every way a man could.

When Lin spied Burton sitting in back of Parish's smoking what was left of a cigar, he approached him and feigned humility. "I gotta beg pardon, my-man for all the noise I raised. It's all my fault. I should've known better. I gotta pint of Canada Dry Bourbon from over at Manby's. You take-a swig, an' let's drink-ta our friendship. Hope we can still be friends."

Burton was surprised as hell, but he wanted to continue the guise of friendship with Lin so he would have a better chance of seeing Bessie. "I go come over an' hear ya out, Lin. But no funny bizzness, now." He kept his eyes on Lin. He knew that he carried a switchblade knife. Other times, he had been known to carry a 22-Pistol in his pockets. "Go ahead, shoot, Homes," Burton allowed.

Lin watched the Herculean frame of Burton inch towards him. He instinctively put his right hand down into his front pants pocket. When Burton got directly in front of him, Lin smiled like an opossum. He gave Burton the bottle. He drained half of it in one swallow.

"Look man. I's been out of it these days. I gotta work at the Mill up yonder an' can't get my games goin' on ever weekends. That's what's got me so worked up. I's just takin' that out on you an' Bessie-that's all. Soon's I get my games on again, I'm go be aw-ight.

"Look, Homes, some-a the boys go be by Sunday mornin'. Why don't ya c'mon by then, bright an' earl,y. I gotta cup'la jars-a Moonshine fresh from the Still. We's go let by-gones be by-gones-we's gon bury the hatchet. We been friends since I got out of the Navy. I ain' go let this little-bitty shit break our friendship down. Whad-da say? Let's shake on it." Lin extended his right hand.

Burton thought he was coming out on top big-time. He shook Lin's hand cautiously at first. Then he became confident that he had landed squarely in the victory circle. He figured that it would only be a matter of time before Bessie would be his gal alone, once and for all times. He wanted her more than life itself.

Lin came home that night drunk as could be. He undressed and got into bed. He breathed harder and harder the more he thought about

Burton on top of his wife humping it to her, making her scream out with delight. That was something she had never done with him.

At about seven in the morning there was a little scratching nose that started near the back of the house that was followed by whistling noises like a black snake's. Then there was a "King Fish Knock-from Amos & Andy" on the front door. Lin yelled out in a loud voice: "Who is it?" He knew very well who it was. Burton always did the same things when he came over to gamble.

"It's me, Lin. Who ya reek-en it is?" Burton replied. "Aw-ight!"

Lin jumped out of bed, pulled on some overalls and ran to the front door. He grabbed his single-shot Winchester from on top of the door frame. He cocked the hammer back, snatched opened the front door and fired! "BOOM!" The shot echoed down through the woods. It was followed by a deafening silence for a moment or two.

The number four shell's load had hit Burton in the forehead at point-blank range. Lin's gun was full-choked. The lead-pellets did not spread or break ranks until they landed on their target.

Bessie ran to the front door. She saw Burton's brains splattered on the left side of the front door, around on the front steps, and a little ways up the pathway to the front door. His body was on the ground in front of the steps convulsing, letting out the remainder of his life's blood. Where his head had been was now only a bloody pulp. It resembled a batch of fresh hamburger.

She screamed at the top of her voice: "Lin, what have ya done? What in the hell's we go do now? Ya didn't have-ta do this-no!"

Without thinking about it, Bessie ran out the door in her under-slip. "Lin, why'd ya do this?" Bessie screamed again and again.

Lin ran back to the bed and sat on the side of it. He hung his head down low. He sobbed. "I lost my head. Lost my temper. He beat me down in Columbia in front-a all the boys. I just wanted-ta talk to 'im.

"Wish I hadn't done it. I ain't never kilt nobody 'fore now, not even while I's overseas, an' all. I kno' I should-a thought 'bout it a little longer. But, Bessie, it's just-a much ya fault as it t'was mine."

Bessie cried like a spanked child. "What the hell ya mean, Lin?" she shouted. She stood right in front of her disturbed husband. The sun was getting higher and higher. The morning was in full bloom.

"I saw Burton right here in this bed on top of you, gal. I ought-a kilt ya both." The gun was leaning against the wall near Lin.

Bessie grabbed her dress off the foot of the bed, threw it on, then an overcoat. She slipped on a pair of flat shoes. She got Alize dressed. They took off heading towards Cora's house.

Lin came to the front door and yelled after his fleeing wife. "Don't worr' little gal. I ain't go never do nothin' toll to ya. Ya ain' gotta run." But Bessie was soon out of earshot of Lin's complaints.

Lin got up and headed over to Mr. Jasper Furman's place just over the hill from his own house. He knew that farmer was up probably eating breakfast.

Furman saw Lin running up the path to his house. He was having breakfast with his wife, Adrienne, and his Daughter, Cynthia. He grabbed his German Luger out of the cupboard-a relic from World War II captured from a Nazi prisoner-and hurried to his front door.

"Adrienne, that shot we heard a little while ago must've come from Lin's 'nem house. I'm ready for whatever may come. That boy's out there on the porch. Get Cynthia and y'all go down to the basement, 'til we see what that boy's up to." Furman didn't want to take any chances. He thought he might have a "Crazy Negro," on his hands.

Adrienne beckoned to her twelve-year-old Daughter, who had buckteeth just like her Father, for her to follow her through the hallway to the back of the Victorian styled house to the stairway that lead to the basement. They were soon out of sight.

Furman clad in his tan-khaki pants and shirt with a safari hat on top of his head snatched the huge green front door opened. He had his left hand behind him clutching the handle of his Luger. "What're you doing out here on my porch so early in the morning? I sure didn't send for you. What's going on?" Furman asked.

"Ah, Mr. Furman. I done messed up," Lin blurted out.

"What you done, boy?" Furman asked. He pulled the Luger from behind him.

"No, I ain't done nothin' toll to y'all. I shot Burton Gaines this mornin'. He's peepin' in my windows. I didn't know who he was at first. He went 'round the house an' knocked on my door real hard. When I yelled out

392

who is it, he ain' say-a word. So-I snatched the door open an' shot. Blew Burton's brains right out."

Furman put his gun in his belt. "Boy, I'm go tell you the truth. I'd have shot that bastard myself if he done the same thing over here.

"Many of us White folk been laying for that Nigger, but he manages to get away ever time.

Glad you finally got his Black ass.

"See, Lin, he been over here peeking in our windows at my wife and Daughter. I could never catch him. My wife can shoot pretty well . . . and my Daughter . . . but they always managed to miss that sly skunk.

"Come on in the house, boy. Lemme call Mr. Bobby Hughes. He'll come right over to your place, directly. He's gonna bring a doctor and a coroner. Now, you just go over yonder and wait a little bit. Everything is gonna be all right; Yaho-0-0-0!" Furman said. The "Rebel Yell" came out like a scream.

Lin headed on back towards his house. That "Rebel Yell" had unnerved him. He hadn't heard anything like that since he had been stationed in Mississippi. Lin knew that the White men around Fluvanna wanted Burton dead. But it sounded like their wives disagreed with them. The Furman women had been missing Burton on purpose--Lin believed that, now. Then-Lin felt like a Negro Fool for killing some Black man the Crackers wanted him to kill.

He dragged himself back through the woods feeling like a cold-bloodied killer. He got to his house and sat on the back steps. Lin didn't want to go to the front of the house to see Burton's lifeless mutilated body. His tears came streaming down his cheeks, because: Lead Pellets fired out a shotgun cannot be called back, and the damage they inflict on a victim is usually permanent and deadly. It was too late to want to take it back after the deed was done. The sun climbed up into the middle of the sky. Lin cried some more.

Looked like it was taking forever for the Sheriff to come. Lin started to vomit when he thought about blowing Burton's brains out.

Bessie ran down the road as fast as her short-fat legs would carry her. She pulled eight-or-nine year-old Alize along with her. "Grandma-ma, slow down. I can't run fast as you," Alize whined.

"No, child. We gotta get ta-my Brother's house. He'll know what-ta do," Bessie whined to her little Granddaughter.

Bessie saw Henry up at the smokehouse and woodshed cutting up slabs into cook-stove wood.

"Bessie, what 'sa matter? Y'all's outta breath. You need-ta let that child rest-a spell. She's red as-a beet," Henry said. He put his Buck Saw down near the pile of wood he had been cutting.

"Henry, Henry!" Bessie shouted. She burst into a fit of crying. She ran to her Brother and he hugged her tightly. "Lin done kilt Burton this mornin' right on our doorsteps. Shot his head 'bout off. Oh, Gawd, I ain't never seen nothin 'toll like that in my life. Burton's layin' out there dead as a doornail."

Henry was excited now too. "Lemme go in the house an' get my hat. I 'ma cut through the woods. You go up to Cora's. Don't go home," said Henry. He was afraid that Lin may be out to get Bessie next.

Henry got on his Jean Jacket and Overalls and a pair of heavy boots. He plopped a plaid cap on top of his head. Then-Henry decided he needed to take somebody with him. He got Billy to go with him.

Judging from the strange way his Daddy was acting, Billy figured something awful must be going on. He saw how hysterical A'nt Bessie was acting when she ran by him into the house to talk to his Mother. He and his Daddy were over to Unc' Lin's and A'nt Bessie's house in about five or ten minutes.

Once they had gotten to the house, Billy was shocked beyond words. He saw a black hearse parked in the yard. Two Colored men dressed in black suits loaded a heavy-green body bag with what seemed like a dead body inside into the back of the hearse. A man wearing a white smock, black trousers, and a red tie over a blue shirt allowed, "We got the evidence you will need Sheriff Bobby. We'll see you later at the Morgue."

"Thank y'all for doing a fine job. I'll see you later on," Mr. Hughes said.

Billy saw what looked like ground beef or hamburger on the doorsteps, and the path leading away from the house. It made him very sick to his stomach. He realized that he was looking at Burton's blood when his Daddy said, "Unc' Lin kilt Burton this mornin'. That's his brains over yonder."

"Dad, why did ya bring me?" Billy asked.

"Boy, you gotta take some things in life like-a-man," Henry said. "Man-up-now."

The blood he saw burned into his psyche an unforgettable image. He turned away from the sight so that his stomach would relax, but he still gagged a little. Then he heard-

"Lin, good buddy, I'm gonna tell you what," Sheriff Hughes said. "Ain't gonna be no further investigation than what you see me doing right now. Way I see it, is, Burton Gaines tried to break into your house early this morning. You warned him to stop, but he didn't. You have a right to defend your home, and you did. Is that the way of it?"

Billy listened carefully. He clearly heard what Sheriff Hughes had said. He knew inside of him that what he was hearing was made-up by the Sheriff, a blatant lie.

"Yes sir," Lin said. "That's how it happen."

"Lemme tell you something else. Many people around here are very grateful to you for ending this Peeping Tom's life. He weren't nothing but a Piece-a-Shit No-count Nigger. Good riddance. I 'ma give you two-dollars and Forty-cents so you can go buy yourself a box of Number Four Shells. Don't you worry about nothing else. Anybody ask you about what happened over here this morning, you send them to me," Sheriff Bobby Hughes said.

"Yes sir," Lin said.

Billy watched as the crooked Sheriff got into his car and drove away. He saw his Unc' Lin standing in the middle of the path waving goodbye, although he was trembling like a dog having a diarrheal attack. Billy knew something very evil had just taken place.

"Bessie, I tol' ya, ya had-da leave Lin, or one-a ya mens fore somethin' bad happen. I don't mean-ta rub it in ya face, but-I tol' ya so." They were sitting on Mabel's front porch.

"I hate this shit, Mabel. I never thought this would happen. I 'ma be a lonely woman again. I think I 'ma go right on back over yonder ta-Lin. Let 'im blow my brains out too. I 'serve it. I feel like the biggest who'e in Fluvanna, Mabel."

"No child. Ya can stay with us long's ya want to. We don't want Lin-ta kill nobody else.

We loves you Bessie. What's go happen-ta Alize ifn you's gone-kilt?" Mabel whined.

Bessie hugged Mabel. Billy and Henry came in the backdoor.

"Bessie, ya ain't go b'lieve what just happen," Henry said. He was out of breath. "What?" Bessie asked. Her eyes spread opened wide like hen's eggs.

"Big Sis, cross my heart and hope-ta die, Lin ain' goin' ta-jail. Sheriff say he ain' go even arrest 'im. Say he 'preciate what he done-ta Burton. Even gave Lin the cost-a box of shells. I ain't seen nothin'toll like that in my life," Henry said.

Bessie grabbed her stomach. Mabel put her right arm on Bessie's left shoulder. "Mabel ... I ain't glad 'bout none-a this," spewed out of the corners of Bessie's balled-up lips. She backed up into Mabel's front door out of earshot of Henry. "I'm goin' back over yonder-ta that old man. I hopes he shoots me. No! ... Don't try-ta stop me. Ya look after Alize till I get kilt or get back whichever come first. I'll come for 'er in a cup'la days. Otherwise, y'all take care of 'er; aw-ight?"

Bessie ran past Henry. She took the little path through the woods Henry and Billy had just used. She was climbing up the steep hill to the larger path to her house before Henry and Billy realized she was gone. She found Lin sitting on the back steps.

"Little gal, I's glad you's back. I don't kno' why ya run. I ain't go never hurt ya. You an' my chillun's all I got in this world that mean anyhin' ta-me.

"That's what I's tryin' ta-tell Burton when he jumped me an' stomped me in front-a all them mens in the Jungle. I knowed he was comin' by here tryin' ta-take ya 'way from me. His own Brother, Marion, tol' me all 'bout his plans.

"I knowed all 'bout it, Bessie. Then, I seen 'im screwin' you-I knew I had-da stop'im-I had-da do somethin'."

Bessie, with tears streaming down her cheeks said: "Lin ... what ya don't know is, I told Burton that I's never go leave ya. I told 'im it was over 'tween us. The day ya seen us together was me sayin' goodbye to 'im. That's why he got so mad when ya spoke at 'im.

"Wish I'd done broke up with 'im sooner. Ya wouldn't 've kilt 'im. His blood wouldn't be stainin' all our lives. We all died a little with Burton," Bessie groaned like in a growl.

"Now, I's so sorry I took Burton's life. 'Jealousy's the rage of a man' . . . that's even in the Bible I done heard; but it would've been better ifn I had just let Burton walk 'way. I didn't know you had ended things with 'im. Ifn they put me in jail I'd feel better. Now, in my mind, I'm go always be in jail. I'll never get Burton outta my mind, Bessie."

Lin went into dead silence. His lips tightened up. He got deep wrinkles all over his face. His hair suddenly turned white all over his head. It seemed like to all who knew him that he had aged twenty years over night. He kept a fixed frown on his face. He stayed to himself wandering around in the woods, but he never again visited the Jungle.

The trauma of the day his Unc' Lin killed Burton was almost too much for Billy. That night he had no appetite. When he tried to eat he vomited up the food right away. He couldn't sleep, either.

Billy watched Gunsmoke, Wyatt Earp, and The Rifleman on TV, then he got into bed with his sleeping Brothers, Dick, Bug, and Johnboy. Alize shared a bed with Julia Mae, Dave and Sammy Lee.

Issues about Sex had not been resolved with Billy. He got up in the night to go to the piss pot. His penis was rigid hard. Like a demon of the night, Billy sneaked over to where Alize slept. He gently eased her awake.

"What you want, Billy," a half-asleep Alize whispered.

"Let's play Momma and Daddy, aw-ight?" Billy suggested in a softer whisper. "How're we gonna do that?" Alize asked.

"Sh-h-h-h, don't talk so loud. We gotta slip into the kitchen. We'll do it in there. I'll show you how," Billy said.

"Okay," Alize whispered. She was about four-foot six. She had a very mature-looking body for a nine-year old. She had on a trainer bra. She wore pink panties. Billy quickly pulled those down to her ankles like he had seen Gene do to Michelle. He got harder when he saw her naked body by the moonlight shining through the kitchen window. "Be quiet now," he whispered to Alize. "We don't wanna wake Ma and Dad up. They will whip us both."

Billy loved Alize's very light skin. She was lighter than Michelle. Alize had very pretty dreamy eyes like her Mother's. Her hair was straight and dark-brown, and fell down on her shoulders in locks. Billy saw the dark-fuzz growing between her legs before he pulled her closer to him. He took her left ankle out of her panties.

He leaned Alize against the kitchen table. He was very excited. He held her left leg at the bend of it and tried to snake his penis up into Alize.

"Ark! Oh-0-0-0!" Alize squawked. The noise she made was almost too loud. Billy had only inserted the head of his penis in her. She felt very wet and warm.

"What's goin' on in there?" Henry yelled.

Alize scrambled back into her panties and made it back to bed. Billy answered his Dad: "Nothing, Dad. I'm just using the pot," he lied.

"What'cha makin' so much noise for boy? I gotta go ta-work in the mornin'. Get back in bed an' be quiet, now," Henry ordered.

"Aw-ight, Dad," Billy replied.

Early the next morning, Bessie came knocking on Mabel's front door. Mabel got up to answer it. "Hi, Bessie. Good-ta see ya. C'mon in. How's Lin?"

"Mabel, when I got home he just cried like-a spanked child. He's goin' over yonder ta Louisa to get his Sister-in-Law ta-Pray for 'im. He left this mornin' I thought I'd come by an' get Alize. Was she any trou'ba?"

Mabel smiled. "No, Bessie. She's the sweetest little gal ya ever did see. She's no trou'ba a' toll." She was thinking: that gal's frisky just like-a Mother was. Bessie go have-ta watch her.

Mabel went into the children's room. "Alize, ya Grandma's here ta-pick ya up." "Bye, Billy," Alize said.

Mabel wondered why she only said bye to Billy?

On this Saturday, Bessie came over to visit with Mabel. She brought Alize along. "You can go on outside an' play, Alize. I'm go talk with A'nt Mabel," Bessie said.

"Yes 'am, Grandma," Alize said.

Billy was up at the woodpile splitting up some wood for the kitchen stove. He spied Alize walking out of the backdoor and across the porch. She was splaying her dress and throwing it up as she walked towards him. Dick and Bug were gone up to A'nt Cora's. Johnboy, Sammy Lee, and

Dave were taking a nap. Billy took in an armful of wood into the kitchen to see where his A'nt Bessie and Ma were. He saw that they were in the front room gossiping. He knew that could go on for hours. They were also watching the Soaps.

Billy took Alize by the hand and led her to a little path behind the hogs' pen. Behind there Henry had made a makeshift bench out of two ten-gallon paint buckets and a six-foot, two-by-ten oak board.

Alize was wearing a red and blue plaid dress. She pulled that up so that Billy could see her black panties. That triggered a hormonal response typical in adolescent boys. He laid her on the bench, pulled her panties down and took them off her. He eased his penis into her vagina slowly until it was half-way into her. He just laid there for a minute.

"Ow, Billy. It hurts. Is it s'pose to hurt like that?" Alize asked. She frowned. "Billy, you gotta take that out. It hurts too bad."

Billy didn't want to, but he got ready to do what she had asked him to do. But a thrill that got started in his spine spread to his balls and caused him to thrust forward without meaning to. His penis seemed like it broke through something-tore through it-or something. He pulled his "Dick" out of Alize. The foreskin was tom. It had a little blood and sperm on it.

Alize had tears in her eyes, but she was not crying. Billy was afraid to look down there for fear of what damage he would see that he had inflicted on his Cousin.

Billy watched Alize get back into her panties. "Alize, Baby, don't tell nobody what just happened. We gotta keep this our little secret. You understand, don't you?" Billy said. He was trembling all over thinking about what kind of beating he would get if his Ma and Dad found out about what he had just done.

"I don't know," Alize said. "You're bleeding, and I'm getting sore down there. Shouldn't we tell somebody?"

"No. That's how it is the first time. We will get over it. I've heard all about this. You will see. Trust me," Billy said.

"Aw-ight. But I'm more worried about you," Alize said. "Don't worry, Baby. I'll be aw-ight," Billy said.

Alize limped away at first, but soon seemed to be walking normal. She turned and said: "I'm not going to let you hurt me like that anymore, Billy. My pussy's sore."

"Baby, I'm so sorry. Just please don't tell anybody," Billy begged. "Okay-I won't," Alize snapped.

That evening he watched his A'nt Bessie and Alize go up the road. Bessie walked in a steady stride while Alize limped every now and then. Then the guilt of what he had done to Alize came to mind. He had taken his Cousin's virginity. He had done to Alize what Peanut had done to Michelle. He wished he could talk to somebody about what he had done. Coming in a girl was one thing, but becoming some kind of monster was another. He felt like he was becoming a dirty sexual predator. He felt like he was on a downward spiral and didn't know how to stop.

After the death of Grandma Maetta, Billy didn't hear his Ma and Dad sexing it up anymore. Henry's fear of "Honor Your Father and Mother...."had been buried with his Mother. He acted as though he felt he was no longer under that "curse." His cruel verbal assaults on Billy got more vitriolic. His ignorance of Mabel became even more apparent. He would leave for work on Friday mornings. He would return home on Sunday nights drunk as a skunk. Rumors spread all over Fluvanna that Henry was seeing every "nasty woman" in Gravel Hill, West Bottom, and Cloverdale. After crying herself to sleep time and time again, Mabel started visiting her Mother's place.

On this Saturday, Mabel took all of her children with her when she visited her Mother. Billy noticed right away that his Ma was flirting with George Mayor. Then he saw George feeling her up. He had a sly grin on his sable face. He was a tall, muscular man, with smooth-Black skin, and straight-ish jet-black hair. He had a physique like a Black Atlas.

After seeing what Unc' Lin had done to Burton Gaines, and hearing about what his Dad had done to Tank Snowvall, Billy filled with a loathsome fear at what his "Mean Daddy" would do to his Ma if he caught her with George Mayor. But he knew that George was slipping around with his Ma.

Billy was confused, angry, and mentally-sick about "Fucking," and he didn't know what to do about the lust that pumped inside of him like the beating of a bass drum at a parade. It was not something easy to control.

On this Sunday, Mabel took Billy and all of her children to visit Agnes. Grandpa Mickens did not come home that weekend from the Mill Crew.

So old man Charles Turpin had happened by to see if he could sneak-it with Agnes a little while. He spent the day hugging, fondling, and teasing Agnes. Billy saw this old light-skinned man put his hand up his Grandma's dress. "Turp," as he was called, was a guitar player. He was playing with more than Agnes's guitar.

A'nt Ginia was up at Gerry 'nem, as was most of Agnes's other children. George Mayor came up the path from Marr' Dee's house. He was delighted to see Mabel.

"Billy, ya take the chillun outside an' play. This's grown-folk bizzness," Mabel said. George had his hands all over her. Then he too put one of his hands up Mabel's dress. She followed him upstairs. Turp had Agnes downstairs and Mabel had her Sister's boyfriend upstairs. That, for some reason, stirred a tremendous bout of lust in Billy. Soon, he heard what was going on and he got a great "Hard On!"

Hazel Scott was around six-years-old. Billy got the kids playing a game of "Hide-and-Go Seek." He grabbed Hazel's hand and held her back when the rest of the kids ran to find a place to hide.

Billy took her to the smokehouse just before he got to the toilet. She had on a white dress. She pulled that up. She slid one side of her panties aside and declared: "This's my pussy. Lemme see your dick." Billy was shocked. How did she know about all that? He wondered.

Billy got very excited at the boldness of Hazel, even though he felt a little tinge in his Conscience. He didn't want to hurt her like he had Alize. He decided he would be very gentle.

He laid her down on the boards in the smokehouse. He took her panties off. He eased down between Hazel's outstretched legs. He was surprised that she knew how to do that. His penis slid into Hazel like he had in Michelle. She felt hot, wet and tight. She groaned and moaned like Annette had a long time ago. Then, Hazel worked it back to him-or she tried to. He came right away. He got up immediately to see if Hazel was bleeding like Alize had. He saw that she was not.

"C'mon, Billy, gimme some more," Hazel said with a giggle. "Wait ... I gotta go see where everybody's at," Billy said.

"Aw-ight," Hazel said. She got up, got back into her panties, let her dress fall into place, and she went out the smokehouse's door skipping along with a sly smile on her immature lips.

Billy heard Turp and George laughing out loud. He sat in the shed for a minute. He wondered how did Hazel know so much? Who had gotten to her first? Then there were a lot of grown boys in that household. Hazel had to hear what her Mother and Daddy did at night. She slept in the same room with them.

When Billy came out of the smokehouse, Hazel sneaked up to him. She said: "Billy let's go back in the smokehouse and play 'Momma and Daddy' again. I want you to do it ..."

"Sh-h-h," Billy said. "Someone might hear you. I'll go to the smokehouse. You come back there when you see that nobody's looking; okay?" They were near the door of the smokehouse.

"Aw-ight," Hazel said. She skipped away singing some song to herself. She came running into the smokehouse, opened the door, pulled her panties down, and laid on the floor. She raised her dress so that Billy could see her nakedness. "Billy, put your big-thing in me," Hazel said with a giggle.

Billy yanked his hard Prick out, got down between Hazel's legs, and got ready to rape this little child again. Before he could get it all the way in her, the smokehouse door swung opened.

Hazel jumped up and grabbed her panties. She ran past Mabel whimpering as she ran around to the back of the house. She stepped into her panties and ran into the house.

Mabel yelled at her oldest Son in a hushed whisper: "Billy! What in the hell's ya doin'? S'pose ya had humped it ta 'er? She'da cried out an' Ginia would-da gone-ta ya ass. She prob be would-a beat the shit outta ya. Who could blame'er? Hazel's only six, or so."

Billy got up. For some reason, his thing stayed rock hard. It was not easy to get it back into his fly. What scared him was how his Ma was looking at it with a sly grin on her face. "I'm sorry, Ma. I won't do nothing like that no more," Billy said. He felt like crying. His Conscience was bothering him. He realized how serious this was.

"Go find the rest of the chillren. We gotta get up the road fore Hazel tell Ginia and George what ya done.'; But, Billy saw his Ma chuckling to herself He didn't know what was funny.

On the way home, Billy saw that his Ma kept a mischievous grin on her face. She didn't say a word about what she had caught him doing. He thought that was really strange. He was still too afraid to ask her anything about "doing it."

Very early the next Saturday morning, a loud knock on the front door awoke everyone.

Mabel got up. She went to the front door wearing a long-flannel housecoat. "Oh. Hi Bessie. What bring ya over here so early in the mornin'?"

"Mabel, Lin's out in the car, but he ain't go get outta it. He's scared shitless. Claim Burton's scratchin 'round the house. Said he kicked the front door in and ran in to grab 'im. So Lin ran outta the house an' took off up the road in his long johns.

"Had-da devil of-a time catchin' that man an' gettin 'im ta-come back-ta the house, Mabel. Finally did, though." Bessie stood at the front door wearing all black like she was in mourning for a lost loved one. "We's goin'ta Rich-men!"

"Why don't ya come on in for a spell?" Mabel asked.

"No Gawd! I just came by ta-say goodbye ta-y'all. And Mabel ... don't let Henry hurt that boy no more. Aw-ight?"

Henry raised up in bed. He grunted loudly, so that Bessie would know that he was home.

Mabel whined: "Bessie, I's go do the best I can." She got a sorrowful frown on her troubled face.

"See ya honey. Take care," Bessie said. Both women clung to each other with tears coming down their cheeks. Mabel watched Bessie run down to Lin's car. She didn't see nothing but Lin and Alize in the car; no extra clothing, bed linen, or dishes and things. She thought that was very strange. She reasoned that they must've left everything back at the house.

Billy heard the motor of Unc' Lin's car revving up. The way that Unc' Lin took off scratching wheels and kicking up a lot of dust meant that he must be in a big hurry to get away from up in Fluvanna. Billy was thinking, "I'm gonna miss Alize."

Around the first of May, 1960, on a Monday, Mrs. Bland handed out a letter at the end of class that day. It said: "We are asking Parents to read and sign this letter giving us permission to conduct lectures on SEX EDUCATION. If you do not wish that your child(ren) attend these lectures, please put a check in the box indicated. We will remove your child(ren) and have he (or they) supervised in the Library during these lectures. Lectures will occur on Friday afternoons. Boys and Girls will attend separate lectures. Your prompt attention is requested."

Billy handed the letter to Mabel as soon as he got home. She read it the best she could. She remembered she had caught Billy trying to "do it" with his Cousin Hazel. She quickly put a check mark in the box allowing Billy to attend the lectures. She handed the letter back to Billy. "Give this back-ta Mrs. Bland tomorrow," Mabel said.

"Ma, what is SEX EDUCATION?" Billy asked. "What's that all about?"

Mabel motioned for Billy to go put away the few books he was toting. "I gotta tell ya somethin' hard-ta take, Son."

"What is it, Ma?" Billy asked. He saw tears gathering in the corners of his Mother's eyes.

Mabel wiped the tears away and dried her hands on her flowery apron. "Tim Adkins's in the hospital. He fell out"

"What! Ma, Tim--our Tim?" Billy exclaimed.

"Buck Payne, Rena's husband, was returnin' home from his job up at the Hospital. He saw Tim standin' near that Great Oak up from what use-ta be Gravel Hill School. Buck say he's wobbly an' sweatin' a who'e lot." More tears came to Mabel's eyes.

"Ma, what was wrong with Tim?" Fear welled up in Billy's stomach. He trembled all over.

Mabel rubbed the sides of her face with both her hands. "Nobody know right now. Buck took Tim up yonder-ta the UVA Hospital. Say Tim passed out in the emergency room. On his way up yonder Buck say Tim allowed: 'Man, I'm not gonna make it.' He tol 'im, man don't talk like that. God's go see ya through.

"When Buck come through this evening, I'm go see how Tim made out. A Lotta people's waitin' ta-find out 'bout that."

Billy went into the boys' room, opened a copy of the Bible and stared at the pages. He was too stunned to read. He wondered: "Why Tim? Why him? What's going on?"

That evening, Lloyd "Buck" Payne, a Son of James Payne, Sr., the Brother of Charles Payne, Miss Payne's Father, came up the road driving a new Four-Door, Chevy Impala. It was green with yellow trim. Mabel flagged him down.

He stopped, rolled the window down on the driver's side, and said: "How ya doin' Mabel?" She came around to the Driver's side and asked Buck, "How's Tim doin'?"

"Mabel, I just left Duke an' Lacy up yonder at the Hospital. They had to give Lacy some treatments. She fainted dead away and almost had a heart attack. They revived her, but had to admit her for treatment. Duke's crying like I ain' never seen-a man cry.

"They had to operate on Tim. They cut his head opened. They found a lotta infection on his brain. Head was full of inflammation. From . . . well . . . Syphilis." He sort of whistled the last words through his teeth. "Tim's dead."

"What!" Mabel shouted. She composed herself a little. "That was the nicest boy I ever seen. I ain't never knowed 'im ta-even have-a gal-friend. I always heard tell that he's savin' his-self for his future wife. He done met a little gal over in Goochland he's go Marr' after he graduated this year.

"I kno' a lotta gals who would've wanted-ta get it on with 'im, but I thought he turned all-a 'em down. I just can't b'lieve Tim caught VD. How? ... Outta the air, or somethin'?" Mabel couldn't fight back the tears any longer.

"Mabel, just 'tween you an' me, now. The only gal I ever seen'im out with was Jewel Patton. Long fore I finished high school, I came home late one night. After taking Rena home, I saw Tim out with Jewel out behind the Chapel. He was near 'bout sucking on'er tongue. He had his hand up her dress. When they heard my car they pulled apart an' ducked behind some Oak trees back of the Chapel. But, I'd already seen 'em."

"I always thought Jewel's a nice gal. She come from a good family. But ya never can tell, Buck," Mabel said.

"Yep-you got that right. Tell Henry I said hello. Gotta go. See ya, later."

Billy watched Buck's car speed on up the road. He listened carefully to everything that Buck had said to his Ma. The more he heard about "Fucking" the more it seemed like a very dangerous thing. He just didn't know what to think.

The next Friday after Tim's death, Mrs. Bland had her first lectures about "SEX." Overall, Billy saw that out of a class of thirty-five pupils, only seventeen of them were permitted by their parents to attend those lectures: ten girls; and seven boys. Mrs. Bland introduced Dr. Snead and his wife Sally Mae, his nursing assistant, to the class. The rest of the children in the class were sent to the Library for the hour of the lecture. The nursing assistant went out of the classroom with the girls to another part of the library, and Dr. Snead stayed with the boys.

"Boys, in light of recent events, members of the school board, and the Principal of this school, Dr. Spraggs, thought it best to educate our young people about the proper functioning of their bodies," Mrs. Bland said to the boys remaining in her classroom. "We have lost one of our precious-young jewels due to ignorance.

"Dr. Snead will talk to you about some very personal and non-personal matters for the next forty minutes. He will leave some very important literature for you to take home to read and study. Without further ado, here is Dr. Robert Snead."

Billy listened attentively to Dr. Snead talk about the real names for Sex Organs: "Vagina for the girls; and Penis for the boys." He explained what an "Egg Cell" was; what a "Sperm Cell" was, and how these had to come together to "create a Baby."

He went on to elaborate on what "virginity" was. Then he talked about the life-threatening presence of "Killer Venereal Diseases, Syphilis and Gonorrhea." He asked Mrs. Bland for permission to show on the green boards the misnomers used out in the world misrepresenting "Sexual Intercourse."

The first word that he wrote on the board and elaborated on was "Fucking." Then he talked about "Getting Some Pussy; Getting Some; Doing It; Humping; Getting Your Jollies; and Coming"; and how all the above were misunderstandings about what was really happening: "Ejaculation." Even Mrs. Bland's cheeks turned pink.

Then-Dr. Snead said something that went deep into Billy's psyche: "Incest is the most common way for children to lose their virginity. Incest is sexual relationships with people who are very close-kin: Brothers and Sisters; Fathers and Daughters; Mothers and Sons; and or, sex with Aunts, Uncles, all Cousins, as well as Grandmothers and Grandfathers. These sex acts are very forbidden in The Good Book-The Holy Bible."

Mrs. Bland waved her hand. The Dr. stopped lecturing for a moment. "Yes, Mrs. Bland, what is it?" he asked.

"Dr. Snead, we can't discuss religion, at all," Mrs. Bland said, shaking her head from side to side.

"Okay, Mrs. Bland. I'm sorry. It's time for the question and answer period. Is there a question at this time?" Dr. Snead asked.

Nobody raised his hand. All of the boys had a sad-to-sorrowful look on their faces. Billy was fighting back the tears of guilt. He got some literature on "Condoms And Disease Prevention," some more on "Teenage Pregnancy," and a pamphlet on "Incest." He felt lower than the swine in the pigs' pen for what he had done to Michelle, Alize, and Hazel.

Billy realized that: *I took something from my Cousins I can't give back; their Virginity, self worth, and innocence I helped to obliterate. I wonder what kind of Monsters are Peanut and Gene? I wonder what kind of Monster I had become? Am I crazy, or something? Oh God-I will never do anything like that ever again! No Incest! And, no child-rape-ever again!*

Mrs. Bland got several scathing letters from the parents of the children who had attended the lectures. None of the parents were too pleased with what Dr. Snead had taught the students during that one Sex Lecture. Dr. Spraggs issued an apologetic letter to the complaining parents, but denied their requests that Mrs. Bland be fired immediately.

It occurred to Billy that he had learned about one of life's Prime Movers: SEX The others were Food and Shelter. He had come by his knowledge about SEX in a most disgusting and degrading way. What he subtly discovered was that most boys that he went to school with had discovered the above same way, and that social convention would see that they remained ignorant about one of life's Major Mysteries: The Creation and Reproduction of Mankind.

Inside of himself, Billy felt like he was Morally Lost. He determined that he would seek Redemption through studying the Bible.

At Central Elementary, students graduated from the Seventh Grade in a ceremony full of "Pomp and Circumstance." While the section of his class was in rehearsal for the upcoming event in June, 1960, Mrs. Bland took Billy aside one day and asked him: "William, what is the matter with you, Son? You have so much potential. Yet, you have no ambition at all. Why don't you at least try to do better? Tell me, what is holding you up? I love you and want the best for you, but your grades and performance in class should make me fail you. I am not going to do that, though. I do not want to know that I got in the way of some Writer, Historian, Scientists, or Musician, who will one day be great. So, I am going to send you over to Abrams. I hope you will pull out of that fog you carry around with you. Talk to me about what is bothering you."

Billy couldn't fight back the tears, but he had stuffed thirteen years of pain deep-down into his "Subliminal Lock Box," and it was going to take a lot more psychological probing than Mrs. Bland was capable of to get to the bottom of all that. So he just got a little misty-eyed, and that was that. He loved Mrs. Bland Dearly for showing that level of concern for him, though.

William graduated June 3, 1960 in the auditorium at Central Elementary. Billy's parents were not in the audience. That hurt him like a punch in the groin!

He walked across the stage, got his diploma, and dashed out of a side door, immediately.

Billy heard through the Grapevine that Jewel tried to kill herself after she found out that she was responsible for Tim's death. She tried to hang herself in her Father's barn. He found her in time, cut her down from the rafters where she had rigged up a rope with a hangman's noose to execute herself. He took his beautiful but wayward Daughter to Berksville Sanatorium in Eastern Virginia. Jewel was treated and cured of her VD, but remained mentally ill. She became a permanent inmate at Central State Mental Hospital for the Insane in Petersburg, Virginia. She was constantly on suicide watch.

The more Billy heard about Sex, the more afraid of it he became. People were dying from disease contracted while doing it. They would kill each other over it or about doing it. They were threatening suicide over it; and, losing their minds after murdering somebody over it. Yet, people wanted to do it, talk about it, and lie about it all the time. The musical lyrics were full of sexual suggestions, so were the movies, and advertisements all over the place on billboards, magazines, and in ads to sell everything from candy to cigarettes. Billy wondered what was going on?

He started reading the Bible more and more to seek an answer to the above perplexing problem. It didn't get too hot for Billy to stay in the house and endlessly search the pages of the King James Version of the Bible that his Parents kept on a shelf at home. But his efforts displeased his Father during the summer of 1960.

One day, "Boy, get the hell outta this house hot as it is an' go play or somethn'," Henry yelled at Billy.

"Dad, I'm just trying to find out ... about saving my Soul," Billy whined.

"I'on care what'cha tryin' ta-find out. Go on outta them doors. From now on, you get the wood for supper. Since ya got so much time ta-sit 'round with ya head in-a book. Go on ..." Henry yelled even louder.

Henry's shouting annoyed the hell out of Billy, but scared him even more. Henry had slapped Billy up beside his head a couple of nights ago. Bug had wedged down in the middle of the bed in the middle of the night. He screamed, "Billy get ya feet off me!" Henry ran into the children's room and assumed that Billy was guilty. He snatched the covers back and walloped Billy on the left side of his head even though he could clearly see that Bug was actually at fault. Then he yelled, "Y'all go on back to sleep. I don't wanna hear no more-a that damn noise."

What Billy could never remember was Henry ever hitting Dick, Bug, Johnboy, Sammy Lee, or Dave up beside their heads, or anywhere else on their bodies, for any reason. He was always the one used as a battering ram.

In the middle of August, 1960, Billy begged his Ma, "Lemme go get Baptized. I'd like to go to the Revival this summer and get Saved. A'nt Cora gets a ride with Deacon Percy Thomas. He's always asking me and Gene to come with him to Church. Please Ma, lemme go this year."

"I gotta ask Henry, first. But ifn it's okay with him, it's okay with me. God said: 'Suffer little chillun ta-come unto me.' So, I's fine with that whole idea," Mabel said.

That evening, after Henry had finished eating his supper, and had gotten out his pipe, retired to the front room to watch the evening news, and got relaxed, Billy timidly approached his "Mean Daddy."

"Dad," Billy spoke in a whisper. "I wanna go to the Revival this year and get baptized, so my Soul will be Saved."

"What?" Henry shouted. "You ain' gotta worr' bout your Soul. All your sins fall on me an' Mabel. So, you ain' gotta think 'bout all that right now. Ya-still-a-child."

"But, Dad, I feel like I need to get Saved," Billy complained. "I feel like ..."

"Get on outta here, boy" Henry shouted. "I'on kno' where ya get half the shit you's talkin'bout-ma-be from ya stupid-slut Momma," he added.

"No, Dad. I'm gettin' it outta the Bible," Billy whined. He walked away from his grimacing Father. Once he was outside near the backdoor he heard Henry growling like an angry dog.

"Mabel. Mabel! Come-the-hell-in-here!" Henry ordered. "What ya want?" Mabel asked.

"Where in the hell's Billy gettin' that shit he's talkin 'bout gettin' Saved?" Henry snapped. "That boy don't know nothin 'bout 'ligion, gettin' Saved, knowin' Gawd-or nothin' like that. That's ser'us stuff, Mabel. Ya can't be playin 'round with that. Billy ain't nothin' but-a boy. Ya gotta be a man ta-get-ta kno' Gawd like that. I don't think that child's read-ta-seek-the-Lord. Mabel, ya can't fool 'round with Gawd-a-mighty," Henry preached at Mabel.

"Henry," Mabel sighed. "Cora go let Gene an' Michelle go to the Revival. Them chillren wanna get Baptized. Cora say she go let'em. Why ya ain' go let your'n?"

Mabel and Billy, with Henry tagging along grumbling behind them, went up to talk to A'nt Cora. Henry broached the subject. "What'cha thinks 'bout chillun gettin' Baptized? I don't think they's read-ta-seek-Gawd till they's grown and know how-ta 'pent-a they sins."

"Henry, let the chillun come to God. Don't try-ta keep 'em 'way from they Heavenly Father.

Ya might as well give'em ta-The-Devil. Ya wanna do that?" Cora said.

"Cora, Mabel. Aw-ight. Let the boy go get Baptized. Don't let nobody say I kept'im from God," Henry said. Tears came to his eyes. "I'm go see ya later, Cora." He left right away.

Mabel came home late that evening with her oldest Son walking slowly behind her. Billy had eaten supper at his A'nt Cora's. He went straight to bed.

"Mabel, come in this kitchen," Henry ordered. Once Mabel eased into the kitchen, Henry dug into her.

"Mabel, ya stupid slut. What'cha kno'bout no chillun gettin' Saved? You ain't shit! Just like ya slut-Momma weren't shit fore ya. Ya don't need-ta be fillin' that boy's head full-a stupid shit. Ya ought-ta be tellin'im how he go help get us outta this shit he got us into. Stead, ya sendin'im ta-join them hypocrites in them churches. So, take his little ass down ta-Columbia Baptist an' let it dip in the water. But let 'im know he gotta get dry an' help me out," was the Gospel Henry James preached.

Billy stayed in bed awake most of the night. He was thinking: *Why's Dad blaming me for what he and Ma did? I don't wanna work at no sawmill for nothing in this world. I would rather die. All I wanna do is get to feeling better about the things I've done wrong. Getting Baptized might help me find a way to do that.*

Billy's determination to never work at a sawmill was heightened in late-August, 1960. His Daddy usually came home from work at around five o' clock each evening. Very rarely did he stay later than five, unless it was on those Fridays when he'd go out and get drunk. He sometimes might come home two days later. But on this Wednesday evening, it was way past five, and there was no sign of Henry James.

Billy was busy hoeing in the garden, a chore he hated, when Mr. Wilfred Kent (a comical copy of John Wayne-the Actor) drove up in his new-blue International Pickup Truck. Kent bolted out of the door of the truck. He trotted over to the porch where Mabel sat. He wore a pair of faded jeans, a Texan-styled shirt, tan cowboy boots, and a beige Stetson hat. "How're you doing Miss Mabel?" he asked in an imitative southern drawl-like John Wayne used.

"Well, I's fine, Mr. Kent," Mabel replied. "What brought ya up here this evenin'? Where's my husband?"

Kent, with a little bit of sadness showing on his square-chin face, put his left hand into his left front pocket. "Miss Mabel, we had a bit of an accident at the mill. Henry got hurt on the job. We took him up to the UVA Hospital, but I think ... he's going to be all right."

"What ... what happened? Man, tell me what happen-ta my husband," Mabel shouted. "Well, he got a little cut on his arm. He ought to be home directly. It's really not that bad.

He is probably gonna be off from work a week or so. I came by to see if you need anything in the meantime," Kent said.

"Yeah. Mr. Kent. I needs some dam-food in this house. So I can feed my chillun. We's all been needin' that for a long time." She looked Kent right in the eyes. Her angry stare caused Kent to look away. He was feeling a little guilty-but not enough to convict him that much.

Kent whipped out his black checkbook. He wrote Mabel a quick check for fifteen dollars.

Then he had the nerve to say: "Ifl can help y'all with anything else just let me know."

Kent jumped back in his pickup and was gone. Mabel saw the measly amount of the check and flew into a rage. "What in the hell we's go do for a couple of weeks on fifteen dollars?" she screamed. "The Cracker could-da gimme at least a cup'la weeks pay for Henry. An' I bet Henry's in a lot worse-a shape than a little cut. He's prob-be might 'near kilt. That's how them Crackers treat us, Billy."

Henry remained at the UVA Hospital for a week. Mabel had to get Rev. Nicholas to take her up to the Hospital to bring Henry home. Kent said he didn't have anyone he could spare. He just sent word by Broadus Jackson that, "Henry's ready to be dismissed."

When Henry arrived home, Billy, and his Brothers and Sisters, saw their Father was in a cast that went around his waist and up to his chest, was connected to a protrusion fixed to his left arm that attached it to another cast that went from his elbow to his wrist. His left arm was fixed in an L-shape out in front of him and across his chest. Henry had to be helped out of the car and almost carried up to the house by Mabel and Rev. Nicholas. The pitiful shape he saw his Father in made Billy a little more sympathetic towards him. All he could think to say was, "How did this happen, Dad?"

"Son," Henry said. (This was one of the few times he called Billy, "Son," instead of "that boy.") "It's just cause-a my evil ways, I reek-en," Henry allowed. "Ya can get Baptized ifn ya wanna. This's prob-be Gawd-a-mighty speakin' ta-me. I's nearly kilt the other day. Saw my life flashin' fore my face-an' it won't pretty." Henry had a terrible grimace on his face. "I hurt all over, Son.

"Mabel, gimme some-a that pain medicine the Hospital sent 'long with me."

Rev. Nickolas excused himself. He refused any money from Mabel. She dashed into the kitchen to get a glass of iced water out of the refrigerator. She had a bottle of capsules in one hand and the water in the other. "What cause this accident?" Mabel asked.

Henry took two pills from Mabel's hand, after she popped them into his mouth. She helped him wash them down with a couple of gulps of water. Tears came to Henry's eyes more from the pain in his arm than any emotional consideration. He calmed down somewhat after the pills kicked in and their effects numbed the pain He felt.

"Mabel, Mr. Wilfred Kent put me in the 'Dead-Man's Hole' that day. See, I done warned he an' Mr. Wally 'bout how unsafe it was down in that bend. Ya gotta bobbin' saw ta-cut the ends off'n planed lumber. The belt on the saw was gettin' worn. It's been bad for over a year.

"Mr. Wilfred got mad at me. Say I talk too much. Put me in that hole 'stead-a one-a his rookies ta-show me that the hole's safe as can be.

"Long 'bout two, I heard-a snap. That's all I 'members. Broadus say that belt slapped me up side my head. It must've burst loose. It knocked me down in that hole with that bobbin' saw bouncing up and down out of control. Could've split my head opened like a melon. But it knocked me out cold. That's what saved me.

"I must've throwed up my arm. The saw hit it. That knocked my arm back 'gainst me with 'nough force so that it threw me 'way from the saw. I stayed down after that. Had I stood up, I'd been sawed half-in-two like a log on the carriage belt. It cut my arm near 'bout in-two. They sewed it back on at the Hospital. But I's lucky ta-be alive."

Billy went outside after he heard what had happened to his Father. He swore: "I will never work at a Sawmill even if I'm nearly starving; here's my hand to God!"

In two weeks time Henry had the cast removed to just one on his left arm from his elbow to his wrist. He went to see Mr. Wilfred Kent to see about getting some Workmen's Comp and to pick up his last paycheck. What Kent said, surprised the hell out of Henry.

"Henry, I gotta take fifteen dollars out of your last paycheck. After all, you weren't at work.

I can't pay you for doing nothing. I've put in for your compensation. You will get a check in the mail as soon as they can process my claim. How's your arm-and when are you gonna be able to come back to work?" was not exactly what Henry had hoped to hear from his Boss.

Henry hung his head. "Well ... thank you, Mr. Kent. My arm ought-a be near 'bout read ta-go in 'bout three weeks. Cup'la my fingers ain' got feelin' in 'em yet. But I's comin' long fair-ta-middlin', go be aw-ight in-a cup'la weeks."

"You'll have one day on hold 'til then. You can collect that, or you can leave it on hold, this coming payday. See ya, Henry," Kent said. He turned up his peckerwood nose like he smelled some foul odor. Henry knew that that meant for him to take his exit.

Cora Winston surprised everyone. Shortly after the Summer Revival ended and Billy, Gene and Michelle had been Baptized, she announced that she had accepted Deacon Percy Thomas's Marriage proposal. She married the Deacon right away in a very private ceremony with just her Sister Cary as her witness. Rev. Lee performed the ceremony.

Billy watched A'nt Cora, Gene, Michelle, Peanut, Lou's children, and all, load the big old truck with all of the belongings the family was carrying with them. Billy waved goodbye with tears streaming down his young cheeks. He thought: "Ain't it funny how life just slips right up on you?"

Mabel and Henry got together like husband and wife after Henry's accident, something that hadn't been happening for awhile. Billy heard them romping in bed-"Disgusting"-together a couple of times. Then-

The daily cussing, cursing, and name-calling got started and went on incessantly between Henry and Mabel James. Billy wondered: "How can my Mother and Daddy ever get to stand one another long enough to manage to SCREW! They did, though, somehow.

September, 1960, right after Labor Day, Billy found himself on the bus on his way to S.C. Abrams. He was glad about that. But the Merchants in Columbia had cut off all credit to his parents.

Henry had to find a way to go to Dillwyn to shop. Hunter Bradford had heard what the Columbia Merchants were going to do. He had expanded his small grocery store to the level of being a small Supermarket. He let it be known that he would extend credit to all comers who were working people regardless of Race. The Columbia Merchants had shot themselves in the foot.

Henry still bought Billy "Farmer John" outfits to wear to school. On this first day at Abrams, Billy got off the bus at Abrams like he had seen students do for years. Like usual, a crowd of upperclassmen collected around the buses to taunt the incoming freshmen. One herculean guy came over to Billy and shouted: "You country asshole. You dared come to this school dressed like a field hand. Nigga, you must be out of your mind."

Billy didn't know what to say. He was so afraid of this huge guy. He was over six-foot tall. He had a square-jaw, was high-yellow, and had a little-red pointed nose. He had bushy straight brown hair, with eyebrows to match. He was wearing a two-piece tweed suit, a red tie over a blue shirt, and black wing-tipped shoes. Billy thought he looked more like someone who should be a teacher rather than a student. He slapped Billy on the left side of his face a blinding lick that jerked his head back.

"I'm Alex Bracket," the Behemoth shouted. "I was made to come over here with you jiggerboos because they closed my school, Evergreen Prep. Now, I be damned if I am going to go to school with the likes of you, Sambo. Don't you ever come back to school dressed like that again-or I'll kick your tar-baby ass every time I see you-you got that?"

The "Abominable Snowman" drew his hand back to slap Billy a second time. Many of the other students were laughing and having a good time watching the spectacle.

A tall, muscular-mulatto teenager, wearing a black suit, ran down the school's front steps. He came over to the big guy from his blind side. He hit Alex ten-or-twenty times like Joe Louis had Max Smelling. Alex hit the ground like Smelling had the ropes. A dark-skinned girl ran into the mix.

"Shirley, I got this," the Mulatto said. "This's my younger Brother."

"No, he's my Cousin, too. I want some of this," Shirley allowed. She stomped Alex several times until he was knocked unconscious.

A tall rotund, White-looking man, wearing a gray suit, a blue tie over a green shirt, and black spit-shined shoes, ran over to the dueling students. A very dark-skinned man, that could have passed for a Zulu Warrior, wearing a blue-gabardine suit, a tan shirt and red tie, and a pair of brown wing-tips, followed close behind the first man.

The dark-skinned man grabbed Shirley. He accidently tore her green-sleeveless blouse. She had lost one of her flats, but was kicking Alex with her bare stocking-foot. She was holding the hem of her gray skirt up above her knees so that she could kick better. She stopped struggling when the "Zulu Warrior" got hold of her.

"I'm Mr. Friend, the Principal. What's going on out here?" the light-skinned man asked. "This is Mr. Williams, my Assistant."

"Mr. Friend, Alex was hitting my younger Brother. I couldn't let him hurt William."

"Mr. Albert Ross, you have to come get me when someone is hitting you or anyone else. I can't let you and Miss James take the law in your own hands. I'm going to have to expel all three of you all."

Mr. Friend looked at Billy. "Young man, what is your part in all of this?" he asked.

"Mr. Friend, all I did was get off the bus. Alex was hitting me because he didn't like the way I was dressed. I didn't say or do anything else to him," Billy whined.

"All right, but I'm going to be watching you after today," Mr. Friend said to Billy.

Billy hated to have met his oldest Brother under such circumstances. He hadn't too long been told by his Mother about Agnes Lewis and Albert Ross, Jr. that they were his older Siblings. When Henry heard what Mabel had told Billy, he cursed and low-rated her to the ground. But now, Billy shook Albert's hand. Albert said: "Hang in there, Lil' Bro."

Albert should have been out of high school, but he had quit school several times to work to help his Mother. Albert, Sr. was an alcoholic that went on months-long binges. Albert, Jr. was about six or seven years behind. He was trying to finish. He had to pay to go to school. He was in the Twelfth Grade. He only needed English and Algebra to graduate. Billy hated the fact that he may be the reason his struggling Brother may not get to finish high school.

By December, 1960, Mabel was showing signs that she was pregnant again. She got more pregnant as August, 1961 approached. She gave birth to a Son she named Cornelius Cery James, August 27, 1961. This child was the only one born in the Hospital. He was Henry's Seventh Son.

Mabel nicknamed her little Son, "Tuck," because he was so tiny when he was born. He weighed just about four pounds and fourteen ounces at birth. Mabel thought the nickname "Tuck" fit him best.

Billy saw Tuck as a tiny-little baby doll. His nickname tickled Billy because of the way he fit into the folds of Mabel's arms while she breast-fed him. Funny too, he rapidly gained weight from day one after he was brought home. Tuck resembled Unc' Charlie more than any of the rest of his Brothers, Billy thought.

PART IV

Henry's First-Born Leaves Home

CHAPTER NINETEEN

"Good morning, class," said the six-foot, athletically-built mulatto standing in front of his classroom that first day of the 1960-61 school-year. "I am Mr. Baylor Easily, your Homeroom Teacher for this year. Welcome."

Billy noticed that this teacher did not have on a suit or tie. He wore a pair of tan-khaki pants, a blue-cotton shirt, and a pair of white-Converse Tennis. The top button of his shirt was unbuttoned, exposing the top of his T-shirt. Mr. Easily had a thick-head of reddish-brown hair that he wore in the new controversial style, called "An Afro." He had very narrow-looking bluish eyes, sitting under thick reddish-brown eyebrows, and a similar thick-mustache. He was one the "Black-Brothers" classically called "A Red-Bone-Brother."

"Good morning, Mr. Easily," the class responded back to their homeroom teacher in unison. Billy heard Mr. Easily say that he had earned a PhD degree in General Science Education, and an MS degree in Physical Education, from Howard University. He claimed that he was a 33rd degree Mason, as well as a member of The Odd Fellows Fraternity. (Billy had never heard of The Masons or the Odd Fellows.) But, he heard Mr. Easily say that he taught Biology and General Science at Abrams, as well as coached the Baseball and Basketball Teams. The man seemed to be in his mid-to-late-forties, or maybe, in his early-fifties.

That school-year, as before, the school required a book fee that Henry could or would not pay.

This was the beginning of Billy's sorrows.

(Billy barely passed his Eighth-Grade classes. He got a "D" in Math; an

"E" in General Studies; a "D" in Agriculture; an "F" in English Grammar; and, a "C" in Physical Education. Most of his lack of academic progress was due to his state of mind. He had come to the conclusion that education would not do him any good, based upon what Miss Payne and Mrs. Thompson had said; and, things at home had gone from bad to the "Pit of Hell!")

Mabel had come home from the hospital after having Tuck complaining about a lingering soreness in her stomach area. One of the reasons Billy thought this happened was because Henry pounced right on his Mother a couple of days after she got home.

Night after night, Mabel groaned loudly, sometimes she let out little screams, and begged, "Henry, take it easy. I tol' ya I's sore." But Henry ignored her pleas.

In October, when Tuck was two months old, Mabel jumped up in the middle of the night, after Henry had finished "molesting her." She ran to the piss-pot. She turned on the kitchen light and screamed hysterically. "Henry, come in here! Somethin's wrong with me. I'm bleedin' all over the place!"

Henry got out of bed and ran into the kitchen area. He ran over to their little pantry, got out a clean sheet and wrapped that around Mabel's middle.

Billy ran into the kitchen to see what was going on. He started to cry when he saw his Ma lying on the floor with a bloody sheet wrapped around her middle. Panic consumed him when he saw that the bloodstain on the sheet was still growing. "Ma, what's wrong with you?" Billy yelled.

Mabel scrambled up off the floor and staggered around for a couple of minutes. She momentarily steadied herself "Son, go back ta-bed. Momma's go be aw-ight. Ya Daddy's go take me ta-the doctor. They'll see what's the matter with me." Then, she got back down on the floor grimacing in pain. She balled up into a fetal position. Mabel passed out.

Billy was overwhelmed with fear. "Ma-get up. Ma, Wake Up!" he yelled.

Henry had purchased an old 1947 Ford with most of the compensation money he had gotten from his accident. He rushed outside, cranked it up, and came back into the house. He put another sheet over Mabel and scooped her up into his arms. "I'ma take ya over yonder to Charles' ville-ta-the UVA Hospita'," he said.

"Billy, ya take care-a the chillun till I get back. Ya know what-ta do," Henry said to his oldest Son.

Billy cooked breakfast in a daze. He cleaned Tuck and fed him his bottle of milk. His Brothers and Sisters got up and asked, "Where's Momma and Daddy?" as they ate.

Billy whined: "Y'all, Dad took Ma up yonder to the UVA Hospital. We gotta wait till he gets back from up yonder. May take him all day long. After y'all eat, go on outdoors and play."

Henry came home that night with a sorrowful frown on his face. He saw Billy sitting at the table in the kitchen. "Ya Ma go have-ta stay up yonder at the Hospita' awhile longa. She's gotta getta oper'rac-ion. She had-da bad 'fection in 'er. They gotta move it outta 'er."

Billy was old enough to know that what his Dad had done to his Ma in the bedroom was to blame. He went into the children's room and wept. He really hated his Dad for what he had done to his Ma.

Mabel stayed at the UVA Hospital until the middle of November. Henry brought her home on a weekend. She got out of the old car and wobbled to the backdoor. Billy saw that she had lost some of her much-needed weight. She was skin and bones. Henry was looking at Mabel like he might be viewing a "Patch of Cow Shit."

Her children ran to hug their Mother. Mabel sat down on the edge of her bed. The children went to stand in the doorway, except for Billy. Henry came in with a snarl on his disgusting face.

Henry commented: "Ya see the house's clean for-a change. That boy cook-a mean meal too. He cook-a lot better'n you," Henry growled. "Ya ain' been that much ta-me nohow. But now ya ain't worth-a shit. Ya ain't even-a real woman no more. All ya womanly inside's gone. Bitch, I don't see what-in-the hell-I need-ya for, now."

Billy's "Subliminal Lock Box" was filled up to the top. His budding manliness made him confront his Daddy. Henry was attempting to walk away from Mabel who was sitting on the edge of the bed crying like a spanked child. Billy stepped in front of his Daddy in a gruff way for the first time.

"Why don't you leave this stupid bastard, Ma?" Billy yelled right into his Father's face. He braced himself.

Henry stepped to Billy. He got so close to his teenage Son, Billy could smell his breath. "Nigga, what ya say? Boy, I'll knock the shit outta you. Then I'll cut ya. Ya don't know who ya be fuckin' with. Fuck you an' ya slut-Momma."

Henry didn't hit Billy. Instead, he ran out to his broken-down car and sped away.

Billy sat beside his grieving, crying Mother. He caressed her. Mabel said: "I hate that son na-va-bitch! I's been tryin' ta-love'im all my life. I want y'all ta-have-a real Daddy. But that bas'sard don't know how-ta treat nobody. I's sorry I ever marri'd'im."

Mabel's inner-longings-the little girl inside of her-that wanted to connect with a father figure-that she hoped Henry would become-were crushed Mortified! Her love and forbearance quickly became a greater hatred than her prior love could ever equal.

By late-December, 1961, Mabel had healed well enough to get around. She flagged down George Mayor one day in front of her house. It was very chilly outside. The air had the feel like it was going to snow. Mayor was driving a car he had put together from parts he had salvaged from a'54,'55, and a'56 Ford. He laughed and called the car "My Ford Thing." The Thing ran fine, and had even passed inspection, somehow.

"Where ya goin' Mabel?" George asked. His eyes shined. He undressed her with his eyes.

"I'm go look round in Columbia, Dixie, or the militar'cademy in Fork Union an' try-ta getta job at a restaurant, as a maid, in a washroom, or some kitchen. Can ya gimme a lift down ta Columbia?" Mabel said.

She saw a strange man sitting in the backseat. "Who is you?" Mabel asked, the carrot-colored man. "I'm Louis Tolliver, Jr. Herman, my Brother, was Queen's boyfriend. My Father Louis married Tank Snownvall's A'nt Eulalia. Tank's my Sister Connie's husband. He is also my Uncle by marriage.

"I just got outta the Army. I got hitched-ta Marr' Dee's gal, Gladys. We're living right side her Ma's house. I got more kicked outta the Army's more like it. I's a Sergeant Major at The Fort Aberdeen Proving Grounds. I was-in other words-a high-class waiter. I had to follow my Uncle Herman's path.

"My friends call me Bo Rabbit because of my big ears and buckteeth." Bo Rabbit reached across the seat to extend his hand to Mabel.

"Hi, Bo Rabbit, my name's Mabel." She was all smiles.

"Please-ta-meet ya little lady," said Bo. He had large teeth in the front and when he smiled he resembled a light-skinned Bugs Bunny.

Mabel lightly shook his hand. "I know where y'all live. I use-ta live on the next hill from over yonder in an old house some people thought was haunted.

"Yeah, I know Herman Tolliver, Sr. and your Brother Herman, Jr. He gotta Son named Herman too ..." she was interrupted.

"Yep. My Brother gotta little gal with your Sister-in-law, Queen. Her name's Shirley. Ya know her?"

"Uh-huh. I know Queen, Shirley, an' all," Mabel said.

"I gotta get goin' y'all. I'm go get a load-a beer for the boys. We's havin' a little game back a Miss Agnes's house. I can get a buck-a-piece for a can of cold beer. I got a tub of ice just ready for the beer to get cold in," George said with a laugh. Then he put his "bucket of bolts" in gear. The car lurched forward and sped down the road.

"Do ya have-ta drive so fast, George?" Mabel whined.

"Gotta, Mabel. That'll keep the motor in this old 'Ford Thing' burnt clean. Will Keep'er runnin' good."

That night, Mabel came home dead-drunk for the first time in her life. Billy had never seen his Ma drunk. She stumbled through the backdoor.

"Bitch, where you been?" Henry yelled. "Why ya didn't come home an' cook for ya chillun?"

"Since Billy's such-a dam-good cook, why didn't ya get'im ta-cook ya supper?" Mabel uttered. She sounded like a sitting hen whining.

"So, I guess ya go add 'drunk who'e' ta-the rest-ta ya shit, huh?" Henry snapped.

"Fuck you! I done took all the shit I's go take from ya, Henry James," Mabel snapped back.

"I done stayed here in this house an' let ya fuck over me all kind-a ways. I ain' go do it no more. I's through with it," Mabel screamed.

Henry was more than a little shocked at Mabel speaking to him that way. He didn't know what else to say so he scratched his head and uttered: "Ya just get-read-ta-help take care all these babies you done dropped."

Mabel put her hands on her hips, and patted her feet. "Don't ya worry. I been all over Fluvanna today lookin' for a job. I'ma get one, so I won't have-ta ask ya sorry ass for nothin' else," Mabel snapped.

Billy expected to see his Dad rush over and at least slap his Ma. He was getting ready to jump in between she and his Dad. But Henry didn't hit Mabel or utter another word.

Mabel said in a slurred voice: "I done had nine chillun for you. I done been knocked-up ten times by you. And you still ain't got no sense. I'm go sleep in there in the front room," then, she went into the front room.

Billy couldn't sleep. He watched his Ma stumble to the front room and plump down on an old sofa Henry had purchased from a second-hand store in Scottsville. After about fifteen minutes he tipped into the front room.

"Ma. Ma. Ma. You wake? Ma ..." Billy asked. "Yeah, I's wake. What ya want?" Mabel asked.

"Ya said you've been pregnant ten times. You only got nine children. What happen to the tenth?" Billy asked nervously. He had gotten bold enough to ask his Ma a question like that.

"Boy, I lost the tenth one. Got knocked-up too soon after I had Tuck. So, that last one just bled 'way. God knows best.

"I'm gon go to work an' help better raise y'all. You go on back to bed."

That Sunday, Mabel didn't utter a word. She cooked breakfast, took a quick sponge off and left out the backdoor. Henry left right behind her. Billy didn't know what to expect.

That Monday, Henry came home in a huff Mabel was in the kitchen preparing a mess of Catfish. Henry stood in front of his wife blocking her way.

"Gal-I done heard that you and Bo Rabbit rode round all over Fluvanna all day long together. You foolin'round with that high-yellar Nigga? That's what you's doin' ain't ya? Ya can't stay'way from them can ya, Mabel?" Henry said.

Mabel moved so that there was some space between her and her husband. She raised the butcher knife threateningly. "Ya been round with

Lavinia-ta-Anna Gray-ta-a lotta other loose gals round here. Hell, I don't give-a damn who ya slippin'round with no more. But, bout me- ya ought not ta-b'lieve ev'thin' ya hear."

"Gal, you's playin' a danger'us game with me. I's soon-a take a stick-a wood-ta ya head. Ya may as well be with-a White man as ta-be with one like Bo Rabbit," Henry growled.

Mabel stood close to Henry. She yelled into his face: "Go-head on! Do it! I don't give-a damn! I'd rather be dead than be livin' a lie with you any longa. I feel dead aw-ready.

"All somebody gotta do is just lay me down in a pine box. Henry, ya done aw-ready kilt me inside." She let big-old raindrop tears rolled down her anxious cheeks. Henry backed away from his depressed wife.

Billy heard his Father uttering something under his breath as he walked out towards the smokehouse that sounded like: "I'ma fuck that yellar Nigga up. He ain't go fuck over me like that. I fucked his Uncle up, an' I'm go get his ass next."

After moving into the old haunted house, Agnes painted the ceilings, and papered the walls. All of the Satanic insignia, signs and the Pentagram were covered over. After a terrific argument, Billy was glad when his threatening Daddy backed out of the backdoor to leave. He knew that Henry would go near the vicinity of Bella's and Gerry's house to pick up some weary gal.

But, Agnes had another one of her house parties going on that night. Henry headed right to it. He had gotten a pint of cheap bourbon from Gerry's, gulped it down, and was feeling no pain when he got to the gaslight Crap Game going on the path leading from Agnes's house.

More people were standing around in the woods watching George Mayor take everyone's money with the dice, than were up at Agnes's house. Bo Rabbit was among the crowd wearing faded Army fatigue slacks and shirt. He wore a pair of brown Army boots and a green cap. He was fading Mayor.

Among the crowd was James, Ma' Dear's Son, now called "Stumpy," because he was short standing at about four-six. John Matt, called, "Matty" stood beside James his Brother.

Henry stumbled down the path towards the gamblers. Once he got insight of Bo Rabbit, Henry yelled out: "Hey, ya yellar Nigga. I done heard what ya done ta-my gal, Mabel. I'ma get ya ass right now!" he barked like an angry dog.

George Mayor dropped the dice on the ground. He ran through the woods. All of the shooters followed behind George, except Bo Rabbit. Bo remembered how scarred up his Uncle Snowvall was after Henry James had gotten through cutting him up. He remembered how Uncle Tank went to Central State Mental Hospital and remained there. Bo Rabbit panicked.

Bo ran to the edge of the woods. He got his hand on a Hickory stick. Henry James was right behind him with his knife opened and ready to stick it in Bo. Bo turned and slammed that stick up beside Henry's head with all of his strength. The lick landed near Henry's temple.

Henry was knocked to his knees. He was dazed. The knife was dislodged from his hand and was lost in the leaves. Henry crawled from where he had been hit to the edge of the path before he completely lost consciousness.

Bo Rabbit ran up the hill towards home screaming, "I ain't go let Henry kill me. I ain't letting that man do me like Uncle Tank. Gladys, Baby, lemme in . . . lemme in"

Gladys came to the door wearing a flannel housecoat. She was pregnant as could be. "Bo, what's the matter with you, man?" she asked her trembling husband.

"I gotta get my shotgun. Henry James might come up that hill and try to stab me to death. I gotta defend myself like any good soldier." Bo was out of breath.

Bo's five-one wife went into the kitchen area of their house that was still being built to get a glass of water out of the water bucket. She was very pregnant and unquenchable-thirst came with that. The walls of the kitchen weren't completely sealed up.

"What? What ya done to Henry'nem?" Gladys asked. "What'cha go need-a gun for?" She sat on an old sofa in the front room. The walls in there were covered with unpainted sheetrock.

"Gladys, I think it's cause-a the other day. I mean, I ain't never touched another woman round here since I got out of the Army. But, somehow, Henry got it in his head that I been with Mabel, his little wife.

"George gave 'er a ride up to Fork Union, down to Columbia, and over to Cary's Brook to look for a job. I rode in the car in the backseat.

Mabel sat up front with George. Somebody must've told Henry Mabel's riding with me."

Gladys got out a quart jar of Peach Preserves and a loaf of bread off the top of a storage shelf in the kitchen area. She put a heaping helping of the Preserves on a piece of bread and gobbled it down. Then she repeated that. She craved Peach Preserves.

"Bo, why'd Henry think you's botherin' Mabel?" Gladys asked.

"I have no idea. We went to Columbia. I got a cup'la fifths from Old Joe Manby. George got a cup'la cases of beer from over at Parish's Cafe. He iced the beer down.

"Mabel talked awhile to Mrs. Parish. I drank a lot of the liquor-almost a whole bottle. I got a great buzz. While we waited for Mabel, I got into a few beers. My buzz turned into a young high."

Gladys looked sternly at Bo. "Why did anybody think you's botherin' Mabel?"

"I was in the backseat getting right high when Mabel came out from talking to Mrs. Parish with a broad smile on her face.

"Gladys, if anything, George might've went with Mabel. See, they drove by Mabel's house an' took me home first. I thought Mabel must've been going to see her Ma. I bet Old G-M took Mabel out in the woods and banged the hell outta'er, an' now Henry's blamin' me," Bo said.

"Bo, you mens is crazy. Ain't nothin'tween-a gal's legs worth killin' nobody over. Don't make no sense. If he kill you, or you kill him, then what? Who go raise ya chillun? Huh? Whose go get 'tween ya gal's legs then? Ya ever thought 'bout that?" Gladys yelled angrily at her scared husband.

"I'm goin' back to bed. You an' Henry, go head on an' shoot one-another, then. Ya gals is just go find another man with some sense."

Bo sat on the sofa and hung his head. He thought about the fact that he had been a Sergeant Major for years. He was used to getting organized and finding solutions. He knew he would do the right thing if push came to shove, but he might be able to go another way with O' Henry.

Henry awoke on the path, but slipped in and out of consciousness until four in the morning. He regained his consciousness enough to hear a faint echo.

"Unc' Henry. What happened to you?" Stumpy asked. "Who hit you?"

"Ain' nobody hit me, James. I's just a little drunk. Gotta get home ..." Henry mumbled.

He didn't remember being hit by Bo Rabbit.

"Unc' Henry, I'm gonna walk you home. You're hurt right bad. Awight?" James said.

Henry squinted through one eye at Stumpy. "Boy you's the spittin' image of ya Daddy. Look just like 'im. I don't need no help. But ya can ... walk long with me." Henry spoke in a low groan. James had a hard time helping his Uncle up on his feet.

"Okay, Unc' Henry. Let's go." James saw a huge knot on his Uncle's head. He figured that Bo Rabbit had to have done that but he was not real sure. He had run away with the rest of the crowd when George Mayor dropped the dice and ran. He ended up over at Annette Nicholas's house. He was able to sneak her out to the barn for awhile. That's where he was returning from that morning.

It was around four-thirty or five in the morning when James helped Henry stagger home. He stumbled through the door of his home, got undressed, and went to bed.

That morning at nine, Mabel saw the knot on her husband's head. Henry yawned and mumbled: "I feel real bad this morning. My head hurts somethin' awful. Must've drank some-a that rot-gut beer ya Momma made," Henry whined.

"No, Henry, ya got a goose-egg knot on your head. Ya been hit in the head." Mabel got out of bed. So did Henry.

He ran into the kitchen area and stood facing the medicine cabinet's mirror. "Somebody done hit me in my head. The last thing I 'member is goin' to the Crap game down the hill from Agnes's house. She got to know who hit me--she or Clemmon. Somebody seen somethin'," Henry exclaimed.

"Another one-a Momma's parties. One-a these days somebody go get kilt at one-a those. It's always somebody gettin' hurt near 'em, but not at Momma's house," Mabel opined.

Henry got a pan of water, put it on the stove, made a fire in the stove and warmed the water. He washed his sore wound. It hurt bad. When he suddenly raised his head he got dizzy. He figured it was because of his hangover. He got his single-shot Winchester, full-choked shotgun and three Number Four shells, that he put in the front pockets of his work pants and headed for the front door. He turned back and went to the children's room.

"Billy, I'm go take ya with me. I's goin' ta-Agnes's house. I gotta find out who did this-ta me. I need-a witness. Get dressed. I'm go take you long with me," Henry ordered.

After getting dressed, Billy allowed: "Dad, can't you do this some other way? Can't we use the nonviolent ways of Dr. King instead of this gun?" He didn't want to witness another scene like the aftermath of Unc' Lin's Killing of Burton Gaines.

"I'm just takin' my gun long so nobody'll try nothin'," Henry said. "I ain't plannin' on shootin' nobody. See, I got the gun broke down. The shells's in my pockets. I just wanna kno' what happen-ta me," Henry said.

"Dad, why don't you go get the Sheriff? Let him find out what went on," Billy whined. "He's the Law. That's his job."

"Billy, you saw what the Law-the Sheriff-did after Lin kilt Burton. The Law ain' go help us. He'll only come after one-a us done kilt the other'n. He ain't studyin' 'bout us Colored folk," Henry snapped. "That's why we gotta settle things the best way we can."

Henry knocked on Agnes's front door that morning and the door opened right away. "Agnes, what happen-ta me last night round here? I gotta knot the size of-a goose-egg on my head."

Nervously, Agnes replied, "I dunno nothin' toll." Seeing the shotgun on Henry's arm, she backed away from her front door. "I's'fraid-a what evil may be sneakin' round out in the dark so, I lock my door, an' don't dare look out at night."

"Agnes, dammit, ya mean ta-tell me, a man get 'tacked outside ya house an' ya didn't even take-a look-see who it was," Henry snapped.

"It tweren't none-a my bizzness what y'all's <loin' out yonder-long's it ain't in my house," Agnes uttered through trembling lips. She clutched her housecoat around her nude frame. She was scared. "Don't shoot me, Henry. I didn't hurt ya."

"I didn't come over here to get after you, Agnes. I just wanna kno' who "

Stumpy came down the little hallway, "Hey, Unc' Henry," he said. "Stumpy, who hit me last night?" Henry asked his Nephew.

"Unc' Henry, I think Bo Rabbit did it. He's scared that you might cut him like you did his Unc' Snowvall. He got a big old stick and hit you with it. Then he ran home. You both was right drunk. I found you on the edge of the path and took you home," James said.

Henry turned away abruptly from James. He got out a Number Four shell out of his pocket, plunked it into his shotgun, and clicked it shut. "Thank you, Stumpy. See you later," he said.

Billy was scared as could be. He felt sick to his stomach, remembering what Burton's brains had looked like after being blown out by Unc' Lin. He didn't want to ever see anything like that again. "Dad, can we come back some other day and see about this?" Billy whined. Then

Billy could've sworn he saw an old Hag dressed in a black-hooded cloak staring at him with icy eyes through an upstairs window. He blinked and the image was gone. He vaguely remembered that he had seen that image before, but could not remember where he had seen it.

Billy watched his Dad walk over the hill to Marr' Dee's house. They went past there to Bo Rabbit's place. Tears came to Billy's eyes. "Dad, please don't," Billy whispered.

Bo saw Henry and Billy coming up the hill. He saw the gun on Henry's arm. He had laid his gun on the floor in front of his sofa. He heard the knock on his front door. He opened the door.

"I came over here ta-see ya bout-a 'portant matter." Henry had completely sobered up, so had Bo Rabbit.

"I'on blame ya," Bo said. He trembled all over. "But ya don't need no gun, man. I's wrong as could be. I beg pardon, I's just drunk. I didn't wanna end up like Unc' Tank, is all. We got, got little chillun to raise. We gotta be there for'em, ain't nobody go be they Daddies like we is."

Tears came to Henry's eyes. The truth had hit home like a Mortar Shell. He took the shell out of his shotgun and put it in his pocket. "Bo, I don't 'member pullin' my knife on ya. I don't recall ya hittin' me neither. I got a knot on my head, but I don't rightly know who put it there. So, I's go shake ya hand an 'cept pardon." He shook hands with Bo Rabbit.

Bo stood trembling and shaking all over watching Henry and Billy walk away down the hill and on out of sight. (A knot remained on Henry's head until he died in 1973 from a blood clot.)

Henry returned home and Mabel was gracious enough to dress up his head wound. He went straight on outside without showing Mabel any gratitude. Mabel cooked brunch, fed her children, and put a tub half-full of water in the middle of the kitchen. She put a large pot of water on the stove to get hot so she would have warm-to-hot bathing water.

Billy went outside to help his Daddy. "Boy, we gotta find some lightwood. We's almost outta it," Henry said.

A terrible fear swelled up from inside of Billy's guts. He had to struggle with that. But he had mastered putting the thought out of his mind that once his Dad had tried to kill him. That reality was locked-up deep within his psyche, residing in the dark recesses of his mentality. With trembling lips, Billy answered his Dad: "Aw-ight, Dad. We gotta be careful, though, so no one gets his finger cutoff."

"What'cha talkin' bout?" Henry snapped. He had hoped that Billy had forgotten all about what had happened in the woods "one day long ago."

"Oh, nothing, Dad. I was just thinking out loud," Billy replied. "Let's go then," Henry said.

They were in the woods for about half-an-hour. They found several lightwood-pine-knots. "Take these into the kitchen an' put them in the wood box behind the stove," Henry said.

Henry could see that the light was on in the kitchen that afternoon, and he knew that was the time when Mabel usually took her weekly full-bath.

Billy had forgotten that his Ma was bathing. He followed his Dad through the backdoor into the kitchen. Mabel was standing in the tub lathering her-self with Dial Soap suds, when Billy walked in. Henry laughed. Mabel covered her tits with her left arm, and her vagina with a washcloth in her right hand. But Billy had seen everything.

"Henry, why'd ya bring Billy in here knowin' I's washin' up?" Mabel snapped. "Ya beat the hell outta'im just cause he asked where babies came from. Now, ya done brought 'im in ta-look at his naked Ma washin' up. Now, he done seen it all. How's that boy go 'spect me?"

"Ya ain't got nothin' he ain't never seen before. He go see-a lot more than that. Don't make a big deal outta it, Mabel." Henry said. He went into the bedroom chuckling to him-self

Mabel wrapped a towel around her middle. Billy ran into the children's room. He hated that he had gotten an erection at the sight of his Ma's nude body. It made him feel disgusted at the thought of INCEST with his Mother-No! Hell-No!

After supper, Mabel said to Billy: "I wanna talk-ta ya bout things. C'mon in the front room an' I got somethin' I need-ta say-ta ya."

Billy sat on the sofa in the front room waiting for his Ma to come talk to him. Finally she came in and seated herself opposite her oldest Son in an end chair.

"Billy, I's sorry for what Henry did. Ya should-da never seen me like that. Ev'thin's different now 'tween us. Don't feel bad when ya think bout how ya feel, it's Henry's fault.

"I'ma make'im sorry he ever did that. He done dropped on me, *The Straw That Broke The Camel's Back*. I don't feel marri'd-ta ya Father no more. So, don't hang ya head down none. A lotta things go change'round here. So, you go on outside an' play. And, Billy, don't rape no more little gals, aw-ight?"

CHAPTER TWENTY

During the 1961-62 school year, Billy not only did not get the good clothes his Father bought for his other school-aged children, he still did not get the schoolbooks, even those his Daddy could afford. Nor did he get the book fees and other materials he needed to do a good job at school.

When teachers started demanding that all assigned books and materials for their classes must be purchased by students for particular classes-especially those teachers who were getting kickbacks from book publishers-Billy's progress ended at Abrams. A Ninth-Grade Civics Teacher, Miss Mango Fleming, was such a one. Dr. Winthrop White, the Agriculture Teacher was the other one.

All students were told at the beginning of these Ninth-Grade classes that they had to pay a fee of nine-dollars for the Civics Text, and Five-fifty for the Agriculture Materials. The fees were mandatory for passing those classes.

Mr. White automatically signed up all male students in this class-and four-years of agriculture were required at Abrams for all Male students-and four-years of home economics were required for all of the girls-into a National rural organization: The Future Farmers of America (FFA). The fee of five-fifty was for the national dues. Mr. White had to pay that out of his pocket for each student, and then seek reimbursement from the students in that class. He would be stuck in the red if a student could not, or would not, pay.

Miss Fleming ordered her Textbooks from a firm in North Carolina where she had attended college. She purchased a relative number of textbooks for the students attending her two Civic classes (morning and afternoon) each day.

Henry never gave Billy the book fee or the dues, and of course he failed the above classes, along with English again. Billy was told that he had to repeat the whole Ninth Grade.

In late July, 1962, on this Sunday evening, Billy was fifteen years old. He was standing at the turnoff to his home when Jesse Shelby drove up in his new-green Ford Pickup.

"Hey Billy Boy," Shelby greeted Billy in his redneck way.

"How you doing, Mr. Shelby. What's happening?" Billy said. "Don't call me Boy, though."

Shelby laughed. "Okay. I hear you all 're a mite touchy about that nowadays. I don't mean no offense.

"I gotta go to work on the Pipe-Line coming through here. I'm gonna need somebody to hoe the tobacco field. It's hard work, but you's a big boy-ah, I mean, man-and I would like to hire you to do the job. I'll pay you fifteen-dollars-a-week. That's all I can afford. All you gotta do is hoe up one side of the row and down the other. It'll give ya some change for school next fall. Are you game?"

Billy scratched his head for a minute or two. "I need a job. When you want me to stall?" Jesse smiled. "You come to my house tomorrow morning. My Dad, Job, will get ya started.

My wife, Bernadette, will fix you lunch every day. I'll pay ya on Friday evenings." "Right-on, man," Billy said.

That evening, Henry came home reeking of cheap liquor. "Dad, I'm gonna work at Mr. Shelby's place hoeing tobacco. Is that aw-ight with you?"

"Hell yeah," Henry said. That was all that he said. Billy was happy about that.

In two weeks Billy had saved up thirty dollars. He got the Sears and Roebuck Catalog and ordered (COD) some clothes: a couple of pairs of pants and a couple of shirts. The order came to nine-dollars-ninety-nine-cents. The order arrived a week later.

On this Monday evening, Henry came up the road carrying a notice from Sears and Roebuck. He was mad as hell. "Billy, who told ya ta-go order them dam-clothes? Ya know we might need that money right here in the house ta-help put food on the table. I'ma tell ya, you ain' go throw all that money'way buyin' pretty clothes."

Billy hitched a ride to Columbia to get out his COD package from the Post Office before Henry got down there and sent it back. Billy had twenty dollars left.

When Billy got back home, Henry was waiting. "How much-a that money ya got left?" he asked.

Billy didn't answer. He just took out the dollar-bills and forked them over to his Dad. Henry stuffed those into his pocket without looking at them. Billy wondered what in the hell was he gonna do now? He wanted some good clothes to wear to school. He wanted to pay his book fees. He wanted to pay Miss Fleming and Mr. White so that he wouldn't fail again. He wanted to just to get one more year over with.

On this night, in August, 1962, Bug cried out in the middle of the night as before, and Henry, as he had done before, came to where the boys slept, snatched the covers back off the bed and walloped Billy, even though, like before, Bug was the culprit. The lick didn't hurt as bad as it had before, but Billy was getting tired of that shit!

The next morning, Billy suggested, "Dad ... why can't we get another bed from somewhere so that we growing boys can stretch our legs out at night?"

"I'ma do somethin 'bout that," Henry said.

They ate breakfast. Henry ordered Billy to follow him. They took a shortcut through the woods to Unc' Lin's and A'nt Bessie's abandoned house. They had left every dish, stitch of clothing, all bed-linen, pots and pans and silverware behind. Billy asked, "Dad why did A'nt Bessie'nem leave all their things behind?"

"Billy, Lin b'lieves that a haunt can 'tach his-self-ta whatever b'longs ta-the place it's hauntin'. That's why they left ev'thin'. That's why nobody who b'lieves in ghosts will come get nothin' from over there. I don't b'lieve in 'em, though."

They hauled an Army-style bunk-bed piece by piece from Lin's place to Henry's house. Even the mattress and box springs were in good shape. Billy loved the bed-his own bed-the only child in the house with his own bed.

The first day at the Shelby Farm had been hot, backbreaking, and hard on Billy. He had never been out in the sun all day long before in his life. Though, the Shelbys grew mostly Soy beans, corn, watermelons, and wheat, they also grew a sizeable Tobacco crop; and raised cattle and horses as well. Billy could not see the end of any one row while standing at the other end of it. On the first Monday that Billy arrived to work, Jesse Shelby looked shorter than he had the first time Billy had seen him-or maybe Billy just had grown that much taller since then.

Shelby was waiting for Billy to arrive early that morning. "The hoe you gonna be using is over yonder on the edge of the field," Jesse said. He took off his Dodgers' cap, and ran his left hand through his rough-red hair. "You start at that row, go up one side, and come back down the other side. Don't leave any grass, Billy. Now, that's very imp0liant. That's why I'm paying you."

Billy observed the endless rows with four-foot plants that stood at about two or three feet apart. Jesse got in his truck and sped away. Billy was minded to quit and go home before lunchtime. Man that was the hottest morning of his life up until then. But he needed money real bad.

At around noon, an attractive woman came out on the veranda that went around the entire green and white wood-frame house. She was about five-three, and looked a lot like Lucy, of the "I Love Lucy," sitcom, except that Lucy never had the body this shapely woman had. An old pointed-nose man on crutches quite startled Billy. He had come up behind him.

"That's Mrs. Bernadette. She's gonna bring ya your lunch ever days. Gonna be bout in the middle of the day like now.

"See that big oak tree over yonder. There's a bench built-in on the other side of it. That's where you gonna take ya meals. You'll have lots of shade and all," the old troll of a man said.

Billy realized that he had just met Job Shelby, Jesse's Father. Polio, or some bone disease, had crippled the old guy. His legs and feet were bent back and resembled a fish's fins. He hobbled very well on his crutches, though. Once he had gotten back up to the part of the veranda that had a ramp for Mr. Job Shelby so he wouldn't have to climb the seven steps in front of the house, Bernadette waved at Billy. He thought she was smiling too brightly and for too long. That made Billy a little nervous.

Two little girls stood beside Mrs. Shelby. She spoke to one: "Suzanne, stay close to Mommy." She cuddled the smallest one. "And you too, Christine. Y'all stay in the shade on the porch. Mommy's got to feed Billy."

Four-year-old Christine squealed, "Why, Mommy? Why do I gotta stay ... on porch?" Six-year-old Suzanne squealed, "I wanna see Billy too, Mommy!"

Mrs. Shelby turned towards her girls and, "Sh-h-h-h. No! Y'all stay up here with your Grandpa. I'll be right back," she whispered.

Billy went over to the bench that had been nailed to the side of a massive Indian Oak. It shaded one side of the whole house. The weird look on Mrs. Shelby's face with her gray eyes shining like a cat's at night made Billy a lot more than nervous.

"Hi, Billy. I can see that you're nervous. Hon, don't be nervous, I won't bite ya," Mrs. Shelby purred. "I got ya some cool milk. I want ya to drink it all up. It's cool, white, and smooth." She giggled.

"Hi, Mrs. Shelby. Thank you," Billy said. He smiled like a little boy with his hand caught in the cookie jar. He took a swig of the fresh milk. He saw Mrs. Shelby sat a brown-bag containing two sandwiches on the bench beside him.

"Billy, this is your lunch. If I can get anything else for you, just let me know," Mrs. Shelby crooned, then she scared Billy shitless.

Mrs. Shelby wore blue short-shorts that she had rolled up even shorter around her thighs so that the edge of her red panties could be seen. She had tied her white blouse into a halter so that her full red bra could be seen. She stooped down beside the bench where Billy sat to pull up her Bobby Socks. Then Billy nearly choked on the egg-salad sandwich he was eating.

He saw the brown-pubic hairs on the crevice of her leg and vaginal region. The way she was stooping also caused her big boobs to lean forward exposing them all the way. She stood up and flicked her Page Boy haircut a little. "Do ya see anything else ya want, hon?" Mrs. Shelby asked in a sultry whisper.

"No Ma'am, I'm fine," Billy said. He lost his appetite.

"Well, if you change your mind, just whistle," Mrs. Shelby whispered through her teeth.

Billy's eyes got glued to her buttocks as Mrs. Shelby pranced away from him gyrating her hips like Marilyn Monroe did on the Ed Sullivan Show. He tried as hard as he could to not notice what Mrs. Shelby was doing or suggesting, but he could not take his eyes off her, and a big lump rose in his pants.

His deep-down lusts came bursting up through his loins, his testicles, his penis, even though he was trying to hold all that down. Then, Mrs. Shelby stopped, turned around and looked right at the lump in Billy's pants, and with her head half-turned, she winked. Billy could feel her eyes burning through his pants. She walked even more seductively, imitating the "Act" itself. When she got to the porch, she turned towards Billy, smiled, and stopped walking. She slowly ran her left hand over her left breast. She ran her right hand quickly over her crotch area. She got a sensuous grin on her full-lips. When she got to the front door, her grin became an ear-to-ear smile. She pranced on through the front door, where her Father-in-Law was standing angrily staring at her.

Then it occurred to Billy: *That's what got Emmett Till, Mack Parker, and the Scottsboro Boys in trouble. I don't believe that Mrs. Shelby wants me. But she wants to know that I want her bad enough to risk being lynched for even flirting with her. My wanting her is something, "She Needs to Know."*

White women probably got that from their men keeping Black men away from them. These women have heard all of their lives how beautiful and desirable they are supposed to be. So, they get disturbed if a Black man does not go out of his way to have sex with them. Then they feel that they have to prove how irresistible, but virginal, they are. So they will seduce a Black man, or put themselves in a compromising position so that they can pretend that they have been violated by a "Black Brute." Anyway that a Black man touches her, "has to be rape!" That's how they intend to remain "Pure!" in spite of them having and expressing very "whorish" ways. "They will scream Rape!" in a minute, and get some hapless Black man lynched This reaffirms their "Need to Know" that "the Niggers" will do anything "to get into their Panties."

One day, Billy saw Mr. Job reach down and fondle Mrs. Shelby. She had been lying out in the sun on a beach towel in a new outfit called a "Bikini." She had not learned to shave her pubic region yet. She was very hairy between her legs, and seemed to be very nude in a Bikini.

Mrs. Shelby got up, folded up her towel and served Billy lunch in her outfit. When she came back up on the porch, Mr. Job grabbed himself a handful.

"Now, you stop that, Grandpa," Mrs. Shelby shouted. "I'm gonna tell my husband bout ya putting your grimy hands on me. You know that ain't right. I'm gonna tell Jesse on you."

Mr. Job leaned on his crutches. "Well . . ." he spat out a big blob of tobacco juice. "What'cha think Jesse's gonna say bout all that shit you're doing round Billy Buck over yonder. I don't wanna tell 'im bout that. He'll shoot that boy an' you too."

"You just gotta keep your hands off my private. That's all to it. That's for your Son, only."

Mr. Job spat out another blob of tobacco spittle over the banister. He laughed out loud. "You're a crazy Cunt. Po' White Trash's all you is. I don't see what Jesse sees in you."

Bernadette swished her hips even harder. "Ya cripple-old-bastard," she said followed by a taunting snicker.

"White Trash!" Mr. Job snapped at his wayward Daughter-in-Law.

Jesse drove up in his Pickup. He got out of it in a hurry. Billy was nervous as could be. The riff had started-he thought-over him. He didn't want to be in the middle of White-Folks' business.

"Hey! Hey! Hey!" Billy heard a dusty-dirty Jesse, who seemed to be covered all over with red mud, yell at his Father and his wife. "What y'all's fussin 'bout?"

"Grandpa's been at it again," screamed Bernadette.

"Pa, what ya got to say for yourself?" Jesse asked, pointedly, but hilariously.

"Well ... that gal ain't doing nothing but misusing her 'magination. She's just tryin' to act like-a-fine-White-Lady-but she gotta long way to go before she'll be there," Mr. Job said in a chortle.

Jesse turned to his grieving wife. "Baby, you can see that Daddy's just an O' Crazy Man. He can't catch you. How'd ya let'im get close enough to you ta-feel ya?

"Next time, Honey, just slap his wrinkled-up old hands away. Shove the old buzzard out of your way. He'll be just as harmless as a eunuch," Jesse allowed. He turned to his little girls.

"Come here, Suzanne. Come here, Christine. Y'all give Daddy a kiss."

Bernadette snapped: "But, I want that old fox to stop trying to feel me up, though, Jesse!" "Sugar, I'll get on him about that later. Right now, lemme go over yonder and pay Billy. I reckon he's a smart enough Boy ta-let what he just heard stay right here where he heard it," Jesse spoke loud enough for Billy to hear him.

Jesse pranced over to where Billy sat on the bench attached to the big Oak tree. "Billy, you're doing a fine job. The field looks good. That's why the tobacco's grown so fast. It's time for it to mature fast now.

"I'ma give ya an extra day's pay. In this envelope's eighteen dollars. Ya come on back Monday morning. I'ma let ya off for the rest-a this evening.

"One thing you gotta promise me is, what ya hear and see round here on this farm about my wife, and all, ya gonna let stay right here where ya heard or seen it; okay?" Jesse said, pointing his finger in Billy's face, a little.

"Yes sir, Mr. Shelby," was all that Billy managed to say. He was glad to get that brown envelope in his hands, to feel the new money, and to savor the scent of it.

But-Henry was waiting for Billy when he got home with his pay. He ordered Billy to fork it over. Billy's pleas about buying school-clothes made no difference to Henry. He took most of Billy's money anyway. That's why Billy ordered stuff from Sears and tried to get it out before Henry had a chance to take all of his money. Other than the two outfits, Billy managed to buy a New Acoustic Guitar. He ordered it out of the Sears Catalog.

The Guitar cost Eleven Dollars. Since there was no more room in his "Subliminal Lock Box," Billy turned to his Guitar to relieve his stress.

That last week of work at the Shelby Farm, Billy did the laying-by rows-on either side of the tobacco plants. After that harvesting the plants from the top down was the only thing left. Jesse wouldn't need him to do that.

On Billy's last payday, Henry took fifteen dollars from Billy. That left him with three dollars. Billy had seen in the Daily Progress an Ad that said that Bradford Dry Goods Store in Dillwyn had a back-to-school-sale-special for $2.98-one-per customer. For that, a customer could buy a sports shirt and a pair of pants for a school-age child. With his last three dollars, Billy came to his Ma.

"Ma, here's my last dollar. Y'all go right by Bradford Dry Goods on your way to his Grocery Store. Please stop and buy the advertised shirt and pants outfit for my first day of school. All I got so far are two outfits and a guitar. Y'all used my pay to buy clothes for my Brothers," Billy pied with Mabel.

Late that evening, Mabel and Henry came home from shopping. They had bags of groceries and some clothes in other bags. They had some notebooks, packs of lined paper, and pencils. "Ma, where's the clothes I asked you to buy with my last dollar?" Billy yelled.

"We had-da use that money, Billy, in the house," Henry snapped. "Now ya knows how it feels ta-never have nothin' toll. I's been feelin' that for years, cause-a you!"

"All-a y' all's crazier than a June Bug in December. Y'all gotta stop this shit! That's all to it," was Billy's heated response.

Billy ran out of the house to down the spring path. He found the old Hickory Tree that he talked to sometimes when he felt he had to contact his Grandma. He knelt down before that old tree and cried out of his heart:

"Granny, I wish you were here. I know you wouldn't have treated me like Ma and Dad are doing. I wish I could leave here and go over to where you are. Then I would be with you forever. I hope you can hear me through this tree. Everybody down here seems to be against me because I am who I am, and because I look the way I do. You're closer to God than I am right now. Please ask Him to help me-because I can't go on like this much longer." The words flowed out of Billy like water over a dam. Then tears came streaming down his cheeks

Billy figured: I won't run away from home just yet. But this is the last year I'm going to put up with Ma's lies, Dad's brutality, and supplying my Dad with money to go out and get drunk on, in the name of "Helping Out At Home." He went back to the house that evening, swallowed his grief, and pride, ate his plate or so of Brown Beans, and said nothing at all. Right then, he hated his Ma and Dad, equally. He just wanted to get away from them both. He wished he was dead-or had never been born!

CHAPTER TWENTY-ONE

In 1962, Labor Day came on a Saturday. So, the schools celebrated it on that Monday. Billy was home reading the Bible when Henry came home from gambling up in Cloverdale with some of his childhood friends. He was tipsy but not drunk. Billy stared Henry in the eye. He was getting a lot taller then and was not as afraid of his Dad as he had been.

Henry had a favorite rocking chair he sat in near his Chest of Drawers at the foot of his bed. He plopped down in that chair and began rocking. Billy approached is Father. "Dad, why 're you so cruel to me?" he asked Henry.

"Iain' no meaner-ta you than Poppa was ta-me, or Unc' Johnny was-ta Poppa. Boy, ya better get use-ta being hard. Ya go have-ta face a lotta shit, ya can't do nothin 'bout.

"Get use-ta dis'pointments. Get use-ta losin' things ya love. Get use-ta the 'Man' takin 'vantage of ya. Get use-ta being hooked-up with some bad Bitches. Cause-dammit-that shit's go happen-ta ya. Less ya go get read-ta-kill a half-dozen assholes, ya go just have-ta take the shit an' move on. It may as well start with me-ya Daddy," Henry preached at his puzzled Son.

"Maybe it'd been better that a Black man was never created than Dad. It's like God has made a mistake, or something. That's how it seems to me," Billy opined.

"Lemme warn ya too, Son. Ya better be ver' careful who ya call 'Black.' Ya say that ta-the wrong one, an' ya liable-ta get ya throat cut," Henry warned.

(The Color Schism Henry referred to was more prevalent during his childhood then during Billy's. In 1962, people of African descent were proud to refer to themselves as Blacks.)

Billy let his Father dose on off to sleep. Mabel got out of a car outside and trotted up to the house. Once she got into the kitchen, she was all smiles. "Billy, gimme a glass of iced tea out of the pitcher in the 'frigerator. I got some good news for all y'all."

"What's happening, Ma?" Billy asked trying to sound hip like those characters he had watched on the "Mod Squad."

"Son, things go change a lot 'round here," Mabel said in a sing-song way. "I gotta job down in Columbia. I been practicin' how-ta drive too. I'm go get my license next week. George Mayor go lemme use his car. I can drive good 'nough aw-ready.

"I'm go make it up-ta ya Billy bout your clothes. You'll see, ya go have clothes-ta wear, an' all ya books, an' ev'thin'. I'm go fix things 'round here, Billy."

Billy watched tears ease down his Ma's cheeks. All of her children gathered around her. The girls cried with their Mother.

"Where you gonna be working at, Ma?" Billy asked.

Mabel took a big sip out of her iced tea. "I'm go be workin' at Mrs. Parish Cafe in Columbia, prep-cookin' and cleanin' up the kitchen after closin'. I get-ta take the leftovers home ev' night.

"Ya bigger chillun go have-ta help take care-a the little ones, but ya ain't go have-ta cook nothin'. Ya go have-ta just warm things up. It's go be plenty of food in the 'frigerator ev' day from now on.

"Mrs. Parish gotta used 1960's Datsun. George know where-ta get the parts-ta fix it an' get it runnin'. Mrs. Parish go let me have it for just twenty-five dollars. She'll take that out of my pay five-dollars-per-week till it's paid off By next weekend, I'm go be drivin'," Mabel said.

Billy was glad to hear what his Ma said. "Ma, when ya go start?" he asked.

"George go gimme a ride down there in a half-hour. I'm go start this evenin'. I gotta cook-a ham and make some vegetable soup. I gotta slice up a roast so Mrs. Parish an' er Daughter can make beef sandwiches tomorrow. What they served today, I can bring most-a that home, or throw it out. I think she got meatloaf, macaroni salad and cress salad seasoned with ham hocks, leftover," Mabel said.

Mabel went into the front room and came back with a large bag. She took out a black uniform that had a white apron sewn onto its front. "Billy put the old flat iron on the stove, I gotta press this uniform. Mrs. Parish gave me two, but only one is clean. I gotta wear one ev' day down there. Things go change 'round here," Mabel said.

That year, Billy found himself in Mr. White's homeroom. Just as soon as Mr. White finished calling the roll that first day, Billy raised his hand. "Yes, William," Mr. White said.

"I want to see you after the bell rings for our first class, Mr. White. Is that all right with you?" Billy asked.

The bell rung. The students got up to go to their first-period classes. Billy knew some of them from last year. They had been underclassmen then. Being in a homeroom with them made him feel out of place. He went to the front of the classroom before it was time for him to leave for his first class of the school year. When he got directly in front of Mr. White, Billy held out his hand to him. In a tight fist, he held six dollars. He dropped the ball of dollars into Mr. White's opened right hand.

"Willaim . . . you could've waited until class this afternoon. But, thank you. I've got the change right here. Your FFA fee is paid in full." He gave Billy two quarters in change.

Billy went to his first-period class, it was English Literature and Composition, one of those he had failed. His second-period class was Biology; next was Music Appreciation, then lunchtime. He had fifty-cents left in change, so he bought a hot lunch from the cafeteria. Then it was Civics again, and on to American History; then Agriculture; and last but not least, Health and Physical Education. Billy had no study period. He had to repeat his English class at that time.

That night Billy heated up Beef Stew for supper. Mabel had brought that home along with a cardboard box, lined with tinfoil, full of Rolls. Henry and the children ate their fill with plenty of scrapes leftover for the dogs: Rat, and Mike-another brown-colored-Hound.

Mabel got her driver's license and car running. She was off from work on Sundays and Wednesdays. Billy got his book fees paid. He got a couple of pairs of decent dress-shoes to wear and a pair of winter boots. Mabel bought him a heavy winter coat as well as several pairs of pants and a half-dozen winter shirts. He started to look like any other student at Abrams. He was never hungry or ashamed of what he had for lunch anymore. Then came: *The Straw that Broke the Camel's Back.*

After the midterm exams, **Miss** Fleming became very distraught over how poorly the entire class had performed. Billy got the only "A" on that exam. Two other students out of twenty had passed the exam. The rest had failed. Most students earned an "F."

What tickled Billy was: The majority that failed was light-skinned Mulatto-types. He had to wonder was there something wrong with Miss Fleming's testing methods?

While passing out the corrected test-papers, Miss Fleming made some very disparaging remarks that grated the nerves of an already disconsolate and emotionally disturbed, teenaged William Anderson James. Miss Fleming harangued:

"I don't know what you 'real-darkies' are going to do anyway. Some of you all don't even belong in high school. High school is not going to do you all any good. It won't stop you from ending up where you are bound to end up.

"You are going to end up married to some nappy-headed slob, and you girls will have a houseful of little snotty-nose tar babies. You're going to work yourselves to death on a farm, in some white-person's kitchen, or at a Sawmill. You're just not going to be allowed to do any better. Why don't you just give me a break and quit, if you are old enough to."

Billy was mad as hell. He was thinking: *That chocolate bitch! She sounds just like Mrs. Thompson and Miss Payne. Why the hell should I stay in school for twelve or more years if all that's going to get me is shitty jobs? I can get them without that much schooling. This is the last year of my pain and suffering and taking shit from high-yellow teachers who wished they were White!*

He whispered aloud to himself: "I'm go leave school after this year."

On this Saturday, Jasper Furman came by to ask, "Billy, I wonder if you would be able to come help me for the rest of the day? I gotta separate out some shoats to take-ta the market. Your Father helped castrate them, but he's gonna be busy today. I'd appreciate it a great deal. I tell you what-I'll pay ya twelve Dollars. We're gonna be busy until way after dark, but it'll be worth your while-I think."

Billy looked at the green International Log truck Furman sat in, and said: "Let me get into some work clothes, first. I'll be right out," he said.

Working in a large pig pen is smelly, slippery, and disgusting work. The hogs are all running every which way. Those pigs designated had to be rundown and forced into a section of the pen that had a ramp where they could be easily driven into the back of a tractor and trailer for hauling to the slaughterhouse in Richmond, Virginia. Each one of them had a metal tag stapled to its ear that had a classifying number engraved on it.

Other pigs were to be loaded onto a smaller pickup. They would be taken to a barn for fattening. These would be slaughtered that winter for the Furmans. The young female driving the truck was Furman's Daughter, Cynthia. Billy was seeing her up close for the first time. She was a strawberry blonde, with :freckles on her face. She had cute buckteeth that made her seem to be smiling even when she wasn't. She was sitting in the truck, but Billy could see that she had a very shapely body.

She pulled the truck toward the hog pen, opened the door, and slid out. She looked Billy up and down. "You're Mabel 'nem Boy, Billy, ain't you?" she said to Billy right away. "I've heard about you." She smiled shaking her head affirmatively.

She was wearing a dress like Billy had seen Dale Rogers wearing on "The Roy Rogers Show." It was gray with some kind of western design on the front of it, like a horse rearing up, and a cowboy throwing a rope after it. The helm of her dress came up above her knees. She wore two-tone black-and-white bucks with bobby socks. She had her hair in a long, bushy, ponytail down her back. She had on a white short-sleeve blouse.

Jasper said: "Billy after we get this truck loaded, ride on the tail-end of it till we get to the barn. Then you jump off and let Cynthia back it up so that we can open the gate and let the hogs unload. We gonna make about five trips fore it gets dark. I'm go ride in the cab with Cynthia."

On their first trip up a little hill at about a half-mile from the barn, near a curve in the road next to a stand of walnut and hickory-nut trees Jesse Shelby came speeding down the road in his Pickup Truck. He jumped out and yelled; "Whoa, Jasper. Whoa." "Cynthia, stop the truck. Let me hear what Jesse's talking about."

Billy jumped off the edge of the tail-end on back of Furman's truck. "Cynthia, you and Billy wait a second. I ain't got too much time to fool with Jesse. Time is money," Furman said.

What shocked the hell out of Billy happened no sooner than Jesse and Jasper had gone around the curve towards some cattle grazing on a nearby field.

Cynthia opened the truck door on the driver's side. "Billy, come around here. I got to show you something," she whispered.

Billy wondered what she was whispering about. When he came from the back of the truck to her side, he found out more than he wanted to know. She pulled her dress up to her thighs exposing her white cotton panties. "Billy, look. You show me yours, and I'll show you mine," Cynthia said in a sultry whisper. She pulled her dress up even higher, then, she dropped the hem of it very quickly. The voices of Jesse and Jasper were heard getting closer to the truck.

"Later, Billy. We'll be going to school together next year. You can see it all then," Cynthia whispered. She got out of the truck to stand closer to Billy. She giggled, mischievously.

Cynthia scurried back to the driver's side got in the truck and eased the door closed so that it did not make much noise. "Sh-h-h-h," she whispered through her teeth.

"We'll be by to get that young bull directly," Jesse said.

"We'll let a couple of familiar cows go with it to your farm. Let them stay for a couple of days. He'll get settled in by then, I reckon. Then we'll get settled up too," Furman said.

"Thank you, Good Buddy. I'll get Bernadette to draft ya a check," Jesse said. Jesse got into his truck and sped off and went back up the path he had come down.

"Cynthia, Billy, we gotta get cracking. We ain't gonna be able to get but a couple-a loads up yonder before it gets dark. Let's go y'all," Jasper said.

"Okay, Pa," Cynthia said. She had a sly grin on her young face. She looked over at Billy and winked. She mouthed, "Later, Hon."

They got to the barn. Billy pulled the ramp from under the barn's edge. Cynthia backed the truck up to the opened gate. Then Jasper placed the ramp. Billy opened the truck's gate. The hogs scampered down the ramp to an opening into a fenced-in area. They ran to a group of other pigs to group-in with them. These were large hogs weighing about ninety-pounds-a-piece.

"We will only be able to round up two other loads fore dark. So, Billy, I won't need ya to help me with that. So, I'll pay ya when I get up to the barn.

"Do you need a ride home? It's getting late. I can let Cynthia take you in the car."

Fear swelled up in Billy's stomach and rushed up to his chest. "No sir. I'm gonna walk. Gotta stop over at my Grandma's house," he lied. He just did not want to be alone with Cynthia.

Furman gave Billy two fives and two ones. "Thank you sir," he said. He heard Cynthia say something that shocked him: "Billy, won't it be nice when our schools mix, huh?" She said.

Billy didn't know whether her Daddy heard her or not. He took off up the road, running until he was out of the sight of the farm. He wondered if White women were out of their minds? He went straight home in case Furman had heard Cynthia and was coming to avenge his Daughter's honor.

Billy got home late that evening. Henry stumbled in behind him. He was drunk as could be. "Boy, I know ya got paid. Furman always pay good. Now, ya give it up. I need some extra money. Ya got any? ..."

"No Dad. I won't do it," Billy replied. "You and Ma got money now. Why you gotta take all my money? I worked too hard for that money. You are just going to go out and drink up every nickel you take from me. I won't do that anymore."

Henry felt like he wasn't going to stand for Billy to sass him to his face. He ran over to Billy and slammed his balled-up right fist into Billy's nose. "You thinks you'sa man, now? Man 'nough-ta sass me ta-my face, huh?"

He was knocked to the floor. Blood came out of Billy's nose in a splatter at first, then in a trickle. He cried out: "Don't hit me no more, Dad."

Mabel, Dick, Johnboy, and Sammy Lee ran into the kitchen and grabbed Henry. He struggled to get loose from them to hit Billy some more. Sammy Lee went into a cabinet in the corner of the kitchen, got out a butcher knife, and ran over to where Henry was struggling to get free.

"Here, Big Brother. Stick 'im with this," Sammy Lee said.

Billy took the knife and threw it so that the tip of the blade stuck into the kitchen floor. He ran out the backdoor. He went to his Grandma house. He had kept his money, though.

For the first time, Billy spent the night drinking cheap wine and beer with Leroy, Stumpy, and Matty. They told him to forget what Henry had done. So, they told him the story about the Witch who had lived in that house, to help him forget about the beating at the hands of his Dad. To some extent, it worked. Billy decided that he would ask some old-reliable person in the neighborhood about the Witch Story and see if there was anything to it.

Billy knew he would be Sixteen soon. He figured he would go back home and stay until June 11, 1963. He would leave home for good then. But he had learn to shoot the shotgun-had shot it, in fact, down through the woods-and he made up in his mind, that he would blow his Father's brains out before he would let him beat him again-and he was not going to give him any of his money, ever again. So with that mindset he headed home.

When Billy walked back through the backdoor that Sunday morning, he was high. Henry was in the kitchen, sober, and nervous. He was sitting at the kitchen table. He looked up at his oldest Son. "Beg pardon," was all he said. He went out to the woodshed and got out a buck saw and cut-up a stack of firewood for the cook stove.

Mabel came into the kitchen. She caressed Billy with tears coming down her cheeks. "I'm sorry," she said.

"Ma, if Dad ever hits me like that again, I'll blow his brains out with that shotgun in there. I'm too big for him to knock around like that anymore. And-I'm not going to give him money so that he can go drink it up-and that's all to it!"

Mabel got very tear-eyed. She ran over to Billy, looked her oldest Son in his eyes for a moment, then hugged him tightly. "Billy, you's my an' Henry's First-Born. I don't wanna lose none-a my chillun. No . . . cause-a lotta the blame's on me. I kno' I ain't been the best Momma y'all could-a had.

"But, killin' somebody ya ain't go never get over that-look at ya Unc' Lin. Billy don't think'bout killin' ya Daddy. I don't wanna lose neither one-a y'all. You might shoot him, or he may kill you first-none-a that go do any of us no good. I love ya with all my heart, but you's wrong 'bout that, now."

Billy pranced around in the kitchen for a minute. "Ma, how am I gonna stop Dad from hitting me, then?" he asked.

"Well, Billy, ma-be it'd be better ifn ya did leave. Ya can better get over that than if ya kilt ya Dad, an' got put in jail. Or he kilt you an' we had that ta-tend with for the rest-a our lives. Who go help me take care-a the rest-a ya Brothers and Sisters?" Mabel whined. She was near tears, looking deep within Billy's troubled, bloodshot, eyes.

"Aw-ight, then. I'm go put up with Dad for a couple more months, then, I'm out of here," Billy said. He went into the children's room and fell across his bed. The alcohol he had consumed made him "drunk as hell" for the first time.

Maury Macklin Paddy was a friend Billy had known since his Shiloh days. His Grandmother was named "Clarita Ester Paddy." Maury and his Grandma lived with his Aunt "Venus Mae," and his Uncle "Chessman Lighthouse Paddy."

Maury was called "Jack Rabbit" because he was no more than four-eleven tall, and was very light-skinned. Everybody called him "Jack" for short. Jack hated living at home because his Aunt was a Pentecostal Minister of a small, rural, Church called the "Burning Bush Church of God," located in Palmyra, Virginia. His Aunt was strict on him. He couldn't drink or smoke, or even look admiringly at a pretty girl. So Jack wanted to quit school and leave home too.

On this Wednesday, Mabel decided to take Billy up to the UVA Hospital to see if he could work there for the summer. Not trusting driving in the street traffic, Mabel and her oldest son waited for the Westbound Local at the bus stop. Billy and Jack had planned to go to the UVA together-though Mabel didn't know about their plan at first.

Buck Payne had told Mabel to "see the Executive Housekeeper, Mrs. Irene Shuffles, and she will probably give Billy a job for the summer, and if he do a good job, he can stay on after the summer-if that's what he wanna do."

Jack got on the bus at the Palmyra stop. He came back and sat across from Mabel and Billy. He walked with Mabel and Billy from the Trailways

Station on East Main Street up to the UVa Hospital. They had traveled for about ten city blocks. They entered the Hospital through its Ground Floor East Main Street Entrance.

They walked up long corridors to the Freight Elevators, pressed the down arrow and waited for those doors to pop open. The elevator ride down to the Sub-Basement felt funny to Billy. It was like when a car suddenly went down a hill leaving your stomach back up the hill.

They got off the elevator and saw a sign that said: "Office of Executive Housekeeper." Mabel knocked on that door. "Come in," a pleasant voice said. "The door is unlocked."

Once inside of the spacious office Billy saw several green file cabinets, a large bulletin board was covered with notices, and a huge, brown, desk was positioned in the far corner of the place. A gray-haired old lady that had been a very-pretty young woman, sat behind that desk. "C'mon in you all. Mr. Minifield told me that Buck Payne was sending me a good worker from Fluvanna. I didn't expect to see two of them. I'm Mrs. Shuffles, the Executive Housekeeper.

"Ma'am, are you the Mother of both of these fine-looking young men?" Mrs. Shuffles asked Mabel.

"No ma'am. Just the tall one," Mabel said with a smile.

"Okay, then. Here's the papers you will have to fill out. What's your names?" Mrs. Shuffles asked.

"I'm Maury Paddy," Jack said.

"I'm William Anderson James," Billy said.

"Mrs. James, fill out this consent form. Sign it, and put your signature on the Social Security Form and William's application. I have to send a copy of those to the School Board.

"Maury, you can take your forms home and have your parents mail them back. Here, use this brown self-addressed envelope. School will close June 10th You all should report to work on June 11th, at seven in the morning I will look forward to working with you all," Mrs. Shuffles said, in her soothing voice.

Billy, Jack, and Mabel filled out the forms they were handed, and Jack took those given to him to take home and put them folded-up in his back pocket.

On their way back down to East Main Street, Billy got to the crest of the

Hill at Forth and Main, and wondered at the abandoned Neighborhood, and empty buildings that had probably been business sites. He wondered what had happened to them.

Because Jack was so light-skinned and had those off-green eyes, straight-blondish hair, and a mouth that was not at all Negroid, Billy thought he would ask him a question he had wondered about but had not dared to ask.

"Jack, my A'nt Cora had a White Daddy ... What about your'n?" Billy asked his friend.

He stopped walking for a minute. Then Jack answered: "Billy, I swear to you, If I ever find out who that son-of-a-bitch is, I'm going to gut him like a hog. No mercy will I show him," Jack spoke in a trembling voice.

"Don't say that," Mabel interjected. "Who-so-never he is he's still your Daddy. How you know he didn't wanna do right by you an' your Ma? The Law might've stopped'im."

"Grandma say, my Ma died in childbirth. My Dad never came forward to help out. He could have slipped around and helped me.

"He slipped around in the woods with my Mother. She was only twelve. He knocked her up and made her promise not to tell nobody. She kept who he was a secret to her grave. So, I hate my Daddy to the grave," Jack said.

"Sometimes, knowing who your Daddy is ain't all that it's cracked up to be," said Billy.

On the bus that evening Billy and Jack sat together. Mabel sat a couple of seats in the front of them. They were all as quiet as a mouse pissing on cotton all the way to their stops.

Very early on this Sunday morning in early-May, a loud knock on the front door awoke Mabel.

It made her mad as hell, because that was one of her days of rest.

"Who is it?" Mabel yelled. She got out of her bed and put on a flannel housecoat. "Oh, Hi, Bessie. How're ya doin'?"

"Hi, Mabel. How's you an' Henry doin'?" Bessie asked.

"Bessie, Why's Matt'nem still out in the car? Tell 'em c'mon in. What brings ya out so early this morning? Must be Matt's new boyfriend driving that new car, huh?"

"Mabel. I go let them stay out yonder in the car. But lemme come in for a minute or two." "Bessie, Why' s ya wearin' all black?"

"Child, Mabel, I got some bad news. Yeah, Matt's got a new man, Blakey." "What done happen, Bessie?"

"Mabel. Mabel, Lin ain't no longer with us," Bessie said with a deep sigh. "Heart attack." "Bessie, what happen-ta Lin's heart?"

A few tears moistened Bessie's big eyes. "He got up Tuesday mornin', ran outdoors and on up the street wearin' only his shorts an' T-shirt. Nobody could catch'im. He ran like a madman for several blocks 'til he dropped dead. Said Burton was chasin 'im!"

"We took'im to MCV. They tried-ta'vive'im, but he was dead when they brought'im in." Tears came to Mabel's eyes. "I's sorry-ta hear'bout it, Bessie."

"Yeah, but Mabel, Lin had that comin'. He didn't have-ta kill Burton like that. Reck-en Lin got what he 'serves. Burton got even with'im even from the grave."

Mabel didn't know what else to say, so she said: "When an' where's the funeral go be.

Henry's go wanna know."

"Mabel, it's go be in a cup'la days. 'Vange'lis Jackson his Sister-in-Law's go preach his funeral. They go have-a grave-side service up at Cunningham Cemetery. Henry know where that is. I can see Henry ain' here. Tell'im when he gets back," Bessie said. "I gotta go Mabel. Matt, Alize, an' Matt's Boy, 'Gook,' send they love-ta ya, bye, child. I just came up here to tell you and Cary. Ya can meet Matt's new man another time. See ya."

Henry came home drunk as a skunk. Mabel told him what Bessie had told her, but he seemed unable to hear her. He climbed into bed and fell off to sleep without saying a word. Later on he awoke.

Mabel got dressed and went up to so-call visit with her mother. She was actually slipping around with Mayor, her Sister's Lover.

"Jenny Ree, I had a dream or somethin'. Thought ya Ma told me that Lin died. She's here this mornin' when I came in. Was I dreamin'?" Henry asked his youngest Daughter.

"Nope, Daddy. You weren't dreaming. A'nt Bessie brought the news this morning. Said she was going over to tell A'nt Cary," Jenny Ree replied.

Judy Mae said: "Dad, I second the motion. I heard A'nt Bessie too.

Bet they'll have Unc' Lin in the ground fore you find out where they're puttin'nem in the ground."

"Y'all heat me up somethin' ta-eat. I's hungry as a dog," Henry said. He got up still wearing all of his clothes. He took a sponge off after eating sliced ham, potato salad, and green peas. He got into his old "bucket of bolts," and took off again. That was how he and Mabel were living: trying to ignore each other, even though they were sleeping in the same bed.

As it turned out, Henry never found out where Lin's funeral was being held. So, he drowned that out with some more cheap liquor, like he did almost everything else.

Later on, in May, 1963, during the Reading Days for the Final Exams, Billy hung out in Columbia that day. He wanted to talk to one of Halle Bland 's Daughters, Virginia, called Gen. But he was too nervous to approach her. He thought that she was so incredibly pretty, though. He'd hang around in Columbia all day long just for the chance to get a glimpse of Gen Gen.

Billy sat in one of a group of chairs at Parish's. He saw this tall, skinny, wizened, very light skinned man limp into the backdoor of Parish's Cafe. He was wearing a brown prison-issue two-piece suit, and brown old folks' comfort-shoes. He had on a white shirt and black bow tie. He walked very slowly like each step caused him a great deal of pain. He used a steady walking cane. His hair was white like snow. His skin was a pallor-tan color. He seemed to be no more than skin and bone.

He went into the Cafe. Billy watched him through the doorway. Mabel came out of a backdoor and jumped for the arms of that 'gray ghost.' Then Billy figured he better keep an eye on this old guy.

"Hi, Wayne, Baby. How ya <loin'?" Mabel asked. The old guy flinched in pain. He backed away from Mabel.

"Mabel, be careful. Don't hug me too tight," Wayne whispered. "What's wrong with you, Wayne?" Mabel asked.

"It's my bones. They ain't no good no more. That's why they lemme out early. I stay in the hospital so much they feel that I'm not pullin' that much time. I'm on my way to my grave Mabel," Wayne said.

"Wayne, ya gotta few minutes? I wanna know what actually happen that night ya got in trou'ba. I kno' ya didn't kill that old man. Fore ya leave this world, tell me what really happen," Mabel paused to frown, "when ... y'all kilt that old man."

"Ifn we hadn't been so close, little gal, I wouldn't tell ya this. But here goes:

"Gus an' I got up-ta Stiles's house in the middle of the night. He's in his bedroom. Iain' had no gun. We weren't s'pose-ta have no guns. We was just go beat-it outta O' Stiles-y'kno' where he hid the money. The old son-na-va-bitch wouldn't tell us nothin'toll. We beat his ass all over the place till he pissed and shitted all over his-self; but he never gave up where he kept his money.

"His blood got smeared all over the house. I found a gallon-size King Syrup can full of small change sitting on a counter in his kitchen-that's all the money we found. Gus got mad as hell.

"Then . . . Gus, pulled that gun out. He punched holes in the old guy's cheeks with that gun. Didn't do no good. Stiles kept his lips shut. Gus knocked out all of his front teeth. The old guy cried out: 'Hitler-Hitler-Hitler-killers-Nazi-killers!' I didn't know what that meant. It made Gus even madder. He yelled: 'I'ma give ya one more chance-ta tell-me where ya got that money hid. Then, I'm go send ya ta-hell.' The old guy screamed: 'Auschwitz!' I didn't know what that meant either.

"Then-Gus pulled the trigger of that gun. More and more blood spurted out of the old guy's head. Three bullet-holes was in his head, Mabel. Stiles slumped to the floor, balled up in a knot and trembled all over. I stood there stunned. I had never been part of killin' nobody before. It made me sick-ta my stomach, at first. Then I 'membered that he's just 'nother Cracker.

"I helped Gus ransack the place. We still didn't find any money in the flooring, ceiling, walls, bedding, or anywhere. I told Gus, daylight is comin' up, man. We gotta get outta here. We cut out of there like two deer. Gus had his gun. I had the can-a change. I gambled that'way up at Lin'nem."

Mabel sarcastically shook her head. "Y'all kilt that innocent old man for nothin'toll. He'sa good man, too. Gave all the little Colored chillun a dime for a ice-cream cone in Columbia. Always spoke to all-a us like we's just-a human as he was.

"Did ya ever think'bout, it? Ma-be he didn't have no money in his house. He could've kept it in the bank; or, ma-be he gave it all 'way ta-charity-least, that's what Lin an' Bessie b'lieve. Don't ya even feel bad bout that?"

Wayne's eyes bugged out a little. "Hell no!" he snapped. "It's payback! That's what that was. Look at all our Boys that done been lynched-for nothin' toll. Lease, we's tryin' ta-take back some-a the money them Crackers stole from us. I'm sorry I didn't kill more-a them Murthers! Gus, got one, though. Got 'way with it, too."

"Wayne, ya can't blame all White folk for what some-a them did ta-us," Mabel said.

"Tell that ta-them, Mabel. A White Bitch get raped-or claim she was-an' ev' Black man gotta pay for it. Any of them might get hung bout it. That's why I ain't sorry'bout-a damn-thing Gus an' I did ta-that old Cracker."

A terrible sadness came down on Mabel. "Wayne, why'd ya'gree-ta-go-ta prison, if ya didn't kill nobody?"

Mabel had touched a nerve in Wayne's psyche. "Mabel, I looks in the mirror, an' I sees the color of the man what raped my Great Grandma. I gotta look at it ev' day. I can't wash it off I look at the Color of mens like ya Unc' Gus, an' wish I looked more like them.

"I hate my Color. I hate what that shit means, Mabel. So, I put that shit on my body through hell. I went-ta prison-ta save-a real Brother-ya Unc' Gus. Them Crackers will lie in a minute ta save one-they own. He only did what I wish I could-a done, Mabel."

She shook her head at Wayne again. "Wayne! Unc' Gus ain't thinkin 'bout you. He talk 'bout you like you'sa dog. He say, he would-da never gone to jail for you.

"Ya done time for a crime ya didn't commit just-a spite ya own skin-color. Ya done near'bout got worked-ta death-for what? Wayne, that all sound a little crazy ta-me."

"Might be crazy to you, but I'd do it again ifn I could. We gotta get even with them Crackers. Malcolm X an' Elijah Muhammad was right. We gotta stop dyin' so much. We gotta start killin' a little more. Ev' one-a us gotta do his part. Don't matter what Gus think. I made a sacrifice for the cause. Didn't have nothin' toll-ta do with Gus, Mabel.

"Ya Son's generation go see things different than you. They ain't go take-a lotta shit that got shoved down our throats. I listen-ta the young Brothers that been comin '-ta the joint. They's on fire. A change go have-ta come."

"Wayne, I ain't go never 'gree with what ya done said. Killin' ain't the answer. We needs more Love in the World, not Hate, that's what I b'lieves," Mabel opined.

"Mabel, I bout-ta die of thirst for-a Budweiser. Gimme-a quart. I gotta go up yonder an' see Momma'nem. Oh, by the way-I heard that you an' Henry once lived in that old house over the hill from us. Is that right?"

Mabel scratched her head. "Yeah, that's right. What 'bout it?"

"A old witch use-ta live over yonder. I seen ghostes in the form of dogs, cats, and big snakes. I seen-a man with a goat's body from his waist down. Ya heard anythin' bout that?" Wayne asked.

She lied. Mabel said: "No. I ain' seen nothin'toll like that." She gave Wayne the quart of beer she had put into a brown-paper-bag. He ambled on out the door seemingly barely able to walk. The screened door slammed shut.

There was that Witch Story again. Billy decided that he was going to get to the bottom of it once and for all.

A couple of days after Wayne Nicholas's unexpected release from prison, Billy, after asking around discovered an old lady-who was then the widow of old Gilliam Langhorne. Her name was Martha. Her skin was raisin-colored, and wrinkled-up like a prune. She wore an old Maid's outfit every day. She even had a little white-bonnet on top of her braided-white-gray hair. Her voice had a scratchiness to it that made her sound wise.

Billy came up the steps to the full-porch, western-style. The whole house was like one seen on "The Bonanza" Western Sitcom. Mrs. Martha came out on the porch, all four-six of her. She wore a pair of brown lace-up old-ladies' comforts. She had a mouth full of perfectly preserved teeth that were as white as pearls.

"Hi, Billy. How are you?" What brings you over here on such a lovely evening?" Mrs. Martha asked. She sat in one of the metal-porch chairs and motioned for Billy to sit in one next to the one next to hers.

"Ma'am, I've been hearing stories about a Witch named Caroline who used to live over the hill over yonder from you. Do you know anything about her?" Billy asked.

"Yes-Lord. I sure'nough do. Child, you sit awhile and I'm gonna tell you the story:

"She's kin to a lady live up near Gravel Hill School, name's Betty Lou. Now, Betty Lou's Tom Wells's Sister. She married Han-y Lee, My Brother. The Witch's name was Caroline Anderson, but she was from a different branch of us Andersons. Billy, there's about ten or twelve different branches of Andersons. But we may all be kin in there somewhere.

"See, most of us Andersons come from slaves off the Furmans' Plantation back in the day. One of the owners of the Furman Farms, used to breed slaves. All of the bred slaves got the last name Anderson. Didn't matter who they was kin to. The slaves was bred like cattle or other livestock.

"One-a the Furman men took a slave gal and slept with her. The little gal got with child. The child grew up along with the Master's son. The old master put his teenage Son with his half Sister.

"That's what happen to Caroline's parents. For the children off the Furman plantation a lot of inbreeding had taken place among these slaves. Brother with Sister; Father with Daughter; and, Grandfather with Granddaughter. Got so most of the children born to them was mental 'flicted, y'kno' crazy. Then after the Civil War the inbreeding kept on going.

Caroline's messed-up crazy inbred-Father got to raping her. He was Caroline's half-White Brother. She got knocked up and had a Son by him. He named him, Waldorf Anderson, Jr. He was only mildly mental 'flcted.

"Caroline was not crazy at all. She hated her Grandma, Lola. She despised her Mother, Nola. And, y'kno' she had to hate her Daddy, Waldorf, Sr. To get even with everybody, Caroline sold her Soul to The Devil for Magical Powers. That woman became a Powerful Conjure Woman. She fixed a lotta mens around here, too.

"During one of her witchcraft rituals, Caroline got pregnant by her Son, Waldorf, Jr. She had to sleep with him to help make him a Warlock. Caroline had a perfectly beautiful little gal she named 'Angel.' A Warlock is a kind of head-witch.

"Soon after the birth of 'Angel' Waldorf, Jr. became a 'Pan Witch.'

He seduced women all over Fluvanna, every which way. Eventually, he murdered four well-bred Church Women.

"Tom Wells say, Caroline was ordered by Satan to sacrifice her Daughter to him as a burnt offering. If the child had-da been mental, or somethin', Caroline wouldn't have had a problem offering her to the Devil. But 'Angel,' they tell me, was gorgeous. Caroline tried to refuse Satan.

"Satan caused Caroline to turn into a ball of fire. She burnt right up. Strangest thing I heard of in the world. 'Angel' ended up with Caroline's Daughter, Eve."

Some kind of strange fear came up from the bottom of his stomach. "Mrs. Martha, what happened to Waldorf, Jr?" Billy asked.

"He remained a Forest Witch, 'A Pan,' I think you call them. He was messin' with half the White and Black women in Gravel Hill. Got to foolin' with four Church Ladies, They say, one of those was A'nt Betty Lou's gal, Tina Marie.

"One day, at a party Waldorf shot Tina, and three other women to death right in broad daylight. He ran into A'nt Betty Lou's house. That's the last anybody ever seen of Waldorf

"Unc' Harry Lee say Waldorf became some kind of Fake Preacher. Some say he joined a Witches Coven in New Orleans, Louisiana. Nobody knows whether he is living or dead to this day. They say Caroline fixed your Uncle Lin Jackson and A'nt Bessie, though.

"William, that's all I know about that old gal. She never bothered me none. I don't think she got hold of my husband, Gilliam-though he's a man, now. You gotta realize, Caroline was a high-yellar, pretty gal. She didn't look like the picture of witches you see today. That's the story, Son, go in peace."

Billy checked with Tom Wells, Unc' Harry Lee, and a number of other old people, and they verified portions of Mrs. Martha Langhorne's incredulous story.

So, what may have been going on, Billy surmised, was that his Mother and Father were full of Demonic Entities. They had moved into a house that was one of the Gateways to Hell! He was brought with them. Then, Dick and Bug were born in that old house. Momma got pregnant with Johnboy in that Godforsaken Den of Satan. "Have Mercy, Father Eloah!"

Billy finished that school year on Friday, June 10, 1963, one day before his sixteenth birthday. He was glad that this part of his life was coming to an end. It had been sixteen-years-of-horror.

But, in fourteen of those years, Billy never saw his Daddy hit Dick, Bug, Johnboy, Sammy Lee, Dave, Judy Mae, Jenny Ree, or Tuck. That night that thought alone made Billy weep like a spanked baby.

He got up early that next morning. He was sixteen. He was carrying that many years of emotional baggage around like a sack of heavy garbage.

Mabel fixed Billy a breakfast of scrambled eggs, bacon, hash browns, toast and jam, and a cup of black coffee. He ate hurriedly. Then, it was time to go.

He reached out and hugged his Ma. "No matter what happened, remember, I will always love you and my Brothers and Sisters. Kiss them for me Ma, when they wake up."

He headed for the backdoor. Billy carried a paper bag with a change of socks, drawers, and a single pair of pants and a shirt. He had outgrown or wore out all of his other clothes. He was leaving home with just about what he had come into this world with.

"Billy, I'm go walk with ya down ta-the bus stop. Wait-a minute. You's my oldest Son, my First-Born Leaving Home," Mabel said. The words came out like each one hurt her throat.

Mabel followed behind her Son with her eyes downcast, not uttering a word all the way to the bus stop. Then she sobbed a little, even though she was fighting back the tears.

As he waited for the bus, as painful as it would have been, Billy wished that his Dad would have come down that road and pled with him to come back and stay at home. He wanted to hear his Dad say, "Son, I'm sorry. I'm sorry for how I've mistreated you for all your life." And, Billy knew he would have forgiven his Father. He would have gone back home, finished school, and let the horrible bygones be bygones. But, the terrible moments ticked by, clicking toward another scenario altogether. He knew his Dad was not going to come and rescue him, and that hurt! He noticed that his Ma kept her eyes downcast like she blamed herself for everything that was going on. Tears eased down her dark-guilty cheeks. Then the bus came around the curve. "Take-care yourself, Son," Mabel whined. Her voice was no more than a whisper, like the wind in the trees after a bad storm ends.

"Okay, Ma." Billy said. He didn't hug his Mother goodbye. He got on the bus paid his fare and took a seat in the back of the bus. He sat down and immediately burst into a fit of crying. He took a sideways glance at his Ma. He extended that glance up the road toward his home. The bus pulled off and a new round of emotions came gushing up out of him through his tears. He was glad no one was sitting close enough to him to see how bad he was crying. After the bus had traveled about fifteen miles, Billy calmed down enough to stop crying.

"Hi, Buddy," Jack greeted his school chum. The bus had made a stop up where Route 53 dissects with Route 15. Jack had come to the back of the bus and sat beside Billy.

"Hey, man." Billy answered his friend back. They both remained silent on up the ten miles to Charlottesville. The bus station was now at a new location. It had been moved from downtown on the very East End up to Ridge and East Main. Everything was newly painted and shiny. There were now four loading docks and these were wider than the one in the old station. Billy had gotten his emotions together enough to ask Jack a very important question:

"Jack, where in the hell are we gonna live, man?"

Jack smiled. "Look, my-man-don't worry. I got that covered. My Uncle Bateman Moore and his wife, Loran Belle, live out on Ridge Street. They got a big-old house with lots of empty rooms because their children are growing up and moving on. We can rent one of those rooms. I already rapped to them. They charge five-a-week for the room and another two-fifty for meals if we want them. So, let's head on over there after checking in with Mrs. Shuffles 'nem up at the UVA"

"Aw-ight, my-main-man, lead the way," Billy chimed.

EPILOGUE

Billy was no longer content to be called, "Belly," as his name was pronounced in Fluvanna. He hated it too, that when he objected to being called "Belly," he was called, "Will James." He wanted to be called **"Bill"** or **"Will"** and or "William." But in Charlottesville, because of his nubby finger, he got the infamous nickname, "Fingers," which he hated worse than, "Belly."

Jack and William remained friends in Charlottesville for only a few weeks. They moved out of Mrs. Loran Paddy's house in one week, to rent a room together with a widow, Mrs. Eunice Lesley. She was a tall-stately, light-skinned, woman, with skin the color of orange-peels. Her shiny-black hair was in long locks down on her shoulders. Though she was still very attractive, her portly figure was wrinkling away. She owned a two-story brick house on Gordon Avenue.

Mrs. Lesley was an avid churchgoer. Billy heard her rehearsing hymns out of a green hymnal and figured she must be a member of the Choir at First Baptist Church up at Seventh and Main, the oldest Black Church in Charlottesville, where she attended.

In about two weeks after William and Maury had moved into Mrs. Lesley's spotlessly cleaned room with two single-beds, a bureau, and a chest of drawers, she suggested: "William. Maury. Y'all are too intelligent-looking to be out of school. If you are not going back to Fluvanna to school, you ought to consider finishing at Jackson P. Burley High.

"I know Mr. John Scott, the Principal, very well. I've talked to him about y'all, and he says you all can go to Burley this fall. All you got to do is have your Moms come up here and give me temporary guardianship of you all. Jack, I heard you and William talking about dropping out of school. Forgive me for eavesdropping. But I raised two boys of my own. One of them dropped-out of school. He's regretted that every since. Maybe you

465

all may have met them, Mann Atlas Lesley, the oldest one, and Ray-Ray Lesley, my youngest one. They're twenty-four and twenty-five years old now. The youngest one was the dropout. Oh-didn't meet them?

"Well, I'll be glad to help you all finish school. I've helped ten or so boys and girls get through Burley the same way. I'd be happy to get an appointment with Judge Melon Ziegler in Juvenile and Domestic Court so we can get you all enrolled at Burley this fall. What 'cha say?"

"Well. I do wanna finish school, Mrs. Lesley," William spoke enthusiastically. "Me too," Maury spoke very unenthusiastically.

Mabel James, Clarita Paddy, Mrs. Lesley, Maury, and William went before Judge Ziegler, in the Midway Building that housed the Juvenile and Domestic Court on the Comer of Garrett and Ridge Streets on this Monday morning.

The Judge had one badly crippled leg. He had braces on it but had a difficult time walking even with the aid of crutches. He looked scornfully around the courtroom at the people assembled before him, staring out of tiny-blue eyes that were like dots in his A-shaped head. He had very bushy-blond eyebrows that matched the color of his close-cut hair. He had a broad nose with big nostrils. With his slight mustache, he reminded William of a picture he had seen of "Groucho Marx." His dwarf-physique in a black robe made him seem ominous and scary.

William and all rose as the Judge entered the courtroom as the Bailiff had ordered. Before the Judge seated himself, he allowed: "I understand that we have one-a you Negresses who want to take charge of two Juvenile-Nigra Boys. I don't know what in the hell you want to do that for. But I can't stop you. So, I'm not going to try." He maneuvered into his leather-bound seat and coughed to clear his throat.

"Y'all may be seated, if you Niggers got sense enough to," croaked out of the side of the Judge's mouth like the croaking of a bullfrog.

Maury jumped up with his fists balled up. The Bailiff approached him. "Be seated, Boy," the Judge ordered, with a sneer. "Y'all are not in a Northern Court, now." Everyone sat down.

"You don't have to insult my Grandma like that," Maury snapped at the Judge.

"Boy, you must think you're up North or something. Now, you jump up one more time in here like that, and I'm going to send you to jail with the rest of those vagrant Negroes. All of y'all Coloreds stand and take the oath before me. I've signed those inferior papers so you can fast get your Black asses out of my courtroom." The Judge slammed his gavel hard on his desk.

They all took the oath-read by the Clerk. While leaving the courthouse, William wondered why that Judge had to be so mean. He was just plain and simply a White-Racist through-and through. He was probably taking his handicap out on Black people. William wished he could have made him Black for just a couple of days. That would change him-he bet. William hated the very sound of the name "Ziegler" forever after that infamous morning.

Maury attended Burley that fall during the 1963-64 school-year for just two weeks. He dropped-out. He and William went their separate ways. Burley was cramped and all, but William loved it. First of all, he was allowed to take a full Eleventh-Grade load of classes. Agriculture was not a required subject at Burley, and Shop was an Elective. So, William had only one English Class to make up. He was allowed to take Advanced English Composition and a Creative Writing class as well. He took Music Appreciation II, and an Art class. He loved Biology, and American Government Systems classes.

William bought decent clothing and looked good in them. He got along well with the other students, especially the girls-who thought he was He cute." Some would say, loud enough for him to hear them, "He's Country, but he's a Cutie." He held his head up high as he walked the shiny hallways at Burley. He made "A's" in all of his classes.

One girl started writing love-letters to William. Her name was Amy Greene. William was a little shy at first, but learned to relax a little around Amy. One day Amy invited William to walk her home. She lived only four blocks from Burley, up on Booker Street. Burley was on Rose Hill Drive and Henry Avenue, on Charlottesville's Northwest corridor.

When they got to Amy's white and green stucco house on Booker Street, she asked William to come in for a moment, because her Dad and Mom were at work. After William had come through the new screen-doors of this fine home into a spacious living room stocked with white leather sofas and end-chairs, Amy dropped her books on the floor, seized William and kissed him in the mouth. She put her tongue in his mouth and played with his tongue with hers.

The pretty light-brown girl with Eartha Kitt's eyes, Lena Horne's shape, and Dianna Ross's sexy-sounding voice whispered, "William, I love you. You are country-sweet, baby."

Amy got out of her blue short skirt. Then she undid her white blouse. She stood before William in her white bra and pink panties. At this point, William got an erection.

Then, Amy pulled off her bra. William was all right up to then. She grabbed William's left hand and placed that on her right breast. He was still all right with that.

"Pull my panties down, William. I'm all yours. I wanna be your girl. We can go-steady.

You are so cute," Amy crooned. William got nervous.

After William's hesitation, Amy pulled her own panties down, and stepped out of them. He panicked. Her naked Vagina reminded him of what he had seen of his Mother's. He didn't feel like having sex. Seeing Amy's fury V-shape-in-the-middle made William feel like throwing up. He turned and ran away. He felt embarrassed. He heard Amy laughing as he ran away from up on Booker Street. Then he ran down Preston Avenue, to Tenth Street Northwest, then to Gordon Avenue. He fell down across his bed. He knew that Amy was a popular girl. She probably was going to tell everyone "that he couldn't do it." He felt that he would never be able to hold his head up at Burley again, so he did not go back.

Mrs. Lesley evicted William after he fell into alcoholism. Out on the streets living from day to-day with the winos, William worked at day-jobs to earn enough money to buy cheap liquor, wine, and beer. Sixteen years of buried pain ached inside of William like Cancer. The Amy Greene debacle was not that big of a deal by itself But on top of all of the other pains from William's childhood, and that one time of seeing his Mother's nudity, had a tremendous psychological effect on him.

The pain-inside of William-had to be anaesthetized. Gallons of alcohol-even though he hated the taste and smell of it-were the anesthesia he thought he needed. He drank until he felt nothing. Then he sobered up. He had to get drunk all over again to get numbed again. He was in a vicious cycle. He ate very little in-between drinking spells. He became like skin and bones.

William's young body paid a toll for his rampant alcoholism. He started to experience stomach pains, tremendous headaches, and blurred vision even after he had been sober for a week. The rotgut beverages he gulped down were consuming him up from the insides out.

By 1966, William knew he badly needed a change of pace; a change of habits; and a changed mindset. He wanted a change of venue to some place where he could find an institution, a sanctuary, of sorts, to heal inside and out. He wanted to hear the soothing voice of someone who understood what he was feeling deep within his Soul. He wanted to go into military service.

The military rejected William because of his missing Trigger Finger. He drank himself into passing out for several days after hearing that he could never be a G.I. Recruit.

In 1966, after three-years of alcoholism, William joined the Job Corps to escape from what plagued his psyche, his Soul, and his Conscience. See, the main reason for so much of William's pain, was that Charlottesville was too close to Fluvanna, the origin of all of his mental and emotional pains. He asked the Job Corps authorities to send him as far away from Charlottesville as they possibly could. He was sent to an Urban Job Corps Center in Battle Creek, Michigan.

The Center was named, "Fort Custer Job Corps Center. It was underwritten by Kellogg's Cereals; Motown Records; Delci Chemical Corp; Ford Motor Company; and Kodak Inc. It received donations from the City Governments of Flynt, Detroit, Lansing, and Kalamazoo.

After sobering up, cleaning out, and getting straight, William took a battery of aptitude tests administered by Job Corps counselors. He was placed in a Clerical Trades Curriculum. The courses of study were after a module, self-pacing, schemata, to allow every individual a chance to develop at his own pace and to give him a chance to learn what to do to get better. Most of the Center's instructors were degreed volunteers. They had degrees in English, Math, Sociology, History, Philosophy, and psychology. The last case was very fortunate for William.

There were about twenty-thousand b9ys in the Center at the time William was there. Every race, creed, and color was represented. The instructors were likewise. Some instructors were retired from the military. Some had retired from academia, and some from The Central Intelligence Agency.

One such instructor as the above was Dr. Wolfgang Burger-Muller. He told William that he was an FBI retiree, who once worked for the Simon Wiesenthal Investigative Unit. He helped locate Nazis who had been smuggled out of Germany directly after World War II ended, and passed on that information to Simon Wiesenthal, who then passed it on to the Israeli Intelligence Agency. Dr. Burger-Muller's position in the FBI was highly classified. The FBI would not claim that he existed as one of its agents. Nor would it admit that it was connected with the CIA in running down Nazis to bring them to justice.

William talked to Mr. Wolfgang daily after class. He told William that he had been smuggled out of Lebenstein, near Munich, from a little farming village in Bavaria, by Mr. Amen Hans Von Hansel and his wife, Greta Frauen Von Hansel.

Mr. Wolfgang's family had been sheep-herders before the Nazis took over. When the SS came to arrest his family, Brothers Kurt, Benjamin, and Jacobi, and Sisters, Gloria, and Maria; his Father Jehu, and his Mother, Elizabeth; Wolfgang hid under the hollow flooring below the kitchen. There was a trapdoor inside of a closet that led to his place of escape. After the Nazi police left his farm, he escaped to a German family that lived over on the next hill.

The Von Hansels had two children, Adele and Hamlet. They had lost an older Son to Cholera just a couple of months before the Nazis stormed into Lebenstein. Because Wolfgang had similar features to the dead Edmund Pryor Von Hansel, and because the Burger-Mullers were such good friends with the Von Hansels, Mr. Von Hansel decided to flee his homeland, and to take Wolfgang along with him, posing as his "dead" Son.

Mr. Von Hansel was a prominent Lawyer before the Nazis took over. He took clients on a first-come first-served basis. He was under investigation for being a Communist sympathizer when the Burger-Muller Family was arrested, and a number of other Jewish families who lived in Lebenstein. They were herded onto trucks like cattle and just disappeared. Von Hansel's wife worked in his law office as his assistant. They knew very prominent German people who had been appointed to the upper-levels of the Nazi-government hierarchy. They were warned that an anti-communist sweep would probably lead to the Von Hansels' arrest. Mr. Von Hansel fled with his wife, two children, and Wolfgang.

Wolfgang ended up in New York via Switzerland. Mrs. Von Hansel had a degree in Psychology from the University of Berlin. Wolfgang learned to speak English in Switzerland, so he could go through school very rapidly in New York. He made high grades all through school and majored in Psychology at Columbia University. His "Sister," Adele majored in the Law, and so did Hamlet. All of them graduated with honors. They all secretly joined the Simon Wiesenthal Organization. They all pursued the whereabouts of Josef Mengele, and Adolf Eichmann. Dr. Burger-Muller retired without knowing success. (These were notorious Concentration Camp officials responsible for the mutilation, torture, and murders of millions of Jewish Inmates, including Dr. Burger-Muller's entire Family.)

On this morning, Dr. Burger-Muller called William aside and told him to see him in his office after classes that day. William wondered what he had done to deserve that. Usually that meant an Instructor was going to write someone up and give him a number of demerits. After classes William reported to Mr. Wolfgang.

"Have a seat, Wilhelm," Mr. Wolfgang said. He still had a slight-trace of a German Brogue. "I see you are looking downcast again. You have a lot of trouble in your heart, yah, Wilhelm. What is it that is bothering you so badly?"

Wolfgang had salt-and-pepper hair he wore like Albert Einstein wore his. He was broadly built and was seated behind a large-brown desk that all Job Corps' officials had. He would be just typically German, except that he had a prominent Abrahamic-nose. He had on a dark-blue suit like he always wore, and a pair of brown shoes. His silk-white shirt was opened at the collar but he sported a loosen-red tie.

Now, William felt like letting go of "all of the shit I've carried around inside of me for all of my life." He cleared his throat. "Dr. Burger-Muller . . . I'm just wondering if any of these classes is going to help me do any better in Virginia. When I go back there, Whites are going to still treat me like a 'Nigger,' like always. I'm too dark-skinned to fit into any of their Color based schemes. Schools down south have been desegregated, but nothing changed for a lot of people like me. I'll still being treated like an outcast by a lot of Blacks, and most Whites who are in power. Whites hate me because I'm Black and Blacks hate me because I'm too Black."

The old guy stood up and walked from behind his desk. "It's not what anyone thinks about you, Wilhelm. It's what you think about yourself This is most important. You are the one who must decide what you are going to do with your life, regardless of what anybody may think about you."

"My people came through slavery," William snapped. "As Field Slaves, we were taught to hate the House Servants. I came from Field Slaves, and unlike the House Servants, my people were not allowed to learn, or do anything. Then after the Civil War, we were just let go. We had nothing to start with, weren't given anything to work with, and were put back into enslavement by the 1890s. It's not my attitude that is at fault, here."

Dr. Burger-Muller turned suddenly to stare directly into William's eyes. Great excitement flashed across his ashy-white face. "Wilhelm ... "He slowly paced around the office but made sure that his eyes stayed fixed on William. "All of my people were killed by the Nazis ... Yah! I had to flee to America-a strange land-to stay alive. I do not know if there are any Burger Mullers still living in Germany. None of my letters have been answered.

"I will go back to Bavaria one day to see for myself if any of my people can be found. But I have not gone so far, because I suspect that I am going to be very disappointed.

"So, Wilhelm, I do the next best thing. I have and will always give-up most of my time and money for the hunting down of the Nazi killers of my people until the day I die. My people's blood cries to me from their graves and that is why I must do this," Mr. Wolfgang said. "What anyone thinks means nothing to me. Nor, should it matter to you."

He was moved by what Mr. Wolfgang said. But he said: "Doc, after all though, you are still a White guy," William uttered.

Dr. Wolfgang Burger-Muller shouted: "Wilhelm! Wilhelm! You must stop talking and thinking like that. A person's skin color should not matter. It is what is in his heart that counts. You cannot condemn an entire people because of the stupid actions of a few among them.

"This was what was the matter with Adolf Hitler. He was offended at

472

a Jew or two somewhere in his early life. His hatred for those drove him in an insane direction toward a holocaust, after he became Germany's Fascist-Nazi-Ruler, then he called for the genocidal removal of all Jews from Europe. No Jew did anything to Hitler worthy of that level of anger and his call for the mass-Extermination of Jews, and his working them to death in Concentration Labor-Camps in Poland and Germany; any more than the rape of a White woman by a Black man somewhere in the South called for the lynching of all Negro men in the South.

"All people are just different colors of Yahweh's Human Rainbow. We are all of one Race: 'The Human Race.'"

It dawned on William that what Mr. Wolfgang was saying was very significant. Jacob Stiles had White skin. He was not a racist. He was not hoarding thousands of dollars in the walls of his home. And, even if he were, that was no reason to rob and kill him.

The old man had tried to tell Gus and Wayne where his money was. He was sending it to the Simon Wiesenthal Fund to help find "Hitler's Nazi-Killers," and to help the victims of "Auschwitz."

What the old Doc had said got down into the bottom of William's heart. He heard him say, "Wilhelm, do you want me to help you?"

"Yes sir," William said with a sigh.

"I'm going to give you a booklist. All of the books on it are in our library. Read every book on the list. Come and discuss any one of them with me at any time. You are going to find out some wonderful things about Black people that I am sure you don't now know. What you find out will give you a better perspective on life and how to live it."

Dr. Wolfgang Burger-Muller had given him three typed pages, back and front. These were books from a wide variety of Black, Jewish, and White Authors. (And William Did Read.)

In January, 1967, William was nineteen-years-old. He had just finished the last Module for a Clerical Trades Certificate. He had one more Module to finish before taking his G.E.D. test. He would graduate in that coming March. Over the intercom this morning an announcement startled and angered everyone: "We will cancel classes for today. All Corpsmen must meet with the Administration in the Auditorium at Nine o' clock."

William cried that morning like he had when he heard that Diana Ross had married a White Dude. He did not want to hear that that Beautiful Black Woman was married at all-but to a White Man!

For some strange reason, the Federal Government was going to suddenly close Fort Custer Job Corps in 45-days. President Johnson had given the order. That was all that was said.

He would see Dr. Burger-Muller no more. The Job Corps focused on getting those who may be ready prepared to take the G.E.D. test at Western Michigan University. William was ready to take the test in February, 1967. He passed.

He left Fort Custer in late-February with a Clerical Trades Certificate, and his G.E.D. Certificate. Every one of his seven Instructors had written very encouraging recommendations that William should seek to enter a Community College, or a Historically Black College or University after leaving the Job Corps.

When William returned home to Fluvanna in February, it felt like springtime. He was so used to the cold winds in Michigan, until the climate felt very agreeable to him. He had had an allotment sent to his Ma of twenty-five dollars-per-month, while in the Job Corps. He sent another twenty-five-per-month of his own money and wrote a letter asking his Ma to put that aside so he would have a little nest-egg when he got back home. She wrote him a reply that she would comply.

The Monticello Community Action Agency (MCAA), of Charlottesville, had an office in Columbia, Virginia just across from Arthur Walton's Store. A Mrs. Susan Cason was the agent in charge. William talked with her about the possibility of going off to college. She said that she had some contacts and would ask around to see what she could come up with.

That next Monday, Mrs. Cason called William at home-by then that neighborhood had phone-lines installed-that she had found a Black College in Georgia that was willing to recruit him-providing that he came up with the first $250.00 of the payment towards tuition. Georgia State College would provide the rest. William asked his Ma for the nest-egg. In ten-months she should have about $250.00 saved.

Mabel's reply: "Billy ... I loaned out the money ta-a friend-a mine, ta-buy tires for 'is car." William blurted out: "Yeah-I bet! That friend was George Mayor-wasn't it?"

"Yep, George done me a lotta favors. I'll try-ta get-a loan from the Virginia National Bank in Fork Union. I got a hundred in savings up yonder. They'll just be loanin' me one-fifty," Mabel said.

William had all of his clothes together folded-up in his green duffle bag. He didn't expect the Bank would loan Mabel any money. William had a few dollars he had saved out of his remaining Thirteen-Dollars-per-month while he was at Fort Custer. He caught the bus to Charlottesville, this time he stood at the bus stop all by himself

He got a job at the University of Virginia, cleaning the showers in the girls' dorms. When he called home, his Ma told him the Bank had turned her down, and so had her Credit Union at Morton's Frozen Foods in Crozet, Virginia-at fifteen miles due-west of Charlottesville. William told her it was all right: "Forget about it Ma;' was William's reply. He slammed the phone down in his Mother's ear. He was wondering: "How could Dad be so ready to kill Bo Rabbit when he only suspected him of being with Ma? Now, he knows that George Mayor is seeing Ma regularly and Dad has never even confronted George. Was he scared of George- must be."

At his new address at Mrs. Sarfonia Jackson's boarding house at 405 Ridge Street, Southwest in Charlottesville, Mabel did send an envelope addressed to William James containing five twenty-dollar bills. That was the money he had told her to keep; but he did not send it back.

He gave up on the idea of getting a higher education. He went to work at the UVA Building and Grounds Department, to clean up the filth White Students left behind in their bathrooms, five-days-a-week. It paid $3.00-per-hour.

Finding himself back in Charlottesville amid familiar surroundings, and fellow drunks, William fell back into his old pattern, of drowning out his disgust and pains with gallons of cheap alcohol. He quit working at the UVA, found a job at a textile mill, called Ix's that manufactured silk cloth.

Inside of Ix's the temperature went from 70 degrees to 125 degrees. The noise was ear splitting, and the floors seemed to be slippery in a lot of places. The work was backbreaking. William had to tote spools of cloth that weighed fifty to a-hundred pounds from the looms to a checking room, where women examined the cloth for flaws. The job paid just Five Dollars an hour: $200.00-per-week. William quit after just two weeks. Ix's paid every two weeks. It had its own business and accounting office on premises, so there was no waiting period. William got his only check from them and was glad to be getting out of that hell-hole.

He had cleared a little over $350.00 at Ix's. He knew that wouldn't last long, even though Mrs. Sarfonia only charged fifteen dollars a-week. He searched for a job all over Charlottesville, in Clerical Trades. He was told he was "Unqualified," or "Overly-qualified," and or, "We're looking for just the 'Right Person' (or White Person) for this Job Opening. We will keep your application on file for thirty days. We will call you if an opening meeting your qualifications should arise. Thank You for Thinking of Us!" William got tired of that shit. He had to find some work before his money ran out and he found himself out in the streets.

He went to the University of Virginia's Employment Department on the corner of Madison Lane and West Main Streets. He filled out a long-detailed Application. He stated that his preferences were Clerical Trades. He sat out in a large waiting room full of White people seeking a job. All of them were interviewed and hired before him. A fat-jolly-looking man wearing a black suit finally came to talk to William.

"Hi there, Mr. James," The Pillsbury Dough Boy-looking man said. "I'm Mr. Pressley.

Please to meet you."

The guy stuck out his fat right-hand. William shook it. The fatty wiped his right hand with a white handkerchief and threw it into a nearby trashcan. "The only job we have open is Janitorial. I see you have done that before. Now we don't pay as much as Ix's. We only pay about half that. $2.35-per-hour until your six months evaluation, then we will raise you a quarter at a time. You will be on weekly pay without benefits until after one-year of good service. Then we will put you on the semi-monthly, every-two-weeks, pay-scale. You will get paid on the first and sixteenth of each month. Then you will get sick-leave, and a one-week vacation every year."

William was disgusted as hell with Pressley. But he needed a job. "Yep. I'll take it," he groaned.

"Go over to McCormick Road. In the basement of Bonnie Castle Dorm, you will find the clothing department. They will have to measure you for your uniforms-we furnish those. You can pick up clean ones every Friday. Or, you can wash them at home.

"Take this Memo with you. Give it to Mrs. Fran Rufus. She's the Maid in charge of giving out the clothes. On your first day of work, we will let you go over and pick up your uniforms. We expect you to show up dressed in one every day after that." Pressley walked away after he said that.

He took the Memo over to the Dorm, got measured, and it made him feel like a head of hog getting its ear stapled for identification. But he signed the slip Mrs. Rufus presented to him. He was given the right to wear a gray uniform with red-lettering (UVA) on the pockets of the shirts. What was ludicrous was that a black tie was part of the uniform. William wondered what in the hell that was for. When he got dressed in his uniform, he felt like he looked like a convict, or something. But that was life, as it were.

On this weekend, William walked up Ridge Street. He got to a boarding house on the corner of Garrett and Ridge Streets. It stood directly across from the Fire House.

This beautiful light-brown-skinned girl was sitting on the steps of her brick house smiling at William as he bopped along. She had long-black hair hanging down her back. Her pretty brown eyes seemed to sparkle when William stopped in front of her to speak. Sitting down, she seemed like she would stand at about five-three or so tall. She was slim but shapely. She looked like a grown-up version of Alize.

"Hi pretty lady," William said. He knew it sounded tacky, but-hey, that's how the homeys in Michigan used to rap.

"Hi. Who are you? I don't remember seeing you around here. Are you from Charlottesville?" the lady asked.

"No, I'm actually from Fluvanna. My name is William. What's yours?"
"I'm from Madison. My name is Sarah Hill. Please to meet you."

William was smitten by her beauty, and soft-spoken voice. He loved her tiny hands and feet.

He loved her bodily curves. He loved too how she never pushed herself on him.

Once he sneaked her into his room at Mrs. Sarfonia's, William overcame his fear and dread of a woman's naked body. He made love-at first-to Sarah in the dark. After a few times he discovered that he could look at her completely nude, and he still desired her, and the sight of her did not make him want to throw up. It got so, William hated to go home and leave Sarah after a date. He wanted her to be with him always. In July, 1968, William asked: "Sarah, will you marry me?"

"First, I got to take you to Madison to meet my Mom. I told her about you and she said she wants me to bring you and let her and the family meet you before I got any more serious about you. I love you very much, but I won't marry you if my Mom doesn't approve of you," was Sarah's reply to William's request.

William agreed to go to meet Sarah's Mom. He bought the first two-piece dress-suit he had ever owned. He got a blue tie with orange pheasants imprinted on it. He found a pair of patent leather shoes, too, at Sears and Roebucks up on West Main.

On this Saturday morning Sarah and William caught the N01thbound Local at the Trailways

Station in Charlottesville. It put them in Madison in twenty minutes. At the Madison General Grocery Store they got off the bus and a young man in an Army uniform was waiting for them in a New Roadrunner Plymouth. They got into Sergeant Joseph Lee Hill's car, and he zipped them up the curvy four miles to where Sarah had grown up.

Sarah had grown up in her Grandmother's home. Sarah resembled the lady they all called, A'nt Janie. She had been married to Lee Rucker, Sarah's Grandfather, for over fifty years. Then William had the great pleasure of meeting Maude Hill, Sarah's Mother. She was a rotund, light brown-skinned woman in her f01ties. She had light-brown eyes, and resembled a darker-skinned version of a picture William had seen of Queen Elizabeth.

The first thing that got William's attention about Maude was how jovial she was. Her husband, Sarah's Father Winfield, Sarah had told William, passed away when Sarah was fourteen. He had been dead for eight years. Maude had moved in with her Father, Lee, and Mother, Janice Rucker.

Maude had six children. She lost two of them in a few years to an epidemical illness. They were Robert Lewis and William Smith Hill. The illness fell upon Sarah's Sister, next to her, Johanna. It left her somewhat disabled. Joe was unha1med, as well as Sarah Elizabeth, and the youngest child, Mary Louise. With that much tragedy in her life, it was inconceivable to William how Maude Elizabeth could laugh, joke and make everybody happy like she did.

SFC Joe Hill was stationed at the Pentagon. He was quiet and stand-offish towards William like he didn't like him, at first.

The table that evening was full of fish, lamb, beef, pork chops; collard greens, green beans, mashed potatoes, and candied yams; and apple, coconut, and chocolate pies; as well as coconut covered and chocolate-icing cakes. William had never seen that much of a variety of food on the table in front of him at once in his life. Unc' Lee said the Grace, and everyone passed every platter by everyone. William didn't eat that much. He was trying to be "proper."

That night, Grandma Janie made sure that William and Sarah slept in separate beds. "Y'all ain't married yet. In my house, only husbands are allowed to sleep with their wives," A'nt Janie allowed. "If you wanna sleep with her, marry her, William." Everyone had a good laugh.

Joe took them to the bus stop early that next morning to catch the Southbound Local back to Charlottesville. Once they were back to town, William made rapturous love to Sarah. He slipped into Sarah's room this time. The other girls were out for the day. While he held her in his arms feeling like she was the most beautiful woman in the world, he asked her, "Baby, are you gonna marry me?"

"Yes, William," she said, with a schoolgirl-like giggle. "Yes, what, honey?" William asked the love of his life.

"I'll marry you. My Mom loves you. Joe doesn't think you're good enough for his Sister but he always say that about the boys I have dated. Grandpa Lee, said he would reserve judgment. Johanna and Mary think you are very cute. Granny wishes you were saved and in a Church somewhere. Other than that, she thought you were a good enough fellow-better than most she's seen me date.

"So, William, Darling, let's get married. I love you."

William was turned on all the way. He couldn't get enough of Sarah. She was on his mind like nothing else in all of his life.

On August 5, 1968, William and Sarah got married at Mount Zion Baptist Church in Charlottesville. Reverend William Hamilton performed the ceremony. A friend that William had met a couple of times, Tony

Ragland, was the witness. William couldn't wait for, "Now, you may kiss the Bride." He did, he did, and he did!

Sarah was a Nurse's Aide at the University of Virginia Hospital. William was a Janitor. Facing the fact that he may be stuck in a menial job for the rest of his life; and the fact, too, that his wife made two-dollars more an hour than he, frustrated William to no end.

They rented an apartment at 526 Ridge Street, a three-room suite, consisting of a bedroom, a half-living room, and a small kitchen. They rented from a Mr. Otis Lee. Sarah told William, "Honey, I think I'm pregnant, in 1969.

"Baby, we gotta get more space. This is no place to bring a baby back to."

Sarah agreed. They moved to a little larger apartment up in the University area at 101 Woodrow Street. Apartment 3. Shortly after they moved to the new place, Sarah lost her baby. It was a boy. Losing that child nearly tore the mental insides out of William. He went on an alcoholic binge, staying dead-drunk for two weeks.

William started yelling, screaming, and cussing at Sarah, and blaming her for everything he thought was going wrong-including losing their first child. What William was becoming was a replica of his Dad.

One day he caught a glimpse of himself in a mirror fussing at Sarah, who sat in the front room crying, but not uttering a word back at her husband, and the negative image of himself shocked the hell out of William. He saw his angry, mean, Daddy, staring back at him. He wondered how Sarah could have remained the kind, patient, loving, person she had been for three years, and put up with the likes of him. But, somehow, she had. She must have inherited that spirit from her Mother, Maude.

On June 11, 1971, while Sarah was about seven months pregnant, she baked a chocolate cake for William's birthday, and before going off to work, she gave him a new watch. "Here, Honey," she chimed, as she handed her husband a colorfully-wrapped package, with a red-ribbon and bow around it.

William hurriedly unwrapped the package to find a golden Bolivar Watch inside. It touched William's heart. He knew that she had to have been saving for a long time to be able to afford that watch.

Tears came to William's eyes, because he hadn't remembered Sarah's Birthdays, their Wedding Anniversaries, or anything like that. In fact, William realized that he had been entirely selfish and arrogant in the way he had been treating Sarah. He felt as though the stress he had been causing Sarah may have contributed to her miscarrying their first child.

With tears running down his cheeks, he called his pretty wife back from the front door. "Baby, come back for a second. Please ... I love you," William said, with his voice choking from emotions. He watched his petite little wife trot back towards him wearing her green and yellow Nurse's Aide Uniform.

"What's the matter, William?" Sarah asked, blinking her light-brown eyes in her customary way like an excited little girl. She smiled pouting her rosy-pink-colored lips.

William bear hugged her. "Baby-I'm sorry. I've been a no-good husband. Been just like my Daddy. But I'm gonna change--right now! I swear to you, from this day forward, I'm going to spend the rest of my life making it up to you for the lousy husband I've been to you for the last three years. Sugar, I love you so much-and I know I don't deserve you," William cried out of his heart to his wife.

Sarah clung to her husband. She had a big emotional outburst. "William, I'm so happy to hear you say that. Darling, I needed to hear you say that. See, I couldn't go on like we were going. I want to be with you, though. I want to stay with you-I love you too much to be without you; but I couldn't take it anymore. I needed to hear you tell me how much I meant to you. I needed to hear you say you love me. I needed to"

"Hush, Baby. I know, I know. I can feel you. Every word you're saying, I feel it way down deep inside. I promise you things are gonna be different," William answered his trembling wife.

They kissed a long, searching kiss, clinging to each other, both crying and searching each other through their kisses, then, Sarah ran out the door saying, "Thank you God for saving my Marriage!"

William sat down on the sofa. He knew inside that he had to quit a lot of things: smoking, drinking, the other women he'd slipped around with, and hanging around with the cut-ups he called his "Boys-his, Walk-Partners." He made up in his mind that day he was truly going to turn over a New Leaf.

On August 21, 1971, Sarah did the most fantastic thing in William's life. She brought into this world a beautiful, brown, little girl that William named, Deloris Anne'.

William stood outside of the UVa' s Nursery on South-One staring through the viewing window at his little baby girl lying in one of the many basinets. She was up on her knees sucking on the top of her left knuckles, rocking herself to and fro. His heart literally melted. He had never seen anyone, or anything, so beautiful in all of his life. He cried out aloud:

"Thank You, God!" He wiped the tears from his cheeks and whispered to God: "I promise You, I'll be a perfect Father to this little girl You have given us. For her sake, I'll be a changed man. I will learn to do all of the things I don't know how to do now to guide this Child in the right way, I promise You, God!"

He ran back to the recovery room where Sarah was lying on a cot in a little-bit of a daze from the medication she had been given. William kissed her face and spoke excitedly. "Thank you, Sugar, for giving me such a lovely Daughter. Thank you, Honey!" he said. Sarah had been through a difficult delivery. She was so much in a daze she didn't respond to William. She just opened and closed her eyes ever so slightly. William decided he would go and let her rest.

William quit his job at the UVA. He got hired as a Short-Order Cook at The Howard Johnson Motor Lodge on the 1300 Block of West Main Street in Charlottesville. He worked the 6:00- 2:00 AM. Morning-shift, Monday-through-Saturday. Sarah worked the 3:00-through-11 P.M. Evening-Shift with varying days off. William made $4.50-per-hour as his starting salary-a dollar increase over his pay at the UVA. Sarah made $5.00-per-hour at the UVA. William didn't sweat it because he figured he would catch Sarah's salary and pass it in a year, or so.

He was content to spend every evening with Deloris. William told Sarah not to have any more children so that he could properly spoil his little "Lo-Lo."

"No," Sarah replied. "I'm not gonna raise no spoiled child. We're going to have at least one more."

"All right," William said. "But the second one has to be a Boy, though."

"William, the second one will be whatever God sends us," Sarah said.

When Deloris was going on two-years old, Sarah announced, "William I checked with my gynecologist and she confirms that I am pregnant."

William waited patiently for the second child to arrive. It did on March 15, 1973. Sarah had another girl. She named her Barbara Elizabeth. She was another beautiful little girl that looked a lot like her Great Grandma, Janice. William was disappointed for a second, but was thankful to God that Barbara made it here healthy and alive. She was a breach-birth. The doctors were able to turn her around and they unwrapped the placenta from around her neck. Both Sarah and Barbara survived the ordeal. William realized that this child was more than a Miracle from God. She looked like an Angel. From day one, she was a happy-smiling, cuddly-child. William nicknamed her, "Bee," because she did resemble a big bumblebee.

Bee's birth signaled to William that it was time to seek Divine Guidance in his life. A disgruntlement with management at the Howard Johnson Motor Lodge caused William to quit his job. He had only gotten a twenty-five cents raise when he felt he should have gotten a dollar.

He went back to the UVA Building and Grounds Department. He was assigned to cleaning the new girls' dorms. His starting salary was $5.50-per-hour. He was still a dollar behind Sarah. He hated that.

Shortly after the birth of Barbara, William looked around for a church to join. He suffered withdrawal for about two weeks, but was able to quit smoking cold-turkey. He had no trouble quitting alcohol. He saw a sign on an old dancehall door that he once visited on Friday nights, at the Odd Fellows Hall on the Corner of Preston Avenue and East Jefferson Streets downtown in Charlottesville. The sign said: "True Holiness Apostolic, Inc. Bishop Robes Mack Pastor.

By the time Bee was ready to come home from the hospital, William had joined the Holiness Church. He had his fill of the Baptist Church in Fluvanna. He heard his Dad, Grandpa, and other people downplay all of the local churches in Fluvanna. So, he had no intentions of joining such a Church in Charlottesville.

He discovered that Bishop Mack's headquarter Church was the one downtown. It was in a storefront he rented from the Odd Fellows. At the time Bishop Mack had about a-hundred members at his Charlottesville location.

William moved his family from Woodward Street to Lankford

Avenue. He rented a four room apartment from Mr. Nate and Mrs. Alia Perlman, the richest Black landowners in the Charlottesville-Albemarle area. Lankford Avenue is on the Southeast Corridor of the Charlottesville area. It is off of Cherry Avenue. (Most of that area was sold to the Perlmans after the first Black family had moved onto Lankford Avenue in 1968. Nate got the property for about fifty-dollars-per acre. He acquired a couple of thousand acres at that time.)

William was still in walking distance to his job and so was Sarah. He was also in walking distance to his Church. The problem:

The place William and Sarah rented on Lankford was once a "White Only" Grocery Store owned by the Perlmans before desegregation mandates demanded that they serve Blacks. All of the Whites moved out of the neighborhood. The one-bedroom house was in bad need of repairs. It needed to be modernized and winterized. When the cold wind blew in the winter it came right through the walls of the house. Complaints to the Perlmans were ignored. William and Sarah stayed in the place because the rent was only fifty-five dollars-per-month. They paid twice that up at Woodward.

William learned to drive soon after he moved to Lankford Avenue. He bought an old-used Ford Falcon for $100.00. He knew a local service station owner who helped him get that old car running like new. (One of Sarah's cousins taught William how to drive.)

By the winter of 1973, William had quit the UVA again. This time he got a job at Morton Frozen Foods in Crozet, a fifteen-mile commute up 250 west. He was an Industrial Cook at Morton's. The position paid Seven Dollars fifty cents-per-hour, with free health benefits for him and his family. Things seemed to be going on the up and up, at first, on the new job, and in the Church. The job paid William a dollar more than Sarah made. That made him very happy.

The first eight or nine months of worshiping with True Holiness were quite an experience for William and Sarah. They had never witnessed the free-wheeling spirituality of absolute charismatic splendor they experienced in that Congregation. Bishop Mack was a young forty something man. So was his wife. On the surface Sister Elvira was a light-skinned beauty with a smile that could melt an ice-mountain. She had natural good-looks that were apparent because one could not spot any makeup on her face at all.

She was soft-spoken and causal when speaking to people about sometimes very caustic problems in their lives. She wore very modest dresses and clothing very befitting of a Church lady; but, she sold Avon Products.

Elder Mack, her husband, was a carbon-copy of Daddy Grace and Father Divine. He dressed in very flashy suits, ties, and jeweled cufflinks. He wore the latest shoe styles, seemingly a new pair each and every week. During the day he worked at a Leggett's Clothing Store. He got his suits, silk-shirts, ties, and shoes at low discounted prices. He looked more like a movie star than a Pentecostal Bishop.

Elder Mack had Churches in South and North Carolina, Florida, New York, and New Jersey. All were storefront establishments; and all had Pastors who had been hand-picked by Bishop Mack. Those in the South were his wife's relatives: her Brother in North Carolina; her Cousin in South Carolina; and in the North, her Sister in New York; and another Cousin in New Jersey. So, Elder Mack was not rich but not poor either.

It was rumored that Bishop Mack was involved in a number of trysts in his Church in Charlottesville, and sometimes, with young women in some of his other Churches. William knew that such rumors always circulated among the members of any Pastor's Congregation, and was usually nothing but idle gossip. But-

While at work one day, William had an unusual experience. He found a comer in the men's room off from the shower, in a closet, where the cleaning equipment was stored. He prayed instead of eating lunch that day. He felt strange all over after he finished praying. The feeling would not stop for the rest of the afternoon.

At about three that afternoon, William looked out of the window on the North Side of the building at a large Magnolia tree. He felt a tingling all over his body. He saw a large ball of fire burning in the middle of the tree. It was raining a downpour outside. The fire should have been extinguished. But it blazed despite the rain.

The blaze quieted down. It became two smaller flames. Then it disappeared. "Father, I have just had my first Vision. Please grant me an understanding of what You are trying to tell me, Your Humble Servant," William prayed. He was nervous as could be. When God sends a Vision, terrible things are getting ready to be unfolded. William wondered how he figured in all of that-he was trying to live as best he could, ever since the birth of Bee.

The Vision troubled William, but he had not been told to tell Sarah about it, so he kept it to himself That night he could not get to sleep at first. He got up in the middle of the night and prayed. When he got back into bed, he dropped into an immediate deep-sleep.

William had a vivid, realistic, dream. In the dream he saw the Bishop, and all of his ministers, missionary women, and choir members in the Church, between the pews engaging in every wanton, lascivious, and lurid sexual act known to man-hetero-and-homosexual embraces as well as sodomy with inanimate objects. The vivid dream shocked William awake.

He fell back to sleep immediately. This time Elder Mack stood in the door of the Church blocking William's entry into the sanctuary. "Get out! Go! Don't you ever come back! I don't want you anyway-I want your wife," the Bishop screamed at William. He stood at the entranceway of the Church and watched Elder Mack return to the orgy as before. He made perverted love to several young women among the pews of the Church, speaking in tongues, and jumping up and dancing and shouting every now and then after each round of unbridled and oral lusts.

He tried to do the right thing. William decided he would tell Elder Mack the whole contents of the dream. He got a special meeting with the Bishop. It was at the Pastor's study after the Sunday Morning Service. He told the Bishop what he had seen in the dream, scene-for-scene.

Elder Mack jumped up and got very close to William. He yelled: "You have been possessed by a 'Demon of Confusion.' You must never tell anyone about this dream because you may cause them to also be confused.

"You go get on your knees and ask God to Cast that Demon Out of your heart. Ask Him to Erase the very thought of that dream out of your Mind, Body, and Soul," Elder Mack ordered William to blaspheme.

For days, William prayed harder and harder, but the essence of the dream persisted in plaguing his mind. Then he fast three-days and three-nights, praying at the top of every hour during the night while fasting; but the contents of the dream became more vivid, more alive, and would not go away.

Just before Christmas, William, with a troubled heart and vexed mind, decided he would go out early one morning and pray until God either took the dream away, or took him away, one or the other. William went to the Dam in Albemarle County. On the banks of the river he prayed.

In what seemed like a few minutes, William felt that same sensation he had felt that day at Morton's, only this time it was way more profound. He felt like he had become weightless. He was praying near a little stream running down hill out of the Rivanna River. Looked to William like the stream reversed its course and ran up hill instead of down it. Then, William heard the voices of millions of people praying. A massive chorus of voices went up, then a voice that was smooth, mellow, peaceful, and full of Divine Love, spoke to William's Soul.

"LITTLE WILLIAM, THERE IS SO MUCH YOU DON'T KNOW. SEEK KNOWLEDGE. COME TO KNOW WHO YOU ARE; AND WHY YOU ARE ON THE EARTH. I WILL GUIDE YOU; AND MY GUARDIANS WILL PROTECT YOU. NOW GO, AND BE."

"Father, please, I don't want to go. Let me stay here. Let me "

"YOU HAVE A LIFE TO COMPLETE. SO, BEGONE!" The still, quiet, soothing voice said.

William found himself again of his right mind. He realized he was running around in a circle, screaming "HalleluYah! Gloria Yah! Gloria!" Then he spoke in many other languages that he understood at that moment. He was laughing and crying at the same time. He was dancing like his life depended on it. He remembered:

I can see all around me at the same time. I can see the earth's future unfolding-events, wars, devastation, famine, and the End of this Age. I can see a New Beginning. I know everything there is to know about Mankind, the animals, and science. I can see the people all around me what they have done, is doing, and will do. I understand all mysteries in the earth. Then he was suddenly back fully in his Human Understanding. His Prophetic Mind was almost gone, only bits and pieces remained.

Then there was the realization that if someone had seen him that morning, William knew he would have thought he was insane. He looked at his watch. A light coating of snow had fallen, but the sun was shining brightly, melting it. What had at first seemed like a few minutes had actually been several hours. He had started at seven in the morning. It was twelve o'clock.

Once the Spirit subsided, for some reason, William became extremely afraid. It felt like he had to get away from that place as fast as he could. He ran the hundred yards to where he had parked his Falcon, got into it, cranked it up, and sped away like someone might come after him.

William felt like something weird had just happened to him, because he was no Prophet, High-Holy Saint, or Great Church-Leader. So he had to wonder why God had chosen him to have such an Epiphany. He drove home as fast as he could.

When William got home that afternoon he knew there was something he had to get out in the open. When he looked at Sarah, he knew he was not looking at the same woman he had been looking at before. A strange but compelling anger surged up in his stomach. A slew of intimate questions plagued his mind.

As William ate brunch, he asked Sarah, "Sugar, you need to level with me. There's something awful standing between us-a terrible secret. What is it? What have you done? Have you been unfaithful to me? Out with it-let's hear what it is. We cannot go forward until we truly clear the air," William said.

The questions seemed to prick Sarah's conscience. Tears came down her rosy cheeks, as she cleared the brunch dishes aside. "William ... I ... I once had an affair," she moaned.

William jumped up from the table. "What?" he exclaimed. "With whom?"

"A. Yates. I was lonely. You were gone all the time. I thought you were gonna leave me. It seemed like you didn't love me anymore. I knew you were seeing other women.

"I gave in to this man I didn't care that much about one night at work. He came up to our apartment on Woodward a couple of times before I realized I couldn't go on with him because I loved you too much. Can you forgive me?" Sarah whined.

William ran over to his grieving wife. He seized the short-sleeves of her blouse. "Where does this scoundrel work? Who is he? Why did you screw him in our home in the bed that we shared? What kind of a slut are you, Sarah?" he snapped at her.

"I'm not a slut, William. You were gone most of the time out drinking with your friends. I had to sit at home alone, wishing I could just see you time and time again. Some man came along with a kind voice. I had sex with that more than with him. I didn't love him-he doesn't mean anything to me. Now that I think about it, I don't know what got into me. The last time he approached me, I told him to get out of my face, or I would tell my husband. That's been several months ago.

"I'm so sorry, William. I messed up. I let a Night Supervisor in Housekeeping step into our lives just like that. I'm not a whore. I promise you, and God, I swear I will never do that again.

"We got girls to raise, William. I don't want us to breakup for their sake. They need their Daddy-you know that. What are we gonna do? Just tell me what you want to do."

William ran out of the house and on up Lankford to Ridge, wondering what in the hell was he going to do now. He understood what his Grandpa and Father went through. Sarah's confession had hit him like a huge stone hurled into his face at full-force.

He wandered the streets of Charlottesville for three days and nights half out of his mind from the emotional distress, inner-turmoil, and psychological pain. He didn't want to end up like his Father, Grandfather, and Great Grandfather had. Yet, he realized that he had been largely responsible for setting the stage for the same adulterous things to tear-up his piece of mind, and good-feelings about life. There was a war going on inside of William.

One side of his nature wanted to kill Sarah. The other side wanted to forgive her, for she was just being human, and he had made his bed hard, and now he had to lay in it. Words like "Slut," and "Whore," came up in his first mind. Words like "Victim," and "Wife," swirled around in his second state of mind. Then That Still, Small, Smooth, Voice, spoke: "LITTLE WILLIAM, GO HOME TO SARAH YOUR WIFE. BE RECONCILED WITH HER FOR SHE IS A GIFT TO YOU FROM THE ELOAH EL SHADDI."

The mental funk broke at that point. After three days and nights had passed, William stumbled home exhausted. He had remained stone-sober, never even considered taking a drink of alcohol. For him, that was most extraordinary. For whenever he had faced a difficult situation in the past he got drunk-real drunk.

He walked through the front door, took one look at Sarah, and "The Forces of Evil," got a hold on him, right away. He grabbed his little wife, slapped her several times in her face, and hit her with his fists a couple more times. Sarah's lips were swollen and bloodied. He put his hands around her throat and started to choke her. Then it dawned on William what he was doing. He released his grip on his wife's throat.

Sarah coughed then spoke in a garbled whine: "I promised God, that if He forgives me this time, I'll never do anything like that to you again. But if you want to kill me-go ahead. I won't fight you. 'Until Death We Do Part.'"

Her words stopped William dead in his tracks. He wept like when his Dad had whipped him with a switch. Sarah had not struggled against him. She didn't try to scratch him. She didn't try to hit him-nor did she scream. She had been knocked to the floor. She laid on it crying and snuffing her nose like a little girl. "Don't hit me in the mouth again, William," Sarah begged.

"Sugar, I'm sorry. I must be some kind of monster or something. I had no right to hit you like that.

"See, I'm guilty of adultery myself. I've been with Josephine C. I've been with Frances N. too, many times. I left you alone to sneak around to be with them. If you can forgive me, Baby, I have forgiven you. Let's start over. Now, I know what being a cheat feels like."

"I forgive you, William, even for beating me. My Mom never beat me, nor did my Daddy.

Let's be kind to each other from now on," Sarah spoke through swollen lips.

Inside of William he heard the Voice: "TAKE STOCK OF YOUR WAYS. YOU WILL RECEIVE CHASTISEMENT, FOR YOU HAVE LAID HANDS ON A CHILD OF THE MOST HIGH." (Elder Mack lost all of his Churches for fornicating with Church-Ladies.) William clung to Sarah. She hugged him back. Then, William whispered into her ear:

"Sugar, I want you to get pregnant again, and this time, have a Son."

"William, I can get pregnant again. But I can't promise you a Son.

Only God can promise you that. So don't hold it against me ifl fail," Sarah said.

"Okay," William said. "Nothing will fail you but a try.

"Baby, lemme get some ice for your lips. I'm so sorry," William said.

In 1975, with Sarah pregnant a fourth time, William had gotten tired of floating from menial job to menial job. He heard of the construction of a new community college: Piedmont Virginia Community College.

In SEPIA Magazine William saw an application for a Basic Educational Opportunity Grant (BEOG). It paid tuition and fees for higher education at the community college level. An applicant had to be enrolled and accepted into a program of study at a college to qualify for a grant. William had traded in his old Falcon for a New Ford Grand Torino. He filled out the enrollment application at PVCC for the 1974-75 school year. William heard back from BEOG in two weeks. He got a $1,500 Grant. The School matched that with a Supplemental Educational Opportunity Grant (SEOG), for two-hundred dollars-per-year.

William dropped out after only one quarter. It was hard to work and study at the same time. But PVCC arranged for William and his wife to work at PVCC as Janitors as Work-Study for William, and a fulltime job for Sarah. He reenrolled at PVCC in 1975.

Sarah had a Son for William on August 12, 1975. He babysat the children in the evenings and Sarah was home during the daytime. He named his Son, William Anderson James, Jr.

All that stuff about race and fearing White Women, William had to make quite an adjustment.

Black men and White women walked around on the Campus of PVCC arm-and-arm every day. One of the faculty, a White Man, was madly in love with another faculty member, a Black women. So, William had to learn to accept interracial relationships.

William had no trouble adapting to the academics at PVCC. With the proper support and encouragement, he became an exceptional student. In 1977 he earned his Associate in Science in Liberal Arts Education. He was encouraged by many of his instructors to seek a higher degree at perhaps a four-year College or University.

He enrolled at Virginia State College in 1977. William and Sarah transported their family to Hopewell, Virginia. They lived at about ten miles from VSC. William met many inspirational people and professors at VSC: such as Dr. Edgar Toppin, and Dr. Oscar Williams in History. He met Dr.'s Perry, Goldberg, Thomas, Baez, and Braxton. These instilled in William that he should seek the highest college degrees (MA, PhD) because of his innate abilities.

William received his BA degree in American History in 1979 at VSC. The College became a University that same year. In 1980, he received his MA degree from VSU. He then enrolled at the University of Virginia that was by then completely desegregated.

In March, 1980, William received a letter inviting him to come to The Corcoran Department of History at the UVA to see Dr. Joseph Miller, Chairman of the Graduate Committee of the Graduate School of Arts and Sciences (GSAS). After that meeting, he was admitted into the UVA as a graduate student.

On the day that William went to meet with Dr. Miller he had an unforgettable experience. Miller's office was on the first floor of Randall Hall. Miller gave William a form he had to take to Dr. Carl Brauer, the Recent American Historian. He had an office just up the steps on the second floor of Randall Hall.

William hurried out of Miller's office and on up the steps at the east end of the building. At the top of the second floor landing were four students. Two of them were a young woman and man who were unquestionably Whites. Two of them were a young man and a young woman who were "mixed."

The mixed young woman had very kinky-reddish-blond hair, a very Negroid nose, and a light-brown hue to her light skin. The mixed young man had curly light-brown hair, and an even more pronounced Negroid nose, large-gray eyes, with a cream-and-coffee color to his skin. They were all staring at William.

The Mulatto Woman whispered loudly, "They're letting anything into this school nowadays!"

The Mulatto man said, "They must be searching way down in the low-income areas to find someone like that," in a louder whisper.

The White man said, "I don't give that Nig, a month. More like a couple of weeks," speaking out loudly.

Then the White woman allowed: "Seems as though the more Negroid they are the more likely it is for them to fail early. It's their brain-size or something, I've been told."

William felt like those people didn't know him from Adam. They didn't know what sort of income group he had come from, whether low or high-income. They were going by skin color alone-nothing else.

Dr. Carl Brauer had satin-blond hair. He wore that sort of long. He was kind of sh0lt with a handsome face resembling Bob Hope's. He wore a two-piece brown suit and a white shirt with no tie. He had on black shoes and white socks. His office was much smaller than Miller's with cheap-looking brown furniture in it.

His big-blue eyes blinked incessantly as he spoke with a northern twang. "Come in. Have a seat, Mr. James. I've been expecting you." He pointed to one of several office chairs along the walls in his office. William took a seat.

Dr. Brauer said, "You would do better at a school like Howard University, or perhaps, Fisk. The skill levels at VSU and those required of a student here are incompatible. I'm not sure you will be able to succeed here, judging from what I've seen of your transcripts. I have to be honest with you, Mr. James."

With some degree of nervousness, William responded. "I noticed that all of the schools you mentioned are 'Black Schools.' Are we still having some problems with race and color, in light of recent litigation and court rulings against racial segregation in Virginia's public schools?"

Dr. Brauer stood up abruptly behind his huge desk. He walked around so that he could sit in a chair next to William's. "Mr. James, I'm simply trying to be realistic with you. I marched with activists in Boston. I believe in racial equality at this University. I constantly work with Dr. Paul Gaston to help bring that about. I have a problem, though, with Blacks seeing everything as racism when it is clearly not the case."

Before William could say more, Dr. Brauer raised his left hand. "Look. I see that there is some element of distrust here between us. I want my decision to be completely unbiased and objective. So I will send you to talk with Dr. Wilhelm Harbaugh, my esteemed colleague. He is two doors up the hallway. Give him this form. If he signs it, I will too."

Harbaugh wore a two-piece seer-sucker suit. He wore his blond hair in a pompadour, but his facial features resembled Clarke Gable's, a little. When William got to his doorway, Dr. Harbaugh said, "Come in Bill James. Dr. Brauer called me about you just a moment ago. I'm delighted to meet you."

William walked into this man's huge office that had two mahogany desks, and smelled the rum-cured tobacco he smoked in his English pipe. "I'm going to sign the form, William. I don't need to see anything other than that you are Black. You can sink or swim per-your abilities. But I want you to have the chance to do so."

William, Sr., and Sarah moved with their children into 17-5 Copley Hill, the family village for married graduate students, May, 1980. Before 1980, Blacks had a hard time getting an apartment at Copley. Now, William figured he was all set.

He received a letter from Dr. Miller just before Labor Day. It instructed William to go meet with Dr. Gaston. On his application essay, William had indicated that he wanted to study Afri can-American History. Since the UVA do not confer degrees in African-American History, a Doctoral Candidate could not major in it. The closest thing was Southern History. The Southern History Professor was Dr. Paul Gaston.

Gaston had an office at Leverhing Hall. He was considered a Premier Historian, and therefore had an office On The Lawn of the Rotunda. The man that played Andy of Mayberry, Dr. Gaston looked just like him, except that Gaston wore a blue blazer, tan slacks and oxford penny-loafers. His white-silk shirt he wore unbuttoned at the collar with no tie. His office was on the second floor of Leverhing.

"So, you're Bill James from Virginia State," Gaston said. His gaze grew narrower. "I have to admit . . . you don't look like the type of scholar who can fit in here at the UVA. But looks can be deceiving. I predict you will suffer some culture shock. Come on in, Bill, have a seat. Let's talk," Gaston spoke in a refined Southern drawl.

The way that Gaston's piercing blue-eyes were looking at him made William feel very uncomfortable. It seemed as though there was something sly, sinister, hateful, and condescending about how he seemed to look right through William.

"Bill, what do you hope to learn here at the UVA in a graduate program?" Gaston asked. He loudly cleared his throat.

"I want to study all I can about 'The Byrd Machine' and the politics of 'Massive Resistance' in Virginia; and, why Byrd, who secretly did a number of favors for Black people in-need, was so opposed to them attending schools with White People," William replied.

Gaston walked around in his massive office with a full conference table with twelve leather bound chairs around it and several other plush leather-bound chairs at various places around the carpeted room. Then he stopped and stood directly in front of William.

"For this reason alone, I'm saying you will have a very difficult time trying to research that particular topic, here. You will find that this University community will see your chosen topic as the most subversive and subjective of topic-choices. Senator Byrd-and now his family-has a large endowment in the millions of dollars here at this institution. I know it will be best if you pick another topic to develop into a dissertation," Gaston said, as casually as Andy of Mayberry would have when talking to A'nt Bee.

William was shocked. "But isn't that academic approach a very subjective one to begin with?" he snapped.

"Bill. Bill, I'm talking about what will work and what will not," Gaston snapped back at William.

"Wait a minute Dr. Gaston. All I want to do is get some advice from an objective advisor. I want the facts to fall where they will or may. I don't want you or anyone telling me that I can't write the truth because it may get in the way of your fundraising politics," William said, just below a 'Rebel Yell.'

An angry scowl came suddenly across Gaston's face. "Well, your academic record does not show me that you have all the abilities you think you have. I am to be your advisor. Carl Brauer would have been if he were not up for Tenure Considerations.

"Bill, we don't have a Black History Department. We have the rudiments of a 'Black History institute.' But you will not be allowed to major in that subject. You will have to major in 'Recent Southern History.'

"This is my gut-feelings: At this institution you will never be a Bonafede scholar, because you come from the poorest academic organizations in the State of Virginia-VSU, PVCC, and the Job Corps. After S.C. Abrams High and Gravel Hill Elementary, these schools and the Job Corps cannot prepare you to face the academic rigors you have to master here at the UVA I can tell by looking at you, you are not one who will make it very far here." Gaston had raised his voice to just below a shout.

William's emotions started to boil over. It was almost as if Dr. Gaston was his angry Daddy yelling at him. His first compunction was to flee-get to safety, run. But, there was nowhere to run to.

"Dr. Gaston," William whined. "I'll do my best and maybe that will pull me through. I should be given a chance to prove myself one way or the other."

"William don't get me wrong. I marched during the early 1960s. I fought for the desegregation of Public school education. I respect your right to be treated equal up here at the UVA But, we still have the right to say no," Gaston said.

"Why are you singling me out? Why do you want to reject me? I'm one of those you fought for, right?" William said.

"All right, William. I'll give-in against my better judgment. But you remember that I tried to warn you upfront.

"You don't have any money, I know. We can't give you a full-scholarship based upon the schools you have attended. You will have to prove yourself first.

"I will send you to Dr. Alexander Sedgwick, Chairman of the History Department, and he is in charge of a scholarship program called the Governor's Scholarship. He and William (Bill) Ellwood, Dean of GSAS, will have to sign-off on it, but it gives $2,500.00 for one-year. If you do well we will give you a full-scholarship that pays tuition and fees, and gives you a $500.00 stipend per-semester, as well.

"Take these forms I'm handing you to Dr. Sedgwick and Dr. Ellwood."

William got the forms signed. He got his class assignments filled out. He got into all of his classes. No Problem-right?

He flunked all of the courses he was signed up for. Gaston had advised William to take classes that even a genius would not have been able pass. He was in two collegial and two seminars the same semester. A collegial is the reading part of the seminar. You take one the first semester and the second part the next semester. You have two semesters to do your dissertation. One Semester for a Collegial; one for the Seminar and annotated outline for the thesis; and two or more for writing and defending the Dissertation. There were six credits for collegial; three for each seminar; and eight-four-per-semester-for writing and defending the dissertation. Thirty credits were required for graduation. A candidate had to take seven or eight electives outside of his major, depending on how soon he successfully completed his seminar.

As could be expected William earned a grade of B- in a seven-hundred level course; and an incomplete for the others. All grades have to be honor grades: A, A-, B+, and B.

The semester had been replete with many raw-racist encounters with White students. They always got around to telling him that he didn't belong at the UVA, and certainly not as a Graduate History Student.

In the hallways, William was fondled, pushed, tripped, and groped by men and women. Some said, "' scuse me," in a ludicrous way imitative of Black dialect. Some White women just stared William down, like they were daring him to say a word. He'd hear the word, "Sambo," hurled through the air when he quickly walked away. "Why don't ya come on back an' rape me?" Then they flipped the bird at him.

There were times during lectures when students and or professors stooped to blatant misuse of the word, "Nigger," while looking at William as they did so. Then there were inequitable grading practices, on the part of the professors, and their teaching assistants, who normally grade most papers. William realized that he made the mistake of his life by coming to the University of Virginia. (William was the only Black person in the above classes.)

In his office one day, Dr. Gaston with tears in his eyes declared: "Bill, I feel for you. But ..

. as your advisor, I have to be perfectly honest with you. You will never be allowed to earn a PhD from the UVA. What would the Alumni think? They would think that Graduate History had lowered its standards. This University-and all of those like it-has an academic reputation to uphold. I regret this fact. But, that's the way it is. There is a certain kind of Black this institution is trying to recruit into its academic ranks."

William interrupted him. "And, who are those, Dr. Gaston?"

"Those people you call 'Mulattos.' Those are the people the Graduate Schools are looking for. They see them as part of the 'Top-Talented-Tenth' spoken of by W. E. B. Du Bios. Even many members of your own race will agree with me on that.

"Don't get me wrong, Bill. I wish all of you 'Coloreds' nothing but the best. It's not me.

Why do you think they have Black Schools? I donate to them every year."

William jumped up from the chair he was sitting in. He wanted to puke. So, this was the Origin of "The Skin-Color Syndrome Among African Americans." This was what had been haunting him and people like him for all of their lives.

He was dropped from the GSAS. He was not allowed back in, though he took classes as an Independent Study Student in '82, '85, '86, and '93. "Maybe, by the time my children have grown up, they will not have to face the White-racism that has gotten in my way," he hoped.

Dick attended Johnston Smith University in North Carolina. He dropped out after one year. He went to work as a Security Guard at The Virginia State Prison System. After twenty years he retired with the rank of Captain. He was married three times and is the Father of five children.

Bug attended Wilberforce University in Ohio. He got his BS and MS in Biology, but ended up working for the UVA as a Physical Therapist. He retired after thirty years.

Johnboy attended the UVA. He earned his BA in American History. He and a group of friends and colleagues founded an Insurance Brokerage Firm in Washington, D.C.

Sammy Lee attended Lynchburg University. He later dropped out. He enlisted in the Army where he retired after twenty-years. He became a Drill Sergeant. His last rank was Master Sergeant. He is currently a Baptist Evangelist.

Dave graduated :from high school. He worked in the UVA Records Room for Twenty-years.

He and his wife live a quiet life in the Louisa countryside.

Julia graduated :from high school. She still works in retail sales.

Janice attended Virginia Tech. She graduated with honors. [She married a drug dealer. He is currently pulling fifteen-years to life in a Federal prison.] Janice is an Administrative Assistant for Louisa County.

Cery graduated :from Norfolk State University. He was hired fresh out of school by the Department of the Navy. He moved up into the position of Computer Analyst, First-Grade, with a salary of $60,000 per-year. Then he contracted HIV/AIDS. He died November 11, 1989. It reminded William of Tim. Both Cery and he died :from a Government runaway experiment.

Finally, I, William A. James, Sr., "Survived the Hard Times," so I am A Writer. What would I be today if I had been given an Equal Opportunity, :free of racism and color-prejudices?

One good thing, though, is I lived to see the Election of America's First Black President, Barack H. Obama in 2008. I got to see the most beautiful, gracious, exquisite, First Lady, Mrs. Michelle Obama, to ever grace the White House, do so with her magnificent Black presence.

So, it is true: "What don't kill you will make you stronger." However, **THIS IS MY MESSAGE TO AFRICAN-AMERICANS: ALL OF US MUST LEARN TO LOVE AND RESPECT EACH OTHER, OR WE WILL SURELY BE THE MAIN CULPRITS RESPONSIBLE FOR OUR OWN GENOCIDE!**

(Henry James died of a Cerebral Hemorrhage in 1973 [53] due to the lick he received from Bo Rabbit's attack of him over ten years earlier. Mabel died in 1979 [48] from Gastroenteritis due to chronic alcoholism.)

Printed in the United States
By Bookmasters